Achim von O

Terms of Trade and 7

The history and contexts of
production around the Upper Zambezi and Kasaı

Studien zur Afrikanischen Geschichte

herausgegeben von

Helmut Bley

und

Leonhard Harding

Band 6

LIT

Achim von Oppen

Terms of Trade and Terms of Trust

The history and contexts of pre-colonial market production around the Upper Zambezi and Kasai

LIT

Die Deutsche Bibliothek – CIP-Einheitsaufnahme

Oppen, Achim von
Terms of Trade and Terms of Trust : The history and contexts of pre-colonial market production around the Upper Zambezi and Kasai / Achim von Oppen. – Münster ; Hamburg : Lit 1993
  (Studien zur Afrikanischen Geschichte; Bd.6)
  ISBN 3-89473-246-6

NE: GT

© LIT VERLAG   Dieckstr. 73   48145 Münster   Tel. 0251-23 50 91
                             Hallerplatz 5   20146 Hamburg   Tel. 040-44 64 46

CONTENTS

Part A:	INTRODUCTION	1
A 1:	Opening the lens: Views of an 'end of the world'	2
A 2:	Choosing a perspective: Origins of peasants and markets in Africa	9
A 3:	Processing the material: Disparate snapshots and their synthesis	29
	3.1 The unit of study	29
	3.2 The sources	37
Part B:	ENTERING THE ATLANTIC WORLD	45
B 1:	Gates between coast and interior (before c.1800)	49
B 2:	The climax and end of slave exports (c.1800-1850)	59
B 3:	Ivory, beeswax and new patterns of trade (c.1840-80)	62
B 4:	The 'Rubber Delirium' (c.1880-1910)	78
B 5:	By the roadside: Services for travellers	87
B 6:	Conclusion Part B: A chronology of market integration	97
Part C:	THE REGIONAL ECONOMY: EXPANDING PRODUCTION AND LOCAL NEEDS	101
C 1:	A prehistory of indigenous productive innovation	103
	1.1 Widening the choice: Early Bantu innovations (up to 1600 A.D.)	103
	1.2 Increasing the productivity: Innovations of the 17th and 18th centuries	108
C 2:	Population and ecology - a changing balance	120
	2.1 A mosaic of ecosystems	121
	2.2 Ecology and food	123
	2.3 Regional sub-economies	130

C 3 :	**Emerging divisions of labour**		**135**
	3.1 The division by gender and age		135
	3.2 The division of knowledge		141
	3.3 The importance of regional trade		143
C 4 :	**The means of export production**		**154**
	4.1 The utility of the honeybee		155
	4.2 The ways of winning rubber		159
	4.3 The dangers of hunting elephants		166
	4.4 the technology of warfare		175
C 5 :	**Adaptations in the regional food economy**		**181**
	5.1 'By-products' of the export sector		181
	5.2 The changing economy of staple food		187
	5.3 'Relish' and 'cash crops'		196
	5.4 The value of livestock		201
	5.5 Changes in the regional division of labour		204
C 6 :	**Use-values and currencies:**		
	the utility of imported goods		**211**
	6.1 Intoxicants		212
	6.2 'Ornaments'		218
	6.3 Textiles		223
	6.4 Imports as 'wealth'		232
C 7 :	**Conclusion Part C:**		
	'Subsistence' and 'surplus'		**236**
Part D :	**THE SOCIAL CONTEXT:**		
	LABOUR, POWER AND EXCHANGE		**243**
D 1 :	**'Owners' and 'villagers'**		
	1.1 Individual ownership		246
	1.2 Villagers' obligations		249
D 2 :	**Sisters and wives**		
	2.1 Claims on labour		258
	2.2 Rights over food crops		260
	2.3 Demands for gifts and sexuality		265
	2.4 Women's autonomy		270
D 3 :	**Children and slaves**		
	3.1 Paternal frustrations and avuncular authority		273
	3.2 Unreliable juniors		280
	3.3 Slaves as 'wives' and 'children'		285
	3.4 Authority and independence		293

D 4 :	**'Strangers', neighbours and 'friends': the importance of non-kinship relations**	**295**
	4.1 Types of inter-village relations	296
	4.2 The costs of inter-village relations	305
	4.3 The utility of neighbourhood: Cooperation, piecework and barter	313
	4.4 The benefits of friendship: credits and compensations	331
	4.5 The meanings of inter-village exchange	342
D 5 :	**Chieftainship and trade**	
	5.1 Chiefs without power ?	345
	5.2 Chiefly revenues	350
	5.3 Politicians or entrepreneurs ?	363
	5.4 Power and accumulation	369
D 6 :	**Conclusion Part D: 'Equity with growth' ?**	**371**
Part E:	**NEGOTIATING THE MARKET: RESIDENT PRODUCERS AND FOREIGN TRADERS**	**380**
E 1 :	**'Extortions, exactions and vexations'**	**381**
	1.1 The language of legitimate demands	382
	1.2 The valuation of respect	385
	1.3 Hospitality and accusations	388
E 2 :	**Business and trust**	**393**
	2.1 Friendship sales	394
	2.2 Credit trade	396
	2.3 The scramble for allies	400
E 3 :	**The right price**	
	3.1 The problem of currencies	406
	3.2 The ideology of fixed unit prices	409
	3.3 Bargaining on the price	417
E 4 :	**Conclusion Part E: Changing moralities of exchange**	**412**
Part F :	**EPILOGUE**	**429**

APPENDIX AND REFERENCES

Synopsis of travellers' reports
on the Upper Zambezi and Kasai, 1794-1907   438
References
1. Oral sources   441
2. Written sources and bibliography   443

TABLES

Table 1:	Approximate population of the Upper Zambezi and Kasai by ethnic group (1940s)	30
Table 2:	'Legitimate exports' from Angola, 1780-1933 (only products of the interior, in metric tons)	64
Table 3:	Exports from Angola 1760-1908 (in current values)	80
Table 4:	Comparison of cassava with millets as staple crop	126
Table 5:	Productive activities around the Upper Zambezi by season and gender	139/40
Table 6:	The processing of *kambungo* (wild rubber)	122/23
Table 7:	The tasks of husband and wife (current village norms)	259
Table 8:	Typical elements of marriage payments among the Chokwe, Luvale and Southern Lunda	266
Table 9:	Composition of the *banzo* ('load'; standard unit of account in West Central African barter trade)	410

MAPS

Map 1 :	West-Central Africa before c. 1900	470
Map 2 :	Ecological zones in the Upper Zambezi and Kasai region	471/2
Map 3 :	Upper Zambezi and Kasai region, c. 1790-1910	472/3

FIGURES

Fig. 1:	Wooden chair of the Chokwe Chief Chipukungu	48
Fig. 2:	Indigenous carriers with foreigner in a hammock	51
Fig. 3:	Slave caravan in the interior, on the main 'watershed' route (1875)	58
Fig. 4:	'Angola caravan' (Chokwe ?) with ivory loads in the Congo (around 1900)	77
Fig. 5:	Ovimbundu *pombeiros* from Bihe (1891)	81
Fig. 6:	Armed Bihe caravan carrier, with typical load (1878)	89
Fig. 7:	Caravan camp on the main 'watershed' route (1875)	90
Fig. 8:	Food sales in a Mashukulumbwe village (1904-07)	95
Fig. 9:	Yowena Samakayi, an aged Luvale trader (1986)	100
Fig. 10:	Cassava (manioc) plant	109
Fig. 11:	Gate on a *wálilo*-dam for plain fisheries, with fishtrap	115
Fig. 12:	Luvale weaponry of local manufacture (1875)	118
Fig. 13:	Indigenous cassava cultivation system (1979)	128
Fig. 14:	The author of this book trying a fish trader's load (1985)	146
Fig. 15:	Chokwe beeswax hunters and beehive (1884/1878)	156
Fig. 16:	Processing *carpodinus* roots to extract wild rubber	161
Fig. 17:	Chokwe big game hunters' camp (1878)	167
Fig. 18:	A Chokwe hunter with muzzle-loader gun (1878)	171
Fig. 19:	A Luvale hunter with muzzle-loader gun (1985)	174
Fig. 20:	A mead or honeybeer brewer, with gathering of drinkers (Chokwe, 1878)	184
Fig. 21:	Chokwe chief with locally made brass crown (1900s)	219
Fig. 22:	*Jimbe* shell and medaillon made of it (1854)	221
Fig. 23:	Chief Kakenge and a slave (1895)	231
Fig. 24:	Small Southern Lunda village, surrounded by cassava plantations (1895)	252
Fig. 25:	Chokwe woman hoeing a young cassava field	263

Fig. 26:	Luchazi woman on the road (1878)	264
Fig. 27:	Stockaded Southern Lunda village, seen from the inside (1904-07)	284
Fig. 28:	Female field labourers, Central Chokwe area (1878)	291
Fig. 29:	Conclusion of a friendship pact (detail from Chief Kakoma's chair)	300
Fig. 30:	Warriors fighting with guns (detail from fig. 1)	356
Fig. 31:	Livingstone's reception by the Southern Lunda Chief Ishinde	357
Fig. 32:	A market place (*chitaka*) in Central Chokwe (1878)	418

LANGUAGE ABBREVIATIONS

sg.	=	singular
pl.	=	plural
lit.	=	literally
Pg.	=	in Portuguese
Lv.	=	in Luvale or Lwena language (chiLuvale)
SL.	=	in Southern Lunda (Lunda-Ndembu) language
Ch.	=	in Chokwe language
Lz.	=	in Luchazi language
Umb.	=	in Ovimbundu language (uMbundu)
Lo.	=	in Lozi language (siLozi)

ACKNOWLEDGEMENTS

This study has been, from its inception, an attempt to transcend various limitations: spatial and historical distance, social and cultural difference, disciplinary boundaries, and sometimes physical limits. As a 'traveller' and 'stranger', I would have been unable to come to reach the spaces 'beyond' without the hospitality, assistance and friendship of a variety of 'residents', i.e. people who are more acquainted with them than myself. I wish to express my particular gratitude to:

* The inhabitants of the Zambezi and Kabompo District with whom I lived, who assisted me in many ways and who, notably the elderly, taught me so much about their history;
* My field assistants, especially David Chishinji;
* The friends and colleagues who exchanged information and shared views as well as experiences with me during fieldwork and evaluation, especially Kate Crehan and the students of the 'Zambia 1986' project;
* The government and project officials in Kabompo and Zambezi who made my field stays possible;
* The University of Zambia and particularly the Rural Development Studies Bureau who affiliated my research;
* The National Archives of Zambia who made accessible to me the written records on Kabompo and Zambezi;
* The Institute for Sociology, Dept. of Sociology of Development with Prof. M. Schulz, at the Freie Universität Berlin, which gave me the space to write and defend the original version of this study as a doctoral dissertation;
* The Professors Georg Elwert (Freie Universität Berlin) and Helmut Bley (Universität Hannover), who encouraged and inspired my work on this study through discussions and reports;
* The Regional Government of Berlin (Senat von Berlin), that awarded me the 'Tiburtius-Preis' for my dissertation (among a total of seven theses) in 1991, together with a grant for printing expenses;
* The scholars and friends, notably Prof. David Birmingham (Kent University), Prof. James C. Scott (Yale University), Dr. Kurt Beck (now University of Bayreuth), and particularly Dr. Beatrix Heintze (Frobenius Institute at Frankfurt/Main), whose encouraging comments

and numerous advices helped me much in revising and updating the original version;

* The Centre for Modern Oriental Studies which provided me with the working time and facilities required to give this book its final shape;

* The Museum für Völkerkunde Berlin (Museum for Ethnography), Staatliche Museen Preussischer Kulturbesitz, for the permission to reproduce some of their collections (see illustrations);

* Heinrich Hattebier, who sacrificed some of his off-time to draw the maps;

* Kate Sturge, who very diligently and efficiently checked through the text in its different stages to correct major English language problems (while any remaining mistakes or lack of elegance are my own reponsibility);

* my close friends and relatives who not only endured, but also supported the finalization of this study, especially during its various 'final stages', in many practical and emotional ways,

* and among them very especially my father Dietrich von Oppen, who sometimes had to conceal his impatience for the appearance of this book. He will discover in it traces of his own thought. I wish to dedicate this book to him.

Part A

INTRODUCTION

A 1 Opening the lens: Views of an 'end of the world'

Field research inevitably leads to some confrontation with current views of the people under study, current among those in the field and also in the researcher's mind. A particularly controversial aspect of the way in which the inhabitants of the region I have studied are portrayed is their attitude towards the market. In 1979, when I arrived for my first spell of fieldwork in that corner of North-Western Province which now forms Zambia's share of that region, backwardness was the dominant theme in conversations with officials and experts who were concerned with raising market production and incomes in the area. Some of them, especially urban Zambians, had a distinctly negative image of the rural producers I wanted to become acquainted with. In official post-colonial language they were called 'villagers', as opposed to 'farmers', or at most 'traditional subsistence farmers' (versus 'emergent' and 'commercial farmers'), because they relied almost entirely on autochthonous production technology and provided the (state controlled) market with only negligible quantities of products.[1] Privately, one could hear them being complained about as more concerned with witchcraft than with farming, as 'mere cassava eaters', because cassava was (and largely still is) the staple crop of most peasants[2] in the area for which there is very little urban market demand (while maize growing is regarded as the essence of 'progressive farming' in Zambia). Among local government officers in general, there was a frustrated feeling of being posted in an utterly remote and hopeless place - very similar to their Angolan counterparts across the international border who used to call this region *fim do mundo,* the end of the world.[3]

Others, including myself, assumed that, rather than innate conservative mentality, the deprivation of productive resources through constant government neglect and widespread labour migration since the colonial period were the main reasons for 'underdevelopment' in this rural periphery. But both views converged in the practical conclusion that outside assistance and careful education were needed for local cultivators, livestock rearers, beekeepers and craftsmen to produce systematically for

---

[1] See for example Government of the Republic of Zambia 1979; Pausewang et al. 1986: 74f; cf. Marter 1978: 1

[2] This term will be discussed in the next chapter; for the time being it is used as a shorthand for 'rural producer'.

[3] These views go back to the colonial period. In 1959, for instance, Kenneth Kaunda, the future first president of independent Zambia, was taken to Kabompo for several months internal exile. For Angola see Pélissier 1977: 396.

the market, thereby raise their income and eventually take a more active and powerful position in the society at large.[4]

During fieldwork, I realized that 'villagers' had a somewhat different assessment of their situation:[5] Most of them saw themselves not as emerging, but as degraded market producers. In fact, they seemed to have ample experience in how to respond in a 'rational' way to market opportunities and constraints. They had all been constantly engaged in various local income-generating activities throughout their adult life. Most of them had been quick to try new forms of production, especially when these promised to open new market opportunities. Cash money was indeed needed, not only for manufactured consumer goods, but also for a large number of petty exchanges of goods and labour within and between rural communities, quite different from what I expected of a kinship-based 'subsistence economy' based on 'traditional solidarity'. The older peasants, in retrospect, felt the first 15 years since Independence in 1964 to be a period when previously good marketing opportunities for local products, mainly cassava, groundnuts and beeswax, declined. When, in the 1980s, new development projects established an extended network of buying stations, villagers saw this partly as an overdue resurrection of earlier marketing opportunities. At any rate, the response to these projects was unexpectedly enthusiastic, and the number of participants grew at a rate that regularly exceeded projections. Within a few years, thousands of peasants became suppliers of the official marketing network.[6]

Whether in response to such overwhelming reactions or to new political priorities, the 'development' discourse in remoter parts of Zambia had changed considerably when I returned to the area in the mid-1980s. 'Villagers' were now widely called 'small-scale farmers' (or 'small-scale producers', when off-farm activities were included); and an active interest of every household head, including the poorest (often female), in monetary income was presupposed.[7] 'Small-scale-producers' were typically imagined as more or less enterpreneurial people who, with the help of their own household's labour, combined market with subsistence production, took rational decisions according to prices, costs and needs,

---

4   For initial project planning see Rauch and Weyl 1978: 209ff; for the use of the term 'market' in this thesis see below, fn.10.
5   Results of this study are included in von Oppen 1981.
6   The story of the most important of these projects, the LIMA, is traced in Crehan and von Oppen 1988 (revised version in: forthcoming 1993).
7   E.g. Honeybone and Marter 1979; Chilivumbo and Milimo 1983; Provincial Planning Unit 1986

and strove for ultimate independence from Government intervention.[8] In short, modernity rather than conservatism had become the official working assumption for the majority of rural producers.

Again, however, this image of the rational, innovative, small-scale market producer did not quite match our observations during fieldwork.[9] For example, in reality it was difficult to make a clear-cut distinction between 'market' and 'subsistence' production, even within the 'household'. Instead of specializing in one particular form of market production (as is quietly assumed in most development projects), many producers tried to combine several forms, and frequently changed from one to another, causing considerable fluctuation in project participation. Between the peasants, market production and incomes were extremely competitive and individualized, even between husbands and wives of the same household. But individual economic success, on the other hand, was met with considerable suspicion and sometimes caused allegations of witchcraft among other villagers. Finally, in meetings with marketing officials, economic demands were put forward very frankly, but often phrased in an idiom of personal rather than market (or power) relations. For instance, in stark contrast with the outstanding sense of independence exhibited on many other occasions, credits are regularly demanded, even without any acute shortage of capital. Peasants often seemed to see credit as a bond of trust and alliance with these outside forces; and when at one point, after considerable patience, some credit defaulters were taken to court, an outcry swept through the area which seemed disproportionate to the actual event.[10]

Such inconsistencies may seem explainable, at the first glance, as typical phenomena of transition: The market, it appears, has not (yet) transformed production and permeated social relations in the area to the same extent as in rural areas of developed capitalist 'market economies'.[11] This, in turn, could be attributed either to time - the evolutionist assumption that the area is still at an early stage of market integration - or to more specific, systematic 'distortions' in this process - an popular argument among neoclassical as well as dependency theorists.

---

[8] In the background, a mixture of farm economics, 'petty commodity production' and 'self-reliant' basic needs producers can be easily discerned.

[9] Results of these two research periods, in 1983 and 1985, have been compiled in von Oppen, Shula and Alff 1983, and Alff, von Oppen and Beck 1986.

[10] More details in Crehan and von Oppen 1993

[11] 'Market' and related terms are understood here as referring to a particular form of circulation of goods, inseparably linked with various forms of production for this purpose, which is situated in the wider historical context of the advancing, capitalist-dominated world economy. The circulation of products and people within the region will be spoken of in more neutral terms, such as 'trade', 'exchange' and the like, although the question of an 'internalization' of market relations will also have to be addressed.

In any of these explanations, there is something like an implicit modernism: 'The market' is seen as a potentially uniform way of organizing production and circulation of goods throughout the globe. In fact, a kindred line of argumentation merged with my own 'africanist' concern at the time when I started research for this study. My initial concern was to demonstrate that, on the one hand, the process of modernization by market integration had started much earlier, and people in this area were much more open and active in it, than assumed by speakers of the 'backwardness' discourse. On the other hand, I intended to show that market producers always had to struggle, with more or less success, against a variety of odds ranged against them by economic circumstances (such as remoteness from major markets) and by non-economic interventions of middlemen, conquerors and governments.

During my last phase of research, which began in 1986, I concentrated therefore on the social and economic history of the area, and collected evidence showing that the inhabitants of this 'lost corner' (Vansina) had in fact been involved in market relations for a very long time. A large majority of them had produced for outside markets not only throughout the colonial period, but had regular direct exchange with the world market from at least the last decade of the 18th century. Through my findings, whose essence is presented in the following chapters, I became aware, however, that there were more contradictions in the process than I had anticipated. Reading the written sources, in the first place, yielded ample evidence that from the beginning the inhabitants of the region impressed outside visitors in much the same ambivalent way as today: as efficient market producers and tough traders on the one hand, and as incalculable and 'traditional' forest-dwellers on the other. As late as by the turn of the 20th century, for example, one of the first British (BSAC) colonial officers remarked on the Luvale that 'except for a little beeswax I know of no natural production that is of any value. ...If there is any trade with the outside world, it ... is very small.[12] A Belgian counterpart of his found instead that

> ...the *Ba-Louéna* [Luvale] are rich and happy; they are very hospitable towards travellers, in their non-fortified villages amidst large and varied agriculture; through their products of cultivation, livestock raising and fishing they largely supply the caravans of black traders coming from the west, who leave with them a large part of their exchange goods...[13]

60 years on, towards the end of the colonial period, observers of the area were by no means closer to a consensus. While the Provincial Commissioner reported bluntly that 'the province generally adheres

---

[12] Major Gould-Adams, Report 24/08/1897, on the Luvale and Lunda (PRO, file 795/107-45080/6, item 12)

[13] Lemaire 1902: 67

rigidly to the traditional forms of cultivation and a restricted subsistence economy'[14], a former district officer with an admittedly much more intimate knowledge of the area concluded:

> 'Unlike some areas where this process has been achieved to a great extent by Government and rural development programmes, the Luvale owe most of their agricultural development to date to their own initiative and enterprise. Strong factors which have operated to produce this result have been the long contact with Portuguese West Africa [Angola], and the egalitarian and competitive values of Luvale society.'[15]

Working through such material, I realized increasingly that the distinction between market-oriented modernity and pre-market 'backwardness', be it self-styled or imposed by 'external' forces, was far too clumsy a tool for analysis. The twisted course of market development in this area, as in any other, clearly unfolds itself only through a synopsis of 'outside' and 'local' influences, prominently including the social relations and struggles 'within' the local population. In other words, the question of how much the development of market relations owes to local relationships and meanings can hardly be tackled on the basis of the evolutionist and normative assumptions outlined above. With regard to Central Africa, this begins with the empirical problem to trace genuine 'pre-market' structures where this would mean going back into times where any kind of memory is fading. More principally, however, the 'local' factors in question here are not necessarily 'older' nor easily distinguished from factors related to the market. Even 'the market', on the other hand, is by no means a ready-made, invariable structure imposed by global capitalism onto local populations who can only adapt to (or try to escape from) it. In a social science perspective, 'the market' as an abstract, and 'the world market' as an empirical entity, consist in a multitude of particular 'real markets' which are constructed in particular local contexts through a dynamic process of interaction between a variety of social forces, as a tangled web of both global and local, capitalist and non-capitalist structures and meanings.[16]

Seen in its historical depth, the course of this construction is by no means a linear process but changes with its particular context. The case studied here, however, exhibits some remarkable continuities in the pattern of peasant market relations, such as innovativeness, unstable social relations, relatively low level of unequality, and an idiom of personal relations in market contexts. It seems that the repercussions of the great historical turning points in the wider context - long-distance trade, colonization and political independence - were mitigated to some

---

[14] Secretary for African Affairs 1961: 9
[15] White 1959: xi; 21

extent by local conditions which changed much less briskly and at a much more slower pace than is often assumed. This study is confined to the pre-colonial section of this long history of market production, but many of the patterns that developed during this period have relevance up to today in the area.[17] This is not to deny, of course, that fundamental changes have taken place during and after that period. One of the decisive differences between pre-colonial and colonial period, for instance, is the greater political autonomy of local groups and institutions compared with the modern central state. The pre-colonial period is therefore a particularly promising field for the study of (probably uneven) interaction, rather than outright domination by outside agency.

However, there is more to the mentioned controversial images which accompanied the area's history (that remains to be told in the following chapters) than a useful key to a controversial reality. At the same time, these images were always expressions of political struggle about the future of the area and its people. Those talking about backwardness and 'the end of the world', and sometimes joked about simply fencing off the whole border area and forgetting about its onerous 'development', clearly represented a lack of central government committment to invest in local resources or loyalty in these now marginal areas. Those pointing at the potential 'modernity' of the population, on the other hand, implicitly argued for an increase in such interest and investments. For some of these foreign observers, this was mainly a matter of justice or development philosophy. Others, such as C.M.N. White, took up an implicitly 'regionalist' line, influenced by strong personal experience. They were also the ones who were in closer touch with the population in general, and with local leaders in particular, through length of stay, position or preference. In this indirect way, also local African views seem to have entered the discourse among experts and writers on the area. I experienced myself the demonstrative hospitality with which visitors and researchers are received, the continuous attempts to enmesh them in lasting personal relations, and the expectation on them to adopt their hosts' demands towards the outside world. I have witnessed how lively an interest Lunda and Luvale notables and elders took in my project, emphasizing the long history of market-oriented enterprise of their people.

In this area, historical research has always taken place in a strongly politicized context. With their main market links pointing first towards the Atlantic coast in the Angolan west, and later towards the urbanized 'Line of Rail' in the Zambian east, the basic experience of inhabitants of the

---

16 Globalization - Localization debate; new market debate (or references below ?); 'real markets': Maureen Mackintosh
17 See von Oppen 1990 and forthcoming

region has been throughout one of feeling remote from the centres of power and well-being, and one of feeling forgotten by those who give access to such resources. They have always been aware of having to struggle for access to political representation and markets. As a part of such struggles, since the 1930s, remarkable efforts have been made by 'peasant intellectuals' from the region to reconstruct the history of Luvale and Lunda chieftainship, as a proof of the level of political development reached in the past.[18]

Efforts to show themselves as dedicated and longstanding market producers must be seen in a similar context. Not very different from the first Luvale who approached Portuguese traders two centuries ago (see below, beginning of Part B), villagers ask visitors for capital and advice as to how they could profitably produce for exchange with his side of the world. Taking wild rubber as an example, once the most important export product of the area, one of my hosts, an elder of about 80 years of age, remarked: 'There are a lot of valuable things in Africa which we don't

Like earlier researchers, I felt sympathetic with this local concern for economic and social history in one of the remotest, yet very remarkable, corners of Central Africa. Nevertheless this book has not become a monument for 'heroic deeds of the past'. The production of scientific knowledge should be conscious of its own political implications, but it cannot allow to be governed by them. I beg for my hosts' and informants' recognition that this book has to ask also for the costs and contradictions of remarkable developments.

---

[18] See Report of the Macdonell Commission, NAZ ZP/5/1/A; Chinyama 1945; Papstein 1978; Sangambo 1979; Papstein 1989

[19] Interview Mr.Sondoyi, 24.10.1986; similar references to historical experience by Senior Chiefs Ndungu [Luvale] and Ishinde [Lunda], audiences on 23.8.1985 and 25.8.1986, respectively.

A 2 Choosing a perspective: Origins of peasants and markets in Africa

Having explained the background of personal experience from which the concern of this book originated - to explore how Central African rural producers have become involved in market production since the pre-colonial period -, I shall try in this chapter to relate this concern to some on-going scholarly debates. It is not my intention here to provide a thorough discussion of the considerable variety of approaches relevant to the problem. I will use this broad overview mainly to develop the wider perspective which structures the following study, and which emerged in a process of learning, thought and discussion. I will come back to the questions raised here, and to some of the more general answers that have already been given by other researchers, in the remarks concluding each part. Another aim of this chapter is to provide a short survey of existing literature with a comparative regional focus. This also illustrates how interdisciplinary an enterprise the study of the origins of rural market production in Africa necessarily is: it brings together historians, economists, sociologists, social anthropologists, geographers and ecologists, and touches on a correspondingly wide range of areas of knowledge.

'Peasantisation' as social history

Debates about the integration of what is now rural Africa into 'the' world economy[1] can be broadly clustered into two sets of questions. On the one hand, there is a focus on the the emergence and potential of rural producers, and on the way in which their social and economic relations, including those with other sectors of the society, are structured.[2] The second focus instead stresses the institutions and rationalities of commodity markets and their spread in the context of modern capitalism.[3] It will be seen further below that these debates in fact represent two sides of the same coin; they seem to be divided mainly by disciplinary discourse and tradition.

Since the late 1960s, the discourse of social historians has tended to revolve around the paradigm of 'the peasant'. The emergence of

---
[1] In fact, only by this very process of integration did these areas become 'rural', as opposed to the urban centres of development inside and outside their territory.
[2] For a recent review of literature on this topic see Isaacman 1990.
[3] See, for instance, the special issue of *Cahiers d'Etudes Africaines*, vol. 77/78 (1980), no. 1-2

'peasants' as a social category, also spoken of as 'peasantisation' (as opposed to 'proletarianization'), in Africa, particularly in the southern sub-continent, has been a contested issue. There has as yet been relatively little controversy about the ultimate destination of this process. In African studies, it has been widely accepted that 'peasants' can, in analogy with the classic definition by Eric Wolf,[4] be seen as

> 'those whose ultimate security and subsistence lies in their having certain rights in land and in the labour of family members on the land, but who are involved, through rights and obligations, in a wider economic system which includes the participation of non-peasants.'[5]

It is usually further assumed that this wider economic system is the capital-dominated world economy, and that economic relations are essentially market or commodity relations with non-rural, capitalist sectors of production, from which at least some consumer goods have to be bought and to which household products are sold in return. Another assumption is that peasant households are more or less independent economic units; and that the state (a centre of political power which does not coincide with the peasants' own socio-economic structures) determines important conditions of production.

It is problematic enough, and not very fruitful, to define which particular groups of African rural producers, and from when, should actually be called 'peasants' (see below). Consequently, I will avoid using this term in the following study, instead taking it up as a question: Rather than taking them for granted, I will ask which particular types of claims were actually being brought forward by market agents on rural producers, and by these on their dependants, and *vice versa*.[6] The historian's task would then be to look at these claims (and those making them) in a process perspective and to find out how they changed; in other words, 'how cultivators became peasants and why they remained so'.[7] Particularly in Africa, this question is a controversial one for several reasons. One problem is the conceptual vacuum which surrounds indigenous forms of production and social organization. Lack of sources and of adequate attention has for a long time led to misleading labels such as 'natural economy', 'traditional subsistence economy', 'communal cultivators' and the like,[8] which have, if unwittingly, reconfirmed inherited prejudices about 'peoples without history'.[9] The other problem is the fact that 'peasantisation' in Africa has been - in evolutionist

---

[4] Wolf 1966: 3-4
[5] Saul and Woods 1971: 105
[6] I was inspired for this perspective by Robert Harms and James Scott.
[7] Klein 1980: 12; see also Post 1977: 243
[8] E.g. Post 1977, Bernstein 1979: 423f
[9] Wolf 1982

parlance - very slow and full of 'diversions' and 'relapses'. Even farm households in the more advanced industrial societies usually depend on various forms of unpaid extra-household labour; in Africa, non- (or pre-) market structures seem particularly persistent in the rural sector.

Doubts about such evolutionist views prompted the rise of another paradigm, the 'articulation of modes of production' (Meillassoux, Rey, Terray and others), which found widespread international acceptance among social scientists and historians in the 1970s.[10] Pre-capitalist societies were seen as geared around human reproduction and 'subsistence production' (the production of use-values, especially food, for consumption within the unit of production), with lineage organization as a mere superstructure of these specific 'relations of production'. Their persistence in market contexts was no longer seen merely as a transitory stage, but as a necessary condition of a form of market integration which rested on the exploitation of 'cheap' African labour. Two variants of 'articulation' have been emphasized, one between rural subsistence production and wage-labour outside the area, and the other between subsistence and 'petty commodity' production of food and raw materials within the rural sector, but for capitalist-dominated markets outside.[11] The first could be called the 'migrant worker', the second the 'peasant' option of rural transformation.

I do not intend to discuss here the many critical comments on the concept of 'articulation' that have been brought forward since the 1970s, especially on its structuralist and sometimes determinist implications.[12] Instead, I propose to take this approach back to where it started from: the empirical and historical study of rural Africa. Along the West African coasts, where the French protagonists of the 'articulation' debate undertook most of their research, the 'peasant' option was clearly in the foreground. This is also an area in which the beginnings of this transformation clearly predated the hoisting of the colonial flag, contrary to still widespread assumptions that market integration in Africa was only imposed on local 'communities' by colonial rule.[13] Numerous historical studies since the late 1950s have shown that systematic production for the world market (mainly palm oil and groundnuts, and often by small-scale producers) had begun here at the latest by the mid-19th century.[14]

---

[10] See the discussion by Raatgever 1985

[11] See Elwert 1984: 384ff for a more complex and dynamic model of the economic as well as social relations between these different 'sectors' of society.

[12] See Raatgever 1985

[13] This assumption was still present in the definition of 'peasants' by Saul and Woods (1971) quoted earlier.

[14] Of more than regional importance among the numerous studies on West Africa was, for instance, the collection edited by Meillassoux 1971 and the study by Curtin 1975 (see pp.

Migrant (wage-) labour, the other variant of 'articulation', appeared as well, but mainly after the colonial conquest, although the 19th-century slave trade, directed mainly at centres of cash crop production in plantations, could be seen in some ways as a precedent of colonial labour migration.[15]

South-Central Africa, where the region discussed in this study is located, is widely seen as the classic case of migrant labour economies. Here, pre-capitalist relations of production seem to have been carried over directly into wage-labour in mines and towns, reducing large tracts of land to subsistence-producing workforce reservoirs for the capitalist sector.[16] Since the late 1970s, however, a number of important studies have appeared that have revealed a forgotten aspect of rural history in that part of the continent: the rise and subsequent fall of an African peasantry in the early colonial period.[17] The authors argue that after the colonial conquest rural dwellers raised their marketable surplus so rapidly that they could supply a substantial share of urban food markets. Only political intervention, mostly assumed to have begun around the Great Depression of the 1930s, spurred on by white settlers' interests, was able to reduce them to subsistence-level and seal their fate as migrant workers.

Terence Ranger, in a contemporary review article on the first collection of these studies, outlined an agenda for historical research on 'peasantisation' in South-Central Africa which seems still valid and inspired much of the work on this book.[18] The first question he raised there was that of chronology: Did the history of peasant market production in the Southern African mining and settler economies really come to an end after the 1930s, and, even more importantly, did it really begin only with the onset of formal colonial rule ? Secondly, there was a call for greater attention to the local (as opposed to the global) dynamics of market integration and agricultural change, without glorifying these. The 'African response' can only be fully understood if, thirdly, 'the' peasantry is not seen as a homogenous entity, but with sufficient consideration of social divisions and struggles within local 'communities', which tie in with external contradictions. If, finally, 'peasantisation' is acknowledged to be a result of multiple social interaction, the question of 'peasant consciousness' must arise: How do the various groups of producers, and indeed the other social actors, see themselves, how do

---

197ff). The decentralized, 'proto-peasant' form of pre-colonial market production in many societies along the Guinea Coast found special consideration in Northrup 1978.

[15] See Meillassoux 1975 (second part); Lovejoy 1983: 159ff, 220ff; for the East African Coast see Cooper 1977.

[16] See for example Wolpe 1972

[17] See Bundy 1979; Beinart 1982; Ranger 1985; and various contributions in Palmer and Parsons (eds.) 1977; Beinart, Delius and Trapido (eds.) 1986.

A 2 : *Choosing a perspective* 13

they motivate and justify their actions and interactions ? More specifically, this is the question of the forms of consciousness under which producers of the region effectively tried to negotiate the terms of their incorporation into the pre-colonial world market.

This last question, I would add, leads to a further one, namely how these diverse forms of consciousness were moulded into discourses and institutions that could frame the interactions (or struggles) of these actors, e.g. the terms of exchanging material goods and resources, be it as commodities through markets or otherwise.[19]

I see my study to a considerable extent as an attempt to take up this agenda for the particular region of the Upper Zambezi and Kasai. In the rest of this chapter, I will look somewhat more closely at the background of debates each of these questions draws upon, and specify their importance in the construction of this book.

On the chronology: Case histories of pre-colonial Central Africa

Despite Ranger's call for more research on the early beginnings of 'peasantization', studies on the pre-colonial economic history of peoples in the interior of that part of the continent which is in anglophone contexts conventionally called 'Central Africa', are still rare and selective in their focus.[20] This macro-region has, since the rise of classic social anthropology, had a reputation of providing textbook examples of segmentary lineage societies with weak political centralization.[21] Precisely in response to these findings, historians who had a primary interest in the question of pre-colonial class and state formation produced a number of excellent works on the Central African interior. At first, they concentrated on the history of the 'kingdoms of the savannah', i.e. on early centralizing polities such as Luba, Nuclear Lunda, Bulozi or the Mbundu states.[22] With few exceptions,[23] the history of societies where

---

18 Ranger 1978
19 For this institutional or systemic axis of thought, I obtained particular inspiration from Georg Elwert.
20 For an overview of this literature for Africa as a whole see references in Isaacman 1990: 23ff
21 Fortes and Evans-Pritchard (eds.) 1940; see also Middleton and Tait (eds.) 1958; Kuper 1983: 137ff
22 See the classics by Vansina 1966; Birmingham 1966 and Heintze 1989 [on the Mbundu]; de Heusch 1972 and Reefe 1981 [Luba]; also Roberts 1973 [Bemba]; Miller 1976 [Mbundu]; Vellut 1972 and Hoover 1978 [Nuclear Lunda]; Mainga 1972 and Clarence-Smith 1979c [Bulozi].
23 E.g. Delgado 1940, Childs 1949 [Ovimbundu Highlands]; Clay 1945 [on the Nkoya, southeastern neighbours of the region under study]

the development of social differentiation and political superstructures was slower came to the fore only in the 1970s; but the question of the conditions (or constraints) of political authority and ethnic realignment mostly continued to predominate.[24] This focus on political institutions in many of the most important studies on the Central African interior meant that social and economic aspects, in varying depth, were dealt with mainly in relation to their implications for political history. Nevertheless, they contain valuable material and conclusions for the early history of market integration, because of the contemporary debate on the economic basis of power in pre-colonial Africa (see below). What I have said also applies to Robert Papstein's study of the Luvale, so far the only major work on the pre-colonial history of the Upper Zambezi and Kasai itself, a region with a remarkably slow pace of state formation.[25]

As indicated above, economic and ecological history remained something of a subsidiary theme in research on pre-colonial Central Africa. It began to receive attention only after the late 1960s, parallel to an increasing interest in 'development'. First, brief general overviews appeared,[26] followed more recently by more comprehensive ones for major parts of the subcontinent.[27] Detailed regional case studies on specific societies exist, for instance, for the peoples east of the Upper Luapula and Middle Zambezi,[28] the inhabitants of the Ovimbundu plateau,[29] the central Zaire basin,[30] and the region around Lake Victora.[31] Most of these studies focus on the development of exchange, with many of the groups concerned specializing in trade, and on indigenous forms of appropriating nature, while there is little material on pre-colonial 'proto-peasant' market production, comparable with or even

---

[24] The question of political development also seems to be the deeper concern in the impressive new *magnum opus* of Vansina (1990) on the central Zaire Basin, or, for instance, in Bhila 1982 [on the Shona], despite rich material on economic history. For less centralized peoples immediately neighbouring the Upper Zambezi and Kasai see especially Kodi 1976 [Pende]; Vansina 1978 [Kuba]; Yoder 1992 [Kanyok]; Schecter 1976 [Lunda-Ndembu]; van Binsbergen 1992 [Nkoya]; and some remarks in Jaeger 1981: 46-68 [Kaonde].

[25] Papstein 1978; his main source, the oral 'History of the Luvale and their Chieftainship' by Moses Sangambo has been published separately (1979^1; 1985^2). Similar oral history projects for the Chokwe, Luchazi and Mbunda are currently being prepared by R. Papstein and G. Kubik (personal communication).

[26] Vansina 1962, 1979 and 1990 (ch. 7); Gray and Birmingham (eds.) 1970; Sundstrøm 1974; Roberts 1970 and 1976; Chrtien 1983.

[27] Notably Miller 1988 (on West-Central Africa) and Koponen 1988 (on what is now mainland Tanzania).

[28] Most importantly Alpers 1975; see also contributions by Roberts, St. John 1970 and Sutherland-Harris in Gray and Birmingham (eds.) 1970.

[29] Heywood 1984 and 1985; Madeira-Santos 1986 (introduction); Soremekun 1977.

[30] Harms 1979, 1981 and 1987 [Bobangi]

[31] Hartwig 1976; Cohen 1983

related to the peoples of the Upper Zambezi and Kasai, except on the Nuclear Lunda,[32] the Kuba peoples,[33] the Lozi-Kololo,[34] and populations nearer to the coast.[35] Only three smaller studies exist, finally, on the beginnings of market production among the peoples dealt with in this book.[36]

Nevertheless, not just long-distance trade, but also production for that trade was widespread even in remote parts of Central Africa long before the colonial conquest (which was completed only in the first decade of this century). As shown in the following part (B), the frontier of the world market, bringing multiple new influences and pressures, gradually moved after about 1500 from the Angolan coast towards the interior, and reached the area under study here sometime during the 18th century. I hope to show later why the cluster of peoples inhabiting this area was a rather remarkable case of early commodity production for external markets, not only of raw materials, but also of substantial quantities of foodstuffs. It was these developments which directly prepared the colonial and post-colonial market production mentioned in the opening chapter.

On the dynamics: Global economy and local development

In this book, however, I will not restrict myself to tracing the beginnings of commodity production in the region, but attempt to find explanations for this process. Since the 1950s, research of African economic and social history has been strongly influenced by a concern with 'development'. Different variants of modernization and world-system theory in the social sciences left a legacy of unilateral stress on 'external' factors. According to the theoretical and political viewpoint, either potential 'development' or actual 'underdevelopment' were seen as a result of the working of industrialized centres with their capital and power, especially under colonialism. But this debate also had its repercussions for historical research into the pre-colonial past. There were, on the one hand, attempts to project the origins of 'underdevelopment', notably as a result of the slave trade, back to the times of mercantile capitalism. For Africa, Walter Rodney's book is the

---

32 Vellut 1972; for the end of the period also Vellut 1977
33 Douglas 1963; see also Vansina 1978
34 Flint 1970; Hermitte 1974; van Hoorn 1977
35 For instance Isaacman 1972 [Mozambique]; Clarence-Smith 1979a [populations east of Moçamedes]; Mbwiliza 1991 [on the Makua in what is now North-Central Mozambique]; Bley 1992 [on the Giriama, in the hinterland of Mombasa].
36 Miller 1970 and 1974 (based on his Master's Thesis); Papstein 1978 in the final chapter of his Ph.D. Thesis (which is almost a study in itself); and Vellut 1979.

classical indictment.[37] He pointed to the massive loss of people, the main force of production, and emphasized the structural effects of the pre-colonial export economy: concentration on extractive technologies for export, destruction of productive domestic industries, dependence on imported goods, and disruption of internal trade networks - in other words, prevention of 'development' in terms of a societal division of labour geared to domestic needs.[38] The 'underdevelopment' hypothesis has subsequently been applied to a series of case studies on pre-colonial African economies. Outstanding examples for Central Africa are the studies by Edward Alpers and E.H. Bhila, who emphasized the emergence of pre-colonial market production but described basically the same negative effects.[39] Others singled out the second half of the last pre-colonial century, the 19th, as the time when capitalist expansion brought havoc to pre-colonial African societies.[40]

The 'externalist' concept, with its tendency to describe metropolitan capitalism as (under-) developing the peripheries, and to see the active forces of history as complex entities such as 'economic sectors' or 'modes of production', has invited far-reaching revisions in recent years. Without denying a general process of subordination of peripheral societies to metropolitan ones, the concrete form of this process is now widely seen as the result of a rather more complex history of interaction and struggles, involving a variety of social forces or actors. In this perspective, African producers by no means merely play the role of passive 'victims', but display much initiative and readiness to experiment, select and adopt innovations.[41] Their strategies can be seen not just as an adaptation to advancing outside markets, but as a continuous, sometimes successful, quest for better terms of exchange with them, while preserving as much autonomy as possible. The work of historians such as those mentioned in the previous section contributed much to this revision. My own study, presented in this book, has been strongly motivated by this concern for the extent to which the course of market integration was influenced by rural producers themselves. Examples to be inspected more closely range from the introduction of new, cassava-based cultivation systems to the continuous re-phrasing of 'legitimate claims' on foreign traders.

In recent years, remarkable pieces of research have been presented, particularly on West Africa, which demonstrate the indigenous

---

[37] Rodney 1973; the most important representative of 'underdevelopment' theories for Africa today is Samir Amin.
[38] See also Amin 1981: 33-38
[39] Alpers 1975; Bhila 1982
[40] E.g. Kjekshus 1977
[41] See Elwert 1981, 1992

innovativeness and adaptability of African producers in response to economic and ecological conditions, both with and without reach of outside markets and government intervention.[42] The potential of indigenous African production, especially agriculture, had already been the subject of the older 'vent for surplus' debate, initially among economists who assumed that the pre-contact economy had sufficient unused land and labour resources (and limited enough local demand) to respond quickly to new export opportunities as they arise.[43] This hypothesis gained additional support from 'africanist' historians,[44] implicitly also from the analysts of early colonial 'peasantisation' in South-Central Africa, who emphasized the entrepreneurial potential of African cultivators.[45]

Critics of such optimistic assumptions have made it clear, however, that such 'africanist' revisions must not push things to the opposite extreme. They have pointed to the lack of historical specification and the diversity of ecological, land and labour situations in Africa. In their view, in some parts (especially in semi-humid savannah environments or densely populated highlands) subsistence production was dangerously fragile and in addition often depended on extended systems of food trade, so that the adaptation to long-distance trade and the siphoning off of 'surplus' production by external market demand, as in the so-called 'cash crop revolution', could trigger serious famines.[46] Much of such criticisms was inspired by the 'ecology control' debate with Eastern Africa as its focus.[47] While some described major economic disasters as the costs of market integration and subsequent imposition of colonial rule, despite remarkable adaptations to it in local production systems,[48] others detected here indigenous limits to 'development' in the local economies. In this view, the widespread disasters and famines of the late pre-colonial period are seen in part as a symptom of vulnerability of indigenous systems of production.[49] The sufferings connected with market integration, at any rate, tend to appear in this perspective as a necessary purgatory on the way to brighter futures.

In the meantime, the 'development' paradigm has become increasingly problematic among historians and sociologists because of its strong

---

[42] E.g. Richards 1983 (with more references) and Richards 1985; contributions to *Africa*, 51, 2, 1981
[43] See Myint 1958
[44] E.g. Hopkins 1973
[45] See Palmer and Parsons 1977
[46] See for instance Tosh 1980
[47] Prompted by Kjekshus 1977
[48] E.g. Giblin 1986; Bley 1992
[49] E.g. Iliffe 1987

normative connotations. The time seems to have come for a more differentiated exploration of both indigenous African economies and the impact of foreign influence. The first and foremost requirement is a stronger acknowledgement of regional specifities and historical situations. Any regional case study which, like this one, seeks to understand the dynamics of productive change and market integration requires, secondly, analysis of the local social context.[50] Such research also allows for a better understanding of how the emerging global capitalism could 'take root' in pre-existing social formations rather than 'penetrating' them; how in fact the global economy was made up from this (and innumerable other) local economies. Areas as remote from, and at the same time intimately connected with, major market centres as the one studied in this book may offer particular insights in the 'localness' of world market development.

This takes up, in some respects, the basic question underlying the 'articulation' model, namely why older forms of production and reproduction were often not destroyed but remarkably persistent, going on to ask how these forms were restructured in the process and why they often even increased in importance in the new (undoubtedly dominant) context of global capitalism.[51] However, both the functionalist and structuralist dangers of the 'articulation' model must be avoided. Instead of trying to isolate structural entities such as 'indigenous' and 'capitalist' relations or logics which interact with each other in more or less predictable ways, a more open, actor-oriented view will be adopted in the following chapters. In this view, both 'indigenous' and 'exogenous' definitions of relationships are available to the variety of social groups[52] in the local arena and are made use of in changing, but not mutually exclusive, ways. Heterogeneous sets of relationships and meanings thus combine to structure the same interactions and struggles between the same social groups, according to particular local interests and historical conditions. In the course of the same process, these relationships and meanings are themselves subject to adaptation and change.

---

[50] Cf. Austen and Headrick 1983; Tosh 1980; a landmark in the debate on the social conditions of technological change in pre-colonial Africa has been Goody 1969. A particularly open model of the connections between 'decision-making' in society and appropriation of nature has been given by Harms (1987).

[51] See Elwert 1984: 387f; see also Geschiere and Raatgever 1985

[52] J.-P. Rey (1973), for example, has spoken of 'classes' as actors of conflicts and alliances both within and beyond pre-capitalist modes of production. I avoid the term 'class' here because it should in my opinion be reserved for social divisions which are unambiguously based on differential access to the means of production.

On social differentiation: Struggle and balance

Critical, 'externalist' statements on the impact of market integration in rural Africa often had a fairly idealized view of African pre-contact societies as their baseline. It was acknowledged that these societies may have had distinct social hierarchies, but for a long time it was widely denied that economic inequality was in any way constitutive of them. This assumption was particularly pervasive for Central and Eastern Africa, from which anthropologists had drawn textbook examples of largely acephalous 'segmentary lineage societies'. As far as economic relationships are concerned, reciprocity and redistribution within kin-groups, and a preference for investment in social cohesion rather than economic accumulation, have been seen as decisive features here. The market consequently appeared as a transformer or destroyer, for good or for evil, of earlier forms of group cohesion or solidarity.

These general assumptions have been subject to considerable debate among anthropologists themselves as well as among historians. Following the French school of marxist anthropology, since the 1960s there has been an increasing emphasis on economic inequality and incipient class formation within pre-colonial African societies and to what extent it subsequently paved the way for capitalist penetration. One central point raised in this debate has been the rise of ruling classes of 'nobles', 'chiefs' or 'kings', warlords and traders, combined with the question of their basis of power and revenues. Broadly speaking, an assumption of 'internal' accumulation based on the exploitation of labour (notably slaves) was countered by the hypothesis that state formation in Africa had to rely on the appropriation of external revenues through warfare, tribute and trade.[53] The latter would comfortably explain the rise of states in the late pre-colonial era of slave trade and world-market integration,[54] but there are too many other examples to generalize this hypothesis.[55] Nevertheless, it drew attention to another aspect of the distribution of wealth, that between populations of different areas as a consequence of long-distance trade, notably from the interior towards the coast, paralleled by an increasing differentiation among trading groups.[56] Another interesting question raised in this context is the extent to which pre-

---

[53] See the controversy over an 'Asiatic' or 'African' mode of production (e.g. Suret-Canale 1964; Coquéry-Vidrovitch 1969; Terray 1974).

[54] E.g. Vellut 1972, Miller 1973, Feierman 1974, Cohen 1983, Giblin 1986.

[55] The connection between long-distance trade, accumulation and state-formation has been also touched upon by the authors mentioned earlier in this chapter in footnotes 22 and 24, and by the contributors to the special issue of *Cahiers d'Etudes Africaines* vol. 77/78 (1980), no. 1-2

[56] E.g. Newbury 1971 and 1972 (discussing the effects of the widespread institution of credit trade in West Africa); Harding et al. 1992.

colonial forms and carriers of accumulation were carried over into colonial ones.[57]

As for the earlier societies, however, the exploitation of juniors by seniors was identified by Meillassoux, Rey and others as the central socio-economic contradiction in African 'lineage modes of production'.[58] Yet another focus of debate has been the character, importance and transformation of 'internal slavery' in Africa. While admitting that there were indigenous origins on which the expansion during and after the transatlantic slave trade could build, and that there was an enormous variety of forms of bondage for which this summary (and eurocentric) term is unsatisfactory, scholars tend to disagree over the economic importance of slave labour for pre-colonial market production and accumulation.[59]

These older discussions about socio-economic differentiation in pre-colonial African societies were echoed to some extent in the more recent 'peasant' debate.[60] There is now little doubt that in many of these societies strata of specialized agricultural producers, working mainly with their own labour, land and means of production, were in fact emerging long before the colonial conquest, although the multitude of social relations and paths of transformation involved still make it difficult to speak of 'peasants' and 'peasantization'.

A criterion repeatedly suggested is by marxist scholars to determine the onset of peasant production is whether economic investments were ultimately made to accumulate material wealth or to strengthen and enlarge the human network of followers ('wives', 'children', 'slaves') 'allies' and the like. A preference for social instead of material accumulation has been cited as an indigenous barrier to development.[61]

The core problem here is the role and status of a variety of claims on land and particularly labour originating from outside the producer's own group or 'household', but often amalgamated with it in various ways. Again, it turned out that many pre-colonial market producers owned or

---

[57] See for example Isaacman 1972 for a positive, and Clarence-Smith 1979a for a negative answer.

[58] E.g. Meillassoux 1960 and 1975 (second part); Rey 1971. For Southern Africa, the appropriation of juniors' labour through the circulation of cattle and wives has been emphasized by Guy 1987. How the juniors/elders relationship tied in with the emergence of long-distance trade has been examined by Terray 1971.

[59] Much of the answer depends, of course, also on the particular part of Africa in focus. Two poles of the debate are represented by Miers and Kopytoff (1977 (eds.)), who emphasize the social marginality, and Lovejoy (e.g. 1983 and 1986 (ed.)), who stresses economic exploitation. See also Meillassoux 1989, and for West-Central Africa Miller 1981.

[60] Cf. ch. A 1 and the first section of this chapter

were unfree labourers or 'slaves'.[62] In this way, the debate on pre-colonial peasantries in Africa contributed to a more general shift in focus in the 'peasant' debate: an increasing awareness of social and economic contradictions within 'the' peasantry, in Africa and elsewhere, and of the ways they were related to older patterns of differentiation as well as to the contradictions in the relations with other sectors of the widening society.[63] This awareness received much additional stimulus from the 'household' debate, which brought the relationship between men and women into focus, including within 'peasant households'. The seminal hypothesis was that female cultivators in Africa lost much of their former position in the process of agricultural market production and were reduced to subsistence work in both production and reproduction, forming so to speak the 'underside of development'.[64] Relatively little work has been done as yet, however, to pursue this aspect of gender relations back into the pre-colonial period of Central Africa.[65]

All these aspects and levels of social differentiation will have to be considered in the subsequent study. As for other parts of Central Africa, most detailed anthropological fieldwork attempting to reconstruct indigenous society and to trace social change around the Upper Zambezi and Kasai was done in the 1950s, published in a number of most impressive classics in social anthropology.[66] Researchers followed mainstream thinking of their time when they presented kinship as the structural core of society, but can in other regards still stimulate research today. Some of these works became most relevant for own research. One was Victor Turner's, who studied the Lunda-Ndembu, closely related to the Southern Lunda on the Upper Zambezi, when he began his scholarship at the Rhodes-Livingstone-Institute. He paid close attention to the fragility of authority and to mechanisms of conflict resolution.[67] There was much less attention, however, to the effects of wider economic integration on these internal social relations, or only for the colonial

---

[61] Guy 1987; Koponen 1988; see also Austen and Headrick 1983; Austen 1987

[62] Isaacman 1990: 23ff

[63] See for instance Cooper 1980; Guy 1987.

[64] For the Northwestern Province of what is now Zambia, but only beginning with the colonial period, see Crehan 1984; Spring and Hansen 1985.

[65] Notable exceptions are the volume edited by Robertson and Klein (eds.) 1983, and especially the new book by Marcia Wright on forms of bondage among women in late pre-colonial Central Africa (1993). Jeff Guy has declared the appropriation of the labour of wives and their children to be the decisive contradiction in pre-colonial Southern African societies (1987).

[66] Central Africa in general, and what was then Northern Rhodesia with its excellent research institutions in particular (notably the Rhodes-Livingstone-Institute), has provided much evidence for this (see van Donge 1985).

[67] Turner 1957

period.[68] This also applies to the other anthropological classic on an area adjacent (and in many ways comparable) to the Upper Zambezi and Kasai, namely Mary Douglas' study on the Lele.[69] Here she even found, in the perspective of the 1960s, a lack of both authority and initiative to be indigenous obstacles for 'development'.

One might have assumed that at least anthropological work on the peoples in the focus of this book would have been forced by evidence to give more prominence to the existence and effects of strong pre-colonial market connections. Yet important scholars studying the Chokwe, while emphasizing their enormous 'assimilative capacities' (Redinha), largely skipped these earlier experiences, and saw the Angolan Chokwe of the 1930s to 60s in a difficult process of transition from and disintegration of 'traditional society', while one century earlier they had been described as 'terribly keen' traders and market producers.[70] The only anthropologist of the late colonial period who systematically integrated this pre-colonial market experience into his social analysis was another (associate) fellow of the Rhodes-Livingstone Institute, Charles M.N. White. He was by background a colonial officer who did the most extensive fieldwork and produced a large number of valuable ethnographic publications on what he called the Luvale or Balovale peoples of the (at that time) Northern Rhodesian part of the Upper Zambezi. He came to conclusions that were remarkably different from the assumptions cited above; his concern was to demonstrate, in contrast to the Turners' findings, that the 'unauthoritarian, competitive and egalitarian nature of society' in 'his' area had allowed for a quick and smooth adoption of productive innovations and market orientation, in other words 'development', since the pre-colonial period.[71]

Any new attempt to reconstruct pre-colonial society and its transformation around the Upper Zambezi and Kasai must appreciate and reconsider these earlier assumptions and findings. It seems a priority, however, to overcome the structuralist bias involved in much of this impressive body of research. In this book, an attempt is made to analyse social relationships, like those between men and women, chiefs and commoners, owners and slaves, as more open and in need of continuous confirmation or re-negotiation among the parties involved, both local and 'external'. Not an intrinsic structure or logic of institutions, but various forms of struggle over resources and power will be seen as the moving

---

[68] Only one article on this problem appeared at the time (Turner and Turner 1955). A broad examination of the long-term effects of 'external exchange' on the 'kinship system' in Central Africa has been presented by Ekholm 1977.

[69] Douglas 1963

[70] Baumann 1935; Redinha 1966; Livingstone 1963: 249 [1855]

factor in the historical process.[72] Struggles presuppose inequality between the parties, and the pre-colonial society in this region was undoubtedly fractured not only by 'vertical' segmentation, but also by emerging 'horizontal' or class divisions in several dimensions. Nevertheless, as the analysis will show, social differentiation in the 19th century seems to have been remarkably unstable, allowing for considerable individual mobility on the one hand, and for ubiquitous threats of conflict and violence on the other. Yet, even if a relative balance in social relations appears in certain respects and periods, it has to be examined as the result of interaction rather than as an expression of structure. Such an understanding of social relations also creates, in my opinion, the basis for a fruitful synthesis between social science and history, between systematic and diachronic perspectives on 'modernization' in pre-colonial Africa and elsewhere.

On the 'embeddedness': Constructing markets in Africa

If social interaction and struggle are seen here as the moving factor in local history, this certainly does not mean that the sociological study of 'structure' as opposed to 'action' can be dispensed with altogether. Interaction and strategies by social actors not only challenge and gradually transform the distribution of resources and the structure of relationships but are at the same time clearly shaped by pre-existing patterns.[73] This also applies to the level of meanings, such as morality, discourse and identity, which appear in a variety of societal institutions and which structure both social action and as material conditions. At the same time, however, meanings also constitute resources which become objects of struggle and negotiation in the course of which they undergo change. In other words, the consciousness of social groups influences the historical process, and new forms emerge and become institutionalized as a result of interaction itself.

The institutional patterns to be addressed in any study of the expansion of market production are clearly those governing the transfer of resources and goods between different groups of producers and traders. A classic in this respect is the volume edited by Bohannan and Dalton on *Markets in Africa* in 1962. In its attempt to classify different forms or logics of exchange as different stages of market development, it draws very much

---

71 White 1961a: xviii; see also the quotations in ch. A 1. See the (incomplete) list of his publications in the bibliography.

72 See, for another area adjacent to the Upper Zambezi and for the post-colonial situation, the excellent analysis of intra-village relations by Kate Crehan (1986).

73 This 'dialectic' view of the connection between structure and action follows the line of Giddens' Theory of Structuration (1984).

on Karl Polanyi's 'substantive school' in economic history and anthropology, but in a more structural than historical way. Polanyi and his students had identified different forms of 'institutedness' or 'embeddedness' of exchange processes.[74] Modern types of transaction governed by price-setting markets were distinguished from processes of centralization and redistribution (in 'early empires'), and reciprocal exchanges of gifts (in 'archaic', i.e. stateless societies). For the concept of reciprocity they drew heavily on much earlier studies by Richard Thurnwald and Bronislaw Malinowski, and on the famous essay by Marcel Mauss.[75] Following the 'substantive school', 'trade', 'exchange', or 'money' came to be seen as universal phenomena with, however, very different functions in different societies.[76]

Historical studies on pre-colonial Central Africa have taken up elements of the 'substantive' concept,[77] mostly in its 'system theory' version which distinguished different, coexisting 'spheres of exchange', such as 'subsistence', 'prestige', and 'market-oriented'.[78] This distinction helped to accommodate the fact that in historical reality different forms of 'institutedness' or 'embeddedness' of exchange usually coexist and even mix with each other. When applied to pre-colonial Africa, it underlined the fact that a wide array of exchange activities, involving both local and long-distance, food and non-food products, had been regularly going on for a long time. 'Subsistence', then, no longer appeared as the trade mark of 'traditional society', but as something complementing market activities. Subsequently, French marxist anthropologists went even further in rejecting the evolutionist implications in the 'substantive' model, with the hypostased 'market' at its apogee. They regarded the spread of market institutions and utilitarian rationality not as a more or less automatic process, but as a product of particular, and area-specific, historical circumstances. The explanation for such structural constellations was sought mainly in the allocation and distribution of productive resources ('relations of production'); the 'substantive' school was criticized for its

---

[74] See Polanyi 1957
[75] Both Mauss (1924) and Malinowski (1926) referred to earlier work on structures of reciprocity by Thurnwald (summarized in his textbook of 1936). The concept of reciprocity has subsequently been further refined and differentiated by Sahlins (1974); see also Servet's study on 'archaic trade' (1982).
[76] See for example the recent collection edited by Bloch and Parry 1989.
[77] See, for instance, Gray and Birmingham (eds.) 1970; Sundstrøm 1974; Hermitte 1974.
[78] See, for instance, Bohannan 1959 and some contributions to Bohannan and Dalton (eds.) 1962. Another structural distinction has been introduced recently by Bloch and Parry 1989 (introduction), between more long-term exchanges serving mainly social reproduction, and more short-term ones ensuring material life.

concentration on the circulation of products through trade, 'gifts' and the like.[79]

The rules of exchange as classified by Polanyi and his followers, however, are by no means irrelevant for material relations of production. Polanyi himself had explicitly included the circulation of resources such as labour and land in his model. Neither do the institutions of exchange simply mirror these material relations. The relationship between 'circulation' and 'production'/'reproduction' is more complex than marxist scholars have tended to assume. For instance, the particular material processes involved in the transfer of goods require 'relations of exchange', in analogy with relations of production, which provide an infrastructure of information, means of transport, capital (credit), labour, safety, and last but not least contract security. These cannot be secured within the realm of economic interest alone - Durkheim has spoken in this regard of the 'non-contractual element of contract'.[80] The particular ways in which scarce goods are distributed, their prices determined and their handing-over assured are necessary, not contingent, aspects of the functioning of any society. In this field, economic and social structures are always interlinked. At the same time, bargaining on the terms of exchange can be seen as a medium through which a variety of relationships and conflicts between different members of that society are negotiated.

This is less visible, but not less true, where apparently anonymous market relations are dominant; 'real markets' are certainly as socially 'embedded' as other forms of exchange.[81] The 'embeddedness' is particularly evident, however, in less stratified pre-capitalist societies, e.g. in Africa, where social relations depended on continual confirmation by material expressions of personal respect.[82] Here, where claims on other people's products and labour did not necessarily depend on exclusive rights over means of production, a 'relative autonomy of exchange relations alongside relations of production' should be acknowledged.[83] The morality of credit, the choice of currencies, and the rules of bargaining prices were important institutional aspects of relations

---

[79] E.g. Dupré and Rey 1973; special issue of *Cahiers d'Etudes Africaines* vol. 77/78 (1980), no. 1-2
[80] Durkheim 1893: 7th chapter (see ch. E 4)
[81] Elwert 1987, 1991
[82] See J. Miller's interesting essay on 'ethno-political economics' (1988: 42ff).
[83] Raatgever 1985: 324

between exchange partners in pre-colonial Africa which were, at the same time, 'embedded' in a variety of other societal relations and practices.[84]

Particularly relevant for the purpose of this study is the question of which significance older indigenous rules and institutions of exchange retained or gained in the context of market integration, and how they eventually changed under the impact of the latter. Often enough indigenous concepts clashed with the ideas of foreigners acting as agents of the world market; on closer inspection, however, it becomes clear that around the Upper Zambezi and Kasai norms of reciprocity (which Polanyi had attributed to 'archaic' societies) and free haggling of prices (normally associated with markets) did not just coexist, as in a transitory state, but overlapped and adapted to each other considerably. Eventually, a fairly durable symbiosis of heterogenous moralities of exchange and modes of negotiation developed over most of the 19th century.

At this point, a structuralist view of exchange relations reaches its limits. The interaction between heterogenous institutional structures can be grasped more easily if these are seen as different normative concepts that are invoked, or different languages that can be used, by the same groups of emerging market producers and traders in different situations, according to need and opportunity. But also implicit in this view is a danger of voluntarism, of projecting utilitarian or 'post-modern' attitudes towards ideology onto pre-colonial market producers in Central Africa . Which set of norms was 'available' to which social actors in which situation was not entirely open to choice. Moreover, beyond the struggles of interest, there was a need to establish some sort of agreement between differing moralities of exchange. The various aspects of 'infrastructure' for commodity transactions, mentioned above as 'relations of exchange', were particularly brittle in pre-colonial Central Africa. The safety of foreign travellers and the necessary trust in contracts were continuously threatened by collapse into violence. More generally, any increase in commodification or 'venality' puts pressure on social actors to adapt their morality of exchange to new challenges within their society.[85]

Consequently, it seems that the institutional framework of market relations was continuously on the agenda of negotiations between pre-colonial exchange partners, at least implicitly. These negotiations seem to have been to some extent successful in this region, not least because both local and market exchanges built on a morality that combined contract and personal relationships in a very similar way. Otherwise, the construction

---

[84] On the social implications of credit see, for instance, Douglas 1963, Newbury 1972, Trenk 1991; on currencies see Vellut 1972 and Martin 1986; on price formation Newbury 1971; for all these (and other) aspects see Sundstrøm 1974.
[85] Elwert 1987

of this section of the pre-colonial world market society would presumably not have advanced as rapidly as it did in the region.

On the structure of the book

The threads taken up in this overview of relevant scientific discussions provide so to speak the warp into which the weft of empirical data will be woven to form the fabric of the following case study. The structure of the study as a whole therefore follows roughly that of the overview given in this chapter.

The next part (B) is a chronological overview of the history of market integration in the area as a process of interaction between various 'market forces', acting from outside the region, and the inhabitants of the region, mainly as producers.

The subsequent parts aim to explain systematically the factors behind the course of events outlined so far. In part C, the the basic material preconditions of commodity production are examined, notably the allocation of natural resources and labour. A long pre-history of indigenous productive innovation and change is traced for the period before the establishment of market relations. Subsequently, the benefits and costs of market integration for the regional economy are discussed, particularly with regard to the relationship with nature and to the satisfaction of food and other essential needs. In this regard, also the significance of imported goods comes under scrutiny, which turns out to be much less physical than symbolical. It becomes clear that changes in production and reproduction cannot be explained solely by an economic logic of adaptation to relative material scarcities, be they indigenous or induced, but are deeply embedded in societal relations of power and appropriation.

This leads into part D, which concentrates on the differences among 'the' inhabitants of the region. Men and women, seniors and juniors, free people and slaves, chiefs, traders and other commoners are looked at in their 'multiplex' relationships and struggles. The question is why changes in production and opportunities to obtain imported goods were so readily taken up by certain groups, and how this in turn changed social relations within the region.

In the last part, E, this kind of social analysis is extended to the relations between different strata of residents and the variety of foreign traders ('foreign' being defined here as 'extra-regional', unless otherwise stated), i.e. to the ways in which the crucial link between regional production and the world market was established and maintained. As in the previous part, however, social structure is approached here through an analysis of processes of interaction and negotiation. In this part, there is a particular focus on the question of how the institutions and meanings of market exchange were constructed between the different categories of actors. As far as they were 'foreigners' and 'residents', the focus is on the extent to which these institutions and meanings were owed to indigenous patterns of exchange or to the pressures of wider market forces. As far as the actors were socially stratified, for instance as 'producers' and 'traders', the question is what ideologies and discourses developed in response to changing relations of power and appropriation. Through this analysis, it is hoped, a better understanding of peasant-market and peasant-state relations during the subsequent, colonial and post-colonial, periods can be reached.

Each of these systematic parts ends with some concluding remarks, addressing some of the more general questions and debates raised in this chapter. In an epilogue (part F), the fate of pre-colonial developments in the region after the colonial conquest will be considered.

A 3   Processing the material: Disparate snapshots and their synthesis

What has been said so far makes it plain that this study is bound to combine heterogenous approaches, not only with regard to disciplines and debates, but also to the material and methods required to reach a better understanding of people in a distant region and time. At this point, therefore, some remarks are due on the pieces of evidence that were used and on the ways in which they were collected and reassembled to make up the mosaic of this study. As with any empirical work, the task of delimiting the 'unit of study' has to be addressed first, and as so often, it turns out to be a difficult one.

A 3.1   The unit of study

The people

In this book, I will often use the sowewhat clumsy paraphrase 'the peoples around the Upper Zambezi and Kasai' to avoid an even more clumsy enumeration of ethnic names currently in use among the inhabitants of that area: Chokwe, Luvale, Southern Lunda, Luchazi Mbunda and Mbwela. It is this cluster of peoples which is in the focus of my interest, even if in the paraphrase my unit of study appears to be defined in territorial and not in ethnic terms.

According to McCulloch's survey in the late 1940s, the population numbers of the groups mentioned, spread over what was then Angola, Northern Rhodesia and the Belgian Congo, were as follows:[1]

---

[1] Given an abnormally low reproduction rate, these figures are probably not much higher than at the end of the pre-colonial era (when the end of the slave trade stopped the continuous absorption of people from the east, especially among the Chokwe).

Table 1: Approximate population of the Upper Zambezi and Kasai by ethnic group (1940s)

Chokwe:	c. 600,000
Luvale:	c. 90,000
Southern Lunda:	c. 63,000
Luchazi:	c. 60,000
Mbunda:	c. 24,000
Total:	c. 837, 000

Source: McCulloch 1951: 7, 30, 54/55

In this book, the territorial criterion 'around the Upper Zambezi and Kasai' is not used for convenience alone. As will be seen further below, the peoples just mentioned draw much of their identity from the particular kind of landscape they share and work on. It is a semi-humid savannah-woodland mosaic composed of remarkably similar ecological elements, and is structured by the two river systems just mentioned.

In the 19th century, when today's ethnic identities in this region were already in the making, outside observers from various sides came to see, for good reasons, more similarities than differences between these groups. By the middle of the last century, for example, the Ovimbundu in the Angolan highlands plateau used to call the entire range of peoples to their east and southeast (beyond the Kwanza river), with whom they conducted regular trade, 'Ngangela'.[2] Portuguese-speaking traders like Silva Porto took over this term and spoke of the *Ganguela* 'people' or 'race', among whom they distinguished different 'tribes' or 'nations'.[3] The original meaning of this Umbundu term was probably simply 'dawn', i.e. 'east',[4] but it included a derogative idea of these peoples' cultural features. Comparing them with what he regarded as a higher level of cultural and political development among the Ovimbundu, Silva Porto adopted its negative connotation along with the term. In 1853, he summarized the specifics of 'the *Ganguela* people' as follows:

> 'They are robust and of a good appearance, and, in general, circumcised; they are arrogant, treacherous, capricious and perverse, albeit weak, because all these defects are readily seen in their faces where the instinct of badness is marked; they are given to drunkenness in all its vigour, and live therefore in

---

2 Magyar 1859: 259; cf. Madeira Santos 1986: 81, fn.3 and 353, fn.39; Bontinck 1974: 18/19; according to Figueira (1938: 331ff), this term was equally applied by Mbangala middlemen to the peoples to their east.
3 Silva Porto 1986: 315ff (diary of the journey to Bulozi in 1847/48)

continuous disorders and arson among neighbouring villages, which are composed of [only] four or five houses... In superstitions they exceed all other peoples, and they are independent. They are given to hunting, fishing, agriculture and to the traffic in beeswax...'[5]

The subsequent analysis will have to decode this devastating picture by exploring the concrete experiences and interests behind it. At this point, some more remarks on the classification problem are in order. Originally, the *Ganguela (grande)* may have included even people as far off as Katanga, Bulozi or the middle Kasai, [6] but with improved knowledge, the scope of the term was increasingly narrowed. The western or 'small' *Ganguela (pequena)* have been defined by 20th century ethnographers as comprising only the Luchazi and Mbunda-Ambwela, as well as a variety of smaller groups nearer to the Kwanza and to Ovimbundu influence who remain largely outside the scope of this study, such as the Nyemba, Lwimbi, Mbandi and Nkhankala or Ngangela in a narrow sense.[7] The Luvale (Lwena) were often, the Chokwe sometimes included in this category.[8] Otherwise, these two have been grouped together with various Lunda groups[9] and may have been what the Ovimbundu themselves sometimes called 'eastern Ngangela'.[10]

Other attempts to fit the ethnic groups of this region into one category came with the onset of colonial rule. In Bulozi, and among British officials operating from that end, the Mbunda, Luchazi, Luvale and Chokwe, who immigrated in increasing numbers from Angola into their area of control, were summarily called *Mawiko*, people from the West.[11] Later, after the consolidation of colonial territoriality, this new grid provided the categories of common classification. C.M.N. White, who undertook extensive research in which he emphasized the common characteristics and history of these peoples, classed them together as 'Balovale' peoples, using the colonial name of the northwesternmost district of what was then Northern Rhodesia.[12] At the same time, White suggested through this term a hegemony of the Luvale (*Balovale*) in this area, which he emphasized even more strongly in his later works where

---

4 Kubik 1981: 1 (citing Pearson 1977: 11)
5 Silva Porto 1938: 70
6 Figueira 1938: 331f
7 Diniz 1918, chapter XVI; McCulloch 1951: 52; Kubik 1981: 1. - Only in this narrow sense will the term Ngangela be used in the following text; '*Ganguela*' (in italics) will represent instead the less specific perspective of Portuguese and Ovimbundu travellers on the peoples to their east.
8 Mendes Corrêa 1943 and 1916; Fonseca Cardoso 1919
9 E.g. Diniz 1918: chapter III; Redinha 1966
10 Schönberg-Lothholz 1960: 112 and fn.4
11 Gluckman 1941; interview Mr.Orr-Ewing, Nov.1987
12 White 1959 and 1949

he spoke of 'Luvale peoples'. José Redinha, his Portuguese counterpart working from the Angolan end, called his unit of study 'peoples of northeastern Angola', also suggesting a cultural hegemony of one particular group, in this case the Chokwe.

Others, finally, approached the area from the viewpoint of the ancient Lunda empire in what was then the Belgian Congo. They included the cluster of groups in the area (including Chokwe, Minungu, Lwena (Luvale), Luchazi, Lwimbi and Mbunda) simply into 'Lunda', or called it 'Southern Lunda and related peoples' (McCulloch).[13] The term 'Southern Lunda' was used as a shorthand here for several groups (mainly Akosa, Ndembu and Lunda of Ishinde) that were in the past politically dependent on, but culturally distinct from, the 'Northern' (Nuclear) Lunda. In this study, I will also speak of 'Southern Lunda', for lack of a more convenient alternative, although my emphasis will be less on the Ndembu and more on the Lunda of Ishinde near to the Zambezi, and on some chieftainships between the Zambezi headwaters and the Kasai bend which were gradually absorbed or pushed back by expanding Luvale and Chokwe.[14]

The observers cited so far all tried more or less to reconcile the (colonial) discourse of ethnicity with the category of territory or region. The most important justification for classing the peoples in this region of Central Africa into one research unit, however, is the fact that intra-regional, trans-ethnic linkages represent an important aspect in the identity of the researched themselves.[15] Among the inhabitants of this region, both the homogenous cultural background and high spatial mobility meant that members of different ethnic affiliation were in constant touch with each other. Today, initiation ceremonies, marriages, friendship, productive cooperation or joint business ventures very frequently cross ethnic boundaries; almost every child can communicate in at least two of the local languages. There are many indications that the same was true in the pre-colonial period. Although ethnic conflicts have sometimes been fierce during the present century, here perhaps more than elsewhere ethnicity appears here as an ideology of struggles for scarce resources and political realignment, like competition between rival brothers, rather than as an expression of real structural difference or

---

[13] Baumann 1935; Murdock 1967: 9; McCulloch 1951.
[14] McCulloch 1951: 5f; his 'Northern Lunda' have also been transcribed as 'Ruund' by Hoover (1978), but in the following text they will be called 'Nuclear Lunda', because this term is more widely known and also expresses better the dynamic relationship between nuclear and peripheral Lunda polities.
[15] See van Binsbergen 1985

distinction.[16] Significantly, such clashes take place mainly on public occasions and mainly among men. Privately, the most militant Lunda or Luvale partisans can be found drinking together, borrowing each other's guns, as in-laws etc.

For members of different ethnic groups within the region it is thus a pervasive everyday experience that they share important cultural characteristics and that real differences start only when they move beyond this common cultural environment. There are, however, few explicit expressions of this feeling akin. In contrast to the most westerly Ngangela peoples, who proudly accepted this Ovimbundu denomination and scorned their eastern neighbours as *mbwela*, the peoples of the Upper Zambezi and Kasai rejected the term Ngangela as derogatory.[17] The single most conscious expression of common, inter-ethnic identity, by which members of these peoples, including women, distinguish themselves from outsiders, is probably *mukanda*, the circumcision ritual for boys.[18] It is no accident, and corresponds to my own experiences from Kabompo and Zambezi, that the author of the most detailed description of *mukanda* found in his research area in eastern Angola in 1965

> 'such a degree of ethnic, linguistic and cultural mixing that it appears more appropriate to me to speak of a **regional culture** with a certain range of variation, often along ethnic lines, than of the cultures of individual ethnic groups.'[19]

The structural closeness between the peoples of the Upper Zambezi and Kasai will become visible in the course of the following analysis.[20] In short, a range of economic, social and cultural characteristics developed in three historical stages, which are common to all the groups mentioned. The oldest was the immigration of early Bantu peoples, amalgamating to some extent pre-Bantu *Khoisan* populations. It resulted, between about 100 and 500 A.D., in a cluster of closely related languages,[21] in an economy based on gathering, grain cultivation and small livestock, a matrilineally-based descent system, similar expressions of religious belief

---

[16] Cf. Papstein 1989; a more detailed discussion of alleged **economic** differences between ethnic groups in the region is found in chapter C.2.
[17] Kubik 1971: 49/50; McCulloch 1951: 52; on the Upper Zambezi, I found the term *Ngangela* used only for a vast, agriculturally sterile and uninhabited plain west of the Zambezi, by the Luvale.
[18] See Papstein 1978: 179 and fn.30
[19] Kubik 1971: 45 (his emphasis)
[20] For details see the respective chapters further below.
[21] Papstein 1978: 70/71; he speaks of a 'Congo-Zambezi-Watershed group'; according to Guthrie's revised classification, this group is located in the centre of Bantu Zone K (Hoover 1978, map 5).

(e.g.the *makishi* masks), and in a superstructure of clans which significantly crosscuts the present ethnic divisions.

The second stage or layer is associated with the immigration of political dissidents and vassals from Nuclear Lunda between about 1500 and 1750, who imposed themselves as chiefs on the existing population (at least among the Luvale, Chokwe and Southern Lunda). They introduced more or less successfully a number of productive, social and political innovations, notably cassava cultivation, new cross-kinship initiation rituals (*mukanda, mungongi*), and powerful symbols of chieftainship.[22] The third layer, finally, was the history of world market integration itself, which increased trade, travel and migrations, and hence the mixture of population, in a region where spatial mobility has always been high.

Discussing the problem of whether to define the unit of study in ethnic terms, van Binsbergen has concluded that any meaningful anthropological (or historical) analysis must emphasize relationships rather than define boundaries.[23] The classifications of the group of peoples under study I have presented so far have underlined not only similarities and linkages among them, but also significant differences vis-a-vis their neighbours. Views from the outside had as their starting points three adjacent centres of pre-colonial state formation and social stratification: the Ovimbundu plateau, the Nuclear Lunda empire, and the Lozi state (from where colonial rule over 'Balovale', today Zambezi and Kabompo, was established). These views defined the peoples of the Upper Zambezi and Kasai as 'non-Ovimbundu', 'non-(Nuclear) Lunda' and 'non-Lozi'. Historically, however, such views resulted precisely from the establishment of relations crossing these divisions. It remains to be seen why, as far as the subject of this study is concerned, the peoples **within** this triangle were homogenous enough to be regarded, if not as a unit, then as a separate entity.

Consequently, one may speak of a regional society for this region in the pre-colonial period, without assuming, however, that this society could be regarded as a world of its own.

---

[22] The introduction of *mukanda*, the boys' circumcision ritual, by these immigrant chiefs is asserted by Papstein (1978: 174ff); this ritual is found, however, even among *Ngangela* peoples not affected by immigrants from Ruund.

[23] van Binsbergen 1985

The region

Due to the considerable mobility of its members, the location of this regional society can not be determined by fixed boundaries. Hence, the territory covered by the following study somewhat changed over time. At the beginning of the period under research, it included the original settlement nuclei of the Chokwe, Luvale, Southern Lunda, Luchazi and Mbunda-Mbwela (see map 1, in the appendix). Until the colonial conquest, it covered much larger spaces in which especially the Chokwe and Luvale gradually came to predominate as a result of migration and conquest. This vast territory then extended over roughly 670 kms between the 8th and 14th parallel in the north-south direction, and over a maximum of about 550 kms between the 24th meridian to the east and the 19th to the west. In terms of current administrative divisions this corresponds more or less to the present Zambezi and Kabompo Districts in Zambia, to the Moxico, Lunda Sul and part of Lunda Norte provinces in Angola, and to the south-eastern stretch of the Lualaba District of Zaire's Shaba Province. More exact topographical limits for the period around the turn of the century are the Lungwevungu confluence to the south, the Kwando and Kwito to the southeast, the eastern Kwanza and Kwango watershed to the west, the 8th parallel to the north, the Luembe and the present Benguela railway line to the northeast, and the Manyinga-Kabompo to the southeast.

For people in the pre-colonial period, however, river valleys and watersheds mattered less as boundaries than as unifying spaces; the former, especially, were preferred areas of concentrated, ribbon-fashion settlement, and some of the originally uninhabited watersheds gradually gained importance as lines of communication because of seasonal floods in the lower parts. Within the designated zone, the numerous tributaries of the Upper Zambezi and Upper Kasai to the south and north, and the crucial east-west 'watershed route' in between, were therefore the real arena of the history traced in this study (see map 3).

The natural environment shaped not only the lines of communication and settlement, but also the opportunities for producing livelihoods. The region inhabited by the group of peoples mentioned features a fairly uniform combination of open plains (*chana*, Lv., sg.) and depressions (*chinema*) on the one hand, and semi-deciduous woodlands (*musenge*) on the other, which are based on a deep layer of fossil windborne Kalahari sands crossed by perennial water courses (see ch. C 2). The Kalahari belt of West Central Africa is wider than this, but the region under study coincides with most of it and can therefore also be regarded as both a cultural and historical and an ecological unit (see map 2, appendix). Because of this criterion, the Southern Lunda group of the Ndembu

(Lunda-Ndembu) have been considered in the following study to a lesser extent than the sources would have allowed: their ecology and economy resembles more that of the Central African plateau, east of the Kalahari sand belt.

The time

The history I intend to trace in this study begins with the establishment of the first direct links between the Upper Zambezi and the lusophone sphere of Angola in the 1790s. It will be seen that the earliest, indirect links to the 'Atlantic Zone' may have to be dated at least some decades earlier, but this prehistory of world market integration remains obscure and was anyway probably marginal compared to the enormous acceleration of development from the end of the 18th century on.

This part of the story ends with the colonial conquest; an epilogue will give some glimpses into the following period, which will be the focus of subsequent studies. However, the date when colonial rule became effective for the rural economy is not always easy to define. The first Portuguese flags were hoisted in this region in 1895 (Mushiku or *Moxico*, Nyakatolo, Kakenge), but large areas further south remained without any colonial outposts until 1903 (Kangamba) and 1908/09 (near the high Kwito and Lungwevungu).[24] On the British side of the future boundary, the *boma* of Balovale (Zambezi) was set up only in 1907.[25] Initially, these outposts were small islands whose commanders lacked support from their centres and had little power to actually penetrate their hinterlands; there, the impact of the new administration was hardly felt except through occasional punitive expeditions to intercept slave caravans or protect white traders' interests.[26] Only after 1910, later than in many other parts of Africa, did colonial domination become effective at the grassroots level. Between 1910 and 1915, three factors brought the late pre-colonial economy to a virtual standstill: the collapse of the rubber market, the effective imposition of taxes (first in kind, then in cash), and the demarcation of the international boundary between British Northern Rhodesia (Zambia) and Portuguese West Africa (Angola).[27] I have therefore taken the year 1910 to mark the end of my period of study.

---

[24] Delgado 1944: 477, 483, 497; Pélissier 1977: 400f, 404, 408
[25] Annual Report District Commissioner Barotse 1906/07, NAZ file KDE 8/1/1
[26] See for example Venning 1953; Relatórios...1905 and 1907 (in: Delgado 1944: 658ff and 652ff); Pélissier 1977: 405
[27] See below, part F

A 3.2   The sources

In historiographical parlance, the pre-colonial societies of the Upper Zambezi and Kasai would have to be called 'pre-historic' because there are no 'sources' in the form of written evidence from the area itself. Any attempt to analyse such societies in detail inevitably meets with some scepticism. I would not have embarked upon such an enterprise if an unexpected richness of information had not turned up from various heterogenous sources. This information, on which the following study is based, is almost exclusively qualitative. This requires some special comments on the familiar problems of any empirical data - reliability and validity - as well as on the ways in which I have analysed and recombined these data.

Oral history 'from within'

The collective or individual memories of the population itself are obviously the first historical source to be consulted by foreign researchers. Remarkable initiatives in recording oral traditions of the peoples of the Upper Zambezi and Kasai, thereby transforming them into written historiography (with all the problems involved), have been taken by local historians themselves. Works already available include the short 'Early History of the Balovale Lunda' by T. Chinyama (in Lunda Ndembu) and the 'History of the Luvale people and their Chieftainship' by M.K. Sangambo (in English).[28] With competent scholarly support, this process is still going on.[29] The use of these works for the purpose of my study was limited and had to be cautious, however, above all because of their strong leaning towards political and dynastic history; their emphasis on the importance of chieftainship must be seen to some extent as the product of attempts to reconstruct identity and legitimize specific power interests.[30]

To obtain more firsthand information on pre-colonial social and economic history, I conducted, in 1986, a series of historical interviews with surviving witnesses and local experts (see list of primary sources at

---

[28] Chinyama 1945; Sangambo 1979 (edited by R. Papstein and A. Hansen), 2nd edition 1985; see also the history of the neighbouring Nkoya by Rev. J.M. Shimunika, edited by van Binsbergen (1992).

[29] Similar histories of the Chokwe, Mbunda and Luchazi are currently being compiled by local experts advised by R. Papstein and G. Kubik.

[30] See for Chinyama (1945) briefly White 1962a: 14f; for Sangambo (1979) in great detail Papstein 1978, see also Papstein 1989, and (for the Nkoya history) van Binasbergen 1992.

the end). I was lucky enough to find a number of aged villagers, former local traders and export producers, who were ready to talk at length about their lives (see fig. 6 and 16).[31] Most of them were first generation immigrants from the Angolan part of the region, which used to be economically more active, [32] and some of them (probably around 90 years old, but mentally very fresh) had vivid memories of the pre-colonial long-distance trade in slaves, rubber and beeswax. Besides questions of production and foreign trade in the pre-colonial era, a particular focus of these interviews was on labour relations, including the rarely examined forms of inter-household labour circulation and their origin. Another concern was to discuss relevant local or 'emic' terminology, as a key to indigenous concepts of the social relations dealt with in this study.[33]

It would have been impossible, however, to accomplish this analysis solely on the basis of oral sources. Fairly accurate information, especially on the level of everyday life, can only be expected from actual eyewitnesses, or at most from their immediate descendants, and this of course restricts the historical depth of information. The testimonies recorded in the 1980s go back hardly further than the rubber boom of the 1880s and 90s, and the number of potential informants on this period is shrinking very rapidly. To complement my own records, I have included some material from life histories that were collected in the 1950s,[34] but these also begin only in the 1890s. In addition, memories tend to fade the further one goes back into the past. Exact dates and figures given are unreliable, although a remarkably sharp memory for prices and measurements of trade goods has been retained. Amnesia of certain facts also has to be taken into account, although, for example, informants spoke fairly freely about slavery, which has been a widely repressed topic in post-independence Zambia.

Thus, I began a systematic evaluation of existing written sources. This work yielded an unexpected wealth of relevant information, despite the

---

[31] I owe the acquaintance with some of the best informants to my assistant David Chishinji, himself an ex-local trader. Most of these interviews were conducted together with an assistant, both as interpreter and partner to discuss results afterwards. My ability to communicate in local languages on my own was hampered by the enormous variety of idioms spoken in the research area, and by the relatively short duration of my individual research stays.

[32] I have not been able to visit the Angolan part of the region myself because of the ongoing civil war.

[33] Relevant dictionaries (Fisher (revised edition) 1984, and especially the excellent Luvale dictionary by Horton 1975^2 and 1978^1) and the valuable linguistic appendices 2 and 3 in J.Hoover's thesis (1978) have helped to complete this task. Existing ethnographic sources were used for cross checks.

[34] Especially a few case studies by Turner (1957) and a very interesting summary of historical interviews with ex-Ovimbundu caravan traders (Chiyaka) by Schönberg-Lotholz (1960).

remoteness of the region. I am convinced, however, that the value of early travellers' and administrators' accounts could only be tapped because I could relate the scattered remarks by these often uncomprehending strangers to my own firsthand experience with the 'view from within' gathered during repeated fieldwork in villages of the area (see below).[35]

Written history: The view 'from the outside'

Reports by Euro-African and European traders, explorers, missionaries and early administrators have accompanied the history of market integration of the region under study. For most of the period under study, these records consisted almost exclusively of more or less detailed accounts of journeys to or through the region. I have tried to trace all journeys on which written accounts exist and have evaluated at least one version of these accounts.[36] A synopsis of these sources is given in the appendix. It shows first of all that travellers' accounts fall chronologically into three clusters: 1795-1805, the years when the slaving frontier reached the Upper Zambezi; 1846-1855, the peak of the ivory boom; and from 1875 onwards, in preparation for the colonial conquest. These clusters, in other words, correspond to periods of European advancement into the interior. Periods of relative stability or recession (from the non-African point of view), in contrast, yielded very few records. There is, unfortunately, no source for this region on the years surrounding the end of slave exports, and only Silva Porto's writings provide some observations (from the distance of Bihe) for the 'strenuous 1860s'.[37] No major gaps in records occur after 1875.

The methodology used while evaluating these accounts was to create a kind of map to be filled by as many relevant statements by pre-colonial visitors of the region as possible. This map was first of all constructed in two dimensions, a topical and a chronological one. Every traveller's account was regarded as a more or less detailed cross-section of the

---

[35] Cf. T. Ranger's remarks on 'the problem of sources' in his review of studies on peasantization in South-Central Africa (Ranger 1978).

[36] For the most important of these, Silva Porto and Livingstone, I consulted the diaries which have been published in very good critical editions by Schapera (quoted as Livingstone 1960 and 1963) and Madeira Santos (quoted as Silva Porto 1986). The editions used for the other travellers are indicated in the list of primary sources. All written travellers' accounts up to 1897, to my knowledge, have been published in at least one version. This can be explained by the continued strategic interest in, and relative scarcity of, information on this region.

[37] See the second volume of Silva Porto's diary, edited by Madeira Santos (forthcoming) ; Silva Porto 1891

regional economy and society which could provide information on different topics. As these cross-sectional observations were made at exactly defined points in history, individual points mentioned by different travellers were then systematically compared in a diachronic way to make processes of change visible. Although I hope the following study will prove the usefulness of this method, a number of difficulties should also be mentioned. One is that the 'unit of study' as defined above, the region and its population, is simply too large and requires further differentiation. In this way, a third, spatial dimension of the map was constructed. If the concrete coverage by travellers' accounts is analysed according to ethnic groups or subregions, a more uneven pattern emerges (see synopsis in the appendix). For instance, written sources on the Southern Lunda before 1895 exist only for the decade between 1846 and 1855; material on the Luvale and Luchazi/Mbunda/Mbwela is most evenly distributed; and records on the Chokwe are largely missing between the mid-1880s and the early 1900s, but are particularly rich for the decade before. In general, as can be expected, areas close to the main caravan routes and hence to the market are covered best by these reports, but conclusions on the other areas are possible as well because some travellers tried precisely to avoid these routes, for 'exploration' purposes and to avoid heavy exactions. All this has allowed some amount of comparison between different subregions.

It has been argued that written travelogues 'tell us more about the travellers who composed them than about the African peoples they aimed to describe.'[38] Also in accounts on the region studied here, as much as anywhere else, the bias of foreigners writing on the peoples of this region must not be overlooked. A special feature of this region is that throughout the earlier period, up to Silva Porto and Livingstone, the travellers' main interest was commerce; most of them were traders themselves, and all were concerned with 'free' trade. They wrote down their accounts as diaries or as reports to the Portuguese administration, [39] and only sometimes and secondarily for a public interested in the 'civilizing mission' of Europe in Africa.[40] These sources are, understandably, particularly rich in information on the authors' often difficult relations with the local trade partners and hosts, and on production, including food, that was relevant for them.

---

[38] Essner 1987: 204

[39] For Silva Porto and Livingstone, the most important written sources on the period, mainly their diaries were used. 'Government Reports', partly in the form of travel diaries, are: Silva Teixeira [1794]; Vieira de Andrade [1799]; *Anonymus* [1803]; Costa [1804]; Baptista [1805-1814]; Graça [1843-46].

[40] Livingstone 1857; Magyar 1859 and 1860; Silva Porto 1885 and 1891

As a prelude to the colonial conquest, scientific interest, increasingly tainted with racism, [41] grew stronger from the 1870s, with new types of travellers arriving: 'explorers'[42] and missionaries.[43] Their experiences, however, were considerably influenced by the fact that they relied on the existing infrastructure of long-distance trade; they were usually regarded as traders by the local population. This demonstrates that travellers' perceptions were never only determined by their prejudices and domestic interests, but also by the encounter with a specific local situation.[44] Another characteristic of travel accounts compensating to some extent for biases in the author's view is that empirical evidence is often presented in a very personal and concrete way, with exact indication of time, place and situation. I have quoted many examples of such concrete evidence in the following study, not only to lend more colour to the analysis, but also to inform the reader about the context of individual pieces of information. Finally, in comparison to in-depth social research, travellers' observations often remained relatively superficial because of the usually short duration of stay at any one place. On the other hand, they have the advantage of covering much larger areas and allow us to compare different locations.[45]

From 1895, with the establishment of the first colonial outposts, a new type of testimony came up: the records of early colonial officers, administrators, experts and missionaries (see list of primary sources). Paradoxically, the first Europeans, both officers and missionaries, who actually lived in the region or rather in their little islands in the middle of what appeared to them as sheer 'wilderness', sometimes seem to have been more distant from the realities of everyday social and economic life than travellers who passed by before them.[46] They were absorbed to a considerable extent in the task of establishing colonial and spiritual authority among a highly mobile, recalcitrant and 'superstitious' population, against Belgian, British or Portuguese rivals. They sometimes resorted to dubious or illegal business practices to secure their livelihood. In consequence, official reports and correspondence are scanty and often of relatively marginal value for the kind of questions asked in this

---

[41] Cf. Marx 1989 [on Pogge]
[42] Cameron [1875]; Pogge and Lux [1875]; Pinto [1878]; Capello and Ivens [1878 and 1884]; Schütt [1878]; Buchner [1880]; Wissmann [1880]; Dias de Carvalho [1885-86]
[43] Arnot [1884-88]; Johnston [1891]; Coillard [1895]. Crawford [1889] is almost useless and very racist.
[44] See Spittler 1987
[45] Ibid.
[46] Much more interesting for this study would have been memories of the first resident European or Euro-African traders in the region, but they generally left no written material (one of the few exceptions is the report of 1905 by the Portuguese trader Frausto

study.[47] More valuable are the personal reminiscences of these early officers and missionaries, again mainly in the form of travel accounts.[48]

Data from social research

The main problem with travel accounts for the purpose of the following study is their lack of explicit and systematic information on relations and discourses within the local societies. This lack was apparently also felt to some extent by early colonial governments in the process of conquest and the establishment of new administrative structures. A systematic collection of ethnographic data in this region commenced surprisingly early, with the expedition of Dias de Carvalho [1885-86] and a survey among 'resource persons' carried out by the first 'Secretary for Native Affairs' in Angola.[49] But up to about 1930, such data were collected mainly by a few resident officers with a personal interest; their accounts were of particular value for this study because they still represented to some extent the late pre-colonial situation.[50] With very few exceptions,[51]

---

prepared for the Belgian 'Compagnie du Kasai', which was found by Jean-Luc Vellut (1972: 153/4)).

[47] I have consulted such sources for the British side which are kept in the National Archives of Zambia (NAZ) and in the Public Record Office (PRO), e.g. the tour reports by Goold-Adams [1897] and Harding [1899/1900], and the first annual reports on the Balovale District.
Contemporary Portuguese records for the remote east of Angola are particularly poor (Pélissier 1977: 395). Because of difficulties of access, but also because of their marginality for this thesis, I have not consulted lusophone archives. Most local Portuguese administrators' records are apparently kept in the 'Centro Nacional de Documentação e Investigaão HistÂrica' at Luanda. Some of the more interesting specimens of officers' and experts' reports, however, exist in print (Ministerio da Marinha 1894; Relatórios...1905 and 1907; Teixeira de Azevedo 1907 and 1909; Gossweiler 1907; Governo Geral 1910; Mello Geraldes e Fragateiro 1910; Teixeira de Barros Carvalhais 1915; see list of primary sources).
For the Belgian side, finally, a few interesting tour reports to the Upper Zambezi have been found by Vellut in the archives of the Ex-'Compagnie du Kasai' (Frausto, Willemoës and Scarambone).

[48] Trigo Teixeira [1894/95]; Coillard [1895]; Lemaire [1900]; Gibbons and Harding [both 1899/1900]; Schomburgk [1904-07]; Venning [1907-12]; and Gago Coutinho 1915 [1913/14]. The diary of the missionary Dr. Fisher [Kavungu and Cazombo 1893-1902] is kept in the NAZ, some of his letters have been published by Singleton-Fisher 1949 (see list of primary sources).

[49] Diniz 1918 and 1925

[50] Fonseca Cardoso 1919 and in: Mendes Corrêa 1916; Antunes Cabrita 1954; Hudson 1930; less valuable, but remarkable are the accounts of Figueira (ex-rubber trader) and Jaspert (adventurer, sometimes working on the construction of the Benguela railway line) (see bibliography).

[51] The only relevant scholarly research before 1930, to my knowledge, was done by Schachtzabel [1913/14], Frobenius [e.g. 1907] and Torday [e.g. 1925], but all on the fringes of the region in question.

professional social anthropological research began in the region only in the 1930s from the Belgian[52] and Portuguese,[53] and in the 1940s from the British side.[54] But colonial officials, with the advantage of staying in their areas for longer periods, continued to do valuable fieldwork.[55] Very little anthropological research has been done in the region since the respective states reached political independence.[56] Between 1979 and 1986, I carried out several spells of empirical social research in Zambezi and Kabompo, together with Zambian and European colleagues, students and experts. Besides my own historical investigations mentioned earlier, their main emphasis was on sociological aspects of market production against the background of various development projects.[57]

I did use data from this research for the following analysis, but again some typical problems must be mentioned. Earlier ethnographic and anthropological studies, for example, tended to emphasize the normative aspect of social relations, coinciding to some extent with a bias towards kinship structures. Another difficulty is often their lack of historical depth or precision, with an emphasis on the unspecified 'traditional' or 'past'. In particular, they rarely made a clear distinction between the earlier and later pre-colonial period. On the other hand, historical processes like migration, the emergence of chieftainship or long-distance trade have always been so evident in this region that most anthropological writers on the area were at least explicit about the notion of external relations and change as such. Most researchers have collected testimonies on earlier situations and made at least some attempts to locate their findings in history.

Combining oral testimonies, written sources, earlier fieldwork data and my own empirical knowledge of the region, I have developed assumptions on production and social relations in the pre-colonial period. By careful formulation I have indicated where these assumptions are made on the basis of plausibility rather than evidence.

---

[52] Dellille; Devers; Montenez
[53] Baumann; Delachaux and Thiébaud; later Kubik and above all José Redinha
[54] Above all Victor Turner and C.M.N.White, both working in the context of the Rhodes-Livingstone Institute.
[55] Especially Milheiros and others publishing in the *Mensário Administrativo* (bibliography in McCulloch 1951) on the Angolan, and C.M.N.White on the Northern Rhodesian side.
[56] Notably A. Hansen, A. Spring, G. Kubik.
[57] Results in von Oppen 1981; von Oppen, Shula, Alff *et al.* 1983; Alff, von Oppen and Beck 1986; Crehan and von Oppen (eds.) 1987

A note on local terminology

One means of making local perspectives as graphic as possible in this book is liberal citation and analysis of local terminology in the languages spoken around the Upper Zambezi and Kasai. Citing terms from non-European languages, however, raises problems of spelling and format:

* In general, English transcriptions recommended by the International Africa Institute (London) are used, unless otherwise stated.

* Place names, political titles and names of political leaders begin with capital letters and are given in their local (indigenous) form, not in their colonial (mostly Portuguese) versions. The only exception here is the town of Viye (today Cuito, Kwitu) which became so famous in pre-colonial West-Central Africa under the name of Bihe that the latter spelling has been adopted here.

* Ethnic denominations, also beginning with capital letters, are given in the most frequent spelling used in international anglophone literature. No plural prefixes are included, again with one exception, the Ovimbundu, in order to avoid confusion with the coastal (A-)Mbundu.

* Non-indigenous versions of local place names, titles, personal names and ethnic denominations are italicized and begin with a capital letter.

* All other indigenous (non-English) terms are italicized and given in lower case.

Part B

ENTERING THE ATLANTIC WORLD

The first personal encounter between representatives of the European-dominated world and people living around the Upper Zambezi in the remote interior of Central Africa was not established by some courageous white 'explorer', but through the initiative of one of these inhabitants of the interior themselves. Around the year 1790, a 'native of *Loval*' (the country of the Luvale) who had reached the Portuguese settlement of Benguela on the Atlantic coast under unknown circumstances, 'instigated' a Brazilian trader from Bahia, José d'Assumpção e Mello, to come with him to his home country. The latter, apparently in 1793[1],

'took the courage to go to that land to conduct trade, taking in his company the afore-mentioned black, and when he went for the first and second time he did a good business, although with considerable hardship and danger; and the third time went with him Alexandre da Silva Teixeira originating from Santarém' [Brazil].[2]

This third journey began on the 23rd December 1794, and afterwards, at the request of the Portuguese authorities, [3] Assumpção e Mello's companion gave the first ever written account on one of the peoples around the Upper Zambezi and Kasai, the Luvale.[4] He describes their productive capacities and their interest in trade in a rather enthusiastic tone:

'...they have a lot of cassava and a lot of *massango* [bulrush millet], *maça miuda* [sorghum] and some maize; there is a lot of fish of various types, a lot of banana of both types [sweet and plantain ?], a lot of sugar cane; they also have game meat from different kinds of animals... The natives are very kind towards the whites, they always want to have trade with them...'[5]

The author's enthusiasm apparently reflects his experience that

'the chief and all his people (were) gentle and amenable, and gave a hospitable reception [*boa hospedagem*] to the two traders, and conducted business with sincerity, and they do not permit robberies, in that part with better faith than in this captaincy [Benguela ?], because the remoter their homes the more honest they are; and they said that they desired very much that many traders come to their country to trade...'[6]

He contrasts the amicable attitude of the Luvale towards foreign traders with their western neighbours, the Mbunda and Chokwe, who practised

---

[1] Madeira Santos 1978[1]: 165f

[2] Botelho de Vasconcellos 1844 [original dated 1799]; also in: Ferreira Ribeiro 1885: 30-1; translation in Burton 1873: p.24-5 (fn.§)

[3] The interest behind this official request was to pave the way into the interior for trade and, from about 1800, for the establishment of a transcontinal route between Angola and Moçambique (Madeira Santos 1978[1]: 165f).

[4] Held in the *Archivo Histórico Ultramarino* (Lisbon), Cx. 87 No.5, dated 2nd January 1798 (personal communication by Beatrix Heintze)

[5] Silva Teixeira 1940: 237

[6] Botelho de Vasconcellos 1844 [1799]

rougher methods, but towards the same end: to obtain foreign trade goods.

> '...these peoples do not allow passage through their country, because they do not like the whites to go from their country to Luvar, since they are very demanding [*ambicioso*]'.[7]

This he gave as the explanation why their new route avoided these peoples by passing in between them, and went for 21 days through uninhabited 'desert' country, roughly along the Luena headwaters (see maps 1 and 3 for the whole of this part).

The reasons why people in one of the remotest corners of Central Africa should show such a surprisingly active interest in becoming incorporated in the pre-colonial world market points at the importance of factors situated in their own society. These factors, which originated prior to or, at any rate, outside the reach of the world market, and were only subsequently reshaped by its impact, will be explored in the later chapters of this book. As a framework for this, however, I shall outline first the course of incorporation of the peoples of the Upper Zambezi and Kasai into the pre-colonial world market in a more descriptive way, as a chronology of events, beginning with the prehistory of **indirect** trade links to the 'Atlantic Zone'. I will focus in this part on the economic and social forces at work in the wider context outside the area, and describe chronologically the ways in which inhabitants of the area in general responded to these forces, acting as slavers, traders, commodity producers etc. In the subsequent parts I will then go on to examine these responses in a more systematical way.

---

7   Silva Teixeira 1940: 236 [1794]

Fig. 1: Wooden chair of the Chokwe Chief Chipukungu, bought by H. Baumann in 1930. Such richly carved 'chief's chairs' became important enough to be carried along during visits to other villages (Frobenius 1988: 75 [1905/06]). The backrest and front side show, from top to bottom, the powerful *chihongo* mask and then scenes related to the caravan trade: Carriers with a hammock (see fig. 2); two foreign traders (*sertanejos*) with hats and beards resting in folding chairs; and carriers with loaves of beeswax. (Photograph from Völkerkunde-Museum Berlin).

B 1 Gates between coast and interior (before c. 1800)

The journey of the Brazilian traders Assumpção e Mello and Silva Teixeira to the country of *Lovar* in 1794 or 1795 was probably the earliest visit of Portuguese-speaking traders to the area. The date of this event was by no means accidental: it fell within a period of rapid eastward expansion of the trading 'frontier' of the 'Atlantic Zone' of the pre-colonial world economy, more precisely of its Angolan section.[1]

The 18th century slave trade

The driving force behind the accelerated growth of long-distance trade in Central Africa in the 18th century was first of all a rapidly increasing world market demand for slaves. With the expansion of sugar plantations in Brazil and the Caribbean, the price of slaves rose steadily after about 1700.[2] Slaves constituted by far the most important export commodity in the 18th century from Africa in general[3], and from Angola in particular. First peaks in the official Angolan slave trade have been noted in the 1740s and 50s, and in the mid 1760s when 14-16, 000 slaves were exported every year through Luanda and Benguela.[4] Around 1780 a dramatic increase in slave exports from Angola began, with peak legal shipments of more than 20, 000 slaves in the years 1792-94, 1804-06 and 1819-20.[5] Up to about equal numbers every year are estimated to have been exported 'illegally', i.e. outside Portuguese control, particularly

---

1 See the excellent map, showing the advancement of the slaving frontier in West-Central Africa, in Miller 1988: 148
The term *frontier* was originally used to designate outlying, contested areas in the United States, Brazil and South Africa. I would follow Jean Luc Vellut, who first applied it to Central Africa, in defining it as the area of 'radiation of the Angolan economy', i.e. a huge arc around the hinterland of the Portuguese colony of Angola, which was closely connected to it by ties of long-distance trade. The boundaries of this area were, of course, not hard and fast ones, and they were historically highly mobile, according to the cycles of world market conjuncture (here expressed in the successive waves of demand for slaves, ivory, wax and rubber). 'From this point of view, the *frontier* is a border zone of the Atlantic economy' (Vellut 1972: 140-41).-
The whole area influenced by the Atlantic economy has been called 'Atlantic Zone' by J. Miller (1983); and Austen seems to have amalgamated both terms when he speaks of an 'Atlantic Frontier' (1987: 81).

2 Austen 1987: 274

3 *Ibid.*: 86

4 According to Birmingham 1966: 141 154/5 157. Cf. the synopsis with figures given by Goulart and Klein for the period 1760-1780 in Miller 1975: 164-5

5 Miller 1975: 166-67

from the northern coast between Ambriz and Loango.[6] The increase resulted mainly (but not exclusively) from the heavy demand for labour in Brazil, partly owing to disruptions in the North American and Caribbean plantation economies during contemporary European wars[7] (see figure 1).

Agents of the world market

In order to understand how the growing world market demand was transmitted into the Central African Interior, however, one has to look at the social subjects conducting the trade. On the Angolan coast, the slave trade was in the hands of three groups of merchants with conflicting interests: Metropolitan Portuguese trading houses, shipping and trading entrepreneurs of other European nationalities, and Euro-African traders.[8]

During the 18th century, the Portuguese trading houses, based mainly in the oldest bridgehead of Luanda, protected by the Portuguese Crown and administration, came increasingly under pressure from British, French, Dutch and Brazilian competitors who 'smuggled' slaves from minor landing sites along the coast which could hardly be controlled by the Portuguese.

On the other hand, metropolitan-based Portuguese merchants were engaged in a long-standing struggle with Euro-African traders. These originated from poorer European settlers of earlier periods. Their strength rested less on capital than on the good connections they had with their African neighbours and relatives. They procured export commodities such as slaves through skillful manipulation of African exchange systems. They had carefully

> 'built connections through marriage and political influence at African courts, engaged in local forms of commerce and production, and employed local slave labour to enrich themselves. The institutions they created remained Portuguese in name, but owed more to Africa than to Europe.'[9]

Therefore, smaller-scale Portuguese-speaking businessmen, mostly Euro-Africans, were a strategic force in carrying trade into the remoter interior

---

6 Birmingham 1966: 157 (for c.1775); Miller 1975: 137 151 and fn.36. Miller emphasizes, however, that 'legal' and 'illegal' export figures were to some extent complementary to each other since they partly drew on the same supply networks in the interior: 'Boom conditions in one market could contribute to slackened offerings of slaves for sale in adjacent systems' - and vice versa, e.g. in the case of Loango during the Napoleonic wars (*ibid*: 161-2).
7 Miller 1975: 149 155
8 Miller 1983: 133f; Miller 1988: 245ff
9 Miller 1983: 131

(in Portuguese: *sertão*). In the Angolan context, these inland traders were known as *sertanejos* (see figures 1 and 2).

Fig. 2: Indigenous carriers with foreigner in a hammock (detail from fig. 1)

The difference is indicated by the head fashions; the hat wearer is either a trader or a chief who has adopted traders' ways of travelling and clothing. See also p.
(Photograph taken at the Völkerkunde-Museum, Berlin)

The *sertanejos*, however, became increasingly dependent on the metropolitan merchants from whom they obtained the necessary trade goods with which to barter slaves (and some ivory) in the interior. The merchants, stimulated by favourable world market prices, imported relatively cheap manufactured goods. In the course of the 18th century, cotton cloth from India, later from England, as well as tobacco and sugar brandy (*aguardente*) from Brazil, European knives and Portuguese wines gradually replaced the intra-African 'commodity-currencies', e.g. palm cloths and salt, previously controlled by the Euro-Africans.[10] Guns, mostly Portuguese and English-made flintlock muskets, first trickled into the Angolan hinterland only illegally and in limited numbers, which then quickly grew when the ban on gun sales to Africans was lifted by a reformist Governor in 1767.[11]

Many of these imports were forwarded by the metropolitan trading houses to the *sertanejos* on the basis of trade credit, a widespread institution along the African coasts.[12] The number of *sertanejos* was

---

[10] Miller 1983: 146
[11] Birmingham 1966: 139 146f; Tylden 1953: 44f
[12] See Madeira Santos 1886: 58f; Sundstrøm 1974

swelled rapidly during this century by poor new immigrants, including deportees (*degradados*), Jews and 'Gipsies'. Driven by permanent indebtedness and the search for independence from the metropolitan bourgeoisie, they contributed much towards the expansion of the 'Atlantic Zone'.[13] At the creditors' end, also non-resident European and Brazilian merchants apparently contributed to this rapid spatial expansion, rather than intensification, of trade relations in the Portuguese-dominated sphere.[14]

One important result of these tensions was the growth of Benguela, a port south of Luanda, which was to play a prominent role in the market integration of the peoples of the Upper Zambezi and Kasai (see map 1). Benguela had been founded in 1617 and soon became dominated by Euro-African and Brazilian traders who tried to escape the grip of Dutch and Portuguese creditors as well as administrators, for instance the heavy taxation on slave and ivory exports.[15] The inhabitants of Benguela, reinforced by Brazilian traders, soon came into contact with their eastern neighbours, the Ovimbundu states (Wambu, Mbailundu, Bihe, Ngalangi, to name only the more important ones) in the densely settled central highlands. These contacts came about through various military expeditions (i.e. slave raids), but also in the form of trade.[16] After the crown had gained control of Benguela, 'deserters' (credit defaulters ?), convicts and African trade agents (*pombeiros descalços*) circumvented the official ban on entry into the *sertão* by Portuguese traders imposed in Angola in 1620. Allegedly, the Portuguese 'traded, raided and even preached in the area that later became Bihe as early as the start of the 17th century.'[17]

In addition, traders from Ndongo, perhaps building on an old network of pre-colonial salt trade, created a second connection between the Ovimbundu plateau and the coast, through the hinterland of Luanda (Kisama) 'during the very early days of the 18th century or even

---

[13] Birmingham 1966: 159; Vellut 1972: 95f, Miller 1988: 273ff

[14] The credit system more or less compelled those established in a particular place to stick to their customary relations there. This, together with the limited flexibility of African suppliers, forced newcomers in times of rising demand into ever new areas (according to Miller 1975: 163).

[15] See Miller 1983: 134f

[16] Childs 1949: 193-195

[17] Heywood 1984: 103, quoting Cavazzi da Montecuccolo (1687); and sources mentioned in Delgado 1944: I, 334

earlier'.[18] (According to one mysterious report, African traders from Angola had even reached the Middle Zambezi as early as 1696.[19])

The Ovimbundu connection

In response to these early trade contacts, the Ovimbundu became known as slave raiders at about the same time. Among their victims in the surrounding areas were no doubt the Ngangela peoples to their south and east.[20] By the early 18th century, Ovimbundu are reported to have been exchanging slaves and ivory with Portuguese traders.[21] The Chokwe, the westernmost group among the peoples of the Upper Kasai and Zambezi who are in the focus of this study, were probably the first to be raided by Ovimbundu in this way, some time during the earlier 18th century. Lacking political cohesion, many of them were exported as slaves to Brazil.[22] But some slaves and most of the ivory seem to have been acquired by the Ovimbundu through more peaceful interaction, since the Chokwe possessed their first guns 'certainly by 1750 or so'.[23] According to other, unnamed sources the Luvale were the next to begin to trade with the Ovimbundu, in the 1770s.[24]

Thus, the Ovimbundu had become important middlemen who integrated the peoples around the Upper Kasai and Zambezi into the frontier of the 'Atlantic Zone' before the end of the 18th century. This process demonstrates that the first stage of the economic 'opening up' of the African interior for the world market happened prior to any direct involvement by non-African traders, through the interlocking of a number of regional trade networks.[25]

After these early beginnings, however, the late 18th century certainly brought a rapid increase in the volume of exports from the Upper Zambezi and Kasai, mainly through the Ovimbundu connection. The decisive stimulus here, besides the growth in world market demand for slave labour, was the permanent establishment of Portuguese-speaking

---

[18] Childs 1949: 196-98
[19] Sutherland-Harris 1970: 239, quoting a Frei Antonio da Conceição, *Tratado dos Rios* 1696.
[20] Heywood 1984: 102; for a discussion of the term *Ganguela* see section A 3.1
[21] Roberts 1970: 730
[22] Their number was sufficient to produce a Chokwe population in Brazil which is still identifiable today. (Miller 1970: 177)
[23] Miller 1970: 177
[24] Papstein 1978: 199, fn.14

traders on the Central Plateau, mainly in the kingdoms of Mbailundu, Bihe and Caconda, from around 1770. This trading community also provided a relay for other *sertanejos* from the coast who were thus able to reach in person the Upper Zambezi in the 1790s, as we have seen. Many of the new white and Euro-African settlers on the Ovimbundu Plateau had been established at Benguela or in the hinterland of Luanda themselves. The number of these first generation settlers, whom Silva Porto used to call 'the first pleiad of *sertanejos* of Bihé', was over 200 around 1800.[26]

Since they relied mainly on Ovimbundu middlemen carrying their business further into the interior, a new class of African entrepreneurs emerged, often called *quimbares*.[27] European customs and clothes, as expressed in the terms mentioned, were regarded locally as the decisive insignia of these traders, much more than the colour of their skin.[28] Significantly, wealthy Ovimbundu traders were sometimes nicknamed *kindele* (*chindele* in Lv.) among their customers in the interior, a term which originally seems to have been reserved for the Portuguese or whites in general, but increasingly came to be applied to any 'civilized' person 'with European ways'.[29]

The Portuguese administration soon began to extend its grip over this new trading diaspora, gave the main centres the status of *feira* (a controlled and protected market) and subjected them to Portuguese exterritorial jurisdiction by installing a *capitão mor*. Nevertheless, the growth of trade through the Ovimbundu Plateau that ensued took place in a context of growing liberalization of trading, at the expense of the established interests of the metropolitan commercial bougeoisie. The drive into the interior by the *sertanejos* was particularly aided by a number of economic reforms introduced by mercantilist governors: the

---

[25] In their overview articles, Vansina (1962) and Roberts (1970) mention the importance of regional trade networks for long-distance trade, but only for its mature phase, not for the beginnings of long-distance trade.

[26] Silva Porto diary 21.8.1888, quoted by Madeira Santos 1986: 36

[27] This term appears already in sources of the 16th and 17th century where it was used for Africans obliged to serve the Portuguese as local subsidiary troops in their wars (see Heintze 1985: 126f). Until the 19th century, a significant shift in meaning seems to have taken place; in 1801 it is translated as 'free or liberated blacks living close to the whites' (Vellut 1972: 96), and in the 1850s, among the Ovimbundu, the term *kimbalo* was applied for local African traders (Magyar 1857: 292). With this meaning, it seems to have been spread further into the interior, where African middlemen coming from the Ovimbundu Plateau came to be widely known as *mambari* (in CiLuvale *vimbali*, sg. *mambali*). On the etymology of *mambari* see also Bontinck 1976.

[28] Vellut 1972: 95

[29] E.g. Cadornega 1940 [1680], vol. I: 15 (fn.1) and 291 (quoting the term *mundele* as being used among rulers in the African Kingdom of Angola in the 17th century); Graca 1890: 382 [1845]; Magyar 1857: 31; Cameron diary, Sept. 1875, quoted by Heywood 1984: 152; Horton 1975^2: 231.

abolition in 1758 of an old law prohibiting Portuguese subjects from trading in the *sertão*, i.e. outside the *feiras*; the legalization of gun sales to Africans in 1767; and the suppression of the old *contrato* system which favoured virtual monopolies on credit and import/export businesses, in 1770.[31] In addition, the *sertanejos* on the plateau continued to play off their two connections with the coast, to Benguela and Luanda, against each other. At least three times they staged a 'shift' (*mudança*) between these two terminals to escape accumulated debts owed to coastal merchants.[32]

Although the relative freedom enjoyed by the newly established Portuguese trading community also included exemption from African jurisdiction, they very much relied on local African support for their further advance into the remoter interior, particularly as their trading partners, for protection, and for labour. The foreign traders were always anxious to maintain good relations with the rulers of the various Ovimbundu states, who in turn increasingly relied on imported wealth and European expertise.[33] As elsewhere in the Atlantic sphere, indigenous rulers were usually the first to trade on their own account with European goods, usually supplied on credit.[34]

Both *sertanejos* and Ovimbundu rulers, however, also depended on the labour of African commoners and slaves for their trading ventures, mainly as caravan carriers and guards. Much of this work was also done by slaves acquired in the interior, or, in the earlier period, by forced labourers to which local rulers and Portuguese army outposts had access. But with the growth of trade, free recruitment for salary played an increasing role.[35] In addition, both European traders and African rulers needed trading agents, in Angola called *pombeiros*[36], trusted relatives, employees or slaves of the entrepreneur who organized and led the caravan on their behalf. Most *pombeiros* also conducted their personal business while leading a caravan, and many of them established themselves subsequently as independent trading entrepreneurs (*moradores, quimbares*). Among the Luvale of the Upper Zambezi, the

---

[30] Heywood 1984: 103
[31] Vellut 1972: 95, fn.66; Birmingham 1966: 147; Childs 1949: 196-7; Vellut 1975: 135
[32] Madeira Santos 1986: 59-60
[33] Childs 1949: 197
[34] See Miller 1988: 173ff.
[35] Heywood 1984: 119f. Their is a good description of recruitment procedures in Magyar 1857: 447f; cf. Soremekun 1977.
[36] See Heywood 1984: 184f, and Vellut 1972: 136f, for definitions.

term *pombeiro* is still known today in the Umbundu form *fumbelo*, 'wealthy man'.37

The Mbangala connection

The Ovimbundu connection in the west became the most important one for the incorporation of the Upper Zambezi and Kasai in the pre-colonial world market; but it was not the only, and probably not even the oldest one. Interestingly, the Luvale word for 'coast' or 'European town' is *mbaka*, apparently a reference to the old Angolan trading town of Ambaca, in the hinterland of Luanda.38 Similarly to in Benguela, Euro-African and independent African traders had settled there in the 17th century, out of reach of the Portuguese administration.39 *Ambaquistas* stimulated trade not only with the Ovimbundu plateau, but also with the Mbangala people on the Upper Kwango further east, who subsequently became the most important suppliers and middlemen for export slaves bound for Luanda and the Loango coast. As early as the 1650s, *Ambaquistas* had become important supporters of the *kinguri*, the Mbangala king, and began to settle in his capital Kasanje, and a *feira* was established there under joint supervision of the *kinguri* and the Portuguese.40 After this time, both Mbangala and *Ambaquista* caravans opened a direct trade route to the emerging Nuclear Lunda empire, which had hitherto been connected with the world market only marginally through a very long route via the Lulua and Zaire rivers to the north.41 The wars of expansion carried out by the rulers of Nuclear Lunda, (called *Mwant Yav* or *Mwata Yamvo*), probably became the biggest single source of slave exports from Central Africa.42 Very soon, the rulers themselves began trading on this route. Already in 1681, Nuclear Lunda caravans to Kasanje are mentioned.43 The existence of early connections between Nuclear Lunda and the Upper Zambezi, which will be examined further

---

37 Cf. White 1959: 38; Horton (1975²: 34) gives the meaning 'foreman, head servant' in Luvale.
38 Horton 1975²: 202
39 Heintze 1979
40 Heintze 1981; cf. Vellut 1975
41 Lacerda e Almeida 1936: 389-90; Redinha 1968: 105; Vellut 1972: 96
42 Birmingham 1966: 133f; Thornton 1981: 7: 'One might see the Lunda expansion as something of an extended slave raid...'. Hoover (1978: 343), in contrast, doubts that slaves were the dominant export article from Nuclear Lunda before the 19th century. Ladislaus Magyar, however, asserted in the 1850s 'that for almost a hundred years the third part of the victims dragged to the markets of Luanda and Benguela have come from the empire of Moluwa [Nuclear Lunda]' (1860: 231)
43 Vansina 1962: 382, fn.49

below, suggests that some of the Atlantic trade trickled through Nuclear Lunda to the area in question.

Besides the connection with Nuclear Lunda, early direct trading contacts between Kasanje and the Upper Zambezi must have existed as well. It seems, for example, that the Chokwe were accustomed to acquiring salt from the Luyi salt pans near Kasanje even before the Mbangala established this capital (after 1630), and that some of the Mbangala political titles were of Chokwe origin.[44] Such old communications may have been activated when *Ambaquista* and Mbangala middlemen - parallel to their Ovimbundu counterparts - pushed forward with the growing demand for slaves in the 18th century. The Chokwe themselves may have initially been the victims of in this advance of the slaving frontier, probably even before they were preyed upon by the Ovimbundu; at least part of their population, as well as their original identity, seems to have been formed by dispersed refugees fleeing 18th century raids from the north-west.[45]

But for those inhabitants of the Upper Zambezi and Kasai who were strong enough to trade with the slavers, rather than to surrender to them, this meant a second, northwestern gateway to the 'Atlantic Zone' via Luanda, besides the southwestern one through Benguela. The early importance of this route is underlined by the fact that in 1797 both the Kinguri of Kasanje and Mujumbo Acalunga, 'potentate and ruler of all Songo' concluded marriage alliances with the holder of the Chinyama title, the senior Luvale chief, 'to unite more closely the bonds of amity with those of relationship.'[46] The immediate motive for the Mbangala and Songo rulers to knit closer links to the Upper Zambezi, however, may have had to do with the increasing competition with both Portuguese-speaking and indigenous non-royal traders in their own territories.[47]

Such competition, in the context of growing world market demand, contributed much to the intensification of trading activities between the hinterland of Luanda and the Upper Zambezi. For example, in 1805, two trusted slave *pombeiros* were sent by Francisco Honorato da Costa, director of the *feira* of Kasanje (which was at that time transferred to Mukari, further west), at the request of the Governor of Angola, to explore a new route to Nuclear Lunda and to the Eastern Lunda kingdom

---

[44] Dias de Carvalho 1892: II, 348; Miller 1972
[45] Miller 1988: 38; he suggests that the name Chokwe (or *Kioko*) originally meant 'those who left (fled)'.
[46] Cunnison 1961; Costa 1873: 201 [1804]
[47] The *kinguri* gradually lost control over the official Portuguese trading agents (who withdrew in 1807 to Mukari, supported by the Portuguese administration), and over a growing (Mbangala and *sertanejo*) unofficial trading network which avoided the *feira* and exported illegally via Kongo and the Loango coast. (Miller 1973: 20f)

of the Kazembe. His aim was to overcome the Mbangala-Nuclear Lunda monopoly on the direct route, and furthermore to explore a link to Mozambique, the other Portuguese colony on the opposite coast.[48] On their way out, the two *pombeiros* passed through Songo and along the northern margin of the Upper Zambezi. When they arrived there they were made aware that they were not the first foreign visitors from the north-west: a Chokwe chief, Mushiku (*Moxico*), tried to detain them and to seize their goods

> 'because, previously to their arrival, a merchant of the same fair [Mukari-A.v.O.] had...taken, on credit, a certain number of slaves, a certain quantity of wax, and some ivory, and had not yet paid the said chief.'[49]

Fig. 3: Slave caravan in the interior, on the main 'watershed' route (1875)

The slaves are all women and children, for which there was higher demand in 'internal' slave trade, and carry oblong transport baskets resembling the *mutonga* type, current among the Chokwe and Luvale. (Engraving from Cameron 1877, vol.II: 147)

---

[48] See Vellut 1972: 99ff; Bontinck 1974
[49] According to the report written up by one of them, Baptista 1873: 199 [referring to the year 1805]

B 2 The climax and end of slave exports (c.1800-1850)

The search for exportable slaves was the main stimulus behind the eastward movement of the trading frontier. Except in the beginning, however, the western middlemen rarely captured slaves themselves. It was the readiness of local leaders in the interior to sell people in considerable numbers to export traders that secured these middlemen an important role in the expanding trade network.[1] The chiefs around the Upper Kasai and Zambezi, through whose areas the first Portuguese-speaking traders from Bihe and Kasanje advanced at the end of the 18th century, soon began to offer slaves in order to gain access to imported goods. Chiefs of the Mbunda and Luchazi, but not the Chokwe, quickly became known among *sertanejos* as bulk suppliers of slaves in return for cloth and guns.[2]

The Luvale on the Upper Zambezi, however, became the most active slave sellers among the peoples of this region. According to J. Miller, the 'slaving frontier' reached the Upper Zambezi only between 1820 and 1850, when slave exports on the whole were already on the decline.[3] Unfortunately, there is a gap in the sources on that region for most of the period, from 1806 and 1846; but judging by oral traditions of the Luvale, Miller's dates probably mark only the crest of the wave.[4] Around 1800, the country of *Lovar* was already the main destination of all Portuguese-speaking traders using the southern (Ovimbundu) route.[5] As a result of their earlier indirect contacts, during their first negotiations with non-African traders the Luvale had a very clear idea of what they wanted from them: no less than five well-defined types of cloth and two types of trade beads (*missanga*) are mentioned in Silva Teixeira's report. What they offered in return was undoubtedly mainly slaves, since Teixeira used the term *negocio*, which was used as an equivalent for slave trade in early Angola, and described his partners as 'very inclined to war in which they do heroic deeds and for which they are feared by their neighbours.'[6] At the end of this phase, around 1850, travellers' reports still mention the Luvale as very important suppliers of slaves to Mbangala, Ovimbundu

---

1 Cf. Gann 1954: 33
2 *Anonymus* 1940: 25/26 [on Mbunda, Mbwela, Chokwe; 1803]; Graça 1890: 409f [1846, on Chokwe]; Silva Porto 1942: 68 [1847, on Luchazi]
3 Miller 1988: 148 and 233
4 Sangambo 1985: 70f; Papstein 1978: 179f
5 See for example Lacerda 1844, quoted in Ferreira Ribeiro 1885: 30
6 Silva Teixeira 1940: I, 237 [1794]; personal communication by Beatrix Heintze

and Portuguese-speaking traders.[7] A remarkable level of violence had been reached in the whole region, 'a system of petty warfare and stealing people between nearly all tribes'.[8] The Hungarian traveller Ladislaus Magyar noted: 'The subjects of the various chiefs are in incessant strife in which their main aim is to cast each other into slave chains.'[9]

The forms and agents of the violence accompanying the slave trade will be discussed further below, but its immediate result was widespread population movements which contributed to the further advance of the 'Atlantic Zone'. For example, two smaller chiefs of the Mbunda, who were involved 'in continual disputes with the peoples of Kuti, Kwando and the Land of Lovar'[10], fled southeastward from these repercussions of the slave trade, and sought refuge under the Lozi king Mulambwa, who reigned c.1780-1830. One of them, Chiyengele, later settled with his followers in the wilderness north of the Kabompo river, under the exiled Lozi chief Masiko.[11] Masiko, in turn, was involved in petty warfare with the Kololo rulers in the Bulozi floodplain[12], with other Lozi exiles[13], with southern Luvale[14], and with the Southern Lunda chief Ishinde[15]. It is no surprise to hear that he regularly sold captives to the *Mambari* (Ovimbundu) for cloth.[16] Luvale chiefs, as the main suppliers of slaves on the Upper Zambezi, caught slaves for a long time among indigenous populations west of the Zambezi, between the Kasai, the Lwena and Lumbala rivers (whom they used to call *VaMbwela*), in the process of establishing their chieftainship. Gradually, they extended their raids to neighbouring peoples in the south and east. Already during Mulambwa's reign, Luvale-Andonyi raiders reached the northern fringes of the Bulozi floodplain, and kidnapped cattle and people, so that the Lozi King had to rely on the Mbunda refugees as allies to repulse these incursions.[17]

---

[7] Graça 1890: 423 [1846]; Livingstone 1963: 72, 254, 259 [1854/55]; Magyar 1860: 234, and 1857: 298
[8] Livingstone 1963: 42, 95
[9] Magyar 1860: 234
[10] Silva Porto, diary entry 30.12.1847 (1942: 72)
[11] White 1962a: 12f; Hermitte 1974: 53f. Another group from the West (*Ambonda* = Mbunda) under Sekelenke sought protection in Masiko's area around 1850 (Livingstone 1857: 269).
[12] Livingstone 1963: 19 [1853]
[13] Livingstone 1963: 264, 272 [1855], referring to Imbwa, a 'brother' of Masiko
[14] Sangambo 1985: 66, referring to chief Chinyama Litapi who obtained captives in return for guns and men provided as auxiliary force to Imbwa - see fn.43.
[15] Livingstone (1963: 264 [1855]) speaks of an 'old feud' between Masiko and Ishinde.
[16] Livingstone 1963: 24, 42 [1853/54]
[17] Hermitte 1974: 50, 53

According to Luvale oral traditions, there was an almost permanent state of war from the late 18th up to the end of the 19th century. These wars, remembered as the 'Wars of *Ulamba*', were according to Papstein

'...actually a long series of raids...The most intensive period of fighting/slaving appears to have been in the 1830s to 1850s - this period in fact coincides with the peak of the Angolan slave trade...'[18]

During these decades, armies or bands of warriors under chiefs adopting illustrious names such as *jindamisa vambwela* ('destroyer of the *mbwela*', = Kayombo kaKutemba) or 'scorching fire' (the ferocious chief Muwema wa Ngambo)[19] raided deep into the south and southeast of the Upper Zambezi, in what is today Zambian territory, '...in the area of Chavuma, moving down the Zambezi, particularly on the eastern side, and then up the Kabompo and Lungwevungu rivers...'[20] As with the Mbunda, this led to another eastward expansion of population. Luvale-speaking refugees increasingly settled further east, up the river and in the woodlands across the Zambezi.[21] In these areas, Luvale warlords probably found most of their victims; but they also clashed increasingly with expanding Southern Lunda chieftainships, especially that of Ishinde, who competed with them for control over resident acephalous populations since the late 18th century. These chiefs, although in a weaker position, also began to participate actively in the slave trade. In 1854, Livingstone discovered that even at the capital of Ishinde, with whom he established very friendly relations, slaves were sold fairly regularly for cloth (and apparently guns) to the *Mambari*.[22] He even met there a Euro-African from the hinterland of Luanda, an army officer on leave, who took 66 slaves to Kasanje despite the declining interest in this business among *sertanejos* at the time.[23]

At least over the last 50 years of the slave trade's existence, the entire region around the Upper Zambezi remained a vital part of the slaving frontier of the 'Atlantic Zone'. Both as victims and as collaborators, its population supplied the last great batch of slaves for export, with peaks around 1820 and in the mid-1830s which were glorified by traders as 'the golden years'. Slaving and slave trade in the region even continued when slave exports from West Africa effectively stopped, but no longer as a direct result of world market demand.

---

[18] Papstein 1978: 180
[19] Papstein: 1978: 184f; Sangambo, n d · 56f
[20] Papstein 1978: 187
[21] Livingstone 1963: 40, 95, 264 [1854/55]
[22] Livingstone 1963: 60, 72
[23] Livingstone 1963: 56, 72, 213 (1854/55). Portuguese army officers were another group that frequently traded on their own account in the interior.

B 3   Ivory, beeswax, and new patterns of trade (c.1840-1880)

Slave exports were officially prohibited in Angola in 1836, and shipments through Luanda effectively phased out between 1844 and 1850.[1] Illegal exports went on for some time, but were reduced to insignificance during the early 1850s when Brazilian ports were closed for slave ships[2], as a result of British pressure and changing patterns of exploitation of labour in the New World. Severe economic crisis now hit particularly the established trading houses at Luanda who already withdrew most of their representatives (*aviados*) from outposts in the interior in 1836.[3] Perhaps different, but related reasons, namely 'situations of insecurity being created for them by the the reigning king, Basso-Gaba', forced many or even most of the *sertanejos* to leave Bihe in the 1830s.[4] In the 1840s, armed conflicts involving African middlemen and unofficial traders sprang up around the *feiras* of Bihe (1843) and Kasanje (1850), resulting in their subsequent closure.[5] In the 1850s, the area of official Portuguese domination in the northeast contracted from the Kwango to the Kwiji, some 150 km further west.[6]

New markets and new agents

One result of these struggles seems to have been a strengthening of smaller scale traders, both Portuguese-speaking and African. Despite the exodus of the *sertanejos* of the 'first pleiad' from the Ovimbundu plateau, their ex-employees remained and started trading on their own account.[7] Around 1840, old and new *sertanejos* began to return to Bihe as commission agents (i.e.debtors) of metropolitan merchants, mainly at Benguela, to form what Silva Porto called 'the second pleiad of the Bihe *sertanejos*'. Among them were Silva Porto himself (1840) and Ladislaus

[1] Vansina 1962: 385; Miller 1973: 23
[2] Roberts 1970: 734
[3] Graça 1890: 396
[4] Madeira Santos 1986: 41
[5] Heywood 1984: 111f; Miller 1973: 22f
[6] In the late 1850s, after the visits by Livingstone in 1854 and 1855; see Lux 1880: 67f
[7] Madeira Santos 1986: 41-45; in 1846, Graça listed in Bihe the names of 101 'natural sons of the Portuguese who emigrated from the two places of Benguela and Luanda, as well as from other *presidios* and districts': 6 'whites', 40 Euro-Africans [*pardos, cabodos*] and 54 'blacks', '...besides the peddlars [*negociantes volantes*] who have established themselves...'(1890: 399f); most of the non-whites seem to have started trading under the *sertanejos* of the 'first pleiad'.

Magyar (1849). These new *sertanejos* were to play an important role among the protagonists in new patterns of trade in the interior, with a focus on the export of 'legitimate goods' (mainly ivory, beeswax and later wild rubber).

But the protagonists were not the inventors of these new patterns of trade, nor were they alone on the scene. Both ivory and beeswax had been exported from Central Africa since the 17th century, although these exports had been overshadowed by the slave trade for a long time. Already in the early 19th century, the principal products leaving Bihe towards the coast had been wax and ivory, rather than slaves, while the main slaving frontiers shifted to the north and east. But this trade had attracted little attention; it was restricted to Africans and to the poorest among the *sertanejos* (so-called *desposadados*) because of the low profit it fetched.[8]

Beeswax from areas nearer to the coast (Kisama) had been sold in Angolan towns as early as 1611, and the use of locally manufactured wax candles, for Afro-christian ritual and home-lighting, was more widespread, it seems, than in contemporary Europe.[9] Since the late 17th century, growing amounts of beeswax were also exported to Brazil, following overexploitation of its own bee population.[10] Between 1780 and 1830, wax exports reached a relatively stable level with 50-90 tons p.a., and their value was about a quarter of that of slave exports at Benguela (see tables 2 and 3)[11].

Ivory exports, in contrast, had been minimal before the 1830s. But then, a rapid rise in world market demand for ivory due to increasing European luxury consumption (piano keys, knife handles and the like), combined with the removal of the Portuguese state monopoly on ivory exports (1836), resulted in prices shooting up by 300%[12], and made ivory profitable enough to become a substitute for slave exports. The growth of ivory exports through Benguela can be inferred from figures available for Luanda which rose from a mere 1, 4 metric tons in 1832 to 100 tons in 1848/9 . This level of exports, which meant a kill of up to 3, 300 elephants every year for supplies to Luanda alone, was roughly kept up during the 1850s (see table 2).[13]

---

8   Silva Porto, cited in Heywood 1984: 104
9   Vellut 1979: 99
10 *Ibid.* 100
11 Childs 1949: 203; Vellut 1972: 120
12 Miller 1970: 178
13 Assuming an average of 15 (12-20) kg per tusk (Lux 1880: 125 [for 1875]). In the 1850s, average weights of tusks coming from the Upper Kasai and Zambezi were probably higher than in the 1870s (see Pogge 1880: 53), which would of course mean that the

Table 2: 'Legitimate exports' from Angola, 1780-1933
(only products of the interior, in metric tons)

Year(s)	Ivory	Beeswax	Rubber	Reference area	Sources
c.1780*		66-88		Angola	A: 100
1810-30*		50-70		Angola	A: 101
1823-25*	38.9			Angola	B: 28
1830-32*	2.3	106		Angola	B: 28
1832	1.4	?	0	Luanda only	C: 178
1840s*		132	0	Angola	A: 101
1844	47.6	24	0	Luanda only	C: 178
1848/9	100.0	84	0	Luanda	D: 437
1854-59*		415	0	Angola	A: 101
1857		770	0	Luanda only	C: 178
1859	86.2	?	0	Luanda	C: 178
1870-72*	51.0	915	?	Angola	B: 28
1870			34	Benguela	E: 172
1884	21	541	222	Benguela	F: 172
1884	23.1	676	?	Angola	B: 28
1887			411	Benguela	E: 172
1888	12.5	459	1052	Benguela	G: 37
1891	19.7	387	1211	Benguela	G: 37
1900	0	?	?	Benguela	H: 207
1933			>1000	Angola	A: 101

*per annum.
Sources:
A = Vellut 1979; B = Ministério da Marinha 1889; C = Miller 1970; D = Livingstone 1857;
E = Heywood 1984; F = Madeira Santos 1986; G = Ministério da Marinha e Ultramar 1897
H = Childs 1949

Shortly after the inception of the ivory boom, in the 1840s, beeswax exports also began to rise as a result of the demand from European industrializing countries supplied through the Lisbon stock market.[14] In 1848/49, at the peak of the ivory boom, beeswax already covered almost 10% of the 'legitimate exports' through Luanda (see table 3). The growth of the beeswax trade was smaller but more sustained. In the 1850s, beeswax seems to have overtaken ivory as the main export commodity in

---

number of elephants killed was lower. But Livingstone's statement of 120 lbs. per tusk as an average weight (1857: 438/9) is probably exaggerated. Magyar (1860: 231, fn. 1) mentions 110-125 pounds (60-65 kg) rather as a maximum size for the same period as Livingstone. According to Portuguese standards, only 15 kg was the minimum, and about 21-43 kg the average weight for *marfim da ley*, prime ivory (according to Heywood 1984: 170; Pogge 1880: 53), with many tusks weighing less than that.

[14] Vellut 1979: 101

terms of quantity (see table 2), and in the 1860s also by value.[15] (cf. table 3). Already in the early 1870s, a level of almost 1, 000 metric tons of beeswax exports from Angola *per annum* was reached, comparable to mid-20th century figures.

The rise of 'legitimate exports' brought an increasing importance to the southern connections between the coast and the interior, via the Ovimbundu plateau and the port of Benguela. When 'legitimate trade' began to boom, in the 1840s, caravans carrying beeswax and ivory left Bihe every day on their way to the coast, but many of them still used the old 'transversal' route from Bihe through Ambaca to Luanda.[16] Only after 1838 did Benguela gradually become the main terminal for shipments of ivory, wax and rubber from the interior.[17] Benguela obtained an additional stimulus when Silva Porto opened, in 1852, a new route through Mbailundu which avoided the losses suffered on the older routes via Wambu or Caconda.[18] But Silva Porto's 'new trail', roughly identical with the track of the later Benguela railway line, became fully viable only in the 1870s.[19]

A related aspect of the development of 'legitimate trade' was the continued social differentiation among its agents. *Sertanejos* and African nobles such as the Ovimbundu rulers sought their fortune mainly in trading ivory (and more slaves).[20] Beeswax, in contrast, continued to be a less profitable business for poorer traders, including increasing numbers of African middlemen, and this was probably the reason why the beeswax trade kept pace with the ivory boom in West Central Africa.[21] This had to do with several economic conditions of the trade. While rising world market prices spurred on the growth of the ivory trade, the shortening of transport distance was the crucial economic precondition for the expansion of beeswax exports. Partly for this reason, the acquisition of beeswax in the interior required much less skill and capital than the purchase of slaves and ivory.[22] Another reason was that unit size and value were much bigger with ivory than with beeswax. In the 1870s, a tusk weighing 21-43 kg on average was worth 1 1/2 loaves of wax (*lipawu*, sg. Lv., from Pg. *pão*, 'bread') of between 30 and 50 kg,

---

[15] Assuming mid-century prices, according to Livingstone 1857: 437
[16] Graça 1890, quoted in Vellut 1972: 127
[17] Route description in Graça 1890: 373ff; cf. Childs 1949: 25
[18] Silva Porto 1942: 19f and 1885: 6; cf. Childs 1949: 201f
[19] Dias, forthcoming, cited in Heywood 1984: 113/4
[20] E.g.Silva Porto 1942: 68, 71/73 (=1847, from Luchazi); Heywood 1984: 152f, quoting Cameron on wax caravans of Silva Porto and the king (*Soba*) of Bihe in 1875. For them, beeswax was mainly a means to diversify the commodities carried by caravans and thereby to spread the risks(Vellut 1979: 103)
[21] Graça 1890: 415 (=1846); Vellut 1979: 100 103

i.e. the transport value of beeswax was only about half that of ivory. In addition, beeswax was often offered by producers only in retail quantities, in smaller balls or pieces (Lv. *mbumbe*, 'a little'), and had to be moulded by the trader into full size loaves afterwards (see fig. 1, detail at front side, bottom).[23] This meant that for big traders larger investments in carriers and time would have been required to reach the same turnover in beeswax as in ivory.[24] And this became more and more difficult and expensive among the Ovimbundu and Mbangala because commoners increasingly preferred trading on their own account.

As a consequence, from the 1850s onwards one could meet two types of caravans on the routes of the interior. There were large *sertanejo* caravans carrying mainly ivory (and slaves), but whose *pombeiros* and carriers bought up small quantities of beeswax as 'by-loads' individually. On the other hand, one could meet small groups of Ovimbundu and Mbangala petty traders, partly combined in larger, 'cooperative' caravans, who searched the interior for retail beeswax purchases. 1854, in *Londa* (Southern Lunda country), Livingstone

'often met strings of carriers laden with large blocks of this substance, each 80 or 100 lbs. in weight, and pieces were offered to us for sale at every village...'; and, southeast of Kasanje, he saw 'many parties of native traders, each carrying some pieces of cloth and salt, with a few beads to barter for beeswax',

i.e. items that could be easily divided into small quantities.[25] Many 'little streams made big rivers', [26] and in the late 1870s an estimated total of 9-11 tons of beeswax passed, for example, through Kasanje every year.[27]

Elephant hunters and beeswax collectors

Since the beginning of their trade links to the Atlantic World, producers around the Upper Kasai and Zambezi contributed to these exports. The westernmost groups, Mbunda-Luchazi and Chokwe, were mentioned by the first non-African visitors from Bihe and Kasanje around 1800 as elephant hunters and beeswax collectors. The lands of the former

---

[22] Cf. *ibid.*: 123 129f
[23] Pogge 1880: 53; Lux 1880: 106; Silva Porto 1885: 24 and 166; interview Y.Samakayi, 24.10.1986.
[24] Heywood 1984: 119f
[25] Livingstone 1857: 614 and 358; see also Magyar 1857: 297; Cameron 1877: II 152 182 186 191 [1877]; Capello and Ivens 1882: I 173 197 [1878]
[26] Vellut 1979: 103
[27] Capello/Ivens 1882: I, 291

were characterized as 'lacking food because they are very sandy, but abundant in honey, wax, ivory...'.[28]

The Chokwe, centred around the Kasai source, were probably the first among the peoples of the region to concentrate fully on 'legitimate exports'. Early travellers had described them as 'extremely brave, totally lacking humanity, very demanding', and at the same time as remarkable because 'they do not have slave trade, almost none, because they don't have war with their neighbours; they are very rich in meat and game, principally elephant...'[29] Chokwe chiefs such as Mushiku, mentioned above, are known to have sold ivory and wax to foreign traders.[30] Men in these areas were used to these activities, and they found them easy to combine, which explains the parallel growth of ivory and wax sales (see part C). Just as collecting bees' products was a typical by-activity of men during their elephant hunting trips, the purchase of wax was a typical secondary business of the slave-ivory-caravans.

As a result of this growth, by the end of the 1840s ivory, beeswax and rhinoceros horns were the most important items of external trade for Ovimbundu middlemen.[31] Most ivory was acquired by them through barter from the local population in the regions to their east, although some was also hunted *en route* by members of their own caravans, who were at that time accompanied and protected by specialized groups of elephant hunters (*vakongo a njamba*).[32] Around 1846, numerous travellers crossed the Kwanza, bound for places such as *Quioco* (Chokwe), *Bunda* (Mbunda), *Quiengo, Bomba* (Songo), *Luenna, Luvar* (Luvale), *Ambuellas* (Mbwela), *Cangilla, Cambaca* (?), *Cassaby* (Kasai) etc., i.e. mainly to destinations around the Upper Zambezi and Kasai. On their return, they would pay the ferrymen in ivory and beeswax.[33]

At the same time, fresh news from the production areas were coming in. Two agents of Silva Porto found supply to be plentiful among the Luchazi-Mbunda, and reported that 'they possess cloth originating from the sale of wax, slaves and ivory'.[34] The Chokwe, in their original country, seem in the meantime to have specialized increasingly in beeswax collection, as Graça, in 1846, remarked about them: 'it seems that the Supreme Architect compensated the sterility of this soil with

---

[28] Vieira de Andrade 1940: 252 [1803]
[29] *Anonymus* 1940: 25 [1803]
[30] Baptista 1873: 199 [1805]
[31] Magyar 1857: 297
[32] Magyar 1857: 448
[33] Graça 1890: 404
[34] Silva Porto diary, entries 12. and 28.12.1847 (1986: 325, 330); also Livingstone 1963: 93 [1854]

abundance of wax in whose collection this whole people is engaged.'[35] The same author confirmed 'with certainty' that these two groups produced at that time most of the wax exported through Luanda and Benguela.[36] In 1860, Magyar described the major export commodity from *Quiboco* (Chokwe) as follows:

> 'exceptionally large amounts of wax, the best of South [i.e. Southern] Africa, which they collect in unbelievable quantities in the dense forests of their country from the hives of wild bees, destroying these by fire; furthermore ivory in smaller amounts, and still less slaves. Except in very rare cases, they do not sell people belonging to their own nation.'[37]

Increasing demand for ivory and beeswax caused local producers to step up their spatial mobility to tap more resources. Once again, a shift of the frontier of the 'Atlantic Zone' resulted in major population movements around the Upper Zambezi and Kasai.

The Chokwe, first the male hunters and wax collectors and later their families, moved along two main axes of expansion. The more important axis stretched northeast, along the Chikapa river and its parallels, and down the Kasai. Since the 1840s, Chokwe had been hunting elephants as far away as the core area of the Nuclear Lunda empire.[38] The other axis of Chokwe expansion led south, through Luchazi-Mbunda territory along the headwaters of the Lungwebungu and several other Zambezi tributaries. This movement may have begun even earlier than that to the north, but was less spectacular because more scattered. By 1878, Chokwe elephant hunters and beeswax gatherers had arrived as far south as the Kubangi.[39]

For a long time, the Chokwe residents maintained good relations with the resident populations in both areas of expansion. Later, however, they adopted more agressive attitudes. In the words of Silva Porto, they were

> '...scattered over all places [east of the Kwanza] for the sake of hunting, and in this way (became) acquainted with the residents with whom they live(d) in perfect peace; and later they dictate(d) the law to their host, entering on woollen feet and coming out on iron ones.'[40]

They achieved these good relations partly because they settled in the remotest places and did not compete with the residents for scarce resources. They recognized local power structures and paid for example every second tusk they hunted to the Mwant Yav, who began to depend

---
[35] Graça 1890: 415 [1846]
[36] Graça 1890: 4159[1846]
[37] Magyar 1860: 229
[38] Magyar 1860: 231
[39] Pinto 1881: I, 271; Miller 1970: 197
[40] Silva Porto 1885: 168 [entry 28.3.1880]

on them for his ivory exports.[41] It is probable that much of the 'great amount of ivory' exported from Nuclear Lunda in the 1850s was actually produced by Chokwe hunters, since the Nuclear Lunda were generally described as being poor hunters and traders.[42] Chokwe immigrants also brought labour which they were willing to hire out locally to the residents, and they knew useful subsidiary skills, such as divining, ironwork and carving.[43]

The Luvale also seem to have been involved in early ivory exports, but to a lesser extent. They apparently gave up elephant hunting within their area before the 1850s; thereafter, they exported substantial amounts of beeswax, but relatively little ivory which was hunted or traded by them mainly among the Southern Lunda populations to their east.[44] This fitted well into the general eastward movement of the Luvale in connection with slave raids and struggles to extend their chieftainships. In 1855, Luvale hunters 'having many guns, enjoy(ed) the privilege of hunting on both sides of the river. The *Balonda* (were) able to do little in comparison'[45]

In the late 1840s, the Southern Lunda populations around the Kasai bend were in fact observed to be making little use of their rich ivory resources.[46] But this was different further south. In Bulozi, certain peoples upstream the Zambezi were known as *kalonda maeo* (tusk seekers)[47]. This may have referred to Southern Lunda of Ishinde and the indigenous populations in the woodlands east of the Zambezi and along the Kabompo river, since these were noted to be conducting a thriving ivory trade with traders 'of light colour' in contemporary sources.[48] At the same time, as has been mentioned, pieces of beeswax cakes were offered to travellers at every Southern Lunda village.[49] Another group of important elephant hunters in this remote south eastern portion of the

---

[41] See Miller 1970: 180
[42] Magyar 1860: 231; Pogge 1880: 77, 237
[43] Frobenius 1907: 329; Delachaux and Thiebaud 1934: 135; Schütt 1879: 179
[44] Magyar 1860: 232/33
[45] Livingstone 1963: 270 [1855]
[46] Graça 1890: 427 [Katende, Chibwika]
[47] Livingstone 1960: 42 and fn. 2 [1851]
[48] Livingstone (1963: 32, 41, 49; 213 [1854/55] mentions regular ivory trade along the Makondo river, the offer of a tusk by Masiko on the Manyinga river, and a sale of ivory by Ishinde in 1853/54 to two Euro-African traders bound for Bihe and Kasanje, the latter carrying away over 50 tusks on the heads of his newly acquired slaves. Magyar mentions the Southern Lunda chiefs Musokantanda, Kapende and Kanongesha [Ndembu] as conducting 'a considerable trade in ivory, and are often visited by caravans' in the 1850s (1860: 233).
[49] Livingstone 1857: 614

Upper Zambezi, which was particularly rich in game, were Mbunda refugees from the West, similar to the Luvale.[50]

The widening of trade networks

The main export markets, especially those frequented by the large caravans of bigger Bihe traders, both African and *sertanejo*, gradually moved beyond the Upper Zambezi and Kasai in the course of the 1850s and 60s. The most important centres became Nuclear Lunda, later Luba to the northeast; and Bulozi, later Samba, Lamba, Katanga to the south and east of the region (see map 1). There were several factors behind this renewed shift of the frontier of the 'Atlantic Zone' which had to do with economic and social conditions within the region; in later sections, they will be examined more in detail.

One explanation may be a depletion of ivory resources, which has been mentioned by contemporary visitors and recent scholars and associated with the increasing amounts of firearms that came into the region since the early 19th century in return for slaves, ivory and wax.[51]

Another problem *sertanejos* like Silva Porto found very cumbersome in this region was the very decentralized way in which trading had to be conducted; buying camps had to be set up throughout the area, tusks of increasingly poor quality had to be bartered here and there individually, and for every transaction the trader had to make a liberal allowance of time for negotiations. In addition, prices and demands for other payments increased rapidly and endangered the trader's profit.[52]

Finally, markets beyond the Upper Kasai and Zambezi provided not only more and better ivory, but also more and cheaper slaves. Despite the end of slave **exports** from Africa, slaves continued to be transacted in large, perhaps even greater numbers within the continent. Some of them, mainly the men, were used as carriers to transport ivory and beeswax down to the coast and were then eventually put to work on plantations there.[53] The greater part, however, especially women and children, was bought by caravans for imported goods in the remote east and north only as a means of payment for ivory elsewhere in the interior. The ivory boom depended to a considerable extent on an increasing demand by

---

[50] Livingstone 1963: 30-31; Livingston 1857: 269 [1854]

[51] E.g.Livingstone 1963: 92f, 240, 249 [on areas around the Kasai bend 1854/55]; Miller 1970: 179; see below, C 4.1

[52] Madeira Santos 1986: 105ff 133ff; the first specimen of a seasonal buying camp is mentioned by Silva Porto (Silva Porto diary, entry 28.12.1847 (1986: 330)); see below, part E

[53] Magyar 1860: 234; the official abolition of slavery in Angola took place only in 1876.

peoples of the interior for slaves. The classic example of this new triangular trade network, operated mainly by the *sertanejos*, is Bulozi.

Throughout the era of slave exports, the rulers of Bulozi had been rather reluctant to enter exchange relations with traders coming directly from the Ovimbundu plateau, partly because these were mainly after slaves, and their own economy depended largely on slave labour. In the early 1800s, king Mulambwa refused to give permission to the first Mambari traders to buy slaves.[54] Therefore, the Ovimbundu trade had subsequently bypassed Bulozi to the north, and intensified the market integration of the peoples around the Upper Zambezi and Kasai.

Direct trade between Bihe and Bulozi started only around 1850, when Silva Porto and his agents, followed by other *Mambari* parties, opened the route through Luchazi territory and proposed a new deal to the Lozi-Kololo rulers: to obtain, rather than sell, slaves in return for ivory, which was still plentiful in Bulozi. The rulers of Bulozi, encouraged by the success of Livingstone's famous experimental journey to Luanda in 1854/55, made some attempts to market their ivory directly on the coast, and later diversified their export avenues via South Africa and the East Coast.[55] But at least until the end of the 1860s they remained largely dependent on the middlemen of the Ovimbundu network. These paid the Lozi-Kololo partly with slaves whom they obtained further east (Samba, Southern Luba (Katanga), Lamba (Kafue), Muchinga) and transported to Bulozi via the Ovimbundu plateau. In addition, they paid with imported goods. For them, and for Silva Porto personally, Bulozi became the 'Eldorado of the Ivory': bulk supplies of best-quality ivory from one single partner, the Lozi king, and very modest demands in return.[56] Only in the 'trying 1860s' did the situation gradually begin to deteriorate and resemble more and more the situation further north. Traders from the Ovimbundu plateau then began to increase their efforts to reach new markets further east, in search of the ideal, original conditions of Bulozi - with less success.[57]

---

[54] Hermitte 1974: 50
[55] Roberts 1970: 733/34; Hermitte 1974: 178 180; Madeira Santos 1986: 117ff
[56] Madeira Santos 1986: 105ff; the biggest ever prchase of ivory was realized by Silva Porto in Bulozi in 1864; it was worth 20.000$000 (20 contos de réis), which would represent the value of over 400 tusks in the late 1870s (Silva Porto 1885: 570 [diary entry 4.4.1880] and 24 [entry 9.12.1879]; cf. Hermitte 1974: 193f).
[57] Madeira Santos 1896: 133ff

From production to trade

Far from being outstripped by the shift of the trading frontier, the peoples of the Upper Zambezi and Kasai were quick to take advantage of this advance. In fact, they played certain strategic roles in it: as pioneer traders, and as customers for slaves from further north and east.

Trade contacts with Bulozi, for example, had apparently been prepared by inhabitants of the Upper Zambezi and Kasai taking the role of middlemen themselves. The Luchazi chief Kisembu [*Quicembo*], who died in 1852, was described by Silva Porto as a 'wholesale trader' between Benguela, the plateau and the interior, [58] and his counterpart Kabita [*Cabitta*], on the Lutembwe,

> 'wanted the exclusive market of the ivory which he traded with the chief of *Lui* [Bulozi] (...[Santuru]) and exchanged with the *sertanejos* of Bihé, similar to the *Jaga* of *Cassange's* [the Mbangala ruler] trade with the *Matiamvo* [Mwant Yav, the Nuclear Lunda ruler].'[59]

It cost Silva Porto's agents much patience and very valuable presents to break this barrier and establish direct trade links between Bihe and Bulozi in 1845 and 1847. On the return trips, their caravan was again heavily taxed by Kabita; the justifications given for such exactions, which Silva Porto compared with those by other *Ganguela* groups (mentioning Luvale, Lunda), remain to be examined later (see part E). At any rate, for his subsequent visits to Bulozi Silva Porto explored a new path to circumvent the Luchazi alltogether.[60]

Based on earlier regional trade networks, Luvale and Southern Lunda had also played a role as middlemen between Bulozi and the 'Atlantic Zone' prior to direct trade. They were accustomed to seek their share of the riches of the Bulozi floodplain, mainly livestock, not only by force but also by some form of trade.[61] In return for animals, mainly cattle, Luvale and Southern Lunda offered perhaps slaves, but at least since around 1830 (King Mulambwa's death) mainly cloth, beads and other goods which they had imported themselves from the west.[62] To reach this avenue of access to imported European goods without having to pay with

---

[58] Silva Porto, diary entry 16.12.1847 (1886: 326)

[59] Silva Porto 1891: 16

[60] Silva Porto 1986: 329ff [diary entries 27.12.1847ff]; Silva Porto 1891: 16f; Madeira Santos 1986: 106ff

[61] Luvale-Andonyi had raided the northern floodplain repeatedly in the 18th and early 19th century - see above (Hermitte 1974: 50). Da Silva Teixeira (1940: 237 [1794]) and *Anonymus* (1940: 24/25 [1803]) mention detailed knowledge of Bulozi and an admiration for its wealth on the part of their Luvale hosts, as well as some slaves originating from there.

[62] Livingstone 1960: 41, , 228, 296; 1963: 56, 83

slaves seems to have been one important motive for the Kololo coming from the South to invade Bulozi in 1840.[63]

Luvale and Southern Lunda middlemen were apparently also the pioneers of long-distance trade on the routes to their east. At the court of the Kazembe on the Luapula, in 1831-32, all traders from the West used to be called '*moçambazes de Caquenque*', i.e. *pombeiros* ('trusted men') of Kakenge, the most powerful Luvale chief.[64] Also the Southern Lunda chief Ishinde, who 'knew all the paths to the Portuguese settlements, having travelled them all when he was a young man' (mainly towards Benguela), was said to to have 'frequent intercourse' with the Kazembe in 1854.[65] It was Luvale bands and caravans, perhaps also Southern Lunda and Lozi, who opened up for trade in slaves and ivory the farthest point to the east that the Ovimbundu subsequently, in the 1850s, were to reach: the Lamba area, near present-day Kabwe on the Zambian 'Line of Rail'. There they met Bisa and Swahili traders who exported ivory and slaves to the East Coast.[66] Here, as well as in Katanga and on the Luapula, Luvale middlemen helped to establish a transcontinental trade connection, or, in other words, the missing link between the 'Atlantic' and 'Indian Ocean' zones of the pre-colonial world market.[67] Arab and Swahili traders subsequently also reached the Upper Zambezi, and some of them are even said to have settled there.[68]

As a consequence of these developments, still in the 1850s, the empire of the Kazembe on the Luapula, and the newly established Katanga (*Garenganze*) kingdom of Msiri, a Nyamwezi trader from the east, were included in the Ovimbundu network.[69] The route from Bihe along the Kasai-Zambezi watershed, i.e. through the centre of the region under

---

[63] Roberts 1970: 732

[64] Gamitto 1937: I, 325. *moçambazes* was the term used for caravan leaders and agents from Mozambique who frequented Kazembe's court, equivalent to *pombeiro* on the Angolan side.

[65] Livingstone 1963: 55 and 67

[66] Silva Porto 1938: 113 (cf.Vansina 1962: 384 and fn. 62); Only early long-distance raiding or trading contacts to areas far to the Southeast can explain the presence of Ndebele slave women as wives of Ishinde and Masiko in 1854 (Livingstone 1963: 27, 54)

[67] It remains unclear whether there were early trade connections between the Luvale and the East Coast of Africa, perhaps through the Lozi and Tonga along the Zambezi river, as is suggested by a mysterious report of 1799 (Vieira de Andrade 1940: 253) : 'The Zambezi river, they say, is rather large, and on it travel large barges, with sails made of straw, and the negroes who come with them to trade with the people of Lovar give notice that from their land, which is situated on the sea (*á Lunga*) one hears artillery shots, bells and war noise, and that they see ships passing which they call *Brica* (brigg)...' - but this was perhaps a misunderstanding, and the informant, a slave, may as well have been talking about another connection between the Upper Zambezi and the Atlantic Coast, different from the Bihe-Benguela route.

[68] Livingstone 1960: 228; 1963: 11 [1853]; Papstein 1978: 243, 245

study, became the most frequented transit route of West Central Africa. But even when Ovimbundu and *sertanejos* frequented this route, indigenous traders continued to be seen along it, mainly Chokwe and Luvale trading in ivory, slaves and beeswax.[70]

Chokwe trading started apparently in connection with the migrations of elephant hunters and beeswax collectors to the north east. In 1855, the boundary between independent Chokwe chiefs and vassals of the Mwant Yav (Nuclear Lunda) reached Mona Kimbundu, on the main route from Luanda-Kasanje to the Musumba, the capital of Nuclear Lunda.[71] The fact that the Chokwe lived there in diaspora may have caused their particular propensity to trade, as it did for so many other peoples in Africa. The commercial traffic passing along this route became a particular attraction for migrant Chokwe, [72] who quickly seized the opportunity of extracting export and import goods from passing caravans by means to be discussed further below.[73] But by the mid 1860s, Chokwe from around Mona Kimbundu also began to carry guns and other imported goods far to the north east beyond the Kasai, and exchange them with the Bena Lulua and Kuba, mainly for slaves, and with the Luba for ivory.[74] Market centres where Chokwe caravans regularly called sprang up at Kalamba's and Mai Munene's capitals. (See fig. 4)

While Chokwe traders were the pioneers who 'opened' the areas mentioned for the 'Atlantic Zone', they also traded on the older market of the Musumba, with whom they had already established exchange relations in the early 19th century, before their migrations began.[75] In alliance with the Ovimbundu, Chokwe traders brought about an increasing control of the Nuclear Lunda market through the southern network (Bihe)[76], which resulted in violent clashes between the Ovimbundu and their Mbangala competitors in the 1850s.[77]

---

[69] Vansina 1962: 384; Cameron 1877: II 140, 208
[70] Cameron 1877: II 139 160 [1875]
[71] Livingstone 1963: 234; Schütt 1881: 131/2; according to Pogge, the first foreign (non-Nuclear Lunda) potentate of Kimbundu was not a Chokwe but a Luvale, a man who had outlived three Mwant Yavs until 1875 (Pogge 1880: 45-51), which would mean he arrived between 1853 and 1857 (according to the dates of reigns presented by Vellut 1972: 163).
[72] Dias de Carvalho 1890: 556-560
[73] Graça 1890: 410, 413, 423 [1846]; Livingstone 1963: *passim* [1854/55]
[74] Pogge 1880: 51 [1875]; Schütt 1879: 182; Vansina 1962: 384; Vansina 1966: 220f; Miller 1970: 182f
[75] Pogge 1880: 51; Nuclear Lunda oral traditions, cited by Vellut 1972: 148
[76] Soremekun 1977: 87
[77] Magyar 1957: 446

Apart from acting as traders, during the second half of the 19th century an increasing number of Upper Zambezi inhabitants also began to sell their own labour to foreign caravans, as 'workers of trade'.[78] Many younger men, due to their geographical position and experience in travelling mainly Luvale and Chokwe, hired themselves out to passing caravans as guides, carriers or armed guards. This happened particularly in important chiefs' headquarters along the main 'watershed' route and on the routes north of the Kasai.[79] But carriers and above all guides for shorter distances were also hired at smaller places in the hinterland, e.g. at Ishinde's and Katema's in the south, at Chokwe villages north of the Kasai (Luachimo, Luembe), and in Luchazi and Chokwe villages along the route from Bihe to Bulozi.[80] With increasing demand for porterage, the number and radius of Upper Zambezi 'workers of trade' increased. Around the turn of the century, Luvale carriers went as far as Benguela, while Chokwe would take contracts only until Bihe at most.[81] What they ultimately strove for, however, was most probably to set up themselves as independent traders. At least among the Ovimbundu, the typical career of a caravan worker was to start exchanging small amounts of imported goods (taken from the part his pay that usually had to be advanced to them) for other trade goods during his employment. Later, he would try to become an agent of caravan leaders or owners, before he could try to start trading on his own account when he had accumulated sufficient capital.

The interest of inhabitants of the Upper Zambezi and Kasai in engaging in the trade-related activities described so far was first of all to increase their access to exportable goods, mainly ivory, but also slaves for sale to other areas within Africa. Their aim, then, appears clearly as an accumulation of imported, manufactured goods. But the example of the Luvale and Chokwe shows that ultimately other aims were also at stake. The Luvale and Southern Lunda interest in using imported goods to acquire livestock has been mentioned already. The Chokwe, in contrast, bought for their ivory, according to Magyar, 'European manufactures of considerable value and slaves' for themselves, from passing Mbangala and Ovimbundu caravans on their return journeys.[82] And the European

---

[78] Coquéry-Vidrovitch and Lovejoy (eds.) 1985
[79] E.g. Livingstone 1963: 242 [1855: Kabango]; Capello and Ivens 1882: I 189 [1878: Ndumba Tembo]; Vellut 1972: 121 [Mona Kimbundu]
[80] E.g. Livingstone 1963: 65, 88 116, 249/50 [1854/55]; Pinto 1881: 272, 278 [1878]
[81] Singleton-Fisher 1948: 90; Relatório do Capitão-mor do Moxico 1905, in: Delgado 1944: 667
[82] Magyar 1860: 229

manufactures were to some extent reinvested in trade to obtain more ivory for more slaves from their north-eastern neighbours.[83]

Similarly to the Lozi, Chokwe unwillingness to sell slaves by no means meant that they were not interested in them; they only wanted to acquire slaves for themselves, mainly women and children. The Luvale had a similar interest in slaves for themselves, but apparently obtained them in sufficient quantity by warfare; this enabled them to spend their export earnings for other purposes and even to export 'surplus' slaves.[84] As everywhere in Africa, prolonged slave trade led to a reduction of population or at least of demographic growth; but in this part this applied only to areas east of the Zambezi and Kasai. To their west, and especially near to the main caravan routes, sometimes rather dramatic population increases may have occurred.[85] In the 1850s, Magyar asserted about *Kibokoe* [Chokwe heartland]:

> 'The population is exceptionally large in relation to the extension of the country, and we can claim with certainty that *Kibokoe* is more densely populated than any other country of the interior of Africa.'[86]

Miller has therefore argued that population pressure from at least the 1850s, exacerbated by epidemics in the 1870s, was one of the reasons for the great Chokwe expansion.[87] Existing data coverage appears too thin to me to prove this hypothesis.

Their demand for, and partly their supply of, slaves, assured the inhabitants of the Upper Zambezi and Kasai an important role in the new trade networks of West Central Africa even without producing for the world market themselves.

But the production of 'legitimate goods' for export remained an important option for this region throughout the century, and the variety and uses of imported goods exchanged for them are yet to be examined. With the decline of ivory exports, beeswax production attained increasing importance. The position of the region was favourable: ample resources on the one hand, and relatively short distances from the West Coast that could be easily covered by small-scale Ovimbundu and Mbangala traders,

---

[83] Pogge 1880: 51; Frobenius 1988: 73 [1905]

[84] E.g. Magyar 1860: 233

[85] Frobenius (1988: 75) observed high numbers of children in Northern Chokwe in 1905 (contrasting with remarkably low birth rates among Chokwe today), perhaps due to the slave status of many women.

[86] Magyar 1860: 229; also *Lobál* (Luvale country) is described as very populous (Magyar 1860: 233). Miller assumes a relatively small demographic impact of slave exports up to 1830 for West Central Africa, and relative 'overpopulation' in various parts (1888: 163-169).

[87] Miller 1970: 187f

and made it still economic to export even lower-value goods.[88] But producers in the region, particularly the smaller-scale and less powerful, were also more than ready to meet this demand. Without their active interest in selling their products, the impressive rise of the beeswax trade and the subsequent rubber boom would hardly have been possible. Assuming a number of 50 hives per beekeeper, as is the average observed in Zambezi District in 1986, [89] the probably over 500 tons of wax exported through Benguela in the 1870s would have been produced by at least 18, 000 Upper Zambezi beekeepers.[90]

Fig. 4: 'Angola caravan' (Chokwe ?) with ivory loads in the Congo (around 1900)

Chokwe were the main suppliers of ivory in West Central Africa, and some of this trade continued after the establishment of the 'Congo Free State'. Note the numerous, richly decorated 'wives' or mistresses accompanying the carriers. (Origin unknown, photograph kindly supplied by Prof. Georg Elwert)

---

[88] Beeswax exports apparently ceased to be economic due to distance eastwards of the Kasai and Kabompo (see Silva Porto 1938: 106).

[89] According to Wendorf 1988: 99, 80% of the hives are occupied, and a yield of 30 kg of wax is obtained by every beekeeper on average (with wide fluctuations). The following calculation is based on the assumption that all wax is produced in hives, and that production methods have remained the same. In reality, a higher percentage than today may have been gathered from wild swarms ('bee-hunting' - see fig. 15).

[90] Vellut (1979: 102f) arrived at a much higher figure of 90-230,000 beekeepers working for export. He may, however, have assumed only one harvest per year (while two seem to be usual) and a lower yield per hive.

B 4 The 'Rubber Delirium' (c.1880-1910)

The developments associated with the beeswax trade intensified and accelerated considerably during the last pre-colonial stage of the economic history of the West-Central African interior. This stage was largely determined by the rapidly growing world market demand for rubber. Following the invention of vulcanization by C. Goodyear in 1844, rubber was needed in vast quantities by the industrializing countries during the later 19th century, mainly for protective clothing (military equipment), tyres and subsequently electrical products.[1] Before the *hevea* rubber plantations of Malaysia and elsewhere went into production (around 1913), all this rubber was collected from wild plants, mainly in Brasil and Western Africa. In Angola, the gallery forests and shrubby plains east of the Kwanza and Kwango turned out to provide excellent resources for wild rubber. Between about 1870 and 1910 the *Ganguela* peoples between the Kwanza, the Upper Kasai and Zambezi were the most important suppliers in Angola. Due to their greater proximity to the Ovimbundu, the Chokwe and Luchazi were the first to enter this form of commodity production.[2]

Two phases must be distinguished. Between 1869 and 1886, only the latex tapped from *landolphia* shrubs, called 'first class rubber', was exported in the form of rubber balls. 1874 has been assumed as the beginning of the era of rubber trade for Benguela and the Ovimbundu plateau. But initially, rubber supplemented rather than replaced ivory and beeswax, the other 'legitimate' export products of the Angolan interior. Only in 1882 did rubber reach the second position in exports from there, after beeswax. (see table 3).[3]

A more dramatic change in the structure of exports, as can be seen from table 3, occurred only in the late 1880s. In 1886, for the first time an Ovimbundu caravan arrived down on the coast with loads of a new type of rubber of reddish colour, packed in bundles of sticks of about candle size rather than in balls. This 'red rubber' came from the roots of *carpodinus gracilis*, a creeper that thrives on the Kalahari sands surrounding the Upper Kasai and Zambezi. With bulk supplies of this new product, which came to be known at the London stock exchange as *Loanda Niggers*,[4] rubber became the absolutely dominant export

---
1 E.g. Hobson 1960: 491; Harms 1975: 74
2 Interview Mr. Sondoyi, 24.10.1986; Arnot 1969: 81 [1884]
3 Childs 1949: 202f, 208; Hobson 1960: 492/3
4 Vellut 1972: 127

commodity not only for the interior, but for Angola as a whole. The rubber boom, or the *delirio de borracha* ('rubber delirium'), as some observers called it,[5] was to last well into the 20th century, with a peak in its first decade when 77% of all Angolan exports consisted of wild rubber (see table 3).

The rather atypical increases of rubber prices on the world market, amidst a general slump of commodity prices after the 1870s, was certainly the basis of this development.[6] But the 'dizzying prices' wild rubber fetched down on the coast oscillated too much to be the only explanation of the dramatic growth of rubber exports from the interior around the turn of the century.[7] At least of equal importance was the social structure of the supply networks and the similarities with the older beeswax trade.

With regard to the trade channels, the rubber boom was 'in its inception and its great development an enterprise of the Ovimbundu'.[8] Consequently, the route to Bihe, Catumbela and Benguela became the main gateway for rubber exports. Portuguese-speaking *sertanejos*, in contrast, were apparently unable to realize the potential of this new trade. In the course of the 1860s, their profits had declined steadily, despite falling prices for manufactured goods. Madeira Santos, analysing the notes of Silva Porto, has explained this by a continuous increase of costs in the interior as a result of clinging to the old pattern of ivory trade. The exploration of ever new and more distant buying markets for ivory, an inability to account for effectively rising producer prices, and compensatory income strategies of underpaid Ovimbundu carriers and agents finally made large-scale trading so unattractive that in 1870, when rubber exports had just began, the two biggest *sertanejos* (including Silva Porto himself) decided to leave the plateau.[9]

---

5 Soremekun 1977: 90
6 Childs 1949: 2; Clarence-Smith 1979b: 175/76
7 Prices paid in Benguela per kg were 1.440 milréis in 1884, 0.800-0.900 in 1885 (probably *landolphia*), but only about 0.600 in 1893 (Heywood 1984: 166f, quoting AHU sources). In the long run, however, world market prices increased considerably. Antwerp prices rose from 100 in 1886 to 102 (1890) 113 (1895) 171 (1900) and 205 (1905) up to 341 (1910), before they fell to 76 in 1913 (Vellut 1977: 301).
8 Childs 1949: 209
9 Madeira Santos 1986: 157ff; see below, chapter E 3

Table 3: Exports from Angola 1760-1908 (in current values)

Year(s)	Reference area	Total (=100%)	Percentages: Slaves	Ivory	Wax	Rubber	Sources
A:	Referring only to products of the interior						
1760-69*	Luanda	304,000 $[a]	80.3	n.a.[b]	19.7	0	A:100
1760-69*	Benguela	149,000 $	94.0	6.0	n.a.[b]	0	B:134
1844	Angola	108,000 $	n.a[b]	70.3	29.7	0	H: 75
1848/9	Luanda	387,620 $	n.a[b]	82.9	17.1	0	C:437
1886	Benguela	290,387 $[a]	0	13.0	64.5	22.5	D:208
1887	Benguela	482,806 $	0	7.6	32.9	59.4	E: 35
1888	Benguela	804,519 $	0	3.7	13.6	82.6	ibid.
1889	Benguela	830,884 $	0	3.8	16.1	80.1	ibid.
1890	Benguela	886,038 $	0	1.3	10.6	88.2	ibid.
1891	Benguela	1211,151 $	0	3.7	10.2	86.0	ibid.
1904-08	Angola	3924,000 $	0	0	?	?	A:101
B:	Referring to all export products:						
1847	Angola	680,000$					F: 27
1848/9	Luanda	726,446$	n.a.[b]	46.5	9.6	0	C:437
1874	Angola	2671,000$					F:27
1884	Angola	2208,000$	02.3		11.7	37.3	F: 33
1895	Angola	?			c35.0		G:167
1904-08*	Angola	4413,600$	0	0	8.1	70.2	A:101
1900-09*	Angola	820,000£[c]	0	0	?	77.0	G:167

Notes:
*per annum;
[a] $ =milréis (=escudos), more exactly 'weak reis' (colonial currency) until 1861 when
metropolitan or 'strong' reis were introduced in Angola, which meant in effect a slight revaluation against the Pound on international markets, but less than the official 35% (see I:xi);
[b] not included in total, but negligible quantity;
[c] Pound Sterling; exchange rate fluctuated between 4.5 and 8 milréis for one £ (I:xi).

Sources:
A = Vellut 1979; B = Vellut 1975; C = Livingstone 1857; D = Childs 1949; E = Ministério da Marinha 1894; F = Ministério da Marinha 1889; G = Clarence-Smith 1983; H = Madeira Santos 1986; I = Clarence-Smith 1979a.

Trained in trading on their own account during service at least since 1855, ex-*pombeiros* and carriers now grasped their chance to establish themselves as independent petty rubber dealers. As with beeswax, rubber presented ideal conditions for them. It could be broken down into very small units and required few overhead costs if bought retail in not too distant areas. The breakthrough for what has been called the 'Ovimbundu miracle' was in 1874 when Ovimbundu traders became directly accredited by the coastal merchants of Benguela.[10]

Fig. 5: Ovimbundu *pombeiros* from Bihe (1891)
Note the conspicuous wealth in clothing of these caravan leaders (Photograph from Johnston 1893: 46)

The social and economic benefits of a reduction of transport distance, hence of costs, time and risk, were felt among the Ovimbundu especially after 1886. The *landolphia* vines, which grow better in a more humid environment, were soon depleted by Chokwe and Luchazi collectors and had to be sought ever further north in the gallery forests along major

---

[10] Hitherto, they had obtained credit only from resident *sertanejos*. See Madeira Santos 1986: 169ff; Heywood 1984: 145ff

tributaries of the Kasai.[11] The roots of the *carpodinus* creeper, in contrast, are more laborious to process, but they thrive everywhere in the Kalahari sand areas which are located much closer to the Ovimbundu Plateau. Consequently, in this period the majority of Ovimbundu middlemen could operate within a reduced radius from home, and concentrated more on the Upper Zambezi and Kasai than they had done in the previous periods.

When Silva Porto returned from Benguela to Bihe in 1879/80, he had great difficulties in recruiting staff for his caravans and realized the changed situation with a good deal of bitterness:

> 'The people from Mbailundu and Bihe have at present turned into traders and therefore care only for their own interests, paying little respect to the interests of the *sertanejos* to whom they owe their advanced position through the many losses they caused them; we [I] know some of these because they were our carriers before we descended to Benguela, and now we find them wearing hats on their heads, shoes, and being carried in a hammock like a European...'[12]

(see also figs. 1 and 2)

Trained in trading on their own account during service at least since 1855, ex-*pombeiros* and carriers now grasped their chance to establish themselves as independent petty rubber dealers. As with beeswax, rubber presented ideal conditions for them. It could be broken down into very small units and required few overhead costs if bought retail in not too distant areas. The breakthrough for what has been called the 'Ovimbundu miracle' was in 1874 when Ovimbundu traders became directly accredited by the coastal merchants of Benguela.[13]

Trained in trading on their own account during service at least since 1855, ex-*pombeiros* and carriers now grasped their chance to establish themselves as independent petty rubber dealers. As with beeswax, rubber presented ideal conditions for them. It could be broken down into very small units and required few overhead costs if bought retail in not too distant areas. The breakthrough for what has been called the 'Ovimbundu miracle' was in 1874 when Ovimbundu traders became directly accredited by the coastal merchants of Benguela.[14]

Some of these newly independent traders grew big enough to compete with the *sertanejos* for bulk business in ivory and slaves far to the East and North, on the markets of Msiri (Katanga) and Mai Munene (Luba).

---

[11] Already in 1875, rubber resources south of Mona Kimbundu were exhausted (Pogge 1880: 46).

[12] Silva Porto 1885: 18

[13] Hitherto, they had obtained credit only from resident *sertanejos*. See Madeira Santos 1986: 169ff; Heywood 1984: 145ff

[14] Hitherto, they had obtained credit only from resident *sertanejos*. See Madeira Santos 1986: 169ff; Heywood 1984: 145ff

But the transit routes through Chokwe and the other *Ganguela* peoples were increasingly difficult and expensive to pass, due to the rivalry of indigenous traders and 'endless questions of debt and credit'.[15] The less distant and less vulnerable rubber business may thereby have gained even more in importance.

> Because of its easy access, almost the entire Ovimbundu population, including children of both sexes and old people (but not including married women), was involved in the 'rubber delirium', and rubber trading began to dominate all other activities on the plateau. By the 1890s, mission schools on the Plateau remained unattended partly for this reason, and frustrated missionaries observed during the dry season that 'many villages were left empty because most of the people have gone inland with their own trade', and that '...the steadily increasing demand for bicycle tyres and other articles...led to the greatest rush to the *Nganguelas* ...'[16]

Heywood estimates that already in the 1880s, some 50,000 Ovimbundu were involved in the export of the products of the interior, mainly rubber, as petty traders and carriers, with a rising tendency.[17] Cloth was again the most important form of payment, similar to wax.

At the producers' end, unheard-of numbers of inhabitants of the Upper Zambezi and Kasai, Chokwe, Luvale, Luchazi-Mbunda and Southern Lunda, were infected by the *rubber delirium*. Digging *carpodinus* roots was for them just another form of collection economy, and so few means of production and skills were required that rubber export led to an even more widespread participation of petty producers in the market than beeswax. If it is true that the average producer was selling as little as one pound of rubber[18], in a year like 1891 about 350,000 people would have produced the supplies of Benguela, at a time when the total population of Upper Zambezi peoples may be estimated at about 800,000.[19] This meant in reality that whole villages, men, women and children, were involved in the processing of *carpodinus* roots, with dispersed groups of Ovimbundu traders in their camps waiting to buy the proceeds on the doorstep.[20].

In 1986, I met a Luvale elder originating from Kayanga on the main 'watershed' route who still remembered the rubber boom. He described rubber as 'the easiest mine we have ever had here', alluding to the far-off wealth of the copper mines which were later to become so influential for them, but on which they had much less control than over wild rubber. In

---

15 Silva Porto diary, 5.5.1885, quoted by Madeira Santos 1986: 185
16 CCFMS Angola mission Annual Report 1898, and Fisher Diary [1893], quoted by Heywood 1984: 181
17 Heywood 1984: 173
18 Silva Porto diary 1887 (quoted in Heywood 1984: 150)
19 See population figures in the introduction, chapter A 3.
20 Interview Mr.Sondoyi, 24.10.1986; Gossweiler 1907: 52-53 (cited in Heywood 1984: 150)

his memory, the people of Kayanga 'were rich only in the times of rubber - afterwards, they had to go to Katanga for work' (as migrant workers).[21]

As with beeswax, local traders, mainly Chokwe from the Northern diaspora, played an important role in collecting retail quantities from individual producers; they sometimes even managed to bypass the Ovimbundu and to sell beeswax and rubber down in Portuguese territory, in order to raise the means to buy ivory and slaves further in the interior.[22] But local rubber trading was also going on among the Luvale. The famous chieftainess Nyakatolo, for example, was nicknamed *Nyakandundu* (or *Nanakandundu*), 'mother of rubber', because her capital at Kavungu was an important rubber market,[23] important enough perhaps to cause a southward shift of the main 'watershed' route leading to Katanga.[24] Rubber and beeswax offered at this and other caravan relays was collected from outlying producers in the woodlands across the Zambezi, Southern Lunda mixed with a rapidly increasing number of Luvale immigrants, by local petty traders, as I was informed by one of them.[25]

The rubber cycle of world market integration was once again accompanied by increased mobility of the populations of the Upper Zambezi and Kasai to the east and the south. They were partly motivated by the search for more rubber resources and by peaceful trading ventures. The main 'watershed' route to the east (Katanga) provided one obvious line of expansion. In 1875, Luvale settlers had already reached as far east as the Luvua headwaters.[26] In 1900, the most advanced Chokwe villages were even found 120 km east of the Luvua, one of them significantly called '*kundundu*'(from the indigenous term for root rubber).[27] Simultaneously, both Chokwe and Luvale advanced rapidly along the Kasai to the north.[28]

But violence had not ceased to play a role in the migrations of the late 19th century. Nyakatolo, for example, had conquered the Kavungu area, formerly under vassals of Nuclear Lunda, around 1875 and pushed rapidly further east as far as today's Mwinilunga and Kasempa Districts of NW Zambia. Her main objective was to capture slaves among the

---

[21] Interview Sondoyi 18.and 26.10.1986
[22] Pogge 1880: 45 [1875; Northern Chokwe]; Capello and Ivens 1882: I, 225 [1878, Central Chokwe]; Silva Porto 1885: 168 [1880; Northern Chokwe]
[23] Interview Sondoyi 14.10.1986; cf.Papstein 1978: 245
[24] Arnot 1969: 162 [1885]
[25] Interview Y.Samakayi, 21.10.1986
[26] At a place called Sona Bazh, probably near the modern Caianda (Cameron 1877: II 187/8).
[27] Lemaire 1902: 50f
[28] Gibbons 1904: 8 [1900]

Southern Lunda populations there, like her rival Kangombe.[29] Lunda-Ndembu leaders near the main route followed their example.[30]

The wealth and population of the core area of the Nuclear Lunda empire had the greatest attraction for Chokwe, who were assisted in the advance to some extent by Luvale. They profited from a state of declining authority of the Mwant Yav, ultimately caused by the changing structure of long-distance trade since the mid-19th century.[31] The rulers of Nuclear Lunda increasingly relied on armed bands of Chokwe as mercenaries for their internal power struggles; the Chokwe were glad of a free hand to raid Nuclear Lunda villages as their pay.[32] Finally, the contenders for the Mwant Yav title 'lost control of their mercenaries and saw their imperial capital fall in 1886 to enormous caravans and armies of Chokwe'.[33] The conquest of Nuclear Lunda resulted in thousands of slaves being taken by the Chokwe, and in 'a reign of terror'.[34]. Although the Chokwe thus reached the peak of their influence and wealth, they failed to erect stable political institutions and succumbed after few years to the combined counter-attacks of exiled Nuclear Lunda forces and troops of the newly proclaimed 'Congo Free State'. Around the same time, Luvale raids to the south east, into the lands of the Southern Lunda chief Ishinde, assumed such dimensions that the latter called on the Lozi for help. In 1892, the Luvale narrowly escaped defeat by Lozi troops by an outbreak of smallpox in the enemy's camp.[35] Temporary setbacks did not prevent further non-violent migrations of Luvale and Chokwe populations in search of more rubber and trade.

From the beginning to the end of the pre-colonial period the expansion of export production in the interior appears in connection with the search for slaves. Raiders and traders from the Upper Zambezi and Kasai, along with the Ovimbundu, used the proceeds of earlier exports to acquire human beings from further east, partly for themselves, partly to buy more rubber or ivory,[36] and partly for export to the coast.[37] My old Luvale informant from Caianda, on the main 'watershed' route, recalls

[29] Gibbons 1904: 8 [1900]; Papstein 1978: 226
[30] Turner 1957: 13 (Ikelenge)
[31] Vellut 1972: 158f
[32] Frobenius 1988: 75 [1905]
[33] Miller 1983: 156; see Vansina 1966
[34] Miller 1970: 198; Vellut 1972: 150
[35] Papstein 1978: 195-96
[36] Interview Sondoyi, 24.10.1986; but very little ivory arrived in Benguela in the 1890s, and virtually none after 1900 (see table 2).
[37] Gangs of slaves, labelled as *serviçaes* or *contractos* (contract labourers), continued to be exported to the plantations along the Atlantic coast, to the first mines of Katanga, and

Ovimbundu flocking along with 'bundles of guns and buckets of gunpowder', mainly as a payment for slaves, when he was a boy in the early 1900s.[38] 'Every caravan we pass has a string of slaves, and Bihé traders say they would rather have slaves than ivory', observed Arnot in 1885 at Kavungu, which was also a major slave market.[39] Around the turn of the century, Portuguese colonial rule was formally established in the area, but in practice it had very little impact (see part A). Alongside a thriving trade in various commodities, mainly rubber, the miseries of long-distance slave caravans remained on record (see also fig. 3).[40]

---

even to the diamond fields of Transvaal (Childs 1949: 213; Soremekun 1977: 88; Clarence-Smith 1983: 167f; Vellut 1977: 300; Cameron 1877: II 140).
[38] Sondoyi 18.10.1986
[39] Arnot 1969: 164 [1885]
[40] E.g.Harding 1904: 207, 211; Lemaire 1902: *passim*

B 5 By the roadside: Services for travellers

The Ovimbundu trade in rubber ended rather abruptly in 1911, before *carpodinus* resources in the interior were exhausted, and even before world market prices were fully hit by increasing supplies of inexpensive, high quality rubber from the new *hevea* plantations in SE Asia[1]. For reasons to be examined later, 1911 was experienced as 'the year of the great hunger in the Ngangela country'. Of the many Ovimbundu caravans that had gone out in that year's dry season towards the Upper Zambezi and Kasai, only 'few stronger members returned to the highlands - mere skeletons and shadows'.[2]

This event highlights the caravans' crucial dependence on food supplies during their journey. For inhabitants of the interior, however, this dependence meant yet another acces to the market, as producers of surplus foodstuffs. Subsequently, in the colonial period, food production for sale turned out to be the dominant form of local commodity production; but it is little known that its roots can be found in the pre-colonial era of long-distance trade.

The problem of provisions

Throughout this era, the procurement of food had been a constant source of worry for caravan leaders. Up to the mid-19th century, the majority of travellers to be fed were certainly slaves on their way to the coast. In general, slaves were actually nourished very poorly during the first parts of their journey, so that many of them died on the roadside; those remaining had to recover before they entered the Angolan markets, in a place where food was plentiful.[3] The Upper Zambezi and Kasai area apparently contained such places. When Pogge, in 1875,

> '... enquired from the leader of a (Mbangala) slave caravan, which came from Southern Lunda, why they had starved their slaves so much, they remarked: that didn't matter, they went to the north to the Chikapa river; there, a lot of cheap

---

[1] See Harms 1975; he explains the premature ending of rubber collection in 'free trade' zones mainly by rising opportunity costs, in contrast to the areas controlled by concession companies in the emerging 'Congo Independent State', where under brutal coercion production could go on until rubber resources were completely destroyed.

[2] Childs 1949: 212

[3] E.g.Baptista 1873: 232/3: '...all the slaves we brought died of hunger; ...with the men ill and dying on the road...it became necessary to stay two months at the river Luburi [now Southern Zaire - A.v.O.] to get the people into condition, who had come in so pale, thin and ill from hunger...'[1812, on return from Kazembe.]

fuba [cassava meal] was available, and there they would soon fatten up the people, in order to barter them away favourably.'[4]

The problem was one of considerable dimensions: Assuming that about half of all export slaves were being driven from or through the Upper Zambezi and Kasai routes, up to about 20,000 slaves would have left or passed the area during peak years in the early 1800s, not taking into account those who perished on the way.[5] In the second half of the century, freely recruited carriers and petty traders probably constituted the bulk of the itinerant population that crossed the Upper Zambezi and Kasai. Those who wanted to conduct business in the area itself, an increasing number when wax and rubber became the staple goods for export, even lived there temporarily, some of them not only during the dry season, but even through the rains, when food tends to be scarce, in order to return towards the coast the following year.[6] If Linda M. Heywood's estimation quoted earlier is correct, some 50.000 Ovimbundu left their homes every year in the 1880s to trade in the interior, most of them to buy rubber from the populations east of the Kwanza, and this figure probably further increased until the Mbailundu uprising in 1902. In September or October 1908, still as many as 400 homeward-bound Ovimbundu crossed the Kwanza every day.[7]

Not only the absolute amount, but also the spatial distribution of food demand is important in an area as thinly populated as the Upper Zambezi and Kasai. In the earlier period, caravans were probably fewer and relatively large, particularly those equipped by wealthy European merchants, and comprised several hundred persons each.[8] The number of travellers was further swelled by the younger relatives, personal slaves and even wives or mistresses who accompanied pombeiros, carriers, and elephant hunters (see fig. 4).[9] When the emphasis of trade shifted to beeswax and rubber, caravans into the interior grew more numerous, but

---

[4] Pogge 1880: 51/2
[5] See figures given in chapter B 1
[6] See for example Cameron 1877: II, 202, who wrote that Bihe carriers stayed in the interior up to two years [1875]; or Magyar (1857: 148): 'the caravans travelling to the remote countries of the interior usually stay away a whole year.'
[7] Heywood 1984: 367
[8] Graça's caravan in 1846, for example, comprised 400 carriers (1890: 382); Silva Porto's caravan going for ivory to Bulozi in 1864, carried goods worth 20 *contos de réis*, i.e. over 400 loads of trade goods; Magyar travelled in 1857 with numerous personal slaves, 250 elephant hunters, and many free inhabitants of Bihe, in all a party of over 400 people (N. de Kun 1960: 632, quoting Magyar's correspondence; Magyar 1960: 229). But smaller caravans occurred as well: the Euro-African trader who left Ishinde in 1854 for Kasanje had only 66 slaves carrying upwards of 50 tusks of ivory (Livingstone 1963: 213).
[9] Lux 1880: 62, and Pogge 1880: 12/13, 68 [both 1875]; Heywood 1984: 176

smaller on average. In 1875 European merchants and nobles from Bihe or Kasanje then sent 50-100 people at a time.[10] In the Chokwe and Luvale areas, people were accustomed to the passing of Ovimbundu caravans of about 100-150 members in the 1880s[11], and after the turn of the century

Fig. 6: Armed Bihe caravan carrier, with typical load (1878)
The load appears to contain import goods, i.e. a *banzo*. For its typical construction cf. fig. 14. Carriers themselves were not usually armed with guns.
(Engraving from Pinto 1881, vol.I: 162)

even smaller parties of 20-70 were usual.[12] Most caravans in this period were in fact cooperative enterprises of smaller groups of individual traders with a joint concern for security.[13]

---

10 Pogge 1880: 58, 69/70; Cameron diary: various entries Sept.1875, quoted in Heywood 1984: 152-3, and Soremekun 1977: 86
11 Arnot 1889: 153, 248 [1885]
12 Statistics from Bihe (1903) and Wambu (1908), quoted by Heywood 1984: 366
13 Vellut 1972: 137/8, speaks of 'caravanes composites'. Cameron 1877: II 139, gives a vivid example of 'the different parties of which the [his] caravan consisted...: my own party formed one camp; Alvez [Euro-African trader] and his people with their slaves formed another; Coimbra [another Euro-african], his wives and slave gang a third; and Bastian a fourth; besides which there were two camps of independent parties from Bihé;

Within the area of destination, caravans would set up a main camp (*otjilombo* in Umb.), somewhere near the main routes, from where they dispersed into many smaller camps throughout the country. There, they often stayed for considerable periods while bargaining and waiting for their products. Da Silva Porto had such a buying station for ivory and wax already in 1847 among the Mbunda, while the main caravan continued its way to Bulozi[14], and Capello and Ivens found in 1878 in central Chokwe that 'the encampments of Bihénos, in search of wax, are dispersed throughout the dense woods of the country'.[15] Further north, at

Fig. 7: Caravan camp on the main 'watershed' route (1875)
At Lupanda. Some negotiations between caravan leader, foremen and carriers seem to be going on. (Engraving from Cameron 1877, vol.II: 145)

the same time, European traders had already begun to set up semi-permanent 'factories' for the purchase of rubber and ivory, manned with

another of Kibokwé [Chokwe] people; and yet one more of Lovalé men, or, as they were usually called, Kinyama [Chinyama] men, after a chief of that country'. The whole of the caravan took more than two hours to pass one spot (*ibid*.: 147). Other good examples are Pogge's and Arnot's caravan of 1875 and 1885 to the east, which were originally quite small, but enlarged by groups of other travellers seeking protection (Pogge 1880: 57f; Arnot 1889: 145/6).
[14] 1942: 71-72 [at chief *Cabitta's*]

agents who stayed several years[16], predecessors of the first permanent shops.

Those caravans, however, which continued to cross the Upper Zambezi and Kasai in search of slaves and the remaining ivory further east or north east, became even bigger and more strictly organized enterprises than before when in those areas trade and war became more and more intimately connected. Chokwe and other parties in Nuclear Lunda towards the end of the century were up to 'a thousand muskets strong'[17]; and on the Upper Lomami, in Luba country, Congolese colonial officers faced in one year (1900) allegedly no less than seven huge caravan-armies coming from the Angolan sphere, each comprising up to 5 or 6,000 men.[18] On their march through the Upper Zambezi, such groups must have had a food demand like small towns, very slowly moving towns indeed, with carriers and traders travelling no more than 7-19 km per day, and perhaps only for 10 days a month.[19]

The *sertanejos* and their *pombeiros* made some attempts to feed their caravans with their own foodstuffs. The slaves they owned personally and who were often settled in separate villages had not only to supply porterage, but also to grow food.[20] But caravans were unable to carry more than a few days' worth of provisions with them. An average Bihe or Mbangala carrier already had to carry about 30 kg of trade goods, plus his weapon, cooking utensils and sleeping mat, in all 35-45 kg.[21] Any more food to carry would have required either an increase in carriers, i.e. more costs and trouble for the entrepreneurs, or a reduction of the amount of trade goods carried or of the speed of travelling. When encamped for longer periods, caravan leaders would even put their slaves to plant crops.[22]

---

[15] 1882: I 197. Cf.Vellut 1972: 138f
[16] Pogge 1880: 59 and 73 [1875, between Kimbundu and the Kasai]
[17] Miller 1983: 156
[18] Report quoted in Vellut 1972: 139; see also the example of Cameron's caravan returning from Katanga in 1875, quoted above in footnote 13.
[19] Livingstone 1963: 234 and 259 [1855]; Magyar, quoted in Kun 1960: 633
[20] Cameron remarked in 1875 about one of the big Portuguese Bihe merchants that 'each of the six villages he owned had to supply a caravan' (1877: 214); see also Heywood 1984: 120f
[21] Magyar 1857: 28; Livingstone 1963: 259 [1855]. In the later 19th century, when transport value was lower (wax, rubber), the weight of trade goods alone seems to have risen to c. 100 pounds = 45 kg (Pogge 1980: 58; Lux 1980: 62). This may have supported the custom of carriers to take with them wives and children for their personal belongings. Arnot (1889: 148f) also gives a good description of the daily routine of caravans *en route*.
[22] Soremekun 1977: 87

Zambezi/Kasai region was particularly important in this respect because it was surrounded by vast uninhabited areas, the 'hunger countries' mentioned in almost every report on journeys to and through the area.[23] Understandably, even the earliest European travellers were enthusiastic when they observed the abundance of cassava, millet and fish in *Quiboco* and *Lovar* which must have appeared to them as something like an oasis.[24] The acquisition of food was therefore the first and most important business of every caravan arriving in the region.

'Terribly keen traders'

The inhabitants were more than willing to share their food surpluses with passing travellers - in return for adequate compensation, of course. The various modes of transaction and payment of foodstuffs between producers and travellers will be analysed below. It may suffice here to mention that the 'eagerness' to sell food, and the abundance of provisions on offer regularly impressed hungry European visitors. They contrasted this phenomenon not only with the 'desert' areas, but also with other populations further east, notably Nuclear Lunda. There, in 1806, even in main road villages it was 'difficult to obtain any mouthful of meal [cassava] or any description of food, and very costly...'[25]; and, in 1875, women were described as being 'too lazy' to prepare food for sale.[26] The peoples around the Upper Zambezi and Kasai appeared most remarkable in comparison, particularly the Chokwe who were more frequently visited by caravans, and closer to the main routes of access to the interior. Livingstone reports on these people that

'men and women came running after us with fowls, [cassava] meal &c... They are...terribly keen traders, and every art is tried to detain us for a single night

---

[23] Examples (see map 1):
West of the upper Lwena: Silva Teixeira 1940: 236; *Anonymus* 1940: 23; and Singleton-Fisher 1948: 79/80 ('For ten days the road lay through uninhabited sandy plains - known as the hunger country - and they had to make forced marches through this in order to reach the villages beyond, where food could be purchased...' [1893]);
East of the Luvale: Graça 1890: 427; Cameron 1877: II 160; Arnot 1889: 164 [1885]);
North of the Kasai River: Livingstone 1963: 238; Wissmann 1902: 45;
On the route Bihe-Bulozi: Pinto 1881: I, 279).
Southeast of the Kabompo River: Capello/Ivens 1886: 425ff.

[24] Silva Teixeira 1940: 237 [1794]; *Anonymus* 1940: 24f [1803]

[25] Baptista 1873: 223, referring to the area of the copper mines and salt pans near the Lualaba, where travellers obtained food mainly through special farms set up by the Mwant Yav for the purpose. 70 years later, Cameron still apparently had problems obtaining food in the same area (1877: 158-160).

[26] Pogge 1880: 79 [on villages situated along one of the main routes Kimbundu-*musumba*]

at their villages in order that they may have the pleasure of trading in meal, manioc roots and groundnuts'.[27]

Groundnuts, according to a visitor of the same area 20 years later, were even exported 'in great quantities to the coast and then for oil manufacture to Europe...', by peoples west of Mona Kimbundu, apparently including Chokwe[28], although transport costs generally seem to have prevented agricultural export production this far in the interior. Food sales to travellers remained the common form of (indirect) crop export. Again according to Livingstone, even Southern Lunda women on the remoter eastern bank of the Zambezi were 'now continually heard carrying on a brisk trade with the Portuguese in manioc meal for little bits of coarse calico 4 inches wide by 8 long'.[29] And in the areas between the Kwito and Kwando headwaters, 'a lot of massango [bulrush millet] was soon brought into camp by negroes', chiefly by Mbunda and Chokwe immigrants, and by Luchazi women (see fig. 26).[30]

In the mainly Luvale-inhabited plains between the Zambezi and Kasai rivers which are less suitable for crops, the acquisition of dried fish, as foodstuff and as payment for more food from the Chokwe further west, seems to have been the main attraction for passing caravans: 'The natives rush to meet us, carrying their baskets of small fish which they barter for four to eight yards of calico per basket'.[31] But cassava and millet meal and other vegetable products were also available in Luvale areas, perhaps partly as a result of regional exchanges for fish.[32]

Major quantities of foodstuffs were transacted at the capitals of important chiefs, namely where main routes came in from or left for the 'hunger countries'. Among the places recorded are the headquarters of the chiefs *Cayanga*, Katende, Katema, Kavungu; places between the Zambezi and Lulua sources along the various branches of the main ('watershed') route, e.g. Kisenge (Chokwe)[33]; and Ndumba Temho, Mona Kimbundu, Ishinde, *Cabitta* and *Cambuta*[34] on important other routes to the north east and south east. Some of these places, notably

---

[27] Livingstone 1963: 102 [1854], 249[1855]

[28] Lux 1880: 115 [1857]; he even alledges commercial exports of groundnuts and palmkernels from Nuclear Lunda.

[29] *Ibid.*: 64

[30] Pinto 1978: 256, 269f, 274, 278 (=1875); see also Silva Porto 1942: 70, 72/3 ([1847]; Arnot 1889: 100 [1885]

[31] Harding 1904: 199 [1899, nearer to the Kasai]; see also Cameron 1877: II 167 169 174 [1875, nearer to the Zambezi]

[32] Graça 1890: 417, 427 [at Katende's and *Quibuica's* <Chifwisha?> 1845]; Livingstone 1963: 83-91 [at Katema's 1854]; Arnot 1889: 166 [at Kavungu=Nyakatolo's 1885]

[33] Graça 1890: 413 [1846]; Cameron 1877: II 160 [1875]; Arnot 1889: 165 [1885]; for others see footnote 30.

Ndumba Tembo and Kavungu, had allegedly developed fully-fledged markets by the 1870s and 80s, where all manner of food was offered to travellers not only by the local people, but also by inhabitants of surrounding villages (see fig. 32).[35] But organized markets seem to have been rather an exception in the area compared to neighbouring areas[36]; they were probably hardly more than a spatial concentration of individual food transactions that occurred everywhere when big caravans arrived. It seems that the decentralized, brisk barter of foodstuffs which was going on in many smaller places was much more typical of the region. The main caravan routes, particularly more to the west, towards the end of the century, began to resemble the long ribbon-shaped spontaneous market we find today along major African highways:

> 'every day in the *quilombo* [camp] and even on the transit road' waiting for the buyer, one can find in abundance wax..., livestock, provisions and other trinkets from the industry of this people; however, while most of them return to their villages because of lack of buyers [after the passing of the caravan - A.v.O.], it must be noted that in those parts the traveller does not need to carry provisions with him, because on his arrival in the *quilombo* he will buy what is necessary for his stay.'[37]

Elsewhere, when not sufficient quantities were not forthcoming, 'some of the more knowing of the party are then told off to scour the country in search of food, and go off foraging for food in villages some distance away.'[38] Other caravans even established depots along the route where food buyers were placed, with sufficient purchasing power to assemble provisions for the return journey of the same caravan from the surrounding areas.[39] All these practices contributed, of course, to a rapid, area-covering spread of market relations over the area.

By the 1880s, practically the whole population of the Upper Zambezi was linked to the 'Atlantic Zone', not only through the long-distance trade in import/export commodities, but also as food producers. At that time, even in the remotest south-east of the area, near the Lunga-Kabompo-confluence, villagers sold food to passing caravans in return for ammunition.[40] Besides the staples mentioned so far (cassava, millet, chicken and fish), a great variety of other foodstuffs as supplied by

---

34 Silva Porto 1942: 72 [1847]; Pinto, 274, 278 [1875]
35 Capello/Ivens 1882: 184-186 [1878, at Ndumba Tembo's]; oral testimony by chief Muwena Toloshi Paciencia 1976, to R.J. Papstein (Papstein 1978: 267, fn.121)
36 For example, there was a daily big food market at the Nuclear Lunda capital, the *musumba* in 1875/6 (Pogge 1880: 88).
37 Silva Porto 1885: 166 [on Chokwe 1880]
38 Arnot 1889: 150 156 [1885]
39 The leader of Cameron's caravan had placed a nephew with 3 bags of beads in southern Luba for this purpose (1877: II 129).
40 Capello/Ivens 1886: 444 [1884] Mbwela-Lukolwe]

inhabitants of the region, according to the travellers' reports: maize (green and mature),sorghum, beans, groundnuts, groundbeans, sweet potatoes, yams, pumpkins, bananas, sugar cane, pineapples; honey and honeybeer (mead); game meat, goats, pigs and ducks.

Fig. 8: Food sales in a Mashukulumbwe village (1904-07)

Women are sitting to the right, behind their crops, and bargaining seems to take place between caravan members (centre right) and both them and local men (left), recognizable by their hairdress. This scene would have looked very similar in villages of the neighbouring Upper Zambezi region. (Photograph from Schomburgk 1928a. 265)

But by far the greatest part of supplies consisted of cassava which was sold in various stages of processing: as raw roots, as soaked and dried roots, as dried chips (SL. *mubobo*, Lv. *lwambalwila*) or as meal, currently known as *fuba* in the Angolan sphere. To the west, *farinha*, a coarse meal of rasped cassava, which was particularly liked by the Portuguese, was sometimes on offer.[41] But *fuba*, beautifully white cassava meal, became the universal standard caravan food in the Upper Zambezi and Kasai region. Ovimbundu carriers and traders had to adapt to a cassava-based diet, probably with some displeasure because at the

---

[41] Nearer to the coast, this term was used, however, not for ground but for grated cassava (Livingstone 1963: 126). This is the main form of processed cassava in Brazil up till the present day.

time they were already used to a diet of maize porridge and beans at home.[42] To make up for the lack of more wholesome foodstuffs, they were 'able to eat an immense quantity' of porridge during their one daily meal, about 5 lbs. per day.[43]

Such information allows for a very tentative calculation of the amount of staple crops that must have been required by foreign travellers and somehow supplied by Upper Zambezi producers during the late pre-colonial period. If in fact some 50,000 Ovimbundu travelled to or through the region every year in the 1880s, and if they spent there at least 125 days, one arives at a demand of over 14,000 tons of staple crops. Assuming a total population of 800,000 (see introduction, A 3) this would have meant an average sale of 18 kg of staple food per head of population to outsiders, probably very unevenly distributed, which is in the same region as 100 years later (in the early 1980s) in the Kabompo and Zambezi Districts of Zambia.

'At the roadside', inhabitants of the region also rendered a variety of other services to foreign caravans. Sales of craft products, 'medicines' and divining services are mentioned repeatedly in the sources. As has been mentioned before (ch. B 3), an increasing number of Upper Zambezi inhabitants also sold their labour to foreign caravans, as 'workers of trade'.

---

[42] Arnot 1969: 150 [1885]
[43] Arnot 1969: 150 [1885]; Livingstone 1963: 220 [1855]

B 6 Conclusion Part B: A chronology of market integration

The starting point of this chronological overview of the spread of market relations among the peoples of the Upper Zambezi and Kasai has been the role of the various forces and agents connected with the 'Atlantic Zone' of the pre-colonial world market.

The region around the Upper Zambezi and Kasai, in the hinterland of Angola and near to the centre of the continent, had been included in the 'Atlantic Zone' since the late 18th century. Apart from supplying slaves for export, the inhabitants of this region also produced 'legitimate' (non-human) goods for sale to foreigners. Prominent among these goods were products of the gathering economy: beeswax and ivory.

Both producers and traders could build on this experience after the slave export finally ended. The relatively high transport value of these goods, and exceptional rises in world market prices even through the economic depression of the late 1870s and 1880s, were major preconditions for the steady growth of regional export production throughout the century, despite enormous distances to the coast. Changing patterns of demand divided the period into three consecutive export cycles, dominated by slaves, later ivory and beeswax, and finally wild rubber.

An additional kind of commodity production for external markets, however, is often overlooked in the pre-colonial history of the interior, although it was bound to become the most important one after the colonial conquest: Considerable quantities of food stuffs were transacted between the local population and 'workers of trade' who collected the export products and transported them down towards the coast. The size of this demand for food had to do with the geographical position of the area, covering all major cross-roads between the remoter interior and the Portuguese colony of Angola and surrounded by almost uninhabited stretches of land; with the scatteredness of production sites in the area itself; and with the character of trade goods (slaves) and transport (carriers), which meant that the country was frequented by numerous slowly-moving travellers.

The chronological account has also demonstrated, however, that affective world market demand was not the only factor helping to push the 'Atlantic Frontier' eastwards, into and across the Upper Zambezi and Kasai. Rivalries between the various social agents of long-distance trade - metropolitan merchants, Euro-African *sertanejos*, and Ovimbundu and

Mbangala middlemen - also determined the speed and direction of advance, as well as the institutional arrangement under which most trade was conducted in the Portuguese sphere: the trade credit. In the process, some of the inhabitants of the Upper Zambezi and Kasai themselves entered the ranks of these agents of the world market, as caravan workers and middlemen.

While the role and strategies of forces outside the region have been explained at least in outline, the responses of 'the' inhabitants themselves have been described only in very broad terms so far. This leaves open a number of important questions to be tackled in the subsequent chapters, which will be grouped in three parts:

Firstly, the very rapid and flexible response of local producers and traders presupposes an **ability** to produce trade goods beyond regional needs, and to integrate the extended system of circulation into the existing regional division of labour. This first of all raises ecological, technological and economical questions - as to what resources and productive knowledge were available in the area, when and how they were effectively put into use, how local needs were met despite export production, and what role imported goods played for consumption. These issues are addressed in part C.

But any decisions on new allocation of resources are also a product of history, a history of social strategies and struggles between different social groups. Key aspects that arise in the chronology are the remarkably widespread participation of large numbers of petty producers, both men and women, the question of slave labour, and the role of chiefs. This social context of production, the fabric of indigenous relations of labour, power and exchange, and how it was affected by world market integration, will be examined in part D. Only through an understanding of these relations and the resulting specific interests of the various social groups in the region can it be understood why and which inhabitants were so actively **interested** in establishing relations with the world market, producing for export and acquiring imported goods and slaves.

The third question, explored in part E, regards those different and contradictory attitudes and strategies of the peoples of the region towards foreign visitors which can be glimpsed through the chronological account. In the beginning, for example, the hostile and 'demanding' attitudes of Chokwe and Mbunda contrasted by da Silva Teixeira with the hospitality he experienced among the Luvale. A few years later, however, another anonymous trader reported that the Mbunda chiefs, tired of (or disillusioned with) of ineffective obstruction, had changed their attitude. These chiefs no longer blocked the more southerly transit route to *Lovár* through their country which was 15 days shorter than the one da Silva Teixeira had used, because of fewer river crossings. They now gave a 'good reception' to white traders, encouraging them to bring more cloth since they lacked trade.[1] But throughout the 19th century, the inhabitants of the region showed themselves not only as 'eager' to be visited by foreign traders, but were at the same time also notorious for incalculable risks, insatiable demands and outright 'robberies', which made trading in or transit through the region at times unattractive for foreign traders. Relations between producers and traders could differ strikingly even within the same area and period.

---

[1] *Anonymus* 1940: 26

Fig. 9: Yowena Samakayi, an aged Luvale trader (1986)
One of the most important informants for this study, he still used to make pottery by himself, as payment for (female) pieceworkers on his fields. (Photograph taken outside his house, his wife in the background)

Part C

THE REGIONAL ECONOMY: EXPANDING PRODUCTION AND LOCAL NEEDS

Surprised or enthusiastic comments about the productive capacities of the peoples around the Upper Zambezi and Kasai, whatever vices were ascribed to them otherwise, were almost commonplace among 19th century travellers, beginning with the report by Silva Teixeira in 1794 opening part B above, at a time when the Upper Zambezi was only just establishing its links with the Atlantic world. Obviously, the remarkably wide range of economic activities, notably food production, which was praised in this report, must have been the result of a pre-history of economic change that began long before this date. For centuries, the inhabitants of the region experimented with their productive capacities and achieved a series of indigenous productive innovations which paved the way for participation in long-distance trade.

The chronology of productive innovation prior to the 19th century can be roughly divided into two phases: the rather slow emergence of an Iron Age (Bantu) economy up to about 1600 A.D., and a period of rapid change after c.1600. In the first chapter of part C I will give a more detailed account of the innovations that occurred during these phases, a sort of prelude for export production in the era of Atlantic long-distance trade. In subsequent sections, I will locate them in their ecological context, and ask about their economic implications in terms of a growing societal division of labour. Finally, the consequences of long-distance trade for productive development and material needs will be examined in detail.

In the course of the analysis, various aspects emerge that hint at the social relations and meanings behind producers' strategies. These will be dealt with in detail further below, in part D.

C 1 A pre-history of indigenous productive innovation

C 1.1 Widening the choice: Early Bantu innovations, up to 1600 AD

'*Mbwela*' is a term applied by today's Upper Zambezi peoples to those living there before the arrival of new chiefly dynasties between the 16th and 18th century.[1] Some of them were subsequently displaced into adjacent areas to the east, south and west, where the term is in use as an ethnic denomination up to today.[2] But the majority of these resident populations seems to have stayed in the area and been subordinated by the new chiefs; they represent in fact the non-'noble' element in the ancestry of the present population.[3] The term *mbwela* suggests multiplicity. For example, there is a Luvale idiom *mushilinjinji kambwela* - as numerous as rain drops[4], an obvious reference to the multitude of small kinship groups that used to live scattered over the whole Zambezi drainage basin, without central political institutions and 'ethnic awareness' or even linguistic unity when members of subsequent chiefly appeared in the region.[5] It seems that these groups can be traced back to a distinct population of Early Bantu speakers who immigrated into the area some time during the first millenium A.D. from a northerly direction. According to lexicostatistical analysis, Papstein assumes a linguistic origin of these '*Mbwela*' populations (in the wider sense) from an early 'Proto-Western Savannah Bantu' language, from which a 'Congo Watershed' idiom (c.100 A.D.) developed that gradually gradually differentiated into presentday Nuclear and Southern Lunda (until c.500) and a variety of 'Lwena' languages,

---

[1] See White, 1949: 28, McCulloch, 1951: 93f; Turner, 1957: 3f, and R.J. Papstein, 1978: 77ff
[2] Among the Mbwela or *Ambuelas* in South-Eastern Angola, who have the same basic cultural institutions as the peoples of the Upper Zambezi and Kasai, e.g. the *mukanda* initiation ceremony (see Kubik, 1971); the same applies to the *Kawiku* and *Humbu* in Mwinilunga (Turner, 1957: 4), and to the *Nkoya-Lukolwe* south of the Kabompo river (McCulloch, 1951: 94f; van Binsbergen, 1985 and 1992).
[3] The term '*Mbwela*' was 'clearly a concept used by the conquerer' (Papstein, 1978: 78), and is apparently understood as pejorative even by those who still bear this name, the Mbwela in Southeastern Angola (according to Kubik, 1971: 49f).
[4] Horton, 1975[2]: 219; White, 1949: 28
[5] See Papstein and Derricourt, 1977: 174; Papstein, 1978: 79f

namely Luvale, Luchazi and Mbunda, as well as into Chokwe (c.500-1000). Subsequently, only minor dialectal variations developed.[6]

The Early Bantu speakers themselves, on their arrival, had found an aboriginal late Stone Age population of Capoids who were physically, linguistically and culturally related to today's Khoisan speaking ¡Kung groups ('Bushmen') of South-East Angola and the Kalahari.[7] They gradually displaced and absorbed these aboriginals through war and enslavement,[8] but only over a very long period that lasted up to the recent past. Khoisan-speakers were still met regularly by mid-19th century travellers between the Kwito and the western Zambezi tributaries, up to the 11th parallel.[9] Today's Upper Zambezi peoples remember the *Sekele*, as they call them,[10] in oral traditions, folktales and enigmas.[11] This suggests that in the relatively infertile wilderness surrounding the Upper Zambezi Bantu immigrants coexisted with the aboriginal Khoisan-speaking population longer than anywhere else in Central Africa.

This may be explained not only by extremely low population density, but also by the fact that the Early Bantu immigrants relied to some extent on the productive knowledge of the ¡Kung *(Sekele)*. Archaeological evidence, travellers' reports and oral traditions indicate that the late Stone Age men of the Upper Zambezi were highly skilled hunters. In addition, they collected wild honey during their hunting trips, both for immediate

---

[6] Papstein, 1978: 67ff, following the methodology of Ch.Ehret

[7] *Khoisan* was originally coined by physical anthropologists for the aboriginal 'bushman' and 'hottentot' population of Southern Africa, and is today used in a linguistic sense for speakers of click sounds. ¡Kung, in contrast, is the ethnographical term for those *Khoisan* (or rather *san*) speakers who were formerly called 'bushmen' (cf. Kubik, 1984).

[8] See for example Magyar, 1860: 228, who describes these aboriginals living in bands as extremely ugly and mentally underdeveloped, but also as very friendly and even polite towards strangers, unable to steal others' property, and being continually preyed upon like game and cast into bondage. Kubik (1971) describes ¡Kung camps that were attached in the way of serf or client villages to neighbouring Bantu settlements in South Eastern Angola.

[9] Silva Porto, 1942: 74; Livingstone, 1963: 102; and particularly Magyar, who gives a vivid description of them (1860: 228).

[10] This term is Chokwe and Luvale and means originally 'porcupine', according to Kubik (1984: 130). Further west, among the western Ngangela, they are called *Chiningi* (with the same meaning, *ibid.*), while again *Sekele* and *Mukangala* are used for ¡Kung groups in Southern Angola (see for example Magyar, 1860: 228; Figueira, 1938: 387ff; Almeida, 1965). The latter term may be a distorted version of '¡Kung'.

[11] See, for example, Kubik (1984: 129ff) for the Luchazi; even today there are sometimes rumours of small men turning up in remote places of the Upper Zambezi (author's personal experience; Papstein, 1978: 77). These are probably unfounded since at the end of the colonial era an identifiable ¡Kung population occurred only south of the 14th parallel in south-eastern Angola, and they may have suffered genocide in the meantime due to the protracted war in the area.

consumption and beer.[12] On the other hand, a wide range of gathering activities were the tasks of women and children. Around the Upper Zambezi, the superior knowledge of the *Sekele* about their natural environment and about the technologies of hunting and gathering is still acknowledged, perhaps even admired by the neighbouring Bantu, despite their general contempt for these people.[13]

Early Bantu speaking immigrants in Central Africa, including those who settled around the Upper Zambezi and Kasai, most probably carried with them, or developed on the spot, a set of rather revolutionary productive innovations.[14] Perhaps the most important one among them was the replacement of stone by iron tools. Weapons were prominent among these. It seems that the immigrants developed a very efficient bow and arrow technology, and began to make knives. They needed these weapons for both warfare and hunting, in which they became even more successful than the *Sekele*.[15] This innovation, however, must probably be seen as a prolonged process rather than a sudden event. Like in other parts of Central Africa the use of iron may have taken some time to replace late Stone Age technologies.[16]

The other major innovation carried by early Iron Age Bantu-speaking immigrants into Central Africa in general was agriculture, with far-reaching consequences for more permanent types of settlement and lifestyle. Iron tools such as hoe-blades and axes (to cut clearings into more fertile woodland areas) were generally used for the cultivation of domesticated plants. The first staple crops grown in the area, including the Upper Zambezi, were millets, most probably sorghum (*sorghum vulgare*) and finger millet (*eleusine coracana*), which were initially mainly used for beer. Others included squash, bambarra nuts (*voandzeia subterranea*) and cowpeas (*vigna unguiculata*).[17]

In the case of the Upper Zambezi, however, the role of Early Bantu speakers in this innovation is not entirely clear. Although the history of Bantu migration is still the subject of a longstanding debate, linguists and archaeologists now seem to agree that grain cultivation was invented somewhere in the central Sudan zone and transported to South Central Africa by Bantu speakers through the savannahs east of the equatorial rain

---

[12] Silva Porto (1942: 74) and Magyar (1860: 228) were offered dried elephant meat and honey by *Sekele* whom they met on the way, besides ivory and wax. See also Vellut, 1979: 95f.
[13] Kubik, 1984: 128
[14] See Phillipson, 1982: 810ff
[15] Papstein, 1978: 83, 142, 169, 217
[16] Cf. Phillipson, 1982: 816f
[17] Birmingham, 1983: 9, 12; Phillipson, 1982: 812; for the Upper Zambezi: White, 1959: 17; Papstein and Derricourt, 1977: 174

forest during the first half of the first millenium A.D.[18] The most likely carriers were those groups who, after their departure from the area of the great east African lakes, became the 'central stream' of Bantu migration and arrived in what is now Zambia by the fifth century. This would confirm a dim memory retained in oral traditions of the Luvale and Chokwe that the ancestors of their chiefs came from 'the north of Lake Tanganyika'.[19]

Linguistic analysis has shown, however, that the area around the Upper Zambezi and Kasai ("Bantu Zone K", according to Guthrie's classification) was apparently one in which Eastern/Central Bantu influences intermingled with others emanating from the Western stream.[20] Cattle keeping, for example, which was regularly associated with grain cultivation in the East, did not reach the Upper Zambezi headwaters before the 19th century. This may be partly explained by a vast tsetse belt in the southeast of the region; but it is also possible that grain cultivation reached the Upper Zambezi as an isolated innovation **before** the actual arrival of Bantu-speakers and was in fact first adopted by Late Stone Age ¡Kung groups, perhaps through contacts to the southeast.[21] Early Bantu speakers, at any rate, seem to have adopted grain cultivation only after their arrival. Western Bantu influence, with which they are associated by linguists, reached South-Central Africa slightly earlier than the Central/Eastern influence, and included a rather different tradition of cultivating tubers (yams) and raising goats, more adapted to the rain forests from or through which its carriers had come.[22] While they apparently did introduce goat and later chicken raising to the Upper Zambezi, the cultivation of tubers ceased to play any significant role after their arrival there.[23] Instead, the collection of **wild** tubers as well as wild fruits, mushrooms, leaves and insects played an important role in the Bantu Iron Age ('*Mbwela*') food economy, even as staple food, and to some extent continues to do so among Upper Zambezi peoples today.[24] This can clearly be regarded as an adoption of existing ¡Kung (*Sekele*) food gathering technologies. It was apparently the background for the disparaging statement in Luvale oral traditions on the pre-chieftainship

---

[18] See Ehret, 1974, partly opposed by Phillipson, 1982: 811ff; Oliver, 1978: 397ff; Birmingham, 1983: 16f

[19] Sangambo, 1985[2]: 1; Redinha, 1966: 3

[20] Oliver, 1978: 401

[21] Cf. Papstein, 1978: 213

[22] According to Phillipson, 1982: 815f; Ehret, 1974

[23] Yams is still known in the area, but grown only on a very small scale near the houses (Livingstone, 1963: 39 [1854, on Southern Lunda]; personal observations).

[24] Personal observations; for a systematic account see White, 1959: 12-16, who mentions for example no less than 18 indigenous terms for edible caterpillars; Hansen, 1977: 235ff; Malaisse, 1979.

population that they were using grain crops only for beer and ate as their staple 'waterlilies and other such food', (see below). Another important heritage of the *Sekele* food production was certainly the collection of bee products, which were to play such an important role in the later economic history of the region.

Little is known about the importance and technology of fishing in either Stone Age (*Sekele*) or Iron Age (*'Mbwela'*) economies. While the former may already have done some fishing in well-watered environments, the scattered Early Bantu inhabitants of the Upper Zambezi, who preferred to settle in more open country along rivers and streams, most probably used spears, dug-out canoes, fish poison, scooping baskets and perhaps even nets.[25] Luvale traditions that the *VaMbwela* 'did not know how to fish properly'[26], but this must be understood as the view of more recent immigrants who made fishing the mainstay of Luvale economy (see below).

Finally, Early Bantu innovations probably stimulated non-food production as well. Iron tools opened the way into woodwork which began to yield a variety of utensils and materials necessary for intensified food production and for a more sedentary, communitarian lifestyle - e.g. handles for iron tools, mortars, canoes, bows, building materials, ritual figures, drums and xylophones.[27] More sophisticated ways of preparing and storing food and seed among the Early Bantu are evident in the emergence of pottery in those few places in this sandy area that have sufficient clay. Excavations near the Lungwebungu river revealed a remarkable continuity of patterns from around the 9th century up to the present day and have therefore been seen as an indicator for the beginning of Bantu settlement in the area.[28]

Despite the very scanty evidence about this early period, there are indications that the process of productive innovation in the Upper Zambezi region can neither be understood in evolutionary terms as a linear spread of 'better ideas' that simply displaced or superseded older forms of productive knowledge,[29] nor as the result of the action of one dominant cultural group alone. It should be regarded rather as a process

---

[25] Papstein and Derricourt, 1977: 174f; Papstein, 1978: 83, 217, 228; MacLaren, 1958

[26] Sangambo, 1985: 30

[27] The Iron Age *'Mbwela'* and their closer modern descendants such as the Nkoya have a reputation as outstanding musicians, e.g. *marimba* players. (cf. van Binsbergen, 1981: 64)

[28] Roberts, 1976: 40. Another excavation of a Early Bantu Iron Age village on the relatively nearby Lukolwe river dated for the late 15th century, however, yielded a different type of pottery, which suggests that different influences were effective in the area (see Papstein and Derricourt, 1977).

[29] Cf. for example White, 1959 (passim) and Papstein, 1978: 213-215

of experimentation, selection and adaptation with productive knowledge (Elwert), which at the same time was a process of communication between different groups.

The innovations introduced by Bantu speakers in the later first millenium A.D. into the Upper Zambezi did not so much revolutionize production methods or productivity, but rather widened the variety of productive activities in the area. The Early Bantu immigrants, while slowly absorbing the aboriginal Khoisan-speaking population of the ¡Kung, adopted much of the highly skilled hunting and collecting economy of the latter, and were apparently even prepared to drop some of the technologies their own ancestors must have been used to, such as the growing of tubers.

C 1.2 Increasing the productivity: Innovations of the 17th and 18th centuries

The historically rather short period from c.1600 to 1900 brought about a series of more rapid productive innovations that shaped the production systems of the peoples of the Upper Zambezi and Kasai in the era of pre-colonial long-distance trade. These innovations had far-reaching consequences for self-sufficiency in food, the ability to produce surpluses, and hence the circulation of products. The most important were the integration of new, non-African crops, namely cassava (manioc), an intensification of fishing, and a professionalization of hunting and ironwork.

The chronology of the introduction of Asian and American crops to Central Africa is still rather obscure because pre-19th century written sources exist only for areas nearer to the coasts. Some types of beans had already been used by Early Bantu settlers, but others were imported from South East Asia, along with taro (a kind of sweet potato), banana, mango and sugar cane. They arrived at the East African coast towards the end of the first millenium A.D. Very little is known about the diffusion process that followed.[30] Banana and sugar cane, as we have seen, were grown in *Lovár* by the end of the 18th century,[31] while 'a kind of apple tree', perhaps mango, and 'peanut potatoes' (taro) were observed for the first

---

[30] See Vansina, 1979: 11; Harlan 1982
[31] Silva Teixeira, 1940: I, 237

time by Livingstone in 1854.[32] Today, these crops are an integral part of many of the small backyard gardens in Zambezi and Kabompo.

Between c.1600 and 1750, a complex of American crops had reached the Upper Zambezi - in order of their importance for local agriculture: cassava (*manihot utilissima*), maize (*zea mays*), groundnuts (*arachidae*), certain types of beans, sweet potatoes and tobacco. *Mandioca* (cassava) was mentioned in da Silva Teixeira's report as the first staple crop in *Lovár*, alongside millets, and well ahead of maize. Subsequently, this crop was to reach a unique importance in the area. As will be shown further below, it revolutionized existing land use systems, meant an enormous increase in productivity, and had strategic implications for the food economy, local circulation and integration into wider markets. Only in very recent times has maize begun to take over its role.[33]

Fig. 10: Cassava (manioc) plant
Stems grow to a height of about 3 m, roots are up to 50 cm long.

---

[32] Livingstone, 1963: 39, 66
[33] The following account of the introduction and spread of cassava cultivation around the Upper Zambezi and Kasai is developed in more detail in von Oppen, 1991 and 1992.

The date and route of the introduction of cassava and the other American crops in Central Africa is very difficult to establish.[34] Drawing together a number of widely scattered sources, they seem to have taken the following course into the Upper Zambezi:

Cassava had been domesticated by Indian cultivators in the tropical forests of South America. In northern Brazil, after the Portuguese conquest, it soon became a staple also for the colonial conquerors as well. The transatlantic slave trade created a very close link between the South American and West African coasts from the early 16th century. The food needs of Portuguese settlers, ship crews and above all slaves, who had to be fed before and during their passage, created the initial demand for cassava in West Central Africa. The account of a British pirate who seized a Portuguese vessel off the Angolan coast in 1593 shows that processed cassava was at that time still being imported from Brazil. He described the cargo as

'...meale of cassavi, which the Portingals call *Farina de Paw*. It serveth for marchandize in Angola, for the Portingals' foode in the ship, and to nourish the negroes which they shall carry to the river of Plate.'[35]

This does not necessarily mean, as Jones assumes, that at that time no cassava was grown yet in Angola, but obviously there was too little. A few years later, in 1608, cassava is mentioned at Loango, north of the Kongo (Zaire) estuary, by a Dutch captain as being available for ships' provisions; but the spread of this new crop was at least very slow, since it does not appear in two other, contemporary accounts of Loango agriculture.[36] While maize and tobacco were adopted by African cultivators very rapidly, not only on the coast but also in the Kongo kingdom in the hinterland from as early as between 1548 and 1583 [37], cassava appears in the Luanda area, very near to the coast, only between 1620 and 1630.[38] Later, in the 1680s, cassava was cultivated 'with great care' by farmers induced by a 'ready market in nearby Luanda'.[39] At the same time, however, cassava was grown in Kongo still mainly by people of Portuguese descent.[40]

---

[34] See Vansina, 1979: 12
[35] Sir Richard Hawkins, quoted after Jones, 1959: 62; italics added. The mentioned Portuguese term must supposedly be read (in modern spelling) as *farinha de pau*, 'stick meal'. In Angola, *farinha* was sometimes used for cassava as well as for wheat meal (see Dias, 1960).
[36] Pieter van den Broecke, quoted in Vansina, 1979: 12; Brun 1983 [1611f]; Andrew Battel [1603], quoted in Jones, 1959: 63).
[37] Miracle, 1966: 93-95; Vansina, 1979: fn32
[38] Redinha, 1968: 96
[39] Jones, 1959: 63
[40] *Ibid.*

It seems from these earliest reports that cassava began its career in Angola as a cash crop to cover the food demand of non-African officials and slave traders. The same report which first records cassava cultivation in Loango in 1608 does **not** mention it in a comprehensive list of food eaten by the local African population. It mentions instead other American crops, such as groundnuts and maize, which was made into porridge. Cassava is reported as a popular staple in Northern Angola (Luanda?) only in the 1660s[41], and in Loango still later, in the 1760s, as 'the bread of the poor'.[42]

A second, somewhat surprising, conclusion can be drawn from these sources. The introduction of cassava on the coast took much longer than maize, groundnuts or tobacco. This delay contrasts strongly with the rapidity of subsequent cassava expansion into the interior. One plausible explanation for the relatively late introduction of cassava cultivation on the Angolan coast may be that a long period of experimentation and reorganization of the labour process was necessary because of the particular processing techniques cassava requires. The crop contains poisonous hydrocyanic acid (HCN) in varying degrees, and the many existing varieties are accordingly subdivided into sweet and bitter ones. The HCN contained in the bitter varieties is most efficiently removed through a fermentation process before consumption. The practice of soaking the tubers, in order to produce fermentation, was apparently the most striking innovation for African cultivators, since the Bantu root *bóób*, 'to be soaked' or 'to become soft', became the word *stem* for cassava in most Central African languages.[43] Thus, processing seems to have been one critical point in the adaptation of cassava to Africa.

Surprisingly enough, the adoption of cassava in the remote interior of Central Africa took on a much more rapid pace than at the coast, and happened about simultaneously with the other American crops. According to oral traditions, the Kuba (Bushongo) on the Lower Kasai river were the first people of the remoter interior to introduce cassava (and groundnut) cultivation - apparently before 1614, i.e. around the time when cassava had only just begun to spread along the coast. Among the same people, maize was introduced after 1630, or even prior to cassava.[44]

Around the mid-17th century[45], or even 'in the early 1600s'[46], in other words with enormous speed, cassava seems to have reached the emerging

---

[41] Hoover, 1978: 332, fn. 14; Jones, 1959: 63
[42] Vansina, 1979: 12 and fn. 36, quoting an 18th century source
[43] Hoover, 1978: 579
[44] Jones, 1959: 63f, and Miracle, 1977: 44, quoting Torday, 1925: 143, and Vansina, 1960: 261
[45] Redinha, 1968: 106

Nuclear Lunda kingdom East of the Upper Kasai. This means a jump over a distance of almost one thousand kilometres as the crow flies, at a time when cassava was just being introduced on the coast. While cassava was never more than an emergency crop among the Kuba, in Nuclear Lunda it became the absolutely dominant staple. In the 19th century, cassava surpluses brought in as tribute from all parts of the empire were the food basis of the rulers of Nuclear Lunda with their large entourage of non-producers. At their headquarters, notably at the *Musumba*, they ran something like state farms which were worked by their slaves and 'poor women'.[47] And today, the terms for cassava is seen by Lunda people in South-Western Zaire as simply equivalent with 'food'.[48]

The Nuclear Lunda state became the major radiating centre for political centralization and ethnic realignment in the Central African savannah. There can be little doubt that its close relationships with a number of subsidiary polities around it promoted the further spread of the 'American' set of agricultural innovations in Central Africa. This applies most probably also to the areas on the Upper Kasai and Zambezi which during this period came under the influence of Nuclear Lunda political emigrants - the new Chokwe, Luvale, Southern Lunda and perhaps Luchazi chiefs. Linguistic analysis has shown a close link between cassava terminology in the languages of the Upper Zambezi and Nuclear Lunda.[49] Oral traditions recorded among Angolan Luvale speak of cassava having been brought to them by *Namuto* and *Samuto*, mythical foreparents whose origin is said to have been around the Lulua river, i.e. in the Nuclear Lunda area.[50] And Zambian Luvale historians hold that their chiefs' clan, Nama Kungu, who immigrated from Nuclear Lunda, taught a more intensive form of agriculture, along with other food production technologies, to the resident acephalous population. The latter is described as having been 'very backward': 'They hardly knew how to cultivate, preferring to eat water lily plants and other such foods...'[51], clearly a reference to the higher importance of gathering in the pre-Nama Kungu food economy (see above). Interestingly, the decisive innovation is reported here to have been mound cultivation (which is characteristic for cassava), as opposed to the earlier form of cultivation on ridges used for millets.[52] This indicates that from the beginning cassava meant not merely a new crop, but a change of the entire production system. (See fig. 13.)

---

[46] Hoover, 1978: 333, fn. 15; based on linguistic evidence and oral tradition.
[47] Baptista, 1873: 169 [1806]; Pogge, 1880: 243f [1875]
[48] Hoover, 1978: 331
[49] Hoover, 1978: 579
[50] Redinha, 1968: 102
[51] M.K. Sangambo, n.y.2: 30
[52] Papstein, 1978: 219

But the Nama Kungu clearly cannot have carried cassava based agricultural technologies in their luggage when they left the Nuclear Lunda area, since their exodus seems to have happened **before** cassava could have possibly been introduced there. The first Nama Kungu clash with resident '*Mbwela*' groups on the Lulua headwaters, near the present Angola-Zairean boundary, has been dated by Pastein in the early 16th century.[53] It must therefore be assumed that the Nama Kungu became acquainted with the new crops and related techniques some time after their departure from proto-Lunda polities on the Inkalanyi-Bushimaye river. This may have happened between 1630 and 1700, after their arrival in the fertile *Kato* area along the river Lwena.[54] The Luvale had frequent contacts with Nuclear Lunda even after their departure, partly through exchanges of 'gifts' or 'tribute', but more significantly through regional trade (see below). Nama kungu (as well as Chokwe and Luchazi chiefs) may have played a more prominent role in such contacts with their ancient home than commoners[55], and this was perhaps the reason why they became the 'transmission belts' for the introduction of cassava to the areas between the Upper Zambezi and Kasai. In any case, it can be assumed that cassava growing was adopted by these chiefs, as well as by the other populations of the Upper Zambezi, through voluntary and decentralized types of contacts, rather than through political or economic pressure from Nuclear Lunda.

The introduction of cassava, however, should not be seen as something that happened all at once. Rather, we can assume, it consisted in a long process of experimentation and selection, in the course of which new varieties were continuously adopted, while others were dropped again. Keen cassava growers make considerable efforts of this kind up to the present day. In the Angolan parts of the Upper Zambezi, 20-35 past and present varieties are known to Chokwe and Luvale peasants; and at least 18 different varieties, both bitter and sweet, are presently grown in Kabompo, on the Zambian side. The importance of the Nuclear Lunda connection is reconfirmed by Angolan Chokwe memories that the earliest cassava varieties came from Nuclear Lunda.[56]

Another route of introduction of cassava and related crops, however, could be hypothesized as well, given the skimpiness of oral tradition and oral history. Due to their greater proximity to the Atlantic coast, it seems not impossible that Luvale and other related chiefs adopted the American

---

[53] *Ibid.*: 120, 133

[54] According to the chronology established by Papstein, 1978: 151f. He mentions that agriculture played an important role during this stage of Nama Kungu expansion.

[55] Against Papstein's assumption that 'by the end of this period [i.e.end of the 15th/early 16th century] the chinyama [i.e.Luvale] chiefs ceased to have contact with Luunda'(1978: 123; see also p.11). Evidence of such contacts is given further below.

crops through the earliest independent trade links more directly from the West, rather than from Nuclear Lunda in the North. More linguistic research could perhaps help to test this hypothesis.[57]

In the case of the Southern Lunda chiefs, however, the import of cassava growing from Nuclear Lunda appears much less disputable. The holders of the Kazembe Mutanda, Ishinde, Kanongesha and Musokantanda titles arrived - via a short-lived Lunda colony on the Mukulweji river (southern Zaire) - much later in their present lands than the subsequent Luvale, Chokwe and Luchazi chiefs, namely some time during the early 18th century when cassava was fully established in their original homeland.[58] In addition, they were fully integrated into tribute circulation with the *Musumba* (the Nuclear Lunda capital).

Drawing together this evidence, the period when cassava began to spread into the Upper Zambezi can be located between around 1620, the earliest date when the crop could possibly have arrived both in Angola and in Nuclear Lunda, and about 1700, when the last of the new chiefs, the holders of the Southern Lunda title of Ishinde, left the Mukulweji colony of the mature Nuclear Lunda state to settle near the east bank of the Zambezi. The importance, i.e. both reasons and consequences of this innovation will be discussed in subsequent sections; but it should be mentioned here that the fundamental qualitative impact of cassava cultivation on the entire food production system corresponded to a quantum jump in productivity, both with regard to area and labour.

Parallel to the spread of cassava came, according to Luvale traditions, a great improvement of fishing technologies.[59] The Nama Kungu are again presented as those who brought these innovations, which turned fishing from a seasonal to an all-year-round occupation, and from an individual to a collective effort. They claim to have introduced highly productive techniques of catching fish along artificial barriers across drainage depressions in flood plains and along smaller rivers and streams. One type is used for the catching of the mud barbel during its spawning run with the rising floods between November and January, called

---

[56] Redinha, 1968: 99-103; von Oppen, Shula, Alff *et al.*, 1983: 108.
[57] The Nuclear Lunda term for 'soaked cassava root', *(f)bwó: bw* (Hoover's orthography), appears to be rather distant from the Chokwe/Luvale term *(lu)pa*. Although some linguistic correspondence between the two word stems may be detected (see Hoover, 1978: 579), one could as well argue that the stem *-pa* is either a parallel, but independent derivation from the same kiMbundu source (*boba* means 'to soak' in kiMbundu) (*ibid.*), or has a completely different origin.
[58] White, 1962a: 14/15; Hoover, 1978: 267, 270f
[59] Sangambo, n.d.[2]: 30; Papstein, 1978: 228f

musuza.[60] The practice is still used in Zambezi Westbank with its large seasonally flooded savannahs. More important, according to my experience, seems to be the catching of fish in traps placed in gates along dams of earth and grass sods called *wálilo* (sg.*ma-*), up to several kilometers long, during receding floods in April to June. *Wálilo* fishing contributes significantly to the several hundreds of tons of dried fish

Fig. 11: Gate on a *Wálilo*-dam for plain fisheries, with fishtrap (1985)
The dams are built communally by several fishermen, but each of them has his own 'gate' where conical fish traps are placed before the flood recedes. (Photograph taken near Nyatanda, Zambezi-Westbank)

---

[60] For detailed descriptions of Luvale fishing techniques see MacLaren, 1958; White, 1956: 79ff; Alff, v.Oppen and Beck, 1986: II, 25ff

exported every year from the area.[61] Today, with virtually unchanged technologies, between 650 and 1.000 kg of dried fish p.a. may be produced by a fisherman using nets in permanent waters (rivers, lakes), but up to 5.500 kg by a *wálilo* fisherman. The yields of the latter, however, are subject to greater variations with the changing height and duration of floods than net-fishing. Nevertheless, these are very substantial amounts, if only 50 to 100 kg are estimated to be the annual subsistence requirements of a nuclear family (5 persons).[62] It may be concluded that the new types of fishing that are said to have been introduced with the coming of the chiefs are not so much a year-round activity in themselves (they seem to be even more seasonal than some of the older indigenous types of fishing - see above), but they allow for fishing when other techniques are at their lowest ebb, particularly in the non-agricultural season (see below, table 5). Their main effect was a considerable increase of surplus beyond subsistence needs of this highly valuable form of animal protein.

A third set of innovations which may have affected the peoples of the Upper Zambezi during this period regarded hunting. There is today a remarkable variety of techniques, both collective and individual,[63] and of hunting rituals among all groups in the area. The solitary professional hunter (SL. *chiyang'a*), who is an initiated member of the hunters' cult, enjoys a particularly high social status among all Upper Zambezi peoples.[64] This contrasts with the gradual decrease in the economic importance of hunting, compared to fishing and agriculture, since the 19th century (see below).[65] At least in the case of the Luvale, immigrant chiefs are again said to have introduced more efficient techniques and devices to the Upper Zambezi, such as stronger hunting gear in connection with their superior skills in ironwork.[66] It should be assumed, however, that many hunting technologies and rituals actually go back to the Iron Age '*Mbwela*' and to the *Late* Stone Age '*Sekele*' aboriginals, with their even greater emphasis on hunting; it seems, for example, that the use of various traps and collective game drives using pitfalls and long fences or nets were devices already used before the new chiefs arrived.

---

[61] Aggregate data on the total fish production of the western half of Zambezi District are still lacking. In the late 1950s over 200 metric tons of dried fish left the area eastwards across the Zambezi river per year (White, 1959: 85), while production was estimated to be over 400 mt in the mid-1980s, produced by about 2300 to 3700 men or 50-80% of all adult men in the area (Alff, von Oppen and Beck, 1986: II, 40ff).

[62] *Ibid.*

[63] Redinha, 1966: 90-93 describes various forms of approaching and pursuing game, the use of dogs, fire, pitfalls, traps and fences up to over a kilometer long.

[64] Cf. White, 1956f; Turner, 1957: 28ff; Baumann, 1932: 42; Redinha, 1966: 90

[65] The higher prestige of hunting compared to fishing is expressed in the Luvale term *unyanga wauleya* for the latter (literally 'the fool's hunting').

On the other hand it is possible that only the Nama Kungu and related immigrants began to attack large mammals more directly.[67]

A widespread and superior knowledge in ironwork, particularly among the Chokwe, Luchazi and Luvale was observed by most 19th century visitors of the respective areas.[68] They mentioned explicitly a kind of steel manufacture,[69] a variety of arrowheads for different purposes that was unique in Central Africa[70], steel for making fire with flints,[71] iron rings, hoes, axes, ornamental axes[72], 'spears, large double-edged knives [*mukwale* - A.v.O.], and besides these they manufacture with perfection the whole range of thrusting weapons.'[73]

Oral traditions of the Nama Kungu also claim the introduction of an iron-made *lupembe*, a double clapperless bell representing chiefly powers.[74] Most of these items, including the *mukwale* and the *lupembe* bells, good axes and arrowheads, and decorative iron rings are also reported from Nuclear Lunda.[75] This suggests once again that important technological innovations - important not only for hunting, but obviously also for warfare - reached the Upper Zambezi and Kasai from this direction. Remaining acephalous *Mbwela* populations between the Kwando and Kubango, in comparison, were described in the 1840s as very poor blacksmiths, depending on imported hoes, axes and spears from the Luchazi.[76]

All these findings on the process of productive innovation in the region, which rest to a considerable extent on oral traditions serving political interests, should be taken with some caution, especially with regard to the dates and reasons given. But in combination with other evidence, it can

---

[66] Papstein, 1978: 137, 217
[67] White, 1956: 77/8; Papstein, 1978: 93, 217; cf. the description of a game drive organized by a party of Mbwela (in the south-west) by the mid 19th century, in Livingstone, 1857: 60 [1851].
[68] Most general statements: Magyar, 1860: 229 [Central Chokwe, 1850s]; Capello and Ivens, 1882: I, 225 [1878, Central Chokwe]; Pogge, 1880: 47 [Northern Chokwe, 1875]; Pinto, 1881: I, 274, 279 [1878, Luchazi]; Harding, 1904: 159 [Southern Lunda, near Zambezi source, 1899]
[69] Best pre-colonial descriptions of ironwork processes for the region: Johnston, 1969: 99 [1891, Ngangela]; Schütt, 1881: 128, 131f [1878, Northern Chokwe].
[70] Silva Porto, 1938: 70 [1852, Ngangela]; Cameron, 1877: II, 163, 165 [Luvale, 1875]; see also White, 1948: 57; Papstein, 1978: 84
[71] Pinto, 1881: I, 255/6 [Luchazi, 1878]
[72] Silva Porto, 1938: 70 [1852, Ngangela]
[73] Silva Porto, 1986: 325 [Luchazi, 1847]
[74] Papstein, 1978: 137
[75] Hoover, 1978: 530; Lux, 1880: 122/3
[76] Silva Porto, 1986: 322

nevertheless be assumed that during about the 17th and 18th centuries a concentration of rather rapid innovations took place which allowed for considerable gains in productivity in specific sectors within the much broader mix of productive activities developed by Khoisan aboriginals and Early Bantu immigrants.

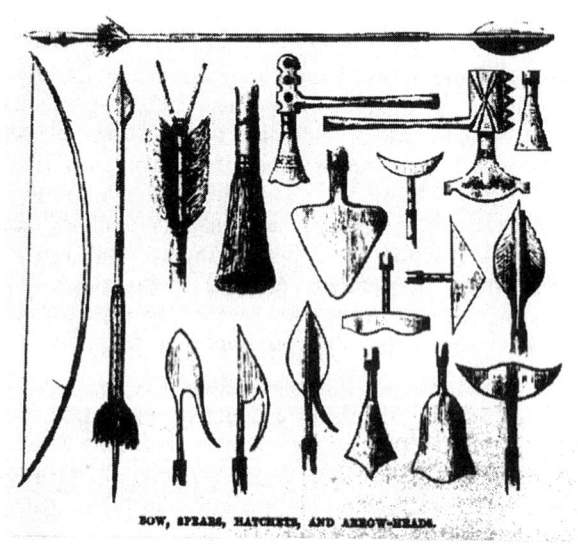

Fig. 12: Luvale weaponry of local manufacture (1875)
(Engraving from Cameron 1877, vol.II: 163)

But the account of this innovative process has so far only **described** the diffusion of new products, techniques and tools in terms of time and space. It has offered little **explanation** as to what the reasons for these innovations in the period up to the late 18th century were. The whole picture presented this far should not be regarded along the lines of a still popular view of innovation: as a more or less automatic spread of 'more productive' techniques as soon as obstacles to communication are removed. Such a view fails to explain under which conditions and for whom an innovation is in fact more productive, and why the recipients are eventually prepared to make the effort of adopting or experimenting with new methods of production. Undoubtedly, the peoples of the Upper

Zambezi were very actively involved in the introduction of far-reaching changes in their production systems. Like other peoples of Central Africa, they showed 'a continued interest in innovation'.[77] The following two chapters try to illuminate some of the factors explaining these early processes of innovation, before attention is turned to the effects of 19th century world market integration.

---

[77] Vansina, 1979: 12

C 2 Population and ecology - a changing balance

Any kind of change in primary production first of all means a change in the relationship between producers and their natural environment. Adaptation to difficult ecological conditions - which themselves are subject to historical change - has been called the chief characteristic of indigenous agricultural change in Africa, as against in Europe and Asia, where often other resources (namely land) were the critical scarcities.[1] But the other, human side of the equation cannot be regarded as a historical constant, either. In the case of food production, population densities and patterns of consumption change over time, and they must be seen in a complex relationship with changing forms of production or 'appropriation of nature'.[2]

For the inhabitants of the Upper Zambezi and Kasai region, the encounter with nature is a matter of everyday life. Their intimate knowledge of this natural environment has resulted in a differentiated terminology which combines geomorphic, edaphic, botanical, and land-use criteria.[3] This truly 'ecological' understanding of nature by those who have to interact with it every day in order to make their living is a useful starting point for the classification of the sharply contrasting ecosystems that exist in very similar types throughout the region. In Upper Zambezi languages, a general distinction is made between **lowlands** ('downstream') that are regularly affected by open water, and **uplands** ('upstream') that are normally dry (for the following overview see map 2).[4] This antithesis of the ecosystems described so far is found throughout the region.

---

[1] Richards, 1987: 1f

[2] See the debate on whether agricultural innovation is a response to growing population (following Boserup, 1965), or perhaps vice versa (quoted in Vansina, 1979: fns.46 and 48).

[3] See Redinha, 1961 [mainly on the Chokwe], the only publication explicitly tackling this question so far, which I could use for comparison with some of my own observations; some expressions were also taken from Horton, 1975^2; White, 1959; and Trapnell and Clothier, 1957^2.

[4] This opposition is expressed by speaking of 'downstream' vs. 'upstream' areas: Lv. (*ku-*)*sango* or *songo* vs. *kato* (or *tunda*, 'land rising above the water'); Ch. *kumuanda* vs. *kutunda*; SL. *kunvungu* vs. *kuntu*, *kundundu* or *kunsulu*.

C 2.1 A mosaic of ecosystems

The latter, to start with, can be subdivided into various ecosystems of woodlands and open plains. The major part of the region is covered by semi-deciduous open **woodlands**[5], for which the most common local term is *musenge* (Ch.,Lv.) or *isanga* (SL.).[6] These woodlands seem to be the 'climax' vegetation of the region, but rather a 'pyro-climax', i.e. a selection of fire-resistant plants as the result of centuries of human intervention through shifting 'slash-and-burn' cultivation.[7] They occupy the vast, gently vaulted uplands between rivers and streams, particularly between the Kabompo and Zambezi; within the bend of the Upper Kasai; and the hilly area, with peak altitudes of about 1600 metres, which Magyar has called 'mother of the Southern African waters'[8], because of its central position between the headwaters of the Zambezi, Kwando, Kwanza, Kwango and Kasai (see map 3). Only in the flat northern half of the present Lunda Sul province of Angola they grade into a moister, more evergreen type of forest which is called *usaki* by the Chokwe.[9]

Otherwise, the whole area around the Upper Zambezi and Kasai is covered by a deep layer of loose aeolic Kalahari sands, the result of hot and dry periods during the glacial periods of the northern hemisphere. The mostly whitish and greyish soils are therefore chemically very poor but have good water retention capacities in the lower horizons.[10] Those few upland areas that are distinguished by a higher clay content, visible as a more reddish colour of the soil, and therefore more valuable for agriculture, are called *mbunda*, 'red', by Luvale and Luchazi. The original woodland vegetation on Kalahari sands may have consisted to a considerable extent of *cryptosepalum* trees, which are now reduced to isolated thickets called *mavunda* (Lv.) or *ivunda* (SL.). The rubber plant *carpodinus gracilis* is originally a liane of *cryptosepalum* forest.[11] This thick vegetation was gradually displaced by more open types of woodland: the more fire-resistant *burkea*, also proper to the sands, which

---

5 Other current phytogeographical terms for the same ecosystem, which covers about 12% of Africa's surface, are: tropical savannah woodland, dry or raingreen forest, forêt dense sèche, forêt claire, forêt tropophile (see Malaisse, 1979: 38).

6 Another Chokwe and Luvale term, according to Redinha (1961: 68f), is *chipapa*; but Horton (1975[2]) translates this as 'any unused ground outside village and fields', i.e. 'wilderness'; he gives instead *litala*, a more open woodland than *musenge* (literally one 'that can be looked through').

7 See Malaisse, 1979

8 L.Magyar, quoted in Silva Porto, 1885: 166

9 See Gossweiler, 1939

10 Trapnell and Clothier, 1957[2]: §24

11 *Ibid.*: §48

forms scattered tree formations along the edge of open plains (Lv./SL. *lusese*); and varieties of *brachystegia* and *isoberlinia* stemming from plateau soils to the east which now dominate the actual *musenge* woodlands.[12] They provide the resources for many forms of craft and food production, both gathering and agriculture, and are famous as 'honey woods'.[13]

Between the woodlands, **flat open grasslands** (sg. *chana*) of often considerable dimensions occur, which are the traditional hunting grounds in the region. They form smaller clearings in the bush, notably around the sources of rivers and streams, but are vastest immediately west and northwest of the Zambezi river. In Zambezi District, these plains are today called *ngangela* and reach several dozens of kilometers in diameter. Tree vegetation is not entirely absent, as there are narrow strips of woodland on sufficiently high river banks, the *lusese* fringes already mentioned, and isolated clumps of small trees on slight elevations within the plains (*lihumbu* in Luvale)[14]. Some creeping shrubs and stunted trees do occur here and there, notably *diplorrhynchus* and a palm tree whose leaf stalks (Lv. *mavale*, sg.*li-*) are used for basketry, and when this type of plant is more frequent among the grass vegetation, the Luvale inhabitants speak of *likundu*[15]. The *chana* strictly speaking, however, is an extremely sandy open grassland with a watertable too high for trees. In years with high floods, the lower parts may be covered by water up about knee depth towards the end of the rains. In the western part of Zambezi District, up to one third of the total area is liable to flooding. This is the area of floodplain fisheries (*wálilo*).

Only the 'downstream' or **low lands**, however, are regularly affected by open water. They have numerous permanent rivers, streams and lakes which are extensively fished. Their water level oscillates significantly, up to several meters, during the year. The rising waters regularly cover a part of the grassy river valleys (often called *damboes* in Southern Africa) and adjacent depressions; this is the place *for musuza* fishing. The whole inundation zone is called *chinema* in Luvale and Chokwe. Due to alluvial deposits, river banks offer prize soils for cultivation, but on the lower slopes only outside the rainy season. River bank gardens are called *litepa* (Lv.) or *itempa* (SL.). Some of their fertile alluvial soils also come from the water that seeps through the valley slopes. The seepage zone itself often forms swampy approaches to the open waters which yield grass for

---

[12] *Ibid.*; Roche, 1979. The *Brachystegia-Isoberlinia-Julbernardia* woodlands of Central and Eastern Africa have also been called *miombo*.

[13] Redinha, 1961: 70; see the useful discussion of its value for food gathering in Malaisse, 1979.

[14] North of the Kasai, these isolated clusters of trees may be surprisingly rich; they are called *matumba* by the Chokwe, 'god's grove' (according to Redinha, 1961: 67-8).

building, fish caught at transverse fences, small animals to snare or trap, certain wild food plants etc. The inhabitants call them *tenga* (Ch.) or *sanga* (Lv.). Rivers and streams in the west and north flowing through appropriate depressions are often lined with dense evergreen gallery forests (Lv.*lito,* Ch. *muchito;* SL. *itu*) which contrast sharply with the surrounding plains or woodlands. They resemble southern extensions of the tropical rain forest, and are used for various gathering activities.[16]

Upper Zambezi landscape can thus be described as a rather small-scale mosaic of sharply contrasting ecosystems. In most parts, soil fertility is very low, but climatic conditions are not unfavourable. Due to the altitude of this part of the Central African Plateau (about 1000 m above sea level), temperatures are generally moderate. However, variations between a cool and dry season (May-August, Lv.*chishika*), a hot and dry season (September/October) and one long rainy season (about late October to early April, Lv.*vula*) are considerable. Precipitations are reasonably high, but it is important to note that there are considerable oscillations in the amount and distribution of rains. Rainfall figures for Balovale (now Zambezi) collected from 1917 to 1963, show variations between 21.5 % and 51 % of the annual total for the first three months of the rainy season (October to December), which are crucial for agriculture. The total was on average 1091 mm, but actually varied between 693 and 1426 mm per year. Precipitation shortfalls resulting in partial crop failure, as well as exceptional rains leading to sometimes devastatingly high floods, occurred about every seven to ten years.[17] According to a long-term analysis of historical sources for West-Central Africa, major or catastrophic droughts, which may last several years, happen on average almost once in a lifetime.[18] Scarcity and insecurity of rains tend to increase towards the South and West of the area.

C 2.2 Ecology and food

The earlier phases of economic history on the Upper Zambezi, in broad terms, can be understood as an increasing adaptation to this highly variable natural environment under conditions of very low population density. Late Stone Age ancestors of the *Sekele*, with their emphasis on hunting and gathering, probably had their temporary camps in the *chana*

---

[15] *Kabengi* in Ch.; SL. perhaps *ikuna*
[16] Cf. Redinha, 1961: 58f
[17] Balovale District Notebook, NAZ file KTW 1, p.201
[18] Miller, 1982: 21f

and along the forest fringes where game abounded.[19] Early Bantu Iron Age immigrants continued these well-adapted, though extensive methods of production, but they widened the choice by additional activities which meant an opening of hitherto almost unused woodland resources. Shifting agriculture needs virgin forest soils, and ironwork relies on fuelwood or charcoal. This may have resulted in a deeper penetration some of the more sedentary Iron Age Bantu groups into the *musenge* woodlands, along smaller rivers and streams. In addition, improved hunting methods with iron tools may have caused a gradual withdrawal of game from the great plains into the woodlands, where it is mainly found today.[20] At the same time, the *'Mbwela'* are also said to have preferred the plains as their habitat, especially those in the south, i.e. perhaps those who followed more closely the *Sekele* type of economy.[21]

Higher variation of production meant more food security, particularly with regard to the low soil fertility and climatic uncertainties. The fact that the Late Stone Age population survived here longer than in any other neighbouring area, and the continued importance of hunting and gathering in the Iron Age economy, shows that their mix of productive activities helped to avoid competition for natural resources, while a very scattered population grew at a rate which was possibly as low as during more recent times.[22]

One open question is the development of a division of labour between different producers. It is possible that in this period it was still essentially restricted to a division of work within the same residential groups; this would suggest that the Iron Age Bantu (*'Mbwela'*) would have preferred selected settlement areas near junction points in the ecological mosaic. It is more likely, however, that ecological diversity early encouraged a tendency towards productive specialization between inhabitants of different ecological environments, with some groups focusing on hunting and perhaps fishing, and others more on agriculture, ironwork and forest gathering.

The innovations introduced since the 16th century, in connection with the beginning of chiefly traditions, then, clearly pointed towards growing economic specialization along the lines of ecological differentiation in the region. Improved iron weaponry for hunting, and intensified fishing activities made life on the plains and along rivers much easier, and probably allowed for greater concentration of a sedentary, surplus

---

[19] See Bisson, 1980: 58
[20] Luvale traditions tell us for the early period (16th century) of strong *'Mbwela'* communities living in the thickly forested countries to the East (Sangambo, n.d.[2]: 27).
[21] Papstein, 1978: 83
[22] See White 1959: 53f

producing population. These innovations allowed the tapping of a much greater part of the potential of animal protein which is embodied in game and in the fish climbing and descending every year with the floods between rivers/lakes and the lower *chinema* parts of the plains.

Cassava-based agriculture, on the other hand, is best suited to the vast, wooded uplands which had probably hitherto been rather sparsely populated. Here, the new crop proved particularly helpful, much more than in the plains: it is fairly undemanding with regard to soil nutrients and copes much better with the acid Kalahari sands than millets; and it can be grown much longer on the same plot than grains, i.e. requires less labour for the shifting and clearing of fields. A high water table is the only environmental condition cassava tubers definitely do not tolerate since it makes them rot; this makes cassava cultivation in the plains impossible unless extra efforts are made to construct particularly high mounds. Besides these specific advantages in the Kalahari sand belt around the Upper Zambezi and Kasai, cassava-based mound cultivation is well suited to the ecological environment of Central Africa in general for a number of reasons. The decisive consideration that first made cassava so attractive to Upper Zambezi cultivators, at least as a supplementary staple, was presumably the fact that it scores considerably better than millet with regard to output of calories per area, and particularly with regard to yield security (see table 4).

Cassava provided Central African millet cultivators with an invaluable hedge against famine. Millet is a relatively nutritious and tasty grain, but its yield relative to area is low[23] and further reduced by the need to store seed, and by pre- and post-harvest losses[24]. Consequently, food scarcity and famine are a more or less regular experience among millet cultivators of this zone. Every year before the new harvest, towards the end of the rain season, some harsh 'hunger months' have to be lived through.[25] In addition, millet yields are highly susceptible to intermittent periods of drought, often accompanied or followed by locust invasions. Cassava, in

---

[23] Bulrush millet (and sorghum) yields are about 600-700 kg per hectare under 'traditional' African smallholder conditions, compared to an average of about 9, 000 kg/ha for cassava (with an approximately 3-year period from planting to complete harvest, i.e.3000 kg/ha per year) under Western Zambian conditions(Minster, 1982: Appendix 7-2; A. Marter, 1979: 32).

[24] Birds'attacks during the weeks before harvest are the most regular threat, but insects and rodents may also destroy up to 30% of the millet in the stores. Frequent shifting and isolation of fields, bird scaring, and curing the harvest by kitchen fumes (cooking places are often placed underneath the grain stores) are adequate, but laboursome and unsatisfactory protective measures. Catastrophic losses occur during locust invasions which are remembered by the peasants as major historical landmarks.

[25] Cf. Richards, 1939: 35, for the example of the Bemba.

Tab. 4: Comparison of cassava with millets as staple crop
(under the conditions of the Upper Zambezi and Kasai)

Condition	Advantages (of cassava,	Disadvantages compared to millets)
Ecology:	Higher/more secure yields:	
Dry sandy (on uplands)	Lower demand in soil nutrients	(except potash) soils
High watertable (in lowlands)		More susceptible to waterlogging
Only one rainy season	Harvest throughout the year; intercrops during first year	
Periodic droughts and locust invasions	Less susceptible to drought and insects; longer storage of crop in the ground	
Cold and long dry season		Prolonged maturation period (c. 2-3 years, according to variety)
Labour:		
Low population density; forest vegetation and low fertility requiring more energy for / more frequent opening of cultivable land	Higher yields (in caloric energy per area) Less frequent shifting of fields required More flexible timing of field operations; no seasonal labour peaks No bird scaring required (as with millet)	More effort in field preparation required (mound building, green manure)

[Table 4, continued:]		
Condition	Advantages (of cassava,	Disadvantages compared to millets)
[Continued: Labour]	No building of stores required (storage in the ground)	More labour for processing required, particularly with bitter varieties (soaking, drying)
	Fewer pre- and post-harvest losses through pests;	
	No deductions for seed (planted with stem cuttings	
Nutrition:		
	Higher caloric yield	Unpleasant taste; low content in proteins and vitamins, therefore more need for supplementary foods
	Leaves are edible	
	Intercropping with supplementary crops is possible.	

contrast, is particularly drought resistant[26] and its main edible parts are the tubers, out of reach of locusts.

Cassava can be harvested and replanted - this is often done plant by plant[27] - at any time of the year without significant impact on yield; this also avoids peak demands on labour and hence risk. In addition, during the first one or two years when the cassava plants are still young, grain crops can be planted in between them. This practice was even more widespread in the past, when freshly opened land used to be planted with bulrush millet and eventually some sorghum first, and increasing portions of cassava with interplanted grains came in only from the second year onwards.[28] This was probably the way in which cassava cultivation was gradually integrated into the older grain-based land-use pattern. Different from the ancient staple crops (millets, sorghum) was maize, which seems

---

[26] See Cock, 1985: 18. Climatic varations do affect the above-ground parts of the plant, but there is no direct relationship to the growth of the tubers (Norman et al., 1984: 230-234).

[27] Even the tubers from the same plant may be harvested at different times, with the biggest taken out first leaving the smaller ones more space to develop. (The practice of piecemeal harvesting is called *kutwela*. Cf. White, 1959: 24)

[28] See Trapnell and Clothier, 1957: 32/33 [analysis from the 1930s]

to have been introduced from Angola along with cassava; it was originally grown only in small patches, purestand and in between young cassava plants, and eaten green as a snack (Luv. *chisakwola*, 'vegetable'), as another means of alleviating the scarcity of food towards the end of the rains.

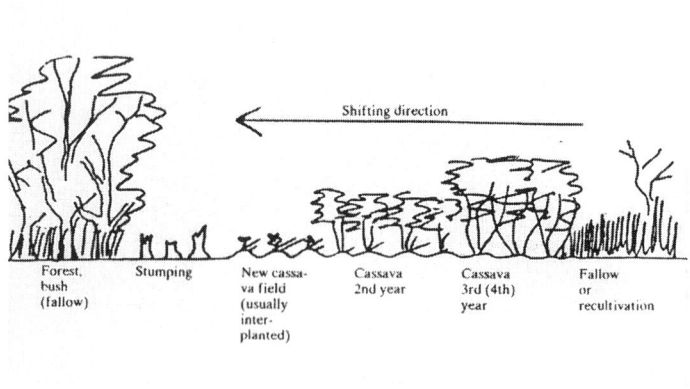

Fig. 13: Indigenous cassava cultivation system ('Luvale System'; 1979)
(Drawing from Schönherr 1979: 12)

Miller explains the introduction and spread of cassava in West Central Africa in the 17th and 18th centuries mainly as a response to the threat of periodic famine.[29] According to his 'chronology of drought and disease in West-Central Africa 1560-1830,[30] there was a period of repeated environmental disasters between about 1615 and 1665. This coincides exactly with the period of rapid spread of cassava cultivation in the interior. The reliability of cassava yields in fact seems to explain to a large extent why cassava began to supplement millet so early and so rapidly around the Upper Zambezi and Kasai. In contrast to most other cassava growing areas in Central Africa, however, the crop subsequently began to **replace** rather than just supplement millets as the dominant staple here. Other, social and economic factors will therefore be examined further below.

Even if cassava cultivation made yields much more reliable throughout the year, it created other, more qualitative food problems. The smell and

[29] Miller, 1982: 29

taste of fermentation in soaked cassava is rather unpleasant, not only for the taste of neighbouring grain eaters, but also for Upper Zambezians themselves. The area's most intimate observer during the colonial period even found that 'the older generation indeed hold that the odour of damp cassava flour introduced into a house will upset the efficacy of protective charms.'[31] He described the invention of specific drying techniques as one way to cope with this problem. High, solid racks for sun drying have replaced the once ubiquitous, sophisticated grain stores in Upper Zambezi villages. For the rainy season, when sun drying may place a constraint on food supply even if tubers are widely available, a system of drying cassava near the fire (*kusota*) was developed which is unknown in other parts of Zambia.[32]

Another difficulty, in comparison to a grain-based diet, is the fact that cassava has a very low content of non-caloric nutrients, mainly proteins.[33] Upper Zambezi cultivators were certainly always aware of this; they say that cassava has to be eaten in bigger quantities, and that satisfaction lasts less long. They do not regard cassava porridge (*nshima*), even to a lesser extent than other staples, as a full meal in itself. Some of them therefore find a mixture of cassava and some millet or sorghum flour more palatable. At any rate, eating a *nshima* makes sense to them only if accompanied by its natural counterpart, a 'relish' (Lv. *ifwo*) rich in those missing nutrients. It consists partly in additional vegetarian foodstuffs; the most important ones probably going back to the pre-19th century being, in order of their importance:

* ground beans or bambarra nuts (*voandzeia subterranea*, Lv. *vyelu vyakeseke*, SL. *katoyo*), and

* cowpeas (*vigna unguiculata*, Lv./SL. *makunde*), both indigenous African pulse crops;

* sweet potatoes (*ipomea batatas*, Lv./SL. (*n*)*tamba*), another American crop which is grown in small patches behind the houses or adjacent to the fields; the roots are also eaten as snacks, particularly by children, and the leaves are a nutritious vegetable.

These and a great variety of smaller crops can be easily combined with the cultivation of cassava, particularly because of the mentioned possibility of interplanting. One important source of protein and minerals is also provided by the cassava plant itself, in the form of cassava leaves

---

[30] *Ibid.*: 21 and appendix
[31] C.M.N. White, 1959: 18
[32] *Ibid.*
[33] Bulrush millet contains about 11% of crude protein, compared to only 1.2% in cassava meal (Minster, 1982: 48).

(Lv. *makamba*) which are used as a kind of spinach. This valuable part of the output should not be overlooked when considering the productivity of cassava cultivation.

By today's standards, however, a proper 'relish' must contain animal protein: fish, game meat, small birds or rodents, caterpillars or, though rarely, meat from domestic animals. In the more distant past, hunting and gathering small animals probably played an greater role than today, although customary standards should not be confused with reality. Such foodstuffs come in fairly often, particularly during the respective seasons, but not every *ifwo* actually contains animal protein.

Consequently, the introduction of a diet based on cassava would have required an intensification of complementary use of other ecological niches offered by the regional environment: fishing, hunting, and gathering, if nutritional standards were to be maintained. It has been mentioned already that an intensification of animal food production seems to have taken place, in fact in the field of fishing, during about the same period as the introduction of cassava. Since they increased both productivity and the need for each other as complementary foodstuffs, cassava cultivation and intensive fishing probably reinforced each other; these innovations were particularly conducive to a growing regional exchange, as will be seen further below.

C 2.3 Regional sub-economies

However, it should be mentioned here that in the course of history certain economic specializations have emerged within this spectrum of productive activities. More recently, they have often been described in terms of 'tribal' or ethnic traditions.[34] On closer inspection it seems that these specializations can first of all quite simply be explained as different responses to different ecological environments (although this is only part of an explanation, as will be seen later). Corresponding to the indigenous classification of ecosystems presented earlier, these responses cluster around the two poles of 'upstream' and 'downstream'.

The **Southern Lunda of Ishinde, the Luchazi, Mbunda and Chokwe** have been known for a long time as growing cassava for their staple food,

---

[34] Strict ethnic categorization prevails in colonial reports on agriculture and other economic activities, even where the evidence suggests cross-ethnic similarity and differentiation along ecological lines (see for example the reports of Diniz, 1918; Trapnell and Clothier, 1937; and McCulloch, 1951, which are mainly referred to in the following account. Only additional sources will be cited explicitly).

combined with bulrush millet and some sorghum (in the case of the Chokwe) as subsidiary crops. This combination suits best the sandy upland forests from which these groups originate. The Luchazi have a reputation for preferring the remotest and thickest bush, which enables them to stick to a relatively large share of millet growing; for their millet fields, they clear virgin soils at short intervals and seek protection from bird damage before the harvest by distance from other fields.[35]

Outside agriculture, gathering is a classic form of production for women of all Upper Zambezi ethnic groups, just as hunting is for men. The originally forest-dwelling Southern Lunda and the Chokwe, however, are particularly renowned as skillful hunters, despite the fact that in the past game abounded in more open landscape. This may indicate that these groups originally settled more towards the margins of the forests; but the importance of hunting could also be reinforced by more recent developments, as mentioned below.

Men of these groups, at any rate, have a good reputation with regard to forest-related activities, notably the collection of honey and beeswax (an activity usually combined with hunting trips), wood and ironwork. The Lunda of Ishinde produce the best dugout canoes, and the Chokwe make the most famous wood carvings of Central Africa, originally mainly for ritual and magical purposes, in which they were regarded as masters. The Luchazi were once famous producers of bark cloth.[36] Chokwe and Luchazi were most well-known as blacksmiths and iron smelters, the latter probably being connected with the occurrence of iron ore in the hilly original Chokwe homeland around the peak of the 'mother of Southern African waters'.[37] Southern Lunda women, in addition, are specialized in mat-making, the raw materials for which they obtain from special grass of the *chinema*. This suggests a greater closeness to major rivers or streams than the Luchazi and Chokwe groups, whose original homes were between the headwaters of the Kasai and Lwena/Lungwebungu etc. (see map 3).

The **Luvale**, on the other hand, represent almost the opposite extreme of ecological and economic specialization. The majority of their ancestors seem to have lived in or near the open *chana* with its annual floods and numerous rivers and lakes. Although in a more distant past hunting was probably the more important means of food production in this ecosystem[38], fishing became the typical Luvale speciality, a year-round occupation that includes both Iron Age techniques and 16th/17th century

---

[35] LIMA Survey 1983, Chikenge area; for the past see for example Figueira, 1938: 361
[36] See Pinto, 1878: 279/80; Figueira, 1938: 361f
[37] Magyar, 1860: 229
[38] See White, 1959: 7

Nama Kungu innovations. Concerning cultivation, the Luvale put greater emphasis on grain crops (bulrush millet,sorghum, today also maize and rice) rather than cassava, probably because of the high watertable. This preference has induced colonial observers to adopt an evolutionist view, and to classify the 'Luvale system' with its higher percentage of millet and frequent shifting of fields as more 'backward' than the land-use pattern of neighbouring groups. But it was the same authors who realized for the first time that 'the practice adopted depends as much on the soil obtained for cultivation as on custom.'[39]

This last remark underlines the fact that economic specialization among the peoples of the Upper Zambezi and Kasai has never been absolute; in principle, all the forms of production mentioned are practised by members of all ethnic groups in the area. Specialization should be seen to a considerable extent as a flexible response to local ecological conditions and potential, rather than as a fixed expression of some 'traditional' cultural heritage of specific groups. This is demonstrated by those people who left their original home lands for various reasons and migrated to different ecological environments, or those who had to face environmental change. For example, agriculture had apparently been the main economic basis of pre-Lunda polities near the Upper Lulua from where the Nama Kungu originally came.[40] In the sandy *ngangela* plains of the Western Upper Zambezi where they then settled, sophisticated methods of fishing began to prevail.[41] Also Non-Luvale groups such as the Southern Lunda of Ishinde, Chokwe or even Luchazi applied the whole range of fishing technologies when they lived close to major rivers or flooded depressions.[42]

Those Luvale, on the other hand, who migrated into upland areas for one reason or another, very quickly became devoted cassava cultivators, beekeepers or woodworkers. If Nama Kungu chiefs, most of whom today reside in the plains west of the Zambezi, consider themselves as the ones who brought the cassava-based cultivation system to the area, this can only refer to a period when they lived in an upland area. This is why it seems most plausible that this innovation was introduced when the Nama Kungu had reached the rather fertile, densely populated *Kato* area along the river Lwena and near its confluence with the Zambezi river.[43] It is also probable that the importance of hunting increased during the 19th

---

[39] Trapnell/Clothier, 1957: § 134
[40] Hoover, 1978:
[41] Papstein, 1978: 152
[42] Personal observations; Redinha, 1966: 94f for the Chokwe; McCulloch, 1951: 17 and 61 [Southern Lunda and Luchazi]; Harding, 1904: 87 [Southern Lunda, near Zambezi source, 1899]
[43] Cf. Papstein, 1978: 151ff

century among those Chokwe who advanced into the plains of the northeast (where they came into close contact with the distinct hunting culture of Nuclear Lunda)[44], and among the Southern Lunda when larger game retreated into the woodlands following increased hunting further west.

The terminology of ethnicity itself reveals the priority of ecological before ethnic identity in the region. Despite all attempts by immigrant chiefs to gain a strong personal grip over the resident *'Mbwela'* population, the emerging new ethnic units designated and still designate themselves primarily in ecological terms that correspond to their economic specializations: *Luchazi* is a small forest stream, a tributary of the Lwena headwaters rivers to the northwest or the Upper Zambezi; the term *Luvale* stems from palm trees typical of the plains that yield the *livale* fibre for baskets; the Luvale in general, who are also called *Lwena* after this major tributary of the Zambezi, are usually subdivided into *Vaka Songo* or *Luvale Lwasango* ('down river people'), *Luvale Lwambunda* ('red soil Luvale' - on the middle Lwena) and *Vaka Kasavi* (Kasai people).[45] The name *Mbunda* again alludes to more reddish upland soils. Only the Southern *Lunda* derive their name from a political structure (Nuclear Lunda).[46]

The logic of the relationship between people and nature, however, cannot explain exhaustively the process of productive innovation on the Upper Zambezi. The importance that was attached to certain activities and technologies apparently exceeds what we can reconstruct as their actual relevance for a sufficient and reliable food base. This applies, for example, to the enormous prestige associated with hunting among the forest-dwelling Southern Lunda. Cassava growing and year-round fishing, on the other hand, would have supported a much larger population than actually lived in the sparsely settled region. In other parts of Africa, cassava was introduced apparently in response to growing population pressure on land, because it allowed for a more stable pattern of cultivation with less frequent shifting of fields.[47] It seems very improbable that this factor played any significant role in the adoption of cassava for the peoples of the Upper Zambezi and Kasai, at least for the period prior to the 19th century. It is well possible that the variety of

---

[44] Cf. Baumann, 1935: 42
[45] Interview Mr. Sondoyi, 18.10.1986; Papstein, 1978: 6-7
[46] There are contradicting etymologies of the name 'Chokwe' (which is pronounced and written in an enormous number of ways - see McCulloch, 1951: 28). The explanation given by Dias de Carvalho (1890: 90), that it derives from a phrase with which the ancestor of Chokwe chiefs was told to leave Nuclear Lunda (*aioko a ku kinguri* - 'go as well where Kinguri [the mythical founder of the Mbangala state] went', i.e. to the west), and therefore carries a notion of 'expatriated', appears far fetched. A different explanation has been given by Miller, 1988: 38 (see above, chapter B 1, footnote 45)
[47] Cf.Jones, 1959: 57

existing food resources would have technically sufficed to bridge at least the 'normal' annual hunger period without resorting to those innovations, particularly if gathering activities are considered.[48] One example is perhaps the case of the Luchazi, who continued to grow much more millet than cassava in an environment which is fully suitable for the latter.

We have to assume that the new technologies were advantageous for subsistence security, but that their actual adoption and spread depended on a number of additional economic, social and political conditions. They had to fit into existing patterns not only with regard to the relationship between producers and nature, but also to various relations between different categories of producers. The social logic at work in relations of production, distribution and power will be dealt with analytically in subsequent chapters. But one basic aspect of these relations has to be introduced already at this stage, at least in a descriptive way, because of its essential implications for economic analysis: the division of labour between producers of different gender, age and location.

---

[48] The collection of certain wild fruits and tubers was an important means of alleviating periodic famine, even after the introduction of cassava (see Schomburg, 1925^2: 67 [1905]; Redinha, 1966: 87f).

C 3 Emerging divisions of labour

Different economic activities, and consequently the changes they undergo, are related to different categories of producers. The most basic of these categories - gender, age and location - seem to be based on certain physical characteristics, namely differential involvement in procreation, differential strength and expertise, and differential access to natural resources. More recent social research has made it clear that in Africa, as elsewhere in the world, even such 'objective' criteria are to a large extent socially constructed and tend to be used in ideological ways to justify social and economic inequality.[1] Nevertheless, on a descriptive level, the division of productive tasks between men and women, between seniors and juniors, and between forest dwellers and the inhabitants of open grasslands are basic realities with considerable bearing on the economy of kinship-based societies in Central Africa. These relations are looked at here mainly with regard to their economic functioning; only subsequently (particularly in chapters D 2 to D 4), the emphasis is turned to how they are formed, and transformed, through social processes of negotiation and struggle.[2]

C 3.1 The division by gender and age

'For the man, huntsmanship; for the woman, procreation' (*nlyulu wubinda, namumbanda lusemu*) is a classic Lunda-Ndembu description of gender roles.[3] It defines the activities of women and men as strictly complementary or even opposed to each other, with destruction versus creation of life as the essence of men's compared to women's roles.[4] A very similar definitin has been reported by Redinha from the Chokwe.[5]

---

[1] See, for instance, the recent critique of the concept of a 'division of labour by gender' with regard to Zambian peasants by Geisler (1990).
[2] This approach has been elaborated more systematically, again with regard to relations between male and female producers, by Crehan (1986: 62ff) for the Kaonde in Northwestern Zambia.
[3] Quoted by Turner, 1957: 27
[4] Cf.Turner, 1957: 28
[5] Redinha, 1966: 39ff

As often in such anthropological analyses, however, the description of village norms tends to be confused with actual reality.[6]

It is true that on the Upper Zambezi a variety of non-agricultural activities have always been clearly associated with male labour, particular those which involved destruction of larger animate beings: hunting, fishing, beekeeping, tanning, building, ironwork and woodwork. All these activities involve male absence from homes for sometimes considerable periods. Particularly hunters and fishermen often stay in temporary grass shelters in the bush or the plains for weeks or even months during the productive seasons. In all these activities, there is a certain division of work between younger men who contribute their strength and endurance, and older men who have more professional knowledge and experience.[7] But the latter tend to leave the village less frequently and for shorter periods and distances, not only because of decreasing strength but also due to their greater social responsibilities.

Another feature of male activities is that they mostly require periodical, relatively short but intense input of labour. Typical female activities, on the other hand, are all those connected with regular day-to-day reproduction: food preparation with all related tasks; bearing and rearing children; keeping the village tidy; also gathering wild fruits, leaves, mushrooms and insects in the bush, and keeping small livestock such as chicken, goats etc. - all these are exclusively the task of women.[8] (see table 5)

But it is difficult to identify clearly separated domains of men and women on a geographical or sectoral basis, as elsewhere in Africa. Women are more closely tied to the village, but they do also go to the forest for day-long gathering trips[9] ; women and children make important contributions to the 'relish' by catching small birds and mammals (gerbils, rats, moles and the like) by snares, traps and digging up on the plains[10] (which, however, nobody would call 'hunting'[11]) ; and women also catch small fish with scoop baskets (Lv.*liyanga*; the method: Lv. *kuswinga*). They also participate in the ancient methods of fishing out

---

6   Cf. the critique by White, 1955: 112, of Turner (1957).
7   See also White, 1956: 76f; Singleton-Fisher, 1948; and Turner, 1957: 29 [on hunting and woodwork]; Wendorf, 1988: 93f [on beekeeping]; Muwika and Chifwisha, 22.10.86 [on canoe-making]
8   Beck and Dorlöchter, 1988: 279
9   White (1959: 12) remarks that in contrast to other Central African peoples with a more 'extreme division of the sexes between forest and village', in the Upper Zambezi 'if the women did not work in the forest, the economic life of the village would collapse'.
10 Cf. White, 1959: 6
11 Lv./Ch. *u(n)yanga*; Nd. *wubinda* - literally 'hunting skill'

ponds at the end of the fishing season using poison or baskets.[12] Both men and women participate in basketry and pottery (see fig. 9), with a certain division only according to raw material and technique: women specialize in coil techniques (used to form certain pottery; tall *ihebi* and *ibango* baskets for meal), while only men make root baskets, bark rope and bark cloth, apparently because these are regarded as wooden products (i.e. cut-off or 'dead' parts of living trees or shrubs). There are also divisions according to product (e.g. mats, different types of baskets) which however vary from area to area. Sleeping mats, for example, are made by men in Mwinilunga (Ndembu) and among the Angolan Chokwe, but always by women in Kabompo/Zambezi.[13]

Agriculture as a whole is a field of joint activity of both men and women. Here, the reconstruction of older patterns of division of work is particularly difficult because of the intensity of more recent historical change. Only the beginning and the end of the crop production process are clearly divided: tree-felling, burning and brushing virgin fields (as well as building the grain stores and drying platforms) are exclusively the task of men, while planting, weeding, harvesting and processing of the crops are always done by women. Clearing and burning of fallows, however, and the laborious process of hoeing up the soil and forming it into seedbeds (ridges or mounds) can be done in principle, according to village norms, by both women and men.[14] But the actual part either group plays in these tasks differs widely. Those statements which emphasize for men's participation the tasks of hoeing and planting[15] in men's participation either refer explicitly to today's situation as different from the past, or to a situation where specialized cassava cultivation had already begun, apparently with strong external market demand.

A careful examination of these statements leads to the conclusion that before the 19th century men tended to contribute very little to any fieldwork after they had completed the task of bush-clearing and -burning, particularly with millet cultivation. If any men, however, it was rather the elderly ones who participated in cultivation, because they are less mobile and have more obligations of hospitality towards relatives and strangers (see below).

---

[12] White, 1956: 80-82
[13] McCulloch, 1951: 17 (based on information from White); Baumann, 1935: 65, 77; personal observations
[14] Thomas Maseka Mbondu, *Kanampumba* (Senior Councillor) of Chief Ishinde, 25.10.1986; Baumann, 1935: 50; McCulloch, 1951: 15, 60; Turner, 1957: 21/2; White, 1959: 21/2; Beck and Dorlöchter, 1988: 224ff; personal observations
[15] Arnot, 1888: 159 [on Luvale and Southern Lunda]; Baumann, 1935: 50 [on Chokwe]; McCulloch, 1951: 60 [on Luchazi]; Turner, 1957: 22 [on Ndembu-Lubnda]; White, 1959: 21

To sum up, agricultural production is basically a female enterprise, but has always depended to some extent on male labour, particularly in the initial task of opening fields for cultivation. Men, on the other hand, have their customary main areas of activity outside agriculture, mainly the provision of tools and protein foods, and are completely dependent on female labour for their reproduction. The supply of starchy foods is entirely the responsibility of women, as is reflected in the strict rule that only women may harvest food crops and prepare meals. Even fermented drinks (SL./Lv.*walwa*, 'beers') from various grains, roots or nuts are always prepared by women, except honeybeer (Lv.*wala wa ndoka*, SL.*wala wa kasolu*) which does not need cooking and is usually prepared by male beekeepers.

Seen in this context, the productive innovations of the 17th/18th century first of all meant a deepening division of labour between men and women. Improved iron tools and weapons for hunting (and warfare) as well as new, more intensive fishing technologies fostered prolonged absences of men, particularly younger men. They helped them to concentrate on typical male products: fish, game meat, honey (mainly for beer), buildings and wooden utensils.

To better understand these implications of productive innovations we must also bear in mind that all productive activities in the region have a strongly seasonal character (see table 5). The main season for fishing at the large *málilo* (dams) in larger depressions in the plains is March to July, that for building these dams is August and September; the building of grain stores and houses, ironwork and woodwork take place during the whole dry season from May to October; and hunting is best in the later dry season (August to October) when hungry game gravitates to those places where fresh shoots are available, often as a result of systematic burning by hunters. Hunting trips are also often combined with the collection of honey, which is most plentiful in March to July and in October and November. There is an obvious clash between these male activities and the season of male participation in agriculture: the laborious clearing and burning new fields, and men's part in subsequent hoeing and mounding, which must all be completed by mid-October before the rains set in.

Table 5: Productive activities around the Upper Zambezi by season and gender

Task	Jul Aug Sep Oct Nov Dec Jan Feb Mar Apr May Jun
Building	(houses) MfMfMfMfMfMf ... (stores) MMMMM
Basketry	fmfmfmfmfm
Ironwork	mmmmmmmmmmm
Woodwork	mmmmmmmmmmm
Saltmaking	ffffffffffffffffffffff
Hunting (bows)	MMMMMMMMMMMMMMM
Collecting:	
Grasshoppers	fcfcfcfcfcfcfcfcfcfcf
Caterpillars	fcfcfcfcfcfcfcfcfcfcfcfcfcfcfcfcfcfcfcfcfcfcfcfcfcfcfcfcfcfcfcfcfcfcffcfcfc
Other insects	fcfcfcfcfcfcfcfcfcfcfcfcfcfcfcfcfcfcfcfcf
Fruits/nuts	--fcfcfcfcfcfcfcfcfcfcfcfc-----------
Beekeeping:	(harvest) mmmmmm (hive-making) MMMMM mmmmmmmm (harvest) MMMMMM
Fishing:	
Weirs, dams	(building) MM MMMMM (musuza) MfMfMfMf (catching) MMMMMMMM
Emptying pools	mfmfmfmfmf
Nets, hooks, traps	mmmmmmmmmmmmmmmmmmmmmmmmmmmm
Cultivation:	
Bush clearing	(cut) (burning) MMMmmmmmmmmmm (cutting) MMMMMMM
Hoeing, mounding	ffmffmffmFmFmFmFm
Sowing, planting	ffffff (bulrush millet) ffff (maize) ffff (fi.millet, gr.nuts, beans)
Same, cassava	ffff (Westb.) ffffffffffffffffff------ (Eastbank) (sweet potatoes) ffffffff------------
Weeding	FFFFFFFFFFFFFFFF
Bird scaring	fcfcfcFCFCFCFCFCFC?

140   C : THE REGIONAL ECONOMY

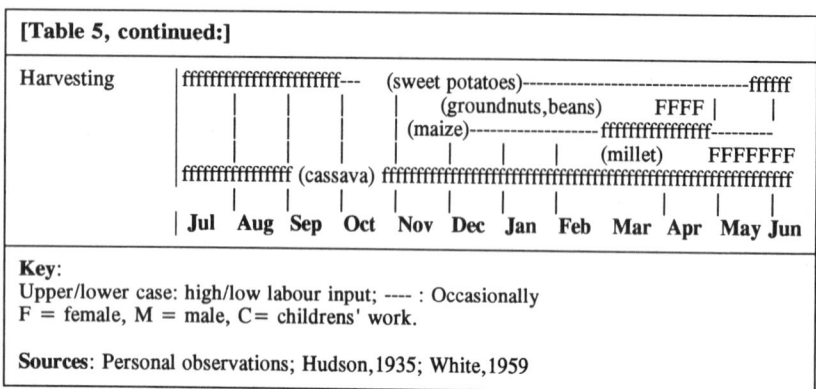

Cassava cultivation, the major innovation in agriculture, appears to have been a solution to men's problems with their labour time. As has been explained in the last section, cassava makes little demand on soil nutrients; it therefore requires less frequent shifting of fields to unexhausted land. It has a noticeably higher output per area than grain crops, which also reduces the labour to be expended on bush clearing. And finally, cassava roots are kept in the ground until needed, and therefore no building of sophisticated stores is required. (See fig. 13 and table 4.) The price for these improvements, on the other hand, was an increased work load for women in crop cultivation and processing:[16] in order to preserve a minimum of soil fertility required for repeated cassava cultivation on the same plot under conditions of heavily leached sandy soils, high seedbeds containing green manure (mounds) are built in a very laborious manner every time cassava is replanted. Prolonged cultivation on the same plot also means a rapid increase of weed growth, hence a need for weeding. Harvesting the tubers is also more energy-intensive than cutting grain. And, above all, the processing of cassava is as a very time-consuming task. All these are in this region considered to be typical female chores (see table 5). It appears plausible to conclude that the introduction of cassava reduced men's labour input and made prolonged absence from home for the pursuit of their own activities even easier. (See fig. 25.)

But this should not lead to the conclusion that the introduction of cassava was in the unilateral interest of male producers. The analysis of social relations of production between men and women in the following chapter will demonstrate that the situation is much more complex and that, on the contrary, women themselves may have had an active interest in introducing cassava cultivation. This has to do with the strategic

---
[16] See also Hansen, 1977: 176ff

importance of power over food which is always linked to power vis-a-vis other people (see below, D 2).

C 3.2 The 'division of knowledge'

Different access to productive knowledge has always been an important basis of the general division of labour by gender and age. It has already been mentioned that elderly people in general were privileged not only with regard to social and ritual experience, but also to technological knowledge. They represented something like the 'libraries' in their communities. For the more widely used and less specialized occupations - e.g. fishing, gathering, hunting small animals or cultivation - such knowledge was passed on to juniors as part of the general education process. Aside from story-telling and talks in the *zango* (the men's meeting shelter in the centre of the village) or near the kitchen fire, boys' and girls' initiation ceremonies (*mukanda* and *wali*) played an important role as places of traditional education. This education included practical skills relevant for production.[17] Among other things, girls were, and are, taught cultivation, fishing and food processing practices during *wali*, and at least in the past boys were taken 'away to the forests for most of the mornings and afternoons to familiarize them with the life of the forest' during *mukanda*.[18] Papstein even believes that 'it was in all likelihood through the *mukanda* camps that the Nama Kungu [Luvale immigrant chiefs - A.v.O.] passed on their knowledge of fishing, iron working and medicines...'.[19] If *mukanda* helped to popularize new production technologies, however, this probably did not include cassava cultivation which was essentially a women's domain.

Much of the transfer of productive knowledge took place individually by training 'on the job'. Boys learnt much about ways of appropriating the wilderness by accompanying elder men during their hunting or fishing trips, and by assisting them in beekeeping or general woodwork. They had to help seniors during this training, e.g. as carriers. This could be seen as an appropriation or even exploitation of the juniors' labour, but in all these cases, training seems to have been regarded only as a temporary, target-oriented form of subordination; juniors always ended up establishing themselves as independent producers. Therefore, these forms

---

[17] Cf. the popular account of Mwondela, 1972, while in older anthropological literature only the symbolism included in this *rite de passage* was in the focus of attention.
[18] Mwondela, 1972: 14
[19] Papstein, 1978: 28

of training should be seen rather as some sort of 'apprenticeship' (on the social relations involved see next part).

Such more general activities therefore established only a temporary 'division of knowledge' between entire generation segments. More restricted was the access to certain activities that entailed a more professional identity: specialized solitary hunters (SL./Lv.*ayi-/vinyanga*), of which a village usually had only one who distributed his kill to other villagers and neighbours; diviners (Lv.*tahi*, SL. *katepa*, sg.); healers or herbalists (sg. *chimbanda, chimbuke*); and 'witch doctors' or 'medicine men' (sg. *-nganga*). Among hunters and diviners, an elaborate form of initiation existed through which only selected juniors obtained access to an exclusive circle of adepts. The knowledge transferred during this training, however, apparently included mainly ritual skills, while technical skills were taken for granted among the applicants. Membership in a hunters' or diviners' cult was relevant for protection against a complex of interlinked material and magical dangers commonly associated with these occupations, and they created a professional identity which was connected to high social status in the village - the highest next to headmanship.[20]

Other forms of professional specialization with more direct economic implications applied among craftsmen. Iron work had probably always been done by hardly more than one specialist in each village who exchanged his products in one way or another with his fellow villagers and neighbours. Similar local specialization may have existed with the more sophisticated wooden products such as drums or dugout canoes, but ironwork is seen as the archetypal form since the term for blacksmith (SL.*muchiji*, Lv.*fuli*) is sometimes used as a generic term for any specialized craftsman (e.g. canoe-makers). The introduction of new expertise in ironwork from the north-east during the 16th-18th centuries helped certain blacksmiths who made good quality raw iron, iron tools, weapons and ornaments, as well as perhaps some canoe-builders, to extend their reputation beyond the boundaries of their home area. The Luvale *Chihuka* clan, for example, claims to have come from the north, the origin of improved iron technology, according to linguistic analysis of the clan formula, in this formula, one of the founders is mentioned as follows: 'Konga left his home and came from a far place; he had forged arrows, and with those he had left he bought meal.'[21] Gradually, their products entered local and regional barter trade, and favoured

---

[20] Some observers have therefore talked misleadingly of a 'hunting class' or 'hunters' guild' for the Upper Zambezi, while McCulloch has suggested 'profession' as a more appropriate term (cf. Baumann, 1935: 42f; McCulloch, 1951: 35f, 16).

[21] *Konga lyavotoka lyafuma kwakusuku; wafulile kwashi jasaala jakulanda unga.* (quoted after White, 1957: 62).

specialization also among their customers: hunters and notably fishermen (see next section).

Differential knowledge on production techniques, to sum up, had always to some extent divided individuals of different gender, age and expertise. But technological and even ritual knowledge did not become a monopoly of certain social categories. This did not change fundamentally when productive innovations, notably in ironwork, deepened this division of labour along the lines of specialist knowledge and professional identity. Such innovations did, however, most probably contribute to an increase in regional trade, because they meant stronger reliance on particular, unevenly distributed natural resources.

C 3.3 The importance of regional trade

Economic activities such as hunting, fishing, agriculture, metal or woodwork, which could provide a balanced livelihood only in combination (see above), were typically divided not only between men and women, elders, juniors and professionals within the same communities. Such a division of labour also occurred on a larger scale between different locations within the region.

Especially fishing peoples and specialized agriculturalists tended to exchange their surpluses across ecological boundaries. This was and is true for Africa in general[22] and for Central Africa with its mixture of drier and wetter areas in particular. There, 'ecological differentiation was the first factor which led to regular trading contacts'[23]. A regional division of labour emerged early, not only with regard to iron, copper and salt, the classical articles of regional exchange, but notably also to foodstuffs.[24] It is even assumed today that 'the interaction between dense riverain and lakeside populations, and dispersed dryland settlements has been one of the basic dynamics of history' in Central Africa.[25]

In the Upper Zambezi, dried fish and perhaps game meat may have already been exchanged for staple crops between different Iron Age

---

[22] See Austen, 1987: 21
[23] Miller, 1983: 127
[24] The importance of food products has long been neglected in studies on early indigenous trade which tend to focus on scarce minerals (copper, iron, salt) or craft products (tools, ornaments, carvings) - maybe because of their greater appeal for archaeologists (cf.Fagan, 1970; Roberts, 1970: 721f).
[25] Reefe, 1983: 161

groups, because crop harvests were always threatened by high floods and scarcity of virgin upland soils west of the Zambezi, and because originally game was relatively scarcer in the East than in the West. But it must be assumed that regional exchanges of foodstuffs greatly increased with the innovations of the 16th/17th centuries. These changes not only gave to upland cassava cultivators and to floodplain fishing people the opportunity to produce more surplus, they also created new scarcities. A cassava-based diet, as we have seen, is particularly dependent on complementary foods rich in protein and other nutrients; a diet of fish (as well as meat), on the other hand, does not provide enough calories and fibre and requires a basis of staple crops. Intensification of cultivation and fishing most probably meant a certain concentration of population in areas ill suited to the production of the necessary complementary foodstuffs: far from permanent or seasonal water surfaces on the one hand, and along lakes and rivers on the other. In addition, the work calendar of fishing and agriculture overlaps to a considerable extent, at least as far as the tasks of men are concerned (see table 4).

Widening the options for obtaining scarce complementary foodstuffs through regional exchange may in fact have been one of the motives for increases in productivity in certain forms of production. In any case, this was certainly one important consequence of flood-plain fishing and cassava growing. Gradually, producers on both sides of the Zambezi became so dependent on each other for their diet that today the Eastbank is nicknamed *nshima* (porridge), and the Westbank *ifwo* ('relish').[26]

'The Luvale have traded fish and cassava for hundreds of years', we are told by their historian.[27] It is likely that floodplain dwellers west of the Zambezi with their surplus of dried fish were the main force stimulating regional exchange around the Upper Zambezi and Kasai. As in other areas of Central Africa, they were particularly prone to shortages in staple food, which could be supplied by upland cultivators who, in turn, 'would travel long distances to barter quantities of this tasty protein.'[28]

Unfortunately, there are no other pre-19th century sources to confirm such oral traditions of the Upper Zambezi and Kasai. During the 19th century, for which a variety of sources exist, certain changes in the functioning and volume of regional trade may have occurred, as will be

---

[26] In the pre-colonial period protein surpluses in the Westbank also seem to have included game meat which was either exported to the East or hunted by Eastbank inhabitants themselves (see for example Livingstone 1963: 30/31 [1854] who met a large group of Mbunda refugees living in the Eastbank who took huge amounts of elephant meat across the river back to their homes).
[27] Moses Sangambo, n.d.[2]: 70
[28] Reefe, 1983: 172

seen in the next section. These changes, however, seem to have been mere adaptations to long-distance trade, regarding volume, carriers and use of additional commodities. Nothing in these sources suggests that direct exchange of basic local products between producers from different areas within the region was a new phenomenon. 19th century travellers' observations therefore seem to permit some conclusions on early regional trade. Magyar, for example, found in the 1850s the inhabitants of the Dilolo and Kifumaji lakes and swamps catching 'many and various fish' throughout the year, 'drying them and conducting a considerable trade with them'.[29] According to Cameron, considerable quantities of fish were caught by Luvale fishermen by 1875 using both lake and flood-plain fishing technologies, 'roughly dried and exported to the neighbouring countries.'[30] Such observations seem to confirm Moses Sangambo, the Luvale historian: 'We used to trade fish with the other peoples between the Lungwevungu and the Luena and even as far as the *Kasavi*' [Kasai river].[31] This clearly refers to the Luchazi-Mbunda and to the Chokwe with whom the Luvale conducted a brisk trade. Fish was also exported to the woodland areas east of the Zambezi which were inhabited by people with Southern Lunda affiliation.[32]

Cassava was obviously the main product which flood-plain exporters obtained from woodland dwellers in return for their fish. Some of this cassava seems to have been grown by 'up river' Luvale groups (see last section) who lived for one reason or another in areas with more upland.[33] Considerable amounts of cassava, however, were also produced and exchanged by Southern Lunda[34]. Luchazi-Mbunda producers even seem to have been able to export millet surpluses to the plains.[35]

---

[29] Magyar, 1860: 230
[30] Cameron, 1878: II, 169
[31] Sangambo, 1985: 69
[32] See for example Livingstone 1963: 49 and 67/68 [1854], who was offered dried fish by Southern Lunda chiefs and headmen. It is possible, however, that a little fish was also caught along the Eastbank rivers since today the Southern Lunda have taken over Luvale fishing technologies in those few places where the environment is appropriate.
[33] See Sangambo, n.d.^{2}: 70
[34] *Kanampumba* Maseka Mbondu, Senior Councillor of Chief Ishinde, 15/10/86
[35] Interview Yowena Samakayi, 21/10/1986

Fig. 14: The author of this book trying a fish trader's load (1985)
The shape (and much of the trade) is virtually unchanged compared to pre-colonial long-distance trade - compare with fig. 7. Note the cooking utensils on top. (Photograph taken by Evans Kavungu near Muyembe, Zambezi-Westbank)

But staple crops, it appears, were not the only products woodland cultivators could offer for precious fish protein:

'The Luchazi and Mbunda used to come into our country to buy fish. In return they brought hoes, axes and castor oil to trade for the fish. Castor oil was particularly wanted by the women who used it as a cosmetic hairdressing. This was considered a sign of beauty. Before the *Chilumbu* dance (mostly performed in distant past) was performed the hair had to be dressed with oil'.[36]

The cultivation of the castor plant, which is still found today in almost every backdoor garden in Zambezi and Kabompo, for purposes of body care in the pre-colonial period is also mentioned by a number of 19th century sources. Near the capital of the Luvale chieftainess Nyakatolo, in 1899, for example, every village was

---

[36] Sangambo, n.d.[2]: 69. A brisk trade in castor oil for fish between Chokwe and Luvale, as well as between Chokwe and Lwimbi, is also reported by Arnot (1969: 249/50 [1888]).

'surrounded with these shrubs [castor],... The beans are gathered annually, and the cultivators travel miles laden with their precious "pomade", dispensing it to those who are less fortunate in its cultivation, in return for meal or fish.'[37]

The ubiquity of castor makes it difficult to believe that it should have been differences in resource endowment which made the oil a valuable item of regional exchange; a more likely reason in this case may have been the high amount of labour required for processing, which not all producers (women) were able or willing to perform.

Another line of specialization which promoted regional exchange, again based on the location of raw materials and furthered by productive innovations, occurred in iron work. Because of the relative scarcity of good iron ore and the strategic importance of iron tools, these were classic items of early trade everywhere in Africa. Around the Upper Zambezi and Kasai, there are various deposits of iron ore in hilly places which were exploited in the pre-colonial period[38], but none in the Luvale plains: 'the Luvale know iron-working, but our country does not have many good places to find the iron ore...'[39] This did not prevent Luvale from producing high-quality iron tools, weapons[40] (see fig. 12), ritual objects including the double clapperless *lupembe* bell, a masterpiece of indigenous craftsmanship, and ornaments such as iron leg or arm rings (Lv.*lisele*, SL. *mubula*), both fashions imported from Luba/Nuclear Lunda.[41] They may have even used inferior laterite iron that is available in many places, so that by the end of the last century Harding found that 'each village has its smelting shed and blacksmith's shop at hand'[42]. But at least for their raw material they had to 'import large quantities of iron from *Kibokwe*' [Chokwe][43].

Highly skilled Chokwe and Luchazi blacksmiths were the real specialists in the area which produced particularly good iron ore, 'not inferior to the Swedish', which they worked into hoe and axe blades, arrowheads, double-edged swords (sg. *mukwale*), a variety of thrusting

---

37 Harding, 1904: 177; see also Graça, 1890: 416 [1846; Central Chokwe]; Pinto, 1881: I, 228, 254, 274 [1878; Luchazi]; Livingstone, 1963: 77 [1854; Southern Lunda]
38 Notably in Central Chokwe (e.g. Magyar, 1860: 229; Capello and Ivens, 1882: I, 225 [1878]), and among the Luchazi near the Kwanavale source (Pinto, 1881: I, 274, 279 [1878]); but also in the *Saloisho* hills, '10 miles east' of the Southern Lunda chief Ishinde (Livingstone, 1963: 267 [1855])
39 Sangambo, 1985: 69
40 Cameron, 1877: II, 163 [1875]
41 See Papstein, 1978: 137; Lux, 1880: 122/3
42 Harding, 1904: 159 [1899]
43 Cameron, 1877: II, 165

weapons, and iron wire.[44] Raw iron, tools and weapons were used both domestically and for export to their neighbours, mostly in return for foodstuffs such as dried fish.[45] According to another testimony, 'hoes and honey' were also exported from an area on the Manyinga River east of the Zambezi.[46]

The distances covered by this regional trade were remarkable: the boundary of the Chokwe core area on the Upper Kasai was 8-9 days' walk from Kakenge, and 2-3 days' more from today's site of Mize.[47] But it seems that regional trade networks based on productive specialization had reached even beyond the boundaries of the peoples of the Upper Zambezi and Kasai from ancient times. For example, there was a lack of good clay for pottery in the sandy, wooded uplands of the Upper Zambezi; this lack was particularly painful in the case of the big vessels required for the preparation of beer from grains or honey which was an important part of the diet and of social life. Clay pots were therefore an important item of barter trade.[48] At least by the mid-19th century, when beer consumption had probably increased significantly, clay pots, particularly the bigger ones, were imported from as far as the Kwanza river.[49] (See fig.s 9 and 20) The Lwimbi people of that area became then known as *Kimbandi*, 'the pot people'.[50] Since the Lwimbi themselves were otherwise specialized in fishing, it seems likely that crop surpluses were given in return for these pots.[51]

In what appears to be a reversal of the customary European sequence from Bronze Age to Iron Age, the body ornaments made from iron wire mentioned before, but not the tools and weapons, were gradually complemented by bracelets and leglets made from copper. One of the earliest written reports, from around 1800, indicates that by that time copper, apparently in St.Andrew-cross shaped bars,[52] was already being imported by Luvale and skillfully manufactured into copper wire which

---

[44] Magyar, 1860: 229 [1850s] and Capello and Ivens, 1882: I, 225 [1878][both on Central Chokwe]; Pinto, 1881: I, 274, 279 [1878, Luchazi]

[45] Interview Yowena Samakayi, 21.10.1986 [Chokwe-Luvale/Southern Lunda]; Silva Porto, 1986: 317, 322, 325 [1847], and Pinto, 1881: I, 250 [1878, both on trade between Luchazi and Mbandi]

[46] Livingstone, 1963: 264 [1855]

[47] See the map of walking distances in Papstein, 1978: 231

[48] Yowena Samakayi, 21.10.1986

[49] Pinto, 1881: I, 280 [Luchazi]

[50] Magyar, 1860: 227; on specialization of the Mbandi on fishing and pottery for export see also Silva Porto, 1986: 317 [1847]

[51] See Arnot, 1888: 250

[52] The Luvale call these cross-shaped copper-ingots *mwambo* (see Horton, [2]1975: 7), from an identical Nuclear Lunda term (see Magyar, 1860: 231). Their shape is explained as making transport in bundles easier (e.g. Lux, 1880: 123/4).

was wound round a core of wood or elephant tail to make those precious wire bracelets still known as (Lv.,sg.) *liseka* among the Luvale, Luchazi and Chokwe.[53] The same copper wire bracelets, called *minungu*, seem to have been widespread in Lunda.[54] Not only the fashion but also the raw material seem to have had a common source: the copper mines on the Lubudi river in what is today Southern Zaire, then part of the Lunda empire.[55] Another early report mentions that copper from there was partly delivered to the Mwant Yav, the Lunda emperor as tribute, but adds that 'the smiths *(ferreiros)* also exchange their bars for flour and other provisions that are valued'.[56] These 'provisions', according to other remarks in the same text, were obviously manioc flour and perhaps dried fish. Seen in this context, intensification and specialization of food production seem to have provided inhabitants of the Upper Zambezi and Kasai with the means to increase their imports of non-food items such as copper, but also the others mentioned above.

Another strategic item of early pre-colonial trade was salt. Like in many areas of Africa, mineral salt was constantly scarce in the Central African interior including the Upper Zambezi and Kasai, and therefore highly appreciated, almost as a titbit.[57] The traditional method of salt production, which is now regarded as a sign of poverty by village women, is a rather complicated processing of the ashes of certain grasses.[58] With regard to ash salt, not so much the availability of these grasses, but again the willingness or ability to carry out the labourious production process, in this case by women, seems to have been different according to region. The most important export area for ash salt in the pre-colonial period, particularly in the North, were the famous salt pans of Kijila, situated close to the copper mines near the Lualaba River. Foodstuffs, notably cassava, are once again mentioned in the earliest reports as what female producers wanted in return for their ash salt, because

---

[53] *Anonymus*, 1803: 24; Arnot, 1969: 249 [1888]; throughout the 19th century, Luvale and Chokwe were known as importers of raw copper from Luba/Nuclear Lunda (see Magyar, 1860: 231; Pinto, 1881: I, 280; Arnot, 1888: 249).

[54] Magyar, 1860: 231

[55] Cross-shaped copper ingots have been exported from the copper mines of Kijila far and wide from ancient times; samples have been found in 15th century excavations as far south as Ingombe Ilede, on the Middle Zambezi (Roberts, 1976: 58). During the 19th century, they were witnessed by Cameron, 1877: II, 149 [1875, at Kwijila], and by Capello and Ivens, 1882: I, 180 [1878, among the Chokwe].

[56] Baptista, 1873: 223 [1810]

[57] Capello and Ivens, 1882: I, 8; Pogge, 1880: 10

[58] Personal observations; see the description of ash salt manufacture in Livingstone, 1963: 31 [1854, Southern Lunda]

'they do not cultivate manioc, it not being the custom of the country: the previous sovereigns of this land did not grow this product, and this became the general habit...'[59]

- a telling description of regional specialization. According to the same source, dealers in salt and other commodities would buy the required manioc flour on the river Lubudi in order to conduct their business. It can be safely assumed, however, that Upper Zambezi inhabitants also exchanged their own surplus produce with the women of Kijila. The Luvale are explicitly mentioned in a later report as importing salt from Katanga (*Garenganze*) in return for dried fish.[60] Another area from which ash salt is imported even today, often in return for dried fish, is located in the Kaonde country northeast of present-day Kasempa.[61]

Whether early trade already gave the peoples of the Upper Zambezi and Kasai access to the even more valuable sodium salt (from rocks or salines), in contrast to ash or potassium salt,[62] is unclear. As I have mentioned in the chronology, the Chokwe may have been accustomed to acquire salt from the Luyi salt pans near Kasanje even before the Mbangala established this capital (after 1630).[63]

A particular kind of regional division of labour developed between the more southerly inhabitants of the Upper Zambezi and the Lozi of the open, seasonally flooded Bulozi floodplain who had access to scarcely any upland at all. They were constantly lacking forest products such as canoes, building materials, bark rope and bark cloth.

'During the flood season, Luvale traders descended to the flood plain in their newly made canoes loaded with forest products; these would be exchanged for animals which were in turn walked back up to Luvale country'.[64]

It seems, however, that southern Lunda speakers from the more wooded eastbank of the Zambezi as well as Mbunda, in the uplands far to the south west, were at least as much involved in this kind of exchange as were the Luvale.[65] In addition to canoes and other wooden items some upland foodstuffs, probably honey and staple crops, seem to have been

---

[59] Baptista, 1873: 223 [1806]
[60] Arnot, 1888: 249
[61] See also Papstein, 1978: 232 and fn. 69
[62] Terminology according to Sundstrøm, 1974: 122ff
[63] Dias de Carvalho, 1892: II, 348
[64] Papstein, 1978: 232
[65] Thomas Maseka Mbondu, *Kanampumba* (senior councillor) of Chief Ishinde, 25.10.86; Hermitte, 1974: 35; Gluckman, 1941: 72

C 3 : Emerging divisions of labour 151

traded with the Lozi, particularly those near to the northern border of Bulozi.[66]

Dried fish seems to have been one important trade item which woodland dwellers in the Upper Zambezi obtained from the Lozi in return for their exports.[67] This far, the Bulozi trade appears merely as an extension of the customary exchanges between woodland cultivators and fishing people. But as the first Portuguese-speaking visitors heard by the end of the 18th century, the Lozi were famous among their northern neighbours for raising livestock, particularly cattle, on their vast flood plain.[68] Livestock seems to have been the real attraction in dealing with Bulozi, particularly for the Luvale, who had abundant fish themselves, but also ample grazing ground. The livestock trade between Upper Zambezi inhabitants and the Lozi certainly dates back to the 18th century at least,[69] although it is possible that the interaction between Luvale and Lozi originally took the form of raids on Lozi cattle.[70] Subsequently, however, it was clearly a regular exchange.

Originally, goats seem to have been given in return for Luvale exports, but from some time around 1800 onwards, cattle was increasingly given as payment by the Lozi.[71] It has been seen in the chronology (B 4) that the trade in cattle, as the most valuable animal form of capital, was closely linked to Atlantic long-distance trade. This had to do with the fact that livestock as a whole, and cattle in particular, was seen as a symbol of 'wealth' rather than a means of physical subsistence (see C 4.2). But below this level, another animal product of the Lozi, beef lard, was highly appreciated as an item for more regular consumption. It was used for hair and body dressing, and Livingstone noted in 1854 among the Southern Lunda that

'a pot of fat, if from the meat or milk of cattle, is an acceptable present to a chief'.[72]

We can conclude that the volume of regional trade within and around the Upper Zambezi and Kasai before the period of long-distance trade should

---

[66] Hermitte, 1974: 145; Papstein, 1978: 191
[67] *Ibid.*: 35 and 39
[68] Silva Teixeira, 1940: 237 [1794]; *Anonymus*, 1940: 24/5 [1803]
[69] Hermitte, 1974, refers in his remarks to the reign of Mulambwa, c. 1780-1830.
[70] e.g. Hermitte, 1974: 50
[71] Papstein, 1978: 232; Hermitte, 1974: 35, 39, 47. In 1854, both the Southern Lunda chief Ishinde and a Luvale chief *Quendende* showed themselves very interested in acquiring cattle from Bulozi through trade. The latter asked Livingstone 'if he should make a canoe and take it down to the Makololo [then ruling Bulozi], would they give him an ox ?' (Livingstone, 1963: 80).
[72] Livingstone, 1963: 32

not be underestimated. Its pattern is typical for Central Africa, but it will be seen below that it appeared on the Upper Zambezi and Kasai in a particularly decentralized form, involving individual petty producers and traders. An important question which remains open at this stage is, however, how important it was to cover the material needs of the local population - in other words, to what extent regional exchange was in fact an expression of an increasing societal division of labour.

The foregoing analysis suggests that uneven distribution of natural resources did play an important role in stimulating regional exchanges of basic goods. However, observations suggest that up to today, with a certainly greater degree of market integration, this division is only limited. Even in fishing areas, millets and cassava are still grown, and concentrations of fishing populations are usually found where some unflooded uplands are near. The forest peoples have their own ways to get access to animal protein through hunting, gathering insects, and small scale fishing. And ash salt, honey, iron tools or wooden items can in principle be produced almost everywhere. It seems that only very few resources were restricted entirely to certain locations (notably copper). Increasing specialization and regional trade in the earlier pre-colonial period can therefore hardly be presented as a result of absolute physical necessity, but rather as an expression of a multitude of strategies for making a living. The logic of such strategies was probably not purely economic, but also social (see next part, D).

More economic 'cost-benefit' considerations come in, however, where relatively richer resources in certain areas allow for better quality and a higher productivity of labour; when certain activities are more compatible with each other than others; or where some forms of food production (such as crop cultivation on the seasonally flooded plains) are not safe enough to be fully relied on. Under this last point fall also 'emergency' exchanges between those who happen to have a surplus and those who suffer from deficit, a fairly regular event given the normal fluctuations in yields of primary production.

Economically relevant exchanges do not only occur between, but also within the same areas. Local exchanges - following rules which remain yet to be examined - are the necessary implication of the division of labour by gender and age analysed above. Regional trade was originally perhaps a mere spatial extension of such normal local exchanges, as crop surpluses came mainly from women's hands, and dried fish men's. In one version of the legend on the origin of Lake Dilolo, for example, a young woman sells cassava meal for fish offered by a stranger. The stranger in this case, however, is presented as an old woman. Since surplus fish is

C 3 : Emerging divisions of labour

almost always a product of men, this seems to suggest that women were already involved to some extent in local trading in remoter times.[73]

Productive innovations, especially cassava growing and improved fishing techniques, thus meant important steps in an emerging division of labour, both on a local and a regional level. Economic specialization and the intensity of early regional trade paved the way for participation in Atlantic long-distance trade - as will be seen in the following section.

---

[73] Quoted in Fonseca Cardoso, 1919: 21-24; confirmed by Yowena Samakayi, Dipalata (interview 21.10.1986).

C 4 The means of export production

The different waves of demand released from the 'Atlantic Zone' meant considerable new strains on the productive capacities of the inhabitants of the region around the Upper Zambezi and Kasai. To meet external demand they had to rapidly increase their supply of ivory, wax and rubber, to switch quickly between these different productions, and to generate sufficient food for the rations of caravan slaves, carriers and other 'workers of trade'. In spite of these new strains, and increased mobility and insecurity as their concomitants, production and circulation of goods for the needs of the regional population itself had to be upheld as well. The transmission belt for this externally induced demand on productive capacities during this period, on the other hand, consisted in new types of imported goods all export producers in the region aspired to.

Both the long-established diversity of production in the region, and the more recent gains in productivity in some of its sectors seem to have provided important preconditions for the inhabitants of the Upper Zambezi and Kasai to cope with these additional demands. This is not to say, however, that the pre-colonial era of intense long-distance trade passed without any major impact: certain changes in production technologies, division of labour and patterns of consumption seem to have been the result or the cost of adaptation to world market integration in the region.

This impact will be scrutinized in this chapter, focusing on a sort of questions that have more often been asked with regard to later periods of the colonial and post-colonial history: was the growth of output for sale the result of 'development' in the sense of a sustainable growth of productive capacities, or did it rather lead to increasing dependence and gradual destruction, also of the environment? What strategies did the producers pursue to ensure their own subsistence, and how successful were they? And finally, what value did those imported goods have for them, once they had undergone so many hardships to obtain them - did they represent 'new needs' or substitute regional products whose production was eventually destroyed?

C 4.1 The utility of the honey bee

Beginning with the question of how the enormous growth of production for export was achieved, beeswax as perhaps the earliest non-human export commodity, along with ivory, will be considered first. When wax export started in the late 18th century (see chronology), it was a mere by-product of the gathering of honey ((w)uchi). It has already been mentioned that honey has been collected since time immemorial from the vast *musenge* woodlands. A considerable number of different insects produce honey, the African honeybee (*apis mellifera* ssp. *Adansonii*) being only one of them, but the only one that also produces wax.[1] Only small portions of the harvest would be eaten raw by the male honey-hunter or his relatives, while its main use was for honey beer or mead (*wala wa ndoka* in Lv., *kasolu* in SL.). Even mead was usually produced by men alone because it normally requires no cooking.[2] As long as no external demand existed, they threw most of the combs away, as far as bee-honey was concerned[3]; only some of the wax was used for making *likishi* masks, maintenance of musical instruments, and mending wooden utensils such as dugout canoes.[4] Thus, there was to a limited extent a 'vent for surplus' in beeswax (*sela*, from Pg. *cera*) to be sold to foreigners.

However, when the sale of wax became increasingly attractive for village men, they probably made special efforts to gather more bees' products. It is not clear to what extent the rapid growth of wax exports after 1850 resulted from increased numbers of men roaming the bush in search of wild bee swarms. The contribution of this extensive form of 'bee-hunting' was perhaps substantial, since simultaneously other forms of appropriating the wilderness (ivory hunting, then rubber collection) brought many more men into the bush.[5] Up to today, the emptying of hollow trees in which wild African bees live is a regular by-activity during hunting trips, canoe making and even beehive inspection tours.

---

1 See Malaisse, 1979: 49; White 1959: 13f
2 Personal experience; according to Silva Porto (1986: 326, fn. 2 [1847, Luchazi-Mbunda]), '*doca*' fermented in the sun or 'at the heat of the fire'. Cooking is a strictly female task.
3 This continued to happen where no market demand for wax existed; for the 19th century see Livingstone, 1960: 44 [Bulozi, 1851] and Silva Porto 1938: 106 [*Bálua*, on the Kafue, 1853].
4 See Baumann 1935: 48
5 Arnot (1969: 148) mentions Chokwe 'bee-hunters'.

Fig. 15: Chokwe beeswax hunters and beehive (1884/1878)
The more destructive form of beeswax hunting was (and is) widespread in the region, but more professional beekeepers have been using hives since pre-colonial times. (Engravings from Arnot 1889: 147 and Pinto 1881, vol.I: 283)

This extensive method is, obviously, fairly time- and energy-consuming, as well as destructive since the swarm is chased away or even killed and the tree that forms its habitat demolished by fire or even cut down. An important step towards intensification of honey and wax production was the construction of artificial hollows, i.e. bee hives to attract and keep semi-domesticated bee swarms. It is not clear when this step was made around the Upper Zambezi and Kasai, but it seems that the technology was developed by Bantu cultivators in West-Central Africa, and applied when the need arose, already before the arrival of the Portuguese.[6] For the peoples of the Upper Zambezi and Kasai, the first written evidence on beehives is found in 1854 for the Southern Lunda of Ishinde:

'In travelling yesterday through dense forest, many hives for bees were observed. These were a piece of a tree, about 10 inches or 15 in diameter and about 5 feet long. Some were made of bark, and a covering put on each end with holes for the bees to enter. They are suspended horizontally on trees...'[7]

The bark hive described here (Lv.*ngoma*, lit. a particular type of drum) became the classic type still widely used in the area today.[8] Undoubtedly, hive-keeping expanded enormously in the interior when the demand for beeswax increased.[9] In the home area of the Chokwe, chief exporters of beeswax in the region (see part B), in 1878 'every tree almost had its hive,... and an immense quantity of bee hives hinted at the wealth of wax and honey existing in the district.'[10] And in 1899, Gibbons, who came from the Lozi, observed near the source of the Zambezi that

'the Malunda cultivate honey more than any other tribe I have met. In addition to wild honey, they procure a very plentiful supply from bark hives which they attach to the branches of trees...'[11]

The intensity of bee-keeping, however, depends on more factors than the use of hives. A crucial question is the method and extent of emptying the

---

[6] Vellut 1979: 95f and fn. 9 (written evidence of bee hives in Angola dates back to 1594).

[7] Livingstone 1963: 45f

[8] Other early descriptions of beehive construction in Pogge 1880: 46 [Northern Chokwe 1875]; Pinto 1881: I, 282 [Luchazi 1878], and Schomburgk 1925: 127 [Southern Lunda 1906].

[9] For Cameron, on his way from the East Coast, the appearance of beehives was associated with the beginning of wax marketing to the West (1877: II, 152 [Fundalanga, in Ussambi = Southern Luba]).

[10] Capello and Ivens 1882: 197 and 214

[11] Gibbons 1904: II, 44f; other references to the numerous bee hives seen in the area, besides those mentioned already, are found in Livingstone 1963: 94 and 106 [South and North of the Kasai, Luvale / Southern Lunda / Northern Chokwe, 1854]; Cameron 1877: II, 186 [Central Chokwe, 1875]; Pinto 1881: I, 254 [Luchazi, 1878]; Coillard 1897: 604 [Southern Lunda on Zambezi River, north of the Kabompo confluence, 1894]; Schomburgk 1925: 127[Southern Lunda, north of Kabompo, 1906/07].

hive, because it decides the fate of the swarm and thereby the sustainability of production. Expert beekeepers today claim that they have long been accustomed to apply smoke rather than fire in the very difficult harvesting operation, and to take out only part of the combs in order not to expel or starve the swarm. In their rush to obtain marketable produce, these rules may not always have been observed by producers, even though they were evidently aware of needs and behaviour of bees, since Capello and Ivens

> 'observed at more than one spot, beneath the hives, a large quantity of dead bees, killed (as we were informed) by the other inhabitants of the hive to prevent an inconvenient consumption of honey.'[12]

Today's experience shows considerable variations in the occupation rate of beehives, depending on ecological and climatic conditions but also on the skill of the beekeeper.[13]

Yet another criterion of the intensity of beekeeping is the number of harvests per year. Trees flower at different times of the year, so that up to two harvests *per annum* are feasible under careful management and increased labour input, mainly through the allocation of hives in different ecosystems.[14] Pre-colonial reports mention both two and one harvest per year for Chokwe areas.[15]

All these observations suggest that professionalization among honey and wax producers of the region already began in the pre-colonial period. In addition to skills, the manufacture, allocation and supervision of hives requires extra labour time; especially the very labour intensive harvesting seasons collide with other male tasks in agriculture and fishing (see table 5). It may therefore be assumed that beekeeping, while rather easily combined with hunting, fostered existing tendencies of a withdrawal of men from agriculture and/or towards specialization among male producers.

The technology applied in the intensification of beekeeping to supply export markets for wax was apparently indigenous; this was not entirely the case with the means of production. Locally manufactured axes and knives are the only tools a traditional beekeeper needs, but wax processing requires additional devices:

> 'They extract the wax from the comb by a simple process of boiling, and then put it through a sieve made from bark fibre, by beating and rubbing. The wax is

---

[12] Capello and Ivens 1882: I, 214 [1878, central Chokwe area]
[13] Wendorf 1988: 97, 99; Riechert 1981: 23
[14] Wendorf 1988: 94ff
[15] Pogge 1880: 46 (Oct. / Nov. and July / August; Northern Chokwe 1875); Capello and Ivens 1882: 197 (July / August; Central Chokwe 1878). This is the situation still observed in Zambezi and Kabompo today (Wendorf *ibid*).

left to gather on the surface of the water, and is then collected, pressed by the hands into balls, cast into large cakes, and sold to Bihé traders.'[16]

The moulds for casting the wax into loaves (Lv. pawu, from Pg.'pão', bread) or cones were mostly formed in the earth, but sometimes also by the excellent baskets, some of them watertight, these peoples were renowned for.[17] Today, iron pots are mostly used. The wax obtained through this process was so impure that the trader had to reprocess it, using imported cotton cloth for pressing. The producers themselves began to use cloth (and thereby obtain higher prices) only during the colonial period, according to one old Luvale ex-beeswax trader,[18] perhaps because cloth was too valuable or otherwise unsuited for the purpose. Among the central Chokwe, however, cloth was already in use for filtering honey (combs?) in 1878.[19]

C 4.2 The ways of winning rubber

The other great export product of the gathering economy in the Central African interior was rubber. Among the *Ganguela* peoples, rubber production even seems to have displaced to some extent beeswax gathering during the 'rubber delirium', although a certain amount of specialization within the region may also have played a role.[20] The collection of wild rubber was so attractive and spread so rapidly because of the 'dizzying' prices it fetched (see chronology), but probably also because it fitted in very well with established patterns of local production. If bee-keeping required little imported equipment, rubber production required none at all: for tapping *landolphia* vines, an axe would do; and for the more complicated processing of *carpodinus* and related gummiferous creepers, only a hoe (to dig up the roots), a wooden mallet (to hammer out the rubber content), and a pot to boil and rinse the resulting cake were needed.

Since the processing of *carpodinus* rubber (Lv.*kambungo*), which was so important in the late pre-colonial economy of the Upper Zambezi and

---

16 Arnot 1969: 147 [1885, Central Chokwe]
17 Samakayi *ibid.* ; Silva Porto 1885: 166 [Central Chokwe 1880]; Capello and Ivens 1882: 197; Lux 1880: 106 [1875, Northern Chokwe]; Johnston 1969 [1891, Ngangela]
18 Y. Samakayi, 24. 10. 1989
19 Capello and Ivens, 1882: I, 197 [Central Chokwe, 1878]
20 Ministério da Marinha 1894: 22; in this report of the Governor of the Districto de Benguela, the Mbwela region (on the Kubangi) is mentioned as main supplier of wax during the rubber boom.

Kasai, is unknown even to most people in the area today, I will give a short description:[21]

Table 6: The processing of *kambungo*
(wild rubber, from carpodinus gracilis)

1.	*Mambungo* plants are searched for in the bush ('growing everywhere') and the roots ['running along for many yards, about six inches below the surface, varying in size from a quarter inch to an inch and a half'] dug up with a hoe.
[2.	The roots are dried in the sun in order to concentrate the latex in the bast between bark and wood.]
[3.	The roots are cut into pieces 30-50 cm long, put into receptacles and soaked for 2 days in water.]
4.	The roots are crushed on a wooden surface with a wooden hammer (Lv. *lindole*) to reduce the bark and the wooden cores to small pieces and separate them from the latex contained in between. This procedure is repeated, after drying, until a sticky sheet of reddish-brown colour emerges (called *chisama chakambungo* in Lv.) which, however, still contains many impurities of bark, wood and dirt. In the past this work was usually done in groups, either in camps in the bush or at home.[22]
5.	The sheets are dried for two to five days [and cut into smaller pieces or lumps]
6.	The dry lumps are thrown into an [earthen] pot of water which is brought to the boil, and cooked for about 15 minutes. This supports the removal of remaining impurities.
7.	The boiled pieces are put in between bundles of grass [and rinsed with cold water, to remove impurities] and then stepped upon to dry them and bind the latex [and to form them into new sheets].
[8.	Steps 5-7 were repeated about three times, with intermediate hammering]

---

[21] I owe great thanks to Mr. Sondoyi, Dipalata Area, Zambezi District, who remembered the processing of *kambungo* from his childhood in Caianda, Angola ('centre of big rubber trade' according to Gago Coutinho 1915: 185), and demonstrated it to me with the assistance of David Chishinji between the 21st and 26th October 1986. [In brackets: additional information from Johnston 1969: 107 (observed among the Ngangela in 1891), and Mello Geraldes / Oliveira Fragateiro 1910: 28 (observed 1903-05 among the Ngangela)].

[22] See also Schomburgk 1925 [1906, Southern Lunda]: 'The roots are cut and carried in bundles to the village'; but the banks of the Kwando near its source were 'lined with small, tempting camps, the casual dwellings of the rubber grubbers.' (Harding, 1904: 246 [1899]).

C 4 : The means of export production

> 9. In the past, in Portuguese dominated territories, the lumps of rubber were taken out of the pot during the last cooking and formed into *mutali* (sg.), cigar-shaped sticks which were the current trade units [about 15-20x1-2cm in size; in the East the were first made into small balls five of which formed a *mutali*[23]]. The British, however, preferred thick sheets.[24]

Fig. 16: Processing *carpodinus* roots to extract wild rubber (1986)
Mr. Sondoyi, another important informant in very advanced age who arranged this demonstration for me, is aided David Chishinji, one of my field assistants, in performing stage 4 - see Table 6 (Photograph taken at Dipalata village, Zambezi, 1986)

This technique, according to the same informant, was learnt from the Portuguese via the Ovimbundu, with the Luchazi being the first Upper Zambezi group to adopt it. But it is quite possible, given that the first red

---
[23] 10 small rubber balls , according to Ovimbundu traders from Chiyaka (Schönberg-Lothholz, 1960: 120).

[24] See also Hobson 1960: 503. Schomburgk 1925: 127/8 (who undertook some processing tests among the Southern Lunda north of the Kabompo River in 1906/7) preferred sheets because they made the degree of purity more visible.

rubber seems to have arrived down on the coast as somewhat of a surprise, that middlemen or even producers of the interior themselves (the first being *'Ganguela'* east of the Kwanza)[25], with their superior knowledge of the natural environment, discovered the utility of *carpodinus* roots. Its processing was certainly not a striking innovation for them. For example, tiresome beating bark bast with wooden mallets was the customary way of obtaining the precious bark blankets (Lv.*chilondo*, SL. *chilondu*), the main indigenous way of making textiles.[26] And the processing of non-food substances through cooking was known, as we have seen, for castor oil and beeswax. Wild rubber, at least the *landolphia* variety, had been used on a small scale prior to European influence for local purposes such as the manufacture of drums and drumsticks, or rubber balls for children's games east of the Kwanza and in other areas of Central Africa.[27]

One crucial problem with indigenous rubber manufacturing was quality. The balls formed of *Landolphia* rubber from vines (Lv. *kandundu*) reached sufficient degrees of purity due to their easier processing, which raised their value even more, but the remains of bark, wood and sand contained in red rubber (*kambungo*) led to continuous complaints and much lower rating on the market.[28] Plans to improve its quality through more careful processing were made by early colonial officers and consultants, but their own findings made it fairly obvious that not the ignorance of the 'natives', and not only their attempts to raise the weight ('fraud' - see part E), were the constraint.[29] Any increase in purity meant additional labour, and labour seems to have been the decisive problem in pushing rubber production up to unheard-of totals.

Tests have revealed that the production of one *chitota* (another customary unit in the Ovimbundu trade, containing 10 *mitali*)[30] weighing little more than 2½ lbs., i.e. 'the usual quantity worked at one time', cost 124 'man-hours', i.e. about a 'man-month' in terms of village labour.[31]

---

[25] Childs 1949: 208

[26] Best description of the production process in Baumann 1935: 61f. Now hardly seen any longer. Mentioned by Arnot 1969: 101 [1884, Mbunda-Mbwela], Cameron 1877: II, 189 [1875, Central Chokwe], and Milheiros 1950: 70 [Ngangela].

[27] Silva Porto 1885: 159 (mentioning drumsticks made by the Ngangela before 1869, the beginning of *landolphia* exports); Hobson 1960: 493

[28] Schönberg-Lothholz 1960: 119/20; see next footnote.

[29] The Livingstone Mail, April 15, 1911 (quoted in Hobson 1960: 503); Mello Geraldes and Oliveira Fragateiro, 1910: 26f

[30] Schönberg-Lothholz 1960: 120

[31] Hobson 1960: 493. According to another calculation, concerning root rubber in the then French Congo, the same quantity (extracted from about 20 kg of roots) took only 36 hours to process, with two cookings. Beating time was over 50% in this example.

The standard payment for one such *chitota* was only one *chilala* (the 'piece' of cloth measuring 8 yards in the interior), at a time of rapidly growing need for imported goods. The question of how individual producers mobilized the necessary work force will be examined in the next part, but on a more general, 'national economic' level it becomes clear what strains this form of export production put on labour resources in the area. Not surprisingly we hear from the Luchazi in 1899 that '...on approaching a *kraal* [derogative term for village - A.v.O.], the drum-drum thump of the native mallet crushing the root is constantly heard...'; and even from an area as remote as the source of the Kabompo in October 1900: 'I found rubber there, and the natives living near were constantly employed in its manufacture.'[32]

High labour input for rubber was facilitated by the fact that this business does not depend on a particular season as do virtually all other forms of production. Every time of low energy requirements for other tasks could thus be used for the manufacture of wild rubber. It seems, however, that in the end even in high seasons of food production, such as around the onset of the rains in October/November, much energy was invested in rubber.[33] In peak times, the daylight may have been entirely used for the collection of roots, and hammering have taken place during the night.[34]

In addition, the gathering of roots and the processing ('cooking') of rubber was much less male-specific with regard to the conventional division of labour by gender than the other forms of export production. Men still seem to have dominated the trade, probably because of the dangers of work in the wilderness during the era of slave trade. But women and children contributed considerably to the work, particularly to processing at home, perhaps not on their own account, but at least as an assistance for men.[35]

These changes in the conventional work calendar and division of tasks suggest that rubber production took place even at the expense of food production (see below). Within an emerging new societal division of labour between export and food producers, the Luchazi had the reputation of being the most specialized rubber makers. An early Portuguese administrator reported:

(Quoted in Mello Geraldes and Oliveira Fragateiro 1910: 24). The effective price for rubber seems to have increased in the early 1900s (see below, chapter E 3)

32 Harding 1904: 238, and 370 [Southern Lunda].
33 Johnston 1969: 107 [Western Ngangela]; Harding 1904: 370 [Southern Lunda]
34 Mr. Sondoyi, 24. 10. 1986 [referring to the short-lived rubber boom during the Second World War, Balovale=Zambezi]
35 Mr. Sondoyi, 24. 10. 1986 [early 20th century, Caianda, Luvale / Southern Lunda]; Harding 1904: 245 [Luchazi]; Arnot, 1893: 32 [Chokwe]

'...the information I have collected tells me that this people [the Luchazi] is the most hard-working devoting itself to the preparation of *borracha* [wild rubber] while apart from this enterprise it exercises no other systematically...'[36]

The scope for productivity increases was obviously low under village conditions. The Northern Chokwe, and apparently also the Luchazi, were to some extent able to concentrate on the more valuable, and much more easily prepared *landolphia* rubber.[37] In the case of *carpodinus* root rubber, to raise both quantity and quality of the product required first of all additional labour for processing, which was notoriously scarce in the area.[38] Consequently, two early colonial entrepreneurs, one Portuguese and one British, tried to introduce industrial machinery in Central Africa.[39] The second attempt ultimately failed because it coincided with the collapse of the rubber market, but the reason for the failure of the first one (in 1905, among the Luchazi) reveals how ecological constraints joined in with labour problems to limit the perspectives of this form of export production:

'One year later, approximately, he was forced to abandon his factory, because the raw material - the roots - was exhausted, and to continue one had to bring them in from other *chanas* [open plains rich in *carpodinus* - A.v.O.], which would have rendered the exploitation impossible due to the high price of labour force and transport.'[40]

Systematic gathering of wild rubber inevitably leads to rapid exhaustion of the required plant population, unless special care is taken to spare some of their parts or replant them. Rubber producers of the Upper Kasai have been persistently blamed for reckless exploitation of the ressource.[41]

'The negro, ignorant and short-sighted, who does not think of the future, and when he goes to the *chana* to manufacture rubber, his only aim is to obtain, with the least effort possible, the biggest quantity of an exchange product of which he knows that one will give him the desired gun, the attractive brandy and the fancy clothes in return,'[42]

was seen as the main threat to economic life in the area which, as far as foreign trade was concerned, revolved entirely around rubber by the turn

---

[36] Relatório do Capitão-Mor do Moxico, 5. 2. 1905, quoted in Delgado 1944: 668
[37] Mr. Sondoyi, 24. Oct. 1986; Harding 1904: 240 [1899]
[38] See for example the considerations of Schomburgk 1925: 128
[39] Mello Geraldes and Oliveira Fragateiro, 1910: 17/18 [1904, near the Cuanavale, Luchazi area]; Hobson 1960: 506f [1913/15, in Northern Province of what is now Zambia, against the advice of the British rubber consultant de Jong who had suggested the area of the present-day Zambezi and Kabompo Districts]
[40] Mello Geraldes and Oliveira Fragateiro 1910: 18
[41] For the Northern Chokwe see Pogge 1880: 27 [1875, six years after the beginning of rubber exports]
[42] Mello Geraldes and Oliveira Fragateiro 1910: 15 (as a solution, they suggested conservation measures promoted by an intensive information campaign).

of the century.[43] Harms has shown for the Congo Free State that in reality coercion by the notorious concession companies forced producers to finish-up all rubber vines in their territories, and that this, earlier than dropping prices, brought rubber exports to a premature end.[44] The case of the Upper Zambezi and Kasai demonstrates that on the one hand even in Harms' contrast case, the so-called 'free trade' areas, *landolphia* supplies could be quickly exhausted, as had happened to the Chokwe around Mona Kimbundu in 1875, only six years after the beginning of rubber exports.[45]

On the other hand, this may have been rather a local phenomenon in a heavily populated area.[46] Given the vastness of open lands in the region as a whole, the usual response to such a dwindling of resources, similar to the case of ivory, was increased mobility. Since rubber production involved the whole workforce, it contributed significantly to the spread of the Chokwe, with entire villages moving north- and southwards along rivers whose gallery forests contained untapped *landolphia* vines (see chronology).[47]

As far as root rubber is concerned, supplies seem to have been even less near exhaustion by the end of the rubber trade, despite the laments of some early colonial officers. De Mello Geraldes and d'Oliveira Fragateiro in their report tried hard to discredit an earlier report by the Anglo-Portuguese botanist John Gossweiler which came to the conclusion that

'it is not at all probable that the production of rubber is diminished in this region because of the destruction of the plants by the exploitation conducted by the natives'.[48]

But their own observations seem to support only the conclusion that a **capitalist** form of exploitation was not feasible, because of the high spatial concentration of demand by industrial processing plants, and the

---

[43] See Relatório do Capitão-Mor do Moxico 1905, in Delgado 1944: 666
[44] Harms 1975
[45] Pogge 1880: 51.
[46] Miller perhaps exaggerates the significance of this observation when he generalizes that 'no rubber remained'(1970: 186f). Rubber varieties tapped from stems called *kandundu*, 'rubber wood' (*landolphia* vines? Certain trees?) still appear to have been present around the turn of the century (Mr. Sondoyi, 24. Oct. 1986; Harding 1904: 240 [1899], both on Luchazi).
[47] According to Pogge (1880: 51) even the people of Mona Kimbundu continued to obtain rubber by supplies from the Chikapa valley to the north [1875, Chokwe]. Wissmann found *landolphia* in the valleys and even the heights around the Chikapa (Chief Kissenge's) in 1880 (1902: 47).
[48] Relatório da missão agrÀcola região dos Ganguelas, Ambuelas e Luchazes, 1907, quoted in Mello Geraldes and Oliveira Fragateiro 1910: 18.

high wage costs involved in transportation (see the example given above). With the highly mobile, decentralized mode of production of Upper Zambezi producers, who hardly calculated labour costs, these problems did not occur, as long as there was a reasonable market price.

It is true that any sustainable form of production of wild rubber in the long run would have required conservation and replanting measures. It seems plausible, however, that the producers of the Upper Zambezi and Kasai with their limited attachment to particular areas found it simply easier to explore more resources elsewhere as long as these existed. In addition, they may have felt little inclination to invest so much additional labour in long-term development of one product as long as market demand in their experience was so highly volatile. If they thought so, they would have been prooved right by history: While the minimum time of growth before harvest for *carpodinus gracilis* was estimated to be between 5 and 15 years[49], the 'rubber delirium' as a whole lasted only about 25 years in this region and experienced violent price fluctuations.

C 4.3   The dangers of hunting elephants

In contrast to beeswax gathering and rubber production, the technology of hunting ivory, the third great form of appropriating the wilderness for export, appears to have been revolutionized by world market influence: through the massive import of firearms.

For the 19th century, however, I have found only one eye-witness report on elephant hunting in the region which describes vividly the dangers and difficulty of indigenous methods, both without and with firearms:

> 'The quantity of elephants is so great in Katende and Quibuica that they go in herds like livestock, because the hunters are few, because many have lost their lives in the hunt on them, which is rather dangerous in consequence of the great instinct with which this animal is endowed...[then follows a detailed description of how wounded elephants attack hunters - A.v.O.] ...Some kill them by shooting, some with poisoned spears, others with arrows, and many die in large pits, big and funnel-shaped, made where they usually pass, and when they pass there many of them fall and are crammed in them, and they finish them with shots etc., but nevertheless woebetide the unexperienced who approaches him and is his [the elephant's] victim if he reaches him with his trunk.'[50]

---

[49] Mello Geraldes and Oliveira Fragateiro 1910: 23; Gossweiler 1907: 48-50, quoted in: *ibid*.

[50] Graça 1890: 427 [Southern Lunda area of Katende's and Chibwika's, Nuclear Lunda vassals, near the Kasai]

Fig. 17: Chokwe big game hunters' camp (1878)
Note the temporary shelters, models for caravan camps, which are protected by animal skulls, and the racks for drying meat. Besides slaughtering, some bargaining over meat transactions seems to be taking place. (Engraving from Capello and Ivens 1882, vol.I: 219)

Nevertheless, hunters of the Upper Zambezi and Kasai were apparently very successful in their battles with the grey giants. The land of the Luvale, which had been trodden by elephants in all directions by 1842, no longer had sufficient ivory to attract traders by 1850.[51] And the Chokwe, along with the Luchazi-Mbunda renowned as the most specialized ivory

---

51 Silva Porto diary, entries 16. 2. 1886 and 17. 5. 1968, quoted by Madeira Santos 1986: 83. See also Magyar 1860: 234

hunters in the region,[52] were expected by visitors to clear certain areas such as the Upper Kasai of elephants soon, and extended their hunting trips to ever more distant places by the mid-1850s.[53] This may also be seen as the beginning of the subsequent massive emigration of Chokwe people to the North-East and South (see chronology, part B). Twenty years on, ivory resources began to disappear even in the Northern Chokwe diaspora, and contemporary observers attributed this to the influx of ever larger quantities of guns:

> 'The elephants have no better fate than the rubber tree. In inhabited areas it is completely exterminated. It only still exists deep in the interior where it has not yet made the acquaintance of the shooting gun. It is therefore not surprising if ivory gets scarcer from year to year...'[54]

In fact, the inhabitants of the Upper Kasai and Zambezi, particularly the more westerly ones, were quicker to acquire considerable quantities of firearms than other peoples of the interior. While no guns appear in descriptions of Luvale and Chokwe weaponry up to the mid-1840s, in 1847 the Luchazi near the Upper Lungwevungu were the first to be mentioned as possessing in their majority 'firearms which they obtain for the commodities mentioned' [wax, slaves, and ivory]. In 1853, 'there is no *Ganguella* who has no firearm...'.[55] At the same time, Livingstone was informed by jealous Lozi-Kololo that all the peoples up the Zambezi 'possess boats and are rich. There is no want of food. Many of these tribes possess guns...', and he was to experience this personally during his following trip to the Southern Lunda, Luvale and Chokwe.[56] At Mai Munene on the Middle Kasai, in contrast, he heard shortly afterwards that 'neither guns nor native traders are admitted into the country, the chief of Luba entertaining a dread of innovation.'[57] His attitude was to change soon, but Southern Luba still had no guns in 1875.[58] And for some Western Ngangela groups near the Kwanza (Mbandi etc.) there is a report

---

[52] In 1878, senior chief Ndumba Tembo of the Chokwe proudly boasted in front of his guests that 'the *ma-quioco* are even now the boldest and fleetest in the pursuit of the *njamba* [elephant]' - quoted in Capello and Ivens, 1882: I, 192

[53] Livingstone 1963: 92/3 and 249 [1854 and 1855, near the Upper Kasai]; Magyar 1860: 231, fn. 1

[54] Pogge 1980: 28 [1875, Northern Chokwe]. The same is said to have happened in the next stage further north: The people around the lower Lulua and Kasai killed elephants by spears, traps and poisoned arrows in the 1850s and tried to impose a ban on gun imports, but by 1880 these animals were finished due to firearms (Livingstone 1857: 458, and Wissmann 1902: 74 and 353).

[55] Silva Porto 1986: 325 and 1938: 70

[56] 1960: 42 [1851]. For the Upper Zambezi and Kasai, see references to Livingstone 1963 in the following footnotes.

[57] Livingstone 1857: 458 [1855]

[58] Cameron 1877: II, 162

from as late as 1878 observing that 'there are but few firearms among them, as they have no means with which to purchase them.'[59]

Miller has therefore assumed, particularly for the Chokwe, a strategy of concentrating on the import of guns (at the expense of other trade goods) in order to produce more ivory, as part of their specific pattern of pre-colonial accumulation.[60] Apart from some doubts as to whether the Chokwe were in fact less interested in other trade goods such as cloth than other Central African peoples, Miller's hypothesis raises first of all the question of the efficiency of imported firearms.

Late pre-colonial accounts suggest that guns in fact came into widespread use for hunting in the region and were responsible for the disappearance not only of elephants but of game in general.[61] On closer examination, however, sources appear too scanty and contradictory to uphold the absoluteness of this assumption. As late as 1878, when the more important ivory markets had long moved to the distant north and east, Capello and Ivens were reassured by the senior hunter at a camp in the heart of Central Chokwe that

'though game was becoming rare in *Quioco* [Chokwe], it still was to be found; that the buffalo, the elephant, and the *chicurro* (rhinoceros) were not yet driven out of the district...'[62]

And in 1906, south-east of Nana Kandundu and the Zambezi, a Danish elephant hunter managed to kill about 20 bulls in a few days,[63] while the Portuguese *Capitão-Mor* of Moxico showed surprise about the Luvale's preference for fishing despite an extremely rich wildlife.[64] What seems to have happened is a disappearance of game in more open landscape in general, and in areas of population concentration (see next chapter) in particular, while in others even big game continued to abound. Game, particularly the long-distance migrating elephant, disappeared probably at least as much through withdrawal into remoter, more wooded places as through extermination. For the hunter this meant that more time and energy was required to approach the prey. On the whole the sparsity of the population probably prevented complete destruction of larger fauna

---

[59] Pinto 1881: I, 230, 243
[60] Miller 1970: 176, 181
[61] Livingstone 1963: 79 [south of Lake Dilolo], 240, 249 [between the Mombo and the Chiumbe, and on the Luembe, Northern Chokwe], 270 [Kabompo-Zambezi confluence, Luvale; all 1854/5]; Lux 1880: 59/60 [general interior, 1875]; Pogge 1880: 46 [Northern Chokwe, Mona Kimbundu, 1875]; Capello and Ivens 1882: I, 214 [Central Chokwe, 1878] - see fig. 18; Schomburgk 1925: 58, 63, 187 [Southern Lunda, Kabompo, 1905/7]
[62] Capello and Ivens 1881: 218/19
[63] Schomburgk 1925: 139
[64] Relatório... , 1905, quoted in Delgado 1944: 667

at least for the pre-colonial period. With and without guns, again, labour appears as the decisive constraint of production.

Where it went on, on the other hand, large-scale killing of game was apparently possible even with traditional knowledge and devices such as the ones mentioned by Graça, and also game drives using dogs, fences, nets and grass fires.[65] Livingstone wrote of the Southern Lunda of Ishinde:

> 'All were armed with large bows and arrows headed with iron. They kill much game, and have many dogs with which to kill elephants... Their bows and arrows have been nearly as efficacious in clearing the country of game as firearms have been in the south [South Africa].'[66]

And Capello and Ivens witnessed an incident during a trip with Chokwe hunters

> 'that proved to us the agility and precision of some of the trained negroes in the management of their arms. A hare was started close to the caravan, and before we had time to unshoulder our guns, a young fellow in front had sent an arrow unerringly through the body of the animal as it was in the act of leaping into cover.'[67]

In comparison to this, the performance of imported guns was remarkably poor. The bulk of them consisted up to the colonial period of flintlock muzzle-loaders with particularly long, grooved or fluted and extremely thin-walled barrels.[68] The type of these muskets, which were currently called *lazarina*, seems to have hardly changed over the whole period of long-distance trade.[69] Ignition was unreliable, target precision may not have gone much beyond 20 metres, and bullets did not reach 150 or even 100 metres by 1906.[70]

---

[65] See section C 1.2 above; McCulloch 1951: 35; Torday 1925 and Hilton-Simpson 1895 (on elephant hunting).
[66] Livingstone: 1963: 32 and 45 [1854]
[67] Capello and Ivens 1982: I, 214 [1878]
[68] E.g. Relatório do Capitão-Mor do Moxico, 1905 [Central Chokwe]
[69] See Livingstone 1960: 42 [Bulozi, 1851]; Lux 1880: 59/60 [Northern Chokwe]; Schomburgk 1925: 119 [Southern Lunda, 1906/7]. The nickname was taken from the producer's brand name 'Lazaro Lazarino Legítimo de Braga', found on the gun even after manufacture had been transferred from Northern Portugal to Liège. After 1854, they were increasingly replaced by British and German equivalents, the former being called *reuna* and 'of indescribably vile quality' (Tylden 1953: 44; see also Madeira Santos 1986: 56, fn. 1; Silva Porto 1891: 23; Ministerio da Marinha, 1889: 20/21). Only a minority of the guns that reached the hands of hunters in the interior were 'good old tower muskets', apparently the 'male' version of the British trade-gun, 'flintlocks of a better sort'(Tylden 1953: 44f; Schomburgk *ibid*. and p. 163 [Kaonde, Mbunda; near Kabompo]).
[70] Schomburgk 1925: 120 [north of the Kabompo River]

Fig. 18: A Chokwe hunter with muzzle-loader gun (1878)
The feathers, bead in the beard, and metal rings around the ankle are symbols of prestige and modest wealth. Note the powderflask at his belt. (Engraving from Capello and Ivens 1882, vol.I: 214)

When hunters used these guns, they depended at least as much on their traditional wisdom, such as careful tracking and approaching, imitation of animal voices, use of disguise, fences and last but not least charms.[71] The use of 'gun medicine' to guide the bullets was widespread in Central Africa 'without which, it is almost universally believed, no one can shoot straight'[72]. The peoples of the Upper Zambezi were well known for particularly trusting this device.[73] Often, the belief in charms actually seems to have overridden technical considerations, when the iron sights of the guns were obstructed by tortoise shells and other medicine.[74] The attachment of magical powers to guns, however, indicates not only a low efficiency of shooting, but also a rather different meaning of this kind of weaponry (see below). The users were certainly not unaware of technological considerations. Gunmen of the region were often described as poor marksmen,[75] but sometimes also as understanding well the handling of guns.[76] They showed great practical interest in the superior breech-loading cartridge rifles Europeans carried after about 1855 and regularly used to impress their hosts:

> '...we met a small party of Lovalé people looking for ivory and beeswax. They were armed with guns, and as always was the case with those possessing them were far more curious with regard to mine than people who had never before seen any firearms. My heavy rifle was examined with much admiration, but they did not consider it sufficiently long, their own weapons being lengthy Portuguese flint locks. But when one of them consented to shoot at a tree distant about fifty yards, I followed with shell... They were then quite satisfied as to the power and accuracy of my firearms.'[77]

They very rarely seem to have been able to obtain breech-loaders or even specimens of the intermediate generation of percussion cap guns for themselves, but their interest in these expensive instruments also seems to have been limited by practical considerations. They meant more dependence on imported spare parts and ammunition,[78] while flint lock

---

[71] Lux 1880: 59/60 [Northern Chokwe 1875]; Schomburgk 1925: 127
[72] Livingstone 1857: 257, also 1960: 143 [Bulozi 1851]
[73] E.g. Wissmann 1902: 93 [on Bashilange comparing themselves with Northern Chokwe; 1880]
[74] Harding 1904: 88 [1899]; see also Papstein 1978: 172 [both on Luvale]
[75] E.g. Silva Porto 1938: 70 [Ngangela, 1852]; Relatório do Capitão-Mor do Moxico, 1905 [Chokwe]
[76] Pogge 1880: 46 [1875, Northern Chokwe]
[77] Cameron 1877: II, 161 [1875]; see also Capello and Ivens 1882: I, 218 [Central Chokwe, 1878]; Schomburgk 1925: 163 [Southern Lunda, 1906/07]
[78] Metal cartridges were very expensive and rare. Paper cartridges, once described as 'cut in the shape of an isosceles triangle, having a bullet at its lower extremity', are mentioned repeatedly in the sources as ammunition and a form of payment (e. g. Capello and Ivens 1882: I, 220 [Central Chokwe, 1878]; Livingstone 1963: 121 [Mbangala traders, 1854]; Arnot 1969: 157 [Upper Lwena, 1885]) , besides the ubiquitous gunpowder. They were obviously used in muzzle-loaders, perhaps a local invention, while

muzzle-loaders could more easily be kept going with local means, despite their deficiencies.

This has to do with the other fundamental problem of imported flintlock guns, besides their low efficiency: a very limited durability. According to sources evaluated by Miller,

> 'only a small percentage of these weapons survived the first attempts to fire them, and a good many were unusable from the start. An official check of the trade guns stocked in Luanda in 1759 revealed that 200 of the 4,000 on hand, or only 5 percent, met the government's standards of military reliability.'[79]

The quality does not seem to have improved very much afterwards, since it was recorded in 1875 that

> 'it often happens that the barrel bursts at a shoot. During the journey I saw several of such partly burst barrels, which however did not prevent at all the owner from continuing to use it. The barrel is tied up with bark strings or, if the native is perhaps in the possession of ropes, even with those, and given the normal way of the negro to use firearms, the fumes flowing out of the barrel do not damage him at all. Since when the gun is brought into the approximate position with streched-out arms, the marksman first quickly turns his face backwards and only then triggers off the weapon.[80]

The barrels, however, remained the critical point, and their weakness often accounted for the firearms' rather short life. A considerable part of new imports probably served in fact to replace broken ones. Miller has estimated the life of a musket at only one year. This may be exaggerated, at least for the remoter areas, where the users had to ensure greater durability, come what may.[81] Already by the mid-19th century, the famous Chokwe and Luchazi blacksmiths were applying their workmanship to this new tool, and were known among travellers as being able to perfectly repair or rebuild virtually every part except the barrel:[82]

> 'On one of my journeys...I handed over to a Chokwe blacksmith a damaged musket without lock for repair, and as a sample a french flintlock on whose cover the word "Laport" was engraved. After some days the blacksmith returned the musket; he had not only manufactured the lock well and neatly, but also faithfully engraved the word "Laport" onto the cover, with the letters being only somewhat less subtle.'[83]

---

metal cartridges also seem to have sometimes occurred and were cut up (Capello and Ivens, 1886: I, 444 [Mbowe, on West Lunga / Kabompo]).

[79] Miller 1988: 88

[80] Lux 1880: 60 [Northern Chokwe]; in other instances the barrel was fixed with brass wire.

[81] Miller 1986: 91

[82] Silva Porto contrasted this with the Mbwela, whom he describes as very poor blacksmiths and completely unable to repair guns (1986: 322 [1847]); also Frobenius, 1988: 131 [1905]

[83] Magyar 1860: 229 [1850s]; also Silva Porto 1986: 325 [1847]

In the end, particularly among the Chokwe, expertise in gun technology was apparently so superior that they managed to sell deficient weapons to Ovimbundu travellers.[84] A proof of the craftsmanship of village artisans is, after all, that functioning flint lock muzzle-loaders are still to be seen on the backs of hunters in Zambezi and Kabompo today.[85] Bullets were another important contribution of indigenous ironworkers towards imported weaponry.[86] Local productive capacities here alleviated the permanent dependence on imports.

Fig. 19: A Luvale hunter with muzzle-loader gun (1985),

of pre-colonial origin, still functioning after many decades and many repairs, photographed in the middle of a vast *chana* (treeless, seasonally flooded plain) west of the Zambezi river.

---

[84] Silva Porto 1885: 574
[85] In 1951, almost 1200 still functioning muzzle-loaders were recorded in the Balovale (Zambezi) district, about one for every ten male adults, which must have all stemmed from pre-colonial stocks (Annual Report on African Affairs 1951, NAZ SEC2/135). This figure may have been closer to reality than the more recent ones on gun licenses issued which appear far too low as an indicator.
[86] Schachtzabel 1923: 142 [1913/14, Southern Chokwe]

In this way, hunters and blacksmiths of the Upper Zambezi and Kasai were able to turn imported guns to some productive use for themselves despite their poor quality. Whether this technology really 'assumed a growing importance in the production of food', as Miller argues, remains doubtful for this region, if normal hunting is meant. More appropriate here seems his second assertion that 'guns surely assumed some significance' in ivory hunting for European demand; they may have made it a much safer business.[87]

C 4.4   The technology of warfare

In view of the rather limited use-value of imported firearms for hunting, the reason for the enormous demand for guns by inhabitants of the Upper Zambezi and Kasai remains obscure. It is striking that really dramatic increases in gun imports occurred in the 1880s, definitely after the end of the ivory boom.[88] Instead, the general increase of violence in the interior seems to have been the main reason for a steady growth of demand. Towards the end of the pre-colonial period, even in the remote Southern Lunda area every able-bodied man seems to have possessed at least one functioning flint lock musket - a frightening level of public armament.[89]

While the Chokwe began to raid the crumbling Nuclear Lunda empire to the North, Luvale gunmen were particularly notorious around the Upper Zambezi, even among well armed Ovimbundu slavers:

> 'The inhabitants [Luvale] carried guns, and the Bihé [Bihe] men, so brave and bold amongst the natives of Urua who had no better weapons than bows and arrows and spears, were here extremely mild and frightened to say or do anything which might offend, and submitted to the most unreasonable demands without a murmur.'[90]

They gladly left the bloody business of procuring slaves for them to buy to the Luvale themselves. The success the Luvale had in raiding mainly the Southern Lunda living to their east and south east (see chronology) has been attributed to their better access to firearms due to their more

---

[87] Miller 1986: 89
[88] Ministério da Marinha 1889: 20/21
[89] Schomburgk 1925: 119 [north of the Kabompo, 1907]; for comparison, in the United States today, notorious in this respect, only just over 20 out of 1,000 residents hold a private firearm (Miller 1988: 91, fn. 56].
[90] Cameron 1877: II, 162

westerly position.[91] In fact, all the numerous warriors of paramount chief Kakenge were reported to wear 'a kind of miniature Gladstone bag' round their loins containing 'powder, bullets and spare flints'.[92] Yet, even their main victims, the Southern Lunda across the Zambezi, had begun to acquire firearms about simultaneously, long before the end of the century, although they probably got fewer of them and were perhaps less efficient marksmen than the Luvale.[93] They seem to have been able to catch up in a kind of arms race during the rubber boom: the first British administrator of Balovale (Zambezi), in 1908, could not discern much of a difference any longer and found both the Southern Lunda and Luvale owning large numbers of guns.[94]

Despite the obvious importance guns obtained in armed conflicts, however, their technical deficiencies affecting hunting were even more important in warfare. For such extremely versatile bush fighters as the people of tis region, slow und unreliable flintlock guns were technically not much of an improvement. On the other hand, it seems that the Luvale had been able to build up a reputation as fearsome warriors without having recourse to firearms before the end of the 18th century:

'...and they are very inclined to warfare in which they perform great exploits, and are feared for that by their neighbours; they fight with bows, arrows, spears and big knives, and shields which they make of wood.'[95]

And another contemporary report describes their courageous fighting using quivers full of small lances, knives[96], bows and arrows, 'but no firearms because they don't know how to use them'.[97] This statement does not actually exclude the possibility that the Luvale did already possess some firearms by that time, it only excludes their use in fighting. Such a situation is confirmed more positively for the Luchazi and Southern Lunda some decades later:

'The majority of them possess firearms...; the weapons of their habitual use, however, are: bows and arrows, big double-edged knives (footnote: ...*macuale*...), and besides these they manufacture with perfection all manner of thrusting weapons'

---

[91] Gann 1954: 36 (quoting archival material of Gibbons, Harding and Goold-Adams); Papstein 1978: 240

[92] Harding 1904: 80 [1899]

[93] Livingstone 1963: 31, 53 and 270 [Southern Lunda of Ishinde, 1854, 1855]; against allegations of Goold-Adams, quoted in Gann 1954: 36.

[94] Venning 1953: 55

[95] Silva Teixeira 1940: 237 [1794]

[96] 'which may be two hands'breadths long of iron, and in the middle more than one hand's breadth wide...'(*ibid.*), obviously the famous broad sword (Lv. *mukwale*) widely used for warfare in the Nuclear Lunda sphere of influence throughout the pre-colonial period.

[97] *Anonymus* 1940: 25 [1803]

and

> 'they were generally armed with bows, arrows and Portuguese guns. They cannot use the latter well...'[98]

Firing abilities may have improved over time, although even the first colonial military officers experienced indigenous arrows as far more precise and dangerous weapons than imported 'trashy guns', at least from a distance.[99] (See fig. 12.)

Nevertheless, guns did play an important role in warfare, but a different one to an understanding of which, although tinged by racism, the colonial officer mentioned came perhaps closest:

> 'The warfare of the Wa'Lunda is noisy but harmless. When two chiefs decide to fight each other, a formal declaration of war is transmitted first; then the two forces turn out against each other... From a safe distance, then, all guns are fired, and the winner is the one who made the biggest hullaballoo.'[100]

His account illustrates vividly the attempts by Southern Lunda warriors to use guns and firing as symbols of power and means of intimidation rather than for actual target shooting; he was one of the few Europeans who consciously countered this type of warfare by systematically mocking the threat.[101] Allegedly, his Southern Lunda enemies at one point sent a message in which they acknowledged the superiority of his firearms and threatened instead to appropriate the magical powers they associated with them:

> '*Chindele* [European, civilized person], we have seen now that we can't kill you with our guns. We will therefore try again to slay you with bows and arrows... Should we ever succeed in catching one of you we will cut him into small pieces so that every man of our tribe may carry one as a charm.'[102]

The function of firearms as means of terror and intimidation rather than precision instruments comes up in many other pre-colonial reports on the region; for example in a sham fight involving the display of a big (empty) powder chest and an attack on a village by a force of 600 out of which

---

[98] Silva Porto 1986: 325 [1847]; Livingstone 1963: 53 [on warriors at reception by chief Ishinde, 1854]

[99] Schomburgk 1925: 57/8, 119, 138/9 [1906/07, Southern Lunda north of the Kabompo River]

[100] Schomburgk 1925: 126

[101] Schomburgk 1925: e. g. 120/1, 175, 191; he claims to have helped the Southern Lunda chief or headman Kakeki [today Zambezi district] to successfully fight off an enemy force by lending him a breech-loader (of which he had removed the lock) for display in the action (*ibid.* 162/3). Similarly also Johnston 1969: 116 [Ngangela, Upper Kwandu, 1891]

[102] Schomburgk 1925: 138

only 8 carried guns which they had to brandish into the air while all of them uttered 'the most frightful cries to intimidate their adversaries.'[103]

Often, however, forces involved in petty warfare or slave raids were much smaller. Chokwe raiding bands numbered hardly more than 10-20 warriors, and yet they were able to march off about 10 times their number in captives after an attack on a Nuclear Lunda village.[104] A fearsome reputation underlined by generous gunfiring seems to have made up for the small scale and fragmentation of political units around the Upper Zambezi and Kasai. (See next chapter and fig. 30.)

The display of potentially powerful weapons had always been an important part of warfare, with the broad *mukwale* knives traditionally being of central importance here.[105] The way in which guns were fitted into this pattern is nicely documented in a clash recorded by Livingstone in 1854:

> 'All seized their arms, and stood on the defense. The young *Bachibokwe* [Chokwe] brandished their short swords with great fury. I called on the chief and my people to sit down. Some obeyed, but the *Bachibokwe* stood flourishing their weapons & pointing their guns at us...'[106]

What made guns so attractive as means of intimidation was not only their theoretical striking capacity, but also their association with fire, and their noise. Johnston's impression of Mbwela warriors was that 'they have a wholesome dread of the guns which they say go "bam, bam, bam!"'[107] And there are revealing desires for more sophisticated European weaponry by chiefs wishing to wipe out their enemies by a kind of 'big bang'. For instance, Sekeletu, the pretender to the Lozi throne in 1853, dreamt of a 'pot (a cannon)...which would burn up any attacking party', and his rival Mpepe actually obtained 'a large blunderbuss to be mounted as a cannon' from Silva Porto.[108] Ndumba Tembo, senior chief of the Chokwe, even asked for 'balls...that were fired off without a gun, and would set fire to the *senzalas* [villages] and forests where they fell' - in other words, hand grenades.[109] For chiefs with their permanent need to underpin their fragile power position (see next chapter),

---

[103] Pinto 1881: I, 230 [Mbandi]; see also Venning 1953: 56 [Luvale of Chinyama Litapi, Zambezi West, 1908]

[104] Dias de Carvalho 1890: 472-75 [1884/5]; see also description of late pre-colonial Chokwe raids in Miller 1970: 191 (citing memories of a Belgian ex-officer).

[105] In Nuclear Lunda, in the 18th century, the first imported guns were allegedly even forged into *mukwale* swords (Hoover 1978: 342, fn. 31).

[106] Livingstone 1963: 103

[107] Johnston 1969: 1220 [1891]

[108] Livingstone 1857: 180 and 216

[109] Capello and Ivens, 1882: I, 181 [1878]

'firearms became an extension of the rulers' supernatural powers, a means of attracting forces in numbers sufficient to overpower opponents in the conventional manner and of instilling in them the morale that enabled them to cow enemies by intimidation at the outset of massed confrontations.'[110]

Consequently, local rulers relied increasingly on the symbolism contained in firearms to demonstrate their power. The incumbent of Kakenge, senior chief of the Luvale, at his court in 1894 surrounded himself by bundles of guns[111]. The Chokwe were known for having their guns richly decorated with imported metals, such as Ndumba Tembo's gun, 'a long musket, plated with tin, and the stock adorned with as many *fuma*, or brass-headed nails, as could find a place' which was shown at a reception in 1878 'by another negroe...of less consequence about the court', apparently a slave.[112]

Perhaps the oldest use of firearms in Central Africa was ceremonial noisemaking.[113] To fire volleys at receptions as a way to pay respect to the ruler was customary at the court of the Mwata Kazembe on the Luapula by the beginning of the last century.[114] The same custom was later adopted by the peoples of the Upper Zambezi and Kasai when important visitors arrived; but sources do not mention it before 1854 for the Southern Lunda, 1875 for the Central Chokwe, and 1894 for the Luvale:

'...bands of armed men kept coming up from various directions. Night fell, the drums began to beat, they fired one gunshot after another; they shouted and yelled; it was an appalling hubbub, the dances had begun...'[115]

These dates may be accidental but perhaps also reflect a more thrifty attitude in the earlier period, given the lower level of accumulation by individual chiefs. Subsequently, the firing of gun volleys became widespread practice in the area at receptions and at ceremonies such as funerals and circumcision.[116] Missionaries remember constant discharge of muskets as a welcome greeting when they opened the station in Dipalata (Zambezi) as late as 1937.[117]

---

[110] Miller 1988: 87

[111] Coillard 1897: 611; the symbolism of 'bundles of guns and buckets of gun powder' for power and wealth was still echoed in 1986 in the words of Mr. Sondoyi quoted above (B 6).

[112] Capello and Ivens 1882: I, 174; Arnot 1969: 156 [1885; Central Chokwe]

[113] See Hoover 1978: 342, for Nuclear Lunda.

[114] E.g. Baptista 1873: 219 [1808/12; Kazembe]

[115] Coillard 1897: 611 [Kakenge]; see also Livingstone 1963: 53 Ishinde, 1854]; Cameron 1877: II, 187 [Peho, 1875]

[116] Harding 1904: 55 [Luvale, 1899]; Fonseca Cardoso 1919: 26 [Ngangela, Moxico, 1903]; see Sundstrøm 1974: : 119 on the same custom for other parts of Africa.

[117] Mr. and Mrs. Finnegan, Dipalata Mission, 11th Sept. 1986

The display of lavishly decorated guns and the massive 'burning of powder'(Henning)[118] resembled a form of 'conspicuous consumption' whose social implications will be examined in the next part of this book. This use of firearms appears to have had little to do with actual warfare. But we should be careful not to overlook the symbolic or 'ritual' meanings which are inherent in the use of sophisticated weaponry (and in fact any 'advanced' technology) up to the present day.

We can conclude that export production in the region during the 19th century relied almost entirely on the use of indigenous technology, mainly gathering, hunting and ironwork, that had been developed in the preceding centuries and proved to be productive enough to enable a remarkable growth of output. Producers remained largely independent of imported wisdom or tools, except for guns which facilitated to some extent the hunting of elephants and people. It is obvious, however, that this 'increase of productivity' was destructive if seen from beyond the hunter's or raider's angle. The main importance of guns, at any rate, cannot be conceived in terms of the technical, but rather of the political economy that will be the subject of part D The negative side of the general reliance on indigenous technology was a heavy dependence by all these forms of production on labour, particularly male labour. In the following chapter, the responses to, and impact of, exports of food production are examined.

---

[118] According to Frobenius, the Northern Chokwe had an immense consumption of powder for their 'greeting and hunting bang-bang' (1988: 73 [1905]).

C 5 Adaptations in the regional food economy

Export growth in African economies, it has been argued, has often threatened the regional supply of basic reproduction goods, notably food.[1] Around the Upper Zambezi and Kasai, the absorption of a large proportion of labour and the exploitation of certain natural resources for the import/export economy during the pre-colonial period seems to have had no remarkably negative effects on regional food production. Except for the late rain season, in the case of natural disasters, and of course for the sparsely settled 'hunger countries', no shortages of food are mentioned for the Upper Zambezi and Kasai by sources on that period.[2] On the contrary, a particularly active food economy here became the perhaps decisive precondition for export-growth.

This is somewhat surprising. Most of the labour directly involved in export production and import trade, was supplied by male inhabitants. Even if men had always been less involved in agriculture (see above), men's efforts had been crucial for the supply of animal protein and other non-vegetable matter. Probably the main factor that cushioned the impact of the world market in this respect was the closeness of male activities for export to those for regional food supply.

C 5.1 'By-products' of the export sector

Intensified hunting of elephants, to start with, undoubtedly resulted in increasing supplies of meat and other raw materials as 'by-products'. Hunters in general were and still are accustomed to cut up and dry by sun and smoke the meat of their prey on the spot in their bush camps, as well as processing intestines, skins, horns, and blood.[3] Elephants' meat was apparently abundant by the middle of last century so that hunters offered

---

[1] For a review of relevant literature see Tosh 1980, Berry 1984: 67ff, and Watts 1989.
[2] Livingstone 1963: 66 [Southern Lunda speaking on Luvale north-west of Zambezi River, January 1854]; Coillard 1897: 605 609 [Locust invasion north of Ishinde, June 1895]; Singleton-Fisher 1948: 80 [Kavungu, January to March 1894]; Harding 1904: 117 [February 1899, near Zambezi source]; Schomburgk, 1925: 67/8 [mid-June 1905; Southern Lunda, near Kabompo River]; on the 'hunger countries' see B 7
[3] See Capello and Ivens 1882: I, 217-19 [Central Chokwe, 1878]; Pogge, 1880: 10 [general interior, 1875]

it to travellers whom they happened to meet on their way.[4] During these hunting trips as well during honey and rubber collection tours and caravan journeys, other game was regularly hunted,too, and sometimes also bartered away to hungry travellers, although this was the only food foreigners could often supply themselves with.[5] In the long run, however, the continuous search for exportable produce in the bush probably contributed significantly to the reduction of game in inhabited areas, perhaps more than gun imports. This reduction may have caused some strain on protein supplies in the most densely populated areas. Already in January 1854, for example, Livingstone noted near Ishinde's 'town' that buffaloes were 'nearly if not quite cleared out of this district. The people eat mice or moles with avidity, and very few small animals are permitted to live.'[6]

But he did not realize yet that such small animals are not an emergency food but a traditional and very popular part of the diet, a dish even for distinguished guests as I experienced personally. Later, in 1907, dried meat was highly appreciated, also at local prices, at Nyakatolo's 'where today no game at all appears anymore'.[7] This may have been the consequence of the probably considerable concentration of population around this important centre, but a craving for meat may have also been motivated by the unilateral concentration on dried fish in the area (see below). None of the later pre-colonial sources on the Upper Zambezi and Kasai suggests a 'chronic food problem' like that in western Bihe, where by 1892 'protein in the form of fresh meat or fish was rarely to be had' resulting in general ill-health.[8]

To the contrary, bushtrips in general, and the search for exportable beeswax in particular, on the other hand, yielded ever greater quantities of another popular and nutritious 'by-product': honey.[9] Some of it was consumed by the hunters, beekeepers and rubber collectors themselves or sold to travellers they met[10], but most was brewed by them into the

---

[4] Silva Porto, 1986: 335 [Sekele, on Luanginga river, 1848]; Magyar 1860: 228, fn. 1 [Sekele, 1850s]; Livingstone 1963: 30 [Mbunda returning from Zambezi West bank, 1854]

[5] E.g. Cameron 1877: II, 144 [Samba, 1875]; Silva Porto 1938: 79 [1852/3, Ngangela]

[6] Livingstone 1963: 50; also 66 [Southern Lunda]; the same misunderstanding occurred to Schomburgk 1925: 187 [Luvale, 1907]

[7] Schomburgk 1925: 186

[8] Singleton-Fisher 1948: 76

[9] E.g. Vieira de Andrade 1940: 252 [1799; Mbunda]; Graça 1890: 414 [1846, Central Chokwe]; Arnot 1969: 146 [1885, Central Chokwe]; honey is a concentrated form of carbohydrates (sugar) and rich in vitamins and other nutrients.

[10] E.g. Harding 1904: 215/6 [1900, Luchazi / Mbunda]; Silva Porto, 1986: 335 [Sekele, on Luanginga river, 1848]; Magyar 1860: 228, fn. 1 [Sekele, 1850s]

honey-beer or mead I have mentioned before (called *wala wa ndoka* in Lv., *kasolu* in SL.).[11]

Alcoholic beverages have always played a considerable role in nutrition in Africa. Most important were the relatively light millet beers which in the past were brewed everywhere by women, particularly after harvest. Around the Upper Zambezi and Kasai, the traditional grain beer is mainly the so-called *wal(w)a wa masangu*, made from bulrush millet. Given the abundance of honey in the *musenge* woodlands of the region, mead always played an important role as a second type of beer, which was prepared mostly by men. With the growth of wax exports, the relative and absolute importance of this 'male' beer must have increased considerably.[12] This type of alcohol was also seen as more valuable, perhaps as a reflection of the greater labour involved, and also because of its sweetness and greater strength compared to the relatively light grain beers.[13] Around 1850, at the time of the ivory and beeswax boom, excessive use of honey-beer was observed: 'The inhabitants of the country are of a turbulent mood, and given to the vice of drunkenness.'[14]

Chiefs particularly appreciated this intoxicant because of its importance for the 'spiritual component of power' (Miller - see below), and regularly presented important guests with calabashes of mead. On one such occasion, according to Livingstone, he was recommended by the Southern Lunda chief Ishinde 'to drink plenty of mead, for it would spread in my system and do me well. I suspect he uses the remedy pretty frequently himself.'[15]

Forty years later, a disgusted protestant missionary rejected an 'immense calabash of *mpote*' ['a very intoxicating beer; Lo.], offered by another holder of the Ishinde title, of which he found him 'inordinately fond'.[14] In the Central Chokwe area, the heartland of wax production, senior chief Ndumba Tembo offered his European guests some special mead for communal 'morning libations' during his audience.[16] But even ordinary beeswax collectors in the bush would brew mead, and 'as they drink this warm in the morning it keeps them in a half-dazed condition all day'.[17]

---

[11] Gibbons 1904: II, 45 [1899, Southern Lunda]; recipe in Schomburgk, 1925: 112 [Southern Lunda, 1906/07]
[12] Cf. White 1959: 29
[13] Personal observations; confirmed also by 19th century travellers: Pinto 1881: I, 282: '... I thought it the most alcoholic stuff I ever tasted'; see also below, section C 6 1)
[14] E.g. Silva Porto 1986: 324/5 [1847; Luchazi-Mbunda]
[15] Livingstone 1963: 55 [1854]
[16] Capello and Ivens 1882: I, 205/6 [1878]
[17] Arnot 1969: 146 [1885, Central Chokwe]

The variety of non-commercial relations through which beers were redistributed among villagers and guests are analysed in the following parts.[18] The new abundance of honey apparently also led to a beer production for sale to strangers and even to local residents. July and August, when wax was melted and cast into moulds, in Central Chokwe was

Fig. 20: A mead or honeybeer brewer, with gathering of drinkers
(Chokwe, 1878)

The original comment suggests that this mead was actually sold, probably upon arrival of the caravan. Note the high stands of sorghum, the main ingredient for beer brewed by **women**, contrasting the scene. (Engraving from Capello and Ivens 1882, vol.I: 185)

---

[18] See Dorlöchter and von Oppen 1989

'the time for the land to flow with mead, and the markets are filled with natives, rolling about under its influence during their intervals of chaffering with the dealers.'[19]

This selling of beer, however, seems to have developed out of the older form of communal drinking (*lizaji* in Lv.), as indicated by a description of one of these 'markets', where the mead 'was "drunk upon the premises", out of basins containing some three or four pints, the customers sitting round the coveted store'.[20] In Upper Zambezi villages, alcohol is still retailed in this way, not at a permanent shebeen but at the *nzango* (central meeting shelter) of the respective hamlet where beer has been brewed.

The descriptions suggest that local customers at these 'mobile shebeens', in contrast to the consumption of free alcohol, seem to have been exclusively men, probably rather those who were engaged in other activities not related to the forests (although non-economic reasons may play a role even when the beer is being paid for). Besides those who obtained money-like goods as warriors, carriers and guides for caravans, fishermen were the most important group which was generally unable to participate in the set of interrelated forest activities mentioned so far. Harvesting beehives and hunting usually have their peaks between May and November, the seasons of late dam fishing and building new dams (see table 5). Above all, fishing takes place in 'downstream' ecosystems which are normally unsuited for bees and deserted by larger game.[21] Root rubber is partly found in plains with stunted vegetation (in Eastern Angolan Afro-Portuguese called *chanas de borracha*), but not in those liable to flooding and hence weir-fishing.[22]

With the reduction of game in inhabited areas, on the other hand, fishing gradually became even more important for the protein supply of the region. What prevented the male-dominated fishing economy from collapsing during the era of pre-colonial world-market production was probably the fact that not only the regional population, but also the foreign travellers who flocked to the country had a strong demand for dried fish (see B 7). In a report of 1905, one of the first Portuguese administrators remarked, after dealing at length with rubber production:

'Another industry exists among the people of a part of this region, especially around Dilolo and Kakenge; it is the fishing industry, however with very limited development prospects. The people of the areas mentioned devote themselves to fishing in order to then dry the fish and go to sell it at more or less distant points in exchange for cloth...; the dried fish constitutes for the people a very

---

[19] Capello and Ivens 1882: I, 197 [1878]
[20] Capello and Ivens 1882: I, 186
[21] These incompatibilities may explain why the Luvale were reported in 1905 not to hunt very much although game allegedly remained abundant in some parts of their country (Relatório do Capitão-Mor do Moxico, quoted in: Delgado 1944: 667).

appreciable food, and a very popular one, which may in situations of scarcity, such as for example the time of the most persistent rains, reach a very high price. I do not know of any other industry in this region.'[23]

This suggests that specialization in fishing had further increased during the 19th century in suitable parts of the region, particularly among the Luvale.[24] Again, the methods developed in the course of preceding centuries proved capable of producing substantial amounts for exchange. All elements of the year-round fishing cycle described by C.M.N. White in 1956 (and witnessed by myself in the 1980s)[25] already appear in pre-colonial sources: the catching of the mud barbel during its spawning run (*musuza*)[26]; the fishing of *tukeya* along fences and enormous dams (*wálilo*) across the flood plains[27]; the bailing of small pools and ponds while they dry up, in which particularly women participate (*kusuhwa*)[28]; the construction of fresh dams and weirs for the next season[29]; the intermediate fishing by traps, nets, and lines using dug-out canoes in permanent waters, rivers, oxbows, and lakes[30]; the drying by smoke and sun, and the packing into oblong bundles fastened by barkropes.[31]

No signs of change in production technology during the late pre-colonial period are found, except perhaps the spinning of fishing lines out of cotton instead of indigenous bast fibres, and the use of imported wire for simple, unbarbed hooks.[32] But it is improbable that such minor innovations meant any significant increase in productivity. The question of the ecological impact of these technologies, in other words whether they potentially meant overfishing, has been answered in the negative even under today's conditions. Only certain techniques, such as *musuza* killing of spawning barbel, and the blockade of rivers by artificial weirs preventing fish migration, have been regarded as detrimental for the reproduction of the stock, but even today, with fish being an important

---

[22] Gossweiler 1939: 130ff
[23] Relatório do Capitão-Mor do Moxico, quoted in: Delgado 1944: 666
[24] Livingstone (1963: 66) was informed by his hosts on the South-East bank of the Zambezi river that he was about to 'enter a country the inhabitants of which did not sow' - i. e. the area of Luvale fishermen near the main 'watershed' route.
[25] White 1956: p. 77ff; White 1959: 8f; see also Maclaren 1958
[26] Livingstone 1963: 22 [Dec. 1853; Banyeti, near Lungwevungu mouth]
[27] Livingstone 1963: 74 [Feb. 1854; Luvale on Lukalwiji]; Cameron 1877: II, 169 [1875; north of Zambezi source];
[28] Livingstone 1963: 261 [June 1855, Luvale, Luvua-Chiambo]; Pogge 1880: 218 [August 1875, Northern Chokwe women]
[29] Arnot 1969: 155 [1885, Upper Luena]
[30] Livingstone 1963: 258 [August 1855; Luvale, Lake Dilolo]
[31] Livingstone 1963: 22 and 74 [1854]; Cameron 1877: II, 175 [Luvale 1875]
[32] E.g. Johnston 1969: 102 [1891, fishermen on the Kwanza]

export commodity from the region, the potential is by no means exhausted yet.[33]

To sum up, the diversion of male labour to export production does not seem to have seriously affected the regional supply in 'male' foodstuffs; on the whole, it may have even slightly increased it. There are two main reasons: for forest dwellers the fact that men's export production by men focused on the same environment in which they were used to producing foodstuffs, and for inhabitants of the lowlands the fact that access to the desired import products could also be obtained through fish production. One could see this as mere coincidence, but might suspect that this compatibility of export and food production was in fact one important precondition for male producers to enter the world market. But what about the compatibility of pre-colonial export orientation and agriculture, the domain of women ?

C 5.2 The changing economy of staple food

When long-distance trade reached its peak, as we have seen in the chronology, cultivators of the Upper Zambezi and Kasai managed to satisfy the food needs of substantial numbers of foreign travellers, in addition to domestic needs. At the same time, raiding, hunting, gathering or carrying for export meant that at any given time, including seasons of food production, considerable numbers of male producers were temporarily on the move. Increased migration (see chronology) meant that entire populations were on their way to new homes where it would take some time for them to reap their own food from newly established fields. The ways in which food circulated between resident cultivators, notably women, and these non-selfsufficient groups will be analysed in the next part. Here it should be emphasized only that there was a need to increase the productivity by those who continued to concentrate on food cultivation during this period.

Growing demand for food during the 19th century probably contributed to an expansion of crop cultivation in general, at least among specialists and near the main caravan routes. According to Silva Porto, the Mbwela in remote areas between the Kwando and Kubango had

---

[33] White 1956: 84; Alff, von Oppen and Beck 1986: II

'limited themselves to the tilling of insignificant patches of land which did not cover their subsistence since they sustained themselves through a major part of the year by hunting, honey fruits and wild tubers'

until they began to trade ivory and beeswax with the Ovimbundu. This allegedly happened only by the mid-19th century, and 'from this same period dates the cultivation of land on a large scale.'[34] Serpa Pinto, in 1878, praised the same group of people as 'the greatest and most successful cultivators of the soil which repays with wonderful prodigality the care and labour bestowed upon it'.[35]

Less remote areas had already been described as relatively rich in staple food by the end of the 18th century, and this favourable situation seems to have endured all through the 19th century. Travellers continually used terms such as 'abundance', 'plenty', 'richness' etc. to describe the food situation in the area; they invariably designated the inhabitants of the Upper Zambezi and Kasai[36] as 'hard-working agriculturalists'[37]; they mentioned 'big gardens' which were 'very carefully grown' and 'beautifully kept free from weeds'.[38] Standards for comparison were apparently the Ovimbundu, Mbangala, and Nuclear Lunda (except near the capital)[39].

Most Upper Zambezi cultivators apparently found it much easier to serve these new demands for food with cassava rather than with grain crops because of its higher surplus potential (see above, B 7). By the mid-19th century, traders on the Ovimbundu Plateau were aware that

'the peoples living further east in the interior produce very little maize and extraordinarily much cassava. Beyond the Kwanza, in general the sandy countries prevail...'.[40]

From an elevated viewpoint, Capello and Ivens, in 1878, found the valley of the Upper Kasai

'clothed with numerous *senzalas* [villages] of *ma-quioco* [Chokwe] and *macosa*, indicated by the white patches of manioc-flour spread to dry upon the *luandos* or mats...[41]

---

[34] Silva Porto 1986: 322
[35] Pinto 1881: I, 339
[36] Such statements include certain neighbouring peoples such as the Western Ngangela or the so called *Balúa* on the Kafue (Silva Porto 1938: 70, 108 [1853]).
[37] Magyar 1860: 229 [1850s, on Chokwe], cf. Capello and Ivens, 1882: 225 [1878, Chokwe].
[38] Silva Porto 1986: 325 [Luchazi, 1847]; Schomburgk 1925: 187 [1907]; Harding 1904: 178 [1900; both at Kavungu, Luvale].
[39] Cf. Pogge 1880: 79 [1875]; Livingstone 1963: 245 [1855]; and above, chapter B 5
[40] Magyar 1857: 300/01
[41] Capello and Ivens 1882: I, 197

In consequence, travellers who were more used to the maize-based diet of the Ovimbundu, Mbangala or Lozi-Kololo,[42] had to suffer from 'long fasting on light disagreeable porridge because in many parts manioc is the chief article of cultivation ...', when they came to the Upper Zambezi and Kasai.[43]

It must be assumed that the increasing absorption of male labour by export production and concentration on fishing for the long-distance trade meant, on the whole, that men had less time for and interest in their tasks in crop cultivation, notably bush clearing and perhaps the construction of storage for grain crops (see table 5). The fact that cassava cultivation requires considerably less effort for men, and can be largely managed by women on their own, was now probably in the foreground and made it particularly attractive during this period.

Unfortunately, observations on the division of labour by gender are extremely rare in written sources on the pre-colonial period. Harding's statement in 1899 may be rather biased:

'here as elsewhere in South (read: Southern, A.v.O.] Africa the women do all the work in agriculture: hoeing, planting, harvesting and 'stamping', while men spend their time 'hunting and paying visits to different *kraals*' [read: villages, A.v.O.],[44]

since he was an agent of South African capital eager to find surplus male labour for migration to the mines. Perhaps more reliable were Capello and Ivens, who during their visit of Central Chokwe in July 1878 saw

'plantations of manioc and *massambala* [sorghum], growing abundantly upon the slopes, and at that time filled with girls and women engaged in hoeing and other field labours.'[45]

This observation is significant because July is normally the time of bush clearing done by men, while hoeing, at least for grain crops, normally takes place later and should involve both men and women. Only women and girls were seen in December of the same year on cassava and millet fields among the Northern Chokwe.[46] The expansion of cassava cultivation and processing undoubtedly meant additional strain on women's labour, alleviated only by the much greater flexibility of this crop with regard to the timing of its many chores, and by the redundance

---

[42] Magyar 1857: 300f [1850s]; Livingstone 1963: 120 [1854]; Livingstone 1960: 40, 45, 130, 144, 145, 147 etc. [1853]. The Lozi King Santuru allegedly even forbade his nobles to eat cassava on the grounds that it 'caused coughing' (Livingstone, 1963: 166).
[43] Livingstone 1963: 85, 46, [1854]
[44] Harding 1904: 56 [Southern Lunda]
[45] Capello and Ivens 1882: I, 196
[46] Schütt 1879: 181

of the very time-consuming task of scaring of birds before harvest on millet fields.

But, as it has been suggested earlier (see C 3.1), women themselves may have had a strong interest in this crop since it gave them greater independence from unreliable male assistance and enabled them to produce larger surpluses of food. Because of the well-established rights of women over their products which will be explained further below (chapter D 2), cassava cultivation became the most important means for women of finding their own access to the market. In 1854, Southern Lunda women near the Zambezi were already 'continually heard carrying on a brisk trade with the Portuguese in manioc meal for little bits of *calico* 4 inches wide by 8 long.'[47] In Capello and Ivens' report of 1878, girls and women appear not only as tillers of the land, but also as vendors of various foodstuffs on the 'market' at Ndumba Tembo's capital.[48] And Harding remarked in 1899 that, when visitors bring grain to camp, 'meal and other commodities of marketable produce is borne, and borne alone, by the "gentler sex".'[49] Senior advisers to the Southern Lunda chief Ishinde put it more bluntly: 'Cassava business is the business of women.'[50]

Despite the clear dominance of women in this field, however, according to several sources men were not completely absent in the cultivation and marketing of cassava among some of the peoples of the region. Near the Kasai, in 1854, for example

'men and women come running after us with fowls, [cassava] meal, &c, which we would gladly purchase had we the means, and when they find we have no cloth they turn back disappointed.'[51]

It must be taken into account that women in remoter areas sometimes had to rely on men for marketing their products, for reasons of distance and safety.[52] But F.S. Arnot, writing in 1885, showed himself pleased with the fact that 'men work in the fields as well as the women' among both the Southern Lunda and Luvale.[53] And another missionary, in November 1891, was

'surprised to see a number of men come round the camp with hoes on their shoulders, and was told that all through the eastern part of *Ganguella* [Luchazi,

---

[47] Livingstone 1963: 64; see also *ibid*. : 256
[48] Capello and Ivens 1982: I, 185/6 [1878, Central Chokwe]
[49] Harding 1904: 56 [Southern Lunda]
[50] Interview 25. 10. 1986
[51] Livingstone 1963: 102 [1854, Chokwe north of Kasai River]
[52] Y. Samakayi, 21. 10. 1986
[53] Arnot 1969: 159 [December; weeding time]

Mbunda, Mbwela - A.v.O.] the men work in the fields along with the women, during the planting season.'[54]

These observations suggest that either women in these parts were particularly successful in soliciting male assistance in one way or another (see below), or that certain men had an active interest in cultivation themselves. It is possible that besides women also some men began to specialize in crop cultivation, in view of growing food markets - a tendency increasingly observed during the colonial and post-colonial period.

Long-distance trade, however, brought not only new opportunities but also new risks for Upper Zambezi cultivators. When violence between and even within ethno-political groups spread as a result of the slave trade, grain stores and even the standing crop in the fields were among the prominent targets. During raids, fields and stores were systematically plundered or destroyed by the attackers in order to starve the owners into slavery.[55] Everywhere in central Africa, food stealing became another threat to independence, particularly in areas where many travellers passed by, that is near the main routes of pre-colonial long-distance trade.[56] One strategy of cultivators to protect their fields against such destruction was to hide them even deeper in the bush (where millet or sorghum fields had to be located anyway because of their greater demand for virgin soils and to avoid bird damage).[57] Removing the fields from the village, however, meant increasing walking distance, risk of animal damage and perhaps even kidnapping, in the case of women. Again, cassava appears to have provided a better solution to these problems. The crop remains unharvested in the ground until it is actually needed, and consequently destruction or theft is much more difficult than with grains. Its reduced demand on soil nutrients means that it can be grown in a semi-permanent way near the village; pre-colonial visitors already found that villages were 'surrounded by gardens of manioc', and sometimes they marched 'half an

---

[54] Johnston 1969: 125. These authors probably used the Western Ngangela and Ovimbundu as a comparison, where 'the men regard fieldwork as humiliating and leave it entirely to the women' (Magyar 1859: 299; Pinto 1881: I, 244).

[55] Papstein 1978: 171

[56] Southern Lunda women, for example, complained about thefts from their fields in 1899 (Harding 1904: 91). But the peoples of the Upper Zambezi and Kasai seem to have been rather successful in protecting their fields by means of charms etc., since examples of actual food thefts come mostly from other areas, e. g. : Cameron 1877: II, 143/4 [Samba = Southern Luba, 1875]); Wissmann 1902: 76 [Bashilanje carriers used to steal sweet manioc *en route* - 1880].

[57] Schomburgk 1925: 105 [1806/07, Southern Lunda]

hour incessantly through manioc fields' before they reached a village;[58] much the picture of today. (See fig. 24.)

One thing that particularly annoyed Angolan visitors to the Upper Zambezi and Kasai from the 1840s on was the predominance of bitter cassava varieties[59], while further down near the coast sweet varieties prevailed.[60] Bitter varieties, as has been mentioned before, require a laborious process of soaking, fermentation and drying before they can actually be consumed, and their flavour of their fermentation is considered as unpleasant even by the inhabitants of the region themselves.In 1800, the *Ganguela* peoples are still reported to have an abundance of cassava producing giant sweet roots which could be eaten raw.[61] One plausible explanation of why Upper Zambezi cultivators nevertheless came to prefer bitter varieties in the course of the 19th century, is precisely the fact that when eaten raw they can produce seriously poisoning of the thief: a protection against both human and animal predators.[62] Even today cultivators usually mix bitter and sweet varieties at random on the same field, partly as a deterrent for thieves and elephants.[63]

Because of these new stimuli following world-market integration, it has even been argued that the very introduction of cassava, along with other crops of American origin, was only 'a by-product of the earliest phases of long-distance exchanges' between coastal traders and inhabitants of the Central African interior.[64] The chronological evidence presented above (chapter C 1) shows that some sort of early exchanges must in fact have been the transmission belt for these innovations; but it also suggests that these crops were introduced in the region at a time when contacts with the 'Atlantic Zone' were still very tenuous and happened through a long series of intermediaries. Even Reports from around 1800, by the first Portuguese-speaking traders who ever reached the Upper Zambezi, emphasize the abundance of cassava and other American crops.[65] It seems therefore seems unlikely that direct or indirect pressures from outside were behind the innovations. The first introduction of cassava in

---

[58] Livingstone 1963: 65 [1854; Southern Lunda near Zambezi]; Schomburgk 1925: 58 [1904, Southern Lunda / Kaonde on Upper Kabompo]
[59] E.g. Graça 1890: 414 [1846]; Magyar 1859: 300/01 [1850s]
[60] E.g. Magyar 1857: 17f
[61] *Anonymus* 1940: 22 [1803]
[62] Bitter varieties also seem to have a higher starch content, and its meal keeps longer than the one from sweet cassava (Mowat 1989: 7).
[63] See Ficalho, 1947: 250; Redinha 1968: 101, 102; von Oppen, Shula and Alff 1983: 108
[64] Reefe 1983: 190
[65] Silva Teixeira 1940: I, 237 [1794] - see quotation at the beginning of part B ; Vieira de Andrade 1940: 253 [1799]; and *Anonymus* 1940: 24-5 [1803]

the remote interior appears to have been quite clearly a response to 'normal' food deficits **within** these societies.

But emerging 'market' demand for food surpluses undoubtedly played a significant role in accelerating the expansion of cassava growing during the 19th century. Cassava, both roots and meal (*fuba* in the Angolan sphere), was the single most important foodstuff that appeared during transactions between residents of the region and their foreign visitors. In addition, as we have seen, the aspect of food security for the population itself also gained additional momentum during this period. Cassava undoubtedly developed into the most important staple crop of the region as a whole during the 19th century.

But within the region there were slightly different responses in different ecological situations. The Southern Lunda east of the Zambezi probably came to rely more exclusively on cassava than any other group in the region. Elder advisers at the court of the Southern Lunda chief Ishinde claim that bulrush millet, some maize, beans and bambarra nuts (ground beans) were grown by their ancestors alongside cassava.[66] In the mid-19th century, when he first visited the area, Livingstone noted in his diary: 'all the Balonda cultivate the manioc or cassava excessively ... manioc is the chief article of cultivation ... which they seem to regard as their staff of life'.[67]

He did also notice considerable quantities of maize (as well as some sorghum and other crops) apparently grown in between young cassava plants.[68] But this seems to be explained by the fact that Livingstone arrived just at the end of January, the season when green maize is eaten in limited quantities as a vegetable to bridge the period of scarcity.[69] Half a century on, the first colonial officers observed that 'native food ... comprises manioc,...and that alone.' Even in remote parts near the Kabompo they found that 'grain is not grown by the Walunda, but only manioc in large, extensive gardens. The manioc thrives excellently in the sandy soil.'[70]

Among the Luvale, cassava is mentioned consistently, also as a major staple, from the late 18th century on, but on about on equal level with bulrush millet (*masangu*),[71] apparently because of the ecological constraints on cassava in the plains which were mentioned in chapter C 2.

---

[66] Interview 25. 10. 1986
[67] Livingstone 1963: 36, 46, 65
[68] Livingstone 1963: 36, 39, 44, 55, 66
[69] See Livingstone 1963: 46, 70
[70] Harding 1904: 163 [1899]; Schomburgk 1925: 128 [1906]
[71] beginning with Silva Teixeira 1940: 237 [1794]; Vieira de Andrade 1940: 253 [1799]; and Graça 1890: 417 [1846]

Change here seems to have occurred with regard to the **intensity** of grain cultivation. On the Chikalueje, an 'extremely fine and fertile country', Livingstone found in February 1854 various grains, including bulrush millet and maize, 'at all stages of growth... the people seem to have no winter and to continue sowing and reaping at all times...'[72] This remark suggests that Luvale cultivators already practised double-cropping techniques here (two harvests per year), which are technically possible in the lower parts of the *chinema* ecosystem.

Another development in Luvale agriculture during the 19th century concerned the **use** of grain crops. While one of the earliest reports calls *masangu* 'the major livelihood of these peoples'[73], millets (bulrush millet as well as sorghum) were reduced mainly or even entirely to a raw material for grain beer.[74] The *nshima* or staple dish gradually ceased to contain anything but cassava.

Similar changes in the use of staple crops may have occurred among the Luchazi and Mbunda to the west. For Luchazi groups on southern tributaries of the Lungwevungu, cassava was mentioned among 'their favourite foods' in 1847, but together with *masangu* (and ground beans).[75] In 1878, in the same area, the importance of *masangu* (bulrush millet) seems by no means to have diminished, perhaps even increased. Every time he asked for food, Serpa Pinto was delivered substantial amounts of bulrush millet by Luchazi and Southern Chokwe women, and lamented:

'the sole article of food they cultivate in any quantity, besides a little manioc, still fewer beans...They do not grow maize, and feed almost entirely on *massango*...that terrible *massango* that literally haunted me...'[76]

His observation may have been biased because he happened to arrive during the grain harvest (June-July); but Luchazi are seen up to today as being particularly 'conservative' because they have maintained a high percentage of bulrush millet.[77] In more recent times, the reason was clearly that *masangu* particularly appealed to Luchazi women as a surplus crop because they could make it into beer which is useful both for sale

---

[72] Livingstone 1963: 74

[73] *Anonymus* 1940: 24 [1803]

[74] Y. Samakayi, 21. 10. 1986; confirmed by the memories of an early colonial administrator in the Angolan section of Luvale country (Antunes Cabrita 1954: 52 [on 1920s]); see also White, 1959: 17. According to him 'the former position of bulrush millet is preserved in the ritual **eating** of the first fruits (*kutoma masangu*), there being no such ritual for cassava' [emphasis added].

[75] Silva Porto 1986: 325

[76] Pinto 1881: I, 270, 274; see also pp. 256, 269, 278

[77] Johnston (1969: 11) confirms for 1891 that the Luchazi had bulrush millet as their major crop.

and for distribution within the village (see next part).[78] This motive was probably already strong in the last century, against the advance of men's honey-beer and as an additional way for women to market crops. Ovimbundu travellers' memories confirm that *Ganguela* women used to sell fermented and unfermented grain drinks, besides the obligatory cassava, along the main caravan routes.[79]

Only some Mbwela groups seem to have followed the example of the Western Ngangela near the Kwanza[80] and increased their cultivation of maize for staple food.[81] The demand along important Ovimbundu routes may have played a major role here; other Mbwela groups came to rely increasingly on cassava only.[82] The first colonial agricultural report came to the correct conclusion that maize was doing fine on the clayey soils near the Kwanza, but was far less suitable than *masangu* for the sandy uplands further east.[83]

In the densely populated highlands where the Chokwe originated, traditional grain crops (sorghum and some millet, both bulrush and finger) also seem to have retained their importance throughout the 19th up to the 20th century.[84] Those who migrated into the flats to the north of the Kasai that were crossed by important trade routes, however, seem to have reduced sorghum cultivation; some of them concentrated on bulrush millet, apparently for beer that was available for sale 'in abundance in big Chokwe villages' by 1880, and on maize.[85]

These changes with regard to grains did not prevent cassava from becoming very clearly the dominant or even sole staple food crop among many northern Chokwe; and also among those who settled rather sparsely in the future *Moxico* (Mushiku) area, along the great watershed route, only *fuba* (white cassava meal) was available for visitors towards the end of the last century.[86] Only later, at the beginning of this century, and then

---

[78] Annual Report Balovale 1932, p. 3 (NAZ ZA 7/1/15/2); LIMA Survey 1983, Chinzombo-Samalesu village (Kabompo)
[79] Schönberg-Lotholz 1960: 113
[80] Silva Porto 1886: 317/18 [1847]; Johnston 1969: 99 [1891]
[81] Silva Porto 1938: 70, 75 [1853]; Pinto 1878: 339 [1875]; Capello and Ivens, 1886: 1, 267 [on Kubango, 1884]; Harding (1904: 237, 240 [1900]), who found no maize any more among the Luchazi further east.
[82] Johnston 1969: 105 [1891]; Silva Porto, in 1847 [?] had mentioned maize meal, millet and cassava as the staple foods in the same area (1986: 339).
[83] Gossweiler 1907: 60
[84] *Anonymus* 1940: II, 25 [1803]; Graça 1890: 414 [1846]; Magyar 1860: 229; Capello and Ivens, 1882: I, 185; see also Baumann 1935: 50
[85] Livingstone 1963: 235 [1854]; Pogge 1880: 46-7 [1875]; Wissmann 1888: 48 [1880]; but Frobenius observed a staple dish (*chintu*) from cassava **and** millet in 1905 (1988: 151).
[86] Arnot 1889: 151-2 [Nov. 1885]; Trigo Teixeira 1936: 22 [March 1895]; Graça (1890: 417 [June 1846]) already spoke of an 'abundance' of maize, besides cassava, sorghum,

only in 'the old caravanseray district of Moxico', does maize seem to have become a major food and cash crop besides cassava,[87] probably in connection with the opening of the main road and future Benguela railway through eastern Angola.

It can be concluded that producers of the region were able to satisfy the additional 'market' demand for staple food during the 19th century through those crops and techniques that they had already introduced at an earlier date with a logic of securing regional food supply. Up to today, a tendency to combine food and market interests in the same crops can be observed in the area. This tendency, however, does not mean that sales were only accidental, a kind of 'normal surplus of subsistence agriculture'.[88] There are signs that already in the pre-colonial period, cultivators on the Upper Zambezi and Kasai deliberately produced surpluses for exchange, and were even prepared to subordinate their preferences as consumers - besides other considerations - to market opportunities. This is reflected in changes such as a greater concentration than before, both in cultivation and consumption, on the more recently introduced crops, notably cassava and maize, and in increased efforts to overcome the seasonal limitations of a grain-based agriculture.

C 5.3 'Relish' and 'cash crops'

Another story of agricultural change in the cultivation systems of the Upper Zambezi and Kasai during the 19th century was the appearance of new pulses, notably beans and groundnuts. At first sight these innovations appear to be perfectly in line with ecological and dietary considerations following the spread of cassava. In grain-growing economies of Central Africa, pulses were already interplanted with maize or millets, but they complement even better with cassava: as intercrops they enrich the poor soils of cassava fields with nitrogen, and as food they enrich the sauce or relish (*ifwo*) that accompanies any dish of staple with the vegetable proteins and fat that cassava is particularly deficient in (see C 2). Because

---

millet and beans, being grown at Katende's, an ethnically mixed area near the Kasai, further east along the southern route to Nuclear Lunda. This is, however, an isolated statement which is not confirmed by Livingstone (1963: 257 etc. [June 1855]) who found hardly anything but cassava and groundnuts in the area.

[87] Relatório do Capitão Mor do Moxico, 1905, in: Delgado 1944: 666; Baumann 1935: 50

[88] Cf. Allan 1965

of the quick spread of the foliage, they tend to protect the soil against leaching and save (female) labour during the second weeding. The cultivation of beans and groundnuts is again mainly done by women.

Cowpeas (*vigna unguiculata*) and groundbeans (bambarra nuts, *voandzeia subterranea*) are the two indigenous pulses of the region (see C 1.1 and C 2.2); originally, they were probably mainly intercropped with millets. By the beginning of the last century, 'not many beans' were mentioned by a Portuguese visitor of the Luvale[89], probably somewhat disappointed because of the importance beans then already had for the Portuguese and the African peoples further west.

In some areas with the subsequent spread of cassava cultivation and perhaps diminution of animal protein (game), there seems to have been an increase of intercropping these 'traditional' pulses on both millet and cassava fields. 'The grain called *bihello*' [*vyelu* (Lv., pl.), ground beans] was mentioned by Silva Porto in 1847 as one of the staple foods of the Luchazi. But he also observed that 'the maize, coarse and small beans are cultivated on a small scale among them'.[90] This distinction makes it possible to identify 'small beans' as the new, American-imported *phaseolus* type.

The Chokwe, who had early been in touch with the Ovimbundu due to their position along major routes to Nuclear Lunda, were apparently quicker to adopt these new American pulse crops. An 'abundance of cassava and sorghum, but little maize' already appear together with 'sufficient beans' and *mondobi* (groundnuts) in 1803, and the latter two continued to play an important role in the region.[91] By the mid-19th century, beans (probably *phaseolus*) were reported in 'abundance' for the people of chiefs Katende and Chibwika, apparently of mixed Luvale and Lunda affiliation, on the Upper Kasai river. Their position was along the main southern route between Ovimbundu and Nuclear Lunda, and a significant comment was added:

'These peoples keep themselves up by meat and fish from rivers and lakes; they plant beans but make little use of them; they sell them to the traders who pass through there, otherwise they keep them until they rot, but they never fail to plant them at the proper time.'[92]

This suggests that *phaseolus* beans and groundnuts, in contrast to cassava, were only introduced on any significant scale when there was a market

---

[89] *Anonymus* 1940: 24 [1803]
[90] Silva Porto 1986: 325
[91] *Anonymus* 1940: 25 [1803]; see also Graça 1890: 414 [1846], and Capello and Ivens 1882: 185 [1878]; Relatório do Capitão-Mor do Moxico, 1905, in Delgado 1944: 666
[92] Graça 1890: 417, 427 [1846]

for them, and ecological and dietary advantages were only of secondary importance, though not unwelcome.

A decade later, between about the same area and the zone of mixed Chokwe and Nuclear Lunda influence in the northern flats, near other routes leading to Nuclear Lunda, groundnuts appeared as one of the main crops. Here, the ecological and dietary considerations mentioned may have played a role, since to visitors 'the population [seemed] large, and the cultivation of manioc greater than any we have seen in [Southern] Lunda'.[93] Apparently, groundnuts were grown in combination with cassava, while excessive Chokwe hunting in the same area may have reduced animal protein supplies (see above).[94] Here, even legumes may have become attractive as 'relish' for cassava, despite their connotation of 'poor food'.

But a second, and approximately simultaneous reason for these 'terribly keen traders ' to introduce groundnut cultivation seems to have been again 'the pleasure of trading'.[95] Livingstone, a very accurate observer on agricultural matters, even remarked that 'in some parts of the country we could get nothing but the manioc and groundnuts'.[96]

The case of the neighbouring Southern Lunda, also devoted cassava growers, seems to support this hypothesis. They had been found by Livingstone one year to be earlier as also growing groundnuts, besides beans (*vigna* type ?) and the traditional groundbeans (*voandzeia*), but only among a whole variety of minor crops.[97] In this remoter area, the adoption of new crops still seems to have followed a main consideration of diversifying food supply, notably protein sources, among which game and gathered forest produce played an important role. They would 'exercise great ingenuity in securing the available wild produce of their country, but do not cultivate what is equal to their needs'[98], and continued to rely on food gathering, including a substantial amount of small animals[99], particularly during the pre-harvest season.[100] Women seem to have been less prepared than elsewhere to devote a great part of their energy to cultivation, with pulses being rather labour-intensive.

---

[93] Livingstone 1963: 246, 247, 249 [1855]
[94] Livingstone 1963: 240, 249 [1855]
[95] Livingstone 1963: 249 [1855]
[96] Livingstone 1963: 257 [1855]
[97] Livingstone 1963: 36, 39, 66 [1854]
[98] Livingstone 1963: 46 [1854].
[99] Livingstone 1963: 46, 50 [1854]
[100] Schomburgk (1923: 67): 'The natives themselves lived on tubers and wild fruits.'[mid-June 1905; Upper Kabompo]

However, these non-agricultural means may not have fully satisfied the need of Southern Lunda for complementary foodstuffs to counterbalance their strongly cassava-based diet. In the last century, there was in addition a permanent threat of being kidnapped as slaves for sale which probably prevented women and children from collecting foodstuffs farther away from their villages. Nevertheless, a lack of references in the sources available suggests that a move towards an increasing proportion of legumes in cultivation did not take place here. One reason may have been the greater distance of Southern Lunda areas from trade routes and market demand.

Along the main routes in the north, in contrast, groundnut cultivation subsequently increased more and more: at Caianda, by the turn of the century, groundnuts and Bambarra nuts were grown regularly by Luvale.[101] And the people around Mona Kimbundu, mainly Chokwe, had apparently already adopted groundnuts both as a cash and as a staple food crop in 1875, and seem to have cultivated it even in pure stand, not just as an intercrop, since they were seen by visitors to have

'little plots on which they grow the mentioned manioca or the groundnut...The blacks in Angola, as well as on the route that I took through the independent countries, enjoy the "*ginguba*" [Angolan term for groundnut - A.v.O.] almost as daily food... The groundnuts are taken in great quantities to the coast and then for oil manufacture to Europe...'[102]

The readiness of cultivators around the Upper Zambezi and Kasai to adopt or experiment with new crops and the required techniques as soon as market opportunities arise, a recurrent feature throughout the region's history, becomes particularly evident in the case of some minor crops. Foreign fruits and vegetables, except banana and sugarcane, seem to have been absent from the region up to the mid-19th century, while Portuguese-speaking traders at Kasanje and Bihe maintained rich orchards and vegetable plantations.[103] In 1854, however, Livingstone was offered near Manenko's, in Southern Lunda area

'a very good pineapple...It was produced by a *Lobale* man, and he states that there are plenty in front [i.e.further north - A.v.O.]. He calls it Lekonda di Ambaca' [*likonda lya-mbaka*, 'banana of the coast' A.v.O.].[104]

One year later, he stated that

---

[101] Interview Samakayi, 21. 10. 1986
[102] Lux 1880: 115 [1875]; also Pogge 1880: 46-7 [1875]
[103] See Livingstone 1963: 128; Cameron 1877: II, 214
[104] Livingstone 1963: 40

'pineapples are reported as existing in the woods in the Lunda country, and are not eaten by the people. Who introduced them?'[105]

In one case, Livingstone himself, who was full of ideas for agricultural development, answered his own question, and

'planted in the yard of one of *Shinte's* [Ishinde, Southern Lunda] principal men two dozen orange trees, three or four cheremoya trees, and one fig tree, besides a number of fruit tree seeds, as mango, ... coffee, *araças* [guava], papaw &c &c' [that had been 'carried on a pole over the shoulder through dense forests' from Angola - A.v.O.]. They will serve as a nursery for future planting',[106]

apparently welcomed by his host. The more interesting question, however, of what such fruits were grown for, would most probably have been answered by 'sale to foreigners'. At Kimbundu, in 1875, saleable fruits were reported as still being absent, but tomatoes were already being grown in backyard gardens.[107] At Kavungu, the other important crossroads for caravans, among the Luvale, agriculture for sale was flourishing by the turn of the century:

'The land is extremely fertile, and big gardens are cultivated most carefully by the natives. Regarding the fruits mainly banana have to be mentioned. Native corn [millets] and vegetables of every kind thrive marvellously'.[108]

In a contemporary early colonial report, (sweet?) potatoes and cabbage are explicitly mentioned as being grown for European transit travellers by local soldiers in their off time and by two chiefs, a Luchazi and a Luvale.[109] Little demand, and the sandy soils which require additional labour for watering and/or fertilization, were seen as the constraints for this type of 'cash crop development'.

My conclusion from this evidence is that not only the 'big' staple crops, but also a variety of minor crops show significant changes and a general expansion of agriculture during the 19th century, notably in the spread of pulses, vegetable and fruit. As against most of the staple cultivation, market demand by travellers more used to vegetarian 'relish' was probably the decisive factor in the emergence of new pulses, mainly carried through women. Their efforts to maintain the ecological and dietary balance vis-a-vis the expansion of cassava-based agriculture played a subsidiary, but increasing role in certain areas. Again, the

---

[105] Livingstone 1963: 228; confirmed by Magyar 1860: 232, for Nuclear Lunda (pineapples and banana).
[106] Livingstone 1963: 266/7 [1855]
[107] Lux 1880: 115
[108] Schomburgk 1925: 187 [1907]
[109] Relatório do Capitão-Mor do Moxico 1905, in Delgado 1944: 666/7

identity of 'cash' and food crops prevented that women's increasing concentration on agriculture (at the expense of other food activities) and market production from resulting in negative effects on regional food supply.

Vegetables and fruit, in contrast, were introduced almost exclusively for sale to foreigners, as the first purely 'cash crops'. They were apparently grown mainly by men, particularly chiefs, because they had better access to such new seed and the relevant knowledge through external contacts, and in some cases to extra labour (see part D). The development of cash crops began to cut through the division of labour.

C 5.4 The value of livestock

Livestock could be seen as another source of nutrients to balance out a diet rich in carbohydrates. The 19th century seems indeed to have brought a remarkable increase in domestic animals around the Upper Zambezi and Kasai. First, there was probably a certain increase in goats, sheep and chicken, the traditional stock already mentioned at the end of the 18th century,[110] since they were reported widely and sometimes as abundant by the mid-19th century.[111] While this increase continued up to the colonial period[112], new animals appeared in the region. An interesting case is pig-raising which was seen first among the central Chokwe, in the 1850s.[113] In 1878 domestic pig-keeping was said to have expanded enormously among 'civilized negroes' on the Angolan coast and in Bihe, but not yet seen north-east of the Kwango, and very seldom among the Luchazi.[114] By the 1880s, also the Luchazi (in contrast to their south-western neighbours, the Lozi), the northwestern Chokwe, and the Luvale possessed considerable numbers of pigs.[115] Since pigs abounded in even

---

[110] Vieira de Andrade 1940: 252/3 [Luvale, 1799]

[111] Graça 1890: 414 [1846, Chokwe]; Silva Porto 1986: 325 [1847, Luchazi, Ngangela]; Silva Porto 1938: 74/5 [Western Ngangela]; Magyar 1860: 229 [Central Chokwe, 1850s]; Livingstone 1963: 50 [Southern Lunda, Ishinde, 1854]

[112] E.g. Schütt 1879: 200/01 [Northern Chokwe]; Arnot 1969: 157 [Luvale 1885]; according to Schomburgk (1925: 113), there were about 3-4 goats per house in remote Southern Lunda villages north of the Kabompo [1906/07], much more than today.

[113] Magyar 1860: 229

[114] Pinto 1881: I, 339; Schütt 1879: 201

[115] Arnot 1969: 105, 157 [1884/85]; Wissmann 1902: 34 [Northern Chokwe, on Kwilu River, 1880]; Baumann 1935: 47 (plenty of pigs among northern and central Chokwe [1930]).

bigger numbers on the Ovimbundu plateau[116], it is more than likely that most of the increase in stocks of swine around the Upper Zambezi and Kasai was owed to occasional sales by Ovimbundu travellers.

The main problem in pig-raising is the fact that pigs compete for human foodstuffs and require considerable care for fencing and/or watching, and for regular feeding. Neither men nor women, who both may own livestock, are very prepared to invest this labour, so that pigs roam around freely and threaten the fields. Silva Porto's people, in 1880, had to catch themselves a pig donated to a Chokwe chief, because

'these are animals which, like wild pigs, live and feed in the forests, and come running to their lord when he has some food to give to them as a recompense, which happens equally when he wants to get rid of them, but disappear in the twinkling of an eye when more than one person turns up.'[117]

The problem of feeding and herding, two activities foreign to the customary division of labour, also seems to have affected the raising of cattle in the interior. The specimens of the bovine race seen in Luvale villages by Lemaire in 1899 were 'erring at liberty on the plains', and when he was offered one of them by Chief Katende, his intimates told him that 'the cow that is intended for us does not want to be brought, and that one of us must go to kill it by a gunshot'.[118]

Nevertheless, cattle, as much more valuable counterparts of pigs, gradually appeared in the region during the 19th century: by the early 1850s, a few cattle were owned by a Ngangela chief on the Kwito, by some Chokwe and southern Luvale chiefs (see C.3), and by Katema near Lake Dilolo.[119] Their high value was probably another decisive constraint preventing a more rapid spread of cattle in spite of the absence of tsetse in most of the region; the stealing of cattle and other livestock by jealous neighbours was a continual threat to the owners.[120] Hence, the ownership of cattle was probably an indicator of both wealth and military power. By the end of the century, the wealth acquired through successful participation in long-distance trade by people along the main 'watershed' route, especially the Luvale around Lake Dilolo, was reflected in rich herds of big and small livestock: 'beautiful sheep and goats', and 'every village has its herd of cattle', numbering between about 25 and 40

---

[116] 'There is no village that does not possess dozens of swine' (Governo Geral 1910).
[117] Silva Porto 1885: 171 [Kawewe, near Luando source].
[118] Lemaire 1902: 54, 138, 142. Similarly, the 'very large herd of cattle' owned by the Mwant Yav, the ruler of Nuclear Lunda, was said to be so wild that 'when slaughtered the gun must be used as if they were game'(Livingstone 1963: 80 [1854]). See also Pinto (1881: I, 231/2 [1878, Mbandi]) on the problem of herding newly acquired cattle.
[119] Silva Porto 1938: 75; Magyar 1960: 229; Livingstone 1963: 83
[120] Pinto 1881: I, 339 [Mbwela, 1878]

animals.[121] Remoter parts were less fortunate, but before the end of the century important Southern Lunda chiefs such as Ishinde also possessed 20 head of cattle, which he had 'received' from the Lozi king Lewanika.[122] Similarly to the Ovimbundu, but on a smaller scale, people of the Upper Zambezi and Kasai invested part of their trade surplus in cattle imports from Bulozi.[123]

The high value obviously attached by the inhabitants to livestock in general, and cattle in particular, had little to do with its meat. Silva Porto remarked in 1852:

'But what all these [Ganguela] peoples are famous for is that they do not kill an ox for eating; instead, their different superstitions require oxen for their ceremonies.'[124]

Many examples in the sources show that even smaller livestock was (and is) generally slaughtered by the owner only on ceremonial occasions; otherwise, it is used for formal transfers such as marriage payments, legal compensations, or hospitality to important visitors (see next part). It is possible that on such occasions a certain redistribution of meat among residents occurred, but in ordinary villages they were, and are, not frequent enough to form a regular part of the diet. In other words, not its meat weight but its value in establishing or cementing social relations was what made livestock so desirable for the peoples of the Upper Zambezi and Kasai in the first place. This value seems to have endured. In 1905, 'the wealth of the different chiefs is assessed among the people by the heads of livestock and the pieces of cloth they possess.'[125] And in 1985, indigenous veterinary assistants in Chinyama Litapi (Zambezi West) remarked of local cattle owners: 'They only trust the number of cattle because of authority in the village.'[126]

Its importance in 'social circulation' paved the way for additional economic functions, but not everyday diet; since the era of long-distance trade, sales of livestock, mostly small, to foreign travellers in return for other imported goods were also an important aspect.[127] Gradually, along

---

[121] Lemaire 1902: 54, 67 and passim
[122] Coillard 1897: 605
[123] Johnston met in 1891, near the Mbwela capital Kangamba, a homeward-bound Bihe caravan from Bulozi 'laden with rubber and over one hundred tusks of ivory... ; they had also about two hundred and fourty head of cattle' (1969: 121). The import of cattle was an important by-business of Bihe *sertanejos* since the 1860s (Madeira Santos 1986: 143).
[124] Silva Porto 1938: 75
[125] Relatório do Capitão-Mor do Moxico, quoted in Delgado 1944: 667.
[126] Sakazanga and Samujima, 4. 9. 1985
[127] E.g. Cameron 1877: II, 178 [ox sale, near Kasai, 1875]; Capello and Ivens, 1882: I, 186 [pig sale, Central Chokwe, 1878]; Silva Porto 1885: 166, 172, 575 [livestock sales along

with other items of 'wealth' (see below), livestock was also used as a currency for various economic transactions within the regional societies.[128] It will be seen how such sales still linked in with social and political considerations.

C 5.5   Changes in the regional division of labour

So far, the question of regional food security has been examined only between the poles of export and 'subsistence' production within the same communities. The fate of regional food exchanges is often overlooked in such analyses. If, however, a certain division of labour within the region existed prior to the advent of the world market (see C 3.2.), the impact of the latter must have been considerable.

For the Upper Zambezi and Kasai, certain problems can be expected: increasing specialization on fishing and agriculture and concentration on cassava cultivation by those living in suitable areas, for example, also in view of growing demand by travellers, may have enforced an increasing dependence on mutual exchanges of fish and staple. Peaceful local exchanges, on the other hand, were probably disturbed by the general level of violence and insecurity.

For example, travellers often complained about the reluctance of local men to guide caravans even to the next villages, often because of the fear of being kidnapped due to some ongoing local feud.[129] An old Luvale, who was a local trader at the beginning of this century, recalled that they were reluctant to conduct business with the Chokwe because they raided caravans.[130] And in 1906, Southern Lunda villagers north of the Kabompo did not know villages within three days' travelling from their own:

'Since they are in continuous strife, individual people who left their villages would inevitably be picked up and sold as slaves to the *Mambari* traders.'[131]

In this situation, foreign caravans apparently became important carriers of essential supplies between different parts of the region. The Chokwe

---

caravan trails, Chokwe, 1880]; see also Ferreira Diniz 1919: 127. Chickens were sold most regularly.

[128] See Mendes Corrêa 1914: 327 [quoting observations by Fonseca Cardoso, Moxico, 1903/04]

[129] E.g. Livingstone 1963: 88, 95, 246 [1854/5, Luvale / Southern Lunda]

[130] Yowena Samakayi, 21. 10. 1986

[131] Schomburgk 1925: 124 [1906, Southern Lunda]

along the main route Bihe-Katanga, for example, seem to have obtained much of their dried fish during the later 19th century, as usual, in return for cassava meal. But this fish now arrived on the backs of transiting carriers hungry for staple food, who had bought it beforehand among the Luvale in order 'to pay (their) way through to Bihé [Bihe]'[132]. Because of its high value and low weight, dried fish was probably the main regional barter food transported by long-distance caravans; according to Harding, by the turn of the century, again on the main route to Bihe

> 'nearly every boy [racist expression for 'employee', here: carrier - A.v.O.] is now armed with a bundle of fish, which bye-and-bye forms his food, and his capital for purchasing more.'[133]

The most comprehensive account of how carriers tried to obtain provisions and accumulate by connecting a whole series of regional trade networks has been given by Arnot, in 1888:

> 'the natives along the road do not expect to get beads or cloth... in exchange for the food which they bring to camp for sale, but look for the produce of the interior. Consequently, I provided my men with large quantities of salt at the *Garenganze* [Katanga], also with copper anklets and finely drawn wire, which are to be had there, and are much valued by the *Lovale* [Luvale] and *Chiboque* [Chokwe] races. In the Upper *Lovale* country, my men exchanged the larger part of the salt they carried for dried fish, which is in great demand amongst the *Chibokwe*. As the *Chibokwe* cultivate and prepare large quantities of castor oil, my men exchanged the fish for castor oil, which is a commodity greatly valued by the *Valoimbe* [Lwimbi, Mbandi] along the eastern bank of the Quanza, and also among the inhabitants of *Bihé*. The *Valoimbe*, too, are great fishermen, and I observed my men again exchanging the castor oil they had just bought for fish which is marketable in *Bihé*. West of *Bihé*, rubber alone counts, and as my men are well supplied with it, they take a little from their loads to pay the expenses down to the coast, where, arriving with 30 or 40 lbs. of rubber, they make a final exchange for cloth, beads, etc., with which they will set out on their long return journey to the interior.'[134]

Nevertheless, direct barter exchanges between neighbouring peoples did go on at some scale throughout the period (see C 3.2.), mainly thanks to specialized local traders (see D 5). Even for them, however, the carrying of dried fish and cassava meal between different ecological environments was integrated into import/export trade networks. To the Luvale trader mentioned before I owe a very instructive illustration of the complicated network of local exchanges he had to operate in order to obtain export products and accumulate:

> When he was a young man, by the beginning of this century, he lived at Caianda, on the main watershed route between Bihe and Katanga. He used to carry cassava to the plains and lakes near the Zambezi in order to buy fish. He ferried the fish across the river to the woodlands south east of it where he

---

[132] Cameron 1877: II, 163; see also 165 [1875]
[133] Harding 1904: 199 [1899]

exchanged it for rubber. He took the rubber back to the main route and sold it to Ovimbundu middlemen for cloth, beads, gun powder and guns. He carried these items to even remoter areas to buy more fish and more rubber...[135] (See fig. 9.)

This example shows that interests in external trade became to some extent instrumental for the maintenance of the established regional exchanges that were vital for local subsistence. But it also illustrates a new twist in the societal division of labour: export producers such as rubber gatherers had to use part of their produce to acquire essential foodstuffs (rather than imported goods); and producers of animal protein such as fishermen were able to demand imported goods for their fish (instead of staple food), not only from foreigners, but also from local customers.

These new types of exchanges are confirmed by other contemporary sources:

* Very early, some time around 1800, the Lozi had begun to sell livestock, notably cattle, to the Luvale for imported goods such 'clothing, crockery, and beads'.[136] The older means of payment for livestock from Bulozi, forest products and staple food, which were to play such an important role in the 20th century, seem if anything to have decreased during the 19th century; certain groups of Mbunda from the woodlands to the west settled on the margins of the flood plain and 'taught' the Lozi how to grow bulrush millet and especially cassava and thereby reduce the threat of famine.[137]

* Another example is the case of the Luchazi, who in the 1870s imported fish from the Kwanza River (Mbandi) for wax, instead of ironware as they had used to.[138]

* After the turn of the century, at the latest, Luvale fishermen west of the Zambezi (Lake Dilolo, Kakenge and further south) sold their fish for cloth and guns (rather than staple food or raw iron) to people in neighbouring areas.[139]

* Vegetable salt and copper from the east (Luburi-Lualaba and Katanga), which were carried to the Upper Zambezi and Kasai by transit caravans, were paid with rubber or beeswax.[140]

---

[134] Arnot 1969: 249/50
[135] Y. Samakayi, 21. 10. 86
[136] Livingstone 1960: 41, 228
[137] Hermitte 1974: 55
[138] Pinto 1881: I, 254/5
[139] Relatório do Capitão-Mor do Moxico 1905, in: Delgado 1944: 666; Venning 1953: 55
[140] Cameron 1877: II, 152; Mr. Sondoyi, 24. 10. 1986

* Increasing amounts of sodium salt from the salines of Kasanje and from the quarries of Kisama (near Luanda), carried by caravans to the *Ganguela* peoples in bark bags containing 1-5 pounds each, replaced the local ash salt.[141] Such 'luxury' salt was partly given free by traders to establish peaceful relations with their hosts, but was also sold for local foodstuffs as well as wax, ivory or rubber.[142]

The existence of food markets is often taken as the strongest indicator of an established regional division of labour. Permanent food markets were mentioned early for the Nuclear Lunda capital, the *Musumba*.[143] Around the Upper Kasai, in July 1878, Capello and Ivens mentioned several instances of permanent markets established at the headquarters of important chiefs, 'frequented by the inhabitants of neighbouring hamlets', which they call *quitanda* or, apparently as a Chokwe term, *t'chitaca*.[144] According to their detailed description of the *t'chitaka* at Ndumba Tembo's, 'a great concourse of people' was attracted and considerable quantities of foodstuffs transacted here, including

'pumpkins, sweet potatoes, manioc, maize-flour, beans, *inhame* [yams], *massambala* [sorghum], *massango* [bulrush millet], earth-nuts, sugar cane, eggs, dried fish, fowls, goats, pigs, rats, *quissangua* [?] and hydromel or mead'[145]

besides some export goods such as ivory and *landolphia* rubber. Lengths of cloth seem to have been the standard means of payment. But their report also suggests that villagers came rather to sell or watch, while carriers and other staff of Capello and Ivens' own caravan seem to have been the main group of buyers. Given that no other references exist for this period, these 'markets' appear rather like concentrations of those transactions that took place regularly at caravans' camps (*chilombo*, sg.). 30 years later, at the beginning of this century, 'markets *(t'chitaca)* by authorization of the chief or headman' were again mentioned for the Moxico District, but again there are no clear indications as to who the

---

[141] See Magyar 1859: 296, on salt from the coast traded by Ovimbundu. For the history of the Kisama salt trade see Birmingham 1970. On salt exports from Kasanje see E.g. Livingstone 1963: 121 [1854, petty Mbangala traders searching for wax etc.].

[142] 'Mbundu salt' was well established in local transactions among the Luvale by the beginning of this century (Mr. Sondoyi, 18. 10. 1986); in 1899 Lemaire was offered by Ovimbundu traders near the Kasai (Luau) 'a dish of coarse salt' - apparently rock salt (1902: 59).

[143] Magyar 1860: 232

[144] Capello and Ivens 1882: I, 197 (notably Shakelembe, Katende, Kasango, (Alto?) Chikapa, Kimbundu; besides foreign places such as Muene Mai and Msiri). Further west in Angola, among the Mbundu and Kongo, the term *quitanda* has been in use for 'market' or 'market place' since at least the 17th century (Heintze 1985: 127).

[145] Capello and Ivens, 1882: I, 185

customers were.[146] The other term given by Capello and Ivens, *quitanda* (apparently a KiMbundu or KiKongo import, see above), by the way, was later adopted in the localized form *chitanda*, at least by the Luvale, for built-up 'shops',[147] i.e. again places where mainly imported manufactures and exports (rubber) or foodstuffs (for sale to non-residents or wage earners) were transacted. (See fig. 32.)

Fully-fledged rural markets have not emerged in the region even up to the present day; they have remained restricted to places with concentrated extra-rural demand and strong political supervision. The earlier examples show, however, that this did (and does) not exclude widespread exchanges between specialized producers on an individual basis. Up to the end of the pre-colonial period, specialization had apparently increased to a point where many export producers were no longer self-sufficient with regard to food, while others produced more surplus food than was required for their own needs and foreign travellers' demand.[148] Imported and exportable commodities began to intervene between partners who had formerly directly exchanged their surplus. These items did not yet fully assume the function of currencies, although they came close to it (see the next chapter). But regional trade networks and hence everyday reproduction were now clearly integrated into the wider world market.

What this new twist in the division of labour could mean with regard to food security is perhaps indicated by increasing signs of food scarcity by the end of the period. At the end of the chronological overview (in chapter B 5), I mentioned 1911 as the 'year of the great hunger in the *Ganguela* country', which brought the Ovimbundu rubber trade to a premature standstill. In his Annual Report for 1912/13, the District Commissioner for the 'Barotse District' (Bulozi) confirmed a disastrous collapse of food production, notably cassava planting, on the Upper Zambezi in the previous years:

'There was a very great shortage of food among the *Malunda* and *Malovale*. It was reported to me that several of the latter on the Kapaku River [opposite Chavuma, on the present international boundary - A.v.O.] had died of hunger. This should be the last year of such shortage, as both last year and this year all the tribes have ploughed...',[149]

and the *Mwanja* (cassava, Lo.) planted the previous year 'had not yet come to maturity during the latter end of the year'.[150] In the

---

[146] Mendes Corrêa 1914: 328 (quoting observations of Fonseca Cardoso, 1903/04)
[147] Horton 1975: 369
[148] 'Self-sufficiency' includes here home-consumption or local purchase of deficit food in exchange for home-produced surplus.
[149] NAZ, file KDE 8/1/4
[150] *Ibid.*

same year, a Portuguese officer travelling to Mona Kimbundu made very similar observations north of the Kasai:

'Famine plagues the whole region passed through and ... we have the impression of passing through a totally devastated and almost deserted region. It normally produces maize, millet, sorghum and some cassava and beans... The plantations of maize, millet and beans which they have are insufficient to stave off the hunger ...; and whether this people will devote itself to work [i.e. to more cultivation work - A.v.O.] is a very problematic matter on which one cannot count.'[151]

The observations of another Portuguese officer charged with the demarcation of the colonial boundary between Angola and Northern Rhodesia in 1913/14 may shed some light on this marked deterioration of food production in the region. Between Moxico and the Lungvevungu River, he saw

'houses of white traders, who live from rubber, which has now such a low price that it hardly pays the transport to the coast; they therefore see themselves forced to give more importance to food, which they are cultivating for their own use and **for sale to the native** ... There are many villages; and we are generally forewarned of their proximity by the noise they make when they beat the rubber with mallets; because the whole region is rich with the creeping plant which yields the rubber, which the native is extracting to carry it to the trader and which he exchanges for the articles he needs, **and now mainly for food**'[152] [my emphasis].

This suggests a new degree of specialization, or perhaps over-specialization, in rubber production. Given the low productivity of the process, it must have largely depended on the labour of women and children. In the last chapter (C 4.), I have presented some evidence that the growing involvement of women in rubber production took place went potentially at the expense of staple food cultivation.

A similar over-specialization may have occurred among fishing people such as the Luvale on the western bank of the Zambezi. Towards the end of the pre-colonial period, there was most probably a certain overpopulation of these areas compared to the scarcity of cultivable uplands, and an increasing absorption of female labour for processing (see above, last chapter).[153] Their staple food supply had always been threatened by high floods; but in addition, excessive rubber production by Luchazi and Southern Lunda may have cut down deliveries from their traditional suppliers in regional trade. In both cases, climatic anomalies may then have triggered off serious famines.

---

[151] Barros Carvalhais 1915: 19/20

[152] Gago Coutinho 1915: 203/04

[153] See, for example, Johnston (1969: 130), who saw 'plenty of dried fish', but 'no meal' in some villages of Southern Luvale or Banyeti, south of Lower Lungwevungu, in 1891.

However, the changed economic and political context of the early colonial period may also have played a part in the rapid worsening of the food situation. Falling rubber prices were most probably countered by increased production to maintain habitual levels of 'income'; and in the Portuguese sphere forced labour as well as rather arbitrary taxation (payable in rubber) may have compelled people to give up food security. Not surprisingly, these tensions finally erupted in the so-called 'Luchazi revolt' in 1916/17, which was primarily directed against resident white traders. These traders were appointed as tax collectors by local Portuguese commanders, and used this as well as their position as creditors to recklessly exact masses of rubber from the local population.[154]

It seems, on the whole, that before these enforced excesses of rubber export the established system of food production and circulation within the region proved sufficiently stable to ensure food security for its inhabitants. They were able to cope with a considerable amount of export production by restructuring their division of labour by gender and area, by adopting or expanding innovations in agriculture and diet, and because gathering for export yielded 'by-products' for nutrition.

---

[154] See Pélissier 1977: 408/09. In the neighbouring territory of the BSAC (now Zambia), taxes were apparently collected in coined money from the beginning; experiments with collection of rubber for tax proved unsatisfactory, partly because of a low-price policy for wild rubber, due to British interests in plantation rubber (Annual Reports D.C. Barotse, 1910/11 and 1911/12, NAZ KDE 8/1/2-3; see also Hobson 1960).

C 6 'Use-values' and 'currencies': The utility of imported goods

At this point, one central question has to be tackled which has remained open so far: Why men and women of the Upper Zambezi and Kasai invested so much energy and hardship in producing goods for export or sale to foreigners, long before extra-economic repression by the colonial state took its grip. In a largely self-sufficient economy, with functioning systems of material reproduction through regional resources, different from our own, the answer is by no means self-evident.

In the last chapter I have presented some evidence that in the end, export products and even imported goods were to some extent used only to obtain certain regional trade items that had formerly been bartered for local products, e.g. fish, salt, livestock or copper - i.e., as a new means to achieve meet old (economic) ends. Local producers may have found trade goods particularly useful for acquiring larger quantities or better quality of these customary use-values.

But the portion of trade goods invested in this way was certainly too small to explain the entire longing for the variety of new imported goods, goods that were more or less implicitly regarded by most contemporary European observers as useless trinkets catering to playful vanity.[1] In this chapter, I will ask about their different utility or 'use-value' for the inhabitants of this region of the interior, and what kind of dependence they created: whether they represented 'new' needs that could not be satisfied locally, or replaced regional production. The foreign goods that were largely unknown or at least unused in the region before its integration into the world market, but then flowed in incessantly, can from the utility point of view be grouped into intoxicants (tobacco, gin), body ornaments (beads, shells, brass), cloth and clothing, and firearms (which have already been dealt with, in sections C 4.3 and 4.4.). The latter two groups are by far the most important for the Upper Zambezi and Kasai, but the role of smaller goods should not be overlooked, and will therefore be examined first.

---

[1] A reformist Angolan Governor, for example, argued (not without interest) in 1884 that 'the native' was more or less being cheated with 'a variety of the most gaudy and fantastic assortment of objects' for his rubber at Benguela (quoted in Heywood 1984: 160).

C 6.1 Intoxicants

At an earlier stage, smoking tobacco had certainly been a novelty in the region. But by 1850, this American narcotic was already firmly established among both Ovimbundu and Mbangala. Mbangala women were seen sitting and 'gazing at one for hours, smoking their long pipes in dreamy indifference. The men, too, are generally seen with pipe in hand, puffing away in lordly leisure.'[2]

Most of the tobacco produced in these areas, however, was exported into the interior in a processed form.[3] From the point of view of the middlemen, tobacco (similarly to salt) played a considerable role as 'small change' and as an initial gift for opening business talks. According to Wissmann, this was a widespread custom in Nuclear Lunda, and 'it is said that by enjoying the tobacco the person will be contented and more accessible for further negotiations.'[4] For the Upper Zambezi and Kasai, in contrast, only few references to travellers actually expending tobacco exist[5]; demand for imported tobacco there seems to have been somewhat limited compared to neighbouring peoples such as the Shinji, Nuclear Lunda or Luba.[6]

This does not mean, however, that Upper Zambezians were not fond of smoking: Indian hemp (*cannabis sativa*; Lv.*lyamba*, SL. *damba*), growing wild in gallery forests along major rivers,[7] was the indigenous substance used universally for smoking in Central Africa before the 19th century, and has remained popular in Upper Zambezi villages up to the present day. In 1985, I found the following inscription carved into a lone sisal plant in a village on Lake Mwange (Zambezi Westbank): 'Let us

---

2   Livingstone 1963: 120
3   The Ovimbundu exported their tobacco 'to foreign countries' in balls that they called *bunge* (Magyar 1859: 301); see also Capello and Ivens 1882: I, 8. At Kasanje, on his return journey to Bulozi in 1855, Livingstone bought up 380 lbs. of Mbangala tobacco for exchanges in 'Lunda' [which in his terminology refers to both Nuclear and Southern Lunda]. On Mbangala tobacco exports to the interior see Pogge 1880: 26 [1875].
4   Wissmann 1902: 55
5   See Silva Porto 1986: 326 [16. 12. 1847; gift to Mbunda chieftainess] and 335 [12. 1. 1848; sale for meat to Sekele hunters]; Livingstone 1963: 170 [1854, gift to Southern Lunda / Luvale chief Katende]; a certain demand for gifts in tobacco (and salt) seems to have existed among Central Chokwe chiefs and elders later in the century: Capello and Ivens recommended in 1878 that 'the traveller who wends his way to the *Quiôco* [Chokwe] should carry with him abundance of powder, brass wire and native tobacco, which he may purchase in the Bihé...'(1882: I, 8); see also Silva Porto 1885: 570 [1880].
6   Livingstone 1963: 220 (see footnote above) [on Nuclear Lunda], 229 [on Bashinji; both 1855]; Cameron 1877: II, 146 [on Luba, 1875].
7   Capello and Ivens 1882: I, 224 [Central Chokwe]

stay well, let us drink well, because if we have no good communication there will be misunderstanding. The *lyamba* is still fresh these days...'[8]

This quotation expresses perfectly the meaning attached customarily to any use of intoxicants in these societies. Smoking hemp or tobacco is essentially a communal entertainment. The water pipe (Lv./Ch. *mutopa*), made of a small calabash with a hollow reed on which a small clay bowl is placed, which is mostly used for the purpose in this area,[9] goes round from mouth to mouth among gatherings of either men or women:

> '...the *mutopa*, as soon as its owner takes the first puff, runs from mouth to mouth without distinction of classes, and when it returns to him and if he still has a piece of tobacco, he has to add it in order to take a new puff and let it go round again...'[10]

This 19th century description emphasizes the redistributive and socially balancing effect of smoking, which was an essential aspect of using intoxicants. It may be significant that in the 1870s, in a context of political centralization and abolition of older hierarchies, collective and compulsory hemp smoking became the symbol of a new social identity among the northern Luba group of the Bashilange, who forthwith called themselves *Bena Riamba* (from *liamba*, hemp).[11]

Concerning the peoples of the Upper Zambezi and Kasai, late precolonial visitors found that *cannabis*, 'the most objectionable form of smoking', continued to play a significant role,[12] which may explain to some extent why demand for tobacco was relatively low in the region. But besides hemp, tobacco was used widely from at least the 19th century on, by chiefs who smoked 'unremittingly the whole time' as well as hunters who each carried their individual, fashionably carved tobacco pipe or snuff box along with their hunting gear.[13] Judging from later statements by the Luchazi and Chokwe, tobacco had a certain reputation

---

[8] Translation from Luvale; 4. 9. 1985

[9] This is the type I have seen personally and which is the only one used for *cannabis* smoking (cf. Baumann 1935: 57/8); it may even have been an invention of the Sekele (cf. Alméida 1965: 7). In the last century, other designs with antelope horns were seen as well (Johnston 1969: 118; Capello and Ivens 1882: I, 166).

[10] Dias de Carvalho 1890: 677 [Northern Chokwe / Lunda]

[11] See for example Schütt 1879: 206

[12] Johnston 1969: 118 [1891, Mbwela on Kwando river]; as a protestant medical doctor, he only considered the individual and physical effect of hemp smoking in the most derogatory way. See also Schachtzabel 1923: 141 [1913, remote Southern Chokwe]

[13] Cameron 1877: II, 170 [Katende, 1875]; Graça 1890: 416 [Central Chokwe, 1846]; Capello and Ivens 1882: I, 166, 220, 225 [Central Chokwe; 1878]; Pinto 1881: 281 [Luchazi, 1878]; Baumann 1935: 57/8. The Angolan Sekele (!*Kung*) were reported as particularly passionate smokers, both of tobacco and of Indian hemp which they used to exchange for wax from the Luchazi even in the late colonial period (Johnston 1969: 118 [1891]; Alméida 1965: 7; Dias da Silva 1949: 36).

of civilization, while hemp continued to be associated with more remote and backward groups.[14] The main reason for a relatively low demand for imported tobacco seems to have been a successful import substitution strategy: by the 1850s, Chokwe and Southern Lunda themselves were cultivating tobacco (*makanya*, 'leaf') in backyard gardens in most of their villages.[15] This enabled chiefs and notables not only to be fairly self-sufficient in tobacco, but also to **offer** it to, rather than ask from, foreign visitors, and enjoy the superior position of the giver to contract new 'friendships', or to 'allay' conflicts by 'presenting some tobacco leaves'.[16]

How close the essential ideas of smoking and drinking are for peoples of the region is demonstrated by the fact that they use the same term (*ku-*) *nwa* for it. In the last section, I have mentioned already the importance of alcohol for various social purposes. Even more than tobacco, it was always consumed communally: in the past, grain beers were usually served by women to the *nzango* and consumed communally by the group of elder men that formed the core of the village (see below); *lizaji* gatherings, which may include both women and men, are special occasions on which grain or honey-beer is shared out; and a variety of ceremonial occasions as well as collective 'work parties' also require libations of alcohol. The task of sharing out alcohol equally is still today regarded as very delicate so that at *lizaji* gatherings a neutral person who does not drink is called in.[17] In the past, important chiefs had a special officer, the 'beer pourer' (SL. *kaseya*) at their court.

The story of what role alcohol played, or rather did not play in long-distance trade of the Upper Zambezi and Kasai is also quite similar to that one of tobacco. In Central Africa in general, the consumption of

> 'psychoactive substances...intensified communication with the spiritual component of power in Africa. Intoxicants also carried strong connotations of status in the political economy of goods and people, confirming the mundane prestige of those able to distribute them liberally among dependants and guests...'[18]

To dispose over great quantities of strong liquor was, therefore, particularly attractive to chiefs and headmen. This was what made *aguardente*, a rough gin or brandy distilled mainly from sugar cane, the

---

[14] Cf. Dias da Silva 1949: 36; Baumann 1935: 58
[15] Magyar 1860: 229, 231; Livingstone 1963: 265 [1855, Ishinde's capital]; Schomburgk 1925: 162 [1904/07; between Kabompo and Zambezi rivers]; description of cultivation process in Baumann 1935: 57
[16] Livingstone 1963: 94, 99 [Luvale, Southern Lunda, 1854]; see also Silva Porto 1986: 327 [19. 12. 1847; Luchazi]
[17] Beck and Dorlöchter 1987: B68; A. Lufuma, personal communication, 30. 10. 1989
[18] Miller 1988: 83

second largest category (after textiles) on the African import ledger already between 1784 and 1823, mainly in return for slaves.[19] From about 1840, it was sold to areas beyond (east of) the Kwanza river, and later became a 'principal product for transactions in the interior', allegedly overtaking even beads and cloth by the 1890s.[20] An increasing percentage of this *aguardente* was produced by enterprising traders on their own sugar plantations within the country, notably on the coast between Benguela and Catumbela, and near Malange.[21] By 1889, even Bihe was found to be a 'gin-soaked' place 'filled up with distillers'.[22]

For the period after 1855, there are various reports on the distribution of firewater at chiefs' receptions and ceremonies such as funerals, e.g. on Nuclear Lunda, Mbangala and Minungu; among the Songo, for example, virtually everybody could drink *aguardente* except pregnant women, and 'the Lunda peoples appreciate *aguardente* preferring it to any other fermented drink.'[23] Chiefs of the peoples of the Upper Zambezi and Kasai, however, do not appear as recipients or consumers of spirits during that time. Exceptions are individual cases such as Mwene Kibawu (Pg. *Quibau*; Central Chokwe) and Mwene Kimbundu, Luvale/Northern Chokwe, on the main route Kasanje/Malanje - Nuclear Lunda.[24] A reception by the latter, witnessed by Pogge in 1875, may have been quite characteristic of the political significance attached to the consumption of gin:

> The first sip had to be taken by Pogge's interpreter, who then had to give the bottle and cup to 'a grande who as usual hands it over to the chief', before it began to circulate. Turmoil broke out when one 'grande' felt he had been skipped during the circulation of bottle and cup.[25]

On the whole, however, there was no demand for *aguardente* in the region.[26] In their great majority the chiefs of the region apparently did **not** agree with the judgement that

---

[19] In this period, imported gin (mainly Brazilian rum) made up about 20 % of imports at Luanda (Miller 1988: 75).

[20] Madeira Santos 1986: 58; according to import statistics for 1884, however, 'aguardente and simple alcohols' accounted only for about ¼ of flintlock muskets, and about 1/20 of simple trade cloth (Ministerio da Marinha 1889).

[21] Schönberg-Lotholz 1960: 120; Lux 1880: 63, Pogge 1880: 22 [both 1875]

[22] Crawford 1912: 41/42

[23] Livingstone 1963: 241 [1855; funeral at Kabango, Western Nuclear Lunda]; Lux 1880: 78 [1875, King of Kasanje]; Wissmann 1902: 31 [1880; Minungu chief]; Lux ibid. : 89 [1875, Songo]; Diniz, 1918: 127 [Nuclear Lunda, 1886-1912]

[24] Capello and Ivens 1882: I, 194 [1878].

[25] Pogge 1880: 54/5 [1875]

[26] Pogge 1880: 63 [1875; for areas east of Kimbundu; information by Malange trader]; Lemaire 1902: 59 and 148 [1899; no spirits were carried by Ovimbundu traders met on the 'watershed' route east of Dilolo]

'the imported distillates contained a much higher alcoholic content than ... local alternatives and were often sharp in taste, which African drinkers took as a sign of strength and quality.'[27]

Instead, they preferred their customary home-brewed honey-beer or mead. The Chokwe senior chief Ndumba Tembo, at a reception in 1878 'after swallowing a couple more cansful of mead, ... launched out into praise of that liquor, which, in his opinion, had no equal save the *aguardente* of the whites...'[28]

19th century European visitors agreed with this view, as they found honey-beer 'the most alcoholic stuff I ever tasted' and as 'intoxicating as any other spirit'.[29] It is therefore very plausible that the availability of domestic honeybeer, which greatly increased during this period as a 'by-product' of wax exports, for a long time prevented dependence on gin imports. (See fig. 20)

Among the Luvale, gin drinking apparently replaced honeybeer consumption only with the establishment of permanent Portuguese forts (1896); their senior chief Kakenge appeared as a fearful ruler to one visitor in 1894, but as a hopeless drunkard subsisting on the Portuguese commander's bottle of brandy to another in 1899.[30] His example, as well as that of Ndumba Tembo's predecessor, shows that alcohol as strong as gin also meant an increased risk of drunkenness, loss of self-control and hence could be counterproductive for the authority for chiefs and headmen.[31]

Another, less spectacular way in which gin finally entered into the Upper Zambezi might have been through the young men who were included in considerable numbers in the ranks of 'workers of trade' for Portuguese or Ovimbundu caravans. They most probably became acquainted with the drink during their trips,[32] and may have gradually built up a demand for gin back home. Such demand by younger men, especially (ex-) wage earners, is widespread today, and still does not lead to any imports of brandy. It is universally in the region by sales of a

---

[27] Miller 1988: 83
[28] Capello and Ivens 1882: I, 207
[29] Pinto 1881: I, 282; Silva Porto 1986: 326, fn. 2 [1878 and 1847/1869, both on Luchazi]
[30] Coillard 1897: 610f; Gibbons 1904: I, 11, 18-19; according to Harding (1904: 80/81) Kakenge drank **both** 'Kaffirbeer'[millet beer] and 'Portuguese Brandy' in 1899.
[31] Capello and Ivens 1882: I, 207, which shows that drunkenness among chiefs was also not uncommon **before** the introduction of gin; see also Silva Porto 1886: 327 [19. 12. 1847; Luchazi].
[32] When Bihé caravans met in the Central African interior, bottles of gin were exchanged and communally consumed between caravan leaders as tokens of friendship. At that time, Ovimbundu carriers often received extradoses of *aguardente* as bonuses and part of their pay (Lux 1880: 101, 102; Schön-berg-Lothholz 1960: 120, 121).

locally-distilled gin which is called *lituku*. This term alludes to the dripping (literally 'sweating') of the liquor from the end of the distilling apparatus into the bottle. The main ingedients of this gin are normally maize, cassava and a certain wild root (SL. *mulaba*), but a variety of other crops and fruits may be used as well. Village women are the exclusive distillers of *lituku*, and it appears that, at a certain point, they have successfully grasped this new opportunity to market some of their crop surpluses and get a share of men's better incomes. When this point was, is not clear. It is possible that those few women who began to accompany their husbands to the Northern Rhodesian Copperbelt, from the late 1920s on, acquired the knowhow of distillation in town, where it was called *kachasu*, and became the promoters of *lituku* back home. Even more likely is that Portuguese traders who settled in Angolan border areas by the end of the last century were distilling *aguardente* locally, for sale and consumption, and that women learnt it there.[33] A colonial report on the Ovimbundu Plateau from 1909, at least, mentioned widespread cultivation of sweet potatoes for distillation around Caconda, and complained that

> 'due to a regrettable indifference on the part of the authorities of that district it was permitted that the traders supplied the natives with distilling apparatuses of a reduced model with a capacity of 300 to 500 litres with which they manufacture a detestable and highly harmful *aguardente*...'[34]

Similar developments may have taken place at that time around the Upper Zambezi and Kasai. Distilling apparatuses there, however, are much smaller and mostly home-made. The only part that can not be supplied from local materials is the distilling pipe. Today, exhaust pipes and the like are used, but in the past, it is said, unused or broken gun barrels did the job.[35]

To summarize these findings, it appears that in order to understand the history of world market integration of certain African regions, it is sometimes also instructive to look at what items of the general range of import goods were **not** in demand here as much as elsewhere. Intoxicating substances, for instance, were widely used to enhance social cohesion and the position of generous distributors, here as everywhere in Central Africa. But in contrast to neighbouring regions, this demand did not result in substantial imports but was mostly met by indigenous means and more or less deliberate 'import substitution' strategies. It looks as if

---

[33] This hypothesis is supported by the fact that Chavuma, the most important border crossing, is something like the capital of *lituku* in the Zambian Zambezi District.
[34] Governo Geral da Provincia de Angola 1910: 82/3
[35] For the *lituku* story see Dorlöchter-Sulser and von Oppen 1989

the peoples of the region wanted to save their purchasing power (food and export commodities, services) for other, more urgently needed items.

C 6.2 'Ornaments'

Some of the manufactured articles the inhabitants of the Upper Zambezi and Kasai strived to obtain for their hard-won export products, foodstuffs and services looked hardly more useful to European observers than intoxicants. The use-value of these imported goods may be described as 'body ornaments'. They consisted of:

* **Brass**, mainly manufactured in the Netherlands', in the form of bracelets (*manillas*), finger rings, wire or nails, which were particularly valued by the Chokwe;[36]

* **Shells** from both the East and West African coasts, notably the highly valued disc-shaped bottom of the *conus* shell (Lv.*jimbe*) from the Indian Ocean which was later substituted by a European imitation in porcelain (see fig. 22);[37] some cowries (Lv.SL. *lupashi*) came from Luanda or overseas, but they never became as popular here as elsewhere in Africa;

* **Beads**, manufactured in various European countries from glass, porcelain or faience, in a wide variety of shapes: *missanga grossa* (big, red), *missanga fina* (small, called 'turtle eye'), *Maria Segundas* (white stones enamelled red), *missanga branca* (big, white, porcelain), *missanga de vidro* (glass; white, black or silver); *avellorios* or *cassungo* (small beads for embroideries); *almandrilhas* (striped, oval shaped) and *coral apipado* were the most current types distinguished by traders in the Angolan sphere in the second half of the 19th century.[38] There are a number of specific terms in Upper Zambezi languages for different types of beads[39], but the generic term is (*w*)*usanga* (orig. perhaps related to 'egg').

The lures of these new, imported goods for the inhabitants of the Upper Zambezi and Kasai are better understood if we take a look at existing fashions and local equivalents. Brass, for example, simply seems to have

---

[36] Livingstone 1963: 111 [1854]; Capello and Ivens 1882: I, 182; Mendes Corrêa 1914: 327 [1903/04]; cf. Sundstrøm 1974: 229, 234

[37] Other expressions in Central Africa were apparently *mpande*, *vibangwa* or *viongwa* - cf. Papstein 1978: 242; Vellut 1972: 85, fn. 48

[38] Lux 1880: 58/9; Pogge 1880: 141; Capello and Ivens 1882: I, 7/8; cf. Vellut 1972: 85ff

[39] See e. g. Fisher 1984: 15, for Lunda-Ndembu

complemented iron and copper as raw material for the various metal adornments that had been popular in fashion and trade of the region long before (see C 3.3). Brass was easier to work than iron and appealed perhaps particularly to the Chokwe because they were more distant from the Lubudi copper mines - in other words, imports offered greater quantities of raw materials for local artisans. Gun clubs ornamented with brass nails and wire have been mentioned already. In 1878, Chokwe hunters, warriors and musicians wore innumerable or 'thick bangles' round their wrists and ankles.[40] And their senior chief Ndumba Tembo, who was a dexterous blacksmith, wore

'a brass crown, not dissimilar in shape to that of the early monarchs of Europe... His fingers, which were covered with brass rings, terminated in long pointed nails of the same metal, which cramped every movement of his hands... His industry and ingenuity appeared to be great, and we were informed that crown, rings and nails were entirely of his own manufacture...'[41]

Fig. 21: Chokwe chief with locally made brass crown (1900s)
(Photograph by Fonseca Cardoso, In: Mendes Correa 1916, fig. 15)

According to a photograph taken by Fonseca Cardoso (who in 1903/04 confirmed this fashion), these Chokwe brass crowns, by the way, resembled very much the shape of the one traditionally shown in pictures of *Chibinda Ilunga*, the legendary forefather of all holders of Nuclear

---
[40] Capello and Ivens 1882: I, 174, 214

Lunda-related political titles.[42] Brass as a new material may have been integrated here into much older political symbolisms. It also added, however, to the fashions of ordinary people. The general population of Central Chokwe, for example, would wear bracelets of brass or copper, collars of small pieces of wood adorned with brass nails, earrings, finger rings, crosses and the like.[43] (See fig. 18.) Luchazi and Mbunda women were very fond of bracelets, earrings and anklets of iron, copper and brass, the latter being perhaps the most common by the end of the century.[44] Brass as a new material may have been integrated here into much older political symbolisms. It also added, however, to the fashions of ordinary people. The general population of Central Chokwe, for example, would wear bracelets of brass or copper, collars of small pieces of wood adorned with brass nails, earrings, finger rings, crosses and the like.[45] (See fig. 18.) Luchazi and Mbunda women were very fond of bracelets, earrings and anklets of iron, copper and brass, the latter being perhaps the most common by the end of the century.[46]

Further east, the older raw materials remained unchallenged, probably partly also because of continued abundance of copper supplies via long-distance caravans. In 1854, the Southern chief Ishinde, for example, wore 'a profusion of iron and copper leglets'; one of his junior chiefs,

> 'in going off was obliged by such large bundles of copper rings on his ankles to adopt quite a straddling walk. When I laughed at the absurd appearance he made, the people remarked "that is lordship in these parts" '.[47]

The favourite wife of a Southern Lunda headman 'had a mass of iron rings on her ankles'; she and other women, Southern Lunda as well as Luvale and Chokwe, had as part of their hair dress little pieces of sheet iron and copper that 'made a tinkling as she went in her mincing African style...'[48]

These quotations suggest that chiefs were particularly rich in these metal adornments, but had no monopoly; ordinary men and women also wore them. Increased trade may have offered them better opportunities to obtain such treasures as well, particularly copper and brass representing

---

[41] Capello and Ivens 1882: I, 177.
[42] Published by Mendes Corrêa 1914: 327 and fig. 15
[43] Capello and Ivens, 1882: I, 224-5; Fonseca Cardoso, quoted in Mendes Corrêa 1914: 327
[44] Harding 1904: 237 [1899]; Diniz, 1918: 381 [c. 1912]
[45] Capello and Ivens, 1882: I, 224-5; Fonseca Cardoso, quoted in Mendes Corrêa 1914: 327
[46] Harding 1904: 237 [1899]; Diniz, 1918: 381 [c. 1912]
[47] Livingstone 1963: 52, 39 [1854, Southern Lunda]
[48] Livingstone 1963: 37; see also Cameron 1877: II, 177 [1875]; Capello and Ivens, 1882: I, 225 [1878]

'cheaper' materials than iron wire. The latter probably remained much more restricted because of its higher value (i.e. labour involved),[49] similar to ivory bracelets (*makai*), a Nuclear Lunda fashion adopted by Northern Chokwe but gradually replaced by brass wire.[50] Among the Southern Chokwe, imported brass or copper wire is even said to have ultimately displaced the 'serious men's task' of indigenous drawing of iron wire.[51]

No local predecessors, in contrast, existed for shells and beads. Generally, shells from different African coasts figure among the earliest 'ornaments' carried by long-distance trade. The high value attached to the *jimbe* medallion (and its later imitation)[52] may indicate very early contacts between the Upper Zambezi and the East African coast. But other shells such as cowries (*lupashi*) were generally low in demand in this region compared to neighbouring ones,[53] probably because there were few trade contacts to the coast before the region was flooded with European made *missanga* (beads).

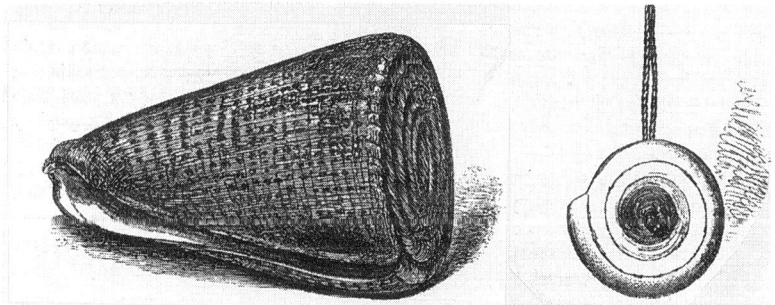

Fig. 22: *Jimbe* shell and medaillon made of it (1854)
This was the friendship gift of the Southern Lunda chief Ishinde to David Livingstone. (Engraving from Livingstone 1857: 300)

---

[49] Iron leglets and armlets, according to Lux, were valued much higher than copper; in Nuclear Lunda, only the ruler (Mwant Yav) was entitled to wear iron rings (1880: 122 [1875]).

[50] Lux 1880: 59 [1875]

[51] Schachtzabel 1923: 143f [1913/14]

[52] E.g. Livingstone 1963: 63 [friendship gift by Ishinde; Southern Lunda], 96 and 103 [an *imbe* shell demanded instead of beads, or as equivalent for an ox, slave or gun by Chokwe; all 1854]; Cameron 1877: II, 163, 169, 175 [1875, payment to Luvale fish mongers]

[53] Cowries are rarely mentioned in accounts of transactions or body fashions (e. g. as part of hair dresses of women) about the peoples of this region, nor were they recommended to be carried by travellers. In 1878, they were rejected as payment by the Luchazi, but 'greatly loved', in contrast, among the Lwimbi (Pinto 1881: 316, 2286); on the Ovimbundu plateau as well as in Nuclear Lunda they were used among other currencies for food purchases (Magyar, 1859: 259 and 1860: 232).

Beads were, and to some extent still are, widely used for necklaces, strings round the waist, hair or beard decoration, also on carved figures of ritual importance. Women were probably the main consumers of these adornments; around the turn of the century, early British officers assumed that 'the one idea of women is to possess and decorate their hair, bosoms and necks with beads to a prodigious and grotesque extent...'[54], and found that, among the Lunda north of the Kabompo, 'the clothing of women (consisted) mainly in glass beads and copper bracelets'.[55] Again, chiefs had no privileged access to beads, but they may have managed to accumulate more substantial stocks of this imperishable commodity which they then used to display in the form of embroideries on their clothing and on their chiefly headdress (SL. *chibangula*, Ch. *ipangula*), again a fashion imported from Nuclear Lunda, perhaps originally from Luba.[56] The earliest description, regarding a simpler version, was given by Graça in 1846:

> 'Their chief [Chibwika, Southern Lunda], sitting on the shoulders of a black, wore a red cloth decorated with beads and corals of different colours, very nicely made ornaments, and had his head girded by a braid of various symmetric beads, adorning his front by a collar of certain distinguished birds [feathers]...'[57]

There were various shapes of these beautiful crowns of several beaded tiers,[58] some of which I have seen personally on ceremonial occasions worn by Southern Lunda and Luvale chiefs. Parrot and other precious feathers, as well as certain baskets, were part of traditional insignia of power in Luba and Nuclear Lunda, and it seems that beads were simply added to embellish them and to mark richness.

At the beginning of the Atlantic trade, beads were acquired by inhabitants of the Upper Zambezi and Kasai perhaps even in return for export goods.[59] Later, they only them for a variety of smaller payments, e.g. presents, retail food or remunerations for dancers and musicians.[60] The general tendency, however, was clearly an increasing preference for cloth (and guns) for all types of transactions, as far as manufactured goods were concerned. David Livingstone, when he reached Luvale and

---

[54] Harding 1904: 206 [1899]
[55] Schomburgk 1925: 58
[56] Hoover 1978: 341, 529; Redinha 1963: 51; the terms mentioned are derived from the Nuclear Lunda original, but in Luvale I know only the term *muchama*.
[57] Graça 1890: 424.
[58] See e. g. Livingstone 1963: 52 [1854; Ishinde]
[59] Silva Teixeira, for example, mentioned in 1794 *Roncalha* [?] *missanga groça e fina*, besides various types of cloth, as principal trade goods for business (i. e. slave trade at that time) in Lovar (1940: 237).
[60] in contrast to the Lwimbi, for example, who around 1878 used to sell wax for cowries and beads to the Ovimbundu (Pinto 1882: I, 250).

Chokwe territories on his way from Bulozi in 1854, could dispose only of a few of the beads he carried for bartering foodstuffs.[61] He noticed 'something like an approach to the market': the people asked higher prices for their cassava meal etc.; and even women mostly refused to sell except for 'little bits of coarse *calico* 4 inches wide by 8 long' (the only other import commodity in demand being gun-powder). On the Chikapa, he offered 'a good return in beads' to a Chokwe man for a fowl and some meal, 'but these he declined saying he wanted a cloth instead.'[62] Cameron, in 1875, had the same experience among the Luvale: 'For a piece of salt I obtained one fowl; but the people would not even look at my remaining beads, being very eager for cloth, of which I had none for trading...'[63], as well as Pinto among the Luchazi and Mbwela to the southwest, who even wanted very specific types of cloth.[64] Only the *Sekele* aboriginals continued to prefer red beads (*missanga coral*) and tobacco as payments, while 'cloth has absolutely no value among them', which Silva Porto had already noted as a curiosity.[65]

This lower valuation of imported ornaments compared to textiles by many inhabitants of the Central African interior also found its expression in the overall figures of goods passing the customs in Angolan ports. *Missanga* (beads, without shells), for example, accounted for only about 7.5 % of Angolan imports via Lisbon in 1803.[66]

C 6.3 Textiles

Textiles were undoubtedly the most important of all imported goods in Central Africa during the pre-colonial period; as Silva Porto put it succinctly in 1880: 'The gold of these areas is cloth, and cloth fascinates the savages.'[67]

Again, there was a considerable variety of types. Non-cotton tissues, such as linen or woollen stuff, had played a role during the 18th century which was largely lost in the 19th; only woollen blankets (sg.*chivundu*, Lv.) continued to be in demand in the region. Cotton cloth had always

---

[61] E.g. Livingstone 1963: 80, 95 [1854]
[62] Livingstone 1963: 64, 96 and 235; he concluded that '... clothing is becoming more and more valuable every year. The coarsest prints & checks are used in the trade.'(*ibid.* : 72)
[63] Cameron 1877: II, 162
[64] Pinto 1881: I, 316 [on Cubangui and Cuchivi rivers, 1878]
[65] Silva Porto 1986: 340 [1847/1869]
[66] Vellut 1972: 87, citing Bowditch 1824
[67] Silva Porto 1885: 606

dominated the scene, and became a universal means of payment for products and services in the interior. By the mid-19th century, Portuguese and Ovimbundu traders made a basic distinction between the simple and rather weak 'trade cloth' (*fazenda da ley*), comprising four varieties, and more expensive printed or dark blue tissues such as *chita fina, lenços, panno da costa, pintado, riscado, zuarte*, with *baeta* as the most valuable type.[68] Around the Upper Zambezi and Kasai, however, people were well aware of differences in quality,[69] but these did not matter as much for them as colours, patterns and above all size.[70]

As a consequence of this widespread demand in the interior, textiles comprised an unusually high percentage of imports to Central (as opposed to western) Africa already in the 18th century, perhaps between 55 and 80 %, much of them from Asia.[71] In the 19th century, when most cloth was in fact European industrial imitations of Asian wares, the percentages of the import ledger were lower, but absolute amounts continued to rise: in 1844, Angola's official cotton imports via Lisbon totalled 140 *contos de réis*, equivalent to about 70,000 'pieces' (containing 560,000 yards or 512 kms of cloth) and representing 37 % of total imports; in 1884, these figures were at about 740 *contos*, or 29 %.[72]

This ardent desire for textiles among Central African peoples, in which the peoples of the Upper Zambezi and Kasai only represented a particularly marked case, appears understandable enough at first sight.[73] Morning temperatures on the Central African plateau are sometimes uncomfortably cool and may reach the freezing point during July and August. And indigenous textile manufacture was not very developed: skins, hides and leathers provided most of everyday clothing; raphia palms only occur far to the northeast, and the high quality cloth woven from its leaves (*mabella*) hardly reached the Upper Zambezi even by trade.[74] Blankets hammered by men from certain bark fibres seem to

---

[68] according to Magyar 1859: 293/94; Madeira Santos 1986: 55, fns. 1-7 [quoting Silva Porto, 1847].

[69] E.g. for the Luvale already Silva Teixeira, 1940: 237 [1794], and Harding (1904: 72), who saw senior chief Kakenge making 'a grab' at a bundle of *calico* [cotton cloth], 'feeling its texture with the air of a connoisseur'[1899].

[70] Madeira Santos 1986: 57 and fn. 1

[71] Miller 1988: 75, fn. 3, citing Richardson 1979; also p. 74, 76f

[72] Madeira Santos 1986: 56 [citing Lopes de Lima 1846] and 100/101 (the size of the 'piece' or *peça* was 8 yards by that time, according to Silva Porto 1986: 330); Ministério da Marinha e Ultramar 1889: 17f

[73] Cf. Miller 1988: 79f, who proposes these material arguments.

[74] It was mentioned, for example, by Baptista 1873: 223 [1805/12] and by Magyar 1860: 231 (erroneously called 'cotton tissues'). According to Silva Porto (1885: 638), who also describes the loom technology, *raphia* cloth was highly appreciated and bought by the

have been the main indigenous form of textile production around the Upper Zambezi and Kasai.[75] But their production was highly laborious, and they were therefore too rare and highly valued to play any role in day-to-day clothing.[76] Only elderly men and women were sometimes seen to have worn them.[77] Otherwise, bark blankets were used mainly for ceremonial purposes, such as initiation of both boys and girls, for ritual masks (*likishi*), and to wrap the bodies of the dead for burial.[78] Finally, cassava meal was traded partly in bags made of bark cloth.[79]

The general absence of any significant weaving industry among the peoples of the Upper Zambezi and Kasai, apparently even before the region was flooded with imported cloth, is nevertheless somewhat surprising.[80] Individual cotton plants, which are now seen in many Upper Zambezi villages, have been cultivated for a long time, at least since some time during the last century.[81] Men spun (and still do so) the cotton (*wanda*) from these plants into threads using a simple distaff,[82] but used them only for fishing lines, to fix decorative beads, cowries and charms, and, more recently, to mend clothes.[83]

The weaving of cotton thread on narrow looms into bands of coarse cloth, similarly to in West Africa, was apparently known in earlier times only among the Lwimbi (Mbandi) south of Bihe, and perhaps some western Chokwe.[84] This technology, which was also known on the Ovimbundu Plateau, may have trickled in from the Lower Kwanza, where it had existed since at least the 18th century,[85] but apparently never contributed much to clothing in the interior. Lwimbi strips of cloth in natural colours were formerly renowned as payment in regional trade.[86]

---

much more distant Ovimbundu - but it is never mentioned by sources on the Upper Zambezi and Kasai.

[75] E.g. Pinto 1881: I, 279 [1878; Luchazi]; Arnot 1969: 101 [1884; Mbunda / Mbwela]; Cameron 1877: II, 189 [1875, Central Chokwe]; Milheiros 1950: 70 [Ngangela]

[76] See Baumann 1935: 61f

[77] Pinto 1881: I, 279 [1878; Luchazi]

[78] On burials e.g. Schachtzabel 1923: 139 [Southern Chokwe, 1913/14]

[79] Yowena Samakayi, 24. 10. 1986

[80] See also Pogge 1880: 47 [1875, Northern Chokwe]

[81] E.g. Livingstone 1963: 77 [Luvale, 1854]; Pinto 1881: I, 254, 279, 339 [1878; Luchazi, Mbwela]; Lemaire 1902: 50 [1899; Northeastern Chokwe / Southern Lunda]

[82] On spinning see Baumann 1935: 76 [Chokwe]; Schachtzabel 1925: 122 [Lwimbi]

[83] Livingstone 1963: 77 [Luvale, 1854]; Capello and Ivens 1882: I, 231

[84] Schachtzabel 1923: 121 [1913/14]; Baumann 1935: 76

[85] Cameron diary, 5. 10. 1875, quoted by Heywood 1984: 36-7

[86] Schachtzabel 1923: 121 [1913/14]; I have not found any references to the use of Lwimbi cotton strips in regional trade with the Upper Zambezi, but the Luvale language has a specific term for them: *lipepu* (cf. Horton 1975: 290).

Among the Chokwe, such strips were used for chiefs' hammocks, which are incidentally also called *wanda* (sg.).[87]

Whatever bark cloth and cotton weaving industry may have existed in Central Africa, textiles made available by Atlantic trade rendered local production unattractive and soon destroyed it.[88] But what was destroyed (and replaced) by imports of *calico* and woollen blankets, at least as far as the Upper Zambezi and Kasai is concerned, was not a manufacture for everyday needs, but at most an indigenous source of 'wealth' (see below). Livingstone, in his diary, tried to explain in very suggestive words why inhabitants of the interior were so impressed by these imports :

'How wonderful is commerce. The prints of Manchester are by means of it brought to the centre of Africa, and seem so wonderful it is with difficulty I can persuade the people they are indeed the works of mortal hands. The *Mambari* told the Makololo, when questioned as to the origin of the prints so curiously written upon, that they came out of the sea. Beads are believed to be collected on its shore. It is now the same with these Africans and the fairy fabrications of cotton mills as it was with our ancestors and the silken robes of the East. The sea is the Tabrobane [classical name for Ceylon - Schapera] of the African, as a strange realm of light whence came the diamond, muslin, and peacock, was to our rude forefathers.'[89]

Livingstone suggests that industrially manufactured cloth had indeed some appeal of novelty and unheard-of quality for inhabitants of the African interior (above all perhaps the patterns and colours). But given the prior existence of indigenous equivalents, the enormous **quantity** of relatively cheap substitutes that foreign trade made accessible may, again, have been of much greater importance for them.

There is no doubt that the wearing of imported textiles as clothes increasingly did impress the inhabitants of the interior. By the turn of the 19th century, the ancient West Central African term for European or White (with *'ndele'* as its root), which had spread in the form *chindele* around the Upper Zambezi and Kasai, was understood by a Belgian officer to mean 'man in cloths' (*homme aux étoffes*); he grasped that it was not the different colour, hair, nose, eyes etc. which struck Africans about European appearance, but the very fact that they wore clothes.[90] This explains why at least since the late 19th century even Africans as middlemen or government employees are called *chindele*, provided they

---

[87] The root of this term, however, denotes simply the idea of something interwoven, and chiefs' hammocks were originally perhaps made of a tissue of indigenous fibres (Baumann 1935: 76f).
[88] Schachtzabel 1923: 121 [1913/14; Ngangela]
[89] Livingstone 1963: 32
[90] Lemaire 1902: 56

present themselves as 'civilized' in the European way, notably by adequate dressing.[91]

But he was wrong when he finally assumed that Ovimbundu visiting the Upper Zambezi and Kasai used to wear European clothes in order to advertise their merchandise.[92] By the 1850s, even at home Ovimbundu commoners would already wear at least a well-sized cloth (Pg. *pano*) round their waist, and perhaps a second one round their shoulders.[93] In the 1870s, carriers from Bihe were 'decked out in print shirts, jackets and red night caps, or felt hats.'[94] And those met by Lemaire in 1899 had even put on 'ceremonial suits', besides 'head coverings as dirty as manifold'.[95]

But many witnesses confirm that, apparently, such 'advertisements' were utterly unsuccessful: while being known for the most extravagant hair dresses,[96] the inhabitants of the Upper Zambezi and Kasai stuck firmly to their traditional way of clothing which European visitors throughout the 19th century found 'rude in the extreme'[97]. According to the following typical description from 1897, Southern Lunda clothing had hardly changed at all since the visit by Livingstone half a century before:[98]

> 'The men, in order to cover their nakedness, wrap themselves in some deer skin which they allow to trail between their legs; while, as far as for the women, they, poor creatures, have scarcely the traditional fig leaf'.[99]

These miniature loin cloths, as well as the slings babies were carried in, traditionally consisted of 'a few small thongs' or a strip of bark cloth. As the only concession to imported fashions, women began to use for these purposes 'a tiny scrap of cloth' measuring 'a foot long and six inches or less in breadth,'[100] and cotton strips. These were at least used as arguments in gift negotiations.[101]

When the first British officers arrived north of the Kabompo, they were still amazed how much 'their [the women's] attire is limited, and chiefly composed of beads and wire ornaments'[102], and that 'although huge amounts of *calico*

---

91 See above, ch. B 1
92 Lemaire 1902: 59
93 According to engravings in Magyar 1859: 451f
94 Cameron 1877: II, 182
95 *Ibid.* See also photograph in Johnston 1969, after p. 44
96 E.g. Coillard 1897: 604 [Southern Lunda, 1894]; a great number of references confirms the importance attached (and efforts devoted) to head decoration.
97 Cameron 1877: II, 165 [1875, Luvale]
98 Livingstone 1963: 36, 39, 57, 64, 256 [Southern Lunda, 1854/5]
99 Coillard 1897: 603 [Southern Lunda, 1894]
100 Cameron 1877: II, 165 [1875]; Livingstone 1963: 36 [Southern Lunda, 1854]

have come to the country through *Mambari* caravans, the people are clothed almost exclusively in antelope skins...'[103]

The Southern Lunda obtained less tade cloth to wear than their Luvale neighbours[104], but even the latter went as late as 1913, according to the Portuguese officer who led the demarcation team for the new international boundary, 'almost naked, and they continued to do so after we had passed, although we had spent in 1913 more than 100 kilometres of cotton cloth in the region.'[105]

At night, not even bark blankets were used, so that 'firewood, they say, is their only clothing', and fire 'the blanket of the rich as well as of the poor'.[106] This situation seems to have remained equally unaffected by long-distance trade; among the Mbunda on the Manyinga River, the Portuguese officer mentioned before noticed in July and August 1913, when morning temperatures were below freezing point, that 'the black, even in the villages, has no stuff to cover himself, and contents himself with fires: one sees men and women with their bellies scorched by fire.'[107]

Almost identical descriptions of local clothing, often emphasizing with a Victorian undertone the 'particularly indecent...state of nudity' of women[108], were also given for less remote areas in the west and north of the region during this period.[109] Visitors became soon aware that this appearance was 'not want in clothing, but a following of what is in their estimation elegance in dress.'[110] Livingstone even heard one Southern Lunda woman, confronted with his better-dressed Lozi-Makololo companions saying that 'she did not like the coverings of our men, it was too large !' 'Poor wretches...', Livingstone added full of contempt.[111] Another traveller argued that women considered themselves 'unworthy' to

---

[101] E.g. Livingstone 1963: 256; Capello and Ivens, 1882: I, 213
[102] Harding 1904: 55 [Southern Lunda, 1899]
[103] Schomburgk 1925: 125 [1906/07, Southern Lunda, north of Kabompo river]
[104] Harding 1904: 124
[105] Gago Coutinho 1915: 509
[106] Cameron 1877: II, 165 [1875]; Livingstone 1963: 36, 39, 64, 256 [Southern Lunda, 1854/5]
[107] Gago Coutinho 1915: 187
[108] Livingstone 1963: 57
[109] E.g. on the Central Chokwe in 1846 and 1878 (Graça 1890: 416; Capello and Ivens 1882: I, 197/8), on the Luchazi-Mbunda-Mbwela (and Southern Chokwe) in 1847, 1878, 1884 and 1891 (Silva Porto 1986: 325; Pinto, 1881: I, 269, 275; Arnot 1969: 101; Johnston 1969: 116); and on the Northern Chokwe in 1875 (Pogge 1880: 91; Lux 1880: 85).
[110] Livingstone 1963: 39
[111] Livingstone 1963: 47

wear the cloth they acquired.[112] Anyhow, there was a remarkable lack of interest in apparel, compared with neighbouring peoples.[113]

Only with the approaching of colonial rule does this fashion seem to have begun to change. Starting in the north-west, among Luchazi, Chokwe and Luvale, ordinary men gradually replaced their leather loin'cloths' by *panos* (Pg., one yard lengths of cloth), and women began to wrap themselves up to their ankles and bust with two smaller or one bigger piece of cloth.[114] (See various figures) This may have partly been a result of greater prosperity due to the rubber boom and other access to the market. A Luvale, who moved around 1920 from Portuguese territory into a remote part of today's Kabompo District to buy up beeswax (which he sold for cloth in Angola), recalls that people there were, in retrospect,

'very poor, they wore only bark cloth and skins. Cloth in this area was introduced by Towulu [local nickname for a British trader who used to buy up substantial quantities of cassava meal - A.v.O.]; and people were caught to work in other countries, from where they brought trousers. It took a long time until they were all dressed...'[115]

Other informants confirmed to me that European fashions of clothing became popular at least in these remoter parts of the Upper Zambezi mainly through labour migration, which began here during the First World War. Missionaries also made their contribution, presumably less through preaching the necessity to cover human nakedness than by establishing new symbols of social status and by paying their employees partly in clothes.[116] Today, trousers and shirts are regarded to be the essential minimum of decent clothing for men, and dresses plus *chitenge* cloths for women. Old women and men are sometimes seen with barely a cloth round their waists, which is now regarded as a sign of abysmal poverty.

It appears that when people in the region finally got accustomed to wearing clothes, they did this not for practical or moral reasons, but as an ostentation to mark wealth and social status. This meaning was prepared by certain developments that had happened already during the pre-colonial period, and qualifies the general statement on people's rejection of European fashions at that time.

---

[112] Graça 1890: 416 [1846, Central Chokwe]
[113] Pogge 1880: 46 [1875, Northern Chokwe]
[114] E.g. Frobenius 1988: 69f [Northern Chokwe, 1905]; Mendes Corrêa 1914: 327 and photographs [1903/04, Chokwe and Chokwe slaves of Luba origin]; Diniz, 1918: 125/6, 381 [c. 1912; Chokwe, Luvale, Luchazi / Mbunda]; Schachtzabel 1923: 121/22 [1914; Ngangela].
[115] Yowena Samakayi, 24. 10. 1989
[116] Cf. the excellent study of the role of missionaries in 'fashioning the colonial subject' through his bodily attire in 19th century Botswana, by Jean Comaroff (forthcoming).

Chiefs, their councillors and important headmen were the only local inhabitants who were prepared to imitate the European fashions displayed by *chindele* visitors to some extent, and wore cloth in various imaginative ways from early in the last century. This may have helped them to distinguish themselves from their followers,[117] but it is more likely that they only 'dressed up' to impress important visitors, notably other chiefs, traders and travellers. From 1846 on, European visitors regularly described the apparel of their hosts during receptions in very constant terms: besides the traditional insignia of chiefly power mentioned before, chiefs and some headmen used to wear a *pano*, usually red in colour, round their waist,[118] and a jacket.[119] Cloaks in black and red also came into use.[120] For the supply of these processed forms of cloth, local potentates depended entirely on their foreign partners. In the beginning, visiting traders were sometimes asked to sew cloth into jackets etc., since tailoring was unknown.[121] Home-made cotton thread was (and is) used at most to fix small beads on ceremonial wear, to stitch together small pieces of cloth ('handkerchiefs') into a *panno*, or to mend imported clothing.[122] From the 1850s, European clothes and a few other luxury articles (e.g. spoons and metal containers) were regarded as necessary for trading in the interior, but as gifts to local potentates, not for sale.[123] In the 1870s and 80s, shirts, trousers, shoes and especially uniforms (which were also often worn by Euro-African traders) came to be increasingly desired by chiefs in the region.[124] The ostentatious role of European clothing is illustrated by a particularly bizarre example, an Mbwela chief on the Kwando river who

'was the happy possessor of four coats, presents from passing traders; and evidently he thought it the proper thing to don them all on this special occasion,

---

[117] This distinction is explicitly mentioned by Lux 1880: 85 [1875, Northern Chokwe]; the same distinction was made in Nuclear Lunda (Pogge 1880: 237).
[118] E.g. Graça 1890: 420, 424 [1846, Southern Lunda chiefs Katende and Chibwika]; Livingstone 1963 [1854; consort of Southern Lunda chieftainess Nyamwana, who herself was, however, dressed in the traditional way]; Cameron 1877: II, 185, 187 [1875, Central Chokwe headmen and chief Peho]
[119] E.g. Silva Porto 1986: 330 [1847, Luchazi chief *Cabitta*, on Lutembwe River]; Livingstone 1963: 52 [1854, Southern Lunda chief Ishinde]; Arnot 1969: 151, 159 [1885, Central Chokwe chief Peho and Southern Lunda / Luvale sub-chief]
[120] E.g. Livingstone 1963: 54, 83, 252, 260; Capello and Ivens 1882: I, 177; Cameron 1877: II, 170, 185, 187
[121] Silva Porto 1986: 327/8 [1847, Luchazi chief *Quisembo*]
[122] Livingstone 1963: 49 [1854; messenger of Southern Lunda chief Ishinde]; Cameron 1877: II, 170 [1875, Southern Lunda / Luvale chief Katende]
[123] E.g. Magyar 1859: 294; Johnston 1969: 11 [1891]
[124] E.g. Livingstone 1963: 52; Cameron 1877: II, 170, 185, 187; Capello and Ivens 1882: I, 184; Arnot 1969: 191; Gibbons 1904: 20

while six of his men were rigged out with one coat among the lot, two of them considering one sleeve each, if properly adjusted, quite sufficient.'[125]

At least from the 1880s, woollen blankets began to be appreciated; in 1894, Coillard found the Luvale senior chief Kakenge 'draped in a thick blanket of coloured wool, under the shade of an enormous blue cotton umbrella held by a slave.'[126]

Fig. 23: Chief Kakenge and a slave (1895)

The young slave, in poor dress, offers snuff to the powerful Luvale chief, whose wealth is underlined by a woollen blanket. (Photograph from Coillard 1897: after p. 614)

Senior chiefs became more and more inventive in the staging of their power, whether real or aspired for; the famous northern Chokwe ruler Kisenge, near the lower Chikapa, presented himself in 1880

'having his hair in tresses two handspans wide adorned with plates of yellow metal, which Chokwe artists manufacture excellently, besides various strings of small beads and small tufts of scarlet feathers from the tails of gray parrots, which adorned the peak of his head. He wore cloths [*pannos*] of fine cloth; printed cotton, handkerchiefs and blankets of the same cloth formed a

[125] Johnston 1969: 11 [1891]

compartment in the centre of which Kisenge was sitting on a bare chair, posted on a lion skin...'[127]

Important chiefs had probably relatively more wealth to display, but they certainly had no monopoly on cloth and clothing. Other social groups possessed them as well, and probably gradually came to display their riches on special occasions. A group of Luvale carriers, freshly returned from the coast with the missionary Dr.Fisher and paid their salaries at Kavungu,

> 'celebrated the occasion by wearing every inch of calico (they) possessed. One had over thirty yards of cloth draped round and round his waist; others had marvellous headdresses. A man with two shirts wore one on his back and another on his head...'[128]

On normal days, and especially during work, however, people did not use their clothes, in order to them.[129] This, along with social differences, is also a reason why it is difficult to assess from traveller's observations when ordinary villagers began to possess European clothes.[130]

Thus, at least during the entire pre-colonial period the wearing of cloth or European clothes clearly represented only the tip of iceberg. So, paradoxically, much of the enormous efforts people of the Upper Zambezi and Kasai invested in export production and trade were devoted to the acquisition of imported textiles for most of which they had no practical use. The solution of this paradox was discerned only by very few observers, for the first time by Silva Porto in scanty words:

> '...although they possess cloth coming from beeswax, slaves and ivory, they keep it for ransoms and other exchanges, and make use of skins...' [follows description of apparel].[131]

C 6.4   Imports as 'wealth'

Some of these 'other exchanges' were clearly of an economic nature. In an earlier section (C 5.5), I have shown that towards the end of the pre-

---
[126] Coillard 1897: 611/12
[127] Silva Porto 1885: 581 [1880]
[128] Singleton-Fisher 1948: 91 [1898]
[129] Dias de Carvalho 1890: 326f [1886, Northern Chokwe / Nuclear Lunda]
[130] Luvale women, for example, on a photograph taken in 1899 show themselves in *pannos*, while more than twenty years later, another woman was photographed during fieldwork with as little clothing as already described by Livingstone (Gibbons 1904: 9; Antunes Cabrita 1954: 48
[131] Silva Porto 1986: 325 [1847, perhaps added to his diary only in 1869]

colonial period imported goods such as cloth began to be used as a means of payment even within the region for basic items such as foodstuffs. Local specialists such as blacksmiths, diviners or herbalists, who had normally received foodstuffs as payment, now often also demanded imported goods: cloth, beads, salt or gunpowder. Even piecework (*njongo*) within the village was sometimes remunerated in cloth.[132] From these observations, it seems evident that the use of cloth came closer and closer to money. According to the classical definition of money functions, it was not only a mode of payment, but also a medium of exchange.

> The importance cloth acquired in these internal transactions is reflected in a complete Luvale terminology of cloth lengths, adapted to current Portuguese and Ovimbundu standards, which White was able to record as late as the 1950s:
>
> '*chitau*, half yard, tip of fingers to elbow joint;
>
> *munjoka* or *mukwambwa*, yard, tip of fingers to middle of chest;
>
> *ngongeke*, tip of fingers to opposite shoulder;
>
> *luvunga*, fingertip to fingertip of outstretched arms;
>
> *chamutatu*, *munjoka* and *luvunga* combined;
>
> *chilala*, two *luvunga* lengths, described as four yards of double-width or eight yards of single-width cloth.'[133]

Already during the pre-colonial period, according to White, these terms

> 'ceased to denote merely a unit of measurement for cloth, and became a **standard of value** at a given time so that any articles could be bartered by fixing their values in this terminology, even if no cloth was actually involved.'[134]

Finally, according to the above observations, cloth was also an important store of wealth. This was obviously not a new aspect, given the use of bark blankets and indigenous cotton cloth described earlier in this section. The generic term for all these types of textiles is the same in the languages of the Upper Zambezi and Kasai: (*l*)*ihina*, pl. *mahina*.

It may thus be argued that cotton cloth became a fully-fledged money or currency in the region. This hypothesis, however, must be qualified in two ways. The amount of cloth circulating was not restricted, as normally with money; permanent imports continuously swelled this amount; the result was a strong pressure for inflation which outweighed the limited durability of cheap trade cloth under village conditions. The other difference is that cloth was not the only 'currency' that circulated in the region. Beads, for example, had a similarly elaborated terminology of

---

[132] Yowena Samakayi, 24. 10. 1986
[133] White 1959: 39; the *munjoka* and *chilala*, equivalent to the Portuguese *panno* and *peça*, were undoubtedly the most important units.
[134] White 1959: 40 (emphasis added)

measurements, and the small wire bracelet called *liseka* soon 'became the standard term to denote a small quantity of a low-priced commodity such as flour.[135]

These currencies, on the other hand, seem to have been mutually exchangeable. One could speak for this region the existence of several 'multi-purpose currencies', different from the findings of Bohannan among the Nigerian Tiv.[136] Cloth and its equivalents could in principle be used not only for 'subsistence goods', but also in what Bohannan called the spheres of 'prestige' and 'rights over human beings': around the Upper Zambezi and Kasai, beads, bracelets and cloth came to be given as marriage goods to future in-laws.[137] But the term 'ransoms' mentioned by Silva Porto in his earlier quotation hints at another use of such imported goods, notably cloth, which was of much greater importance here, namely as compensations or as payment to redeem hostages taken as pawns in the very frequent event of legal arguments:

'In every village one finds in the huts larger or smaller stocks of *calico*, carefully pleated and piled, which is never worn, but kept ready only for this purpose.'[138]

Finally, the importance of a goodly stock of cloth was noticed on yet another social occasion: 'But when they pay a visit to a friendly village, they absolutely overload themselves with cloth in order to make a good impression.'[139]

The importance of these social relations and situations under the specific conditions of Upper Zambezi societies are explored in the following part. Suffice it to say here that imported manufactured goods such as cloth, beads (and firearms) became highly useful for the inhabitants of the region in these respects, replacing or rather supplementing older regional products such as livestock, iron tools and metal ornaments.

This type of goods was commonly meant when people spoke of someone having *luheto* (Lv.; SL.: *maheta*) or *upichi* (Lv.). These terms may be translated as 'wealth' or 'riches'; etymologically they denote the idea of ownership, like in 'possessions'. A third equivalent (in Lv.) is *vikumba*, which originally suggested the idea of competition, 'goods surpassing in greatness'.[140] The division of labour and exchange within the region was sufficiently developed to enable an early integration of

---
[135] White 1959: 39/40
[136] Bohannan 1959
[137] Mr. Sondoyi, 24. 10. 1986; Yowena Samakayi, 24. 10. 1986
[138] Schomburgk 1925: 126 [1906/07, Southern Lunda]
[139] Schomburgk 1925: 125 [1906/07, Southern Lunda]

'wealth' into everyday exchanges, as a kind of currency. This led to improved possibilities of accumulation, which typically carried both economic and social meanings, and accelerated further market integration: 'A Chokwe measures his importance by the number of bales of cloth he possesses', reported a Portuguese trader in 1905.[141]

---

[140] According to Horton 1975: 142
[141] Quoted in Vellut 1972: 153

C 7 Conclusion Part C : 'Subsistence' and 'surplus'

After this rather detailed analysis of what happened to the regional economy in the era of 'Atlantic' long-distance trade, some answers to the question raised earlier in this book can be tried (see introduction, A 2): How the expansion of global markets in the 19th century took root in this particular local economy, which preconditions it found and which consequences it produced. Much of the pertinent debates on dependency and (under-) 'development' was referred to a model that distinguished 'subsistence' and 'surplus'. In my opinion, the results of the foregoing analysis illustrate fundamental difficulties with such a dichotomy.

One of the assumptions underlying this model was that production in pre-capitalist African economies was an essentially static, 'traditional' affair, and that its main rationale was the satisfaction of the basic material (or subsistence) needs of the producer and his/her nuclear group ('family' etc.). Alternatively, it has been assumed that the rationale of securing subsistence developed in African communities when they became part of a wider division of labour, ultimately the capitalist world economy. Their integration in, or 'articulation' with, the wider economy would thus require the existence of a 'surplus', either products or labour, beyond the 'subsistence' needs of the rural producers themselves which could be appropriated by non-producers through unequal exchange or coercion. Since the 'traditional' forms of production are widely assumed to have been transformed little in the process, this appropriation would inevitably result in a clash between subsistence needs and outside demands. This contradiction has been called, for example, 'the peasant dilemma', 'overexploitation of labour' or 'subsistence squeeze'.[1]

The myth of the 'subsistence economy'

In contrast to the first of these assumptions, producers in the Upper Zambezi and Kasai have appeared in the preceding chapters as remarkably innovative and open to experiments with regard to ways of procuring a livelihood. Major areas of innovation were ironwork, hunting, fishing, gathering and crop production; the latest and perhaps most important step was the introduction of cassava cultivation. It amounted to something like an 'indigenous agricultural revolution' as well

---

[1] I am aware that this is a simplifying synthesis of many versions of this hypothesis. One of the earliest and two of the later versions are: Wolf,1965, Meillassoux,1982, Bernstein,1979

as a 'revolution of diet' , and began before any significant impact of market forces, let alone planned intervention, can be suspected.[2]

Paul Richards has drawn our attention to such processes of indigenous productive change and advocates a non-evolutionist view seeing them rather as highly flexible attempts to respond to specific ecological and demographic conditions.[3] The cases presented here can in fact be seen as very efficient adaptations to a specific regional situation, characterized by low population density, marked climatic variations and relatively poor soils. But the example also shows the need to look at specific **historical** contexts. Productive change in rural Africa cannot be seen merely as a response to particular environmental and dietary constraints, as ultimately conservative attempts to find new equilibria between producers, their environment and 'subsistence' needs.[4] Even in the earlier pre-colonial economy of the Upper Zambezi and Kasai, substantial amounts of foodstuffs and tools were produced beyond the individual needs of the producer, not only as a 'normal surplus' (to cushion food crises), but also for various types of exchanges within and between different groups. A societal division of labour, first of all by gender and ecological subregion, most probably existed which individuals must have experienced as part of the normal meaning of their production and not as something alien to an 'attitude of self-sufficiency'.[5]

Attempts have been made to integrate such day-to-day exchanges, which must be assumed for virtually all precolonial African societies, into an extended model of 'subsistence', and to distinguish a 'subsistence sphere of exchange' or 'subsistence-oriented trade' from a sphere of 'wealth' or 'prestige', and from 'market-oriented trade'.[6] These latter are then usually assumed to be 'surplus'. Significantly, however, a separation between the circulation of 'wealth' and 'subsistence goods' can hardly be upheld for this region: iron tools, as central means of production, were at the same time important symbols of 'wealth' and, along with other such symbols (e.g. copper), regularly exchanged for food.

Since even 'prestige' goods were apparently part of (collective) 'subsistence', as they supported the necessary social conditions of production, 'substantive' economists of Karl Polanyi's school have

---

[2] See von Oppen 1991 and 1992
[3] Richards,1983:24f
[4] Cf. for example Coquery-Vidrovitch,1985:147f; Austen,1987:13 and 16f; the element of choice, resulting from social interaction, is emphasized by Harms 1987.
[5] Miller,1988:48; such attitudes certainly existed, but rather as an ideal than a reality. An attempt to reconstruct the forms of consciousness, under which local exchanges took place is made in the following part (chapter D.4.3.).
[6] Bohannan,1959; Gray and Birmingham,1970: introduction, p.3f

proposed to dispense with the 'surplus' concept altogether.[7] This would, however, also mean losing the critical intention behind this concept: that of explaining the material basis of exploitation by stronger social classes. The distinction between 'necessary' and 'surplus' labour probably retains some merit as an analytical tool for developed commodity economies with more or less uniform class-standards of life. Also, unilateral appropriation of labour and its products undoubtedly took place in pre-colonial societies as well, despite ideologies of reciprocity. But something like standards of 'home consumption' is very difficult to determine in the kind of economy analysed in the preceding chapters. Moreover, they would probably have had little bearing on the everyday consciousness of the producers.[8] In the following Part (D), an attempt will be made to show that for the inhabitants of the pre-colonial Upper Zambezi and Kasai the distinction between what they produced 'for themselves' and what 'for others' hardly mattered. Even if one insists on the question of inequality, it is necessary to reconstruct the very complex web of everyday transactions which took place under a pervasive ideology of reciprocity and were essential for both physical and social reproduction.

The costs of market production

The second of the assumptions mentioned above was that the production and accumulation of any substantial 'surplus' began only with the establishment of market relations. But the analysis suggests that in the eyes of local producers the coming of foreign traders and middlemen was not so much the arrival of a strange new 'market sphere', but merely an opportunity to widen the scope of existing exchange relations and accumulation strategies. The kind of goods demanded by these new partners did not require much qualitative change in the existing regional division of labour. Men found it easy to produce ivory, beeswax and fish or to carry loads to or from the market since their main sphere of activity had always been in the wilderness, outside agriculture. It is possible that already in the pre-colonial period certain groups of men, mainly the elderly, were drawn more into agriculture than hitherto; but this did not upset the basic complementarity between male and female producers. Female cultivators at upland locations, on the other hand, had long been used to producing crop surpluses for exchange with hunters and with fishermen in the lowlands. 'World market integration' simply meant, at

---

[7] See Pearson,1957
[8] See the attempt by Meillassoux,1979

the level of both female and male producers, that a part of the yields of their gathering and cultivation was diverted to new partners.

What they obtained in return was often not very new, either. Besides regional foodstuffs (carried as payment by caravan staff), it included traditional forms of 'wealth' from neighbouring regions (copper, shells, textiles, livestock), and imitations of these. The main attraction was undoubtedly that of new types of manufactured 'wealth' goods, and the fact that 'wealth' became much more widely accessible in the process.

Even if market integration, seen from the interior of Central Africa, meant economically mainly a spatial expansion of the existing division of labour, the structural implications or 'costs' of this process still need to be discussed. For pre-colonial Africa two crucial aspects of such costs have been mentioned: a growing dependency on unreliable, expensive and/or unproductive supplies of imported goods, and a lack of incentive for, or even a prevention of, concomitant increases in productive capacity. Both would have failed to 'produce healthy economic, social and political development' and possibly threatened the satisfaction of basic needs.[9]

It is in fact striking how little an increase in productivity occurred in the context of export production, mainly the domain of men.[10] The only major exception was the introduction of firearms which did facilitate ivory hunting to some extent. But firearms were 'means of destruction' rather than production, as they contributed to (though did not cause) the dispersal and decimation of once substantial elephant populations in the region, not to mention the exacerbation of social relations through extended violence and warfare. Nevertheless, the productive knowledge and the organization of labour the inhabitants of the region had developed in the course of the centuries evidently enabled them to respond very quickly to an enormous and fluctuating external demand for their products. Except in the case of ivory, natural resources were rich, the population scattered and mobile, and apparently extractive methods 'appropriate' enough to avoid destruction to a point where ecology would become a constraint of export production.[11]

Export growth seems to have been compatible to a considerable extent with increasing demands on food production. Men's tasks in cultivation did not clash seriously with the peak seasons of their non-agricultural forms of export production, except for fishermen who were specialized food producers themselves. In addition, export production yielded valuable by-products for the local diet, especially game meat, gathered

---

9   Alpers,1975:xviii, also 29-31; see chapter A.2.
10 This point was emphasized by Alpers,1975:29-31; cf. Rodney, 1973
11 Cf. the contrasting example of rubber exploitation in the 'Congo Free State' (Harms,1975).

'relishes', and honey- beer (mead). Female cultivators, the producers of staple food, were less marginalized by men's 'purely extractive activities', and less condemned to technological stagnation than has been described for other regions.[12] In spite of a fairly fragile savannah environment, and certainly without any outside support in production technology, they successfully began to grow substantial amounts of their staple food as 'cash crops', without experiencing for most of the period the kind of disastrous famines described for comparable environments in colonial Africa.[13]

The 'secret of their success', besides the social position of women which will be examined in the next part, was a continuing increase in productivity and diversity of cultivation along the lines of earlier innovations, especially the expansion of cassava growing for staple food, the spread of legume interculture, and the release of millet crops for beer. It must remain somewhat open whether such growth of output entailed costs in terms of quality of diet. It is possible that the dwindling supply of protein and other essential nutrients (in which cassava is particularly deficient), following the depletion of game in inhabited areas and the high risk for women going unprotected for extended gathering trips into the bush, could not be sufficiently compensated by the accumulation of small livestock (mainly for exchange) and vegetable protein (pulses).

It is fairly certain that world market integration, in this context, meant an accentuation of existing specializations, i.e. of the division of labour between men and women, uplands and lowlands. Consequently, the importance of intra-regional exchanges for access to essential consumer goods must have increased. At the same time, however, widespread violence threatened safe travelling for local producers and petty traders, and a certain part of regional trade began to be channelled through the hands of foreign caravans.

Virtually all essential consumer goods and means of production continued to be produced within the region, as imports were restricted to expressions of 'wealth'; producers even substituted successfully a part of these imports themselves (e.g. intoxicants, repair of firearms), and concentrated on only a few others (mainly cattle, guns and cloth). First and foremost, they were instrumental in a variety of transactions that ultimately ensured mutual claims on other people's labour and loyalty (see part D). But these imported 'wealth' goods also had material importance: They became important media of exchange within the region, gradually also in local and regional barter exchanges. These beginnings of

---

[12] Alpers,1975:30f
[13] See Tosh,1980

'monetization' provided an extremely powerful incentive for participation in trade with the 'Atlantic Zone'.

It was therefore in the sphere of circulation, much more than in production itself, that world market integration led to a kind of dependency which could eventually disrupt the bases of livelihood. Such disruptions are recorded, however, only for the very end of the period in question. The serious famines around 1911 may have resulted from a kind of 'overspecialization' in rubber production, in order to maintain a certain level of export earnings (cloth etc.) in spite of falling rubber prices, aggravated perhaps by pressures of taxation. As a result, producers of both sexes may have come to rely excessively on the purchase of staple food and have given up too much of their own cultivation.

However, changes in the division of labour, which are the necessary concomitant of any widening production, are never determined by economic conditions or developments in the 'forces of production' alone. They also represent changes in a variety of social relationships between producers and other economic actors involved in this division, both within the regional society and at the level of the wider market. There has been a structuralist tendency, for pre-colonial Africa, to see these relationships as more or less pre-determined. The paradigm of the 'subsistence economy' often went along with an emphasis on social balance and solidarity within more or less egalitarian 'communities', subsequently subdued and exploited by outside agents, while more recently the inequality of exchanges and power has been prominent on the research agenda (see chapter A 2).[14] Inequality is undoubtedly a regular feature in societal divisions of labour. But this does not render unnecessary the question of how the relations between its participants are actually constructed, what social meanings are attached to material production and (often uneven) exchange, and how these change in history. In pre-colonial Central Africa, it seems, there was particular scope for the re-negotiation and re-interpretation of social relations, which were in a remarkable state of flux. This scope is explored in the following Part (D) for relations within the regional society, and subsequently (in Part E) for relations with foreign visitors, mostly agents of the world market.

---

[14] See, for instance, Guy 1987, and the critique of equilibrium models for pre-colonial regional trade in Pottier, 1986.

Part D

**THE SOCIAL CONTEXT :
LABOUR, POWER, AND EXCHANGE**

One of the characteristic experiences of foreign visitors in the Upper Zambezi was that it was ordinary villagers, women and men, who tried in great numbers to find a market for their products and services. For reasons to be examined in this part, market integration around the Upper Zambezi and Kasai was, probably from the onset, socially decentralized and involved large numbers of petty producers. This leaves, however, the fundamental question of who ultimately had control over 'wealth' acquired by transactions with foreigners. This question is raised, for example, by a small but significant incident noted in Livingstone's diary:

'They have many fears, and ... but little reason to trust in man, for they are not permitted to possess much. A man who got some beads by barter from my people was seen passing us in order to dispose of them, for it was not safe to shew them at home.'[1]

Livingstone's observation is confirmed by inhabitants themselves in a sentence I heard repeatedly in the Zambezi and Kabompo Districts as an explanation for a variety of social tensions: 'We are too jealous !'

'Jealousy' (Lv. *lisungu*) in this context of control over material possession has a twofold meaning. On the one hand, it hints at the strong desire for, or claims on, other individuals' assets. Further below, I will look at the variety of social relationships which provide the material and normative basis for such claims. On the other hand, 'jealousy' also means the strong tendency by the individual owner to resist such claims and guard 'jealously' the rights over the asset for him or herself - just as Livingstone describes in his note. In a number of proverbs, social cohesion is invoked to counter the ever-present danger of jealousy and strife.[2] The individualism among the peoples around the Upper Zambezi and Kasai later became *topoi* in colonial anthropological literature, particularly with regard to economic behaviour.[3] Remarks on individualism, or fear of jealousy, already abound in pre-colonial reports on the region. Livingstone was particularly puzzled by his observations of eating habits:

'They will not eat in the presence of others, but retire to some distance or into the hut, carefully concealing the face in the operation... They believe that if seen eating certain kinds of food, porridge especially, they will become sick and die'.[4]

This custom is confirmed by Diaz de Carvalho for the Chokwe/Lunda area further north, and explained as follows: 'For the natives it is a point of belief ... that the looks of strangers on their meals and drinks can

---

[1] Livingstone 1963: 95 [1854, near Katema, Southern Lunda/Luvale]
[2] See White 1959: 13f
[3] E.g. Redinha 1966: 37; White 1960: 14; White 1959: xi
[4] Livingstone 1963: 57, 86/87 [1854, Southern Lunda]

transform these into poison.'[5] When offered meat prepared by his own people, Livingstone's Southern Lunda companions would only accept it raw to cook it for themselves at home.[6]

It has been argued that individualist tendencies were only the result of integration into the colonial 'cash economy'[7]. I will subsequently present arguments in favour of the hypothesis that personal independence and competition between individuals are rooted to a considerable extent not only in pre-colonial caravan trade, but even in earlier indigenous structures.

In the following chapters, I will try to disentangle the variety of social relations which form the reference framework for claims of individuals on each other - on their productive and reproductive capacities as well as their products. In this first chapter of part D, I will attempt to outline the two basic social positions of individuals with their respective normative bases as conceptual foci of 'society' in the region: the individual with his or her rights of personal ownership, and the 'villager' as the archetype for networks of mutual obligation or claim.

---

[5] [1885/86], quoted in: Diniz 1918: 131f
[6] Livingstone 1963: 81, 85
[7] E.g. Turner and Turner 1955: 36

D 1 'Owners' and 'villagers'

D 1.1 Individual ownership

Communal ownership within kinship units, with certain powers of group elders over labour and products, is a widespread stereotype in models of pre-capitalist, kinship-based modes of production.[1]

Around the Upper Zambezi and Kasai, however, as a general rule both equipment and natural resources brought into use by human labour are owned by individual men and women. Hoes, axes, fishing gear, weapons, household equipment and the like always belong to individuals.[2] Beehives and the trees on which they are suspended (though not the surrounding natural resources) clearly belong to the individual beekeeper who made and put up the hive.[3] *Málilo* fishing dams, pools or portions of a stream are in the first place appropriated by the fishermen working on them.[4] Last but not least, the same applies to agricultural land, for which personal ownership rights are acquired by bringing bush into cultivation through clearing.[5] In this case, the owner would speak of 'my field' (Lv. *wande wami*), rather than 'my land', because his ownership only refers to the product of his labour, not to the land as such. In other words, land is an abundant resource, access to which really depends only on labour.

The generic term used for such 'ownership' rights in Upper Zambezi languages is Lv.*wenya*, SL. *weni*. This term denotes a kind of fairly equal relationship, a strong personal link between the owner (Lv.*mwenya*, Nd.*mweni*) and other entities, material objects as well as human beings, with which he or she forms a union. It seems that, in the case of material objects, this link is thought to have originally been established by an initial investment of the owner's labour. If 'ownership' is essentially established by labour, individual rights of usufruct may be assumed to

---

[1] This is, for example, still the emphasis of Terray's famous attempts to conceptualize pre-capitalist modes of production in Africa (see Terray 1969).
[2] See Beck and Dorlöchter 1988: 255f; 2771
[3] Wendorf 1988: 160
[4] Cf. White 1956: 83; 1959: 10/11; Antunes Cabrita 1954: 41/42 [data from the 1920s]
[5] Cf. White 1959: 32; according to Antunes Cabrita, among the Luvale rights over agricultural land adjacent to a stream may also be acquired by the establishment of fishing rights over that portion of the stream (Antunes Cabrita 1954: 41/42 [data from the 1920s]).

have existed as long as essential tasks could be performed by individual producers. It is important to realize that, based on this situation, individual 'owners', men and women, have probably been the basic 'units of production' or decision-making since the beginning of Upper Zambezi economic history.

There are, of course, a number of productive tasks which cannot be accomplished by one individual alone. If others are involved on the basis of some form of assistance, they may also claim rights over the products (see below). Producers often try to avoid sharing their ownership rights by establishing some form of cooperation with other individuals, which means only sharing the labour but not the produce, or they resort to paying their assistants (see below) in order to preserve their status as independent 'owners'. Turner has rightly emphasized that 'the majority of productive activities involving collective work are carried on by men'.[6] This has partly to do with the shortlasting but intensive character of many tasks conventionally done by men (see above). But it would certainly be exaggerated to style the Upper Zambezi division of labour along the lines of 'female' (or agricultural) individualism and 'male' (or hunting) collectivity, let alone to explain this as an expression of virilocal residence patterns, i.e. a village 'community'.[7] As will be seen later, only some production processes are done communally when this is technically required, and both men and women are involved in communal as well as individual work; the product, however, remains always at the individual producer's disposal.

Widespread individual production can be seen as an important basis of the growth of market production. Developed rights of personal ownership undoubtedly already existed even in remote areas before the colonial period.[8] Foreign traders sometimes profited directly from the respect paid to individual property, since 'the natives (were) scrupulous in guarding all that has been entrusted to them.'[9] But many travellers became aware of the respect paid to individual property rights in a more painful way, when they were legally prosecuted because of allegedly infringing some of these rights. For example, to cut the tree marked by a beekeeper or even to touch his hive,[10] or to pick up a knife or gun (which was sometimes placed deliberately on the path)[11] resulted in heavy demands for compensation (*milonga*) by the owner. Such disputes with foreigners seem

---

6   Turner 1957: 31
7   Cf. Turner 1957: 20-31; and critique by White 1955: 112; 1956: 85f)
8   E.g. Schomburgk 1925: 127 [1906; Southern Lunda, north of the Kabompo]
9   Silva Porto 1885: 607 [Chokwe, north of Kasai; 1880]
10 E.g. Cameron 1877: 165, 186
11 E.g. Livingstone 1963: 96 [Southern Lunda, near Kasai, 1854]; Antunes Cabrita 1954: 70

to have been welcome because they constituted virtually a kind of taxation (part E), but measures were taken to prevent violation of property rights within the local community: 'No one seems ever to touch his neighbour's property through fear of the medicine or charms placed near them', observed Livingstone in 1854 with regard to Chokwe beehives.[12] The protection against thieves by charms is also reported for standing crop in the fields.[13] Theft from cassava fields was regarded as an offence, among the Northern Chokwe even as a particularly serious crime.[14] And among the Luvale it is bad manners to enter the house of somebody else, in order to avoid the slightest suspicion of theft. But the assumption that, in the 1920s, 'theft and robbery within the tribe [Luvale - A.v.O.] were completely unknown until a few years ago' seems to be an overestimation of the efficacy of these sanctions.[15]

Rights over various means of production meant first of all rights over the product, and, by extension, rights over goods exchanged for these products. These rights were the precondition for the vivid interest of individual petty producers in participating in the market, which regularly appears in 19th century sources. By the beginning of the colonial period, among the Luvale, the following were

> 'in fact considered as property of the individual: the house he built, his clothing, the weapons and all the objects he uses, the cattle, the fish he has fished, the game he has killed, and the food stored or ready for harvest. And of his rights over such property the Luvale has a very clear idea.'[16]

In theory, even the 'fields', i.e. the labour of clearing, can be sold. This does happen in the more densely populated areas today; in the past, transfers of rights over fields practically referred to the standing crop, and ended when it was harvested.[17]

The essential consequence of the concept of personal ownership as established by one's own labour is that the individual owner is basically under no obligation to transfer any part of the product to anybody else. All subsequent transfers of products to others, however socially imperative they may be, do not arise out of the production process itself, and do not infringe the concept of individual ownership. The idea of an

---

[12] Livingstone 1963: 106; also p. 94: 'Hives of bees are seen on the trees close to the path, and no one thinks of disturbing them except the owner. All fear the medicine which he has placed there.' [1854]. See also Capello and Ivens 1882: I, 197 [Central Chokwe].
[13] Ibid. , p. 120; Cameron 1877: 159
[14] Dias de Carvalho 1890: 685; Antunes Cabrita 1954: 69 [1920s]; according to the latter's own account, however, no Luvale hesitated to take a cassava root or an ear of millet during journeys, i.e. far from home.
[15] Antunes Cabrita 1954: 69
[16] Antunes Cabrita 1954: 54
[17] Antunes Cabrita 1954: 53 [Luvale; 1920s]

'inalienability of the product of one's efforts' (Miller) inherent in this concept of ownership has been referred to a context of production for one's own needs ('subsistence production' in the narrow sense).[18] But at least in historical practice this idea does not seem to have impeded the establishment of exchange relations, but was extended, probably from early times, without difficulty to goods which were acquired through 'gift' or barter in return for personal products (see above).

But apparently a difference was seen for goods that could not even in theory be obtained by one's own labour, but had to be acquired from strangers, and which had no immediate use-value, but were used mainly for circulation. This was the case with imported 'wealth' goods. Significantly, as already mentioned, there are special terms for ownership of 'wealth', notably Lv. *luheto* or *upichi*, SL. *iheta* or *chikumba*. It seems that these terms, instead of denoting equality or even identity between producer and product, emphasize the acquisition by purchase etc., and a certain notion of power or dominance, i.e. unequality.[19] A very similar difference is made in European languages between 'property' (from Latin *proprietus*, 'own'; cf.'ownership') and 'possessions' (from Latin *potis*, 'able','in power'). Unequality undoubtedly increased with the massive influx of imported 'wealth' during the 19th century.

D 1.2   Villagers' obligations

As I have mentioned in the previous section, the terminology of 'ownership' (*wenya*) around the Upper Zambezi is not only applied to the material objects of a person's labour, but also to other people with whom he or she is equally closely identified. The most prominent application is found in the term *mwenyembu* (Lv.) or *mwenimbu* (SL.) for 'villager', i.e. a person with inalienable relations to (and certain legitimate claims on) the others with whom he or she lives.

In Upper Zambezi indigenous terms a 'village' (Lv./Lz. *limbo*, pl.*membo*; Nd.*mukala*, pl.*nyikala*; Ch.*chihunda*) is not primarily seen as a spatial or residential unit, but as a group of kin residing together.[20] In

---

[18] Cf. the section on 'ethno-political economics' in West-Central Africa by J. Miller (1988: 42ff)

[19] See Horton 1975: 54 and 294/95

[20] The following account of the 'village' is based on data collected by myself, but also on ethnographic literature published since the early colonial period, particularly where it explicitly refers to 'older' structures (Schachtzabel 1923: 137 [Southern Chokwe, data from 1913/14]; Antunes Cabrita 1954: 37-42 [on Luvale; data from 1920s]; Baumann

pre-capitalist, agricultural societies, kinship is the most important set of relationships people enter in the process of production and reproduction. Kinship norms define the legitimacy of claims on others' assistance (labour) essentially as the most important 'force of production', and, even more importantly, rights over **future** labour, i.e. descendants or 'children'. Around the Upper Zambezi and Kasai, unilateral, matrilineal descent rules are clearly dominant, today as well as according to pre-colonial travellers' reports.[21] The affiliation to some matrilineal ancestor is an essential part of village identity, expressed up to today in the *muyombo* tree which is re-planted every time a settlement is newly established. In the last century, these shrines were apparently even more carefully attended to, and were brought regular gifts of food, at least among the Southern Lunda.[22]

Consequently, the male core of a village consists of a group of brothers born of the same mother ('uterine' or primary brothers), or at least of sisters ('classificatory' brothers or parallel cousins). The mother's brother (Lv. *natu*, SL. *mandumi*), if he is still alive, otherwise the eldest of the brothers, is usually the headman.[23] Other male members are typically comprise sister's sons and sometimes matrilineal grandsons. The female members of such a 'matrivillage' (Hansen) are mainly 'mothers' and 'sisters' (both primary and classificatory)[24] of the headman's generation, who were married in other villages and have returned to their sons or brothers after being divorced or widowed. They take the place of matrilineal nieces and grand-daughters who went away from the village after their own marriage, following the second dominant principle, that of virilocal residence: married women usually have to live at their husbands' villages.

Only these matrilineally related inhabitants of a village, i.e. the members of a localized 'minor' matrilineage, call themselves 'villagers' (*venyembu*). The wives of the male inhabitants (SL.*ngoji*, Lv.*vapwevo*), who according to virilocal residence rules live with their husbands as long as they are married, are not considered to be members of the 'village', their 'home' being where their brother/mothers/maternal uncles live. The same applies to their children. As long as they live in the village, they do

---

1935: 125 [Central Chokwe]; Turner 1957: 61ff [on Lunda-Ndembu]; White 1960a: 1ff [on South-Eastern Luvale, Luchazi and Chokwe]).
[21] E.g. Livingstone 1963: 216; Pogge 1880: 45
[22] E.g. Livingstone 1963: 275/76 [1855]; Cameron 1877: 159
[23] (Nd. *mwanta-* or *mweni-mukala*, Lv. *mwenyalimbo* (ancient forms); Nd. /Lv. *chilolo* (more recent form); Ch. *kalamba*; Lz. *mukuluntu*).
[24] In Upper Zambezi languages, parallel cousins are also called 'brothers' and 'sisters', and mothers' sisters as well as fathers, brothers are equally called 'mothers' and 'fathers'. This is what has been termed 'classificatory' relations.

belong, however, to the 'house' (Lv. *zuvo*, SL. *itala*) of their respective husband or father. This is an intermediate social entity between the level of the 'village' and the individual, roughly equivalent with the nuclear family ('household'), but centred around an in-married wife, or an unmarried female 'villager'. The children of the 'house', who are regarded as members of their mothers' matrilineal villages, tend to move there after they have reached a certain age (in the past earlier than now, at about six years), but at latest when their mothers return to 'their home' after divorce or widowhood. Only the children of sisters or sisters' daughters of the male core village members are customarily 'at home' in the village.

This pattern, based on matrilineal descent and virilocal residence, is remarkably uniform among the various ethnic groups living around the Upper Zambezi and Kasai. Only minor variations may occur, for example in the percentage of primary as compared to classificatory kin, or in the incidence of (always rare) cases of patrilocal or uxorilocal residence. For the Lunda-Ndembu, Turner emphasizes the matricentric (nuclear) family, i.e. 'the mother-child bond (as) perhaps the most powerful kinship link...'[25] For the Luvale, Luchazi and Chokwe, in contrast, White has underlined 'linear unity rather than a matricentric family',[26] and pointed to a higher percentage of nephews living with their maternal uncles, and at the fact that classificatory mothers outnumber primary ones. For him,

'the important and binding elements are the sibling ties between men, and in later life between them and their sisters, and their attachment to their mothers' brothers, and again later in life to their mothers.'[27]

Patrilineal influence from Nuclear Lunda and from Angola seems to have had a certain impact among the Southern Lunda and the westernmost groups of the region. There, adult sons tend to stay more often with their fathers than among other Upper Zambezi groups, particularly if their fathers are headmen, and at least as long as their mother stays there; patrilineal succession in offices or inheritance occurs more frequently.[28] Among the Southern Lunda a newly married husband is expected to live with his in-laws during the first few years after marriage.[29] Such differences in the composition of 'the' village, however, seem to vary according to a number of factors, not just ethnic affiliation. One of them is certainly the age of a village, since long-established settlements tend to

---

[25] Turner 1957: 62
[26] White 1960a: 6
[27] White 1960a: 7
[28] E.g. Turner 1960a: 7; Schachtzabel 1923: 137; Baumann 1935: 130
[29] Interview with D. Chipoya, Dipalata 14. 10. 86

contain more classificatory kin, i.e. a more ramified local matrilineage. Older villages are also generally bigger in size.[30]

One obvious implication of this structure of social relations within the village is a continuous change in village composition and a very high residential mobility of individuals, particularly of women: children move with their mothers from their father's to their step-father's, or, after infancy, are sent to their mother's brother's village - 'their home'[31]. Girls and young women marry out to various 'in-law' villages before they finally join their brother or son; young men usually leave their natal father's village to live with their maternal uncle and/or brothers, but often only until one of the brothers has succeeded to headmanship; at this or another point the other brothers tend to split off and to establish their own

Fig. 24: Small Southern Lunda village, surrounded by cassava plantations (1895)

The photograph features two men, possibly matrilineal brothers, sitting near to the men's shelter (*nzango*) at the village centre; two boys below a drying rack for cassava, women in the kitchen shelter (left), near to one of the main houses, and mature cassava plants in the background. (From Coillard 1897: after p. 604)

---

[30] Cf. Turner 1957: 63, 74
[31] Cf. McCulloch 1951: 25 (based on information by White)

village(s). This individualist tendency of village fission (see below, D 3), again, seems to be by no means new in the region; according to Livingstone, the inhabitants of the areas he crossed

'are scattered over the country, each in his own little village. This arrangement pleases the Africans vastly, and anyone who expects to have a village gives himself airs in consequence, like the heir presumptive of an estate.'[32]

Matrilineal kinship may be seen less as a firmly established reality than as a normative attempt to bind together individuals whose relations are often fairly strained. In this context, spatial mobility regulated by virilocal residence rules appears as a means to resolve or avoid social conflicts which always threaten village cohesion. Mobility seems to be one of the most archaic features of social life throughout the region, but particularly marked when reinforced by the strong background of hunting among 'upland' groups: 'Like all hill-men, they are wild and troublesome, continually roving about.'[33] In a somewhat exaggerated way, the Chokwe, to whom this remark referred, have even been called 'the incorrigible nomads of the *sertão*, the bantu gipsies'. That some normative value was attached to mobility even among the inhabitants themselves is reflected in the Luchazi song *tuvangendzi, vachokwe valema kwenda* (we are strangers, Chokwe, fond of travelling).[35]

Another corresponding feature of this structure of village social relations is a fairly high degree of personal independence, quite contrary to popular ideas of 'close-knit traditional communities'. Based on their personal 'ownership' rights mentioned above, both men and women, seniors and juniors interact to a considerable extent as individuals, not as group entities, although their relations are structured by different sets of expectations or norms of mutual obligation.

The most visible part of these obligations is the traditional pattern of communal consumption, which can still be observed in remoter villages. adult (i.e.circumcised) men usually eat and drink communally at the *nzango* (Ch. *chota*), the open shelter at the village centre. At least in the past, the beekeepers, hunter(s) and fishermen among them were expected to distribute part of their catch in the village in the form of mead and contributions to the 'relish' (*ifwo*).[36] But the idea behind this redistribution of 'male' foodstuffs was apparently not communal ownership, but that the producer 'shared out' (Lv.*kwazana*, SL. *anjana*)

---

[32] Livingstone 1963: 248
[33] Arnot 1969: 105 [1884]
[34] Figueira 1938: 334
[35] Quoted after White 1960a: 3
[36] Interviews with Headman Munyawu, Dipalata, 7. 10. 1986, and L. Chinzombo, Chitokoloki, 30. 10. 1986

portions of his own product to individual recipients, the in-married wives and other women of the village, i.e. to the individual 'houses'.[37] Among Lunda-Ndembu, 'a good deal of grumbling over the precise division of the meat and over the amount of food cooked for the men's group' would go on after a successful hunt, an illustration of the tension between 'the individual producer or killer of food and the group who by custom have claims on it.'[38]

Women usually eat separately at their individual kitchens together with their uncircumcised sons and unmarried girls. This is regarded as the traditional observance, although it is possible that in the past Chokwe and Luvale women also used to eat communally in a women's circle, even with their own separate '*nzango*' (shelter) next to that of the men.[39] In turns, they are expected to prepare their 'shares' as well as staple food from their individual fields (or those owned jointly with their husband) for the group male 'villagers'. This seems to reflect a basic idea that even in case of communal consumption at least staple crops are kept separate and are meant mainly to feed the members of the same 'house'. Even if wives cook for the group of village men each on particular day, this may be seen only as a way of the wife discharging her individual obligation of 'feeding the husband'. This observation, and a prevalence of joint field ownership by spouses (see below), has induced White to see nuclear or 'garden families' as 'the essential agricultural units in Luvale [read: Luvale, Luchazi, Chokwe - A.v.O.] society.'[40]

The relative autonomy of the 'house' within the village should not lead to the assumption that it is a homogenous unit. It will soon be seen that 'the garden family' rather embraces a set of particular obligations between individual men and women related in a particular and often conflictual way, namely by marriage (see chapter D 2).[41]

But the relative autonomy of the 'house' observed by White in the 1940s and 50s, and the concomitant tensions or 'jealousy' with the other members of the small village community are apparently not a recent development. They were already described by Livingstone among the Southern Lunda by the mid-19th century:

---

[37] This term was used by L. Chinzombo, Chitokoloki, 30. 10. 1986; cf. the translation of *kwazana* by Horton: 'to apportion part of what one possesses' (1975: 12); see also Turner and Turner 1955: 21; Turner 1957: 31/2.

[38] Turner 1957: 32

[39] Dias de Carvalho 1890: 467 [1885/6, Northern Chokwe]; Antunes Cabrita 1954: 39 [1920s; Luvale]

[40] White 1959: 29 and ff.

[41] On the application of the 'household' concept in this region see Beck and Dorlöchter 1988: 57ff.

'Each house has a palisade round it, and the door so made it resembles the rest of the palisading. They are never seen open.... They appear to be without a sense of security with regard to their fellow men... Each house makes fire for itself, and will not light its fire from a neighbour... Each digs his own little well and puts a shed over it, and strangers ask where these are...'[42]

The most important economic implications of the localized kinship structures 'villagers' are involved in are undoubtedly not communal production or consumption, but the distribution of rights over actual and potential labour. These will be the focus of the two following chapters. A certain function is also assumed by the village with regard to the allocation of other productive assets. Even if 'ownership' is in principle individual, complications with this principle arise when the resources or means of production are commonly used for more than a few years and may even outlast a human life. This applies to the sites of big fishing weirs (*málilo*), ponds and agricultural land, after they have been appropriated by an individual 'owner' through dam building, fishing with poison or bush-clearing.[43]

In these cases, more permanent land or water rights are established which may be transferred from the individual owner to others. A peculiarity of the Upper Zambezi, according to White, is the fact that even rights over resting land (fallows) are maintained: 'True abandonment occurs only when a whole village moves too far from a former site to make it worthwhile maintaining rights over **resting** land'.[44] According to White's survey of land tenure among the Luvale in the late 1950s, unused fallow land of individual village members, particularly after death, may be identified as belonging to the village as a whole. From this pool of land, held in trust by the headman, in-marrying wives and young or newly immigrated village members may be supplied 'The land of the village is potentially open to all lineage or clan members'.[45] A similar emphasis on communal kinship property sometimes seems to apply to water rights: fishermen in Zambezi Westbank told me they would allow (only) relatives to fish in their ponds or oxbows.[46] According to one early 20th century source, among the Southern Lunda

---

[42] Livingstone 1963: 45, 67
[43] The particular importance of ownership in these cases may also have to do with scarcity of suitable water or land resources in certain areas, but only more recently, since population density has always been extremely low in the area, and water and land abundant. The decisive aspect is apparently a long-lasting initial impact of labour.
[44] White 1959: 32; his emphasis
[45] White 1960a: 27
[46] Interview with Mr. Kandala, 5. 9. 85

even beekeeping and hunting was limited to 'the districts which belong to the respective village'.[47]

Even so it appears exaggerated to me to speak of the village matrilineage as a 'land-holding unit'.[48] In general, land is too abundant to cause any strong cohesion in this respect since individuals can always establish their own fields outside the village land; and in the case of fishing sites these are often too far off to suggest any close connection with a residential group.[49] In an earlier report on the Luvale, any maintenance of rights over fallows is denied, and individual land and fishing rights are emphasized.[50] Village rights over fallow land or fishing sites are probably claimed only under local scarcity of open land, as a means of excluding 'strangers' (unrelated immigrants) from the benefits of labour already invested in cleared land by the residents.[51]

'Strangers' have always had little chance of obtaining access to land over which rights are already established, unless they agreed to some sort of payment. This payment, however, was originally understood as a compensation for the labour invested in cutting the trees rather than for the land itself. It is always made to the individual owner of a weir, pool or piece of land, and the consent of the village head is not even required.[52]

On the whole, even more permanent land rights are predominantly kept individual. There are various forms of transferring such rights to other individual owners, and not necessarily only among members of the same 'village'. Both *málilo* and cleared fields or fallows may be inherited by close matrilineal kin of a deceased owner (siblings or nephews/nieces). Land gifts between matrilineal relatives occur more often than inheritance. Even more frequent, however, according to a sample of cases in the remoter Kabompo District in the 1950s, are 'gifts' of fallow land between unrelated 'friends'.[53]

The purpose of this chapter, to conclude, was to introduce the two conflicting poles of basic social relations around the Upper Zambezi and Kasai, individualism and the network of obligations and claims focussed in localized kinship units ('villages'). This polarity, in which the

---
[47] Schomburgk 1925: 127 [1906/07; Upper Kabompo]
[48] White 1960a: 12
[49] Personal observations; interview L. Chizombo, 30. 10. 1986. Many *málilo* and pools in Zambezi Westbank, for example, are owned by individuals from Chavuma, up to c. 100 kms further east, near the Zambezi (see also Hansen 1977: 226).
[50] Antunes Cabrita 1954: 53/4 [data from the 1920s]
[51] The Land tenure survey of White quoted before (see White 1960b) had apparently a bias towards the unusually densely populated Chavuma area.
[52] Antunes Cabrita 1954: 53/54 [1920s]; see also White 1956: 83; 1959: 33.

individual villager finds him or herself placed, has strong implications for struggles over the sources of economic survival and wealth, particularly labour. I have used the 'ethnographic present tense' here because I wanted to emphasize the basic 'logic' of this social structure. Pre-colonial sources confirm the continuity of these basic structures. It was not my intention to put forward any hypothesis on historical origin and change. Such changes will be discussed in the following chapters, when the relations outlined above are analysed in more detail. I do assume, however, that the fundamental structures of this society, individual ownership and dominance of localized kinship segments, combined with very high spatial mobility, which have been observed at different times until recently, go back to before the 19th century.

---

53 White 1959: 32

D 2 Sisters and wives

D 2.1 Claims on labour

The crucial relationships within the village are certainly those between men and women of the same generation. They first of all concern the distribution of potential labour force (descendants). Here, the deeper and permanent link between 'brothers' and 'sisters' (both primary and classificatory) must be distinguished from relations between husbands and wives. According to the basic norms of kinship and residence, siblings are separated after initiation, when the sisters marry out virilocally. But both sides ultimately strive to reunite because it is the sisters who provide men with their descendants (matrilineal nephews or nieces) on whom they have certain claims (see D 3). After a sister has returned to her 'home', it is the brother who is expected to support her economically in a similar way as previously the husband did, although this obligation is less strong and does not entail the same rights over her labour.

The scope of marriage relations, on the other hand, is much more limited, because they do not include rights over descendants, even when children stay for some time in their father's village. As a consequence, marriage usually lasts at most for the reproductive age period of the wife. Divorce in the case of sterility is frequent and apparently an ancient feature in this area; at least among the Chokwe it was rather ascribed to the man than to the woman.[1] Thus, marriage relations are much more a temporary agreement than in other cultures.

This does not prevent marriage from being an economically and sometimes also emotionally strong tie.[2] The main obligations involved in marriage regard claims on actual rather than potential labour, namely that of the spouses themselves. At least in theory, these obligations are not

---

[1] See Diniz 1918: 147 and 392 [Northern Chokwe / Lunda / Luvale and Luchazi / Mbwela; referring to pre-First World War data]; Baumann 1935: 124 [Central Chokwe]. Baumann assumes that divorce increased only with colonial rule, due to an alleged decay of 'ancient, severe marriage laws'(1935: 130), but this statement seems to refer only to the rare case of divorce following adultery - see below. According to recent data, over 80 % of all completed marriages end in divorce (Turner 1957: 62 [Ndembu], and Spring 1976: 188 [Chavuma Luvale]); and according to Beck and Dorlöchter (1988: 150), husbands in a Southern Lunda-dominated and in mixed Luvale/Mbunda/Luchazi/Chokwe village were on average already in their third marriage.

[2] E.g. Turner 1957: 78, on the Lunda-Ndembu.

unilaterally on the wife's side, but mutual, following the basic division of labour by gender (see C 3.1). The customary norms of conjugal life may be listed as follows:

Table 7 : The tasks of husband and wife (current village norms)

The **husband** has to	The **wife**, in contrast, has 'to maintain day-to-day life':
- cut and burn the trees on the fields	- cultivate the land
- to build a house for her	- offer sexual services
- respect the in-laws	- respect the family of the husband, treating them well [e.g. prepare food for them], as well as the visitors;
- procure cooking pots and other household utensils	
- make her a gift (e.g. a goat or a cow) when she gives birth to a child	- prepare the meals for the husband
	- care for the children
- give her a hoe for field cultivation	- keep house and utensils clean
- supply firewood (only Lunda)	- firewood (Luvale)
- supply honey as a snack and for beer	- fetch water
- supply meat or fish for the 'relish'	- harvest, soak, treat [peal] and pound the cassava.[3]

---

[3] After Milheiros 1948: 36; interview with Chieftainess Nyakulenga (Southern Lunda) on 23. 10. 1986; cf. also Beck and Dorlöchter 1988: 271 and 279

D 2.2   Rights over food crops

This normative context may shed some light on the social significance of the economic changes described in the preceding parts. At first glance, for example, the introduction of cassava with a subsequent increase in the number of intercultures such as pulses seems to indicate a shift in power relations among spouses in favour of men, because of its much greater stress on female labour (see C 3.1 and C 4.2). Cassava cultivation probably enabled husbands to pull out from the production of staples even more than before, because their intervention in fieldwork, notably for clearing virgin bush, is less important with semi-permanent cassava cultivation. Especially in the age of 'Atlantic' long-distance trade, it allowed them to stay away from home for longer periods in order to hunt slaves and ivory, to collect beeswax, rubber or fish for export, or to work for salaries as carriers and guides, without endangering the village's food supply.

Men, particularly those with wider social obligations (headmen etc.) may have had additional interests in cassava cultivation with its greater surplus potential. As so often, they could hope to convert power over food into increased power over people: to attract newly arrived relatives in order to boost the size of the village, and to entertain 'friends' and 'strangers' in order to improve their political authority (see below, D 3), and to establish valuable external relations (D 4). Cassava is particularly suited for building up food reserves because it may be 'stored' safely in the ground for several years. The more wives a man has, the more and bigger fields can be grown to improve such 'socio-economic' opportunities, e.g. to grow more millet fields (in addition to cassava) for beer brewing.[4] To expand their food-generating capacities through female labour was apparently the first reason why in the past, more regularly than today, important and/or wealthy men were polygynists.[5] At one of the first Lunda villages they approached, Livingstone's caravan was welcomed by 'the headman and his wives bearing a handsome present of manioc',[6] and this experience was repeated by him and other travellers many times afterwards. With the growth of caravan trade, it seems, wives of both commoners and chiefs were increasingly asked, even against their will, to devote labour time to feed their husband's foreign 'visitors'. In a Lunda/Luvale village, in 1854, Livingstone found that

---

[4] See for example Antunes Cabrita 1954: 42 and 52 [data from the 1920s]
[5] See for example Diniz 1918: 145 [quoting Dias de Carvalho] and 392 [on Chokwe/Lunda and Luchazi]; Baumann 1935: 124 [on Chokwe]; White 1960a: 9; Turner 1957: 281, 283
[6] Livingstone 1963: 36

'their generosity [in food - A.v.O.] is remarkable. This afternoon a woman refused some of our people, but her husband called out, "Give,give". She obeyed, scolding all the while.'[7]

And in 1880, a Chokwe chief apologized to Silva Porto for presenting him only with cassava chips, rather than meal, because all his wives had gone to chase the birds from their millet fields.[8]

Such observations led Harding, in 1899, to a very gloomy conclusion: 'Here as elsewhere in South Africa the women do all the work', while men passed their time 'hunting and paying visits to the different *kraals*.' Male visitors of his camp only carried sticks and guns, 'while the meal, and other commodities of marketable produce, is borne, and borne alone, by the "gentler sex".'[9]

It seems as if cassava cultivation marks the beginning of a history of women's subordination as 'subsistence producers', at most as 'unpaid family labour', to subsidize male export production, as happened in many parts of Africa after market integration began.[10]

But there are indications that women felt less disadvantaged by switching to cassava than the observations mentioned suggest. The crop became so much a part of female identity that, for example, the cassava root is used in girls' initiation rituals.[11] The 'subordination' hypothesis is also contradicted to some extent by the marked interest women themselves around the Upper Zambezi and Kasai showed in marketing cassava meal and other crops to foreign caravans (see part B 7). It is very likely, for example, that the 'gentler sex' in Harding's quotation above were actually women selling their own produce on their own account. Women may in fact have found some advantages in the new balance of power by gender brought about by cassava-based cultivation and by market integration.

Here we must look first of all at how the complex network of mutual claims between spouses over each other's labour worked in the field of agriculture. Particularly here, the general norm of individual field ownership is qualified by the strong interdependence of male (bush-clearing) and female (most of the cultivation, harvesting and processing work) labour input. Today, a confusing mixture of joint and individual field ownership between men and women exists. The older situation is probably a loose idea of joint ownership between husband and wife, based

---

[7] Livingstone 1963: 79
[8] Silva Porto 1985: 571
[9] Harding 1904: 56
[10] See Spring and Hansen 1985, who see the beginning of 'subordination' in the colonial period.
[11] See the description of the *wali* ritual in White 1962: 10

on the mutual claims of bush-clearing (for men) and of cultivating and processing the crops (for women).[12] As a rule, a husband has to supply his wife regularly with newly cleared fields on which she cultivates vegetable foods for the (nuclear) family. This means that, if fields are owned and worked jointly with their husbands, 'the basic principle is...that both have equal rights over crops', regardless of their actual labour input.[13] Even in case of divorce, or death of the husband, usually with subsequent return of wife and children to her brothers' (or maternal uncle's) village, she can still claim half of the produce from her fields.[14] Only the other half remains with her husband or his family, on the basis of his land rights established through the initial act of bush clearing.[15]

Husbands may, however, have their own separate fields whose products are only partly used for the family, but more for hospitality and gifts towards his matrilineal kin, 'friends' and 'strangers'. This is particularly important for elders and headmen.[16] Their wives are obliged to prepare food for such purposes, but they are not necessarily expected to take the crops from the joint fields. It seems that in situations where men develop an increased interest in such personal fields, or where bush-clearing becomes less necessary for some reason, separate field ownership for men and women emerges. As a rule, women may dispose independently of the products of their individual fields after they have fed the family, but they (or their heirs) obtain only half the yield (or value) after divorce or death, still under the assumption that the husband or his family originally cleared the field. Individual compared to joint field ownership thus means for the wife increased control over her products, but also higher risk. But both variants of land ownership mean, on the whole, that within the marriage agriculture is a basis of both economic security and independence for women, which is all the more important because of the high instability of marriage.[17]

In contrast, single women living in their home village before or after marriage only have individual fields. Their matrilineal male relatives are to some extent obliged to provide them with cleared land, taking the role

---

[12] Advisers to chief Ishinde, 25. 10. 1986 [on Southern Lunda], confirmed by Arnot 1969: 159 [1885; Southern Lunda/Luvale, north of Dilolo]; Johnston 1969: 125 ['all eastern Ganguela']; Pinto 1881: I, 255 [Luchazi]; joint cultivation by husband and wife seems to have remained most persistent among the Luchazi (see McCulloch 1951: 60/61), perhaps because millet, which requires regular bush-clearing, retained more importance.

[13] White 1959: 21; confirmed by Frobenius (1988: 75) on the Northern Chokwe [1905].

[14] Ibid.

[15] Beck and Dorlöchter 1988: 53f, pp. 81f. See also White 1959: 21f; Spring and Hansen 1985: 63

[16] According to the councillors of Chief Ishinde (ibid.), these fields are called iha da wuta (Nd.) - 'fields of the bow (or gun)', as the symbol of manhood.

[17] Cf. White 1960a: 40f; Spring 1976: 187f

of a husband; but this obligation is often limited to the first field when she takes up cultivation, and often fulfilled by merely handing over less fertile fallow land.[18] Unmarried women, who form a considerable part of adult producers within the villages around the Upper Zambezi and Kasai, therefore combine a maximum of economic autonomy with a minimum of security with regard to access to cultivable land.

Fig. 25: Chokwe woman hoeing a young cassava field (1930)
(Photograph from the Angola-Expedition of the Museum für Völkerkunde Berlin, reproduced in Baumann 1935)

Seen against this backdrop of customary mutual claims on agricultural labour and products, cassava-based cultivation offered certain advantages to women, too. On the one hand, it made them less dependent on always unreliable male support, particularly bush clearing, because cassava copes much better with poorer fallow soils and may be grown much longer on the same plot without significant loss of yield. This may have been particularly important for singles with weaker claims for male support.

---

[18] Beck and Dorlöchter 1987: B54f

Precisely the higher amount of labour involved, on the other hand, strengthened the bargaining position of women, particularly of married women. Firstly, cassava cultivation increased the amount of surplus staple food women had at their own disposal; they could use this surplus, if necessary, to acquire goods owed to them in theory by men, e.g. 'relish', tools or 'ornaments', and even labour (see below, D 4), and became less vulnerable to divorce or neglect. In this way, cassava significantly increased women's options of finding an independent access to outside markets, and ultimately helped them to consolidate their economic independence within the regional society.

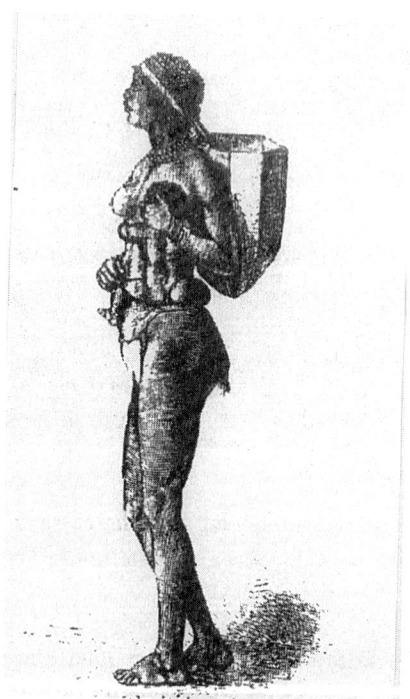

Fig. 26: Luchazi woman on the road (1878)

The type of basket on her back, for crops used at home or for sale, is not known in other parts of the region. The scarcity of ornaments underlines the young age and market distance of the woman. (Engraving from Pinto 1881, vol.I: 257)

Secondly, the monopoly of women over harvesting[19] and processing cassava meant not only more work, but also more influence. This monopoly, and the increasing scarcity of non-vegetarian foodstuffs in general, made men more dependent on the goodwill of their wives or sisters with regard to food supply. In the early 1930s, for example, Chokwe men were someimes seen begging for food at mission stations complaining: 'My wife doesn't give me enough !'[20] Men are particularly dependent on female labour if they want to give or sell cassava from their own fields or their share of the harvest to outsiders. Otherwise, they can only transfer the standing crop.[21]

Several potential uses of women's improved bargaining position vis-a-vis men can be imagined. One of them may have been demands for assistance with regard to access to markets, i.e. for protection and transport of their marketable produce, because of the distances and the difficult security conditions of the 19th century.[22]

D 2.3 Demands for gifts and sexuality

Another area of women's demands was almost certainly the redistribution of imported goods, i.e. attempts to get a share of the incomes of their husbands and brothers from participation in export trade. In theory, these 'incomes' in kind belonged to the individual male producers, carriers or traders themselves, just as the results of other non-food production. But they were potentially subject to a number of claims by their wives, according to the norms of conjugal life presented earlier in this chapter. Marriage payments may be seen as the beginning, and in some way as symbolic for this type of obligations on husbands.

Marriage ceremonies actually happened step by step over a considerable timespan, from betrothal (which in former times took place before puberty, when the girl was about 8 years old) until the bride was finally established at her husband's village, up to several years after the actual marriage. Each of these steps was accompanied by marriage payments, which traditionally consisted in series of distinct transfers of goods and labour, some of which were made to the family of the bride, and others to the bride herself. A compilation of data from the colonial

---

[19] See for example Livingstone 1963: 249
[20] Quoted in Baumann 1935: 124
[21] E.g. Antunes Cabrita 1954: 53/54; White 1959: 32
[22] Interview with Councillors of Senior Chief Ishinde, 25. 10. 1986; Headman Munyawu, Dipalata, 7. 10. 1986

period yields the following list of typical examples of marriage payments in the region:

Table 8 : Typical elements of customary marriage payments among the Chokwe Luvale and Southern Lunda[23]

Significance (occasion)	Item	Giver	Recipient
Betrothal (Ch./SL. chijikilo)	W	G	B
Visits during engagement	F(W)	G	B+P
Bridewealth proper[a]	W	G	B's U/F/R
'Pledge of good faith' (Ch. upite)[b]	W	G's R?	B's R
Support of in-laws during stay there[c]	L,W	G	B's R/F
'Taking up the bride'(Lv/LNd/Ch.kazundu)	?	G	B
Journey to groom's village (Ch.mishinga)	?	G	B
'Welcome presents' (SL.kusomwene)	W?	G's R.	B
'Opening the oil flask'(Lv.kavuku)	?	G	B
'Lighting the cooking fire'(Lv.kauku)	F	B's R	G+B
Presents to groom's family	W?	B	G's U/R
Gift exchange between families (Ch.yonda)	F	G+B's R	

Abbreviations:
W = wealth goods; L = Labour (fieldwork); F= Food; G = Groom; B = Bride
R = Relatives (matrilineal); P = Parents; U/F = Uncle (maternal)/Father

Notes:
a: Lv.matemo, mwivwi; Nd. nsewu; Ch. chihako
b: Only reported for Chokwe
c: Only reported for Southern Lunda

The bridewealth (Lv.*matemo, mwivwi*; Nd. *nsewu*; Ch. *chihako*), which was paid at the time of the actual marriage, in the past normally at the end of the girl's initiation ritual (Lv. *wali*),was always remarkably modest in this region compared to in neighbouring patrilineal societies, because no transfer of rights over dependants was involved.[24] The bridewealth was also modest in comparison to the variety of other

---

[23] Sources: Baumann 1935: 123/4 [Chokwe]; Delille 1946 [Chokwe]; McCulloch 1951: 23/24 [Southern Lunda]; 44/45 [Chokwe]; 65 [Luvale, Luchazi]; White 1955: 108; see also White 1962b: 9ff; A. Spring 1976: 178ff
[24] See Pogge 1880: 40 [1875]; White 1959: 51

transfers between the groom and his family on the one hand and the bride's family on the other. For example, the amount paid as *kazundu* to the 'guard' of a Chokwe bride by the turn of the century was considerably higher than the *chihako* ('bridewealth') paid to her parents.[25] The rationale of these payments must be sought primarily in a policy of establishing inter-family links (see below, D 4).

Nevertheless, they may also be seen to some extent as a test of the groom's ability to fulfill his obligations towards his prospective wife:[26] The bridewealth proper originally consisted, as indicated by the Luvale and Lunda terms, in a hoe or iron arrowheads; it may have also included an axe.[27] These can be seen at the same time as proof of the groom's ability to work iron (or to obtain iron tools and weapons by barter), to supply his wife with the required tools to till the land, and to hunt or eventually to defend her, e.g. against adulterers.[28] 'One or two metal bracelets and a genet cat skin' have also been mentioned as tokens used for bridewealth in the remoter past;[29] a similar meaning may have been attached to them. In addition, small livestock (goats, chickens) used to be provided by the groom and the families involved for the various meals during the ceremony; later, during the marriage, he was expected to present his wife with such prizes on certain occasions, e.g. childbirth (see above). The Lunda custom that the groom was expected to clear a field for his parents-in-law, or to go hunting or fishing with his father-in-law, while being rather resented by younger men, was explained by elders as a similar kind of test, although it was also justified as a kind of training: 'Our grandfathers wanted the husband to stay in their village in order to show that he was able to care properly for his wife and children.'[30]

The various presents grooms were expected to make to the bride herself before and during marriage ceremonies were clearly an even more direct prelude to future conjugal obligations on their part. These payments included fresh meat or fish during the period of engagement,[31] and clothing (originally perhaps home-made textiles such as bark cloth) for the bride at the onset of the marriage ceremony.[32] This corresponds to what today is regarded as a particularly important obligation of husbands towards their wives: 'to clothe her' (see above). I found no references as to what items the series of presents (later mainly money) that

---

[25] Fonseca Cardoso 1918: 26f; cf. Baumann 1935: 123
[26] Cf. Baumann 1935: 122
[27] Interview Mr. Sondoyi, 24. 10. 1986
[28] Turner (1957: 265) gives this last aspect as the meaning of the 'arrows'(*nsewu*).
[29] White 1955: 108 [Luvale etc.]; interview Chipoya 14. 10. 1986 [Southern Lunda]
[30] Interview David Chipoya, Dipalata 14. 10. 1986
[31] Costa Maciel 1948: 32
[32] White 1962b: 9

accompanied the various subsequent stages, from 'lifting the bride' to 'consummating the marriage' may have consisted of in the past.[33] Body 'adornments' regarded as 'wealth' may have figured prominently among these presents. Among the Southern Lunda, for example, iron rings seem to have been a frequent gift by husbands, since the favourite wife of a headman was seen, in 1854, with 'a mass of iron rings on her ankles.'[34]

It is significant that transfers of 'wealth' goods as marriage payments seem to have considerably expanded during the 19th and early 20th century, and that they increasingly consisted of imported goods. Copper bracelets, necklaces, 'white stones'(*missanga branca*), cowries, enamel plates, cattle, guns and above all cloth are remembered to have successively become important forms of bridewealth.[35] The continuous growth in the circulation of these goods may have contributed to a certain inflation in the bridewealth. By the beginning of this century, the bridewealth among the Luchazi and near the main 'watershed' route (Chokwe and Luvale) had risen to between 12 and 80 yards (10 pieces or *vilala*) of cloth, or one to two head of cattle.[36] At the same time, the value of other marriage payments continued to be higher than the bridewealth proper.[37] Such material obligations on male suitors towards their wifes continued during marriage, particularly if they were wealthy. The Lunda wives of Northern Chokwe were, in the 1880s,

> 'very well treated by them, and after a short time... distinguish themselves ... by the enormous quantity of beads they wear over their bosom, by their hairdress and their clothing...'[38]

The Luvale chief Kakenge, in 1894, demanded additional gifts from a foreign visitor on the grounds that he had already distributed the beads of the first shipment to his wives.[39]

These observations suggest that men often felt obliged to pass on to their wifes a share of what they obtained through their better external links , and such obligations may have been **one** of the stimuli for them to establish such links. The question remains unanswered whether this was just a new way of discharging their old obligations, or whether women

---

[33] The most detailed account of this series of transfers I found in White 1962b: 10-12
[34] Livingstone 1963: 37
[35] Interviews D. Chipoya 14. 10. 1986; Yowena Samakayi, 24. 10. 1986; Fonseca Cardoso 1919: 26f; Baumann 1935: 122 [speaking on the past]; Turner and Turner 1955: 19 [dto.]
[36] Interview Yowena Samakayi, 24. 10. 1986; Fonseca Cardoso 1919: 27; Baumann 1935: 122; see also Torday 1922: 268 [Northern Chokwe]
[37] Fonseca Cardoso 1919: 26f [Chokwe/Luvale]; Torday 1922: 268 [Northern Chokwe]; cf. Baumann 1935: 123 [Central Chokwe]
[38] Dias de Carvalho [1885/6], quoted in Diniz 1918: 144
[39] Coillard 1897: 614

acquired additional 'bargaining power' vis-a-vis men during this period. Besides their strengthened position in agriculture mentioned above, another resource comes to mind in which men depended almost entirely[40] on women and which may have become more precious than before during this period: sexual satisfaction.

Extra-marital sexuality ('adultery') was (and is) frequent and seems to be experienced as a continual threat by men who traditionally have no rights over their children and whose rights over their wives' sexuality are anyway temporary. Several early colonial administrators of the region showed themselves bewildered by what they saw as 'an exciting life of sexual luxury of which we cannot explain the origin': 'There is unmistakable proof that the morals of this community were of the lowest possible kind.'[41] What they referred to was clearly the unusually high divorce rate, the apparent tolerance of extra-marital relations, as well as to the deliberate use of contraceptives and abortifacients.[42]

It seems to be true that adultery was not usually a reason for divorce, which rather followed from apparent sterility of either partner, or from misbehaviour (i.e. non-fulfilling of obligations) by the husband. But early anthropologists described at least Chokwe men as particularly jealous, which was used as an explanation for the particular generosity towards their wives mentioned above, as well as for outbursts of rage in case of adultery or 'breach of faith'.[43] Adultery may have sometimes resulted in punishment or even murder of the wife,[44] but what it invariably led to were legal claims for compensation by the husband on the adulterer (see below, D 4). Such compensations were high, so that some men allegedly even tried to instigate their wives to commit adultery, as another way of access to others' wealth.[45] Luchazi men were known as being particularly liberal with their wives' sexuality; for example, they were reported as willing to share or exchange their wives with cross-cousins, 'blood brothers' or 'friends' (see below, D 4).[46] It is interesting to note the

---

[40] Homosexuality seems to have played a minor role, especially among the Luchazi (Diniz 1918: 391)
[41] Diniz 1918: 391; Harding 1904: 56
[42] The richness of medical and ritual treatment controlled by women, another indication of their relatively great social independence, has been examined by Anita Spring (1976).
[43] Dias de Carvalho [1880s], quoted in Diniz 1918: 144; Baumann 1935: 131
[44] Dias de Carvalho [1880s], quoted in Diniz 1918: 144; Baumann 1935: 131. Adultery by a selected wife of a Chokwe hunter (called *na kayanga*, 'woman who shares the vow') during his absence was regarded as a particularly serious crime, because this could result in unsuccessful hunting, and was liable for compensation or even sale as a slave (*ibid.* : 130); This example underlines the importance given to 'faith' between spouses. - Luchazi women were allegedly punished only when they got pregnant (Diniz 1918: 392).
[45] Diniz 1918: 392 [Luchazi]; Schönberg-Lotholz 1960
[46] Diniz 1918: 392; McCulloch 1951: 65

conditions of such arrangements: the co-husband had to maintain the wife for the period she stayed with him, i.e. had to take over some of the husband's economic obligations towards her.[47] As even within the marriage there is evidently some connection between the husband's transfers of 'gifts' and the wife's offer of sexual services, the step from such arrangements to prostitution does not seem great, and has been suggested for the colonial period.[48] But at least in the pre-colonial period, such exchanges of rights over married women were apparently confined to the local network. A systematic 'marketing' of women's sexuality to strangers along caravan routes, partly on their own account, but mainly as a form of exploitation, has only been recorded for unmarried girls of slave origin.[49] With regard to their freeborn wives or other female relatives, Chokwe and Luvale men rather tried to avoid the complications of such exchanges. The Luvale chief Kakenge, when he welcomed visitors from Bulozi in 1894, warned them: 'only do not take the *Balubale* for women.'[50] Despite the continuous import of female slaves, the presence of enormous numbers of male visitors (belonging to trading caravans) at the same time may have even increased the 'value' of women's sexuality.

D 2.4 Women's autonomy

The rather exceptional position of women around the Upper Zambezi and Kasai, to conclude this chapter, was ultimately based on their relative independence with regard to procreation, and on their marked personal rights over the products of their labour. On a logical level, these were implications of ancient kinship and residence structures.[51] But historically, they were probably the result of a balance of power which was continuously reproduced through social struggles, and which found new stimuli during the era of long-distance trade. Agriculture in general, and cassava-cultivation in particular, may then be seen as an important

---
[47] McCulloch 1951: 65 (quoting a manuscript by C.M.N. White)
[48] McCulloch 1951: 65 (quoting a manuscript by C.M.N. White); Philpott 1945: 52
[49] Dias de Carvalho [1885/6], quoted in Diniz 1918: 145
[50] Coillard 1897: 614; Schütt (1881: 125) mentions actual cases of such legal desputes over 'love affairs' with foreigners.
[51] A certain structural weakness in the position of women may be seen, however, in their relative isolation from each other. According to virilocal residence and the frequency of divorce, girls and women move even more often than men. This prevents sisters to establish as stable personal links as brothers in their home village; in their husband's village, they are as wives in a position of potential rivalry with his sisters, mothers and eventual co-wives.

scene of such struggles between gender, and as the economic basis of this remarkably strong social position of women in the region even during the era of pre-colonial market integration.[52] As a consequence, arduous cultivation work, skillful harvesting of cassava roots, and to have big, well-tended fields are important sources of prestige vis-a-vis men, but also among women themselves, while others are called 'lazy' or 'wild pigs'.[53]

It seems that this comparatively high status and independence of Upper Zambezi women was not seriously affected by male-dominated market integration during the late pre-colonial period; in some ways, their strong stand in agriculture even enabled them to take their share of the new gratifications offered by the market. This applied to both married and unmarried women. There was a probably a good deal of truth in the blunt note of Pogge's, otherwise not a very careful observer, in 1875, that 'the woman is free, and she keeps her own economy besides the one of her husband'.[54] 'The husband has no rights over the liberty of his wife', concluded another observer around the turn of the century.[55] Frobenius, writing on the Northern Chokwe shortly afterwards, came to a slightly modified conclusion: 'Women are respected, but removed from tribal life', i.e. presumably from the public sphere.[56]

There were also distinctions to be made among women themselves. Older women used to smoke hemp and tobacco and to drink beer at *lizaji* gatherings and 'work-parties' (see below, D 4) together with men even in the past.[57] Female chiefs are frequent, particularly among the Luvale, Luchazi and Southern Lunda.[58] Because of their claims on their husbands, married women seem to have been, on the whole, in a better position than unmarried ones, despite their own greater obligations. Similar as today, they may have used the period of marriage to prepare for their future period of divorce or widowhood by trying to find their own access to imported commodities. Single women had to rely even more on their own income generating capacity, because they had to fulfill

---

[52] Diniz 1918: 393 [Luchazi]; Baumann 1935: 124 [Chokwe]
[53] Beck and Dorlöchter 1988: e.g. 146; interview Chieftainess Nyakulenga [Southern Lunda], 23. 10. 1986
[54] 1880: 40 [on Northern Chokwe]
[55] Mendes Corrêa 1916: 329 [quoting Fonseca Cardoso, c. 1903, Central Chokwe, Luchazi and Luvale]; Diniz 1918: 393 [Luchazi; data from c. 1912]. Similar statements of subsequent dates are cited in McCulloch: 24, 45, 65
[56] Frobenius 1988: 75 [1905]
[57] McCulloch 1951: 65 [Luchazi]; communication by A. Lufuma, 30. 10. 1989 [Luvale/Chokwe]; according to L. Chinzombo (interview 30. 10. 1986), Southern Lunda women in the past used to drink only at home.
[58] This prompted Gibbons (1904: 8) to speak confusedly of 'pure gynocracy' [on the Luvale]

those needs on their own for which a married woman could make claims on her husband: the procurement of assistance and of those consumer goods she could not produce on her own,[59] and the satisfaction of a variety of social demands which increasingly required imported goods.

Seen from the opposite end, the relatively strong position of women was an important condition of pre-colonial agricultural change and market integration. Comparing with neighbouring regions,[60] it is doubtful whether the food basis for export production and caravan trade would have been as readily forthcoming, and whether market relations would have spread as widely without these marked ownership rights of women.

If the assumption of a potentially conflictious relationship between men and women is correct, however, it may be assumed that Upper Zambezi men were not very pleased with this strong position of women. They seem to have been prepared to accept the full rights of their first wives or favourite, but sought to expand their claims on the productive and reproductive capacities of eventual additional wives. The only category of women that could be forced to give up their normal rights were female slaves. This relationship will be looked at in the following chapter.

---

[59] Cf. Beck and Dorlöchter 1987: B76
[60] See above, chapter B 7

D 3   Children and slaves

D 3.1   Paternal frustrations and avuncular authority

What husbands of free wives perhaps found most irritating was the lack of control over their physical offspring. They could not even slap a naughty child without facing demands for compensation by its mother's brother, the legal 'owner' of the child.[1] All children's affection accrued to the wives or sisters-in-law of the father; even adult men 'talk(ed) perpetually of their mothers, "mama a me" [*mama yami*].'[2] Out of affection or fear of her magical power, even chiefs felt compelled to compliment their mothers with generous gifts which they tried to extract from foreign visitors.[3] Fathers, in contrast, could hardly command any such support from their wives' children. As long as his children were young boys or girls, the father could expect them to contribute in some way to the upkeep of the family, e.g. to fetch water and firewood, catch fish, mice, or moles, 'plait grass' (basketry?), to help in fieldwork (girls) or to accompany their father during hunting/beekeeping or even rubber trips in the bush (boys; see above, C 3.2).[4]

Juniors had to help seniors during these trips, e.g. as carriers. But in all these cases this was clearly only a temporary form of subordination. It had to some extent a meaning of training 'on the job', some sort of 'apprenticeship'. In more recent times, there seems to be strong tendency for fathers to be the main trainers of their sons.[5] One could assume that the relationship between father and son is preferred because it is more personal, and less formal and potentially tense than the one between uncle and nephew (see below). One consequence is that no specialization of entire lineage groups occurs. There are other cases, however, where beekeepers, carvers, hunters and fishermen have been trained by their

---

[1] Antunes Cabrita 1954: 37 [refers to the 1920s]
[2] Livingstone 1963: 95 [Southern Lunda / Luvale, 1854]; he also noted an incident where a young man physically attacked another who had dared to mutter some impatient words about a 'mother' of the former, an old woman who had continued to 'belabour' him for hours (*ibid*: 249/50). See also White 1960a: 36; Turner 1957: 62, 66
[3] Silva Porto 1885: 604 [1880; Northern Chokwe, Kisenge]
[4] Dias de Carvalho 1890: 467 [Northern Chokwe 1885/6]; Livingstone 1963: 249 and 263 [1855; Southern Lunda]; Schütt 1879: 181 [Northern Chokwe]; see also White 1959: 21
[5] Turner 1957: 29; Wendorf 1988: 94; Schmitter 1987: E13f. .

maternal uncles, even by fathers-in-law or unrelated men.[6] The factor deciding who becomes the trainer of a youth seems to be quite simply, with whom he (or she) lives, particularly during childhood. This is (and was) most often in the village of the father, but the latter can be certain that the growing capacities of his children will soon be lost to some other village (in the past even earlier than today). This was either the village of another husband of his wife (in case of early divorce), or the mother's brother's village, their 'home', where at least boys used to go around the age of circumcision, i.e. often at about 8 or 10 years.[7]

The maternal uncle (Lv.*natu*, Ch.*matu*, Lz. *nentu*, SL.*mandumi*), who was often the headman of their mother's village, has been described as the chief authority figure for juniors in the region.[8] In recent times this authority seems to have decayed, but there are indications that in the pre-colonial period sisters' children were in fact a more reliable source of authority for men than their personal children. The question is to what extent the relationship between mother's brother and sister's children included forms of exploiting juniors' labour by seniors, as described for other African societies by Meillassoux, Rey and others,[9] which could eventually be brought to bear on the emerging market.

Unmarried youths very seldom work for senior relatives today unless they are paid for it. In the past, this may have been different. As long as they were children, the tasks mentioned above must have accrued to their uncle's home after they had left their father's. The period during which the uncle could actually claim part of his children's growing labour force, however, was usually very limited in the case of girls since they were soon married off to other men, in the past immediately after they had passed their puberty ritual (Lv.*wali*). Young men, in contrast, tended to marry relatively late.[10] Old informants claim that in the past young unmarried men were expected to work for their father or uncle.[11] Such assistance in fieldwork was probably limited to bush-clearing., Like other men, juniors rather tended to concentrate on non-agricultural activities. According to a report from the 1880s, the more grown-up Chokwe youths spent their day

> 'with hunting, building or repairing the houses, with disputes, in which they are assiduous, trading the produce or the cassava meal and *farinha* prepared by the

---

[6] Turner 1957: 29: 'In his lifetime a hunter may train a number of apprentices: sons, matrilineal kin, and even the junior relatives of his friends and neighbors.' See also testimony by D. Chipoya, 14. 10. 1986; Chifwisha and Muwika, 22. 10. 86
[7] E.g. Antunes Cabrita 1954: 37; Fonseca Cardoso 1919: 25
[8] E.g. Diniz 1918: 147; White 1960a: 39; Baumann 1935: 125
[9] E.g. Meillassoux 1960; Dupré and Rey 1973
[10] E.g. Schachtzabel 1923: 137 [Southern Chokwe; 1913/14]
[11] Interview Mr. Sondoyi, Dipalata 18. 10. 1986

women, and during the hot hours they entertain themselves smoking, talking or playing games.'[12]

Here, again, the labour of young men was apparently of some benefit, not only for their mother, but also for their mother's brother. Among the Lunda-Ndembu, for example, village headmen presided over the obligatory distribution of game meat after a hunt, and the hunter himself was only entitled to keep certain parts of his kill.[13] The other parts were distributed in a strictly hierarchical way, with certain parts being reserved for the headman himself, the hunter's mother's brother, the hunter's mother, brother and even father.[14] It is likely that this Ndembu custom corresponded to the obligation of hunters further west to submit 'the major portion of every piece of game belonging to the chief of whatever dominion';[15] these 'chief's parts' (Lv.*usapu*), which are clearly distinguished from 'tribute' (*mulambu*), were due to 'the owner of the land', really the title of the (head)man who can claim to have first settled in the respective area, or his heirs.[16] Nevertheless, it is doubtful whether such claims were seen as based on ownership rights, or rather on the magical powers associated with headmen and chiefs.[17]

Magical capacities associated with village headmen around the Upper Zambezi and Kasai undoubtedly hint at a powerful social position. For example, during slave raids, according to Livingstone, elders used to be 'slain as likely to give troubles afterwards, if not by actual fighting yet not less certainly by means of enchantments in revenge for having lost wives and children.'[18]

The central theme of Central African 'ethno-political economy' (Miller) has always been the ambition to increase control over people, as the decisive form of 'capital', or better: as the main force of production and source of reproduction.[19] What ambitious men mainly struggled to achieve was, therefore, in Miller's words,

'not direct supervision over others, and still less stocks of the physical products of their labour beyond immediate needs, since both people and their fabrications were all too perishable, but rather a general claim to unspecified future labour

[12] Dias de Carvalho 1890: 467
[13] Singleton-Fisher 1948
[14] Turner 1957: 31
[15] Silva Porto 1986: 333 [diary entry 2nd January 1848; Luchazi/Mbunda area on Lutembwe]; also Livingstone 1963: 34 [1854; Southern Lunda]
[16] Silva Porto, in his last mentioned remark, compared such claims on part of the game hunted in an area with the claims of the owner of a herd of cattle (*ibid*). More on *usapu* in part E.
[17] Horton gives as the first meaning of *usapu* 'blood from slain animal, to be splashed on fetish' (1975: 321/22).
[18] Livingstone 1963: 94

and its product at whatever moment need for them might arise..., primarily the "symbolic" tribute usually glossed in modern Western languages as "respect".[20]

In the case of headmen, this meant that they continuously strove to increase or at least preserve the size of their village. It was mainly towards this end that headmen around the Upper Zambezi and Kasai demanded support from their young men.

Some of this support seems to have fallen under Miller's category of 'symbolic tribute' or 'respect', but headmen apparently needed support also for more 'immediate needs' in the context of strengthening their village: for the provision of food for fellow villagers in need, for visitors and for 'strangers' who could thus be attracted to join the village. This concerned 'relish' (meat, fish), but also staple crops. 'Headmen differ from others in using their garden resources to perpetuate their villages.'[21] Local power figures and their wives tried to satisfy their particular interest in increasing food supplies not only by putting more people to work (e.g. junior men or women), but also by investments in productive innovation.[22] The introduction of improved hunting and fishing techniques is one example, cassava cultivation another. I have found on various occasions that those producers who own the most numerous and sizeable cassava fields with standing crop are old people, often polygamists or single elderly women, who have not migrated for a considerable time. Particularly headmen are more involved in cassava cultivation than other men. The introduction of cassava cultivation served the interests of such resident elders in particular because it enabled them to receive more visitors. At the same time, it may have increased and prolonged their control over newly established young people and immigrants.

This again has to do with ecological conditions and the biological properties of the crop. The physical conditions of the Upper Zambezi and Kasai- sandy soils, altitude and distance from the equator, which result in relatively long and cool winters - have the effect of slowing down the plant's growth. In most local cassava varieties, the roots reach their full size only after 24-28 months,[23] and stay in the ground for sometimes as long a period again because they are harvested only for immediate consumption. Therefore, a full cassava cycle, from field preparation to

---

[19] Cf. Miller 1988: 42ff
[20] Miller 1988: 47
[21] White 1959: 29
[22] Cf. Miller 1988: 42, who assumes that greater labour investments were the main strategy of increasing the output.
[23] Cowsey, Shaw and Lesslie, no year: 46. In tropical lowlands the maturation period is only 12-15 months. (*ibid.*)

the end of the harvest, may last up to four years. During this period, new portions of cassava are planted annually. Four fields in all stages of growth are regarded by Upper Zambezi cultivators as a minimum requirement for economic self-sufficiency.[24] (See fig. 13) This means that cassava cultivation requires considerably more initial investment in both time and effort than grains until a new producer becomes independent of supplies of cassava and planting material (cuttings) from others with a more established cassava base. Thus, cassava cultivation became a means for seniors to attract more dependants (because it provided them with disposable food surpluses), and at the same time prolonged their dependency. In addition, it enabled them (or rather their wives) to reserve greater amounts of any grain crops for beer brewing in order to entertain their visitors, potential allies (see above, C 5.2). It will be seen in the next chapter that elders used their power over accumulated food reserves again not only for 'unspecified claims over future labour' (i.e. feeding allies or dependants), but also turned them into some immediate material benefit.

Headmen's most important demands on young men, however, were different. White has emphasized repeatedly that

'in the past a young member of a village would hand over any wealth or money to his mother's brother so that it could be used to pay compensation for a member of the lineage if the need arose.'[25]

This need arose in the case of legal disputes, which have already been listed among young men's activities. Such legal disputes were ubiquitous in the region and at least during the 19th century resulted with increasing frequency in violent feuds (see below). On these occasions, which could endanger the village's very existence, junior men, as warriors, were required to provide the fighting or threatening potential. Even without actual fighting, legal disputes threatened the size of villages because they usually resulted in demands for compensation, particularly for slaves or human 'pawns' (see next chapter, D 4). Only imported or exportable goods (cloth, guns, cattle, ivory, rubber loads) were accepted as equivalent to slaves; and if these were brought in by young men, they provided headmen with a precious alternative to giving up human life (i.e. both productive and reproductive capacities) from their village.

The question is, however, what means of coercion village elders had at hand to force juniors to actually comply with their demands. One could think in the first place of elders' powers over means of production. By virtue of being regarded as the first settler who cleared the bush in the area (or his heir), a headman in fact often holds the position of 'owner of

---
24 J. Beck and S. Dorlöchter 1987: B33
25 White 1960a: 27; also: *ibid.* : 39, and 1957: 73

the land' (Lv. *mwenya lifuchi*, SL. *mwini itunga*).[26] In practice, however, this position hardly amounts to more than a kind of trusteeship over any village land, a trusteeship directed mainly against 'strangers'. To deny access to land or productive fishing sites to junior village members is almost inconceivable, and would not be a very effective sanction anyway, as has been shown earlier (section D 1.2).

Another kind of dependency on seniors concerned newly established juniors' dependence on food and planting material, which was probably prolonged by the spread of cassava as a staple (see above). This may in fact have been a material reason why, according to old informants, young men did not have their own fields until two years after marriage, during which time they were expected to stay with their uncle, father or father-in-law and work for him.[27] But this kind of dependence could result at most in a delay, not a definite loss, of young couples' independence.

Access to wives was another central concern of young men as marriage was the key to greater social independence.[28] Wives had to be solicited from, and bridewealth usually paid to, the mother's brother (or the brother) of the woman.[29] But this means of authority could obviously not play such a key role in a strictly matrilineal society as it has been assumed for example by Meillassoux. Marriage payments were probably too little (see last chapter), and too easily accessible even for juniors, to create any major dependence of the juniors (and interest of seniors).

Yet another concern that could tie ambitious young men to their maternal uncles or senior brothers was the hope of inheriting headmanship from them, particularly if they had a powerful name. Headmanship in the region usually descends matrilineally, mostly upon a sister's son, often but not necessarily the senior one present in the village.[30] Less frequent is succession by junior brothers of the deceased headman, except among the Ndembu where adelphic succession between uterine brothers seems to be the more normal case.[31] But as matrilineal succession usually leaves several choices for successors, and as these were normally chosen by the other village members and not by the previous office holder, ambitions for headmanship increased tension rather than cohesion in the village.

---

[26] Such titles are frequently mentioned in 19th century sources, e.g. by Silva Porto (1885: 572 [Chokwe]) or Arnot (1969: 159 [1885; Luvale/Southern Lunda])
[27] Interview Mr. Sondoyi, Dipalata 18. 10. 1986
[28] Dias de Carvalho [Chokwe; 1880s], quoted in Diniz 1918: 143
[29] E.g. White 1955: 106; Pogge 1880: 40 [1875; Northern Chokwe]
[30] Silva Porto 1986: 326 [diary entry 16. 12. 1847; on Luchazi, Ngangela]; Pogge 1880: 227 and 243 [1875; comparing Chokwe with patrilinear succession in Nuclear Lunda]; Baumannn 1935: 125; White 1960a: 8

Two forms of such structural power-conflicts have been described in colonial anthropological literature: Among the Luvale and related peoples, conflicts tend to arise particularly between brothers of the same generation whose relations are said to be 'characterized by much suppressed rivalry and hostility'.[32] Authority conflicts between elder and junior brothers may also play a role, but authority is marked only when age difference is considerable. Conflicts may induce individual brothers who are excluded from succession to headmanship to move off and establish a new minor lineage with themselves as headmen. This type of village fission along lineage lines has been called 'vertical' by White.[33] A second type of tension has been identified among the Lunda-Ndembu, that between sisters' sons and mothers' brothers which may lead to the exodus of whole generational segments (groups of brothers etc.).[34] This 'horizontal' form of village fission, according to Turner, corresponds to the adelphic form of succession, the emphasis on generational affiliation as opposed to the mother-child bond and to lineage structures, and to the more pronounced authority of headmanship among the Ndembu.

However, the major threat village headmen could effectively bring to bear on their juniors was probably that of being given away or sold as a slave, in case of disputes, if no other goods were at hand. It seems to have been the practice, and right, of maternal uncles to fall back on their own nieces or nephews to pay for their 'crimes' or debts.[35] On the other hand, juniors themselves depended on their fellow villagers for protection and redemption when taken hostage or slave. Without clear affiliation to some authority, they could be subjected to what Masiko, an exiled Lozi chief near the Manyinga, was accused of in 1853: 'Masiko ... is guilty of seizing all the orphans , or those who have no powerful friends to look after them, and selling them to the *Mambari* for clothing.'[36]

On the whole, the increase of external threats to the very existence of villages during the 19th century may have helped headmen to assert their authority vis-a-vis juniors. They may have managed more than before (and afterwards) to turn this authority, if not into personal benefit, then into a strengthening of the village as a whole and hence of their power base. The prominent position of senior men in a local hierarchy found its expression in a complex system of prerogatives in eating, sitting and

---

[31] Turner 1957: 87ff; Schachtzabel 1923: 137 [1913; Southern Chokwe]
[32] White 1960a: 38
[33] White 1960a: 10
[34] But elsewhere Turner states that also among the Ndembu 'fission occurs most frequently between uterine siblings' (1957: 82).
[35] Livingstone 1963: 216; cf. White 1957: 71; White 1960a: 27 and 39; Turner 1957: 189
[36] Livingstone 1963: 24

greeting.[37] Younger men, for example, had to content themselves with elders' leftovers after these had eaten, and they were allegedly not allowed to drink alcohol, lest 'nobody would give him *nshima*', i.e. staple food.[38] White, in contrast, has denied that there was such a formalized recognition of junior and senior status through eating and drinking habits in Luvale as opposed to Lunda villages,[39] but the fact that he wrote in a different period may be a better explanation of this difference.

D 3.2 Unreliable juniors

I have my doubts as to the ultimate success of elders in appropriating the labour and allegiance of their juniors. For a start, high mobility and prolonged periods of absence due to the very nature of 'male' production meant that seniors' control of junior men's labour and income must have been fairly difficult in practice. This applied to work at home, but particularly to production or services for export. For instance, elephant hunters and rubber collectors, who often operated far from their homes, usually preferred to conclude their sales 'on the spot', when they met caravans *en route* or at some outlying buying camp, at their own production camps, or at far-off markets.[40] Their interest was most probably not so much in saving transport time and not only in obtaining better prices, but precisely in avoiding potential claims by village or lineage elders by hiding their income.[41] Guides and carriers would demand additional payments *en route*, even when their salary had previously been settled with and pre-paid to their 'father or owner' (village headman or real owner, in the case of slaves).[42] Employment by caravans was particularly expedient for juniors to start conducting their own business.[43]

The situation regarding access to the labour of juniors was perhaps slightly different with women. A stronger obligation was, and apparently

---

[37] E.g. Livingstone 1963: 56 and 81
[38] Interview Mr. Sondoyi, 18. 10. 1986
[39] White 1955: 99; see also Dias de Carvalho, who does not suggest such subordination of young men in Northern Chokwe villages either (quoted in Diniz 1918: 467 [1880s]).
[40] Capello and Ivens, for example, met a group of five elephant hunters 'belonging to *Mwene Chinyama*' (i.e. Luvale) far from their home, in a most remote area on the Kabompo River, on their way to Bulozi (1886: I, 440 [1884]; interview Mr. Sondoyi, 24. 10. 1986; Cameron diary 1875, quoted by Heywood 1984: 151).
[41] See also the note in Livingstone's diary quoted at the beginning of this part.
[42] E.g. Livingstone 1963: 242
[43] See below, D 5

is, felt by older children above ten years or so to help their mother, and the older a woman gets, the more respect and assistance she can command from younger relatives of either gender, even adults, finally even from daughters- or granddaughters-in-law. For young women, this obligation to help elder female relatives in domestic and agricultural work can today be rather burdensome.[44] But the decisive limitation of access of women to these services is 'proximity of kin', i.e. the fact that they often live distant from their family because of virilocal residence.

Contradictions in the kinship system itself also provided other defences against legal claims by lineage elders. For instance, as long as a child stayed with its father, the latter, without having any legal basis for it, could sometimes resist attempts by his brother-in-law to use the child as a pawn or slave to settle some dispute.[45] In other words, due to residence rules there was a certain factual balance of power between lineage and marriage authority, i.e. between (mothers') brothers and fathers, which juniors could play off against each other.

If both factual and legal 'children' were a somewhat unreliable source of authority for elders, they could try to fall back on other categories of juniors. One potential such category was, in the past, prospective sons-in-law or bridegrooms, especially among the Southern Lunda. As one of their elders put it: 'Our ancestors wanted the husband [of a daughter] to stay in their village in order to show that he was able to care properly for his wife and children.'[46]

Between the betrothal and/or up to about two years after marriage, i.e. for a period of up to about seven years, the groom could be induced to stay with his in-laws, to clear fields for them, to accompany them during fishing trips etc. He would also learn certain skills during this period, but his independence and rights over his products were clearly reduced during this time.[47] Older men therefore remember how they resented this custom, which is nowadays extinct: 'The husband was like a slave as long as he stayed with his parents-in-law'.[48] ('Slavery', as will be seen below, meant above all a state of being cut off from one's family and to be deprived of the rights of fully fledged village members.) If this was a kind of exploitation, however, it was certainly a temporary one, and therefore of limited use to elders in search of reliable dependants. A son-in-law

---

[44] See Beck and Dorlöchter 1987: B62-64
[45] Such a case is mentioned in Turner 1957: 189
[46] Interview D. Chipoya, Dipalata 14. 10. 1986
[47] Interviews Mr. Sondoyi, 18. 10. 1986; D. Chipoya, 14. 10. 1986; communication by White, quoted in McCulloch 1951: 23. The existence of such claims on 'grooms' labour' was denied, however, by L. Chizombo, an expert on Lunda traditions (interview at Chitokoloki, 30. 10. 1986).
[48] Interview D. Chipoya, 14. 10. 1986

cooped up in his wife's village could, in the long run, even turn out to be a cuckoo's egg: 'He could also try to kill the father-in-law [or wife's uncle ? A.v.O.] by witchcraft and take his position, if he was for example a famous headman...'[49]

Potentially tense relations between adjacent generations seem in fact to have been the reason why a special relationship between grandparents and grandchildren developed.

> 'To maintain its [the headman(ship)'s - A.v.O.] authority within the village on the one hand, and to prevent a disruption of the village as the result of struggles between different matricentric families on the other, an alliance develops between the senior and the second descendant generation.'[50]

Turner has termed this phenomenon, which is also expressed in the spatial pattern of opposed semicircles in Ndembu villages, the 'generational linking'.[51] Among the Southern Chokwe, this link played a role in succession to headmanship:

> 'In the first place, his [the dead headman's or chief's] own brother is considered, but if he doesn't exist or is too poor to hold such an office, one falls back on the male children of the sons [??] of the deceased, regardless of whether they are still young. But never can a physical son follow his father in headmanship.'[52]

At least in more recent times, however, the special interest of grandparents in their grandchildren rather seems to have worked in favour of the latter, implying generosity on the part of the former: 'The grandchildren receive a "subsidy" to the extent of being fed from their grandparent's garden even after they have grown up.'[53]

On the whole, village headmen were therefore forced to come to terms with their unreliable juniors. Even in the 19th century, much depended 'upon the tact and skill of a headman in maintaining harmony and hence stability of residence among those who live(d) together', and this wisdom has found expression in a variety of proverbs in the region.[54] As Turner put it in the 1950s,

---

[49] Ibid.
[50] Turner 1957: 79; among the Lunda, still today children have often much greater confidence towards their grandparents than to their parents, and they can talk to them much more openly.
[51] Turner 1957: 79f
[52] Schachtzabel 1923: 137 ['sons' may actually be translated here, according to the indigenous matrilineal concept of descent, as 'maternal nephews']
[53] White 1959: 30
[54] White 1960a: 14

'much depends in this society of individualists, only too ready to take offence, on the tact and diplomacy of individual headmen, whose best hope is not to browbeat or domineer, but to persuade and reconcile'.[55]

Without such skills, a village headman risked the dissolution of the village. Mobility of villages is generally very high in the region, and intra-village social tensions seem to be a far more important reason for this than the exhaustion of game or soils through extensive forms of land-use. The abundance of open land due to low population density is certainly the decisive material precondition for this tendency, but what usually triggers off the shifting of villages is either the death of the headman (i.e. fear of the spirit of the dead - an expression of past social tensions), or village fission due to actual conflict.[56] A typical event is that discontented junior men split off to found their own village in which they can be the headman.

Village movements and fission was probably no less frequent in the pre-colonial period than afterwards. Silva Porto, for example, described the Luchazi as 'excessively superstitious, and, similarly to the other tribes described [*Ganguelas*], they rarely stay in a place for a period longer than three years'.[57] In 1880, when he remarked to a solitary Chokwe headman north of the Kasai on the scarcity of food in his village, the latter replied in a talkative mood: 'Such it is; it stems from the moving away of my sons who dislike my peevishness...'[58]

The most reliable indicator of the authority of headmen, or alternatively of the frequency of village fission, is the average size of villages. Today, an average family 'village' or rather hamlet (Lv.*limbo*, SL. *mukala*) in Kabompo contains less than three households (Lv.*mazuvo*, SL. *matala*), i.e. around five actual houses, and the smallest are found in the remoter parts.[59] In the 1950s, Turner has put forward the following hypothesis on historical changes in Ndembu village size:

'...before the period of the slave raids most villages were about the same size as those found today in areas remote from European settlements, and ... during those raids some villages tended to unite into larger concentrations while others dispersed into still smaller units.'[60]

Reports on various parts of the region from throughout the 19th century emphasize the scatteredness of the population and that villages, except

---

[55] Turner 1957: 79
[56] Cf. McCulloch 1951: 24 (based on communications by White); White 1960a: 4, 6; Turner 1957: 41ff
[57] Silva Porto 1986: 325 [diary entry 12. 12. 1847]
[58] Silva Porto 1885: 570 [diary entry 5. 4. 1880]
[59] Alff, von Oppen and Shula 1983: table 0. 4. 1 (older boys and girls tend to have their own houses).

around important chiefs (see below) were usually quite small compared to in neighbouring areas such as Nuclear Lunda, between four and about 30 houses.[61] This suggests that, on average, village size and the authority of headmen were slightly higher than today, but remained very limited even during the 19th century. Only towards the end of the century, and only in certain areas close to the main caravan routes (e.g. Northern Chokwe and around the Kasai bend), bigger villages between about 35 and 150 houses were observed.[62]

Fig. 27: Stockaded Southern Lunda village seen from the inside (1904-07)
(Photograph from Schomburgk 1928b: facing p. 241)

As also suggested by Turner in his last quotation above (footnote 60), there seems to have been less linear correlation between village size and defence needs than is often assumed for Central Africa.[63] Throughout at least the second half of the 19th century, both big and small villages were usually fortified with palisades, trenches (Lv.*kembwe*, SL. *kembila* - a

---

[60] Turner 1957: 43-44

[61] Silva Porto 1938: 70 [1852, Western Ngangela]; Livingstone 1963: 36, 65, 275 [1854/55; Southern Lunda]; Magyar 1860: 229 and 232 [1850s; Chokwe, Nuclear Lunda]; Cameron 1877: 158/9 and 162 [1875; Southern Lunda, Luvale]; Pinto 1881: I, 273 [1878; Luchazi]; Arnot 1969: 156 [Central Chokwe, 1885]; Harding 1904: 204 [1899; Luchazi]; Lemaire 1902: 60-65 [1899; Luvale on Lake Dilolo]

[62] E.g. Livingstone 1963: 116 and 264 [North-eastern Chokwe and Luvale; 1854/55]; Wissmann 1902: 46f [1880; Northern Chokwe]; Lemaire 1902: 50-57 and 139 [Chokwe and Southern Lunda, near Kasai bend; 1899]

[63] See for instance Koponen 1988: 345ff

Nuclear Lunda technology), even pitfalls and sharpened sticks, if they were located in dangerous areas, particularly the Southern Lunda villages between the Upper Zambezi and Kabompo.[64] Among the Luchazi, in contrast, only the few capitals of major chiefs were fortified by 1850.[65]

The main factor in village size, however, was clearly a different one: the availability of domestic slaves.

D 3.3 Slaves as 'wives' and 'children'

According to Papstein's informants, Luvale villages prior to 1920 were larger than today because they contained many slaves, and in some large villages 'only three or four people were slave owners', the others slaves.[66] The unusual size of Chokwe villages around the turn of the century was apparently the result of their particular interest in acquiring slaves, and their reluctance to sell them, which has been remarked on by visitors since the beginning of the last century.[67] For the Chokwe, this interest was perhaps the strongest incentive behind both participation in trade and warfare: 'The Chokwe esteems above all the slave as possession. ...therefore in the Chokwe country travellers are offered slaves for sale only in exceptional cases.'[68]

The Chokwe were, however, only the most outstanding example among the peoples of the region. As described in the chronology, inhabitants of the other parts of the Upper Zambezi and Kasai did not only provide substantial numbers of slaves for export, but also kept many of those they had captured during raids for themselves. All groups bought slaves retail from caravans coming from the east or south, in return for ivory, rubber or even foodstuffs and imported goods.[69] Slaves were in effect yet

---

[64] E.g. Livingstone 1963: 45, 47, 60 [1854]; Cameron 1877: II, 158/59 [1875]; Harding 1904: 125, 137 [1899]; Schomburgk 1925: 56, 105, 125 [1904/07]; Venning 1953: 53/54 [1908]

[65] Silva Porto 1986: 332 [1847]; 1938: 72 [1852]

[66] Papstein 1978: 250/51. Cf. White (1957: 71) who asserts that the abolition of slavery during the colonial period resulted in a steady shrinking of large villages. For definitions of 'slavery' see below.

[67] See *Anonymus* 1803: 25; cf. Vellut 1972: 153 [on Chokwe villages]

[68] Pogge 1880: 45-46

[69] E.g. Livingstone 1963: 56 [Southern Lunda, 1854]; Cameron 1877: 167 [Luvale, 1875]; see the demands for slaves as 'toll' Livingstone faced when he crossed the Northern Chokwe areas in 1854/55 (see part E). During his anthropometric studies among the Chokwe around 1903, Fonseca Cardoso found that most of their slaves were of Luba origin (Mendes Corrêa 1919: 329).

another important 'import commodity', besides the ones mentioned before, which stimulated export production and became a kind of currency in intra-regional exchanges. Domestic demand for slaves explains a good deal of pre-colonial market integration in the region.

Slaves were, however, not only imported from abroad, and not only circulated through barter exchange. Although the number of slaves probably increased enormously, and their status may have somewhat changed during the 19th century, 'lineage slavery' (Lv.*undungu* or *upinji*; SL. *wundungu* or *wulamba*) as such can be assumed to be older than the Atlantic market for plantation slaves, although the latter may have had a certain impact.[70] An important indigenous source of slaves was provided by inter-village disputes. For any act causing death or injury, the aggressor's life (or the one of a substitute person from among his followers) could be claimed as compensation, usually in the form of enslavement. Increasingly, these claims could also be satisfied through the delivery of precious imported goods. If they were rejected, open violence could ensue, with captives being taken as satisfaction.[71]

> 'In the past the number of slaves in a village was to some extent a reflection of the strength of the village as a unit, since it showed how far it had been successful in exacting redress from other villages or groups which had committed wrongs against it.'[72]

In a rather different category of bondage, at least in theory, were human 'pawns' or hostages. Originally, they were handed over by debtors to their creditors as a guarantee for later repayment, or more precisely as a substitute person to take on the state of personal subordination created by unreciprocated 'gifts'.[73] The kind of people transferred in such cases were preferably young children.[74] During the 19th century, their status began to resemble that of actual slaves (Lv.*vandungu* or *tupinji*), involving permanent separation from their families and the danger of being sold to traders. The difference is still reflected in a special term

---

[70] The main anthropological sources I have used for the following discussion of 'lineage slavery' in the region are Turner 1957: 188ff [Lunda-Ndembu]; White 1957: 71ff and Papstein 1978: 222ff and 250ff; unlike Papstein (1978: 223), I found these descriptions to be well comparable, regardless of eventual differences in the 'superstructure' of chieftainship. On the relation between slavery and the lineage system in West Central Africa in general see Miller 1981.

[71] This difference seems to be preserved in the Ndembu language, as Fisher (1984: 87/88) translates *mulamba* as a 'captured slave', and *ndungu* as a person born or 'bought' as a slave.

[72] White 1957: 71

[73] On the institution and logic of pawnship in West Central Africa in general see Douglas 1964, and Miller 1988: 51f; and the detailed case study by Douglas (1963) on the Lele (northern neighbours of the Chokwe).

[74] Turner 1957: 189

(Lv. *topo*) (see more under D 4.4).[75], but during the 19th century, the boundaries between different categories of bondage became increasingly blurred.[76]

Out of the slaves who could be acquired by the inhabitants of the region in one of the ways described, women were particularly sought after, while men were more often sold to caravans going west.[77] (See fig. 3) It was estimated in the early 20th century that 80% of the women in some Chokwe villages were slaves.[78] At that time, most men seem to have tried to obtain slave women, either as a way to early overcome bachelorhood, or as concubines to a free wife who, however, would retain a privileged status.[79]

The widespread occurrence of slaves within the population of the Upper Zambezi and Kasai led Dias de Carvalho to the conclusion that slavery was, by the 1880s, 'a social necessity for these peoples'.[80] If this was anything more than an apology for the slowness of Portuguese authorities to effectively suppress slavery in their colony, the question arises of what exactly made the possession of slaves so attractive for the inhabitants of this region: were slaves a better alternative, in the eyes of seniors in general and men in particular, to find obedient wives and faithful children ?

Similarly to in other parts of the world, slaves were permanently unfree and legally regarded as chattels or material wealth which could, for example, be transacted and inherited at will, and for whose deeds the owner (Lv. *mwata*) was fully responsible.[81] In other words, slavery meant strictly unilateral, non-reciprocal claims between the owner and the slave.[82] The other decisive legal aspect of indigenous slavery was that it cut the person off from her or his own kinship and its claims; slave status meant in fact being forced to adopt a completely new social identity, one which was determined entirely by the owner. The 'social death' implied in enslavement often meant an enormous psychological strain (see next

---

[75] Cf. the difference between *dungu* and *fuka* made among the Ovimbundu in the 1850s (Magyar 1859: 286).
[76] See also van Binsbergen 1992: 126f (on the neighbouring Nkoya)
[77] e.g. Magyar 1860: 234 [Luvale; 1850s]; Pinto 1881: I, 257f
[78] Miller 1970: 181 (quoting Mendes Corrêa 1919: 329; but this quotation is incorrect)
[79] E.g. Dias de Carvalho [1880s], quoted in Diniz 1918: 144; Schütt 1879: 202; Baumann 1935: 124 [all on Chokwe]; Turner 1957: 190 [Lunda-Ndembu]; cf. Magyar 1859: 286f [1850s, on Ovimbundu]
[80] Dias de Carvalho 1890: 676
[81] White 1957: 71-72 [Luvale]; Turner 1957: 190 [Lunda-Ndembu]
[82] Papstein 1978: 225 [Luvale]

chapter), although under particular conditions some people may have also found a certain comfort and protection in it.[83]

Slave wives and children in a matrilineal society undoubtedly offered a man unique rights over descendants. Slave wives, their children, and other slave children were personal property of their owner, and did not become members of the village lineage; but they did increase the number of people living permanently in the village, and hence the following of the headman.[84] This is why the Chokwe used to distinguish between the 'wife of the marriage' and the 'wife of the village' (*pwo lya ha chihunda*).[85] Equally, the children of slave wives and free fathers, who retained slave status, were called among the Luvale *vana vahembo*, 'children of the village', while a free person was called *mwana kachisemi*, 'a child of its parentage'.[86]

To have children from slave wives seems to have reduced tensions between free juniors and seniors in the village. For the headman, it was a welcome increase of dependent village members, while at the same time it meant additional independence for the father of these children, if he was not the headman himself. He no longer depended on his maternal uncle to arrange marriage for him. To acquire or redeem[87] a slave wife cost him a modest price he could earn by export production or work for a caravan, or a venture into inter-village fighting, but she bore him children of his own and freed him from paying bridewealth and the other, rather more burdensome obligations towards his in-laws.

A male slave could be allowed by the owner to marry a free wife, but had to pay bridewealth for her. In this case their children were free, but the wife had to stay with her husband, i.e. in his owner's village, again augmenting the number of people under the latter's control.[88] This arrangement was particularly beneficial to the owner if his slave married his own sister's daughter; he was then entitled to both the bridewealth and

---

[83] See the remarks of Magyar on Ovimbundu slavery: '... even free people make themselves voluntarily into slaves of some powerful lord, if they are poor and persecuted due to some crime or debt, in order to escape the danger. For from the moment when they renounce their freedom and become slaves, they are seen as dead with regard to everything that has happened before, and a veil is thrown over all their previous offences' (1859: 289).

[84] White 1957: 71/72

[85] Dellille 1946

[86] White 1957: 71-72

[87] If a Chokwe man wanted to marry a woman resident in the village who was a slave, he needed the consent of her owner and had to pay for her redemption (Baumann 1935: 129).

[88] Baumann 1935: 129 [Chokwe]; Turner 1957: 190 [Ndembu];

permanent control over that daughter and her children, since they would not have to live in a strange village during the marriage.[89]

Obviously, slaves became fully integrated into the system of matrilineal descent and virilocal residence rules in order to turn slave ownership into power over dependants. The transformation of slaves into peripheral 'relatives' with a permanently junior status[90] is also reflected terminologically, as slaves referred to their owners as *nkaka* (Lv.*kaka*), 'grandparent', and applied corresponding kinship terms to the relatives of their owner.[91] Schütt saw the fact that 'bought or captured slaves are immediately incorporated into the family of their owner' as one reason why cultural differences between the peoples around the Upper Kasai were so small.[92]

Besides the more unspecified claims on their slaves as 'children' and 'wealth', i.e. to provide a prestigious retinue of faithful followers or means of payment should the need arise,[93] owners could expect more immediate economic benefits from them. One use of slave labour was warfare, as 'the presence of slaves in a village increased the number of able-bodied persons who were obliged to support a feud initiated by their owners'.[94] In peaceful days, slaves, even men, had to work the fields of their owners, even after they had married. And 'if they became hunters they had to give the whole of their kill, with the exception of the sacred portions reserved for the hunter, to their owners.'[95] Among the Luvale, slaves were also employed as fishermen, honey gatherers and beeswax producers;'the fruits of their labours had to be presented to the *mwata* [owner]'.[96]

This raises the question of a link between slave labour and the growth of production for trade. Papstein, who strongly argues for the labour value of slaves,[97] holds that 'substantial amounts of *vandungo* labour' had been used already for local and regional trade in fish (as producers ? as carriers ?) among the Luvale; he suggests that, in the era of long-distance trade, 'slaves played an important role in production of agricultural

---

[89] White 1957: 72
[90] See Papstein 1978: 224
[91] Turner 1957: 189-190; Horton 1975: 96/97
[92] Schütt 1879: 202
[93] 'Slavery was commonly recognized as a source of great wealth and social prestige; the importance of a man was judged in part by the size of his travelling retinue' (Papstein 1978: 251).
[94] White 1957: 71; Turner 1957: 193
[95] Turner 1957: 190
[96] Papstein 1978: 251; Y. Samakayi (interview 21. 10. 1986) told me that they used a lot of slaves for fishing and cassava cultivation.
[97] Papstein 1978: 227

products and fishing' as well as exportable goods for sale to caravans. They would have thus enabled their owners to avoid certain types of heavy work (e.g. bush-clearing)[98] and to pursue more lucrative activities (e.g. trading) away from home even over peak seasons, and ultimately to accumulate slaves and further expand their capacity for production.[99] An aged Luvale trader confirmed to me: 'Those who (were with) slaves could produce more.'[100]

The exploitation of slave labour undoubtedly played a role in market production during the 19th century; but it is almost impossible to assess how important a factor this actually was. There are a number of indications that the economic role of slave labour should not be overestimated. In particular, the effective control of slave owners over means of production seems to have been too small to make this the basis of slave exploitation.[101] Although in theory all products of slaves belonged to their owners, besides working for their *'nkaka'* (*mwata*) they also had their own fields, their own game meat, their own bundles of fish.[102] The immediate reason for this was that slaves had to feed themselves, but they were apparently even able to produce a surplus for themselves, since they seem to have been accumulating property which enabled them to pay bridewealth or to redeem themselves or their relatives; 'in some cases slaves owned other slaves, making the master even richer.'[103] At least Chokwe slaves, around the turn of the century, lived 'in a certain autonomy, established families, and were not distinguishable from their masters, not even by their clothing.'[104] Frobenius has pointed out with some admiration the 'assimilative capacities' (which he called *Nationalisierung*) of the Chokwe vis-a-vis the masses of strangers that came to them as slaves. According to him, the possibilities of male slaves for upward social mobility were so considerable that flight never happened.[105] But also Chokwe slave wives originating from Nuclear Lunda, although not being entitled to, were allegedly treated so well with presents and attention by their free husbands that they were soon glad to give up their former identity.[106]

---

[98] Frobenius 1988: 71 [1905, Northern Chokwe]
[99] Papstein 1978: 226, 229, 232, 250-51
[100] Interview Y. Samakayi, 21. 10. 1986
[101] Cf. Papstein 1978: 224ff
[102] Interview Y. Samakayi, 21. 10. 1986; Papstein 1978: 225/6
[103] Turner 1957: 190ff; Papstein 1978: 251
[104] Mendes Corrêa 1919: 329 [referring to studies by Fonseca Cardoso in the early 1900s]
[105] Frobenius 1988: 67f [1905]
[106] Pogge 1880: 45-46; Diniz 1918: 144 [quoting Dias de Carvalho 1880s]

D 3 : Children and slaves

Fig. 28: Female field labourers, Central Chokwe area (1878)
If one can trust this representation, the greater amount of clothing worn by these women, even during fieldwork, seems to hint at greater market proximity and wealth. Nevertheless, they may well be of slave status, or pieceworkers, as the original title suggests. Double-handled hoes were used nearer to the western borders of the region only. (Engraving from Capello and Ivens 1882, vol.I: 195)

Turner assumed that 'slaves were not remarkably exploited' because this would have contradicted the tendency to integrate them rapidly into the owner's family, through 'classificatory kinship'.[107] My aged Luvale informant confirmed this to some extent when he made an interesting distinction: 'A slave was effective [for the owner - A.v.O.] only when he was young; later he married and could produce for himself, no longer for the owner.'[108]

With prior consent by their respective owners, slaves seem in fact even to have been married among themselves frequently. This relative independence even in reproduction could result in the emergence of 'slave lineages' within the village, which could, because of endogamy and the prohibition of moving away, eventually outnumber their masters' free

---
[107] Turner 1957: 189
[108] Interview Yowena Samakayi, 21. 10. 1986

lineage.[109] If slave labour and fertility was fully available only from young, freshly acquired persons, this could be yet another reason why the free inhabitants of the Upper Zambezi and Kasai had to continuously acquire new stock of slaves through purchase or war, simply to maintain an accustomed level of services.

Except for young, newly acquired people, slaves often seem to have been able to set themselves up as relatively independent petty producers or 'owners'. This background may also explain why Luvale slaves, for example, were regarded as particularly motivated hard workers, compared to those originating from neighbouring regions, such as Lozi or Luba (Tushilange).[110] Some of Magyar's Luvale slaves accompanied their master repeatedly back to their home, but instead of using the occasion to desert, they even brought him presents from their relatives.[111]

In everyday life, slaves may have felt their inferior social position less economically than in the restrictions on their movement, and in

'their exclusion from the decision making of the village, from certain of the most desirable selections of foods, seating privileges and the host of petty social expressions which form the routines of village life.' [112]

The personal treatment of slaves could be bad enough at times, as witnessed by the missionary Fisher, at Kavungu in 1894, who had to redeem a young slave wife in order to rescue her from the maltreatment of her husband. The latter was outraged, because she was already the second slave wife who had successfully tried to flee him.[113] The flight of slaves seems to have been a certain threat to the owners in the region, although all owners were obliged to cooperate in hunting down and severely punishing fugitive slaves.[114] The success of such a flight, however, was often in effect a change from one owner to the other, perhaps by the clever use of the legal system.[115] The most effective threat owners could use against disobedient slaves, however, was sale to the next foreign caravan, and as this opportunity of exerting 'extra-economic'

---

[109] Turner 1957: 190

[110] E.g. *Anonymus* 1803: 25; Pogge 1880: 183; apathy and distress may partly explain why Schütt, in 1878, found a group of Tushilange slaves among the Northern Chokwe who were 'terribly skinny', unarmed, and 'without any rag of cloth round their loins' (1879: 182).

[111] Magyar 1860: 234

[112] Papstein 1978: 227

[113] Singleton-Fisher 1948: 81; not surprisingly, slave wives were the group from which he drew most of his early converts.

[114] Papstein 1978: 227; Turner 1957: 188

[115] Magyar (1859: 287) has described a successful strategy of Ovimbundu slaves who deliberately committed offences against other lords who would then demand them as compensation from their present owners.

power certainly increased in the 19th century, the social position of actual or potential slaves probably declined during this period:

'The excessive punctiliousness shewn by the poor to the richer persons is probably the production of selling them for slaves. A very small offense is punished by chaining the person and sending him off by the first opportunity to be sold. The inferiors in meeting their superiors in the street at once go down on their knees and rub dust on the upper part of their arms, clapping their hands till the great ones have passed.'[116]

D 3.4 Authority and independence

In many African societies social inequality between people of different gender and age have been the starting point of social differentiation. Having examined the economic implications of gender relations in the previous chapter, the question how seniority linked up with market integration around the Upper Zambezi and Kasai has been the topic of this chapter.

Comparing them with the Bemba, White came to the conclusion that

'in Luvale [short for: Luvale and related peoples - A.v.O.] society there is a greater degree of egalitarianism between males and females...; Luvale society does not exhibit overall regard for authoritarianism, and is not greatly influenced by a hierarchy of age.'[117]

Historical and anthropological evidence suggests in fact that the authority of seniors, particularly headmen, over their matrilineal fellow 'villagers' has always been rather brittle. As soon as juniors, both men and women, had become adults through passing their respective initiation ritual, claims of seniors on their labour and allegiance were limited by a remarkable degree of mobility of juniors. Their relatively great independence may be seen as an indigenous tendency, ultimately the result of individualised production processes and abundance of open land in combination with a particular combination of contradictory rules of residence and descent.

During the era of pre-colonial long-distance trade, roughly the 19th century, a certain increase in wealth, closely linked to power over dependants, of some headmen seems to have occurred temporarily. This was visible in a growth of village size in areas near to the main transit routes. This growth of authority, however, was apparently built less on the appropriation of freeborn juniors' productive labour than on a need

---
[116] Livingstone 1963: 56 [1854; at Ishinde's capital]; see also the description in Schomburgk 1925: 110-111
[117] White 1962b: 18

for military and legal defense of the village as whole. The ability to organize such defense against outside threats was the main basis of authority to which youths were subjected as potential fighters or pawns; but their continued or even increased mobility through warfare and trade apparently prevented any significant enrichment of elders as a social class. The acquisition of slaves may have been also a strategy to find more reliable dependants. But different from neighbouring societies, even unfree 'wives' and 'children' were able after some time to establish themselves soon as to some degree independent producers.[118] In the concluding chapter for this part (D 6) I will adress the question of a 'slave mode of production' and ask whether the phenomenon of restrained social differentiation or class formation can be attributed to the assimilative strength of inherited kinship structures.

---

[118] See for example Clarence-Smith 1979; Miller 1973

D 4 'Strangers', neighbours and 'friends': The importance of non-kinship relations

If the strains of the 19th century could not forestall the mobility and economic independence of juniors and to some extent even of slaves (as 'classificatory juniors'), the social framework of the village remained simply too restricted and brittle for all the problems an individual had to cope with in order to engage with the wider world. Members of highly segmented matrilineal residence groups have apparently tended over centuries to build a variety of reciprocal relationships across village boundaries which play an important role as subsidiary social networks in the region. In contrast to the intra-village kinship relations analysed in the preceding chapter (and to the chieftainship relations dealt with in the next one), which were at least in theory unequal, the inter-village relations described in this chapter included a strong notion of equality.

A general distinction is made in all Upper Zambezi languages between the 'villagers' (Lv. *mwenyembo*, SL. *enimbu*), who belong to the village matrilineage, and their wives (Lv. *vapwevo*, SL. *angodi*) on the one hand, and 'strangers' or 'visitors' (*va-/a-ngeji*) on the other. The term *ngeji* is applied to any person living in other villages, including distant or absent relatives. What this chapter deals with are, in short, strategies to convert 'strangers' into 'friends' (one extreme case of such conversion has already been dealt with in the last chapter: the integration of unfree 'strangers' or 'slaves').

Surprisingly, the classical anthropological literature on the peoples of the Upper Zambezi and Kasai has paid little attention to non-kinship relations except those between chiefs and commoners. Instead, it has showed an overriding interest in the structures of kinship, the dominant theme particularly in Radcliffe-Brown's school of British social anthropology. The Upper Zambezi seemed to present researchers with an excellent example of what came to be called 'segmentary lineage society', including notions of 'productive individualism' that seemed conducive to 'development' (see introduction, part A). But the structural need in such societies for complementary networks has tended to be overlooked.

I will first describe these inter-village relationships in their historical and institutional background, and then try to demonstrate their particular implications for economic history: the mobilization and redistribution of free labour; the absorption of a considerable part of imported 'wealth'; and the provision of security against the ever-present dangers of war, ruinous legal disputes and economic disaster.

D 4.1 Types of inter-village relations

Lineage and clan

Although matrilineal groupings are highly segmented and dispersed through fission and other forms of mobility, members of individual villages do retain a memory of belonging to a wider (maximum) matrilineage. Usually it is elderly experts who retain a sometimes considerable genealogical memory of common matrilineal descent from a historical ancestor; in the 1950s even young men in their twenties could sometimes still recall up to 17 ascending generations.[1] Hansen and also I myself have found in the 1970s and 80s, however, that only three to four generations are remembered by ordinary headmen - perhaps an indication of increasing genealogical amnesia.[2] According to White, such knowledge mainly served as a kind of 'genealogical charter for present social relationships'.[3] Among the Lunda-Ndembu, according to Turner, there was a stronger emphasis on the village (minor) matrilineage, whose magnitude and stability was the 'ideal to which ambitious headmen aspire'; but he also states that the

> 'Ndembu possess a lineage group wider than the village lineage within which genealogical linking is possible. This group extends beyond the village matrilineage and includes all, or nearly all, of the living matrilineal kin of the village matrilineal core...The continual flow of visits between matrilineal kin, however far apart in space, serves to maintain their connection. These dispersed matrilineal kin constitute a pool which may at some time be drawn upon to supplement and replenish the village of the nuclear maternal descent group.'[4]

An important question of wider kinship orientation, particularly among the Southern Lunda, is seniority and juniority between spatially separated members of the same wider matrilineage according to their generational position. But it seems that this only refers to relations between individuals, while villages (matri-segments) as a whole are regarded as equivalent, regardless of their different genealogical point of split-off from the maximal lineage.[5] The non-hierarchical relations between kindred villages are also underlined by the absence of the institution of a maximal lineage head.

---

[1] White 1960a: 17; see also Turner 1957: 83
[2] Hansen 1977: 57
[3] White 1960a: 17
[4] Turner 1957: 84, 86/87
[5] See White 1960a: 2; Turner 1957: 175

An even wider projection of kinship links is the clan (Lv./Ch./SL. *mu(n)yachi*, Lz. *munyati*, SL. also *muchidi*), which links a number of extended matrilineages by claiming a common matrilineal origin further back in history. An accurate genealogical knowledge of the link between lineage ancestors and the mythical clan founder does not exist, a fact which led White to the statement that 'clanship is scarcely different from putative kinship'[6]. Nevertheless, traditionally every child in the Upper Zambezi has to learn the names and formulae - phrases containing a very short version of the clan origin - of both their mother and father. Common clanship involves strict exogamy. There are twelve clans which are common to all peoples of the Upper Zambezi and Kasai, cross-cutting ethnic and linguistic differences. This suggests a common ('*VaMbwela*') background of the population which was only subdivided relatively recently with the immigration of a new political elite. In the preceding period, clanship had probably been the apex of 'political' organisation, creating a kind of loose federation of widely dispersed residence units. Today, the terms for clanship (see above) are also used to denote 'ethnic group' or 'tribe', the more recent model of political centralisation (see below, D 5).[7]

In-laws

Marriage relations between different villages and lineages, as has been shown above, had no importance for the 'circulation of descendants' in this matrilineal society, and only a temporary one for the circulation of female labour. Instead, one of its decisive functions was apparently to create social links between the respective in-laws (sg. Lv. *nyali*, SL. *muku* or *ishaku*, according to generation). On a higher political level, for example, marriage alliances between different kinship groups played a significant role in establishing friendly relations between different rulers.[8] Among the Luvale, in-laws may joke with each other and have extra-marital sexual relations, which denotes at the same time closeness and a need to channel potential tensions.[9] The same may be the original rationale for the distinctive custom of avoidance between husband and

---

[6] White 1960a: 19
[7] White 1957: 60ff; 1960a: 18ff; McCulloch 1951: 19/21 (based on manuscript by White); Turner 1957: 85f; Papstein 1978: 77, 150f and fn. 16 [on Southern Lunda]
[8] E.g. between immigrant Luvale Nama Kungu chiefs and resident '*Mbwela*' leaders during the 16th and 17th centuries (Papstein 1978: 129f); between the Luvale senior chief Chinyama and the rulers of the Mbangala and the Songo in the 1790s (Cunnison 1961; Costa 1873: 201); or between the Southern Lunda chief Manenko and a Kololo noble in 1854 (Livingstone 1963: 40).
[9] White 1958: 29; cf. Turner 1957: 253f

mother-in-law.[10] The most important point, however, is that in-law ties were formerly regarded as permanent and not severed by the almost inevitable dissolution of marriage. This is expressed by the Luvale saying that 'marriages may break up, but the in-law relationship is permanent'.[11]

There was even a marked desire to carry on these interlineage ties into the next generation. In the past, marriages between crosscousins, i.e. children of a father's sister and a mother's brother (Lv.*vasonyi*, SL.*asonya*) seem to have been preferred by village elders, as a device either to create even more permanent links between distant villages, or to strengthen cohesion within the same village.[12] Customarily, crosscousins have a particularly robust joking relationship.[13]

But kinship, clanship and marriage bonds apparently proved insufficient to provide the social integration and support required by individuals in this highly dispersed, mobile and volatile society. Throughout their history, not only in the colonial period, the inhabitants of the region were 'greatly given to forming friendships of a voluntary nature outside the limits of their kin'.[14] In contrast to extended kinship and marriage relations, which created links between groups of common descent, unrelated individuals connected themselves through various more or less formalized types of 'friendship'.

Friendship

Friendship in general (Lv.*usepa*, SL. *wubwambu*[15]) is the most significant example of contractual social relations in a society allegedly based on kinship. Friendship contracts consisted in 'a compact of mutual assistance, sealed by some exchange of goods and services'.[16] They could be concluded between any two persons, both men and women, of the same gender and about equal status.[17] Mobile people such as carriers held

---

[10] E.g. Baumann 1935: 129; White 1960a: 35; personal observations
[11] *Wafwa ulo, unyali kaweshi kufwako* (quoted after White 1960a: 35)
[12] White 1960a: 30, 31/4; Turner 1957: 176, 199, 254/5; Baumann 1935: 125; Schachtzabel 1923: 137
[13] White 1960a
[14] White 1958: 30 [Luvale]
[15] *Wubwambu* seems to be the more general Lunda-Ndembu term according to Turner (1957: 286, 307), while according to Melland (1923: 109-117) this term was applied specifically to blood-friendship.
[16] White 1955: 106
[17] According to Baumann, blood-friendship was sometimes also concluded between spouses to reinforce their relations, but he saw this as a more recent development (1935: 133).

friendships over distances of hundreds of kilometres.[18] The importance of formal friendship ties in the pre-colonial past can be inferred from the frequency with which they appear in 19th century travellers reports.[19]

It is possible that the Luvale even believed that 'the value of a friendship compact is greater than that of kinship'.[20] There was sometimes a tendency to integrate, on a terminological level, friendship to some extent into the dominant ideology of common descent, apparently to emphasize the lasting and reciprocal character of these bonds. Interestingly, only those kinship terms were adopted for friendship relations which had a strong notion of equality,

> 'especially [those] associated with joking relations between kin. In the most intimate cases they like to call each other *musonyi* (cross-cousin)... Equally common, but perhaps a little less intimate is the use of *nyali* [in-law, A.v.O.] between such friends.'[21]

A Chokwe chief, in 1880, explicitly distinguished the friendship he proposed to Silva Porto from the typically hierarchical relation that exists between uncle and nephew.[22] On the other hand, friendship was seen as binding equal but unlike positions together, for which the right of joking with each other is a good indicator, in contrast to relations between siblings, for instance, who were seen as 'alike and equal'.[23] Joking relations customarily exist not only between cross-cousins, but also, for example, between unrelated people who bear the same name or were born on the same day.[24] A joking relationship (SL. *wusensi*, Lv.*usese*) involves not only a (secondary) right of assistance and hospitality, but above all a permission to behave, at least in theory, to each other in a way which would be normally considered as offensive and lead to sanctions (e.g.extra-marital intercourse, taking the other's property etc., or at least joking about such offenses). This suggests that *usese* could also be seen as a means to control potential rivalry or hostility for which it represents a safety valve.[25]

The more formal type of friendship involving stronger commitment, however, was concluded through a ceremony of mixing blood, and was called (Lv.) *usendo* or (SL.) *ulunda*.[26] The earliest description of such a

[18] Baumann 1935: 132.
[19] See references further below
[20] White 1955: 106
[21] White 1958: 30
[22] Silva Porto 1885: 164
[23] Cf. Turner 1957: 254
[24] White 1958a: 32
[25] White 1958a
[26] Or SL. *wubwambu*, according to Melland 1923 (see footnote 15 above); significantly, however, in the case observed by Livingstone in 1855 among the Southern Lunda of

ceremony is given by Livingstone in 1855 among people under the Southern Lunda Chief Ishinde:

'...the ceremony of *Casendi*...consists in making small incisions on the joint hands of the parties and on the pits of the stomachs, right cheeks, and foreheads. The blood is taken off by a bit of grass. That of one party is put into one cup of beer, and that of the other into another. Each drinks the other's blood, and then they are bound to disclose to each other any evil which may be coming against them.'[27]

Fig. 29: Conclusion of a friendship pact (detail from Chief Kakoma's chair)

Baumann, who published this detail in his expedition report, called it an 'eating ritual', but declared himself unable to interpret its meaning (1935: 64, 226). The descriptions of the ritual conclusion of friendship or 'bloodbrotherhood' compacts which he cites elsewhere (*ibid.*: 132f), however, resemble very much the scene represented here: The two men seem to press their (incised) hands against incisions on each other's forehead while eating from the same basket. A woman (distinguishable by her hairdress), sitting next to another food basket, offers them a cup for drinking or mixing blood. (Chair bought in 1930, photograph taken at the Museum für Völkerkunde)

Ishinde the same term as the Luvale was used (*kasendo*) - see the following quotation. - Cf. White 1960a: 25; Turner 1957: 286, 307; Figueira 1938: 348; Baumann 1935: 132-33

[27] Livingstone 1963: 271

Although mainly an alliance between individuals, even across ethnic boundaries, friendship obligations were to a limited degree extended to the following generation.[28]

Initiation classes

Similar types of strong friendship relations, but more exclusive ones, usually arise out of joint participation in rituals. Turner has proposed a distinction between life crisis rituals and cults of affliction.[29] The former category includes the boys' initiation and circumcision ritual called *mukanda*, a famous cultural institution common to all Upper Zambezi peoples which is still widely practised.[30] The initiates of a *mukanda* (Lv. *tundanji*; SL. *mwaadi*), who come together from different villages, were in the past older than today, usually around puberty age, between 15 and 18 years of age, and consisted of groups of 30-40 boys.[31] They stayed together in seclusion in a camp for between a month and a year.[32] 'All the novices are regarded as having a formalized blood friendship with each other and with their keepers as a result of common participation and suffering in the rites'.[33]

Having passed the *mukanda* together thus creates an intense bond between adult men which is comparable to age classes in other African societies. The reconfirmation of male gender roles and of seniority, as well as education have all been emphasized as functions of the ritual by different authors; but the integrative function of the ritual seems to be an equally important one.[34]

---

[28] *Ibid.*; White 1960a: 25 (he speaks of 'sons' (i.e. patrilineal descendents) of friends in his example)

[29] 1957: 292ff; Turner 1953

[30] *Mukanda* is mentioned repeatedly in pre-colonial traveller's accounts, e.g. in Silva Porto's diary 4.12.1847 (=1986: 320)[*Ganguelas*]; by Pogge 1880: 40 [1875; Northern Chokwe]; Couceiro 1892: 49. Subsequently, it always found particular attention among social anthropologists; as a consequence, this is probably the best-documented aspect of Upper Zambezi society. The most important accounts are, in chronological order of publication: Fonseca Cardoso 1919: 24ff [data from 1903/04; *Ganguelas* of Moxico]; Dellille 1930 [Lunda, Luvale]; Baumann 1932 [Central Chokwe]; Gluckmann 1949 [Upper Zambezi immigrants in 'Barotseland']; McCulloch 1951: 85ff; White 1953a [all Upper Zambezi groups]; Kubik 1971 [Luchazi]; Mwondela 1972.

[31] Silva Porto's diary 4.12.1847 (=1986: 320) [*Ganguelas*]; Couceiro 1892: 49 (quoted in Madeira Santos 1986: 384 = fn. 284)

[32] White 1953a: 42

[33] White 1961a: 14

[34] In addition, *mukanda* creates an identity of the circumcised in general in contrast to all the uncircumcised, i.e. younger boys and other peoples outside the Upper Zambezi (White 1953a: 44). Papstein (1978: 179) concludes that '*mukanda* ... provides an

Female puberty rites (Lv.,Ch.,Lz. (v)*wali*, SL. *nkanga* or *wadi*)[35] are much less spectacular because they do not include any surgical operation, and girls are secluded and educated individually, after their first menstruation. This is perhaps a reflection of the greater individuality of women's life as compared to men`s.

Both male and female puberty rituals have in common a final ceremony of emergence from seclusion (Lv.*kulovola*, SL. *solola*). Like the organization of a *mukanda*, it is an important occasion for bringing together neighbouring villages and inviting relatives and friends, even from very far away, and thereby re-emphasizing social links.

Cult membership

Today almost extinct following the decline in ancestor worship,[36] but in the past of an importance similar to that of *mukanda*, are men's funerary associations called *mungongi*, and their female equivalent *chiwila*. These associations performed ritual functions during the obsequies of fellow *mungongi* / *chiwila* members or other important persons.[37] But another important aspect might have been that membership in this 'brotherhood' (White), which was acquired through painful initiation rites in an enclosure[38] outside the village, served to 'provide a bond outside the limits of kinship which binds people together in the same way as male circumcision rites or blood-friendships do'.[39] The institutions of *mungongi* and *chiwila* were thus comparable in both form and function to West African secret societies.

Cults of affliction, to end this survey of inter-village, non-kinship institutions, comprise a large variety of rituals most of which are directed against evil spirits of ancestors who wish to harass ('catch') their descendants, usually in revenge for neglect or social misbehaviour. The generic term for such evil spirits, as well as for the ritual and the cult

---

important mechanism of ethnic realignment and ... is the second cross-tribal feature, after the clan, to give visible form to the cultural unity of the Upper Zambezi.'
[35] White 1953b; 1962: 1-26; White, Chinjavata and Mukwato 1958
[36] Spring 1976: 57
[37] According to Turner 1953: 28ff, to prevent the 'shades' (spirits) of the deceased person from returning and troubling his or her relatives. White (1954: 114/5) has his doubts about this hypothesis. See also Dellille 1944; Baumann 1932; McCulloch 1951: 90f; Turner 1957: 298
[38] The term *mungongi* means 'crying out'. Sometimes, the ritual has been called after the enclosure in which initiation takes place (Lv. *muzembe*, SL. *izembi*, Ch. *zemba*).
[39] White 1954: 115

which cures them, is (*m*)*ahamba*, and there is a profusion of ancient and more recent *mahamba* in the Upper Zambezi, to which new ones are continually added.[40] Affliction becomes visible in all manner of physical and psychological illness, particularly in disturbances of women's reproductive capacities, and therefore *mahamba* rituals include most of the autochthonous medical knowledge and healing practices. At least today, mostly women are involved in *mahamba* and related rituals, but others affect mainly men.[41]

Again one important aspect of *mahamba* and related rituals, besides curing the individual patient and reconciling any social tensions within the village which may have been connected with it, is the

'special form of friendship similar to blood-brotherhood and blood-sisterhood (*wulunda*) which is made between adepts and those who have been candidates in the ritual, called [in Ndembu] *wubwambu* or *wulunda waChihamba*... This *wubwambu* provides yet another means of interlinking different members of different villages'.[42]

Anita Spring's 'informants stressed the friendships made by cult participation and also declared that oaths of truthfulness were sworn by using the society's name by members.'[43] She found membership in *mahamba* cults to be particularly important for women, as

'dispersed matrilineal women become reintegrated through their participation, and in this sense spirit possession and ritual become the vehicle for bonding women of a matrilineage.'[44]

It seems that the *mukanda* ritual, the *mungongi/chiwila* associations, and the *mahamba* cults all originate from the Congo basin to the North. Both White and Papstein assume that they were among the important cultural innovations that were imported parallel to productive innovations by the immigrant chiefs from Nuclear Lunda in the 16th to 18th centuries.[45] They were probably used to consolidate chiefly power because they enhanced ethnic or even cross-ethnic realignment among Upper Zambezi peoples; but they were also taken up and re-valuated by the inhabitants

---

[40] See Turner 1953; 1957: 292ff; 1962, 1968; White 1949; 1961a: 46-49; McCulloch 1951: 76f; Spring 1976: 60-73
[41] Spring 1976: 73ff; White 1949: 326f.
[42] Turner 1957: 307; see also Spring 1976: 87
[43] Spring 1976: 57
[44] Spring 1976: 88; White confirms both aspects: 1961a: 48
[45] White 1954: 115; Papstein 1978: 137, 174; for example, there is up to today a conspicuous absence of circumcision in all groups associated with remnants of the Late Iron Age '*Mbwela*' population, at least for those residing in Kabompo/Zambezi (see also McCulloch 1951: 100).

themselves because they provided them with new devices to cement inter-village and cross-kinship links.[46]

Neighbourhood

Even in the past, before the colonial imposition of administrative villages which each comprise a number of matri-villages, the inhabitants of the Upper Zambezi and Kasai rarely lived in complete spatial isolation. Unrelated individual settlement units of circular shape (*membo, nyikala* etc.) always tended to cluster in areas of good ecological potential, usually in a ribbon fashion along rivers and streams. The extra-village and non-kinship links mentioned above do (or did) not, however, show any preference for nearby villages. On the contrary, it seems people were more interested in creating bonds with others in a much wider spatial radius. This may have been following the perhaps realistic rule that 'too much close and constant proximity between friends leads to estrangement and hostility'.[47]

But it also appears very plausible that day-to-day contacts between neighbouring villages were so close and regular that they did not need as much formalization as between people far apart. This assumption is supported by the existence of specific terms for 'vicinage' or 'neighborhood' (SL. *chitungili* and Lv. *mbweli*). The individual hamlets making up a neighbourhood may be matrilineally related, e.g. if they stem from village fission, but often they are the result of migrations bringing together groups without any kinship ties. The *chitungili* 'becomes visible as a discrete social entity in several situations, and a particular headman within it usually exercises moral and ritual leadership'.[48] It is, for example, within such neighbourhood clusters that *mukanda* is organized, and that the highest incidence of economic cooperation occurs.

---

[46] Papstein 1978: 176ff
[47] White 1960a: 36
[48] Turner 1957: 47; according to McCulloch (1951: 67), cohesion within neighbourhood clusters was particularly marked among the Luchazi who even knew a particular position (*ntsenkulu*) for the headman of such a cluster; the holder of this position was not necessarily one of the individual village headmen.

D 4.2 The costs of inter-village relations

While the economic benefits of relations between individuals from different matri-villages remain yet to be assessed (see next sections), they certainly implied a variety of costs. The amount of material goods invested in inter-village social relations may at times even have exceeded redistribution within the village kin-group. They were, at any rate, big enough to absorb a considerable part of the goods available through production or trade. If the hypothesis is true that non-kinship links considerably gained in importance during the 19th century (see below), these social investment costs may have provided an important stimulus for increasing the amount of goods at hand.

A substantial part of inter-village gift circulation was in foodstuffs, while the use of objects of 'wealth' seems to have been even more typical. Marriage and friendship, as the most explicit forms of cross-kinship bonds, have been mentioned already as being always accompanied by a variety of transfers.

Friendship gifts

'Friendship' between two individuals (either men or women), to start with, was not actually 'sealed' (White), but in effect proposed and started by a valuable gift, which mostly consisted in 'wealth', e.g. some chickens, goats, pigs, an ox, precious skins, hoes, axes or a load of rubber, but could also include staple food (cassava meal).[49] It was socially inopportune to refuse such a proposal. Acceptance of this gift meant conclusion of the friendship, and acceptance of an obligation on the part of the receiver to return a similar gift. Additional smaller gifts, notably food, may have been reciprocated immediately or jointly consumed, but the reciprocation of the actual friendship gift was expected to take place only at some later point. (See fig. 29) A significant Chokwe saying cited by givers on such occasions, in 1880, went as follows: 'Free in the eyes, sold in the heart',[50] apparently implying an idea of personal mutual obligation as opposed to immediate reciprocation. This did not mean, of course, that the giver did not expect a counter-present; in fact, outstanding counter-presents were regarded as formal debts in the legal

---

[49] Baumann 1935: 132; Livingstone 1963: 69, 85, 111, 268 [Southern Lunda, Chokwe; 1854/55]; Silva Porto 1885: 583/84 [1880; Northern Chokwe]; Schomburgk 1925: 55 [Southern Lunda, near Kabompo; 1905/06]

[50] Quoted by Silva Porto 1885: 583/4

sense.[51] But there was an implicit interest in maintaining this credit open for a certain time, because it meant a particularly strong claim on the debtor that the creditor could try to make use of in various ways (see below). I have personally experienced repeatedly that elders in the region still regard it as bad manners to immediately hand over counter-presents in return for welcome gifts and the like; they insisted that it should not look as if one wanted to **pay** for their presents (which did not preempt a variety of later claims and demands). There is also no idea of material equivalence between these gifts; their amount rather depends on the wealth of the respective individual.

Formal friendship continued to be expensive after it had been actually concluded, as 'friends' were expected to invite and compliment each other (e.g. at important ceremonies in which one of them participated), and to support each other whenever the need arose. Certain groups around the Upper Zambezi (Luvale, Luchazi, Lunda ?) also had a reputation for 'blood-brothers' or 'friends' exchanging their wives between them.[52] It was this continuous need for reconfirmation of friendship which made up not only the costs but also the real benefits of friendship.

Marriage payments

Marriage payments, as mentioned already in chapter D 2, were due not only between the groom, the bride and her uncle or father, but significantly also involved a variety of other relatives and even friends on both sides. The meaning of bringing two disparate groups together is evident, as, for example, in the case of the Chokwe *upite* present, translated as 'pledge of good faith' (see table 8). These presents seem to have outstripped the actual bridewealth since the pre-colonial period, and gradually raised the price of marriage considerably.[53] White's observations in the 1940s and 50s appear quite applicable to the late pre-colonial period, when he asserts that marriages

> 'are usually marked by a lavish expenditure on the part of both bridegroom's and bride's family in order to make a display. The bridegroom's expenses in such weddings are often two to three times as much as the formal marriage payments which he makes to his bride's family.'[54]

---

51 See McCulloch 1951: 23
52 See Diniz 1918: 392; Baumann 1935: 133; McCulloch 1951: 65. This custom, however, is found abhorrent by neighbouring groups such as the Lunda-Ndembu (cf.Turner 1957), and has contributed to regular accusations of immorality by colonial officers against the Luvale/Luchazi.
53 See for example Fonseca Cardoso 1919: 27 (quoted in D 2).
54 White 1962b: 33

These expenditures first of all consisted in food: numerous baskets of processed cassava, calabashes of grain and honey-beer, goats, chickens and game meat were (and still are) transferred in this way in the course of marriage ceremonies. As far as such foodstuffs were concerned, these transfers may have strained existing food reserves as a whole, but they probably had only little effect on the economic balance between the social groups involved; both families and both sexes were involved in production as well as consumption of these foods (see further below).

There appears to have been more of a redistributive effect in the case of non-food gifts, whose size depended much more on the 'wealth' of the respective giver. It has been mentioned already how imported goods of European manufacture began to replace indigenous types of wealth goods such as iron and copper ware, and how this led to an inflation in the amount of these payments. This must have affected especially men with access to export earnings and wages. By the 1880s, among the Northern Chokwe, wealthy suitors were expected to clothe not only their bride, but also her parents, the closest relatives and even friends. In addition, substantial amounts of livestock, *aguardente* and/or gunpowder (for salutes) were expended during marriage ceremonies.[55] It is also possible that already in the pre-colonial period wealthy bridegrooms began to pay imported goods to their senior in-laws or to feel responsible for repayment of their debts, as a welcome substitute for unpopular labour services, another part of customary marriage transfers, particularly among the Southern Lunda.[56]

Factual inequalities reflected in marriage payments, however, remained veiled by the idea of reciprocity, or rather social balance, between in-laws. Only the 'hard core' of these payments, the transfer of bridewealth and of a woman, were not seen as being directly reciprocated in the course of the ceremonies. Any idea of bridewealth being a 'purchase' of the wife was strictly rejected. According to Dias de Carvalho, by the 1880s the Chokwe allegedly even tended to avoid any form of payment to the parents or relatives of the wife because they feared this might be interpreted as purchasing her, like a slave woman.[57] With regard to these essential transfers, the balance between givers and receivers was redressed only after some delay, at divorce, when the wife returned to her home, and the bridewealth (but none of the other payments) were due for repayment. This provides a particularly clear illustration of the argument of Meillassoux and others, that bridewealth actually constituted

---

55 Dias de Carvalho [1885/6], quoted in Diniz 1919: 144; this statement refers to a mixed population of Northern Chokwe and Nuclear Lunda; gunfire is mentioned by White 1962b: 11.
56 This tendency is reported for the 'Balovale Lunda' in McCulloch 1951: 23 and 24 (based on communications by C.M.N. White).

only a token to maintain the memory that a woman has been received, which ultimately can only be reciprocated by a woman.[58] In this particular matrilineal society bridewealth was hardly more than a kind of receipt over a debt incurred by the kin group that was to enjoy temporarily the labour (not the fertility) of a female member of another group. The idea that a free wife is a woman 'lent' to her husband and his family[59] is expressed most strikingly in the ancient rule that a husband has to pay compensation to his wife's family if she or one of her children should die while in his village. These 'death payments' (Lv.*jipepi*, SL. *mpepi*) in the past included a series of transfers to the in-laws, e.g.

> 'upon sending word of her death; another payment when he goes to their village to the mourning rites (*chipeji* [SL. *chipenji*]); another for the lighting of the cooking fires at the *chipeji*; a payment for the carrying cloth, symbolic for her children; a payment to the buriers; and payment "for the house", i.e. for the services rendered by the wife in his house... In addition he must pay the relatives of his deceased wife for a ceremony of medication by which he is cleansed from the pollution of her death.'[60]

Colonial anthropological sources agree that these payments were very heavy in the pre-colonial past; statements vary between 25 calves (in cattle owning areas), 'a gun, many yards of cloth and a slave', and 6-10 times the value of the bridewealth for the *pepi* proper, which was subject to negotiation between the two kin groups.[61] It is very likely that the amounts demanded for this kind of compensation increased considerably during the late pre-colonial period with the spread of imported goods and slavery, and these heavy claims on husbands certainly made it even more attractive for them to marry slaves instead of free women. Possibly even new types of death payments were invented during this period, as the original meaning of the term (*m*)*pepi* seems to refer only to the ritual cleansing from the shades of the dead.

Ceremonies

It seems that at some point the actual (*m*)*pepi* payments were separated from contributions towards the cleansing ceremony after the death of a spouse. These latter mainly consisted foodstuffs (beer, meat, livestock) to be consumed during the funeral gatherings. The amount of food expended for these purposes seems to have varied, with Lunda influence

---

[57] Diniz 1919: 143 [quoting Dias de Carvalho 1885/86]
[58] Meillassoux 1975
[59] First expressed for the Northern Chokwe by Torday and Joyce 1922: 268
[60] White 1948c: 152, and 1955: 110; see also Turner 1957: 263, 269f; Baumann 1935: 126
[61] Baumann 1935: 124, 126 [Central Chokwe]; White 1955: 110 [Luvale etc.]

representing perhaps one extreme, as noted by Livingstone in his travel diary in 1855:

> 'A person having died in the village, we could transact no business with the chief until the funeral obsequies were finished. They occupy about four days, and during these there is a constant succession of dancing, wailing, and feasting. Drums are beat during the whole night, and the whole of the relatives, dressed in fantastic caps &c, keep up the ceremonies with spirit according to the amount of brandy, beer, and beef, expended. When these are large, a remark is made afterwards, "What a fine *batuque* that was." ...Much time is spent in these funerals and weddings, which, too, are conducted with great ceremony.'[62]

Among the more southwesterly peoples (Luchazi, Mbunda, Mbwela etc.), on the other hand, there was allegedly no 'ancient custom' of 'great ceremonies on the occasion of the death of whatever person'.[63] For them, instead, puberty rites and cult initiation ceremonies may have been the more important occasions on which, as everywhere in the region, substantial amounts of food and above all beer were expended.[64] Significantly, *mukanda* ceremonies were only held in years after a good harvest,[65] and the availability of greater amounts of surplus food (grains for beer, cassava for *nshima*) was certainly a welcome development in this context.

This form of circulating goods during ceremonies clearly had a social meaning which went beyond the protagonists of the ritual. Initiations, weddings (which in the past coincided with female puberty rites) and funerals brought together even more distant relatives and far off friends as well as the inhabitants of the entire neighbourhood cluster. The sharing out of food (a ritualized and careful procedure in which certain social distinctions were made)[66] reinforced existing bonds of various kinds, and at the same time meant a certain redistribution of food surplus. Expenditure for the ceremonies of 'coming out' from female initiation, for weddings and funerals is met only by the individuals and groups in their focus. *Mukanda* (and possibly other initiation rituals) are in theory communal enterprises to which all villages in the neighbourhood who send candidates and even their relatives and friends are expected to contribute food and drink; but according to earlier anthropological sources a major contribution came from the 'holder of the rites' (Lv.

---

[62] Livingstone 1963: 241/42 (*batuque* = Angolan-Portuguese word for ceremonial dance); also *ibid.*: 251; according to Turner, funeral obsequies among the Lunda-Ndembu could last three and more months in the past (1957: 270).

[63] Diniz 1918: 393

[64] The communal preparation and consumption of (grain?) beer is the most recurrent feature in oral traditions as well as early colonial ethnography on both male and female initiation ceremonies (see accounts in Fonseca Cardoso 1919: 22f, 25ff; White 1962b: 9ff).

[65] Silva Porto 1986: 320 [diary 4.12.1847; *Ganguelas*]

chijika mukanda) and his village, who provided the drinks for the opening and for the 'coming out' (Lv. *kulovola*) parts of the ceremony. This person was usually the headman of the village with most initiation candidates, or the local chief, which suggests that he represented the biggest unit with the most solid food reserves.[67] Specialized beekeepers supplying the world market may have found an additional attraction in their activity as it provided them with unusual amounts of honey-beer to show their generosity during ceremonies.[68]

Even if during ceremonies the more general inter-village social relations were enhanced mainly through distributing locally produced foodstuffs, especially drinks, market relations also came to play their role in this. Certain consumer goods stemming from foreign trade, such as gunpowder (for firing volleys)[69] or in some areas *aguardente* (as mentioned by Livingstone above), began to enter these ceremonies. Individual sponsors sometimes had to raise substantial amounts of foodstuffs for such occasions, which could sometimes arrive unexpectedly (e.g. in the case of death), or for which they could not mobilize sufficient labour (e.g. their wives). They were then forced to pay for the purchase of such foodstuffs, e.g. for the ingredients of beer.[70] At least today, the purchase of grains such as millet, rice or maize for ceremonies is an important stimulus for intra-rural food trading, and an important source of income for women. It is quite possible that imported goods already began to be used for such rather sudden expenses during the 19th century, since there were also other expenses during ceremonies which were increasingly met in the form of imported goods, especially cloth.

These expenses were remunerations for various specific ritual functions performed during ceremonies. One is tempted, of course, to regard such remunerations as actual pay for specific services, but this may have been true originally only for the real specialists among them whose services were in constant demand, such as, in the case of *mukanda*, the medicine man (*nganga*) or the circumciser.[71] But there were a variety of other ritual functions for which fewer skills were required, e.g. musicians, mask dancers, initiation 'teachers', or interventions by members of the

---

[66] See White 1961: 3, 6; senior relatives, men and women, and formal friends enjoyed certain eating and drinking privileges (communication by A.Lufuma, 30.10.1989).

[67] White 1961: 1 and fn. 2; Fonseca Cardoso 1919: 25-27

[68] Specialized beekeepers today are known as sponsors of various ceremonies (Wendorf 1988: 118).

[69] See e.g. Fonseca Cardoso 1919: 26 (saying that a firing volley usually ended *mukanda*); White 1962b: 12, 32 (*idem*, during wedding ceremonies).

[70] E.g. Turner 1957: 270; White reports the bridegroom's relatives being obliged to 'buying the beer' for the bride's instructress when they want to drink at her village during wedding ceremonies.

[71] White 1961a: 2

mungongi / *chiwila* associations during funerals, and for these, payments were expected. The terminology used for these payments is not the same as that used for actual specialist services (*fweto*, 'pay' - a rather impersonal, object-centered type of exchange, see below), but ranges among the highly diversified terminology of 'gifts', 'presents' and 'fines' to be handed over on specific occasions between specific actors.[72] That such transfers in this case were seen in a context of inter-village redistribution and networking is illustrated, for example, by a Luvale saying which seems to express some opposition to this strategy: 'Presents from kindred people to a *likishi* dancer who is one of themselves keep the presents in their own kingroup.'[73]

In the era of long-distance trade, such specialist performers apparently began to expand their functions, even beyond the actual ritual, and to use them them as yet another meands of obtaining valuable goods. *Mungongi* / *chiwila* members (l.v. *kadangu*), for example, began to use their right to obtain food donations (small livestock) from the community, and extract forfeits from anyone who broke their rules, in such an excessive way that this is said to have been one of the reasons for the ultimate disappearance of the ritual.[74] Foreign caravans were more or less regularly given performances of music and mask dancing, and they may have been the first groups prepared to pay 'wealth' for such services, even if only to stop what they sometimes experienced as a serious test of their patience. On such occasions, payments in cloth, tobacco, salt, goats, fish, beads, cowries and copper bracelets were made.[75] At any rate, payments for ritual performances began to be settled in cloth even within the local society.[76]

---

[72] *Kusomwena* seems to be the most specific term for a 'gift' given to a performer such as a *likishi* dancer among both Luvale and Southern Lunda of Ishinde. *Nshinga* (SL.) and *nyembu* (Lv.) are other terms used for this as well as for other specific ceremonial occasions on which 'presents' were to be handed over. The payment for a doctor or diviner, in contrast, is *mwivwi* ('arrows') in Luvale, synonymous with one of the terms for bridewealth (cf.Horton 1978: 66, 114; Fisher 1984: 46/47).

[73] *Likishi lyausoko, kumukina muusoko, kumuzamba muusoko* (quoted by White 1960a: 12).

[74] White 1954: 113-116

[75] E.g. Cameron 1877: II, 158, 176, 188; Lux 1880: 89; Capello and Ivens 1882: 226; Silva Porto 1885: 581; Singleton-Fisher 1948: 84; Frobenius 1988: 77 observed payments of beads to a *likishi* dancer, regarded more as an entertainer (much like today), by other villagers [Northern Chokwe, 1905].

[76] By the turn of the century, a circumcision 'teacher' (*chilombola*) in central Moxico, for example, could expect a payment of 16-40 yards, definitely more than, for example, bridewealth payments (Fonseca Cardoso 1919: 26).

Everyday costs and long term-benefits

Finally, inter-village relations, especially neighbourhood, were reconfirmed outside these ceremonies, on more day-to-day occasions of village life. For example, when a successful hunter returned home, he or his headman would share out the kill not only among the individual 'houses' of his village, but also to important headmen (SL. *chilolu*) of neighbouring villages whose adherence or faith a powerful headman wanted to secure.[77]

As I have mentioned before (C 4.3), alcohol was regarded as particularly conducive not only to spiritual powers, but also to smooth social relations. When beer had been brewed in a village either from grains or from honey, neighbours and friends, both women and men, were (and still are) sometimes invited to partake in a *lizaji* (Lv.) gathering. Sitting in one or two rounds (separated by gender), these guests were entertained by receiving shares of the drink. A fair share was seen as a sign of social recognition, and quarrels could break out if one participant felt neglected. Therefore, a good deal of care was devoted to the exact apportioning of the shares, usually by a specially appointed, neutral person.[78]

Imported goods, again, began to play a role in more regular occasions of gift circulation as well, and were apparently saved for this and other 'social' purposes at the expense of consumption; even at this level generosity seems to have been remarkable towards the end of the pre-colonial period. The first colonial officer who reached the remote Southern Lunda area north of the Kabompo River around 1906 remarked:

> 'Although huge amounts of calico have entered the country from the West Coast through *Mambari* caravans, the people hardly wear anything but antelope skins... But when they pay a visit to a friendly village they almost overburden themselves with cloth in order to make a good impression.'[79]

It may be concluded that the fragmented individuals and groups living around the Upper Zambezi and Kasai were prepared to invest considerable amounts of goods in the the establishment and maintenance of inter-village relations that went largely beyond kinship ties. These investments probably provided a powerful stimulus to surplus production

---

[77] Interview Headman Munyawu, 7.10.1986; Turner 1957: 31

[78] This could be, for example, a young man (communication by A.Lufuma, 30.10.1989); Chokwe chiefs and the rulers of Nuclear Lunda used to employ a special officer for this task whose title is translated as 'cup bearer' or 'beer pourer' (Hoover 1978: 529; Jaspert 1929: 209); descriptions of sharing out at chiefs' receptions and subsequent quarrels are found in Capello and Ivens 1882: I, 205/06 [Central Chokwe]; Pogge 1880: 54 [Northern Chokwe/Luvale].

[79] Schomburgk 1925: 125

and market exchange, and at the same time made up a substantial part of local circulation. Indigenous types of circulation with a prevalently economic character, however, (which will be looked at in the next section) were at least originally to some extent distinguished from the transactions with a predominantly social meaning that have been focused upon in this section. Their primarily 'social' significance does not mean that these transactions were less binding. On the contrary: an idea of strict reciprocity runs through all of them, and interestingly even creditor/debtor relations probably originate in this sphere of mutual social obligations. The underlying concern seems to be the preservation of a precarious balance of power between theoretically equal partners.

It appears that this concern was to some extent put into practice, since 'gifts' and other payments of food and 'wealth', the size of which depended largely on the capacities of the person involved, effectively had a redistributive effect in the region. But this egalitarian picture fades somewhat when one puts aside an economistic view and looks beyond the values of the physical goods involved. Generosity was not only, as we tend to see it from a European point of view, an immediate, voluntary sacrifice to the benefit of the recipient, but at the same time a demonstration of power (based on 'wealth') on the part of the giver. Material goods could enable 'conspicuous consumption' by the wealthy (see earlier quotations), and particularly the 'purchase' of obligations for future personal allegiance which could perhaps be turned into some sort of benefit in the long run. The decisive use-value of both food and wealth was the acquisition of rights over people. Material investments in friendship and neighbourhood played an important part in a pattern of accumulation based on control over living people rather than over dead capital. In the following two sections I will examine the nature of rights that could eventually be acquired through 'generosity'.

D 4.3 The utility of neighbourhood: Cooperation, piecework and barter

The essential meaning of individual ownership in the Upper Zambezi is, as we have seen, individual work. This does not mean, however, that the 'owner' always works alone without having recourse to other people's labour. The size of a job, time pressure due to seasonal change, other important commitments, or infirmity due to age or sickness can always cause individual producers to require labour assistance, even without any intention of producing substantial surplus. In the preceding chapters, the possibilities and limitations of claiming other people's, both freeborns' and slaves', labour within the 'household' and the village have been described. The limitations may explain why aged informants insist that various labour arrangements originated in the pre-colonial economy which were not based on kinship or slavery, but on contractual agreements between formally equal partners. Similar *adhoc* agreements, which do not involve any longer-term personal commitments of the types described so far, also seem to have been concluded with regard to the exchange of goods (barter) since before the world market period in the region. Such transfers of labour and goods, which will turn out to be interrelated, and which play a decisive role for any growth of production today, are analysed one by one in this section. The question is whether and how they were distinguished, and to what extent they were embedded in more binding social relations of the neighbourhood type.

Models of cooperation: *Chilimba* **and 'companies'**

Production by individual 'owners' is difficult firstly as regards production processes which are too difficult or not very productive when done by single producers. For example, catching fish at the fences during *musuza*, at the large *wálilo* weirs which are up to several miles long, or in ponds or oxbows by poison or baskets at the end of the season, requires the cooperation of larger groups of producers. Up to ten or twenty men combine their efforts in constructing dams, and both men and women cooperate in driving and killing the fish at fences and in ponds.[80] Cooperants may come from the same *limbo*, but often they are related only by neighbourhood or other non-kinship links. 'The builders of a *wálilo* may be linked matrilineally, patrilineally, by marriage or merely by a close friendship.'[81]

White has also argued that 'fishing ... lays emphasis on joint activities and cooperation rather than on individualism'.[82] In connection with the growing demand for fish by caravans, such cooperation must, if anything, have increased during the 19th century. But while collective fishing techniques in Nuclear Lunda did perhaps facilitate political centralization at an early stage, they obviously did not among the Luvale of the Upper Zambezi, although fishing has always been central to their local economy.[83] One reason seems to be that work there was collective only in a technical sense while appropriation remained clearly individual. Every

---

[80] Interviews Mr.Likomeno 13.8.1985; Mr. Sakutohwa 15.8.1985; Mr. Muyembe, 26.8.1985; personal observations.
[81] White 1959: 11
[82] *Ibid.*

participant in collective fishing uses his or her own gate in the fence or dam, baskets, traps etc., and may have quite different results.[84] (See fig. 11)

Hunters, in contrast, are around the Upper Zambezi customarily regarded as archetypal individualists,[85] surrounded by fears of jealousy and accusations of greediness, probably because of their privileged access to the most highly prized form of animal protein.[86] According to indigenous thinking, the owner of the spear, bow or trap that killed an animal may dispose of it, within the limits of certain general rules of meat distribution. Nevertheless, cooperation between hunters seems to be a fairly frequent feature:

> 'A *chiyang'a* may lead a small band consisting of men and boys of his own village or of contiguous villages into the bush on quite long expeditions lasting a week or more. On such an expedition the party build grass or leaf huts near an area known to be frequented with game and continue to hunt until they have killed several animals'.[87]

Such cooperation is technically crucial with regard to dangerous large animals such as elephants, and as general insecurity increased with distance from home, it is plausible that during the 19th century communal hunting was even more regular than today. As hunting was often combined with beeswax collection, groups of *Sekele*, Chokwe, Mbunda and Luvale elephant hunters and beeswax collectors numbering up to several dozen, who would stay away from home for up to several months, were met by various travellers.[88] A lively description of one of a Chokwe hunting camp has been given by Capello and Ivens.[89] (See fig. 17) But in this description nothing indicates a communal use of the meat, skins and horns. A communal use of yields is even less to be expected among the

---

[83] Papstein 1978: 216

[84] Interview with fishermen at Nyamhingila 18.8.1985; Samungole, 3.9.1985; cf. White 1956: 79

[85] According to Turner, the majority of hunting activities in the Upper Zambezi exhibit 'a pattern of productive individualism', and White asserts that 'the specialist hunter is a solitary hunter, not the leader of a band of hunters' (White 1956: 85). Folktales often tell of 'a mysterious lone hunter at his shelter surrounded by meat and far from people. This archetypal hunter, particularly well characterized in the *liyambi lyangongo* ('great hunter of the wilderness') of Luchazi folktales is the antithesis of cooperation between a group of related males all cooperating in hunting. The professional hunter, inducted by ritual into the association of hunters is the actual realization in society of this mystical great hunter.'(White 1956: 86)

[86] See D 1.2; White 1956: 76; Interview G. Munyawu and relative, 4.10.1986

[87] Turner 1957: 29; the same procedure is still practised in Zambezi-East (Interview G. Munyawu and relative, 4.10.1986).

[88] Silva Porto 1986: 335 [diary, entry 12.1.1848; *Sekele*]; Livingstone 1963: 30/31, 106 [1854; Mbunda, Chokwe]; Magyar 1860: 229 [Central Chokwe] Capello and Ivens 1886: 440, 443 [1884; Luvale, '*Mbwela*'-Lukolwe]; Arnot 1969: 184 [Chokwe 'bee-hunters']

strictly private owners of beehives. Another form of cooperation in hunting, game drives, did play a role in the past, but has virtually disappeared today.[90] Up to about 30 men participated, organized by any headman who took the initiative. In this case, the neighbourhood again seems to have been the relevant unit within which cooperants were found.

Ironwork is another indigenous example of cooperation out of technical necessity. It was once widespread in the region and required many hands for work on the furnace.[91] In specialized areas most of the male village population, including the 'notables'(seniors) could be required to fulfill this task.[92] It seems that usually only one blacksmith was the 'owner' of the smelter, the others only helpers. Usually, there was only one blacksmith in the same village.[93] But where, in specialized areas, many blacksmiths worked close to each other either in the neighbourhood or in seasonal camps, mutual assistance during mining and smelting must surely have taken place.[94] Such forms of loose cooperation were also applied to new forms of production that came in with the world market, such as rubber collection. Around the turn of the century, rubber was often processed at camps set up in the bush by groups of 10-20 people.[95] But old people told me that the hammering 'was done by everyone individually - we are too jealous !' Cooperation during the work process itself was restricted: 'One could be helped by wife and children.'[96]

Security seems to have been the overriding motive for cooperation in this case, and security was indeed an even greater concern for another group of market activists: petty traders used to combine themselves into groups with some degree of organization (groups which at that time often simultaneously pursued other activities during their trips, e.g. hunting, wax collection and raiding).[97] They often attached themselves to a bigger long-distance caravan but maintained their group identity within it, e.g. by taking up separate spaces within larger camps from which they would

---

[89] Capello and Ivens 1882: I, 217ff [journey in 1878]
[90] See Singleton-Fisher 1948; also Turner 1957: 29/30
[91] For description of the process see Schütt 1881: 128, 131f [Northern Chokwe]; Johnson 1969: 99 [Western *Ganguela*]; Baumann 1935: 80ff [Central Chokwe]; White 1948: 56f. I still saw a few functioning furnaces in remote parts of Kabompo in 1979, and obtained some information on smelting work during the Luvale *Likumbi lya Mize* Festival in 1986.
[92] Schütt 1881: 128, 131f
[93] Harding 1904: 159: 'Each village has its smelting shed and blacksmith's shop at hand' [1899; Luvale].
[94] Schütt 1881: 128, 131f [Northern Chokwe]; Johnson 1969: 99 [Western *Ganguela*]
[95] Interview Mr. Sondoyi, 24.10.1986 [Luvale/Southern Lunda]; Harding 1904: 212, 246 [Mbandi, Luchazi]
[96] Interview Mr. Sondoyi, 24.10.1986 [Luvale/Southern Lunda]
[97] Such not clearly identifiable 'roving parties of robbers etc.' were met by many 19th century travellers. Cf. Miller 1970: 190f

radiate as sub-units.[98] The caravan as a cooperative enterprise has been seen as an Ovimbundu invention,[99] but Ovimbundu caravans were apparently based much more on kinship structures than trading groups from the Upper Zambezi presumeably.[100] Here, indigenous structures of cooperation among independent, equal and usually non-related partners may have paved the way for later successful attempts to unite vis-a-vis the market forces: 'joint ventures' between share-holders in village shops, 'African Trader's Cooperatives' or 'companies' of canoe-builders or oxcart-transporters were to function at various times during the colonial and post-colonial period through initiatives 'from below'.[101] However, envy, jealousy and distrust tend to create considerable tensions between individual participants in such cooperative enterprises in the region.[102] Unfortunately, for all these examples no information exists as to what mechanisms were used between cooperants to stabilize their ventures internally.

More information on the actual relations between cooperants is available for other fields of cooperation where technical ('external') advantages are less obvious: housebuilding, canoe making and agriculture (clearing and hoeing). Besides forms of collective labour for remuneration (*chenda, liyamba*), which will be examined subsequently, a agreement of mutual assistance between otherwise independent producers, both men and women, related and non-related (neighbours, in-laws, 'friends') can be observed here which may be seen as a model of formalized cooperation. In the past, it may have been applied to other activities as well. This arrangement is called *chilimba* and is considered by Upper Zambezi peasants to be of ancient (pre-colonial) origin.[103] The essential meaning of *chilimba* is that different independent producers join forces and work communally on the production site (the house, the field, the

---

[98] These 'caravanes composites' (Vellut 1972: 135/6) including Ovimbundu, Chokwe and Luvale have been described for instance by Cameron 1877, II; Silva Porto 1885; Arnot 1969: 145f; Arnot 1893: 34.

[99] Heywood 1984: 178ff

[100] Cf. Soremekun 1977: 84f

[101] E.g. White 1959: 42; interview D. Chishinji, Dipalata, 16.10.1986; NAZ file SEC 2/155 (Annual Report on African Affairs, Balovale 1948); the term 'company' is most frequently used in local languages for this kind of enterprise (e.g. interview Muwika and Chifwisha, 22.10.1986, on canoe production).

[102] Such difficulties today inhibit various recent cooperative projects in the region (personal experience); it is very unlikely that this as a new phenomenon.

[103] This term is apparently of Luvale origin, related to the verb *kulimba*, 'to entangle, enmesh (as in net)' (Horton, [2]1975: 176), and was taken up by other groups. Today it is sometimes confused with the above-mentioned terms (SL.)*chenda* or (Lv./Ld.) *liyamba*; but these denote essentially the unilateral invitation of other people to work for beer ('work party'). Y.Samakayi, 24.10.1986, on the antiquity of this form.

canoe etc.) of each individual member.[104] The eldest member of the *chilimba* group decides on the order in which the different sites are worked, but much grumbling arises over this question; others are often suspected of working only until their own field has been collectively worked. The idea and moral norm, however, is that each member receives and gives an equivalent amount of labour.[105] 'It's like a company', two canoebuilders explained to me.[106] It is not entirely clear what the economic relevance of this form of cooperation is. One effect may be an increased efficiency and speed of work, particularly with heavy or urgent tasks; the impact of ambition and competition on labour productivity during work in a group should not be underestimated. Another effect may be a redistribution of labour between weaker and stronger participants, e.g. between juniors and seniors. In reality, against the norm, the actual amount of work to be done (size of field etc.) can vary considerably between individual members of the same group[107], but not very much in correlation with age.

Cooperation among individual producers is particularly efficient as a way to cope with labour peaks when these bottlenecks do not occur simultaneously for all participants, e.g. during particular seasons. This is particularly true for cooperation between women, which is less spectacular than that of men or mixed parties, but probably no less relevant for them. Individual women, both within and between neighbouring villages, form personal alliances to assist each other with day-to-day duties, especially food processing, in order to balance out temporary indisposition, e.g. due to illness.[108] But rarely were women, who came regularly from other villages, friends enough with each other to share millet or cassava fields.[109]

Because of the basic idea of a direct reciprocity 'labour for labour' it involves, the amount of **additional** labour it makes available to the individual member of the *chilimba* group remains within narrow bounds. Furthermore, *chilimba* and similar forms of cooperation still imply a certain stronger personal commitment, as individual labour inputs are (in theory) balanced only in the course of longer periods. Wider, more long-lasting social relations may in fact sometimes be an additional motive for

---

[104] Muwika and Chifwisha, 22.10.86; Beck and Dorlöchter 1987: B65f; 1988: 237f; Y.Samakayi (24.10.1986) considered house building to be perhaps the earliest occasion on which *chilimba* was practised.
[105] Beck and Dorlöchter 1987: B65, 66
[106] Interview Muwika and Chifwisha, 22.10.1986
[107] Beck and Dorlöchter 1987: B65, 66
[108] Communication by Fine Beck and Sabine Dorlöchter, who called these alliances 'cassava groups'; see Beck and Dorlöchter 1988: 236
[109] Frobenius 1988: 75 [1905, Northern Chokwe]

individuals to enter such arrangements. In the following sections, I will examine a number of other forms of mobilizing assistance which may have been more effective devices for individuals to increase their productive capacities in the pre-colonial period.

Chenda - the 'work party'

The only form of non-kinship labour which anthropologists of the colonial period, both White and Turner, mentioned are the so-called 'working parties' - collective work by a group of both relatives and neighbours in return for the joint consumption of beer.[110] The terms used today for this form of remunerated work are *chenda* (SL.), *liyamba lya wala* (Lv.) and *nkuta* (Lz.).[111]

Work parties in the past were apparently more regular than today, and were sponsored for various tasks which were particularly labour-intensive: in agriculture bush-clearing by groups of men, the breaking-up of land by mixed parties, and weeding by groups of women; work parties for the construction of houses were also typical.[112] Participants usually come from the same vicinage, and again include both relatives and unrelated neighbours. Some informants claim that in the remoter past only adult men participated in work parties - which would then have mainly covered bush-clearing - because women and boys were not allowed to drink beer in public ('those were the good old days', one old man sighed).[113] But others say that this applied only to some areas while women and men used to drink jointly in others; or even that weeding (done only by women) was the most important occasion on which assistance called for in return for beer and other payment.[114]

The basic idea is that, with a few days' notice, a considerable number of people are called in to work collectively and very intensely for one morning. Again, as in the case of *chilimba*, a kind of sporting spirit of competition between the participants spurs on their work - 'it's like a race', as a young peasant put it.[115] The amount of work to be done is

---

[110] See White 1959: 21; Turner and Turner 1955: 20; Turner 1957: 22

[111] The term *liyamba*, perhaps related to a stem *-yamba* denoting confusion, is also used of old by the Southern Lunda of Ishinde in the form *iyamba* and may be applied to both working parties for beer and cooperative work (*chilimba*). (Discussion between advisers to Chief Ishinde, 25.10.1986; L. Chizombo, 30.10.1986; Kanema women, 8.10.1986; Muwika and Chifwisha, 22.10.1086).

[112] White, Turner, testimony by L. Chizombo, 30.10.1986; advisers to Chief Ishinde, 25.10.1986

[113] Sondoyi 18.10.1986 (Lv.); L. Chizombo, 30.10.1986 (Ld.)

[114] Y.Samakayi, 21.10.1986; advisers to Chief Ishinde, 25.10.1986

[115] Interview G. Munyawu, 9.9.1986

indicated by the sponsor and does not depend on the number of participants, but on the amount of beer served.[116] This relationship was more obvious in the past when the beer pot used to be placed in the field and people worked until the pot was empty or until the sun was too high and people had drunk too much to work. In the past, it is said, the beer was not divided equally between participants, even non-participating relatives could partake (the taking out of the beer pot to the field being perhaps an attempt to avoid this),[117] and the sharing out was organized by the workers themselves. Today, in contrast, this is expected to be done by the sponsor himself or herself, observing strict fairness.[118] This suggests that *chenda* is beginning to resemble a payment for individual labour (see below), while it was originally closer to general.

The type of beer served today is mainly mead made of honey. This is most probably a result of growing wax production for export, of which honey-beer is a by-product (see C 4.1). As honey-beer is directly available only to male beekeepers or honey-hunters, and since the purchase of ingredients for a *chenda* is unusual even today, such male specialists are the main group sponsoring work parties. Only their wives are sometimes given comb honey to brew for a *chenda* (these being the only occasions when women brew honey-beer), but this depends on the individual inclination of the husband whether he wishes to discharge some of his duties of assistance towards his wife in this way, and not on any village norms.[119] Beekeepers and their families were presumably one of the groups which could successfully turn world market integration into better access to labour, though not for beekeeping itself.

An alternative type of beer for work parties, to which women have far better access, is made of bulrush millet. One of the incentives for women to reserve a growing part of their millet crop for beer brewing during the 19th century (see section C 5.2) may have been to keep pace with men in their ability solicit additional labour for heavy tasks in fieldwork independently. Today, only Luchazi women continue to brew millet beer for work[120]; other women now rather use cassava as a payment for this purpose (see next section).

As long as millet was dominant, it is possible that nearly every adult sponsored a working party every year, with the other adults in the vicinage participating, so that in effect the *chenda* system was something like an attempt to combine 'generosity' (such as on *lizaji* gatherings) with

---

[116] See also Turner 1957: 22; Beck and Dorlöchter 1987: B67
[117] Sondoyi 18.10.1986
[118] *Ibid*; discussion by women of Kanema village, 8.10.86
[119] Beck and Dorlöchter 1987: B68
[120] LIMA Survey 1983, Chinzombo-Samalesu village (Kabompo)

chilimba, the communal exchange of labour mentioned earlier. The same was apparently true more recently among adult men in areas specialized in honey production (today mainly in the East).[121] *Chenda* would thus have been an attempt to pursue at the same time short-term 'economic' and more long-term 'social' ends. But the 'economic' aspect, an idea of directly exchanging food for labour, may already have gathered momentum in the pre-colonial period, in connection with the growing division of labour. Specialist hunters and beekeepers could thus perform their domestic duties despite prolonged absences from agricultural work, while women, both single and married, could eventually re-invest part of their produce in an expansion of food production without being dependent on husbands or brothers actually assisting them.

But *chenda* is only of limited use for individual accumulation. According to Turner, an adult man is expected not to sponsor more than one work party per year, and he mentions 'grumbling and mutual recriminations over the amount of work to be done, which takes place between the sponsor of the *chenda* and the volunteers who attend'.[122]

Villagers interviewed on this topic declared that 'working parties are difficult to manage' - apparently because of the mixing of redistributive, cooperative and accumulative motives involved. A much more straightforward form of recruiting additional labour for productive work, especially in agriculture, is analysed in the following section.

Njongo - piecework

Under this concept, a certain payment is made by the owner of the field for a certain amount of work agreed upon with individual labourers who may be either neighbours or relatives, and may work either in (small) groups or individually. The work is divided into individual portions (e.g. a part of the field marked by sticks, or a number of seedbeds to be built), which can be managed by a person in a day or more, although time is not relevant as a parameter. The payment originally consisted in some rarer form of food, especially animal protein as in meat or fish. Both these portions or 'shares' of work **and** the portions of payment (chunks of game meat or plates of small *tukeya* fish) equivalent to them are called *njongo* (Lv.,pl. *jinjongo*) or *njongu* (SL.).[123] Therefore, 'piecework' seems to be the best translation for what appears as a most explicit form of contract which is restricted to the immediate exchange of material goods for

---

[121] Cf.Turner 1957: 22

[122] Turner 1957: 22

[123] '*Njo* denotes the idea of being many, close together' (Horton 1975: 256), referring to the cutting into portions.

objectified services and involves no longer-term commitment for the partners involved. As *njongo* is the most widespread form of mobilizing extra-household labour in the region today, I was surprised to find during fieldwork that this 'modern'-looking concept has in fact been an integral part of the regional economy since time immemorial. 'Our old old fathers already used to work for fish, meat etc.' asserted the oldest of my informants, almost 100 years old,[124] although another added that its importance had considerably increased during the 20th century with the expansion of crop cultivation.[125]

Today, a large variety of village tasks can be done in principle by such pieceworkers, but the concept is said to have originated from the *vaka mbunda* , those Luvale who live on the reddish, relatively fertile soils around the middle Lwena river and are well-known as specialized cultivators. This coincides with the statements that clearing fields, hoeing and weeding, along with building houses were the original and are still the typical occasions on which *jinjongo* are given.

These are the same tasks for which work parties were organized. In fact, the only difference that seems to have been seen originally between *njongo* and a work party (*chenda, liyamba lya wala*) was the form of payment - meat or fish for the former, honey or millet beer for the latter.[126] Only gradually, and first among the *vaka mbunda*, was a distinction between these two concepts made, with a stronger emphasis on the exact individual portioning of *njongo* (both labour and payment), perhaps as a result of growing difficulties in finding people for working parties.[127]

But the relation between those who pay and those who work also seems to distinguish *njongo* from work parties. From the point of view of the owner of the field etc., the position was not very different from someone organizing a work party. He or she would have passed round word, a 'call' that may have sounded like 'I have fish, meat, beer etc. for cultivation'(this, according to elders, being the formulation used before the actual term *njongo* was introduced) to advertise for people to come and help him or her with a job in order 'to make things faster' or 'to finish a big field in time'.[128] In such a case, the owner is still expected to have his or her own portion to work (which also facilitates control over labour), and it is effectively only an extension of his or her limited labour

---

[124] Interview Y.Samakayi, 21.10.1986
[125] Sondoyi 18.10.1986
[126] Advisers to Chief Ishinde, 25.10.1986; Mr.Sondoyi 18.10.1986; Y.Samakayi, 21.10.1986
[127] Cf. Chifwisha and Muwika, 22.10.1986
[128] Interviews Samakayi, 21.10.86; Sondoyi 18.10.86; advisers to Chief Ishinde, 25.10.86

force.[129] This is apparently what is meant by a number of proverbs which a peasant used to explain to me the character of piecework, e.g.: 'When a hand is short, a stick should be added to it';[130] or: 'Slowly slowly the frog caught the young one of a duiker' [antelope]. [131] Another peasant put it in less poetic words: '*Njongo* is the result of someone's failing to do his job'.[132]

As such failure can befall virtually every adult at one point or another, it appears possible that, from the 'owner's' point of view, *njongo* has developed from forms of collective work described earlier, as a means of soliciting extra labour on an effectively reciprocal basis to even out individual labour shortages. But there were other, particular motives involved in this arrangement. For example, a person could offer *njongo* to accomplish a task for which he or she was not sufficiently skilled or otherwise suited, e.g. for bushclearing in the case of women. In such a case, the owner has never been expected to participate him/herself.[133]

Another difference is that, compared to other labour relations, the idea *of njongo* seems to imply a stronger material interest of the pieceworkers themselves in obtaining certain scarce goods. At least today, the workers themselves may play sometimes play the more active role:

'When someone wants something, e.g. a pair of shoes, he goes to somebody who has some, and asks: "What can I work for you so that you give me the shoes?" That is *jinjongo*.'[134]

The consumer goods villagers have always been most regularly short of at some point are fish or meat for the 'relish'. As these are precisely the goods most often offered for *njongo*, this is why virtually all groups of adults except full-time hunters and fishermen are potential pieceworkers, since they are likely to be short of 'relish' at least sometimes. Both women and men of any age participate, and 'if a young man has *jinjongo*, an old man has to put down his beard to get this *njongo*'[135]. This places *njongo* in the context of the emergence of a new societal division of labour which is no longer generational or gendered.

Even today, most villagers have access to fish or meat through other means at least sometimes, so that no permanent status of wage labour has

---

[129] Discussion with D. Chishinji and J. Sakutadika 18.10.1986; interview Samakayi, 24.10.1986
[130] Interview Samakayi, 24.10.1986
[131] SL. *Chovu chovu chula wakwatili mwana kankayi* (interview G. Munyawu, 9.9.86).
[132] Interview Mr.Sondoyi 18.10.1986
[133] Interview Samakayi, 24.10.1986
[134] Interview G. Munyawu, 9.9.1986. My attention was drawn to this aspect by Josefine Beck and Sabine Dorlöchter, cf. 1988: 243.
[135] Interview Sondoyi 18.10.1986

yet been able to develop through this type of contract. People who are able to offer *njongo* at one point may be forced to work for other people's *njongo* at another. Piecework in its original form is seen by the pieceworkers mainly as a means of 'buying' essential foodstuffs when the need arises. In fact, when Upper Zambezi inhabitants talk about *njongo*, they often use a terminology of buying and selling. For example, they complain that 'certain [mean] people buy things only for *jinjongo* and never give any goods',[136] or declare plainly that *njongo* means 'to buy people'.[137] The term used here is *kulanda*, the generic expression for any act of bartering, buying or selling of goods within the region (see next section).[138] In effect, individual piecework is closely linked to other forms of local exchanges between producers.

This analysis of the 'essence' of piecework allows to draw some tentative conclusions as to its historical development in the pre-colonial period. Individual piecework may have been for a very long time just one alternative access to scarce goods and labour between individuals, mostly of different villages, within the local economy, and may have had a socially balancing effect between the individuals and groups involved to even out temporary shortages. Increasing specialization and productivity in hunting, fishing and agriculture following the productive innovations of the 16th to 18th centuries, then, led to a deepened societal division of labour of which piecework arrangements may have become a part.

Specialized male hunters and fishermen can be assumed to have been the first or main group to employ others (both men and women) as pieceworkers and thereby discharge their agricultural duties of assistance towards their wives, and possibly to work their own fields. Plain fishing coincides largely with the season of bush-clearing, and hunting with field preparation (see table 5, above). Some of those employed by hunters and fishermen in forest areas with little fish or game resources, especially men, began to travel to the open plains either to hunt and fish themselves or to barter crops (especially cassava) and other surplus products for fish and meat. They are likely to have been driven not only by their own food needs, but also by the possibility of using these highly demanded protein foods as payment for pieceworkers in cultivation back home, a widespread practice today.

But if only meat and fish were in fact the typical payments for piecework, the female half of the population was put in a weaker position by these developments. Male informants emphasize that both women and men did work for *jinjongo* even in the past, and one told me that 'even

---

[136] Interview Sondoyi 18.10.1986
[137] Interview Headman Munyawu, 8.10.1986

men could work for women [laughter]. They had no right to stay [at home] if they had nothing to eat'; but then he went on to admit that 'in former times it was mainly women who worked for fish and meat'.[139] The problem is that women have hardly any direct access to these forms of payment for piecework according to the division of labour by gender. Women never hunt any game that can be cut up into 'portions', and their fishing efforts rarely bring forth any surplus for paying pieceworkers. Unmarried younger women are in a particularly weak position as they have little claim on men to supply them with free 'relish' even for themselves.

One way for non-hunters and non-fishermen to procure payment for pieceworkers through their own production today is to raise small livestock, especially pigs, among the Luchazi. This possibility may have prompted women in particular to invest export incomes in the acquisition of such animals already during the last century, and may explain some of the growth of small livestock during this period (see C 5.4). But agricultural crops have certainly remained the most important product women can dispose of relatively independent; at the same time women are particularly dependent on assistance by men and often by other women if they want to guarantee or increase their production of these crops. In the past, working parties were frequently called in by brewing millet beer, but this was probably only of limited use (see above). In addition, millet surplus must have often been insignificant or unreliable. Cassava cultivation, it seems, must have appeared to women as a particularly attractive alternative in these respects, especially to singles who have no rights to assistance by a husband. It provided them with more significant and reliable surplus food, not only to exchange with fishermen, hunters or regional traders for 'relish', but also with others for labour. Today, 'of all possible means of payment for piecework, cassava is the most important for women'.[140]

There are two groups of villagers who are potentially in need of extra caloric food for their subsistence: resident women who have failed for some reason to grow enough crops themselves, and recently established producers, either newly married or immigrants just settled, who cannot yet reap their own harvest. Failure to grow sufficient food can be the result of drought (particularly with grain crops) or of some other calamity (e.g. illness) resulting in labour constraints. Drought is a collective fate, and prolonged sickness or infirmity due to age are about the only reasons for relatives to help free of charge, but all other cases tend to be

---

[138] Also interview with advisers to senior chief Ishinde, 25.10.1986; Y.Samakayi equated *njongo* with the verb *kutekela*, the Mbunda synonym for *kulanda* (interview 24.10.1986).
[139] Interview Sondoyi 18.10.1986
[140] Beck and Dorlöchter 1988: 245

condemned as 'laziness' in the village context: to be hard-working and to grow a sizeable crop for food is regarded as one of the prime virtues of a woman. Consequently, piecework for crops is seen as shameful in village eyes. One of the conventional standard measures for payment of cassava meal is a certain basket (SL. *ihebi*, Lv.*mutonga*) which is nicknamed *wayileyi* (Lv.; SL. *wahileyi*), a term which

> 'translates literally as "where were you?", and is an abbreviated form of the derogatory unspoken question that accompanies this basket. "Where were you when your friends were out working ?" '[141]

In practice, many or even all women may have to work for food crops at some point so that piecework of resident women can again be seen to some extent as a means of evening out temporary food shortages. Cassava cultivation increased the amount of crops available for both food and employing pieceworkers; but it did not remove temporary food shortages altogether, because of the protracted treatment cassava tubers require. Often, women are short of **processed** cassava, and have to ask others for chips or meal in return for piecework. (See fig. 28)

Much less balanced is the piecework relation in the second case, in which established residents, both women and men, employ newly settled villagers such as young married spouses or immigrant 'strangers'. In the vernacular languages the term *ngeji* ('stranger') may be used not only for people outside the kingroup but even for a village member, e.g. a nephew, who has been away for some time and just returned[142], i.e. it applies to any newly arrived inhabitant of the village, and distinguishes immigrants from residents. This former group always comprised a considerable percentage of Upper Zambezi population, particularly younger people, due to the high mobility in this society which is its most important means of coping with the social tensions mentioned above (see D 3). The frequency of transferring homesteads undoubtedly increased during the 19th century as a consequence of slave raids, wars and dwindling resources for export production (see chronology, part B). New immigrants or refugees initially often depend entirely on the food and the seed or planting material they are given by elders, hosts or new neighbours. Although these are usually glad to see their number swelled, there are certain limits to the willingness and ability of residents to supply numerous such dependants for longer periods. Besides other forms of payment, to asking 'strangers' to do piecework has probably been found by these residents to be an excellent solution to the problem: without having to appear stingy they can replenish their food reserves for various future occasions. One pragmatic farmer remarked on his extended

---

[141] Hansen 1976: 219; see also J. Beck and S. Dorlöchter 1988: 248
[142] Horton, 1975[2]: 243

relations: 'You can help them as much as you want, they won't remember it. It is better to let them do some work for it'.[143]

Given the very subordinate power position of newly established villagers and neighbours it can be expected that the terms of pay were similarly unequal. At least today, refugees from the Angolan civil war (who are now the most numerous group of immigrants in Zambian villages of the region), do work their hosts' fields at a fairly exploitative rate: two days' food for one day's work.[144] This practice sheds some new light on the introduction of cassava cultivation. Seen in this context, cassava increased, first of all, the food surplus available to feed visitors and immigrants to a certain area or village, and thereby made the place more attractive and populous. If new settlers could be put to work for food after a certain period of grace had elapsed (today only about two weeks), they helped to increase the production of residents before they could build up their own. To resident elders cassava may have appealed at least as much for this second reason as for the first. The increase in number or size of fields was again particularly valuable in the case of cassava because it can be stored in the ground until needed for up to several years, much longer than any stock of millet can possibly last in a village grain bin. Old cassava stocks can later be used to attract more people and pay more pieceworkers.

Cassava, in other words, opened a way for individual accumulation of food in the form of unharvested cassava fields. And power over food could not only be transformed into wealth (through interregional trade - see above), but, as usual, also into power over people, in an area in which this has always been a key problem. Cassava as a form of payment for piecework made women economically less dependent on their male partners, and increased the very limited possibilities of elders in the Upper Zambezi of appropriating juniors` labour, but, characteristically, only during the transition period until these juniors had established their own food base.

Little is known about the extent to which piecework was also more directly involved in or affected by world-market integration. Some remarks suggest that pieceworkers were also employed in export production. I was told, for example, that a hunter may have taken some people with him on his bush trips to dig rubber roots which he would then pay for with meat and give to others for hammering, whom he would again pay in meat.[145] More recently, a beekeeper may have paid his son or nephew to empty a hive for him by giving him a share (between half

---
[143] Interview J. Sakutadika 18.10.1986
[144] See also Hansen 1976: 217

and one fifth) of the yield; and an elderly hunter may give his gun to young men for a hunting trip who may then retain half the kill (or only a leg, if they borrowed even the ammunition).[146] These variants of payment for labour may well have already existed in the last century, although I have no direct proof of this. In these last examples, however, the 'payment' consisted in reality in access to individually owned means of production.

When private capital begins to play a role in production, actual wage relations may gradually emerge. Developed forms of wage labour came into pre-colonial Upper Zambezi and Kasai only through foreign capital, by caravan entrepreneurs employing carriers, guides, interpreters ('workers of trade' - see parts B and E). Another group of foreign entrepreneurs who prepared wage relations was that of missionaries. F. Coillard, for example, employed Lozi women to work his gardens for beads.[147] But inhabitants of the region clearly distinguish work for pay or wages (*fwèto*) from *njongo*; elders say that *fwèto*, consisting in 'wealth' goods, is due for the completion a big job, while the term *njongo* retains the idea of directly exchanging small quantities, 'bits' (of work) for 'bits'(of pay).[148]

This again emphasizes the closeness between the indigenous concept of piecework and barter exchange of local products, which will be looked at in the last section of this chapter. Nevertheless, both types of exchange did to some extent integrate payment in imported goods. Elders say that tobacco, Ovimbundu (rock) salt and cloth were later added to meat and fish as payment for pieceworkers.[149] As with obligations towards other partners (e.g. their wives), men seem to have gradually substituted the products of their labour with what they earned from it on foreign markets. Today, pieceworkers employed by men are frequently paid in cash. In this way, the employment of pieceworkers gradually changed from an aspect of the local and regional division of labour into an expression of income inequality. In the end, the capacity to employ pieceworkers 'depended only on wealth', not on other social categories, as Yowena Samakayi put it.[150]

---

[145] Interview Mr.Sondoyi, 21.10.1986 (but this referred to the short-lived second rubber-boom during the Second World War).

[146] Interview Kasanjilo, Kamenga and Chiwafwa, 28.5.1983; Wendorf 1988: 127; interview G. M., 4.10.1986

[147] Coillard 1897: 524

[148] Interview Y.Samakayi, 24.10.1986; according to Horton (1975: 41) *kufwèta* is said to originate from Ovimbundu; the term seems to be etymologically related to *kuhèta*, to acquire possessions or 'wealth'.

[149] Interviews Mr.Sondoyi 18.10.1986; and Y.Samakayi, 24.10.1986

[150] Interview 24.10.1986

Kulanda - barter exchange

The increasing exchange of products within the region, between different categories of producers at different ecological locations, as a consequence of productive innovation and specialization, has been described earlier (see chapter C 3). An open question is how such transactions were actually realized. Given the high degree of segmentation in these societies, it is certain that a substantial, perhaps major, part of these exchanges went across 'household' and village boundaries. An unidentifiable proportion was undoubtedly channelled through reciprocal arrangements of various kinds, i.e. defined as 'gifts' or 'friendship presents' (see the preceding sections of this part). Gluckman has argued, for instance, that much of the regional trade between the Lozi and their northern neighbours, especially the Nkoya, was realized through 'friendship' arrangements. [151]

The analysis of 19th century travellers' reports on transactions in the region (see part E) allows equally little doubt, however, that another substantial portion of foodstuffs and other local products was transacted between individual producers under the label of 'barter exchange', i.e. a momentary relationship based in principle on the idea of equivalence between certain goods, and not on more long-term reciprocal ties between certain persons. This idea of objective equivalence is precisely what is expressed by the indigenous term *ndandu* (SL.; Lv. *lando*, related to the verb *kulanda*) which was mentioned above in connection with piecework; its meaning comes close to what economists call a 'commodity', goods seen as exchange-value, but also includes the notion of its counterpart: 'price', 'value' or 'payment'. Competent informants consider *kulanda* to be a very ancient practice in the region.[152] The distinctness of this object (and not person-) centred concept of local exchange relations is shown by its central idea of standard exchange ratios between standard amounts of goods. For example, the same type of basket called *wayileyi* full of cassava meal, which was used as a payment for a certain portion of fieldwork (see above), is also seen as equivalent for a certain piece ('bit'- *njongo*) of meat or fish.[153]

How this concept was effective in exchanges with the foreign agents of the pre-colonial world market integration will be analysed in the following part (E). It should be stressed that the indigenous concept originally did not accommodate price fluctuations. The idea of a 'right (or just) price'

---

[151] Gluckman 1941: 72

[152] Interview with advisers to chief Ishinde, 25.10.1986; cf. J. Beck and S. Dorlöchter 1988: 243

[153] See Beck and Dorlöchter 1988: 168; Horton (1975[2]: 247) translates *njongo* as 'small measure or portion for sale or sold'. See also Douglas 1963: 64f

was apparently an essential part of the local barter economy. The advent of the wider market and increasing pressure on certain local resources, because of foreign demand and disruptions of regional trade, most probably meant a serious strain for the local 'moral economy' of prices already in the 19th century. Producers of potentially scarce local products such as game meat, fish, and perhaps iron goods may have felt inclined to ask for greater amounts of products in return. As these were all male producers, such price increases would have been primarily at the expense of women.

No contemporary evidence is available about to what extent exchange rates for local products did in fact change before independence. The issues at stake in such a case are illustrated, however, by recent village studies in the region.[154] Josephine Beck and Sabine Dorlöchter found that such price increases for basic foodstuffs (staple, 'relish', beers) today are expressed in monetary values, although actual money is still not always used in local exchange; the standard measurements mentioned remain important reference units. A doubling of the monetary price appears to be an easier way of saying that for a chunk of meat now two instead of one basket of meal are expected to be given. In this way, the intrusion of pre-colonial currencies (body ornaments, cloth), which were apparently used to some extent also in local exchanges by the end of the 19th century (see chapter C 6) may already have helped men to argue for such price changes.

Furthermore, the two researchers have shown that village women tried to counteract these attempts by demanding a doubling of the price for a basket of cassava as well. Their argument was precisely the customary exchange rate of one to one between the standard units: 'men always destroy the old prices', some women complained.[155] It seems that the women's argument reveals some of the original meaning of barter relations: they took place between individual producers, but were embedded in a context of societal division of labour. Significantly, only products of different categories (crops, 'relish', drinks), usually associated with different categories of producers, are locally exchangeable. Goods of the same category, e.g. different crops or meat and fish, are never bartered for each other.[156] Barter rates of exchange express not only equivalence between certain types and amounts of goods, but at the same time the balance of power between different social groups of producers, above all women and men. It seems that success in such struggles over prices always depended very much on the actual economic

---

[154] The following account is a synopsis of Beck and Dorlöchter 1988: 167-169 (also 1987: 21-23)
[155] Beck and Dorlöchter 1988: 168
[156] Cf. Beck and Dorlöchter 1988: 163

position of the parties involved; today, women tend to be the losers, but this may not always have been so.

These implications of barter exchange explain the social importance of price control mechanisms. Today, prices are discussed once a year at more or less formal meetings attended by both male and female inhabitants of a neighbourhood (today the administrative headman areas). For the pre-colonial period, there are only a few references to formal price control with regard to foreign trade exercised by chiefs (see below, E 1), but this may be a different case. Effective price control, at any rate, seems to have been rather difficult in practice.

Kulanda, barter exchange, thus seems to have an indigenous origin which was distinct from the circulation of 'gifts'. Its functioning, however, did depend to some extent on social networks beyond the individual exchange act. Peaceful neighbourhood relations, for example, were conducive to 'price control' mechanisms. Producers and traders tried to turn these and the other, stronger personal bonds, which cost them substantial parts of their wealth, into benefits which could be decisive also for their economic enterprises.

D 4.4 The benefits of friendship: Credits and compensations

'Friendship' and business

A crucial precondition even for local exchange was trust between the individual exchange partners as to the fulfilment of their contractual obligations. At least in some cases, payments for goods or piecework were made in advance, and the giver had to put his faith in the recipient's reliability.[157] When a man gave his meat first and waited until the pieceworker had time to work, he was considered to be 'generous'.[158] Such short-term 'credits' may have been given deliberately to create or maintain personal bonds with certain people. They may, however, also have resulted from various older claims on the part of the recipient. Such claims are today a constant problem for people who want to conduct business in the local barter economy; female sellers of fish or beer, for

---
[157] An example of a portion of game meat given on credit to a Chokwe slave is mentioned in Dias de Carvalho 1890: 695.
[158] E.g. Interview Mr.Sondoyi 18.10.1986

example, complain about regularly being asked by relations and 'friends' to serve them free or add a bonus 'on top' of the standard unit. In effect, the theoretical 'right price' is in reality often undercut by such manipulations of standard measurements.

Personal 'generosity' in a context of theoretically impersonal exchange, however, was not necessarily onerous for the giver, while often being conducive or even vital for business itself. Trust had to be built, not only to ensure reliability of contracts in a society without state, but also to bring exchange partners together in the first place. This second aspect arose partly from potential competition for scarce goods and services; it may well have appeared as a privilege to be offered a rare piece of meat in return for other goods before others; and in certain seasons and areas it may have been as difficult to mobilize sufficient pieceworkers in time as it is today. In a highly mobile and scattered population like the one around the Upper Zambezi and Kasai, there has always been the problem of actually finding a partner who was able and prepared to offer sufficient quantities of certain goods for exchange. These problems were likely to increase considerably when exchange relations extended beyond the neighbourhood cluster, as it often necessarily did because of ecological differences.

One case where these problems can still be studied is the widely scattered population of the western part of today's Zambezi District who, despite their remoteness, export large amounts of dried fish (see fig. 14). The customers' (petty traders', cultivators') main risk is of spending considerable periods wandering about in search of fish ready for sale or waiting for produce. The inhabitants' main risks, in contrast, are either not being visited by customers when they have substantial surplus fish to sell, or being short of staple food due to unexpectedly high floods. The second problem is exacerbated by the fact that the seasons of food shortage and fish surplus do not coincide, and that floods make the area virtually inaccessible during the hunger months.[159] The solution to these risks that has been successfully applied between Eastbank petty traders (perhaps also cultivators) and Westbank fishermen in the last few decades gives an idea of how regional barter trade may have been conducted in a more distant past:[160]

> The Eastbank buyer of fish selects one or several fishermen whom he has known as reliable for a long time, and whom he calls *vakufwelela* (Lv.,'the trusted ones'). He supplies them with staple food (cassava meal) on credit before the peak of the floods, in November or December, and promises to come back to

---

[159] See Alff, von Oppen and Beck 1986

[160] Y.Samakayi, who had been a petty trader when he was young around the turn of the century, confirmed to me that the *vakufwelela* system was practised then (interview 24.10.1986). It also closely resembles the much better documented arrangements between producers and foreign traders in that period (see part E).

their fishing camps during the peak fishing season, between about March and May. If he is a trader, he promises to bring his *vakufwelela* more goods according to their wishes (e.g. blankets). In return, he expects his fishermen to pay him the value of his supplies in fish. The fisherman may also give additional fish to a trader 'on credit', for additional purchases of goods for him in town. He may furthermore act as an agent on behalf of a trader, and connect him with a number of other fishermen ('friends').[161]

The *vakufwelela* case suggests that credit and debt, which seem to originate in the sphere of personal reciprocal relations (see elsewhere in this chapter), may have also been applied for a long time to the distinct sphere of intra-regional trade. Here, the debt relation responded not only to economic requirements (seasonal food shortages), but also to a strong need for security which could only be achieved through personal networks of 'friendship' and trust. In reality, such relationships at least today appear to be much less mutually beneficial than suggested in the above presentation of the case by an ex-trader, the trader being usually in a much stronger position, but they obviously correspond to security problems felt on both sides. Personal bonds between people from different areas seem to have played an important role as a kind of infrastructure for regional exchange for a long time, presumably since the earlier pre-colonial period.

Hospitality and trade

Another example of this infrastructural role of personal bonds is the hospitality they secured. Hospitality has always been considered a fundamental virtue of inhabitants in the West-Central African interior. The Upper Zambezi term for 'stranger', *ngeji*, has a significant second meaning of 'guest' (like the Latin *hospes*). Popular tales such as that on the origin of Lake Dilolo emphasize the obligation of hospitality towards strangers.[162] This general obligation increased if personal relations with the 'stranger' existed. 'A kind of hospitality and inclination to make gifts to his relatives and friends' was observed by 19th century travellers.[163] Common clanship, in-law status, joking relations, friendship or common cult membership all involve strong obligations to give and rights to demand assistance and hospitality. White has asserted for the Luvale and related peoples, for example, that formerly 'the knowledge of ...

---

[161] I owe this information to David Chishinji, Dipalata, an ex-trade assistant to his grandfather (interview 18.10.1986). 'Trusted friends' are today also employed, for example, to care for distant fields when the owner (a trader) is frequently absent (interview L. Kaloza, Chingalala, 22.10.1986).

[162] Several versions of this legend were reported by 19th century travellers; the first, to my knowledge, is found in Cameron 1877: II, 171f.

[163] Pogge 1880: 6

genealogical links determined how far a man could travel in safety',[164] since common kinship carries with it strong obligations of mutual hospitality and aid. A 'stranger' (*ngeji*) who arrives in a village and, in addressing the *muyombo* tree, is able to prove that he belongs to the same clan as his hosts by reciting the clan formula, can be sure of being given shelter and food. The only expectation on the part of the hosts would be that the visitor hand over a token of respect before departure which may have consisted in some salt or cloth.[165]

The same rules of hospitality applied to the other categories of inter-village relations. To have 'relatives' and 'friends' etc. in distant places or even among other ethnic groups would then also mean to have a reliable network of relays for the numerous journeys a man had to undertake in the past (and still today), e.g. for regional trade. Trade has always meant a considerable amount of travelling in the region, and this tendency undoubtedly greatly expanded during the 19th century. The strength of inter-village networks, the strong cultural, linguistic etc. similarities between the groups, and the incidence of regional trade seem to have been closely interrelated characteristics in the history of the region.[166]

Debts and defaulters

The key benefit of inter-village networks, however, was the obligation of mutual 'assistance' they involved. This assistance seems to have most often consisted in the provision of goods that were suddenly required on various occasions and which could not be procured by the recipient him or herself. One of the oldest such occasions was probably famine, the permanent threat in grain-based economies, in which a 'friend' was expected to help out with food as gifts or loans.[167] Taking credits from 'friends', in fact an essential part of friendship contracts (see above, D 4.2), has always included 'wealth' goods of various kinds.[168] This aspect of friendship must have expanded considerably with the growing demand for imported goods in the era of Atlantic long-distance trade. To seek such goods on credit could be imperative, for example, when a major gift

---
[164] White 1960a: 16
[165] See Antunes Cabrita 1954: 60f
[166] Cf. Gluckman 1941: 72/73; Papstein 1978: 233-235
[167] Cf. McCulloch 1951: 22 [Southern Lunda]. Against Miller (1982: 29), I assume that various forms of borrowing food, as well as 'food for work', were probably the most important arrangements for redistributing food in case of famine in the drier and thinly populated parts of Central Africa, including the entire Upper Zambezi region. The loss of personal freedom and enslavement which he mentions may have been more typical reactions to crop failure around fertile river valleys with intensive cultivation.

was required to appease a close relative.[169] But a need for credit also often arose as a direct consequence of commercial undertakings, e.g. when boats or oxen were unexpectedly required for transport, or when somebody wanted to use an advantageous opportunity to buy cloth without having sufficient rubber ready for sale.[170]

Such indigenous credit relations, however, often seem to have put the 'friendship' in whose name they were concluded under serious strain, as the fear of defaulting was great despite all precautions. The often frustrating experiences of foreign traders with their debtors among the local inhabitants may have held true among these themselves as well (see below, chapter E 2). Disputes over repayment often arose, and creditors resorted to robberies and kidnapping in order to recover their credit, which usually resulted in armed feuds and taking slaves.[171] Credit conditions were often generous for the reasons mentioned, and repayment could be delayed for years or debts were even be passed on to the heir.[172] But ultimate failure or outright refusal to pay back was regarded a serious offence in the local context, for which the highest compensation was due. Defaulters then had to surrender either a dependant or themselves: 'If you took a credit, e.g. *kambungo* [root rubber], and didn't pay back in time, you could be taken a slave yourself.'[173]

In effect, credit relations could become costly, rather than beneficial, for both sides and be rather counterproductive for friendship relations. Significantly, there is no vernacular equivalent for 'credit' (from Latin 'something entrusted to someone'), but a generic term for 'debt' (*mukuli*) which emphasizes the burden or obligation rather than the trust involved.[174]

This was apparently the reason why pledges or pawns were often asked in return for a credit as a recognition of the debt. If the debt was of major value these pawns were in human beings (hostages), while material tokens were used on other occasions, e.g. cattle, amounts of cloth or enamel

---

[168] A detailed anthropological analysis of village debt relations has been provided by Mary Douglas in her book on the neighbouring Lele on the Middle Kasai (1963: ch. IX)

[169] E.g. White 1960a: 37 (a more recent example)

[170] Livingstone 1963: 269 [Southern Lunda, 1855]; Baumann 1935: 132 [Chokwe/Luvale, late pre-colonial period]; Rapport Frausto, quoted by Vellut 1972: 154; interview Mr.Sondoyi, 24.10.1986

[171] E.g. in the case of a Southern Lunda who emptied the beehive of his 'friend' as a return for his 'friendship gift' consisting in some goats (Livingstone 1963: 268 [1855]).

[172] E.g. Antunes Cabrita 1954: 57 [Luvale, 1920s]; Dias de Carvalho 1890: 694 [Chokwe]

[173] Interview Mr. Sondoyi, 24.10.1986

[174] Horton assumes that *mukuli* contains the idea of a heavy load; 'he gave me a credit' would be expressed in Luvale as 'he incurred an indebtedness to me' - *alile mukuli wami* (1975: 139).

plates.[175] Wealthy and powerful creditors such as certain chiefs even seem to have charged 'interest' on such credits as they are said to have demanded double the amount of the loan for the redemption of a hostage.[176] It has been mentioned already that in indigenous terms people given as hostages or in compensation for some offence were distinguished from other unfree persons taken as captives or bought (see D 3). Mary Douglas has argued that this status, in contrast to actual slavery, meant that the person was not completely severed from his or her original lineage identity.[177] I find this distinction difficult to verify for the peoples of the Upper Zambezi and Kasai at least for the second half of the 19th century. Debt pawns seem to have been fully absorbed into the recipient lineage if redemption was not forthcoming after some time,[178] while people given or taken in compensation for debt defaulting or some other offence were usually regarded as proper slaves and were even frequently sold off to foreign traders.[179] Livingstone's statement on the neighbouring Mbangala held probably, to a lesser extent, also true for this region:

'The sons of a sister belong to her brother, and he often sells his nephews to pay his debts; and by these customs more than by war is the slave market supplied.'[180]

Cases and compensations

According to indigenous concepts of law, there is a striking closeness between debt and other outstanding obligations. In the past, the compensation or 'fine' (see below) resulting from a verdict, for example, was regarded as a debt if it is not paid on the spot, and a material token or recognition of this debt has to be handed over by the convict.[181] The

---
[175] See for example Antunes Cabrita 1954: 57 and 71 [Luvale]; Diniz 1919: 397 [Luchazi etc.]. The transfer of a slave as security is mentioned, for instance, in the example decribed by Frausto, a Portuguese trader (quoted in Vellut 1972: 154). On non-human pawns see below.
[176] White 1960a: 51
[177] Douglas 1964; see also 1963: ch. IX
[178] E.g. Antunes Cabrita 1954: 63
[179] E.g Livingstone 1963: 251/2, 268 [Southern Lunda, 1855]; Silva Porto 1885: 146 [1880; Luchazi]; neither Turner (1957: 189f) nor White (1957: 71f) confirm such a special status of 'pawnship', although they both suggest that most 'lineage slaves' were actually obtained through legal cases; White (ibid.: 72) gives only as an exception the case of a captive who is taken as compensation to substitute a man killed during the raid and is then regarded as free (called *kahinga*, 'replacement').
[180] Synopsis of two corresponding passages in Livingstone 1857: 434/35 and 1963: 216. Confirmed by van Binsbergen 1992: 126, for the neighbouring Nkoya.
[181] White mentions *kapopo* as a Luvale term for such a material recognition of the debt of a convict who is unable to pay immediately (communication cited in McCulloch 1951: 49); other Luvale terms are *chisupo* and *chijikilo* (cf. Horton 1975).

D 4: Inter-village relations 337

Luvale word *kuli* (related to *mukuli*, debt) denotes 'one who pays another's fine or debt'.[182] A variety of violations of legitimate claims were seen as 'debt defaulting' and could be sued for, e.g. failure to return a friendship gift; failure to do a job which has already been paid for was regarded as equivalent to theft.[183] Finally, the same kind of ritual was performed to declare a protracted legal dispute settled, an outstanding debt paid, or a commercial transaction sealed (see below).

Defaulting such 'debts', or rather: failure to fulfill formal contracts, however, was only one among a variety of offences according to customary law. Typical others were, according to various sources:

* violations of property rights (e.g.theft, unauthorized grazing of animals on fields, etc.);

* lack of respect for chiefs and headmen (e.g. in greeting ceremonies, failure of a visitor to make the customary gift to his host, refusal to surrender a tribute or pawn to a chief);[184]

* disturbance of ritual processes (e.g.quarrels, disregard for certain rules during circumscision, funerals, hunters' absence...)

* adultery;

* assault;

* manslaughter and murder;

* death of a person regarded as being under the culprit's responsibility (e.g. a wife during marriage, a warrior assisting another village or a chief in a feud, or a carrier while employed in a caravan)

* witchcraft.

The generic term for all these offences, *mulonga*, was at the same time applied to the case or law suit arranged to correct them.[185]

Jurisdiction in these Central African (and other) stateless societies had no penal law; all kinds of offences, including manslaughter and murder, were regarded as 'damages', i.e. as private delicts, liable for

---

[182] *Ibid.*

[183] "Notes on customary law: Manyinga Native Authority (1949)", in: Kabompo District Notebook, vol.II, NAZ KTV I/I, p.6. Among the Southern Lunda, such breaches of 'friendship' were dealt with at 'Native Courts' as late as the 1940s (McCulloch 1951: 23).

[184] Antunes Cabrita 1954: 72f, 62

[185] An idea of 'putting in order' or 'instructing' (cf. the Lv. verb *kulònga*) seems to be the etymological origin of this term (cf. Horton 1975: 184-85).

compensation rather than punishment.[186] Claims by the damaged party thus created were regarded, as long as they were unsettled, as 'debts' or 'blood debts'. As mentioned earlier, either junior dependants or the convict himself were handed over on many occasions as compensation, especially to settle 'blood debts'.[187] As elsewhere in Central Africa, legal disputes may have been the main indigenous source of unfree status ('slavery') in the region.

The Luvale historian M. Sangambo, however, has emphasized that the majority of cases was settled by payments in foodstuffs and other non-human compensation, and that the payment of *vandungo* (slaves) was restricted 'by self interest to the most serious transgressions'.[188] This may have partly been said with an apologetic intention, as any form of 'slavery' assumed a very negative connotation in the area after the colonial period. But it is still likely that compensations really originally consisted mainly in foodstuffs and non-human 'wealth'. Apart from the actual compensations, mutual 'gifts' between plaintiff and defendant (as means of reconciliation and recognition of guilt) took place as well as other payments to the arbitrator (Ch.*ngaji* - usually a local headman or chief) and, if applicable some, advocates (Ch.*haku*). These gifts consisted in food, small livestock (chickens, goats), and later an enamel plate, a cup, or some cloth.[189]

Important changes occurred, however, from the late 18th century on, in connection with the beginning of world market integration. It is plausible, for example, that the frequency of legal disputes increased with the social tensions accompanying pre-colonial world market integration. At any rate, the peoples of the Upper Zambezi and Kasai were notorious among 19th century travellers as being continuously entangled in eternal *milonga* or 'palavers'.[190] It seems that most violent incidents in the area were actually sparked off by protracted legal disputes.[191] Continual petty warfare, stealing of people, 'disorders' and arson between neighbouring villages were described as endemic in many parts of the region in the

---

[186] Pogge 1880: 7 and 36-39 [Chokwe, Songo]; Dias de Carvalho 1890: 687 [Northern Chokwe]; Schomburgk 1925: 126-27 [Southern Lunda]; Diniz 1918: 398 [Luchazi/Mbunda]; Montenez 1937 [Chokwe]; Antunes Cabrita 1954: 57ff [Luvale]

[187] Frobenius 1988: 76 [Northern Chokwe, 1905]; "Notes on customary law: Manyinga Native Authority (1949)", in: Kabompo District Notebook, vol.II, NAZ KTV I/I, p.4. For a detailed analysis of 'blood debts' see Douglas on the neighbouring Lele (1963: ch. VIII).

[188] Papstein 1978: 226/27

[189] Descriptions of the proceedings are found in Wissmann 1902: 34-36 [Northern Chokwe]; Dias de Carvalho 1890: 399ff [Chokwe]; Montenez 1937 [Chokwe]; Antunes Cabrita 1954: 58f [Luvale]; Baumann 1935: 147 [Chokwe]

[190] E.g. Silva Porto 1885: 169 [1880; Chokwe]; Frobenius 1988: 270 [1905, Northern Chokwe]

1850s.[192] (See fig. 27) The basic condition for these tensions and the very complicated way of regulating them is clearly an indigenous one: the fragmentation of this society without a powerful state. Long-distance trade, however, seems to have put the indigenous, decentralized forms of regulating conflict under excessive stress. This is borne out, for example, by a remark by Pogge who found crime and accusations to be much less frequent in Nuclear Lunda than among the Chokwe.[193]

Highly formal rituals were apparently required to declare protracted legal disputes closed and to interrupt potentially endless chains of claims and counterclaims. Several versions or components of this ritual appear in sources on the Chokwe in the 1880s, e.g. to notch a tree, to break a twig, to mark crosses on the mouth with white clay, or to divide a goat into two equal parts between the parties; but the essence was invariably to declare publicly 'the question decided and forgotten, for even to refer to a matter after it has been formally settled in this way is considered by the *Chibokwe* as scandalous.'[194]

The incidence of certain material offences requiring compensation may have increased objectively during this period, e.g. through debt defaulting, property disputes, deaths of dependants during absence from home, or manslaughter during wars. In addition, however, the inhabitants of the region were frequently described as extremely superstitious and afraid of what appeared in European eyes as imagined threats, called 'witchcraft' or *feitiço*. It was observed that no death, except of very old persons, was accepted as having natural causes, but divination and ordeals were resorted to in order to find the 'witch' or 'wizard' (*muloji*) behind the death.[195] Witchcraft may be seen here as a shorthand for magic capacities which are associated with power, 'jealousy' and 'stinginess', in other words, indicators of increasing social inequality and threats to an ideology of reciprocity. Significantly, witchcraft was also held responsible for economic performance. In one case, 'the wrath of the *Valovale* was roused' when their manioc withered due to poor rains, a

---

[191] E.g. Livingstone 1963: 268, 275 [1854/54]
[192] E.g. Silva Porto 1938: 70 [*Ganguelas*, ; 1853] Livingstone 1963: 42, 95 [Southern Lunda]
[193] Pogge 1880: 88
[194] Arnot 1969: 155 [C, Chokwe 1885]; more detailed descriptions for the Northern Chokwe in Dias de Carvalho 1890: 407, 410/11 and 415; he mentions similar customs for Nuclear Lunda, only that instead of notching the tree a banana shrub is planted after the blood of the divided goat has been let into the pit (ibid., 415).
[195] E.g. Diniz 1918: 393 [*Ganguelas*]

victim was saught and found through administration of the hot water ordeal, tied to a tree and allegedly burnt alive.[196]

Capital punishment was apparently not a general device of indigenous jurisdiction. According to White, even in cases of homicide or alleged witchcraft (murder) only particularly heavy compensations were due; feuds and bloodshed (revenge) are said to have been only a last resort when it was impossible to settle cases peacefully.[197] But reports from the late pre-colonial period mention a number of exceptions in which the convict was killed rather than forced to pay compensation: theft of standing crop in the fields[198], adultery with a chief's wife, plotting against a chief,[199] premeditated assassination[200], and above all witchcraft murder[201]. This is a strong indicator of the general increase in social tensions and violence during the period. The intrusion of open violence into law suits meant not only victimization of certain social groups, but also economic damage. It destroyed the human productive and reproductive capacities of the 'convicts' rather than reallocating them as in the customary legal system. Significantly, the 'witches' killed in the most brutal way after their 'trial' seem to have been women in most cases: 'The victims are generally sought among women of advanced age, who are sacrificed together with their single daughters...'[202]

The vast majority of cases, however, continued to be settled with compensation until the end of the period. On the whole, the value of these compensations seems to have increased considerably with the massive import of 'wealth', notably slaves, cattle, guns and cloth. The original meaning of 'compensation' implied in the term *mulonga* (see above) logically suggests a 1:1 rate between damage and compensation. Such a rate was still applied sometimes by the mid-19th century.[203] But in 1875, in the 'wealthier' areas near to northern trade routes, the convict had to pay

---

[196] Harding 1904: 68-70; I have personally witnessed accusations of witchcraft because of uneven performance of crops between different peasants which ended in sudden death of the accused.
[197] White 1960a: 28, 23; M. Douglas (1964: 311) has shown that (originally?) accusations of witchcraft murder in Central Africa were related to the transfer of pawns.
[198] Dias de Carvalho 1890: 437
[199] "Notes on customary law: Manyinga Native Authority (1949)", in: Kabompo District Notebook, vol.II, NAZ KTV I/I, p.4
[200] Baumann 1935: 147
[201] E.g. Pogge 1980: 36f [1875, Songo, Northern Chokwe]; Diniz 1918: 398f; Venning 1953: 53 and Schomburgk 1925: 126f [Southern Lunda, around 1907]; van Binsbergen 1992: 125 [Nkoya, oral traditions]
[202] Diniz 1918: 399 [on *Ganguelas*, including Luchazi, Mbunda, Mbwela]
[203] E.g. in a case of alleged witchcraft murder reported by Livingstone (1963: 251 [1855, Southern Lunda])

'according to circumstances the double to quadruple value in slaves, livestock or current trade goods to the injured party... But the degree of punishment is mostly different among the different tribes.'[204]

The amount of compensation demanded appears to have depended more and more on the wealth of the culprit. Unfortunately, written sources give only few examples of compensations paid within the societies of the region. The payment of 20 slaves (men, women and children), four kegs of powder, four muzzleloader guns, six yards of various various types of cloth and four earthen plates for the accidental killing of the first wife of a Chokwe chief by a Nuclear Lunda youth at the court of the Mwant Yav is the most exorbitant rate I have come across.[205]

As to the form of payments, it seems plausible that, on the one hand, slaves (hostages) were used as payment more and more often. They are the type of compensation mentioned most frequently in the sources. Violence and accumulation of dependants may have enabled many headmen to give away more slaves than previously. But every such case meant a blow for village headmen's ambitions to build up large followings of dependents, and for the weaker and smaller villages such loss of people through legal dispute could shatter the very basis of their existence and independence.

There was only one way to avoid this loss of human labour and independence: to offer instead an equivalent which had usually to consist in the most valuable imports (cattle, guns, bales of cloth) or exportable goods (ivory tusks, rubber loads).[206] The particular importance of always having goodly stocks of cloth ready for this purpose has been illustrated already (see section C 6.3). Schomburgk gives some vivid descriptions of the more or less regular redemption of captured wives for goats, cloth and powder in the course of petty warfare among the Southern Lunda.[207] It is the equivalence between human beings and these trade goods in the circulation of 'compensations' which was perhaps the decisive stimulus to participation in long-distance trade in one way or another and to concentration on the acquisition of these goods.

Legal disputes were also the crucial test of friendship and the other inter-village bonds. The matrilinear village was the decisive unit of jurisdiction, with the headman, sometimes another experienced headman from the neighbourhood, being the representative and arbitrator in most cases.[208] The amount of compensation at stake also depended on the

---

[204] Pogge 1880: 7
[205] Dias de Carvalho 1890: 410
[206] On equivalence between human beings (slaves) and imported goods see below, part E
[207] Schomburgk 1925: 118, 126, 146, 175 [1906/07, north of the Kabompo River]
[208] E.g. White 1960a: 12, 22ff; McCulloch 1951: 71; Baumann 1935: 147

social distance between the parties. Quarrels within the village were settled with much more modest payments than those with individuals from other villages.[209] The most prominent tasks of 'friendship' were to avert such costly disputes and feuds, to provide an intelligence network against enemy attacks, and to provide assistance if such a legal or military attack occurred. As violent clashes happened most often between villages near to each other, more distant friendly villages were called in to mediate.[210]

Not every village head always had the necessary amount of 'wealth' at hand to pay a compensation or a debt, or to redeem a fellow villager taken as captive or hostage. Credits to pay compensations were the most typical kind of 'assistance' expected from 'friends'.[211] The same applied to other types of inter-village bonds such as in-lawship or distant kinship. Significantly, the only term for (matri-) 'lineage' in Upper Zambezi languages is *(w)usoko* which does not refer to any idea of common descent, but denotes a much more concrete relationship: 'those who have to redeem each other' from slavery or pawnship.[212] Occasionally, distant clan members could 'combine to redeem from slavery a fellow clansman even though he was a stranger to them.'[213] As mentioned before, there is a Luvale term (*kuli*) for someone who pays another's compensation or debt, apparently suggesting that the redeemed person is thereby enabled to grow old in his or her village (instead of being enslaved).[214]

D 4.5 The meanings of inter-village exchange

Contrary to widespread assumptions on 'traditional subsistence economies', the relations between individuals of distinct 'communities' involved a considerable amount of exchanges of material goods. Various forms of inter-village circulation were an essential feature of the pre-colonial economy around the Upper Zambezi and Kasai. This feature explains a good deal of why world market agents obviously found the ground so well prepared for their business. There were a number of

---

[209] White 1960a: 11f, 23
[210] White 1960a: 28
[211] E.g. in the example by Frausto mentioned above (Vellut 1972: 154). See McCulloch 1951: 21 (based on White); White 1960a: 19, 51; Turner 1957: 176.
[212] Cf.Horton, [2]1975: 339; Baumann (1935: 126) mentions an additional Chokwe term for one's own matrilineage: *mwiya umuweka*, which he translates as 'one single belt', i.e. body or womb. White (1960a: 17) mentions similar terms for the Luvale, like *lijimo lyetu* (our womb or *membu etu* ('our villages').
[213] White 1960a: 19
[214] Horton 1975: 138/9

characteristic issues involved in these circulations which pervade the sections of this chapter.

One is that transfers of goods were closely associated, and often set as equivalent, with transfers of labour, both voluntary (piecework, cooperation etc.) and forced (pawns, slaves). This 'proximity between the value of material goods and people', which has been analysed by Joseph Miller for the wider regional context,[215] seems to reflect the basic experience of labour as being the decisive force of production. In the context of beginning world market integration, this proximity facilitated first the slave trade (an exchange of imported goods for people), and then the demand for ever larger quantities of imported goods, increasingly through 'legitimate' export production. The possibility of using these imported goods as a defence against loss of labour, freedom and life in escalating inter-village strife was as least as strong a motive for market participation as their investment by the better-off to build up retinues of dependants and followers.

Another observation is that inhabitants seem to have distinguished two root forms of exchange relations. One of them was spoken of in a language of 'presents' and 'debts', and focused on personal reciprocity between the partners who called each other 'friends', 'cross-cousins' and the like. The possibility of making claims on each other's assistance at some future point, e.g. in inter-village disputes, counted here for more than the actual equivalence of the goods exchanged. The idea of short-term equivalence was much more prominent in what I consider to be a distinct second form of exchange, the concept of barter (Lv.*lando*). The roots of indigenous barter exchange can be located in the ancient division of labour by gender and ecological zone. The existence of a customary fixed rate between the standard units of the typical barter products - 'relish' and staple - is closely linked to a strong ideology of balance or equivalence between these categories of producers. Most barter and piecework exchanges took place within the neighbourhood, but they required in theory no further criteria like status or special personal relations. In reality, however, 'gift' and 'barter' relations often complemented each other because of the geographical distances and the insecurity which trade in this region had to cope with. During the 19th century formal inter-village bonds of the 'friendship' type may even have become increasingly important as an infrastructure and a kind of general insurance for conducting business (See ch. E 4 for some more theory-oriented reflections on these issues).

The impact of these strategies on relations with foreign traders remains yet to be seen (see part E). Another question is, however, the social

---

[215] Miller 1988: 40ff

impact of these patterns of circulation in the context of world market integration. The enormous investments in inter-village networks and disputes, which probably absorbed the greatest part of imported 'wealth', certainly provided a decisive stimulus for market participation. It seems possible that these kinds of investments had rather redistributive effects within the regional societies and limited the accumulation of wealth and power, in other words social differentiation, in the region. The social groups with the greatest potential for accumulating imported 'wealth' in the pre-colonial period, chiefs and local traders, will be therefore in the focus of the next chapter.

D 5 Chieftainship and trade

D 5.1 Chiefs and power

Pre-colonial visitors of the Upper Zambezi and Kasai were more than once bewildered about the position of local political rulers. According to Graça, for instance, in the 1840s, Chokwe chiefs' capitals were very unimpressive compared to those of other potentates he had seen further west:

'Not even the chief himself has a capital which could make him respectable like all the others; he lives in a big forest, and with him his people; he only has a hut in which he and his wife resides, but in summer he orders to remove the roof and remains uncovered...'[1]

For Silva Porto, in the same decade, the *Ganguela* peoples (under which term he usually subsumed the entire region - see introduction, A 3) were entrenched 'republicans'.[2] And Livingstone plainly stated in 1854/55 that 'they, the chiefs, are without power', about the Southern Lunda and Chokwe, whom he contrasted with what he had just learnt on Nuclear Lunda, where 'the sway of the chief is absolute'.[3]

A very different picture was drawn by Capello and Ivens when they visited the Central Chokwe district in 1878: 'Great respect is shown by them for their chiefs, whose power is almost always absolute and admits of no questioning.'[4]

They described a strictly hierarchical political system analogous to other Central African states, with elders (village headmen) being elected by their people but subordinate to one central chief (*mona*), advised by a group of dignitaries (*sg. mwenengana*), by whom they were 'placed in command over each little community'.[5] Pogge confirmed this:

'Each of the individual villages has its small chief [village headman] who has to pay tribute to the Mona ... The small chiefs are mostly simple sons of the

---

[1] Graça 1890: 416
[2] Silva Porto 1942: 53 (diary, entry 14.3.1847); see also Silva Porto 1986: 372, footnote 189
[3] Livingstone 1963: 232, 42, 80/81
[4] Capello and Ivens 1882: I, 225
[5] Capello and Ivens 1882: I, 187, 198

wilderness; they mostly lack the big *fazenda* cloth and the umbrella; their clothing normally consists of animal skins.'[6]

Even where political centralization was less advanced, however, many chiefs appear in pre-colonial accounts since the mid-19th century as fearful power figures boasting about their rights over their subjects' life and death.[7] According to Magyar, in the 1850s,

> 'the country of *Lobal* [Luvale] is ruled by several ... cruel and tyrant chiefs of lower and higher rank who are partly independent from each other and among whom there are also several princesses...'[8]

Luvale chiefs (sg. *mwangana*) used to call their subjects 'slaves' (Lv. *vandungu*).[9] Silva Porto mentioned on the Mbunda ('mixed with the Bambueira [Mbwela], Luchiaje [Luchazi] and Luvar') that at their chiefs' fortified headquarters 'human skulls are found at every step', while the Southern Lunda chief (SL. *mwanta*) Katema recommended himself to Livingstone saying that he would see 'no human heads lying about' at his capital.[10]

On official occasions, an elaborate performance of power was staged, refining old power symbols such as sitting and greeting privileges and inventing new ones using imported goods and manners seen at Portuguese traders' visits. By the end of last century, for example, chiefs preferred to be carried in hammocks (called *tipoia* or *machila* in Angolan Pg., hence Lv. *chipoya*) accompanied by yelling and the firing of volleys during journeys;[11] they were seated on wooden chairs as a 'throne' under some sort of canopy, wearing fancy crowns and colourful cloaks and jackets during 'audiences'.[12] (See figs. 1, 2 and 21)One newly invented tradition

---

[6] Pogge 1880: 47 [Northern Chokwe 1875]

[7] E.g. Capello and Ivens 1882: I, 179/80; Coillard 1897: 606 and 611ff [on Ishinde (Southern Lunda) and Kakenge (Luvale), in 1894]; Dias de Carvalho 1890: 692 [Northern Chokwe 1880s]

[8] Magyar 1860: 233

[9] White 1957: 62, 71; this may have been, however, an older attitude, an emphasis of the new supra-kinship and -clanship allegiance demanded of resident Late Iron Age populations (cf. the clan formula of the Kaposhi clan, who claims to have built a big tower to avoid being called 'mere slaves' by the immigrant Nama Kungu (White 1957: 62).

[10] Silva Porto 1986: 332 (diary 1.1.1848); Livingstone 1963: 84 [1854]

[11] See e.g. Capello and Ivens 1882: I, 214 [Central Chokwe]; Harding 1904: 64/65 and 84 [Luvale]; Lux 1880: 40-41 [Angola, Songo, Northern Chokwe]

[12] See above, C 6; on seating and greeting privileges for powerful Luvale chiefs such as Nyacatolo in the early colonial period see for example Antunes Cabrita 1954: 46f, 49f.

was the chief's miming a wild beast at receptions, quite literally a highly suggestive performance on the stage of power.[13]

What these observations do seem to suggest, at first glance, is a progressive stratification between chiefs and commoners during the 19th century. A parallel centralization of political power also seems to have taken place in the region, but with greater intra-regional differences, the Luchazi-Mbunda occupying perhaps the lower,[14] and the Chokwe apparently the upper end of the scale. But even for the Chokwe, experienced travellers such as Silva Porto had their doubts as to the power of senior chiefs; his impression, by 1880, was that grand receptions, sophisticated rules and tyrannical orders by potentates such as the famous Kisenge in no way matched their actual power; he saw them rather as attempts to deceive visitors, followers and subjects about their lack of influence. He found that simple chief's messengers pursued their individual concerns in a way that would have been inconceivable under the Lords of Bulozi or Nuclear Lunda.[15] The independence of smaller chiefs and headmen boasting themselves 'owner of the country', with sometimes no more than a couple of villages and an area of two miles under their jurisdiction, was such that Silva Porto in the 1880s repeated his old argument of 'the constitution of this race in small republics'.[16]

What probably did increase during this period was differentiation among the leaders of these 'republics', and even among senior chiefs, with regard to the number of people under their control. New political structures and a greater degree of centralization probably emerged during the 19th century, with ethnic identity gradually becoming its focus,[17] but this was not a uniform process. Certain powerful chiefs may have claimed supremacy, but in reality, serious power struggles were going on between local potentates without clear hierarchical position, with varying results. Significantly, travellers frequently mixed up the relevant terms in their reports: 'chief', 'potentate' and 'headman' in English, *chefe, soba, dona* or *dono da terra* in Portuguese are hardly distinguished, although in the local languages they are. The independence of junior chiefs and headmen increased with distance from the headquarters of the more powerful rulers.

---

[13] E.g. Coillard 1897: 615 [Kakenge, Luvale, 1894]; Pinto 1881: I, 238 [Mavanda, Mbandi, 1878]

[14] According to McCulloch (1951: 67, 69, 70 - sources not mentioned), Luchazi chiefs may have been only heads of lineages, neighbourhood clusters or 'federations of tribes'; Dias da Silva (1949: 40), however, mentions a class of nobles (chief's kin) using the prefix *mwé-* before their names.

[15] Silva Porto 1885: 581-586

[16] Silva Porto 1885: 164

[17] See Papstein 1989

The struggles for chieftainship may have been exacerbated during the 19th century, for reasons excamined below, but they clearly began much earlier, at the latest when carriers of new political traditions began to radiate from the evolving Nuclear Lunda empire between about 1500 and 1750 (see chapter C 1.2).[18] Characteristically, the imported Nuclear Lunda system of 'positional succession' and 'perpetual kinship', i.e. a fixed hierarchy, based on generational seniority, between a limited number of hereditary political titles (positions) never fully worked in this region. Among the Luvale, their Nama Kungu chiefly clan facilitated its expansion by proliferating the number of sometimes shortlived political titles, 'but never succeeded in establishing, indeed never tried to establish, a centralized state system.'[19] Actual power did not correlate with theoretical seniority, even where it existed, as is illustrated by the rise of Kakenge and Nyakatolo at the expense of the ancient Chinyama senior title.[20] (See fig. 23) At least among the Luvale and Luchazi, incumbents of chiefly titles could be women, which underlines their social position in these societies.

The Chokwe ruling dynasty remained practically divided into rulers (always male?) of independent districts, despite claims of the superiority of the senior *ndumba tembo* title, with growing differences in influence between them.[21] After the death of an incumbent, his or her successor always had to assert his or her position anew; similarly to among the Luvale, there was considerable social mobility as new or junior titles could rise, and senior ones decline.[22] Southern Lunda rulers, who arrived when the Nuclear Lunda empire had already reached its mature form, tried to realize the most differentiated power hierarchy. According to Turner, it consisted of senior titles (sg.*mwanta wampata*), junior ('branch') chiefs (*mwanta wamutayi*) or senior headmen (*chilolu*), headmen of vicinages (*mwenimbu*) and ordinary village headmen (*mwanta wamukala*). But in reality, senior titles did not automatically convey maximum power; the Kanongesha functioned in practice as a *primus inter pares* among his junior chiefs and headmen, while the incumbents of his counterpart title Ishinde seem to have concentrated considerable power on themselves during the second half of the 19th century. The actual power

---

[18] Papstein 1978; Miller 1972; Hoover 1978: 249f, 270f; White 1962a
[19] Papstein 1978: 147; also White 1957: 65
[20] The former since around 1800, the latter in the 1860s (Papstein 1978: 181, 187).
[21] Magyar 1860: 229; Pogge 1880: 47; Capello and Ivens 1882: I, 180; McCulloch 1951: 46
[22] Silva Porto 1885: 604; an example is the decline of the Pehu title.

of the senior chiefs depended on a voluntary recognition by local headmen.[23]

Migration movements helped to multiply the number of contenders and to stimulate these struggles around chieftainship. F.S. Arnot, visiting the Northern Luvale in 1885, was highly surprised when in one place

> 'no less than three chiefs turned up. One called himself the chief of the Lunda residents, another, the chief of the Lovale residents, and the third, the "man of the country" or land.'[24]

The latter was obviously the representative of those who considered themselves to be the firstcomers on the local scene.[25] The title 'owner of the land' was probably the much older one held already by local leaders in the largely acephalous resident (Late Iron Age) society, before the bringers of the new chiefly traditions originating from Nuclear Lunda began to immigrate. Among the Lunda-Ndembu, this title seems to have been partly appropriated by the new rulers, as the chief called himself 'chief of the land' (*mwanta wampata*), while headmen were called 'owner (or chief) of the village' (*mweni-mukala*).[26] The title 'lord of the land' for chiefs appears many times in pre-colonial reports on the Luvale and Luchazi-Mbunda.

Another observation is that 'wealth', usually measured in cattle and a variety of European manufactured goods, increasingly appears in 19th century reports not only as a standard of social differentiation in general, but also as an epithet of political power. Already in 1854, Livingstone observed an 'excessive punctiliousness shewn by the poorer to the richer persons' at the capital of the Southern Lunda chief Ishinde.[27] Ndumba Tembo, the senior chief of the Central Chokwe, when receiving Capello and Ivens in 1878,

> 'launched out into praises of his own person, dwelling more particularly upon his greatness which he averred was without a rival in the country; **upon the wealth he possessed**, and the powers over the lives of his vassals...'[28]

---

23 This paragraph follows Turner 1957: 323-325, and Schecter 1976: 214-26, as cited in Hoover 1978: 272/73.
24 Arnot 1969: 159 [1885, Northern Luvale]
25 A clash between resident and immigrant headmen is also mentioned in Silva Porto 1885: 572
26 Turner 1957: 323/24
27 Livingstone 1963: 56 [1854, Southern Lunda]
28 Capello and Ivens 1882: I, 179/80 (emphasis added)

And the most important Northern Chokwe chief, Kisenge, in 1880, 'wanted the travellers to pass his locality. because they are the ones from whom he receives the objects indispensable for his power.'[29]

This last observation brings us to the economic basis of chieftainship, which will be the focus of this chapter. In the following section I will examine what specific resources and revenues may have accrued to chiefs in pre-colonial history which may explain the mentioned contradictory statements on their position. After that, I will ask what use they made of these revenues and try to identify different paths of accumulation.

D 5.2   Chiefly revenues

Arbitration

The special link between chieftainship and the land by no means implied that chiefs, any more than village headmen, had any prerogatives on the use of natural resources. Part of this special relationship had to do with the magical powers that were usually ascribed to political rulers. Chiefs were seen as capable of bringing fertility to the land, and did perform various agricultural rituals in the past.[30] It is possible that they took over some of these functions from indigenous 'owners of the land' (e.g. rainmaking).

Otherwise, chiefs merely extended the headman's role of distributing land and water rights among 'villagers'. Anybody who wanted to set up a new 'village' was (and is) required to report to the chief who would formally designate to him the land and the adjacent stretch of water he may use.[31] This function was only of practical importance in case of local land scarcity. An appeal to chiefs could (and can) be a made when disputes over land or water rights arose between members of different villages, residents and newcomers. In such a case the chief would play the role of an arbitrator between the parties involved.

This role of arbitration resembles the vital one headmen and, by extension, chiefs used to take on in legal disputes.[32] It seems plausible

---
[29] Silva Porto 1885: 585 (diary, 26.4.1880)
[30] See below and Papstein 1978: 137
[31] E.g. Antunes Cabrita 1954; advisers to chief Ishinde, 25.10.1986; interview L: Chizombo, 30.10.1986
[32] White 1960a: 23-25

that skills and powers of arbitration, an incipient state function, were among the first and most important functions immigrant chiefs had to offer in return for the allegiance of strife-ridden resident populations.

The only personal advantage chiefs enjoyed from their role as arbitrators was receiving special tokens of respect which were sometimes called 'fees'.[33] For both their symbolical and their material value, this right may have spurred on the chiefs' zeal to expand their onerous judicial functions. At the same time, they tended to increase their demands for such such gifts, which were increasingly payable in 'wealth' or slaves.

Tribute

One of the political innovations immigrant chiefly dynasties had apparently carried with them from Nuclear Lunda was the institution of royal tribute (*mulamb*). There, food, export goods, and even goods imported by his subjects were appropriated by the king in this way. The tribute was collected by his headmen (*vilol*) and special messengers, the *tukwata*.[34] It included cassava, which was carried to the capital (*Musumba*) in great quantities, as well as copper, ivory, cloth, beads, salt, palm cloth, slaves, cowries, etc.[35] Tribute was the basis for the monarch's control over all exports of slaves, ivory and copper to foreigners and for his monopoly on domestic caravans.[36] When market conditions changed, as around 1850, the Mwant Yav decreed that ivory rather than slaves must be collected.[37] He called in Chokwe elephant hunters who had to submit one tusk to the Mwant Yav from every animal they killed.[38]

Similar practices were also used in the Bulozi kingdom. 'Gifts' (*limpo*) from Lozi areas and 'tribute' (*namba*) from subject peoples had to be sent regularly to the court of the Litunga. In addition, food from the Litunga's gardens, worked by his subjects, had to be supplied. The collection was supervised by representatives called *lindumeleti*.[39] Silva Porto wrote in 1848 on the Litunga:

---

[33] Porto 1885: 575 [1880, Northern Chokwe]; Arnot 1969: 248 [Luvale]
[34] Vellut 1972: 82-83
[35] Baptista 1873: 169, 203, 222, 229, 231 [1805ff]; Graça 1890: 426 [1847]
[36] See Vellut 1972: 84, 90ff: In Nuclear Lunda, a whole infrastructure existed to facilitate commerce and to ensure the monopoly of the Mwant Yav. Only very little private business was conducted during caravan stays and was considered to be illegal or 'smuggling'. See also Hermitte 1974: 145, 209/10.
[37] Bastin 1966: 61, cited in Miller 1970: 180
[38] Magyar 1860: 231, fn. 1
[39] Hermitte 1974: 45, 141

'Every year, the chiefs of his dominions, followed by many people, present themselves in the capital with tributes of ivory, slaves, canoes, pottery, skins, grains, meat, honey, salt and fruits of the season'.[40]

Royal plantations were worked by state slaves and corvee labourers.[41] State monopolies existed for the export of rubber, wax, and skins, which were largely procured through tributes; consequently, the ruling class could also gain monopolies over certain imported goods such as firearms.[42]

For the immigrant chiefs who imposed themselves in the 16th to 18th century on the pre-existing peoples of the Upper Zambezi and Kasai, these practices in Nuclear Lunda or Bulozi may have been a dreamt-of ideal, but reality was much more modest. Chiefs did obtain tribute (*mulambu*) , but to a very limited extent. It consisted mainly in foodstuffs, especially fish, meat, cassava or honey.[43] For example, levies on fish caught in traps along privately-owned dams (*málilo*) were demanded. The owner of 'every wálilo along the river had to give a full basket to the chief'.[44] According to my informants, the *mulambu* was rarely fixed in quantity or time, but rather due when there had been a good kill, catch or harvest.[45]

The idea of tribute was thus still rather close to the probably much older concept of the *musapu* : in essence, it was the gift of certain parts, usually a leg, of a killed game to the 'owner of the land'. Originally, the recipient was probably the senior headman,[46] but later the chief.[47] Judging from the etymology of the term *musapu*, this gift was initially seen as a kind of sacrifice to the ancestors of the wider lineage and perhaps to fertility, represented by the senior headman (see above, D 3). An additional aspect of tribute, however, probably came in with the advent of chiefs: according to White, fish levies, for example, were given

---

[40] Silva Porto diary, 22.1.1848 (1942: 77)
[41] For Nuclear Lunda see Pogge 1880: 243-44 : the farm of the Mwant Yav was worked by tribute slaves and 'poor women'.- On Bulozi, see Hermitte 1974: 45, 141, 208: The Litunga 's gardens which were established everywhere in his dominions, were worked by large numbers of young men and women and were also called *limpo* or *liketiso*, later *lifunga*.
[42] Hermitte 1974: 209/10; Clarence-Smith 1979: 225
[43] E.g. Sangambo 1985: 55
[44] Sondoyi, 24.10.1986
[45] See also, for example, Capello and Ivens 1882: I, 214; this contradicts White (1957: 66), who holds that in the past villages sent food twice yearly to the capital of their chief.
[46] In Nuclear Lunda, significantly, the term *nsapw* designates the emblem of a *kabung*, originally one of the lineage headmen and independent local rulers in proto-Lunda history whose position was associated with the fertility of the land and the lineage (see Hoover 1978: 527 and 530; Papstein 1978: 91). For the Lunda-Ndembu see Turner 1957: 31.
[47] Antunes Cabrita 1954: 50; Sangambo 1985: 55 (see chapter E 1).

D 5 : Chieftainship and trade

to the chief as a kind of preventive recognition of his role of an arbitrator, because chiefs had to ensure that property rights over the fishing dams were not infringed.[48]

'Wealth' goods were not normally surrendered as tribute. Only indigenous wealth, such as goats, animal skins or parrot feathers were allegedly sometimes given to Luvale chiefs as *mulambu*,[49] no imported goods. Only White holds that a travelling chief, 'on reaching a village, he would not dismount until a gift of a gun or a goat had been made to him,'[50] but such 'gifts' seem to have been demanded rather under the title of 'hospitality'. Eyewitnesses explicitly denied that exportable products entered *mulambu*: 'We never paid rubber to the chief.., never the very profitable things, only things to eat'.[51]

An Upper Zambezi chief also demanded corvee labour to some extent; Luvale commoners are said to have 'cultivated his fields and built his house'.[52] But the amount and frequency of such services cannot be ascertained and was hardly fixed. The chief's demands on outlying villages to supply foreign visitors with provisions on his behalf, a very normal thing in Nuclear Lunda, here met with little enthusiasm and were sometimes outrightly rejected.[53] The assistance in production commoners were prepared to render their chiefs did not, at any rate, include any kind of export products, only foodstuffs. Although the *musapu* custom would have provided a good legitimation for this, I have found only one reference suggesting that elephant hunters were asked to submit one tusk on every animal to a chief (Chinyama Litapi), like in Nuclear Lunda, and these were Lozi refugees.[54] Today, assisting the chief with foodstuffs through both 'tribute' and labour services is mainly justified by his or her public duties as representative of the population, e.g. entertaining visitors, and this 'democratic' view is probably older than it appears.

These findings suggest that in this region, the main justification for demanding tribute (*mulambu*) seems to have been provided by 'respect' for the chief, an attitude which appears closer to the older rights of senior headmen as 'lords of the land' (with emphasis on the function of arbitration), than to an actual centralization of power.[55] During the 19th

---

[48] 1957: 66
[49] Y.Samakayi and Mr.Sondoyi, 24.10.1986; cf. White 1957: 66
[50] White 1957: 66
[51] Interview Mr. Sondoyi, 24.10.1986. It is possible that chiefs used the wax contained in tribute honey for sale - although the quantities are unlikely to have been big.
[52] White 1957: 66
[53] E.g. Livingstone 1963: 45 [Southern Lunda]
[54] Sangambo 1985: 66
[55] Cf. Turner 1957: 325: 'The giving of tribute was regarded as a moral obligation rather than as a compulsory matter'[Lunda-Ndembu]

century, chiefs tried to expand at least these rights of 'respect', but they remained ultimately in a much weaker position than the ruling classes in the neighbouring states of Nuclear Lunda and Bulozi with regard to extracting surplus products and especially the fruits of foreign trade from their 'subjects'.[56]

Production

The only reliable domestic source of revenue for chiefs would, then, have been production by themselves or at least within their own villages. There are in fact many instances in 19th century records of chiefs being personally active as producers, especially in the more prestigious fields. The distinguished Ndumba Tembo, for instance, designed and forged his royal headdress by himself.[57] And Katema was out hunting the skins required as tribute for the Mwant Yav when Livingstone visited him the second time, but 'five large baskets of manioc meal, a fowl, fifteen eggs and some beer', later 'more meal, some fish and fowl, with earth nuts and compliments' were supplied to the visitors by 'his domestics' and 'his wife',[58] which suggests that even food for visitors was home-produced. As ivory for export, let alone wax or rubber, could not be obtained through tribute, foreign traders could buy only small quantities at a time from chiefs and were irritated by the delays caused by waiting even for a single promised tusk to turn up.[59] Chiefs had never a monopoly on foreign trade as in Bulozi and Nuclear Lunda, so that foreigners had to deal directly with great numbers of petty producers.[60] And with regard to production itself, it seems that chiefly producers faced in principle the same problems of claiming assistance from others as did ordinary producers in the region.

Nevertheless, chiefs were, on the whole, in a better position with regard to mobilizing extra labour, at least for food production. The occasional tribute labour on their fields has been mentioned already. The size of their own villages was swelled not only by bigger numbers of dependent kin, but also by numerous wives, pawns and slaves. Some of these were acquired in one way or another through their wealth (see below), but chiefs had also special opportunities to appropriate unfree labour which resulted, again, from an extensive interpretation of their function as arbitrators. Several sources mention the custom of senior

---

[56] Silva Porto 1985: 577 [1880]
[57] Capello and Ivens 1882: I, 177
[58] Livingstone 1963: 259 [Southern Lunda, 1855]
[59] Silva Porto 1985: 608 [Northern Chokwe]
[60] See Dias de Carvalho 1890: 692

chiefs, on their accession to office, being given one or two youths from each village under their jurisdiction.[61] This custom has been explained as a kind of preventive pawnship, an attempt to guarantee peace between the villages, but it also resembles early strategies of building a power base through systematic marriage alliances known, for example, from the Luvale Nama Kungu.[62] Most of these pawns certainly seem to have been girls and women who were eventually taken as chiefs' wives. This explains the remarkable number of wives surrounding important chiefs at formal receptions, and suggests a particular strength of food production in their villages.

There were other ways for chiefs to use their special position for the appropriation of unfree labour. They could try, for example, to declare themselves as entitled to compensation when one of their subjects, even unrelated, had been killed:

'"You have killed one of my children; bring all yours before me, that I may choose which of them shall be mine instead"'.[63]

Warfare

Real or forged accusations brought before the chief were probably the most frequent pretext for him or her to pounce upon some less powerful individual, family or village 'with few or no connections elsewhere' among their own population, to kill the headman and enslave 'the whole of the dependants and children', many for sale.[64] This was, however, an ambivalent strategy because it effectively reduced the number of vassals and people under his or her political control. Energetic chiefs therefore transferred these raids from isolated villages within their realm to other areas under neighbouring chiefs, with whom they anyway competed for power and followers. The most prominent example, as mentioned before, are the 'Wars of *Ulamba*', actually a long series of raids by which prominent Luvale war chiefs extended their jurisdiction to Late Iron Age '*Mbwela*' groups under independent or Southern Lunda rulers between c.1720 and 1890 (see chapter B 2).[65]

---

61 Silva Porto 1885: 604; Schütt 1881: 116 [Kimbundu, from c. 100 villages); Dias de Carvalho 1890; White 1957: 66
62 Papstein 1978: 148ff
63 Livingstone 1963: 251/52 [Kawawa, Southern Lunda, 1855]; see also van Binshergen 1992: 126f [Nkoya, oral traditions]
64 Livingstone 1963: 84 [Luvale/Southern Lunda, 1854]; Baumann 1935: 147 [Central Chokwe]
65 Papstein 1978: 179f; Papstein assserts that '*ulamba* is thought to be an old word for chieftainship'; according to Horton (1975: 161) it denotes 'magic used in catching

Fig. 30: Warriors fighting with guns (detail from fig. 1)
(Photographed at the Völkerkunde Museum Berlin)

At least among the Luvale, chiefs are said to have had, again, special opportunities to claim support from their headmen (*vilolo*); for example, they were apparently not liable for compensation if one of the warriors (*wakajita*) suffered damage during the war, as was the case with alliances among headmen in inter-village warfare.[66] There was a fixed procedure to be followed by chiefs issuing a 'call' (*mutambi*) to mobilize warriors (*wakajita*) for warfare. Papstein, however, who has given a description of such a 'call to arms', suggests that it was successful not because of superiority but only when it could appeal to local self-interest and reciprocal obligations of allied headmen and chiefs.[67] The warriors on whom powerful chiefs relied were apparently themselves tied to their war leaders, usually the chief himself, less by respect than by the prospect of obtaining captive wives and other spoils, in other words, a patron-client

---

people' - perhaps this is what chieftainship was seen as being about even before the age of slave exports.
[66] White 1957: 66
[67] Papstein 1978: 168

relationship.[68] Among all peoples of the region, the chief's warriors and their weapons regularly appeared at receptions for foreign visitors. On one such reception, given by the Southern Lunda chief Ishinde, for example,

> 'the numbers of soldiers who came running, roaring & capering into the enclosure was between 200 & 300. They were armed with bows & arrows. Three lads sat behind him [Ishinde] with large bundles of arrows on their shoulders'.[69]

Fig. 31: Livingstone's reception by the Southern Lunda Chief Ishinde

A substantial crowd, including warriors with bows, musicians with *marimba*, and the chief's numerous wives has been arranged to impress the visitor. In the background, besides buildings drawn in exaggerated height, a fortification in wood and earth around the chief's houses can be discerned (Engraving from Livingstone 1857: 290)

---

[68] Papstein 1978: 167; the same has been said of the notorious bands of Chokwe raiding Nuclear Lunda (Dias de Carvalho 1890: 487).
[69] Livingstone 1963: 53 [1854]

Later, at Katema's court, about 300 armed men were present at the reception;[70] and at Kakenge's, in 1894, Coillard was received by

> 'a mob of young men all armed with guns', and 'bands of armed men kept coming up from various directions. Night fell; the drums began to beat; they fired one gunshot after another... the place was full of men, decked out in their war paint, and surrounded by bundles of guns'.[71]

For these young men, war was undoubtedly an opportunity for early escape from their elders to achieve their most important objective more rapidly: that of building up their own little following of slave wives and descendants that would stay with them and not leave them some day in the future.

But only some of these captives, especially women, were kept by successful chiefs and their raiders themselves. 'Surplus' slaves, mainly men, were used for various exchanges, e.g. compensations, and above all for export. Especially among the Luvale with their host of rival chiefs, but to some extent also among Luchazi and Southern Lunda, slave sales became the typical form of chiefs' export 'production' in order to obtain the desired foreign goods. 'Chiefs were only engaged in slave trading, after that in no other business',[72] Yowena Samakayi put it. This does not mean that chiefs had any monopoly on the slave trade; retail buying and selling of slaves with caravans had been going on at least since the mid-19th century.[73] But chiefs were attractive partners for foreign traders because they could supply in bulk.

When large scale slave exports were suppressed, this was certainly a serious blow for chiefs'revenues, particularly among the Luvale, who were most specialized in this business.[74] Chiefs continued to find customers for the victims of their raids within the continent, but had to think increasingly about other avenues to imported 'wealth', especially with the mounting inflationary pressure on internal circuits of this 'wealth'. Examples of such other avenues are found particularly among the Chokwe, who were located nearest to the main trade routes and had constantly acquired but never exported any amount of slaves, perhaps because of a collective trauma of ancient victimization by slave raids.[75]

---

[70] Ibid: 83
[71] Coillard 1897: 610-12
[72] Interview Y. Samakayi, 24.10.1986
[73] E.g. Arnot 1969: 164 [1885]; Lemaire 1902: 138, 140, 148
[74] Magyar 1860: 234
[75] According to J. Miller, the ethnic identity of the Chokwe or Kioko ('those who fled (or left)') originated by the 18th century when victims of slave raids retreated from further west into the then extremely remote Chokwe highlands (1988: 38).

Chiefs' chances of producing sufficient quantities of exportable products have been discussed already; it seems that even with widespread use of slave labour, chiefs were at most able to boost their food production, but faced the same difficulties as village headmen in controlling the labour of male juniors or slaves who could hunt or collect export goods. The appropriation of foreign revenues through other means than simple exchange or sheer force was the key issue for chiefs under these circumstances, and this dilemma explains a good deal of their behaviour vis-a-vis foreign traders. This behaviour will be examined in the following and last part (E). Only some of their structural and ideological foundations, which are to be sought largely in the indigenous prerogatives of chieftainship, remain to be explained here.

Trading

Since the earlier pre-colonial period, rulers in the Central African interior seem to have been engaged in a continuous exchange of presents, especially 'wealth' such as livestock, parrot feathers, rare skins or copper items, to consolidate and probe their relations. Essentially, this was an extension of earlier exchanges of 'respect' between elders of local communities, but with increasing aspirations to political centralization these exchanges gathered momentum and sometimes covered considerable distances. In Nuclear Lunda, a prominent example of this tendency, the new trade goods which came with the advance of the 'Atlantic Zone' were subsequently fitted into pre-existing networks of 'luxury' circulation; just as indigenous 'wealth', they were not regarded as 'merchandise to be bought and sold, but as tribute to be exchanged.'[76]

'Tribute' was the term the rulers of Nuclear Lunda and also Bulozi preferred to use for what they received from lesser potentates, especially export products, to emphasize their power. However, the loyalty of these smaller chiefs, especially when they were located at the periphery of emerging 'empires', could be secured only if other 'tribute' was returned to them, usually imported goods. What outlying chiefs often liked to describe as a more or less voluntary reciprocal exchange of tokens of respect came in effect closer and closer to a form of trading:

> 'In reality, however, their so-called tribute, the ivory and the slaves Mwant Yav required for the purpose of his own trade, is regularly bought. ... Even of *Mona Kissenge*, the nearest and most powerful of the Chokwe princes, one can hear in *Musumba* that he pays tribute. This is because he sends ivory to the Mwant Yav from time to time in order to barter slaves for it. In turn, the Mona Kissenge

---

[76] Hoover 1978: 341

will then perhaps regard the slaves obtained as a tribute from the Mwant Yav.'[77]

Later, in order to underline their territorial claims, colonial officers would try to misinterpret such payments of 'tribute' by Upper Zambezi chiefs as an expression of permanent subordination to neighbouring 'states'.

Much greater, though, was their significance for the opening up of new areas for the 'Atlantic Zone'. The region of the Upper Kasai and Zambezi itself may have obtained its first specimens of European manufactures through redistribution as 'tribute' from the rulers of Kasanje, Nuclear Lunda and/or Bihe (see B 1). Subsequently, chiefs of the region seem to have played a prominent role as brokers between western traders and rulers of peoples further in the interior. It has been mentioned already that in the 1830s western middlemen were known at the court of the Kazembe as *moçambazes de Caquenque* [Kakenge, senior Luvale chief]. Luvale and Southern Lunda chiefs seem to have been exchanging livestock and ivory for cloth and beads with the Lozi king (Litunga) prior to the Kololo invasion. And the Luchazi chief Kabita was described as a 'great trader between the town [Benguela] and *Lui* [Bulozi]', before his monopoly was broken by Silva Porto's agents after 1847.

A part of trade within the region seems also to have taken the form of exchanging 'tribute', although it was not necessarily beneficial for either of the chiefs involved as long as they were in an approximately equal position.

On the areas north and east of the Kasai, Buchner has concluded that around 1880

> 'everywhere in the interior known to me the princes, with the *Muatiamvo* (Mwant Yav) and the *Lukonkessa* at their head, are at the same time the most prominent merchants. Each of them entertains according to his possibilities business relations with a number of traders from the coastal areas...'[78]

This statement appears exaggerated to me if applied to areas outside Nuclear Lunda, especially the chiefs of the Upper Zambezi and Kasai. Here, too, chiefs were apparently engaged in some sort of trading, but they definitely did not have the power to enforce a monopoly on foreign trade, or to extract the required amount of tribute from their followers.[79] Their opportunities to derive major revenues from trading deteriorated when the tide of the 'Atlantic Zone' had swept over their areas making people further east directly accessible to western caravans, and particularly after the end of large scale slave trading. As had probably

---
[77] Buchner 1883: 63 [1879/80]
[78] Buchner 1883: 62

been the case already with regional exchange in earlier times, it became more and more evident that, in the absence of strong means of extra-economic coercion, successful trading had to be backed up in some way by control over production itself. Given the dispersion of the population and the decentralized form of the most important types of production (gathering, shifting cultivation), trading was open to almost every enterprising individual. Small groups of petty Luvale and Chokwe traders frequented the major routes of long-distance trade between Katanga, Nuclear Lunda and the emporia of Angola at least during the second half of the 19th century.[80]

Commoners had certainly already dominated the scene of early regional trade. According to Luvale traditions, there were certain people who had become seasonal specialists in trading and used slave labour for their domestic duties during their absence.[81] One typical entrance into petty trading in this region has always been that specialized fishermen, bee-hunters or -keepers, game hunters, crop cultivators, castor oil producers, potters and blacksmiths started to carry with them products of their wives, brothers and friends, in addition to their own, when they undertake a journey to neighbouring areas. A part of the goods they receive in return may then be taken back to buy more of the original products. Specialized fishermen, used to exchanging their products with high transport value over long distances, may have always been particularly well-prepared for this business.[82] In the 19th century, similar practices were applied by export producers; for example, Chokwe raiders and hunters began to buy up more slaves and ivory abroad when opportunities declined at home.[83] The Luvale ex-trader Yowena Samakayi mentioned above (section C 5.5) has illustrated how a young man could acquire the 'initial capital' for small scale import-export trading through producing surpluses of food.

A rather different way in which Upper Zambezi traders emerged without recourse to the privileges of chieftainship was employment in foreign caravans. Linda Heywood has provided ample evidence that many Ovimbundu traders had acquired their initial capital (imported goods and personal slaves) and trade skills as agents (*pombeiros, quissongos*) and carriers for Portuguese-speaking or noble African caravan entrepreneurs.[84] During their service, agents and carriers would trade on their own account; therefore, caravans always carried besides their main

---

[79] E.g. Sangambo 1985: 57, 64; Papstein 1978: 233
[80] E.g. Cameron 1877: II, 139, 160; Poggo 1880: 45; see chapter B 4
[81] Papstein 1978: 233
[82] Cf. Vansina 1979: 10
[83] See chapter B 3
[84] Heywood 1984: 146f 175, 179, 184f

cargo a variety of other products in smaller quantities, e.g. beeswax in the era of slave exports, and individual slaves (often for the personal use of the employee) when 'legitimate goods' were officially traded.[85]

There is some evidence that very similar attitudes were adopted by Upper Zambezi 'workers of trade': Livingstone's Southern Lunda guides, for example, 'eagerly' bought as much beeswax *en route* as they could during their employment, 'in order to sell it to the Portuguese in front'.[86] As finding food for the caravan was one of the main functions of a guide[87], it is likely that people with experience in regional trade were preferred as guides. Guides were relatively well paid in this sparsely populated and dangerous area - over 16 yards plus beads being the 'cheap rate' for the relatively short distance from Kabango to Katema.[88] Around the turn of the century, carriers were paid 20 yards for a trip to Bihe lasting one to two months.[89]

Little is known about the social origin and position of Upper Zambezi carriers and guides, as would-be local traders. They were certainly young men, called 'children' (either junior kin or slaves) by their headman who seconded them to a foreign caravan.[90] The prospect of a personal income and of escaping the personal subordination in everyday life for some time may have been a motivation for these young men, as it was later labour migration. At least in the early period, junior relatives and potential successors of chiefs seem to have accompanied foreign caravans, although it is unclear whether as employees, pawns or apprentices.[91] It is thus possible that even chiefs who wanted to engage in trading acquired their knowledge and some initial capital during service in foreign caravans.

'Hospitality'

If chiefs' opportunities to appropriate foreign revenues through trade were limited, they could finally resort only to use (or abuse) of the 'ancient law of hospitality' (Livingstone) mentioned before (D 4.4). As

---

[85] See for example: Arnot 1888: 163, 185; carriers hectically buying slaves retail at Kavungu and in Katanga. Other examples are mentioned by Heywood 1984: 147.
[86] Livingstone 1963: 106, 109 [1854]
[87] E.g. Livingstone 1963: 90/91
[88] Livingstone 1963: 242 [1855]
[89] Interview Yowena Samakayi, 21.10.1986
[90] E.g. Livingstone 1963: 242; 99
[91] E.g. *Anonymus* 1803: 23, who mentioned 'sons' of Luvale chiefs sent with him to the coast; the incumbent of the Ishinde title (Southern Lunda) in 1854 'knew all the paths to

representatives of the villages under their jurisdiction, chiefs demanded certain rights as brokers between their people and outsiders. A visitor or stranger could not only expect to be given food and shelter, but was also obliged to pay his 'respect', usually a material token, to the elder of his hosts. Chiefs increasingly competed with local headmen for these hospitality gifts. This usurpation of the rights of a host, not only those of a 'lord of the land', probably explains why immigrant 'strangers' who wanted to set up a new village were expected to pay homage to the chief. Failure to do so could result in demands for compensation, even in enslavement of the offender, and provide yet another pretext for appropriating slaves for the market.[92]

The most profitable application of hospitality rights, however, was made towards foreign traders. In areas near the main caravan routes, chiefs demanded increasing amounts of 'respect' from caravan leaders, usually in addition to and more than their, in theory subordinate, headmen. These demands and the way in which they were justified are dealt with in more detail in the following part (chapter E 1). What should be explained here is that in reality, they seem to have been only a compensation for the inability of chiefs to tap domestic revenues or become producers of 'legitimate exports' themselves on any larger scale. Even through the devices of 'hostship' and 'arbitration' rights, however, chiefs' possibilities of extracting revenues from foreign visitors often went hardly beyond their capital, and sometimes not even that.

D 5.3 Politicians or entrepreneurs ?

The unspoken assumption behind this survey of chiefly incomes has been that chiefs had indeed an outstanding interest in or demand for surplus food and 'wealth' goods. In this section I will raise the question of why they may have developed such special material needs, in other words, in which particular ways chiefs tended to invest whatever extra income they may have been able to acquire through their political position or personal initiative. I would argue that there were at least two alternative strategies of accumulation chiefs were likely to pursue. Ideally, they could perhaps be distinguished into a strive for political domination (state formation), and a more entrepreneurial strategy of accumulation within the chiefs' own residence groups. In practice, there was certainly some overlapping between these two, but 19th century

---

the Portuguese settlements having travelled them all when he was a young man.'(Livingstone 1963: 55)
[92] Livingstone 1963: 72

sources do contain empirical examples which illustrate the extremes. One such example is the contrast seen by Livingstone between the individuals holding the titles of Katema (originally Lunda, near Lake Dilolo) and Kakenge (Luvale, on Lumbala/Zambezi confluence) in the mid-1850s.[93]

Investments in state formation

The incumbent of the Katema title at that time seems to have been really only a junior classificatory brother of the actual heir or 'appointed successor' (Swana Mulopwe) to the title, but he had managed to outstrip the latter and reach his present dominant position by investing imported 'wealth' goods obtained as 'presents', from trade or other from sources:

'*Moropo* [Swana Mulopwe] is the elder of Katema, but the latter by purchasing cattle and goats had secured the birthright in as far as influence in the country went.'[94]

The way in which he achieved this dominant position was generosity:

'He raised himself to eminence by good policy in the treatment of his people. He has more people and is richer than any of his family, and is liberal to his dependants, giving food &c to them on much more bountyful style than any other we have seen. He bought a bull & cow from the *Balobale* when young, and has now a large herd [of about thirty[95]] of most beautiful cattle, all the produce of these.'[96]

The number of followers Katema could immediately mobilize was displayed at his first reception for Livingstone, who

'found him surrounded by about 300 men and 30 women, said to be his wives, behind him. The main body of people were about 50 yards from him, forming a semi-circle, each clump of men having their headman in front of them.'[97]

His liberality was particularly conducive to attracting 'strangers' in need of hospitality; Livingstone, who was extremely well treated himself, arrived at a moment when Katema

'was engaged in discussing the arrival of a large body of people who had fled from *Kangenke* [Kakenge], chief of the Lobale. They had fled because their

---

[93] Livingstone's account is certainly biased in favour of Southern Lunda views, but the point is that his informants apparently wanted to propagate a certain option of chiefly behaviour against another, more current one.
[94] Livingstone 1963: 77; see also Livingstone 1857: 313/14
[95] Livingstone 1857: 321
[96] Livingstone 1963: 83
[97] Livingstone 1963: 83

chief sold them to the bastard Portuguese who frequent their country. Many of them were fine young men.'[98]

But subsequently, Livingstone discovered that the opportunities of Katema to make counterclaims on his followers in return for his liberality, i.e. his actual authority, were rather limited:

'Katema's rule is not very stringent, for he ordered the Balovale who have fled to him from *Kangenke* to do the work [to go with L. as carriers, A.v.O.], but they will not obey. ... He was distributing dried buffalo meat and handed three pieces to me, saying the carriers would follow me presently, but though the chief guide chased some with drawn sword none obeyed.'[99]

The redistribution of tribute and other income by chiefs to their followers and allies seems to have been a widely accepted norm in the region. It is expressed, for example, in the Luvale saying 'where tribute is there is hunger, too', in other words: the one who brings presents to a chief expects presents to receive presents in return.[100] Apparently, there was not much difference between exchanges between chiefs and commoners, and those continuously going on among chiefs.[101] The ability to distribute exceptional amounts of food and 'wealth' to a variety of visitors was a decisive precondition for accumulating followers and allies. This is most probably the explanation why immigrant chiefs are said to have introduced to the resident population, among other things, new technologies for intensified food production (see chapter C 1.2).

In the case of famine and later slave wars, plentiful food was a good condition for attracting refugees. To flee and seek protection with 'powerful friends' was commoners' only reliable insurance against enslavement.[102] During the 'Wars of *Ulamba*', including practically the whole 19th century, there was a constant coming and going of refugees between enemy chiefs on both sides of the Zambezi.[103] In the 1850s, at Katema's, some people even wished to send their children with Livingstone, 'in order that they might escape being sold'.[104] In reality, even flight was often of little help, since for many chiefs refugees from other 'tribes' were another source of exportable slaves.[105] But this was apparently a matter of some embarassment for chiefs, since the Lozi nobleman Masiko, in his exile on the Manyinga River, defended himself against such accusations by asserting that he only sold 'captives from

---
[98] Livingstone 1963: 83, also p.259 [1855]
[99] Livingstone 1963: 88
[100] Interview Y.Samakayi, 24.10.1986; also Dias de Carvalho 1890: 694
[101] E.g. Silva Porto 1885: 148; Livingstone 1963: 42
[102] E.g. Livingstone 1963: 24 [1854, Masiko]
[103] E.g. Livingstone 1963: 40, 83, 213, 259
[104] Livingstone 1963: : 86.

other tribes'.[106] Refugees, as 'strangers', had a customary right of asylum and were in addition an asset rather than a burden for their hosts whom they could assist as pieceworkers or warriors.

Subsequently, generosity as a means of extending power over a highly independent population also made chiefs particularly interested in imported goods. Chiefs were the first to not only possess but also wear European clothing etc. for ostentation (see chapter C 6). Vis-a-vis foreign visitors, chiefs increasingly insisted on obtaining special personal gifts, distinguished from what was to be immediately redistributed to their followers, in order to protect them from devaluation through vulgarization of imports and to secure themselves the prerogative on the latest luxury fashions. This strategy required the continuous invention of new demands (see E 1). Silva Porto was 'stupefied' when, in 1880, a messenger demanded for his host, the Chokwe chief Kissenge, a double *quibanda* [Umb., 'hospitality gift'], 'one for the day and one for the night, the former being ordinary goods to distribute to his people, and the latter consisting in refined objects for his person'. The second gift, a coat of fine cloth, five pieces of fine cotton, a blanket and two barrels of powder, was then handed over secretly at night by the backdoor of the village.[107]

The problem with the 'generosity' approach to power was obviously that the chief and his own village could end up with very little 'wealth' for their personal use. In addition, as the example of Katema has shown, actual commanding power was not guaranteed by this soft approach. These were presumably the considerations that induced other chiefs to put greater emphasis on coercive strategies - for which they had to pay a different price.

Investments in personal possessions

A number of chiefs, especially among the Luvale, surrounded themselves with a rather different reputation than people like Katema; names like that of his contemporary neighbour Kakenge apparently aroused first of all fear among those who heard it. To Livingstone, in 1854/55, Kakenge was described first of all as a tyrant chief preying upon his own people and driving them off his area in large numbers:

'We passed through many large villages of the Balobale, the inhabitants of which have fled from the chief Kangenke who is favoured with the visits of

---

[105] E.g. Livingstone 1963: 72, 213
[106] Livingstone 1963: 42
[107] Silva Porto 1885: 582

Mambari from Bie, and as he sells his people to them, a great part of the population escapes to *Shinte* [Ishinde] and Katema.'[108]

Chiteta Kayenge, who was probably the incumbent of the Kakenge title at that time, is described also by M. Sangambo, the Luvale historian, as

'a fierce chief. ... He is remembered for guns and gunpowder. He had many, many slaves and he bought and sold many people. He is the one who cut off many heads and placed them on sharpened poles of his royal fence (*lilapa*, *chipango*). The chief also travelled widely. He was accompanied by many headmen and servants (*tutumwa*)... He took trade goods to Lobito on the Atlantic Ocean and passed through the area of Bihe.'[109]

This suggests a strategy which aimed at maximising revenues from abroad, through war and trade in a rather entrepreneurial way. Both the means and probably the end of acquiring these revenues was an accumulation of personal followers, mainly warriors, slave wives, their children, and other dependent labour that could be put to work, for instance, as carriers. Up to the 1890s, the power of the Kakenge and a group of other war chiefs, especially Luvale, seems to have rested mainly on their military strength. The recruitment of warriors not as conscripts, but rather as mercenaries in return for a share in the booty has been mentioned already. This booty, of which the leader reserved a goodly share for himself, both for sale and domestic use, consisted mainly in slaves. (See fig. 23)

Military strength was based not only on the number of warriors, but also on magical powers, another typical ingredient in the mixture of qualities that made up chieftainship.[110] In theory, these magical powers were to some extent claimed to benefit the entire community, by extension of the older functions of headmen. Chiefs used to perform, for instance, certain fertility cults.[111] But fertility cults seem to have decreased with the spread of cassava-growing, and chiefs' abilities to prepare hunting and war medicine became more and more prominent; chiefs of the region even made the sale of such medicine to foreigners a profitable business.[112] An important expedient for such magical powers was obviously slave raiding, ivory hunting and the introduction of guns, which chiefs probably controlled first and in the largest numbers.

These war chiefs probably spread considerable terror in the population. Their subjects' main fear was the prospect of being sold to foreign

---

[108] Livingstone 1963: 264; also p.83, 88, 213, 254; also Magyar 1860: 233

[109] Sangambo 1985: 44. According to Papstein (1978: 195), Chinyama Mushindwa held the Kakenge title from 1835-75, but this contradicts the narrative of Sangambo.

[110] E.g. Dias de Carvalho 1890: 432 [Chokwe]; White 1957: 67 [Luvale]

[111] White 1959; Dias de Carvalho 1890: 464 (ritual of sowing the first seeds)

[112] E.g. Livingstone 1963: 72 [Ishinde]; Sangambo 1985: 42 [Kakenge]; Dias de Carvalho 1890: 702 [the Mwant Yav owed a Chokwe chief two tusks for medicine] and 402

traders, probably much more than ending up as captives or hostages among neighbouring groups of the same cultural background. Villages passed by peaceful travellers were often 'found deserted, a sudden panic having seized the inhabitants',[113] or with closed gates and weapons pointing at the visitors.[114] When caught unawares by Livingstone's caravan, in one instance the villagers 'were terrified by our presence, and one woman seemed as if she would go into fits from fear'.[115] The deepest expression of these fears was a widespread belief that slaves would be eaten by the slave traders.[116] Whether or not cannibalism was actually practised by some of the chiefs or middlemen, these rumours certainly helped to underline the power of chiefs over the lives of their 'subjects'. The treatment of export slaves was certainly much harsher than that of 'village slaves'[117], and mortality much higher. One should also consider the cultural alienation and loss of kinship identity that slaves suffered, which for them came close to a social death. Such beliefs were certainly also systematically promulgated by slave dealers in Central Africa.[118]

But the imposition of military power was clearly not conducive to gaining political recognition in the wider population. Due to their customary high mobility and the rivalry between chiefs, frustrated subjects tended to move away when they felt too 'molested' by their chiefs.[119] To obtain non-human revenues, chiefs adopting this strategy of threats could count even less on any followers in case of need.

Many chiefs, it seems, invested their material incomes, mainly from trade and production, in their own group of dependants. For example, chiefs were in a particularly strong position to redeem pawns and slaves; they tended to redeem even unrelated persons threatened by export, especially women, whom they wanted to include in their own villages.[120] Chiefs' capitals became pools of surplus food, largely of their own production, which not only facilitated their trade exchanges with foreign traders but above all backed up the growth of the capitals themselves. The

---

[113] Livingstone 1963: 47
[114] E.g. Cameron 1877: II, 146
[115] Livingstone 1963: 76 [1854]
[116] Livingstone (1963: 119) observed 'the sense of insecurity felt by those who may at any time be seized by the chief and sold to the slave merchant, and, as all imagine, at some future time be by him fattened and eaten, ...' This was a very common idea in Central Africa - 'they all have the idea that those who are sold to the whites are eaten' (Livingstone 1960: 42 [1851, on the Lozi]). And Silva Porto noted in his diary in 1847 on the Luchazi-Mbunda near the Lutembwe that 'cannibalism is one of their predominant vices' (1942: 72).
[117] See Sangambo 1985: 72
[118] Cf. for example Cameron 1877: II, 142; Arnot 1969: 143 [1888]
[119] E.g. Silva Porto 1885: 577
[120] E.g. Dias de Carvalho 1890: 692; Porto 1938: 72 [*Quiengo*, Western *Ganguela*; 1853]

gifts chiefs received from foreign visitors were redistributed first of all to their relatives, wives, slaves and friends.[121] In terms of material wealth, even the private accumulation option for chiefs required costly investments.

D 5.4 Power and accumulation

19th century travellers often spoke about the number of people individual chiefs were able to muster. These reports permit a tentative comparison between different sources of power among local rulers. In general, the areas around the capitals of powerful chiefs seem to have developed by the mid-19th century into relatively dense agglomerations of population. Graça, for example, when he was received by chief Katende on the Kasai in 1846, estimated about 3-4,000 persons to be present at the reception[122] ; according to Silva Porto, the capital of the Mbunda chief Kabita on the Lutembwe was 'rather populous, despite of the *Ganguela* race not staying more than three years in the same place';[123] and Livingstone reported that the Southern Lunda chief Ishinde 'had according to my imperfect numeration 900 to 1,000 souls around him. Many more were reported as occupying the surrounding vicinity'.[124]

Most of these attendants, however, seem to have insisted on a certain independence from their chiefs. Quite different from, say, the capital of Nuclear Lunda ,the *Musumba*, which was estimated to have a population between 2,000 and 50,000 inhabitants in the later 19th century[125], Upper Zambezi inhabitants apparently did not change their basically centrifugal attitudes and preferred to settle near to, but not in the village of the chief himself, thereby forming agglomerations of villages rather than actual 'towns'. On a local chief in the Northern Chokwe diaspora, for example, Livingstone wrote that

'his village consists chiefly of huts of his wives... His people are scattered over the country, each in his own little village. This arrangement pleases the African vastly, and anyone who expects to have a village gives himself airs in consequence...'[126]

---

[121] Various travellers' reports, *passim*
[122] 1890: 422; see also p.424 on Chibwika, also on the Kasai
[123] 1942: 72 [1847]
[124] Livingstone 1963: 53
[125] Vellut 1972: 74
[126] Livingstone 1963: 248 [Bango 1855]

And F.S. Arnot, in 1884, noted on the 'straggling towns of *Bambunda* and *Bachibokwe*' :

'I speak of "towns"; but though the people are in considerable numbers, gathered close together under their chief, their huts are so hidden and scattered in dense wood, that to a passer-by the only signs of the presence of human beings are certain narrow and winding foot-paths here and there'.[127]

The chiefs' own villages or 'capitals', in contrast, i.e. the number of wives, children, slaves and hostages under his personal control, were mostly quite modest, as illustrated by the remark by Graça in the beginning of this chapter. In addition, it seems that every individual incumbent had to build up his retinue of allies or dependents afresh. Ishinde's capital, for example, had around 100 houses in 1854, but only about 15 huts in 1894 , after he had fled to his present site on the mouth of the Makondo river, nearer to Lozi protection against Luvale raids.[128]

Not the building of political hierarchies through redistribution or force, but successful accumulation strategies by certain individuals and their followers, with emphasis either on warfare (especially Luvale) or trade (especially Chokwe), were probably the main factor behind the differentiation among chiefs described in the first section of this chapter. New opportunities to accumulate imported wealth and dependents enabled these individuals to consolidate their personal political power, and allowed for increased social mobility. Junior titles could rise against senior ones, new titles could be invented, junior contenders or even commoners could accede to power. 'Wealth' as a means to control dependents became the main criterion of social differentiation, including access to power.

It seems that chiefs were able to mobilize some of their political power, in turn, to promote their personal economic accumulation. But the specific revenues they could draw upon as chiefs came mostly from outside their jurisdiction, and consisted mainly in captives, exchanges with other chiefs, and payments of 'respect' by foreign visitors. On the other hand, their special position also meant that they were exposed to numerous additional claims by their unruly allies and followers. The 'wealth' accumulated by chiefly 'entrepreneurs', measured in dependents and imported goods on stock, was not necessarily greater and more durable than the one enterprising commoners could achieve, through production and/or trade, without access to political titles.

---

[127] Arnot 1969: 102 [1884]
[128] Schapera 1963: 65; Coillard 1897: 606

D 6 Conclusion Part D: 'Equity with growth' ?

Historians and social scientists working on Africa have come to share the assumption that unequal relations between producers, allowing for the accumulation of others' products (be they 'subsistence' or 'surplus') are a critical precondition for economic development (see introduction, ch. A 2). At the same time, it is believed that the expansion of market production has supported or even created processes of socio-economic differentiation within the societies affected. Research in the pre-colonial has therefore focused on the more stratified social formations, as potential forerunners in various aspects of 'modernization'.

The limits of accumulation

In the last chapter of this part, I have tried to show the relatively weak position of chiefs (the potential ruling class) around the Upper Zambezi and Kasai, politically as well economically. They apparently had considerable difficulties to exact export goods as 'tributes' from their followers, and were under considerable pressure to redistribute their wealth. In the course of the pre-colonial period, opportunities to improve their position arose temporarily, but mainly through the appropriation of external revenues, in the form of slave raids, privileged access to certain imported goods, exactions from travellers, and trading. This seems to confirm Cathérine Coquéry-Vidrovitch's argument, presented in her classic essay on an 'African Mode of Production', that aristocracies or privileged classes in subsaharan Africa depended on foreign bases of accumulation, at least initially.[1]

Critics of this argument have pointed out the importance of large-scale exploitation of slaves in the formation of practically all major African states.[2] Indigenous forms of bondage, mostly resulting from captivity (war), existed everywhere in Africa (as in most pre-capitalist societies), but they expanded and were transformed considerably in the context of slave exports and pre-colonial trade.[3] Slaves could be useful in a variety of ways for emergent ruling classes, but in the 19th century the systematic use of their labour for the production of 'legitimate goods' for

---

[1] Coquéry-Vidrovitch 1977 (first published 1969)
[2] First by Terray (1973)
[3] See Lovejoy 1983: 269ff; Wirz 1984: 69ff; Meillassoux 1989: 45ff

the world market became the dominant mode of exploitation in many African societies.[4]

In West-Central Africa, which was one of the areas most intensely affected by the slave trade, the institution of 'internal' slavery was predictably widespread. Miller has described the accumulation of dependent people, rather than land or goods, as the main rationale of the indigenous 'ethno-political economy'.[5] When the Atlantic slave trade offered new opportunities to acquire dependants, new strata of slave-owning nobles and traders emerged, both African and European, at the expense of older elites. After the end of slave exports, they employed slave labour for carriage and commodity production, especially on plantations in areas nearer to the coast.[6] Miller has therefore compared the large-scale appropriation of slave labour in West-Central Africa with what has been called 'primitive accumulation' in Europe.[7] Lovejoy has spoken of the same process as a transformation towards a 'slave mode of production', articulated with capitalism. The question is whether such transformation also occurred in the societies around the Upper Zambezi and Kasai.[8] The intensity of market production, and the continuous influx of slaves through trade and war *prima facie* seem to confirm those who have thought so.[9]

Undoubtedly, the acquisiton of productive and reproductive capacities embodied in substantial numbers of slaves was a precondition of export growth in a macro-economic perspective. It meant that the region experienced a net growth of population, despite ongoing exports of human beings. Some of this growth was probably due to the typical selectiveness of slave exports throughout West-Central Africa, with emphasis on youths, men and older women, while young women able to bear children (and to grow food) remained in the region as slave wives.[10] But since birthrates around the Upper Zambezi were unusually low at least by the end of the pre-colonial period,[11] demographic growth would have

---
[4] See Lovejoy 1983: 274ff; Meillassoux 1989: 141ff and 257ff
[5] Miller 1988: 43-47
[6] E.g. Miller 1973 and 1983; more generally: Miller 1988: 136-38
[7] Miller 1988: 137
[8] A 'slave mode of production' has been defined as a social formation in which the exploitation of slave labour prevails in vital sectors of the economy (see Lovejoy 1983: 1ff, 269).
[9] Papstein 1978: 250/51; he concedes, however, that a 'slave mode of production' was more advanced in neighbouring social formations, such as the Lozi.
[10] Miller has estimated, on the basis of census figures for the colony of Angola in the late 18th century, a high percentage and fertility of women resulting in a net growth of population in West Central Africa between 13 and 19 per 1,000 p.a., in spite of massive loss of life and people through the slave trade (1988: 153ff).
[11] See Spring 1976: 32ff

depended more than elsewhere on a continuing influx of people from the east. Chokwe and Luvale with their economic and military power apparently came out as the strongest in this massive redistribution of population; according to contemporary sources the population of *Quiboco* and *Lovar* was growing fastest by the mid-19th century.[12] Southern Lunda and unconquered remnants of the Iron Age *'Mbwela'* populations, on the other hand, may have belonged to those peoples who paid for the others' strength with demographic decline - although they tried, in turn, to make good for their losses by raids further into the interior (see part B).

It has been argued that African 'internal' slavery, as a way of labour mobilization under conditions of open access to land, led to the emergence of a class of unfree labourers, below the classes of free commoners and 'nobles' or 'chiefs'. Even where slave women and children were amalgamated into the existing matrilineal kinship system, in a legal position of permanent dependents, this would have been gradually reduced to an ideology concealing the fact that the exploitation of slaves was becoming the basis of economic reproduction. The 'lineage mode of production' would have thus been transformed into a 'proto-slave mode'. The labour of slaves would have freed their owners (glossed as 'husbands' or 'grandfathers') from physical labour, in both food and export production and in trade, from the need to be present at home, and from customary obligations vis-a-vis their in-laws, and hence enabled them to accumulate more wealth and more slaves.[13]

To prove this hypothesis is difficult, however, for the Upper Zambezi and Kasai. The evidence presented earlier in this part suggests, in contrast, that a specific exploitation of slaves in production was not easy for their owners, or was restricted to a transition period after the slaves' acquisition. The material value of slaves was apparently realized more in external than in internal activities, notably in warfare and legal compensations. Although their status remained subordinate and often humiliating enough for at least one generation, slaves seem to have been able to quickly establish personal rights over land, tools and products, and to engage in market production on their own account. Production and procreation were important tasks of slaves, but their deliveries of products and services seem to have soon begun to resemble the customary obligations of wives and juniors. As in other parts of the West-Central African interior, the transformation towards a class division between freeborn and slaves remained limited; the expansion of slavery apparently

---

[12] Magyar 1860: 229, 233; Miller has therefore assumed a relative 'overpopulation' in the Central Chokwe highlands which he thinks contributed to the great Chokwe migrations (1970: 182).

[13] Papstein 1978: 250/51, 254; Miller 1981: 65/66

'reinforced a social order based on dependency but not on the exploitation of slaves in order to produce commodities.'[14]

This 'restrained transformation' towards a slave society hardly allows to conclude, on the other hand, that kinship-based forms of dependency and exploitation were particularly strong here. Gender and age relations were probably never as hierarchical and exploitative as has been described for other parts of Africa.[15] The massive expansion of slavery, especially the introduction of slave wives, was to some extent nothing other than an attempt to break the norms of reciprocity between free kinspeople, especially between spouses and in-laws. The main interest in slaves, however, probably remained the accumulation of dependants, the real 'wealth' in the region. To have a slave wife enabled a man to keep his own children, against the rules of matrilineal descent. The greater the number of dependants the villagers could rely on as warriors or pawns (hostages), the greater their security against military attacks or legal prosecution with subsequent enslavement which could mean the end of the entire village. Market activities, especially credit business, may have benefited to some extent from this kind of insurance, but most of its importance must be seen in the context of an enormous increase in inter-village disputes and violence, a less direct result of long-distance trade. The specific claims on unfree 'wives' and 'children' remained largely confined to what ambitious men had long been struggling for :

> 'not direct supervision over others, and still less stocks of the physical products of their labour beyond immediate needs, since both people and their products were all too perishable, but rather a general claim to unspecified future labour and its product at whatever moment need for them might arise.'[16]

In other words, people of unfree status were mainly exploited to strengthen the village in outside relations. Increasing outside pressure, especially the threat of enslavement, could certainly be turned by freeborn elders against their dependants or juniors, both free and slave as a powerful means of intimidation; but with regard to relations of production, slaves in this region were apparently in fact absorbed into an existing 'social order' which was not favourable for accumulation, but for some individual autonomy. This has to do with the fact that kinship and marriage were probably never the only principles structuring this order, but overlapped with other networks of personal relationships. On the one hand, producers, including women and juniors, were used to controlling their own labour and products as individuals. On the other, they were used to securing their requirements for food, assistance and security to a

---

[14] Lovejoy 1983: 239
[15] Meillassoux 1960, 1972; Rey 1971
[16] Miller 1988: 47

considerable extent through circulation of goods and labour. Such transfers took place not only among relatives and in-laws, but also with a variety of 'friends' and other partners.

The dynamics of reciprocal relationships

Absence of economic accumulation in pre-colonial Africa has been explained, if not by lack of productivity, by the persistence of traditional patterns of redistribution[17] and social control based on personal dependence rather than property.[18] At any rate, the relative absence of exploitation has been associated with a 'suboptimal use of resources' (Austen) and lack of productive development, particularly in the remoter parts of the continent, nearer to the main sources of enslavement than to the Atlantic commodity markets. This argument is complementary to the one mentioned at the beginning, which emphasized the importance of slave labour in pre-colonial centralized states; but it contradicts the fact that a number of less differentiated societies, even in the remoter interior, have been very dynamic world market producers.[19] This was precisely the case around the Upper Zambezi and Kasai. Does this reconfirm demand-side economics with their theories of 'growth and equity' or 'redistribution with growth' for pre-colonial Africa ?[20]

It is obviously necessary to adopt a less mechanistic approach in order to understand the connection between productive growth and pre capitalist social relations. In the example presented in the preceding chapters, a relative social balance in economic relations does not seem to have stemmed from a conservative logic of redistribution and 'subsistence security', let alone 'egalitarian values' (C.M.N. White). The absence of any marked and sustainable degree of inequality rather appears to be a fragile result of continual negotiations and struggles between different categories of producers. This context seems to have favoured processes of productive innovation and market integration which can be observed up to the present day.

The norms of reciprocity involved in kinship, friendship and neighbourhood, which were regularly invoked in all acts of transfer within the regional societies, should not be taken as fixed obligations that

---

17 See end of chapter C 5 (referring to Austen 1987: 16ff; Coquéry-Vidrovitch 1985: 147ff)
18 Lovejoy 1983: 275
19 Cathérine Coquéry-Vidrovitch acknowledges such cases in the beginning of her article on an 'African Mode of Production', but only to assert bluntly one page later that 'Africa is the one place in the world where agriculture was least liable to produce a surplus' as an explanation why African rulers had to resort to foreign revenues (1977: 82/83).
20 See for example Adelman and Morris 1973; Chenery 1975

had to be strictly observed. They should rather be seen as languages in which, given the absence of strong sanctioning authority, social relationships were negotiated from which, in the longer run, supplies in food and other vital goods, assistance and loyalty could depend. Transfers of material goods, beyond their immediate use-value, were to a considerable extent instrumental in these negotiations. 'Wealth' goods attained a particularly strong bargaining power in this context; they could help to increase power over people, as clients, juniors or slaves, but they could also help to avert the threat of enslavement and establish greater autonomy of subordinate people, both women and men. It must not be overlooked that these struggles about claims for loyalty and assistance through the medium of 'gifts' and 'payments' took place also on a smaller, more day-to-day scale. Massive imports of 'wealth', in return for decentralized natural resources, therefore attracted widespread interest not only among elders and chiefs, but also among ordinary male and female producers (see also ch. E 4, below).

Economic inequalities certainly did arise in this dynamic process, notably between chiefs, elders and commoners, and between producers of freeborn and slave status; they also occurred between residents and immigrants; bridegrooms and parents-in-law, husbands and wives; junior and senior women; debtors and creditors; plaintiffs and defendants. However, the economic differences between basic social categories were mostly not permanent and did not increase very much with market integration, despite an apparent concentration of means of physical coercion. Women were undoubtedly put in a disadvantageous position by male warriors and export producers; but they succeeded in making up for some of that by increasing and using their power over scarce food. Holders of chiefly titles could rise to some importance even from non-noble origin, but their wealth, on which their power increasingly depended, could rapidly be exhausted by substantial claims for redistribution by unruly allies and followers. Village elders who showed themselves greedy or incapable of securing peace and income could be left out in the cold by their juniors. Slaves and hostages could gradually emancipate themselves by establishing their own economy, acquiring their own offspring and even slaves, and were sometimes redeemed through their own, or some relative's or friend's, means.

If in this case marked and sustainable social differentiation did not take place in the process of market integration, this can not be simply attributed to a persistence of older social structures. The continuity of social mobility and negotiability of relationships rested on continuing specific material conditions in the region. These can be roughly described as a combination of two factors: an abundance of open land with a scattered and highly mobile population, allowing for individual appropriation of resources; and a continuing dominance of labour-intensive production technologies combined with scarcity of labour.[21] These conditions were to some extent reinforced, rather than upset, by a pattern of world market demand which addressed a highly decentralized gathering production. At the same time, it is important to note that the continuity of a certain degree of social balance was not simply given, but only the result of continuous negotiation and struggle within the regional society. Under different conditions, these could as well have resulted in more permanent structures of economic inequality and accumulation. The picture emerges of a society in continuous flux but without clearly directed transformation.

It is particularly interesting to see how these indigenous ways of negotiating social relationships were extended and adapted to the relationship between producers and their foreign trade partners. But this relationship was about different resources: access to imported commodities, on the one hand, and to export products, on the other. In this case, negotiations and struggles were primarily about the conditions of access to these material goods, within the 'terms of trade' set by the wider world market. But one of these conditions was again the establishment of a sufficient degree of 'trust' amidst highly volatile terms of trade and highly heterogeneous moralities of exchange. An exploration of the strategies and understandings that shaped this relationship will follow in the next part (E).

---

[21] Cf. Miller 1981

Part E
NEGOTIATING THE MARKET : RESIDENT PRODUCERS AND FOREIGN TRADERS

In the preceding chapters, only actors within the regional arena of the pre-colonial Upper Zambezi and Kasai have been looked at. Crucial relations of labour, power and exchange within the regional societies have been examined in order to explain the different positions, interests and strategies of these actors vis-a-vis pre-colonial market production. It has been left open, however, how the various categories of residents actually realized their ambitions towards market participation, especially their growing demand for imported goods.

In this last Part, I will ask about the ways in which residents of the region voiced their demands towards the agents of the pre-colonial world market who had brought the wished-for riches since the late 18th century. The hard core of these negotiations was, undoubtedly, the question of price relations or 'terms of trade' between imported goods on the one hand and export or food products on the other. A basic antagonism of interests as to which party would get which profit and take on which costs of the transaction certainly existed. Tough bargaining undoubtedly went on in the region throughout the period, with varying results. But the concepts and language used between residents and foreigners to justify their claims were often quite different from what we would expect from market participants in antagonistic positions. There is relatively rich data in early travellers' reports on that discourse which, however, has found little attention in existing literature so far.[1] 19th century travellers mostly regarded this language as mere sweet words, as an attempt to conceal exceptional 'greed', because local business partners often used it to demand a whole range of other payments in addition to the actual price of their products.[2] On the other hand, they sometimes showed themselves surprisingly generous towards their foreign visitors. In reality, more than just the question of 'a good price' was at stake; there was a structural need for both residents and foreign traders to establish some sort of personal relationship in order to participate in an ultimately anonymous and risky market. The analysis of this interaction between residents and foreigners will not only yield additional insights into the conditions of pre-colonial market integration as such, but also show to what extent indigenous understandings of circulation entered and shaped this process.

---

[1] One notable exception is the compilation of sources on pre-colonial trade by Sundstrøm (1974).
[2] 'Greed' (ambição, cobiça), besides curiosity, was seen by Portuguese-speaking traders as one of the outstanding characteristics of the people of the region throughout the 19th century (e.g. Silva Teixeira 1940: 237; *Anonymus* 1940: 25; Silva Porto 1885: 585).

E 1   'Extortions, exactions and vexations'

Before they could engage in any serious negotiations over the purchase of export goods or bulk provisions, European travellers unfamiliar with the customs of the Upper Zambezi and Kasai were faced with what they obviously experienced as rather arbitrary kinds of demands, as innumerable 'extortions, exactions and vexations'[1] by resident chiefs and headmen. As the number of more or less independent local potentates in the area was legion, these demands multiplied, and presented a solid cost factor for any journeys to or through this part of the interior.

The professional traders and middlemen of the 'Atlantic Zone', who were better acquainted with local customs than 'explorers' and missionaries, would set aside special funds to 'pay their way through' the interior. Already the 'Two *Pombeiros*', the first Portuguese-speaking trade agents who managed to cross the continent between 1805 and 1814, had carried with them goods worth 2,000 *milreis* 'to provide and pay the chiefs for safe-conduct' and kept a minute record of every 'present' they expended.[2] Between 1846 and 1881, *sertanejos* such as Silva Porto included a fixed amount of four pieces of cloth, equivalent to 1.6 *milreis* or nearly 5 % of the total value, in every load (*banzo*) of a carrier going from Bihe to the interior for *quibanda* or 'hospitality gifts'.[3] In addition, he would overrate the value of goods issued as payments for slaves, ivory, wax or rubber in his accounts, apparently as a kind of insurance against irregular damage suffered by his caravans.[4]

It was not only the amount, but above all the unpredictability and rising tendency in these constant 'embarassments to which the commerce is subject' that prompted the Angolan Government to support an expedition under the trader Rodrigues Graça along the Upper Kasai to Nuclear Lunda in 1846, in an attempt to reduce or at least standardize these demands.[5] Bigger European and Euro-African traders, such as the *sertanejos* from Bihe and the hinterland of Angola, were particularly subject to such demands outside the actual price for export goods; they were a prominent reason why, since the inception of the ivory boom in the late 1840s, traders constantly tried to extend their radius to new markets beyond the Upper Kasai and Zambezi where they could deal with

---

1 Livingstone 1963: 116
2 Baptista 1873: 200; Vellut 1972: 107
3 Silva Porto 1885: 24
4 Madeira Santos 1986: 103
5 Graça 1890: 368 [1848]

one big bulk supplier instead of wasting their time with petty chiefs and producers, and/or profit from the more modest demands for 'gifts' by local notables that prevailed everywhere at the beginning of long-distance trade. But in the long run it was difficult for them to avoid the region of the Upper Zambezi and Kasai because it cost less time and expenses to reach, because it was more productive with wax, rubber and food, and because practically all major trade routes to and from the remoter interior passed through it.[6]

E 1.1 The language of legitimate demands

The 'presents' that were demanded by local potentates consisted of imported manufactures from caravans on the way up from the coast, but also in export commodities from further into the interior on the way down. Livingstone, for example, on his way from Bulozi to Luanda, was regularly asked to give 'a man, a tusk or an ox'.[7]

European visitors, it seems, did not find it easy to define the title under which these demands should to be seen. François Coillard, writing on the Luvale senior Chief Kakenge, for example, called it 'the homage or rather a *tax* he exacts from black Portuguese traders who enter his country'.[8] Livingstone mostly spoke of 'gifts' or 'presents'.[9] Graça, Silva Porto and F.S. Arnot, instead, called what they had to pay to the chiefs *tributo* (*de passagem*) or '(transit) tribute'.[10] But Cameron found this term inappropriate:

'No tribute is demanded as in Ugogo [East Africa], except by one or two chiefs, but they invent many claims as a means of extorting goods from those passing through their villages'.[11]

In the eyes of the local proponents, these claims were not at all arbitrary, but quite legitimate. The local term used for such 'presents' to resident chiefs was, according to a number of sources, not *mulambu*, the word for tribute. One indigenous term that appears instead is *musapu*, the customary present to the owner of the land after a successful hunt.[12] Even transitory foreign traders and travellers, who were conversant with local

---
6   Madeira Santos 1986: 116, 133ff. See chapter B 3
7   Livingstone 1963: passim [1854/55]
8   Coillard, 1897: 611; emphasis added
9   Livingstone 1963: *passim* [1854/54]
10 Graça 1890: [1846]; Silva Porto, 1986: 322ff [1847]; Arnot 1969: e.g.249 [1888]
11 Cameron 1877: II 164 [Luvale]

customs would submit a part of their prey to the local elder;[13] but obviously this was not the essence of what was expected from them as a gift, as an incident noted by Livingstone illustrates:

> 'I ordered a tired riding ox to be slaughtered yesterday evening, and according to custom sent the hump and ribs attached to the chief of the *Chibokwe* [Chokwe]. He thanked me and promised to send me food tomorrow. This morning after service we received an impudent message scorning the meat and demanding either a man, a tusk, a gun, powder, cloth, an ox, a shell (part of the nautilus [Lv.*jimbe*, see fig. 22]) for in the event of refusal he would prevent further progress.'[14]

'The gift called *o-sapo* for the chief [*chefe*] of the country', which Silva Porto's agents for example had to pay on their first journey to Bulozi, consisted of 'cloth, powder, guns and beads'.[15] At any rate, traders had to send the *musapu* gift in advance, to ask permission to enter the area under the chief's jurisdiction or his capital.[16] While the right to demand gifts from foreigners under the title of *musapu* was apparently appropriated by senior chiefs, additional gifts were demanded under different titles by all categories of local leaders. Silva Porto, for instance, while he sent the *Uçapo* (*musapu*) to Mona Kisenge, simultaneously presented the local Chokwe chief with what he called, in Umbundu, a *quibanda*. Elsewhere, he explained this customary gift, usually paid in cloth, by 'the constitution of this race in small republics, why it is not surprising that tribute is paid to the [every] village headman where one sets up the camp'.[17]

No particular indigenous term seems to exist for this most general type of gift; but resident headmen and chiefs clearly fitted their demands into the current category of 'respect' (Lv./SL. *kavumbi*). Rights of 'respect' (see above, section D 5.2) could be regarded by local chiefs as being due from foreign travellers on at least two grounds.[18] Firstly they

---

[12] See above, D 5.2
[13] E.g. Silva Porto 1942: 73 [1847]
[14] Livingstone 1963: 103 [1854]
[15] Silva Porto diary, entries 17th and 22nd January 1848 (1986: 336/37) [south of Lungwevungu confluence, to Imbwa, northern Lozi ruler]
[16] Silva Porto 1885: 577 [1880, Kissenge, Northern Chokwe]; Coillard 1897: 611 [1894, Kakenge, Luvale]; Vellut mentions the same custom for travellers approaching the Nuclear Lunda capital, the *musumba* - unfortunately without mentioning his sources (1972: 93), while Dias de Carvalho was told that the Pende chief *Cumbana* admitted to his region only 'some *quilolo* [headman] or other subject who gives him a good present (*mussapo*)' (1890: 708).
[17] Silva Porto 1885: 577 and 164 [1880]. The *pombeiros*, who also travelled along the southern fringes of the Nuclear Lunda empire mentioned a similar term, *quipata* [Bangala?], 'which is a gift to the Lord of the Land'(Baptista 1873: 207 [c.1806]).
[18] Such a gift may have been called in Luvale *chitumbwisa*, 'a present given in greeting a visitor, relative etc.'(Horton 1975: 401). A particular term, *quizeza*, 'which the traders

temporarily entered the jurisdiction of a local 'owner' or 'lord of the land', and could therefore be expected to ask permission for the use of paths and bridges, for the building of shelters and even to be allocated land for cultivation, when encamped. As strangers, they had to establish such a usufruct relationship through the payment of 'respect' gifts, and in the case of a trader these gifts obviously had to be his trade goods.

Local chiefs and headmen in the region drew the other legitimation for demands on foreign travellers from their role as hosts, according to the rules of hospitality or 'the ancient law towards strangers'.[19] By these norms, they felt entitled to demand a token of respect from their guests. But by the same norms they felt obliged to give food and shelter to the visitors. In fact, during a stay in a village or chief's capital, caravan leaders were according to all travellers' accounts invariably presented, sometimes repeatedly, with some of the following food items: baskets of cassava meal or millet, dried fish or chunks of meat, eggs, chickens, goats, pigs or even an ox, and calabashes of grain or honey-beer. Again, no particular term in Upper Zambezi languages for this gift is known to me, apart from the general expression *chisambu* ('hospitality'). Lozi visitors, however, seem to have used a special term *liyumbu*, translated by Coillard as 'the food of hospitality'.[20] Local leaders felt embarrassed when for some reason they were unable to fulfill this duty, and then sometimes gave hoes, axes or cloth instead, in order to enable their hosts to buy their 'hospitality food' by themselves from the local population - in another form of redistribution between chiefs and commoners.[21]

In such cases, the gifts also covered expenses for the ordinary caravan members. In most cases, however, the 'hospitality food' of the local leader was only meant for their counterparts in the caravan, while the lower ranks relied for their provisions directly on purchase or hospitality from commoners. Livingstone noted in his diary:

> 'The chiefs and headmen attend to me, but my party is supplied by the common people... My men do a great deal in the begging line. As soon as we come to a village, all run up to it, calling out to everyone they meet:"Give me something to eat, I come from afar", ...and they very seldom come away unsupplied...'[22]

---

from Ambaca call *traquinada* [lit. stroke, noise], and which consists in a portion of beads, bells, powder, brass nails etc., and in two yards of any cloth except cotton' is reported for an extra payment, besides the actual price for export goods, due among Pende of Canhima, by Dias de Carvalho (1890: 707).

[19] Livingstone 1953: 253 [1855]
[20] Coillard 1897: 609, 613
[21] Livingstone, 1963: 41 55, 111 [1854; Masiko, Ishinde, Chokwe near Chiumbe River]; Cameron 1877: II 187 [Mona Peho, Chokwe, 1875]
[22] Livingstone 1963: 79 [1854, Chikalweje, Luvua, Luvale])

Important chiefs sometimes already sent food presents through their messengers already before the caravan had actually reached the place.[23] In such a case, the presents were also a material sign of agreement to the caravan's previous request for access through a *musapu* gift.[24] At any rate, the handing over of the foods mentioned is a well-established rule which is still regularly experienced when being welcomed in Upper Zambezi villages. It was (and is) clearly seen as a kind of counterpart for the gifts a visitor was equally invariably expected to offer, but good etiquette demands that some time, usually at least a night, should elapse before giving the counter-present in order to avoid it looking like a sale.[25]

E 1.2 The valuation of respect

Travellers have always been struck by the strong imbalance in real market value between these gifts, usually at the travellers' expense. Livingstone, for instance, repeatedly complained about the 'exorbitance of demands' by local elders and chiefs for gifts which were usually worth a multiple of the value of the 'hospitality food', and firmly propagated an idea of equivalent payment.[26] He tried to counter what he saw as 'exorbitance' with a mixture of 'good old custom' and 'fair trade' arguments:

> 'The chief Bango came at midday with a present of meal and pallah [Impala] meat. I gave an equivalent and told him the objects of our journey &c. He appeared pleased so far as that went, but objected to a crack in the pannikin which formed part of the present. I exchanged it. He then wished double the amount of cloth, but to this I objected as it was not trade.'[27]

Returning through the areas north of and near the Kasai, he complained that

> 'where slave-traders have frequently been, the negroes do not seem to have the smallest idea of presents being reciprocal', and that the people are 'less liberal' than the Luvale and Lunda further south, although 'there is no lack of food in the country,...they will not sell...except for very large prices.'[28]

Only charismatic persons and non-commercial travellers such as Livingstone were sometimes able to remain firm in such bargaining, and

---
[23] E.g. Livingstone 1963: 49 [1854, Ishinde];
[24] Coillard 1897: 611, 614 [Kakengc 1894]
[25] I was instructed accordingly by village headmen in several cases.
[26] Livingstone 1963: 234; 68, 247, 253
[27] Livingstone, 1963: 247 [Nuclear Lunda/Chokwe, on Luembe river; emphasis added]
[28] *Ibid.*: 253 and 97

to claim the traditional right of reciprocity also for themselves.[29] But most Portuguese, Euro-African and *Mambari* traders usually gave in and paid what they were asked.[30] This shows that in reality, the power position of the agents of the world market was much weaker in the Upper Zambezi than was claimed by some of their spokesmen.[31]

It is therefore necessary to look also at local reasoning behind the size of these demands. A certain correlation seems sometimes to have existed with the amount of hospitality or land rights requested. The Luchazi chief Kabita, for instance, had to be given two payments of gifts, one for for the transit stay of Silva Porto's main caravan, and one for the agents (*pombeiros*) who wanted to set up a buying camp for a longer period.[32] But a main criterion used as to the size of the gift demanded was clearly the power and wealth attributed to the receiver. 'Because I am a big man and lord of these lands', was the argument given by one Chokwe chief to support his demands;[33] and another emphasized his worthiness of presents to an uncomprehending visitor by pointing out 'his three mothers and two fathers with an ingenuous logic' - i.e. his noble descent.[34]

Demands for presents were usually negotiable, and this may have been part of the game of probing relative social status between parties hitherto unconnected, even among friends and relatives. The 'presents' were meticulously examined before they were accepted by the chief or headman, and quite often the whole or some component of it was rejected with demands for more or better. But outright refusal to submit such a gift, even if the caravan only passed the place at a distance, was regarded as an offence liable for compensation. Every chief and headman of any importance *en route* wanted to be asked permission to pass. Otherwise he would declare that 'he felt himself very ill-treated in being passed by' and try to detain the caravan by force.[35] This was not always an empty threat. Destruction was in fact the fate of some caravans in the Upper Zambezi who refused to pay homage to local chiefs. Chiefs of the Upper Zambezi

---

[29] Livingstone 1963: 253
[30] *Ibid.*: 231/2 103; Cameron 1877: 168 178 187
[31] E.g.Livingstone (1963: 252): 'They have not the smallest idea of European powers...'; Graça (1890: 410, 422 [1846]) tells that Katende, after a long exhortation, would have admitted that 'no one of them could reject the orders of *Mane Puto* [the king of Portugal, A.v.O.]; that they needed cloth and other commodities; that the *Mane Puto* did not need them [i.e.their exports of wax etc.]'.(my translation)
[32] Silva Porto 1942: 72 [1847]
[33] Graça 1890: 413 [1846]
[34] Arnot 1969: 151 [Mona Peho, 1885]
[35] Livingstone 1963: 113 [1854]. See also Livingstone 1963: 113 [on Luachimo river, Headman Ionga Panza, Chokwe] and 116 [Chikapa, Chokwe]; Arnot 1869: 248/9 [on Chongo river, small chief under Kangombe, Luvale]

and Kasai, especially Luvale, were notorious in this respect;[36] even members of Bihe caravans who had terrorized the populations further east adopted very modest attitudes when they reached the region.[37] This suggests that military strength and strategic considerations (trade competition) also played their part in determining what extra payments foreigners had to make.

The most important factor, however, was most apparently the status ascribed to the caravan leader, which significantly was measured by the total value of trade goods carried by the caravan[38]. Graça, who in 1846 tried to impose a standard amount of 'tribute' (at a value of 40 *reis* to every chief *en route*) was scolded thoroughly by the Chokwe chief Kanyika:

'I have received what the *chindele* [white] sends me, but I am not satisfied, because what they bring me is little, in view of so much merchandise he carries, is he not ashamed to send me only this ? He shall send me two barrels of powder, two bales of fine cloth (*baeta*), eight guns, one coat, one military uniform, and a hat, a sabre, and he shall send me clothing for my sons, *macotas* [messengers] and friends...'[39]

At least *de facto*, demands for 'gifts' indeed came close to a kind of taxation. It is therefore surprising that, instead of making a low-key entrance, which would have been perhaps more profitable, traders would show their status and wealth upon arrival at a chief's capital in a very ostentatious way, by wearing fancy uniforms, carrying flags, sounding trumpets, and firing guns.[40]

When it came to negotiating their hosts' demands, most Portuguese-speaking traders were apparently 'glad to submit to anything for peace with the inhabitants', and free-trade advocates such as Livingstone noted angrily that the latter were 'not slow to take advantage of it'.[41] This willingness to pay on the part of professional traders in the region, however, was by no means 'cowardliness', but resulted from a profound knowledge of the indigenous 'rules of the game': the more important a caravan's presentation, the more attention it could attract among dispersed producers to speed up business, and the more counterclaims it could make on local potentates some time in the future. In contrast to

---

[36] E.g. Arnot 1969: 248/49
[37] Cameron 1877: II, passim
[38] E.g.Livingstone 1963: 242 [1855]
[39] Graça 1890: 410 [1846]
[40] E.g. Livingstone 1963: 52f [1854, Ishinde]; Cameron 1877: 187f [1875, Peho]; Arnot 1969: 152ff [1885, Luvale]; cf. Miller 1970: 185. Other traders are said to have resorted to a strategy of playing down their wealth and importance (Miller 1970: 194, quoting Marques 1889: 501).
[41] Livingstone 1963: 243

'explorers' who usually visited an area only once, traders and middlemen depended on their local partners in a much longer run.

Of course, Portuguese-speaking traders continuously lamented about these costs, particularly for this region. Rodrigues Graça, in his attempt to curb the practice of demanding exorbitant 'presents', started a series of fundamental debates on realistic terms of trade with his hosts along the Upper Kasai.[42] It is interesting how explicitly both sides tried to argue their relative market strength in terms of the other's dependence on their respective export goods (cloth against beeswax), up to threats of boycott. But in reality, such threats were never carried out, and Portuguese-speaking traders continued to be normally very generous, for good reasons; they nevertheless seem to have secured, in the long run, more than satisfactory profit rates (see below). In the following section, I will ask about the full extent of the value this expensive 'hospitality' had for both sides.

E 1.3 Hospitality and accusations

Clearly, all foreign travellers were, at least potentially, very much in need of more material support than just a gift of food, and claims on this support was what they hoped to obtain in return for giving in to their hosts' demands. When the 'lord (or lady) of the country', after staging an elaborate welcome ceremony[43] (see fig. 31) and accepting their gifts, had permitted a foreign caravan to stay and conduct trade or 'given them the path' to continue their journey, this meant, at least in theory, that he or she was responsible for the well-being of these 'guests'. He (or she) would not only help to provide food, but, if necessary, also arrange for the employment of local caravan staff. Carriers were often difficult to find in this region (see below), and guides were absolutely essential to find the hidden forest paths, the fords, ferries and locally made bridges across major rivers[44], and also to introduce the strangers to the people along the road so as to dispel their suspicion.[45] A chief would also have to help in the tracking down of run-away slaves and carriers.[46] He could also be expected to be more willing to conduct actual business, especially to part with precious goods which he could use himself, such as slaves, or

---

[42] Graca 1890: 409/10 and 422 [1846, Katende and Chibwika, Southern Lunda]
[43] See for example Silva Porto 1942: 70 [1847]; Cameron 1877: 58
[44] E.g. Livingstone 1963: 94, 99 [near Katende]; Arnot 1969: 154 [Luvale, 1885]
[45] Livingstone 1963: 76, 91
[46] E.g. Livingstone 1963: 232, 242

sell more profitably nearer to the coast.[47] Finally, the chief would guarantee damages incurred by the visitors during their dealings with his people, in case of injury, theft and default on a trade contract (i.e. credit, see below).[48]

In other words, the payments made to local chiefs and headmen were, in the traders' perspective, at bottom a systematic building of an infrastructure and a security system for trading where none of these existed for them. It is evident that foreign traders were here yielding to indigenous practices of the region. To some extent they accepted being described as the representatives of a foreign community, and such outsiders probably always had to pay their respect to local leaders before any exchanges could begin. If caravans did not comply with their demands, they could be regarded as enemies, and chiefs repeatedly tried to organize their people to boycott food sales to them.[49] But around 1880, chiefs' claims had clearly expanded; travellers began to dwell on the 'caprices' (Silva Porto) of senior Chokwe chiefs such as Ndumba Tembo or Mona Kisenge. These, for example, insisted on formally giving their permission to start retail trading between petty producers and caravan members at the camp; they forbade buying agents to swarm out to remoter villages before the official introduction had taken place and without being accompanied by a chief's messenger; they confiscated trade goods from either party that had been exchanged without explicit permission for this particular trade; and they claimed the authority to fix the prices of export goods (e.g. rubber for cloth) during a particular stay.[50]

Chiefs even seem to have used their role as guarantors of damages or 'trade insurance', however, as a justification for additional claims on both their visitors and their people. By the 1880s, Northern Chokwe and Nuclear Lunda informants pointed out that

'without this [the chiefs'] intervention, or even permission, trade between tribes, which is principally on credit, .. would always run the risk of lack of guarantee... The ruler guarantees only the obligations incurred under his authorisation, and he draws a share from this.'[51]

They presented this as a reduction of chiefs' customary rights; while this may have been true for Nuclear Lunda, it was probably a rather

---

[47] E.g. Livingstone 1963: 104
[48] For example Livingstone 1963: 268 [1855]; Arnot 1969: 248 [1888]; Dias de Carvalho 1890: 692
[49] E.g. Livingstone 1963: 103 [1854; Chokwe]; Singleton-Fisher, 1949: 101 [late 1890s, Luvale]
[50] Capello and Ivens 1882: I 185 [1878]; Silva Porto 1885: 584/85 [1880]
[51] Dias de Carvalho 1890: 691/92

expansive interpretation of the role of chiefs by aspiring Chokwe power figures. The point was that such claims meant new demands on foreign visitors. When Silva Porto arrived at Kisenge's, he was informed by a messenger that

> ' "*it was necessary to open the door* !" We tried to find the solution of this enigma and found out that it was necessary to give some *pannos* [yards of cloth - A.v.O.] to obtain permission for the people of the caravan and of the country to buy and sell provisions and other commodities, without which nothing could be done.'[52]

Chiefs of the Upper Zambezi and Kasai were probably already very inventive with regard to their rights when the first Portuguese-speaking traders arrived, because these complained about the 'ambitions' (i.e. 'greed') of Chokwe and Luchazi/Mbunda chiefs.[53] But in the course of the 19th century, a multiplication of such demands for permission seems to have taken place which was a good opportunity for chiefs not only to impress foreigners with their apparent power, but also to increase their revenues.

Despite such precautions, countless *milonga* (pl. of *mulonga*) or legal disputes would arise between caravan members and the resident population. Again chiefs tried to benefit from the resulting trials. If the damage was on the side of the visitors, a chief might help in the prosecution, but often demanded generous payments of 'court fees' ('respect' for his arbitration in indigenous terms), which could be much higher than the value in dispute from the successful plaintiff.[54] Much more common was the opposite case, that caravan members were accused of some offence liable for compensation. Powerful chiefs could try to claim such compensation by declaring the damaged party one of his 'children'. But in general, the compensations resulting from *milonga* seem to have had socially a more redistributive effect. Virtually everybody could accuse a foreigner of some offence liable for *milonga*.

All groups in the region were renowned for their passion for entrapping foreigners in some *mulonga*, effectively a form of extorting a share of traders' profits, but the Chokwe were particularly notorious.[55] The accusations were clearly taken from the large arsenal of day-to-day village quarrels, which probably increased anyway at this time. But to foreign visitors originating from a different legal system they appeared as mere flimsy pretences invented anew every time. All travellers' reports contain numerous examples of 'the most frivolous pretences of crime' (Livingstone), e.g.: spitting at someone unintentionally; calling someone

---

[52] Silva Porto 1885: 580 [1880]
[53] Silva Teixeira 1940: 236 [1794]
[54] E.g.Arnot, 1969: 248 [1888, Luvale]

by the name of somebody else; unexpected death of the local business partner, his assistant, slave or even dog; passing fields and houses in a hammock; alleged theft by a caravan member, often provoked by placing the 'stolen' object somewhere as a bait; injury; failure to pay respect to a headman; placing a gun or a spear against a hut; using for camp building a fire-marked tree which was claimed as private property by some bee-hunter or cultivator, etc. etc..

An extreme example of how ordinary villagers used *milonga* as a 'macchiavellian ruse' to milk passing caravans has been given by Silva Porto:

> 'In a Chokwe village through which we passed there was a long trail of cassava meal over a blank space which crossed the path, and the natives of both sexes themselves had their attention fixed on that space so that if anybody during his passage should step on it they could jump on him and accuse him of *milonga*, synonymous with *mucano*, with the exacerbating fact of forcing the caravan to return and stay the day in that place, in order to find an outlet for their products, because no *mucano* is resolved quickly, and in this way they carry out the plan of their devilish invention.'[56]

Particularly damaging for the traders' interests was the application on them of the local rule or at least pretence that chiefs were liable for any 'crime', outstanding compensation or debt of one of their people towards foreigners. Caravan leaders were regularly asked to pay whatever *milonga* members of their party had allegedly incurred, and often they were even held responsible for offences some fellow countrymen had committed earlier.[57] Old disputes and open debts between inhabitants and foreign traders or middlemen were often pursued over many years, as among the inhabitants themselves, before they were formally settled in the ritualized way described earlier (see D 4.4). The 'injured' resident did not always feel strong enough or was not even interested in demanding compensation immediately; he or she may have often preferred to save this open claim for future occasions when the need or opportunity might arise.

Such future occasions often consisted in negotiations over various commercial and legal matters, into which at least the Chokwe tried to include claims from old *milonga* like open invoices.[58] As the only legal way out of unexpected, often excessive demands from some old dispute,

---

[55] See especially Dias de Carvalho 1890: 401ff

[56] Silva Porto 1885: 573 [1880]

[57] The first example recorded is the arrest of F.H. da Costa's 'two *Pombeiros*' by chief Moxico in 1805 as hostages for the debts of another trader 'of the same fair' (Mukari) (Baptista 1873: 199), mentioned above at the end of chapter B 1.

[58] Silva Porto (1885: 146ff[Luchazi]) and Dias de Carvalho (1890: 401-415 [Northern Chokwe]) give various examples of how such protracted disputes were mixed with negotiations over commercial exchanges.

experienced negotiators could try to suddenly present counterclaims against the plaintiff, 'to reverse the *milonga*' - apparently a current practice in indigenous jurisdiction.[59] 'It is in commerce that this way of carrying out justice is felt most strongly...', Dias de Carvalho concluded his account of Chokwe jurisdiction.[60] If no agreement was reached, self-help through armed intervention was regarded as legitimate just as in local disputes. Most of the notorious 'robberies' of armed Chokwe, but also Luvale and Mbunda-Luchazi bands on foreign caravans were probably seen as such self-help actions.[61] Only as long as they were backed up by military superiority, whether ostensive or real, could demands by residents on foreigners for legal redress ultimately be successful. Both means appeared to foreign visitors of the region as mere attempts by its inhabitants to obtain a share of others' riches by force.

One should, though, perhaps not underestimate the potential of residents feeling dispossessed of their rights and therefore justified in their claims. The incidence of *milonga* can also be taken as a symptom of authentic tensions and anxieties which probably increased considerably due to ubiquitous violence, market integration, and social differentiation, particularly in the later pre-colonial period. After all, residents were continuously entangled in legal disputes among themselves. They also realized that excessive demands could kill the goose that laid the golden eggs, and prompt traders and middlemen to look for other routes. Towards the end of the 19th century, however, the latter were looking for even more radical ways out of the continuous 'extortions, exactions and vexations'. In fact, Portuguese-speaking traders such as Silva Porto ultimately prepared the colonial takeover which was to reverse the relations of power in the area, although not with the results they had hoped for.[62]

---

[59] Examples given by Dias de Carvalho 1890: 405; Wissmann 1902: 34-36 [1880]
[60] Dias de Carvalho 1890: 687-691
[61] Graça 1890: 415-16 [1846, Chokwe]; Cameron 1877: II 164 [1875, Luvale]; Arnot 1969: 99 102/3 [on Mbunda-Luchazi 1884]
[62] This seems to have been one factor behind Silva Porto's suicide in 1890.

E 2   Business and trust

No clear trend of development can be observed through the 19th century with regard to the forms or extent of the exactions analysed in the preceding chapter. More or less forged accusations leading to open violence against passing caravans appear to have occurred in the rather remote Mbunda-Luchazi area, for example, soon after the very beginning of long-distance trade as well as towards the end of the century.[1] On the other hand, even among the Chokwe and Luvale, who were regularly described as being 'turbulent', greedy or just 'robbers',[2] travellers were sometimes received in a remarkably generous way.[3] They were not only entertained by their hosts with food, drinks, salt, tobacco and cannabis,[4] but also presented with the most valuable goods such as copper crosses[5], white beads,[6] leopard skins,[7] oxen, loads of rubber, wax cakes or child slaves for their personal service.[8] In 1878, the senior Chokwe chief Ndumba Tembo, for example, received Capello and Ivens so hospitably that they were inclined to take stories of extortion as mere tales.[9] And F.S. Arnot in 1885 passed by a young Chokwe chief, 'a sensible looking man, who was very anxious that I should accept an ox as a present.' In the same area, along the main 'watershed' route, Arnot experienced similarly generous attitudes by the common people. Instead of devising extortions and attack,

'crowds of people came to the camp and were most intent on giving presents. Two pigs, a goat and fowls were thrust upon me, and not content with feeding me they made an entertainment with drums and dancing which was kept up in my camp the whole night long...'[10]

---

1   Silva Teixeira 1794: 236; *Anonymus* 1803: 25/26; Arnot 1888: 102/3
2   E.g. Crawford, 1912: 163 [1889]
3   E.g. Arnot 1969: 102/3 [Luchazi 1884]; Capello and Ivens 1882: I 183 [1878, Ndumba Tembo, Chokwe]; Livingstone 1963: 83, 259 [1854/5, Katema, Luvale]
4   Silva Porto 1942: 70 [1847, Kisembo, Luchazi]; Livingstone, 1963: 94 [1854, Kabinje, near Kasai River]
5   Capello and Ivens 1882: I 180 [1878, Ndumba Tembo, Chokwe]
6   Livingstone, 1963: 56 [1854, Ishinde, Southern Lunda]
7   Schomburgk 1925: 55 [1905, Southern Lunda, on Kabompo R.]
8   Livingstone, 1963: 63 [1854, Ishinde; Southern Lunda]; Silva Porto 1885: 579, 583 [Kisenge, Northern Chokwe, 1880]; Arnot 1969: 102 160 [Mbumda; Katema; 1884 1885]; Coillard 1897: 605 [Ishinde; Southern Lunda]
9   Capello and Ivens, 1882: 183
10   Arnot 1969: 152 154 [Central Chokwe, on Lwena headwaters, 1885]

E 2.1 Friendship sales

Such generosity, a widespread phenomenon in the region throughout the second half of the 19th century, was regularly explained by the givers in a discourse of 'friendship' (*usepa*). Chiefs and other elders solemnly delivered 'tokens of friendship',[11] and asked to be 'included in the number of our [the trader's] friends in order to avoid one party being the sons and the other the uncle', i.e. aiming at a non-hierarchical relationship.[12] Commoners adopted the same language when they presented foreign visitors with food and other goods. Silva Porto remarked on the Chokwe during his journey to Mai Munene in 1879/80:

> 'They are fairly sociable, and never fail to pronounce the word *sepa, sepa liangwe*, which means 'friend, my friend'; but they become rather unpleasant because of the peculiarity of the *mucanos* [*milonga*, law suits]...'[13]

A little later, however, he explained the meaning of *sepa* (= *usepa*) in a more pragmatic tone:

> 'This term, commonly used by the Chokwe when they address travellers, and which means *amigo* ['friend'], does not correspond to its real meaning, because benefit is its principal motive. Those who live at some distance from the camp introduce themselves in arms, in front of their wives and children with the products they want to advertise for sale,... and the word *sepa* by such guests constantly resounds from all corners of the camp.'[14]

It is true that in most cases counterpresents seem to have been expected in due course. Near Lake Dilolo, in 1854, for example, Livingstone noted that

> 'a great many friendships are formed when we have meat, and exchanges of meat for meal take place, thereby affording a stock of provisions for some days after we leave.'[15]

It thus looks as if 'friendship' was merely the terminology in which many of the normal commercial transactions, especially food sales, between local producers and foreign traders and other travellers were clothed. This terminology for exchange appears to have appealed particularly to commoners; but also chiefs and elders usually had an **exchange** of 'tokens of friendship' or 'goodwill' in mind when they made gifts to their hosts,

---

[11] E.g.Livingstone 1963: 56 [1854, Ishinde]; Cameron 1877: II 186 [Mona Lamba, Chokwe 1875]
[12] Silva Porto 1885: 164 [1880; Mbandi or Western Chokwe]
[13] Silva Porto 1885: 169 (diary, 28.3.1880)
[14] Silva Porto 1885: 608 (diary 6.5.1880)
[15] Livingstone, 1963: 85 [1854]

even when they explicitly denied this intention.[16] It has been shown earlier (see chapter D 4) that the conclusion of 'friendship' between individual inhabitants within the region essentially included the exchange of valuable gifts.

But it has also been shown that there is a decisive difference between actual payment for goods and friendship gifts with regard to standards of value. This difference may have made friendship a particularly attractive device for bargaining prices in the eyes of the inhabitants: the size of a friend's 'gift' depended not on the material value of what was given by his or her counterpart, but on the giver's personal status and wealth. When poor inhabitants traded with wealthy, possibly European, travellers, they often tried to bring this difference to bear as a criterion for the price, and the ideology of friendship was particularly conducive to this kind of bargaining. F.S. Arnot, for instance, finally resigned himself:

'I have given up buying anything myself from the natives, as whenever I offer to buy they double their price right off: "Is it not a white man ? Will he cut his cloth up into little pieces?" '[17]

The same strategy had been observed by Livingstone some 30 years earlier. On the south eastern bank of the Zambezi, among Southern Lunda, 'presents of food were brought, and one lady gave me a fowl for friendship. These are usually very expensive friendships to the white man, but I gave the price and parted.'[18] And further north, on the Chikapa, an old chief or headman of a large Chokwe village 'wished to give us food, but the food thus given is very dear: they demand quadruple its price, very soon after it is given, by way of custom.'[19]

It would be premature, however, to assume that 'friendship' was nothing more than a disguised form of trading and an ideological device for bargaining with foreign traders in order to improve the 'terms of trade' in the producers' favour. On the one hand by no means all commercial transactions were conducted under the label of 'friendship'; and on the other, additional issues than just the question of prices were apparently at stake for the inhabitants of the region when they concluded 'friendships' with foreign traders and travellers.

---

[16] E.g. Livingstone 1963: 116 [Chokwe 1854]; Cameron 1877: II 186 [Mona Lamba, Chokwe 1875]; Silva Porto 1885: 583 (diary 25.4.1880) [brother of Kisenge, Northern Chokwe]
[17] Arnot 1969: 153 [1885]
[18] Livingstone 1963: 69/70
[19] Livingstone 1963: 116

E 2.2   Credit trade

The indigenous concept of 'friendship' included a strong notion of indebtedness, as I have shown earlier. It is therefore interesting to note that credit relations played a decisive role in long-distance trade in the West Central African interior, not only between coastal merchants, *sertanejos* and Mbangala/Ovimbundu middlemen, but also between producers and traders.

In the sources on this region, commercial credit relations are explicitly mentioned for the first time in 1805, when the Chokwe chief Moxico (Mushiko) detained the Two *Pombeiros* on their way across the continent as hostages for an unpaid debt in export goods (slaves, wax and ivory) which he had advanced to an unknown trader from Kasanje.[20] Surprisingly, the chief appears in this case as the creditor, contrary to the general rule in pre-colonial Africa that advancements went always from the coast towards the interior. The situation suggests that Mushiko gave his credit out of a fairly weak position: his products were at that time of low value (since the chief was Chokwe, slaves may have been only a small part of what he had given). The chief handed over his products to a stranger before payment was made, which indicates a remarkable amount of trust. In this case the advance may be explained as a kind of advertisement to come back for more trade in a situation of emerging and still very unreliable connections to the market. According to village norms, to give a credit (or to hand over a 'friendship' present) creates a very strong obligation on the part of the recipient, and the chief seems to have used this obligation as an insurance against the unreliability of the market and its agents.

In reality, he obviously had no means of making sure that the trader would actually comply with village norms, i.e. return and pay the debt at a later date. It is possible that the chief was subject to some illusions as to the effectiveness of indigenous normativity in improving his market position. Nevertheless, he was ultimately successful in recovering his debt by applying another indigenous legal norm: the right to make 'relatives' of the defaulter (here extended to all travellers coming from the same place) liable for the damage and ultimately to take them as pawns. Later, this practice of 'recovering from future traders the losses, debts and exactions suffered in whatever transaction' was described as universal and as the main reason for the 'assaults on caravans and the lack of security on the routes' in the interior.[21]

---

[20] Baptista 1873: 199; see the quotation at the end of chapter B 1
[21] Dias de Carvalho 1890: 693/94

This is of course only one poorly documented example, but the strategy of granting 'credits' to strangers, under various denominations (e.g. 'friendship'), may have been a fairly widespread form of entering long-distance trade in early times. Around the same time, a similar example was also given about senior Luvale chiefs. They would send 'some sons [slaves? hostages? A.v.O.] ... in company with the Whites, perhaps to induce them to return there with their business.'[22]

At any rate, producers around the Upper Zambezi and Kasai probably suffered a series of disillusions about the application of indigenous concepts to trade with foreign traders during these early years. They may have gradually arrived at 'prejudices' similar to those 'which the blacks entertain ... against the whites' according to a report of a leading expert, the Portuguese director of the *feira* of Kasanje, to the Governor of Angola from 1804:

'they imagine that the latter (whites) never do anything except for their own profit, and to their (the blacks') disadvantage, that the whites have no sincerity, and only turn their actions to their own advantage against them.'[23]

For the later 19th century, exchange practices in the interior are better documented, and they show a very different pattern of credit. In 1879/80, Buchner asserted on the regions north and east of the Kasai:

'Among the princes of the interior as far as it is known to me, who are outstanding sellers of both slaves and ivory, the old trade custom rules that the traders from the coast have to submit all their goods upon arrival. The prince receives these goods as a debt which he pays back only later and gradually, by receiving ivory and slaves through his hunters also only gradually . The trader often has to wait a long time and be patient...'[24]

Dias de Carvalho, a few years later, confirms this practice as the main reason for long delays of the caravans,

'and nevertheless, the trader sees himself forced to give credits, and this is indispensable for anyone who takes the risk of trading in such a region, if he wants to do it with any success'.[25]

Obviously, in the meantime producers in the interior had turned themselves from creditors into debtors. This apparently applied not only to chiefs, but also to individual petty export producers in the bush:

' The native would be little inclined to gather the products of his country, were he not given the payment in advance ... [*Ambaquista* middlemen - A.v.O.] can buy some products in the interior, these being brought to them by the natives and paid in the customary way. In general, however, they cannot purchase very many commodities in this way but instead give the native credit. Where rubber

---

[22] *Anonymus* 1940: 23 [1803]
[23] Costa 1873: 202
[24] Buchner 1882: 88

occurs in the forests, and where the elephant occurs, the *Baptist* [*Ambaquista*] gives payment in advance to the elephant hunter for so and so many tusks, and to the one who wants to bring rubber or beeswax payment for so and so many pounds of rubber or wax. These people [the middlemen] then have to wait for months and years until their debtors satisfy them, since in most cases waiting is the only means at their disposal. Where the caravans feel strong enough, they also enchain the debtors and sometimes take them with them as slaves. But in general one can say that the natives pay better than one would expect from the negro.'[26]

Sometimes, these credits for common producers had to pass through the hands of the chief and headman, but this again only ensured his arbitration and that he would take liability in case of disputes between trader and producer.[27]

It is not known whether any 'interest' was charged by the creditors; but these credits could at any rate become rather costly because of the delays they involved, especially for caravans containing large numbers of dependants to be paid and fed. Often, the caravans seem to have given up waiting in the end and kept the debt open for later visits. As already mentioned, the debtors and their heirs honoured these debts; when some chiefs were asked to pay, 'no one showed himself ignorant of the origin of the debt and the circumstances that motivated it, all promised to pay and some actually paid...'[28], but often they paid only after many years and reminders. Silva Porto, in 1880, had a very low opinion of the creditworthiness of the Chokwe, and therefore outrightly refused a request for a complete dress and a blanket on credit by a chief who wanted to pay him with an ivory tusk on his return journey. Although he regularly accredited his *pombeiros*, he was allegedly 'not in the habit of such transactions' with producers in the interior, with whom he would only barter directly goods for goods, because, as he asserted, 'they never pay back their debts, and when they are prosecuted, they pay very badly besides making an enemy out of bad payer.'[29]

Nevertheless, many traders were willing to extend credit to their suppliers. The overriding interest of the latter, however, was apparently not purely economic, but rather strategic. It seems that the objective had remained the same as at the beginning of the century; in Dias de Carvalho's words:

'Neither the *Muatiânvua* [Mwant Yav], nor the chiefs in general complete the payment of their transactions, and this is, they say, with the aim that the leaders

---

[25] Dias de Carvalho 1890: 700 [observed in the mid-1880s]
[26] Pogge 1880: 16; see also Dias de Carvalho 1890: 699; Schönberg-Lothholz 1960: 116; Gossweiler 1907: 36/37 (cited in Heywood 1984: 149/50)
[27] See Schönberg-Lothholz 1960: 116 [testimonies of ex-Ovimbundu traders in the interior, for the period after 1890].
[28] Dias de Carvalho 1890: 702

of the caravans with whom they negotiate should return to them with more business. They fear that if satisfied the leaders will not come back, and that in consequence they would be deprived of more trade in cloth, beads, powder, guns, and salt which they need, always assuming that anyone who comes trading from afar must gain a lot in every object he sells. And if in fact this system of conducting trade does not suit the civilized man, we have to remind ourselves that it can also be observed among the peoples of the same family with whose habits it is well compatible, since they find reciprocal advantage in it.'[30]

This 'reciprocal advantage', in the eyes of the producers, clearly consisted in reliable business relations with individual traders under highly unreliable conditions of market access. Every one of the chiefs in the northeast entertained business relations, carried on over generations, with a number of specific Mbangala or *Ambaquista* traders.[31] It is very probable that enduring business relations based on credit or 'trust', similar to those customary within the region (see D 4), were also frequent on the lower level, between middlemen and ordinary producers. In the 1860s, even small-scale Western Chokwe beeswax exporters entertained personal relations with Silva Porto, their wholesale buyer in far-off Bihe, and when he visited their home a decade later, his 'old clients' rushed to exchange presents with him.[32]

But the means of pursuing this persistent aim of stable business relations evidently changed in the course of the century. Producers realized that to take, rather than to give, a credit was a safer way of creating dependence, by casting the creditor into a kind of 'debt-servitude in the reverse'.[33] For the producers themselves, this new strategy demanded perhaps a certain departure from earlier ways of thinking; seeking a debt deliberately was a fairly risky strategy in village terms, because of the obligations and sanctions involved. But as indicated by the last quotation, personal relations based on debt were so common and frequent within these societies that their adaptation to the concrete conditions of external trade must have been easy. Under the concrete conditions of the later 19th century, the market position of producers was in fact relatively strong so that taking a credit did not involve not much of a risk for them. It is true that their dependence on imported goods had increased in the meantime, and acute needs for such goods may have also prompted them to ask for credit. But world market demand for the products of Central Africa was high, competition among traders continuously increased, and the inhabitant's possibilities of exerting extra-

---

[29] Silva Porto 1885: 577/78 [diary, entries 19. and 20.4.1880]
[30] Dias de Carvalho 1890: 693
[31] Buchner 1983: 62
[32] Silva Porto 1885: 165/66 [diary entry 21.3.1880]
[33] Miller 1970: 193

economic pressures (such as the ones analysed in the last chapter) on the traders was considerable.[34]

These Central African producers' attitudes towards credit may appear paradoxical to us, being used to seeing the creditor as by definition in the stronger position because of his larger stock of capital. At the beginning of long-distance trade, economically rather weak producers seem to have generously extended credit to European traders, and later, when their market position was certainly stronger, they used this strength to force such traders to become their creditors. The explanation of this paradox requires a wider understanding of the motives and conditions of credit relations. To incur a debt or to grant a credit in a market context has first of all much to do with different access to capital by the parties involved. Other aspects of commercial credit relations are sometimes overlooked which often play a role even in fully capitalized societies. Credits are often partly an attempt to win reliable business partners in a context of gross imbalances between supply and demand or high market insecurity. In addition, a certain amount of contract security or 'trust' is normally regarded as the necessary precondition of a credit, or even as one of its aims.

It was these additional aspects that made the widespread use of commercial credit in Portuguese-dominated Africa and beyond, sometimes called 'trust trade', so compatible with indigenous African concepts of indebtedness.[35] Throughout pre-colonial Central Africa, commercial credit was largely understood as a personal bond of mutual obligations, a relation of 'trust', between otherwise anonymous market partners, similar to 'friendship' between 'strangers'. Credit relations here should therefore not only be seen as the result of social inequality and economic imbalance between supply and demand; they also represented strategies on the producers' part to create reliable market access and contract security in a situation where both were enormously fragile.

E 2.3   The scramble for allies

The earlier of the two credit strategies mentioned above - to look for debtors - may have survived in the exchanges of 'friendship gifts' between producers and foreign traders. But during the later 19th century,

---

[34] See for example Sundstrøm (1974: 39): 'credit became in many parts a necessary evil as the result of European rivalry'.
[35] Soremekun 1977: 85, and footnote 12; the system itself is perhaps a product of centuries of Euro-African and Arab-African symbiosis.

these exchanges around the Upper Zambezi and Kasai apparently did not include any bulk transactions nor any export goods. In addition, if these were 'credits', they were so only on a very short term. The goods involved were advanced to the visitors, but counterpresents were expected soon afterwards and delay until a further visit was not allowed.

On the whole, 'friendship gifts' to strangers during this period were either confined to business with petty quantities, mainly food, or they were increasingly divorced from actual business altogether. This second trend is particularly visible in various cases where these gifts were explicitly declared by their givers to be an expression of authentic respect, not bound to the giving of a 'counterpresent'. For example, in one case near the Kabompo confluence, in 1854, an individual Lunda hunter offered part of his prey to Livingstone and his companions without asking for pay. He explained his gift as a kind of equivalent to the *musapu* custom, since he called it the 'lords' part', i.e. the part of a game traditionally owed to the 'lord of the land'.[36] Another example of authentic generosity was a junior Chokwe chief near the Luena headwaters who, in 1885, wanted to prove to a suspicious F.S. Arnot that he really meant to present him with an entire ox as a free gift, without expecting any direct reciprocation. The chief decided to give him a receipt for the ox as 'if I [Arnot] had bought and paid for it, in the way that is the custom amongst the *Chibokwe*', i.e. by formally declaring the matter definitely settled as the Chokwe and their neighbours used to when balancing out old cases or debts (see above, D 4).[37]

The fact that no material 'debt' resulted from such free presents does not mean that no expectations were involved at all. These were only less specific and based less on material values. In broad terms, it was hoped to win the foreign visitor as an ally for various purposes. In some cases, free presents could perhaps be seen as a kind of voluntary payment of tribute, as an attempt to assign a superior position to the foreigner and seek his protection against powerful overlords or his assistance in struggles with rival chiefs and inimical headmen. This may have been the motive of the Lunda hunter mentioned in paying *musapu* to Livingstone. Another example occurred at Graça's visit in 1846, when the Nuclear Lunda vassal Katende appeared interested in paying tribute to the *Mane Puto* (the Portuguese Government) and getting its assistance to preserve his independence against the annual devastations and kidnappings by the *tukwata* (tribute collectors) of the cruel Mwant Yav.[38] And in 1885, the Luvale chieftainess Nyakatolo sought the allegience of Ovimbundu

---

[36] Livingstone, 1963: 34
[37] Arnot, 1969: 154 [1885]; exactly the same experience is reported by Johnston (1969: 100 [1891, Ngangela chief on the Kwanza]
[38] Graça 1890: 419, 423

caravans and of F.S. Arnot's party in her struggle against Kangombe, allegedly to protect the 'down-trodden Lunda tribes along the Upper Zambezi'.[39]

Smaller Southern Lunda leaders seem to have felt a particular need for war allies, and they saw the exchange of generous gifts as a cement for such alliances. In 1855, the consort of chieftainess Manenko, near today's Zambezi township, concluded blood-brotherhood (*kasendo*), including the exchange of valuable presents, with a Kololo noble in Livingstone's company, who would then be obliged to inform his friend of any hostile intentions on the part of the king of Bulozi.[40] In 1906, chief Kakeki, on the Lunyuwe river, after a military defeat by the first colonial patrol with subsequent exchange of hostages for valuable ransoms (including a cow and calf) and additional gifts, presented this defeat as a contract of alliance:

'From that day he [Kakeki] regarded us as his protector lords [*Schutzherren*], since the custom of the Walunda has it that the winner later helps the defeated and lends them protection against their enemies.'

Shortly afterwards, envoys of the chief claimed assistance against an enemy, insisting

'that we [Schomburgk, the officer in charge of the patrol] would now be their *Schutzherren* since we had exchanged gifts. If I could not come myself I should at least send my breechloading rifle...'[41]

Another purpose for which allies were of more immediate economic importance has been mentioned already: that of obtaining better access to the market. More specifically, the conclusion of 'friendship' with foreign visitors, particularly with Europeans, can mostly be regarded as an attempt to build more direct links to the Atlantic coast.

From the very beginning of long-distance trade, inhabitants of the Central African interior were aware of their peripheral position vis-a-vis the market and of the restrictions and deductions by various groups of middlemen; continuous competition for limited access to the market was the consequence. Nearer to the coast, these struggles were in the beginning blamed mainly on European and Euro-African *sertanejos* who at that time had monopolized most of the trade between coast and interior. In the words of the director of the *feira* of Kasanje, reporting on the feelings or 'prejudices' among the 'blacks':

'Another great reason for the strife and jealousy existing among the black nations is that the whites endeavour to profit by their superiority of situation and power, to subject other nations inferior in force and position. They are

---
[39] Arnot 1969: 248
[40] Livingstone 1963: 271

jealous lest the blacks should enjoy the same privileges, and thus be able to remove the yoke under which they labour. They supply them, themselves, with those few things that they think necessary, anything that they think proper to their cost; preventing the others from obtaining the same articles first hand from whence they themselves obtain them, and which they thus have the power of supplying them with.'[42]

Inhabitants of the Upper Zambezi and Kasai were equally aware of the even greater remoteness of their region, its long and vulnerable transport routes to the Atlantic; first of all, they had to struggle to get traders to come to visit them at all. Secondly, as they could not hope to take over trade to the coast on any large scale themselves, they tried to establish at least direct communication with coastal 'white' traders and bypass to some extent the brokerage of Ovimbundu/Mbangala who had become the main middlemen in the meantime. European travellers were, on the whole, treated in a more amicable way than African trade partners by chiefs and headmen around the Upper Zambezi and Kasai. Ovimbundu traders from Chiyaka, for example, remembered decades later that they were never regarded as friends by the Chokwe and were consequently never given one of their wives during visits, as it was the custom among 'friends'.[43]

There was great 'strife and jealousy' among Upper Zambezi peoples themselves for direct communication with coastal traders. When *sertanejos* began to trade with Luvale in the 1790s, this 'did not please' either Chokwe or Mbunda on the route, and 'these peoples did not allow them to pass through their land...because they are very ambitious [or: demanding]'.[44] A few years later, when the traders had reacted by abandoning the better Mbundu route and using the 'desert' route through Munyango/Moxico, the Mbunda chiefs were 'disappointed' and changed their strategy. They called the traders back, and when 'one white and two blacks wearing clothes and shoes, whom they also treat as whites' (sic!) followed this call, 'they gave them a good reception and instigated them to come back there with commodities, so that they should not lack business.'[45]

Luvale chiefs had not only invited the first *sertanejo* caravan to the Zambezi (see the beginning of Part B), but continued to be particularly active in trying to establish strong links with non-African traders. In 1854, for instance, a Luvale delegation sent by 'their chief' (probably an incumbent of the Chinyama title) enquired of Livingstone at the capital of

---

[41] Schomburgk 1925: 146 162/63
[42] Costa 1873: 202 [1804]
[43] Schönberg-Lothholz 1960: 117
[44] Silva Teixeira 1940: I, 236 [1794]
[45] *Anonymus* 1940: II, 26 [1803]

Ishinde whether he would proceed through their country.[46] The Chinyama who died in 1858 at the age of almost 100 years old was very popular among foreign caravans because of his generosity. His upstart rival Kakenge, however, allegedly adopted a different attitude; he resorted to heavy 'taxation' and robbing of foreign visitors, and allowed trade with the Southern Lunda east of the Zambezi only through his own brokerage.[47] Again, caravans responded by avoiding Kakenge and used the route through Katende and Katema which Livingstone also followed.

The generosity of Katende and Katema has been mentioned before. Ishinde, the most important Southern Lunda chief on the eastbank of the Zambezi, ordered a junior chieftainess to escort Livingstone to his capital and showered him with presents. His interests were quite obvious:

'he appeared delighted with the idea of being visited regularly by white traders in his old age. ..."These *mambari* cheat us with little pieces (of cloth); I shall send people with you next time you pass to trade for me in Luanda"'.[48]

In 1878, Capello and Ivens were addressed by an extremely generous Chokwe senior chief Ndumba Tembo in very similar terms:

'"I thank you for the favour you have done me in coming into my dominions. Never has a white man been seen here before, and I believe his coming will bring us good fortune. The *bin-delle* [*vindele*, i.e. Whites, civilized persons] reside far from here, near the *kalunga* (great water), and I wanted some of them to come and trade in my territory. I have tried everything to induce them to visit me.."'[49]

By that time, some Chokwe chiefs had learnt to use European etiquette to approach foreign travellers: Mwene Quibau, on the Kwango, invited Capello and Ivens to visit them by sending them a written letter, formulated by his *Ambaquista* secretary.[50]

The other side of the coin was that chiefs and commoners of the region showed much less friendly attitudes towards their neighbours to the east than towards European traders. Here, Upper Zambezi inhabitants adopted the same strategy of trying to

'keep all advantages to themselves, either by preventing traders from passing their territory, or refusing their fellow countrymen [other African peoples] going seawards',[51]

---

[46] Schapera 1963: 56 [1854]
[47] Magyar 1860: 233
[48] Livingstone 1963: 55, 264 [1854/55]
[49] Capello and Ivens 1882: I 179
[50] Capello and Ivens 1882: I 194
[51] Livingstone 1963: 255/56 [1855]

i.e. to get up trade monopolies, which on the other hand they condemned in the case of the middlemen further west. Various attempts by Luchazi, Luvale and Chokwe to establish themselves as middlemen with peoples to their east have been mentioned earlier. When caravans from the remoter interior intended nevertheless to reach the coast directly, Luvale and Chokwe chiefs tried to exact as much of the export goods they carried with them as they could, in the form of homage (*musapu*), compensations (*milonga* etc.) or forced sales. Livingstone himself, heading from Bulozi to the coast in 1854, had the bitter experience that the people around the Upper Zambezi and Kasai 'compel strangers to part with their ivory at their own prices, under the most frivolous pretences of crime.'[52]

As a consequence, caravans sent out by the rulers of Nuclear Lunda, Katanga (*Garenganze*) and Bulozi never gained any significant share of the trade, although such caravans did occasionally reach Luanda and Benguela down on the coast. Msiri of Garenganze was particularly enterprising in these attempts from at least 1874, but finally had to give up sending his own caravans, after a futile request to the governor of Angola to take care of security on the routes in 1888, because they were too badly harassed by Luvale and Ovimbundu middlemen.[53] Such struggles, exacerbated by protracted *milonga* for compensation of damages, even occurred within the region. Luvale ex-traders from the main route remember that they did not like to trade with the Chokwe because these raided so many caravans.[54]

---

[52] Livingstone 1963: 114 117 [1854]
[53] Arnot 1969: 157 [1888]; Madeira Santos 1986: 181-185
[54] Interview Y.Samakayi, 21.10.1986

E 3 The right price

E 3.1 The problem of currencies

> 'It is laborious and even tiresome for the European trader to conduct trade in the *sertão* [interior]; he has to equip himself with much patience, subject himself to many demands and even caprices, and has to be prepared to lose one, two or more days to conclude an at times insignificant transaction, especially if it is with Chokwe...'[1]

With these words Dias de Carvalho begins a detailed account of the way in which exchange was negotiated between foreigners and Northern Chokwe in the 1880s. Livingstone, some 30 years earlier, put the problem more concisely: 'but little business can be transacted in Africa without a liberal allowance of time for palaver.'[2]

The preceding chapters have shown a variety of 'gifts', compensations and debts that could be subject to lengthy negotiations. An additional motive for chiefs and village elders to entangle visitors into protracted bargaining should not be underestimated: they often simply wanted these visitors to stay as long as possible in, and as near as possible to, their place because this would inevitably increase the opportunities for petty barter exchanges between their people and ordinary caravan members. Livingstone pointed out that

> 'they are ... terribly keen traders, and every art is tried to detain us for a single night at their villages in order that they may have the pleasure of trading in meal, manioc roots and groundnuts.'[3]

Silva Porto, in 1880, was constantly invited to stay with his caravan in various Chokwe villages for various reasons

> 'which resulted in benefit for the inhabitants and their chief: he through the *quibanda* [hospitality gift] that he receives, and they through the exchange of their products with the people of the caravan.'[4]

For the same reason, in his experience,

> 'these people [the Chokwe] only feel in a decent position when the travellers camp in their surroundings; in return they take care of guarding the [old] camp,

---
1 Dias de Carvalho 1890: 695
2 Livingstone 1963: 33 [Southern Lunda; 1854]
3 Livingstone 1963: 249 [Chokwe, 1855]

it being regarded a crime or *mucano* [liable for compensation] if others, either natives or even travellers themselves, burn a camp down.'[5]

Even the exchange of retail quantities between ordinary caravan workers and villagers often involved tough and protracted negotiations about 'guns, slaves, rubber, wax, food and livestock' which often lasted into the night and sometimes ended in violence.[6] This bargaining was, however, not about exchanges of gifts, i.e. the valuation of personal respect, but about the right price for trade goods. I have already shown (D 4.3) that a concept of bartering goods for goods (or services) at a certain rate probably did exist within the societies of the Upper Zambezi and Kasai before the advent of mercantile capitalism. In terms of quantitative turnover this concept was probably the most relevant one for transactions between producers and foreign travellers, despite the variety of other forms of exchange described so far.

Interestingly, much of the bargaining around barter exchanges was concerned with the type, quality, and measuring standards of imported goods on offer as payment for export products and food, rather than with the quantity of this payment, the price proper.[7] The enormous variety of forms of payment (imported goods) has been described in chapter C 6; although there was a certain, and increasing, concentration on cloth in the later pre-colonial period, livestock, copper, salt, tobacco, shells, beads, firearms and ammunition were still accepted alternatively as payment by producers for any food or export product; slaves were exchanged for either import goods, export products or even food, according to the occasion.[8] In addition, there was the variety of different fashions among these goods, notably beads and cloth. The type of payment producers desired varied considerably by area and time, and these preferences were mostly very definite, so that if the 'right' kind of payment was not forthcoming, the inhabitants would simply refuse to sell.[9] It was therefore vitally important for traders and travellers to know what was currently demanded in which area, and a list of relevant trade goods was standard in every traveller's report, from the beginning to almost the end of the period.[10]

---

4 Silva Porto 1885: 576; also 574, 569 etc.
5 Silva Porto 1885: 170/171
6 Silva Porto 1885: 575 (diary 15.4.1880); Livingstone 1963: 233 [1855]; Arnot 1969: 164 [1885]
7 Magyar (1857: 294/5) observed the same for bargaining among the Ovimbundu.
8 Cameron 1877: 167 [Luvale]; cf.Papstein 1978: 248
9 E.g. Pogge 1880: 29 [1875]
10 E.g. Silva Teixeira 1940: 237 [1794]; Capello and Ivens 1882: I, 6ff; Johnston 1969: 343f [1891]

Travellers crossing large tracts of Central Africa including the Upper Zambezi and Kasai regularly experienced marked regional variations in the mode of payment. Vellut has argued that the pre-colonial long-distance trade in Central Africa had to pass through a succession of relatively discrete 'price zones' [zones de prix] or 'locks' [écluses].[11] The classic example is the triangle trade described in the chronology, in which imported cloth and guns were exchanged in Katanga etc. for slaves and sometimes copper, and these were then, on the return journey, given for ivory in Bulozi, and beeswax or rubber in the Upper Zambezi and Kasai, before exports through Bihe and Mbailundu could actually take place.[12] But the different goods required in different areas along the route between Bihe and Katanga for the purchase of foodstuffs, which has been described by Arnot, is an even better illustration of the system of 'price zones'.[13]

In addition to differences by area and time, individual preferences could vary considerably and handling them required plenty of skill and patience. The payment of Chokwe carriers, for example, often raised 'complicated questions' which could be resolved only by experienced travellers, such as 'a native of Ambaca' employed by Capello and Ivens:

'He would give a couple of bracelets and four yards of *zuarte* to one; ten *cargas* of powder and five yards of cotton to another; forty strings of red beads and four yards of *gingham* to a third, and so on. If one man wanted to exchange beads for cowries, or another did not want a particular kind of cloth, Francisco arranged it all and made everybody satisfied.'[14]

And Pogge found that

'the natives of the same place usually demand just about equal prices, but often they demand different commodities, for example one woman demands for her basket of meal 1 yard *of fazenda* [cloth], and the other powder, beads etc. as equivalent.'[15]

When a foreign caravan arrived in a Chokwe settlement, much time was spent by the hosts and prospective sellers of local produce in an inspection of the goods it carried, to find out whether these were in line with current fashions. Distrust in measurements was apparently an additional reason for this inspection, according to the lively description by Dias de Carvalho that follows his introductory words (quoted at the beginning of this chapter):

'This begins immediately after the preliminaries, which mean a long discussion and are followed by the choice of cloth and its valuation in *peças de lei*

---
[11] Vellut, 1972: 81; 1979: 104
[12] E.g.Cameron 1877: 140f 152, 204, 214
[13] see Arnot 1969: 142 145, 248/49 [1885/1888] - see quotation in section C 4.2
[14] Capello and Ivens 1882: I, 211

['pieces', i.e. the older standard, while by this time only the yard was the current measurement in Angola]..., by the selection of the *missangas* [beads], counting of the strings [of beads], choice of the guns, opening of the barrels of powder to see whether they are full or notand whether the powder is in a good state, demands for which purpose they are emptied completely, regardless of the fact that they come from their origin by weight. - After having reassembled everything they reject part of what they had chosen and begin then to exchange that and a new selection of articles for its replacement... To negotiate one tusk of ivory for 60 *peças de lei* really costs an enormous effort; the trader has to delay his journey for several days which brings him unexpected expenses. With small business, for example with meat, fish, or cassava chips [*bombó*], in short foodstuffs, it is just the same...'[16]

E 3.2   The ideology of fixed unit prices

From the era of slave exports on the basic unit of account or 'trade money' used by *sertanejos* and *pombeiros* for the purchase of export commodities in the interior was the *banzo* or *banso*.[17] This was essentially a load of assorted trade goods to be shouldered by one carrier. In the 1840s, the *banzo*, which had formerly bought one slave, was used only for the exchange of ivory, one *banzo* for one tusk weighing at least 32 pounds (*marfim da ley*). Later, a slightly lower valued *banzo* was introduced which bought one load of wax or rubber, or one *serviçal* (euphemism for slave after the official abolition of slavery in Angola in 1876). About half of both types of *banzo* consisted in cloth. Their full contents were, in the 1879, described as in Table 9.

The formal exchange rate of one *banzo* for one tusk, one load of wax or rubber, or one slave remained unchanged from 1840 to at least 1881, according to Silva Porto's notes. The composition of the *banzo*, measured in cloth lengths, also remained unchanged during this period.[18] This remarkable continuity in prices apparently suited the thinking of producers in the interior. 'A man (i.e.slave), a tusk, an ox and a gun' was the standard repertoire of demands faced by Livingstone among the Chokwe, and in the interior these items seem to have been widely regarded as equivalent, at least during the period of ivory exports.[19] The

---

[15] Pogge 1880: 29 [1875]
[16] Dias de Carvalho 1890: 696 [1880s, on Chokwe and *Lundas*]
[17] According to Soremekun (1977: 85, quoting a Portuguese publication of 1903), *negocio da banzo* was translated as 'trust trade'.
[18] Madeira Santos, 1986: 398ff
[19] Silva Porto 1986: 330 [diary entry 28.12.1847; Mbunda]; Magyar 1857: 296 [Ovimbundu, 1850s]; Soremekun 1977: 88 [quoting Bastos 1912, referring to 1864-74];

Table 9 : Composition of the *banzo* ('load'; see also fig. 6)
(standard unit of account in West Central African barter trade; values in cloth lengths)

Amount of import goods needed to obtain one unit of:	Ivory	Wax, rubber, slaves	
Trade cloth [*fazenda da ley*]	56	40	*pannos*
One packet of *missanga*, worth	8	8	[yards]
One packet of *roncalha fina*, worth	8	-	
Two strings of *coral* and *almandrilha*	4	4	
One pound (459 g.) gunpowder, worth	4	-	
Total value of barter goods:	80	52	*pannos*
(Same, in percent of total payment:)	(64.5%)	(56.5%)	
Payment of the *pombeiro*:	8	8	
Payment for carrier of the export goods:	12	8	
Payment for carrier of the *banzo*:	4	4	
Hospitality gifts [*Quibanda*]:	4	4	
Cloth for provisions	8	8	
One bundle of *missanga* for provisions	8	8	
Total costs of transport:	44	40	*pannos*
(Same, in percent of total payment:)	(35.5%)	(43.5%)	
Total value of *banzo*	124	92	*pannos*
	(100%)	(100%)	

Sources:
Silva Porto 1885: 24; cf. also Graça 1890: 466 [1846]; Vellut 1979: 104; Madeira Santos 1986: 102f

Pogge 1880: 51 [Northern Chokwe 1875]; Cameron 1877: II 178 [Central Chokwe, 1875]

same equation was extended to wax and rubber, after the 1870s, when one load of either of these was regarded as equivalent to an adult slave woman, a gun or an ox.[20]

Such simple rates of exchange probably owed much to the rules of earlier barter exchanges (*kulanda*) of food and craft products within the region, which have been analysed earlier (see section D 4.3). The important question at this point, however, is how this 'law of the fixed price' worked in a market context. It has been argued that through the *banzo* system in the Central African interior, 'the producer was to some extent isolated from market fluctuations'.[21] Such fluctuations, however, did exist on the world market into which African producers were gradually drawn (see Part B). The world market value of imported manufactured goods, especially cotton cloth, decreased continuously during most of the 19th century.[22] Export prices paid for the products of the interior, in contrast, had a generally rising tendency. After they had shot up by 300% in 1836, ivory prices continued to rise steadily, e.g. from 1$100 to 1$600 réis between 1846 and 1870.[23] Later, the price of rubber went up enormously, by more than 300 %, between 1886 and 1910.[24] In addition, prices for beeswax and rubber were subject to considerable oscillation (see chapter B 4).

In this context, it must be asked to whose benefit the rule of a fixed or standard price affected the terms of trade between the coast and the interior. It has been seen in Part B that this exchange circuit was divided into at least two stages: between coastal merchants and traders (*sertanejos*) or middlemen on the one hand, and between middlemen and the producers of the Upper Zambezi and Kasai on the other. Coastal merchants, probably with some delay, passed on some of these improvements in the terms of trade to their *aviados* and other debtors in the interior, although transactions with them were exclusively in kind.[25] At the *feira* of Kasanje, for example, the amount of cloth paid for a slave increased from 30 to 50 *beirames* between 1792 and 1830.[26] And Silva Porto reduced in his accounts the value for trade cloth from 400 to 250

---

[20] Silva Porto, diary entry 17.11.1860 (quoted in Madeira Santos 1986: 169, fn.1); Pogge 1880: 51 [Northern Chokwe 1875]; interview Sondoyi, 24.10.1986 [early 1900s]
[21] Vellut: 1979: 104
[22] Vellut 1979: 104; Madeira Santos 1986: 160
[23] Miller 1970: 178; Madeira Santos, 1986: 160, fn.1
[24] Clarence-Smith 1979b: 176
[25] Madeira Santos 1986: 99 (for the entire lifetime of Silva Porto, up to 1890); in 1875, cash money could be used along the northern route only up to Sanza, some 80 kms. east of Malange (Lux 1880: 57).
[26] Vellut 1972: 86/87; this still meant a price decrease in world market prices.

réis (0.25 milréis) a yard in 1859, which suggests that his creditor in Benguela had also reduced the nominal value some time before.[27]

During the heyday of the ivory trade, coastal merchants were apparently fairly successful in using the credit system means to keep benefits resulting from export price increases to themselves. In 1875, for example, Silva Porto still only obtained the equivalent of 1$450 per pound in Benguela, whereas the monetary value had reached 1$600 réis in 1870 in Benguela, and 2$300 in Lisbon in 1875.[28] In addition, these merchants would charge 100% usury interest, allegedly to cover the credit risk.[29] Profit margins realized on the coast only fell dramatically during the rubber boom, despite the 'dizzying prices' rubber fetched on the world market, because competition between coastal traders increased tremendously. In order to attract sufficient quantities of rubber, they began to offer sometimes ruinous prices, 'equal to or even superior to the price listed in the Lisbon market'.[30] Interestingly, most of these price increases seem to have been given to the suppliers in the form of 'advertisement gifts', i.e. lavish presents and meals, while the official price remained rather fixed.[31]

It seems that particularly the increasing number of smaller scale Ovimbundu middlemen stood to gain by this discount system, called *cambulação* (approximately 'helter-skelter', feverish speculative buying). The prices paid to larger suppliers, in contrast, even tended to decline, in compensation for the ruinous prices paid to the smaller ones.[32] When 'the terms of trade in the world economy moved temporarily in Africa's favour' between 1870 and 1900,[33] it looked as if only the trading sector, whether merchants or middlemen, would benefit from the change. Both Portuguese-speaking *sertanejos* and Ovimbundu/Mbangala middlemen were unwilling to pass any of their hard-won gains on to the

[27] Madeira Santos 1986: 160 and 399
[28] Madeira Santos 1986: 160, fn.1, 196/97
[29] Madeira Santos 1986: 98/99
[30] Heywood, 1984: 165; in 1900, for example, 1 pound rubber fetched the equivalent of 15 pence on the Angolan coast, only 2½ pence less than on the London stock market (Clarence-Smith 1979a: 68).
[31] For a description of this competition between the Benguela trading houses for incoming caravans bringing rubber in the 1880s and 90s see Heywood 1984: 160ff 170. The same practice is reported for Dondo and other places on the northern coast by Pogge (1880: 17) for caravans coming directly from the interior, but he mentions 'good business' for the merchants in such a case.
[32] The Portuguese authorities attempted in vain to contain this breakthrough of free market economy by reintroducing controlled prices in the 1890s. They were most concerned about the frequent bankruptcies of less wealthy European traders, but argued also that Africans, not knowing the 'real' (monetary) value of things, were being cheated by *cambulação* (Heywood 1984: 163-166).
[33] Miller 1983: 156

interior. In their exchanges with producers in the remoter hinterland they systematically tried to exploit the customarily fixed barter rates of exchange. From 1846 to 1881, *sertanejos* like Silva Porto strictly insisted on the exchange rate of one *banzo* for one tusk etc., on the composition of the *banzo* (see table 9), and on the assumption of a nominal value of 40$000 milréis for one *banzo*. This value had been established in the 1840s, and then already represented a certain overvaluation, justified as a kind of insurance against losses. In 1881, due to the decrease of import prices, the overvaluation of the *banzo* in the interior had reached 266% compared to current prices in Bihe.[34] If these artifical rates had been effective, it would indeed have been more probable that the producer would neither have benefited from the price depression of import commodities, unless in the form of an extension of exchanges'[35], nor from the rising world market value of their products.

It is true that producers in the interior obtained only a small fraction of what their goods would fetch for the middleman upon his arrival at the coast. As far as can be concluded from scattered pieces of information, this percentage may have usually been somewhere between 10 and 25 %.[36] The confessed profit margins *sertanejos* were able to realize through ivory trade in the 1840s was between 80 and 100 %, after deduction of costs for caravan transport which were also included in the *banzo*; if the overvaluation mentioned is taken into account, profits may have actually been up to 400% under optimum conditions.[37] A successful Ovimbundu petty rubber trader, exploiting his own labour and that of his family and slaves, may have reached similar figures.[38] But the profits of both *sertanejos* and African middlemen were not only subject to considerable oscillation and losses; there are also indications that producers, at least those living around the Upper Zambezi and Kasai, gradually managed to increase their share of the cake, .[39] An interesting question is how

---

[34] Madeira Santos 1986: 102/103 and 398ff
[35] Vellut, 1979: 104
[36] See following footnotes.
[37] In 1846/47, in return for one pound of ivory worth 1$200 réis on the coast, the seller would receive the equivalent of 80 yards of trade cloth, which had cost the trader probably 117 réis. This corresponds to 13 % of the export value. In addition, chiefs and food sellers on the road would receive another 3.2 %, and carriers and staff 3.9 % (estimated on the basis of figures given by Graça 1890: 466; Madeira Santos 1986: 100, 103, 398-400; see table 9).
[38] In the early 1880s, a retail quantity of 100 balls of rubber weighing perhaps 5.5 lbs., worth between 1$650 and 3$300 réis in Benguela, would bring a Chokwe producer at most 4 yards (=289 réis), i.e. between 8.5 and 16.5 % of the export value (calculated using figures given by Madeira Santos 1986: 102; Heywood 1984: 167; Silva Porto 1885: 585 [diary entry 26.4.1880, Northern Chokwe]).
[39] According to calculations corresponding to those in the preceding footnotes, the producer's share in sales on the coast had reached between about 16 and 26 % for ivory

producers could press for improved terms of trade in view of the dominance of an ideology of fixed rates of equivalence.

One answer is that many demands for better payment were voiced in a veiled form. Nominally, the quantity of imported goods offered per unit of export products remained fairly stable. It has been mentioned that in the interior, at least up to the 1880s, one tusk of ivory was paid for with 80 yards of cloth, and one loaf of wax or load of rubber with 52 yards. Up to the end of the period the standard load of rubber consisted of 10 bundles at 100 balls or 10 candles each (*mitali* - each formed of 10 little balls) of 'red rubber'.[40] Retail amounts were fixed at four yards per bundle of 100 balls among the Northern Chokwe, and at only one yard further east, in Luba.[41]

Since it was obviously difficult to change these established prices or the customary standard units of export products, producers began to reduce the actual size of these units, at least with weaker trade partners. After 1861, Silva Porto complained bitterly that his *pombeiros* brought home smaller and smaller tusks from their journeys to the interior. In reality, this effective price increase had already begun in the 1840s. In return for the same size *banzo*, the *sertanejo* obtained on average 30-60 pounds of ivory before 1846, then 25-50 pounds with a slowly decreasing tendency, 15 pounds in 1868, and only 5-8 pounds in the early 1880s.[42] Some of this higher price may have been appropriated by the Ovimbundu middlemen and carriers, whom Silva Porto suspected of being 'thieves', to make up for their fixed, artificially low rates of commission and pay; but it is very likely that producers themselves were involved and reacted in this 'market rational' way to increasing scarcity of the product and high competition among buyers.[43]

The same strategy was used by other producers. For example, Chokwe gatherers began to reduce the size of their rubber balls so that one kg. of rubber was made up of 8-10 balls in 1876, of 40 in 1882, and of 100-200 from the late 1880s on.[44] Another example is the standard loaf or bar (Pg. *pau*) of beeswax worth a *banzo*, an ox or an adult slave. This bar weighed in the interior on average 80-100 pounds in the 1850s, 60 to 70 in 1860, and apparently only 30 pounds in 1880; Ovimbundu middlemen

---

in the 1870s, and about 20% for rubber in 1900 (same sources as above; Clarence-Smith 1979a: 68 [quoting Harding]).

[40] Pogge 1886: 187/88; Schönberg-Lothholz 1960: 120; interview Sondoyi, 24.10.1986

[41] Silva Porto, diary 26.4.1880 (1885: 585); Silva Porto, diary 1887 (cited in Heywood 1984: 149)

[42] Madeira Santos 1986: 162/63 and 398-400

[43] Madeira Santos 1886: 161/62, 175

[44] Pogge 1886: 187/88; Silva Porto, diary 1887 (cited by Heywood 1984: 149); Schönberg-Lothholz 1960: 120

therefore tried to cheat their creditors by adulterating the bars using alien objects thus doubling their weight, and then stopped buying wax for some time.[45]

Obviously, producers were to some extent able to turn the ideology of fixed unit prices against traders and middlemen. In the 1880s, Mbangala middlemen felt squeezed between their Chokwe suppliers and their creditors in the hinterland of Luanda, and complained, as Dias de Carvalho reports:

> '"We are accounted here [in the hinterland of Luanda] in weights, and among the Chokwe in *bandos* [local standard for cloth]." - In reality they have long been used to packing the rubber in bundles, and they do not know the size of the packet or the weight, as the Chokwe prepared it, and they draw little profit from it on the balances of the merchants; and with respect to the measures of cloth they find fixed units in the merchants' shops, while the Chokwe are increasing them continuously, thus raising the price of the product in which they trade'.[46]

This refers to another means by which inhabitants of the interior tried to increase their pay. They would remeasure the imported goods offered by traders according to their own standards. Until the beginning of this century, they insisted on cloth being measured by the old standard *peça* or 'piece' (Lv. *vilala*) of 8 *pannos* or yards, while nearer to the coast it had first been increased to 12 or 18 *pannos*, and then been given up altogether.[47] Remeasuring may have been partly an expression of insecurity vis-a-vis frequent changes in foreign measurements. But at least the Chokwe used the opportunity to impose a more generous standard for cloth:

> 'they demand to be paid in conformity with their *bando*, which they substitute for the yard, and which goes from one side of the belt to the hand of the opposite side, having the arm stretched out upwards and passing the cloth to be measured over their chest curved in front. In other tribes the *bando* is smaller...'[48]

This may have been giving short measure even by local standards; a *munjoka* (local equivalent to the yard) was defined among Luvale and Chokwe as 'tip of fingers to **middle** of chest'.[49] In general, petty fraud was not unknown, probably not even in local exchanges, but certainly towards foreign visitors. Cameron, for example, found in 1875 in the Luvale plains that

> 'the art of cheating is very well understood by the native fish-mongers, for in the centre of some of the baskets I found earth, stones, broken pottery and

---

45 Livingstone 1857: 614 [Southern Lunda]; Silva Porto diary, 17.11.1860 (quoted in Madeira Santos 1986: 169); Silva Porto diary, 15.4.1880 (1885: 576)
46 Dias de Carvalho 1890: 704
47 Pogge 1880: 14 and 28; Dias de Carvalho 1890, 696; interview Sondoyi, 24.10.1986
48 Dias de Carvalho 1890: 697

gourds so stowed as to make up the proper weight and bulk. Indeed, as far as my experience goes, the noble savage is not one whit behind his civilized brethren in adulterating food and giving short measure, the only difference being in the clumsiness of his method.'[50]

And Schütt was deeply annoyed about a young girl who came to their camp

'to offer us a basket of meal. We agreed and she received the price asked; but when we poured out the maize meal, which had been very pure on top, it was only a layer, the rest was dirt. The young, pretty seller sat quietly at the side and laughed about our anger; she had sold the things and received payment, the rest did not matter to her.'[51]

Although traders and middlemen were generally aware of these tactics, apparently they were either not able to resist these concealed demands for higher prices or found it was not in their interest to do so, probably in order not to spoil the transaction as a whole, in view of the pressures of competition, credit repayment, and time. But significantly, they tried to resist an open abandonment of customary exchange rates for as long as possible. Instead they granted hidden price increases in the form of bonuses or advertisement gifts on top of the customary price, similar to the *cambulação* system down on the coast, in order to create durable links with their suppliers. This practice of giving something 'on top', originally mainly a drink of gin, was widely known as as *dash* along the Guinea Coast down to the mouth of the Congo, and *matabish* or *matabicho* in Angola.[52] Among the Luvale, the practice is still remembered as *matambwishi* by petty traders who used to sell to Portuguese-speaking traders; they preferred this to the more straightforward cash payment at current market prices which they received later from British traders.[53] Among the Chokwe, similarly, in the 1880s the 'very bad custom' of the *malufo de quitanda* was observed, which consisted in a valuable gift (often worth 5-7$000 on top of the price) to seal the sale's contract.[54]

---

[49] White 1959: 39 [my emphasis]; Pogge 1880: 28; see section 4.3.3.
[50] Cameron 1877: II 175
[51] Schütt 1881: 129 [Northern Chokwe]; Silva Porto also mentions that Chokwe men often cheated Ovimbundu traders with broken guns (diary 15.4.1880; Silva Porto 1885: 575).
[52] Sundstrøm 1974: 3-4; Horton (1975:368) gives a more detailed etymology: 'Said to come from days when a tot of rum was given to one buying or selling in the stores, *para matar o bicho* - to kill the insect (craving).
[53] Samakayi, 24.10.86
[54] Dias de Carvalho 1890: 696

E 3.3 Bargaining on the price

Nevertheless, producers around the Upper Zambezi and Kasai gradually got used to negotiating commercial transactions not only in a hidden way, i.e. by disputing the kind of payment, sizes, measurements or gifts 'on top', but by entering open bargaining on prices.[55] This occurred even within the highly standardized 'big business' in export goods. Kisenge, for example, used his powers of arbitration to raise the price of rubber to four yards per unit (100 balls) in 1880; Luvale rubber producers remember having been able to obtain up four times this amount in the end.[56]

But interestingly, it was the prices of food and small livestock which rose and varied most and perhaps earliest.[57] In the mid 1850s, for example, staple food was considerably more expensive around the Upper Zambezi and Kasai than near the Angolan coast or in Nuclear Lunda; in addition, prices varied considerably within the area. At that time, the price for a standard amount of food, about 20 lbs. cassava meal and one fowl, enough to feed about four people for one day, ranged from about two inches of cotton cloth (worth c.10-20 *réis* at that time) in Central Nuclear Lunda and about 10 inches between Benguela and Bihe to about 24 inches in the Lunda area of Kawawa and as much as 54 inches (1½ yards) in the Northern Chokwe diaspora near the Luachimo river.[58] According to Capello and Ivens' description at the *chitaka* ('market' at the caravan's camp) near Ndumba Tembo's capital, where a considerable variety of food products was sold to caravan members by individual producers, in the late 1870s new retail prices given in cloth lengths were fixed every day:

> 'On one side of the motley crowd we observed a group of girls, vendors of maize flour, who were in hot discussion with a stalwart buyer, whose main object we were told was to fix the market price of the day - for whatever the figure accepted on the first transaction, it becomes a rule or standard for remaining purchasers.'[59]

---

55 In earlier chapters I have shown that such bargaining was already usual, but only with regard to gifts.

56 20 *vilala* à 8 metres for one load of 1,000 balls or 100 *mitali* candles (interview Sondoyi, 24.10.1986). According to the Ovimbundu informants interviewed by Schönberg-Lothholz, however, a load could contain in the end 2-3,000 balls (1960: 120).

57 Outright bargaining had been common much earlier with regard to exchanges of 'gifts', in which not the value of goods (Lv. *kulanda*), but the valuation of respect was at stake (see earlier chapters).

58 Magyar 1859: 30; Livingstone 1963: 256, 240; Livingstone (1963: 220) also mentions the 'very great cheapness of food' in Nuclear Lunda.

59 Capello and Ivens: I 185

Fig. 32: A market place (*chitaca*) in Central Chokwe (1878)
(Engraving from Capello and Ivens 1882, vol.I: 184)

This formal procedure shows a certain concern among inhabitants to keep prices under control, at least for staple food. On public occasions like the 'markets' mentioned, this control was relatively easy to impose, and this seems to have been done by the local chief (see above, E 1). In the villages, customary methods of collective price control (see section D 4.3) continued to be effective to some extent so that inhabitants of one village would demand roughly the same prices.[60] (See fig. 8.) Sales at camps or production sites outside the capitals and at villages, on the field, at hunters', fishermen's or rubber collectors' camps, or even 'at the beehive', probably offered the best opportunities for individual negotiation of prices.[61] This is perhaps one reason why markets have always been unpopular in the region, although individual bargaining

---

[60] Pogge 1880: 29
[61] E.g. Cameron diary, quoted by Heywood 1984: 151; cf. Schapera 1963: 106

occurred even there:'A pig for which they had the face to ask a piece of 18 yards, when it would have been dear at five...' [62]

It remains to be asked what the criteria involved in this new, more flexible kind of price formation were. As far as export goods were concerned, improved communication and information on market prices nearer to the coast certainly played a role in rising demands:

> 'The negro has no fear of distances; for one or two pieces of cloth more he will travel 10-20 German miles [about 70-140 km - A.v.O.] farther, especially since he knows that his commodities acquire a higher value the closer he gets to the coast.'[63]

When Chokwe travellers had reached the coast, around 1880, Silva Porto lamented that it was difficult to conduct any business with them at home except at prices current on the coast, or else when they suddenly needed cloth for some *mulonga* (legal case).[64]

Prices for foodstuffs differed significantly in prices within the region, as mentioned before. Lower prices were generally demanded off the main routes, e.g. among Mbunda and Southern Lunda.[65] Not only a concentration on cloth (at the expense of beads, shells etc.), but also the rising prices were recorded at that time in the more frequented Chokwe and Luvale areas: 'Here, we perceive something like an approach to the market. The people ask higher prices, & in powder [and cloth - A.v.O.] for their meal &c.'[66] Livingstone therefore suspected the emergence of a kind of market rationality, a response to growing demand that drove prices up: 'They will not sell ... except for very large prices. They seem to know we are hungry'.[67] But as a general tendency in the region, the production of foodstuffs seems to have increased along with demand sufficiently to offset such inflationary effects. In the remote areas, in contrast, where population was usually thin and more mobile, often much less food was available for sales to caravans.[68] However, when food was scarce, producers reacted simply by offering smaller quantities for sale or refusing to sell altogether, and not by raising prices.

What probably played the greatest role in inducing producers to try to raise their prices, more than an abstract knowledge of real terms of trade on the world market, or a 'rational' assessment of the supply and demand

---

[62] Capello and Ivens 1882: I 186
[63] Pogge 1880: 17
[64] Silva Porto, diary entries 28.3. and 5.5.1880 (1885: 168 and 608 [Northern Chokwe]); Dias de Carvalho 1890: 711
[65] Silva Porto 1942: 72/3; Livingstone 1963: 64; Arnot 1969: 100 [1884]
[66] Livingstone, 1963: 96/7
[67] Livingstone 1963: 64 [1854, Luvale on Kasai river]
[68] E.g.Capello and Ivens 1886: 444; Pinto 1881: 271/72 [Luchazi, Southern Chokwe]

situation, was their growing dependence on imported goods for all kinds of transactions within their own society (see Part C). This would also explain why within the region prices were highest in the most centrally located, most market integrated areas.

But the conditions to realize higher prices also had to be given. On the whole, Upper Zambezi producers were apparently rather successful in this respect, not only with food, but also with export products, as long as competition between buyers was high. Another important factor was probably the potential of 'non-economic' coercion: Luvale and Chokwe were militarily more powerful than neighbouring peoples. Cameron noted that harsh slave dealers returning from the east suddenly became much more compromising here than they had been before.[69] When world market demand and prices for rubber finally declined after the turn of the century, however, producers around the Upper Zambezi and Kasai had little defence. This time, market price changes were quickly passed on to both traders/middlemen and producers, and both reacted by greatly increasing the quantity of rubber exported, in order to remain accredited or to keep up customary levels of revenue.[70] This is a clear indication of the dependence on imported goods, an early form of 'monetization', that had been greatly accelerated by the rubber boom. The pressure was exacerbated by European traders and the beginning of colonial taxation, with severe consequences for regional food production (see section C 5.5). Producers still tried to protect themselves by supplying a 'greatly debased product', i.e. reducing the quality.[71] But the consequence was a lower grading for Benguela rubber on international markets which only precipitated the final collapse of the market for wild rubber.[72]

---

[69] For comparison: Cameron noted in 1875 in *Ussambi* (Southern Luba area) that 'people were so delighted with the extraordinary circumstance of a caravan being ready to pay for what was required [rather than just looting their food reserves - A.v.O.] that they allowed us to buy at most moderate prices.' (1877: II 144)

[70] Childs 1949: 211/12

[71] Childs 1949: 211; Heywood 1984: 167. She mentions also that wax was adulterated by producers and traders by mixing different qualities and by impurities, as a response to falling prices.

[72] Heywood 1984: 212

E 4   Conclusion Part E : Changing moralities of exchange

The 'embeddedness' of material ('economic') transactions in social relations and institutions that emerges from the foregoing chapters has been a central concern of economic sociologists, anthropologists and historians since the beginnings of their discipline. Both the functioning of the economy, and the possibility of a social order, in spite of growing fragmentation and inequality, were at the background of this concern. One of its earliest expressions was Emile Durkheim's question for the 'non-contractual elements of the contract'.[1] The most concise formulation, however, including the 'embeddedness' paradigm, is owed to Karl Polanyi and his 'substantive' school.[2] In their effort to to show that western utilitarian rationality is by no means as universal as presupposed by 'formal' economics, many relevant authors have contrasted market-type economies with older ones, and developed an increasing interest in so-called 'archaic' or 'primitive' (pre-capitalist and pre-state) social formations.[3] The notion of 'reciprocity' was, implicitly or explicitly, central to their theories.[4] As the same concept is also prominent in the foregoing analysis of pre-colonial exchanges around the Upper Zambezi and Kasai, some more general conclusions can be drawn now with regard to theories of 'embeddedness', notably on the character of 'reciprocity' in economic transactions, and on its transformation in market contexts.

Classical approaches to 'embeddedness' converge on the assumption of a close structural affinity between exchange and society. For 'segmentary lineage societies', as opposed to 'early empires' and 'market societies', more or less homogeneous and autonomous kinship groups were assumed in and between which reciprocal exchange took place as a condition for both physical reproduction and social stability.[5] Sahlins, who developed a differentiated taxonomy of 'reciprocities', assumed that within nuclear groups reciprocity was 'generalized', i.e. material transfers were made without expecting immediate reciprocation by the particular recipient. According to his model, the more distant the relationship was, the more

---
[1] Durkheim 1893 (7th chapter)
[2] E.g. Polanyi 1957; see also the introduction in ch. A 2.
[3] The best known contributions are by Mauss 1973 (first edition in French 1923/24), Polanyi 1944 and 1957, and Sahlins 1974; see also Servet 1981.
[4] The idea has been looming in the social sciences, under various terms, since the end of the 19th century; Durkheim spoke of *mutualisme* (1893), Thurnwald of *Gegenseitigkeit*, translated as *reciprocity* (1916; see also 1932), Malinowski also of *reciprocity* (1926).
[5] Polanyi 1944 and 1957

'balanced' were exchanges, i.e. the more they carried the expectation of more or less immediate repayment in some material item or labour regarded as equivalent to the good transferred in the first place. Beyond the outer limit of the social networks thus created or reconfirmed, 'negative' reciprocity would be likely, i.e. a lack of commitment to reciprocate transfers or honour exchange contracts.[6]

What has been said in earlier chapters (Part D) about indigenous forms of circulation around the Upper Zambezi and Kasai seems to agree at least with the basic assumptions in these approaches to economic anthropology. In referring to them, however, attention is due to the regional and historical specifics of the societies in question. In this area, at least two different regimes of exchange can be traced back into the 19th century. On the one hand, much of the circulation of material goods took place within a language of 'gifts' or 'presents'. Such transfers were, however, not as voluntary and altruistic as the language suggests; the giving, accepting and reciprocation of gifts, though not necessarily their amount, were subject to strong obligations.[7] Among these transfers, a certain amount of generalized reciprocity (in Sahlin's terminology) can be discerned: relatives, in-laws, friends, neighbours and strangers received 'gifts' and assistance, glossed as 'generosity', 'hospitality' or even 'tribute', without any definite and immediate reciprocation being expected. The yardstick for the value of these gifts was the affection for, and the status of, the recipient, i.e. the personal relationship involved or intended. Nevertheless, unspecified returns in assistance and loyalty were expected for future situations of need. The giving of 'gifts' was a symbol of confidence that such returns would be forthcoming one day, and the (more or less obligatory) acceptance of such gifts was seen as incurring an indebtedness (*mukuli*).[8] An ideology of gift circulation between individuals, at any rate, presupposes the general existence of individual control over one's labour and products.

The scanty evidence on the earlier pre-colonial period around the Upper Zambezi and Kasai suggests that this absence of immediacy and equivalence in 'gift' exchanges was by no means confined to local or nuclear communities, as Sahlins has suggested. Social bonds across village and kinship boundaries were very common and important in this highly segmented and mobile society. Marriage alliances and a wide variety of friendship compacts were sealed by series of gift exchanges across large distances which usually involved an element of deferred reciprocation. The idea of 'debt' in these exchanges may have been in the

---

[6] Sahlins 1974: 196f
[7] Mauss 1973: 161ff
[8] Cf. Mauss 1973: 199

interest of both parties, since they increased longterm mutual interest and obligation, i.e. stabilized the social bonds involved.[9]

An idea of immediate exchange and material equivalence ('balanced reciprocity'), on the other hand, does seem to have existed since before world market integration in the form of barter (*kulanda* and *njongo*). Typical was the exchange between 'relish' and staple food or cultivation labour, based on the idea of complementarity between 'male' and 'female' products, a reflection of the complementarity of gender in the division of labour. Barter exchanges of products and labour occurred both within and between (extended) kinship groups, but the strongest expression of the underlying idea is probably found in relations between spouses within the 'household'. These were governed by principles of equal sharing of the yields from complementary work tasks on the fields, and of exchanging equivalent products, services and gifts. Again, social distance does not seem to have had any impact on how 'balanced' an exchange was. More decisive was apparently whether socio-political interests in a personal relationship, or material interests in reproduction were in the foreground - although material and social reproduction were probably never completely divorced.

In both variants of reciprocity, however, a strong element of accounting the mutual obligations was involved, even in close personal relationships, contrary to earlier assumptions of a 'mechanic' or 'generalized' solidarity (Durkheim, Sahlins), or of a 'pooling' of income (Polanyi), in pre-modern societies. This was expressed, for instance, in the legal provisions against violation of rights acquired through transfer of goods, be it barter or 'gift'. Failure to fulfil reciprocal obligations inevitably led to demands by the 'damaged' party for compensation. These compensations (*milonga*) were in principle commensurate to the 'damage' itself, but if the 'culprit' proved unable to pay he or she was threatened with 'pawnship' or debt slavery. Inability to reciprocate was an acceptance of inferiority up to the point of losing social identity.[10]

This brings up another critical point in current understandings of exchange in pre-market societies. Most authors have tended to equate rules of reciprocity with social reality, i.e. to assume some sort of structural equality between partners in exchange acts. Some of the classic authors themselves, however, seem to have pointed beyond such a structuralist discourse. Mauss, for instance, emphasized already that 'gifts' could be used in power struggles.[11] The transfer of material tokens, especially 'wealth' goods, without immediate reciprocation (i.e.,

---

[9] Sahlins has mentioned this aspect, but only for marriage alliances (1974: 222).
[10] Cf. Mauss 1973: 212
[11] Mauss 1973: 199

in order to cause someone to become 'indebted') can be seen as an attempt to establish social dominance in a society in which rights to potential services of others weighed more than material property.[12] This seems to reflect very well the situation around the Upper Zambezi and Kasai. Here, in the course of the 19th century, imported 'wealth' was increasingly used in the local circulation of 'gifts', 'payments', 'debts' and 'compensations', as new means to strengthen existing position in the indigenous political economy (see ch. D 6). Inflation in these internal transfers was the inevitable result of massive imports, but also of an increasing incidence of violence, legal disputes and demands for compensation, which further spurred on the process of market integration. It must be emphasized again, however, that the specific material conditions in this region allowed for fairly widespread access to these goods (see D 6). Consequently, this stimulation of the 'gift economy' offered not only opportunities for new upstarts to rally dependants around them, but also some chances for less powerful groups to defend their autonomy.

A careful reading of Polanyi and the earlier classics in economic sociology (Durkheim, Weber, Mauss) suggests that their deeper concern, beyond the structure of society and the functioning of the economy, was the possibility of social integration amidst a multitude of diverging interests. Their interest in social rules and institutions and in the way they govern economic activities was therefore, at least implicitly, also a moral question. Even if the normative connotations of 'social integration' are dropped, the conclusion remains that the meanings of exchange (as of social action in general) are neither the sum of individual interests, nor can they simply be derived from the structure of society. Bloch and Parry have therefore recently spoken of 'moralities of exchange' which are specific, and continually being constructed, in every social and historical context.[13] This approach seems fruitful for the case studied in this book.

The pre-colonial morality of exchange around the Upper Zambezi and Kasai, i.e. the rules according to which reciprocal claims were settled, was strongly contractual. Contracts were hardly sanctioned by central authorities, such as the state in other societies, and individual interests widely differed, as in any society. There was, therefore, a constant need for negotiating not only the terms, but also the conditions of exchange contracts. At least in these particular societies, there seems to have been a remarkably wide range of claims and rules that could enter these negotiations. Which 'register' was invoked depended very much on the particular situation, but claims belonging to different registers

---

[12] Cf. Sahlins 1974: 204; Miller 1988: 50/51
[13] Introduction in: Bloch and Parry (eds.) 1989

(compensations, payments, gifts...) could be stored for considerable periods of time and balanced out against one another. These negotiations about prices and contracts were conducted in a highly ritualized way. Implicit in these practices is a concern to construct a more encompassing moral order, a 'moral economy' (Thompson) in the strict sense, i.e. a vision of trust and justice in a real society ridden by divisions and insecurity. The basic element in this vision seems to have been not some kind of close-knit nuclear community, but a strong and reliable, often dyadic, relationship with particular persons. 'Strangers' had their place in this order, as they could always become exchange partners and be converted into 'friends'. The proliferation of various types of personal relationships resulted in a multitude of overlapping social networks, which the individual could manipulate to some extent, and which was at the same time the fabric of society as a whole.

This leads to the second conclusion on 'embeddedness' and reciprocity, regarding the problem of their transformation in market contexts. For classical authors such as Weber, the anonymous market and personal non-market relationships, seen in an evolutionary sequence, were fundamentally incompatible.[14] Polanyi and his students, in contrast, did allow for the possibility that different forms of 'embeddedness' or 'institutedness' of the economy could coexist in market contexts, but tended to associate them with different sectors of the economy.[15] In their (critical) view, the assumption that the market economy is 'disembedded' from society seems to have been crucial. But this assumption obviously contradicts the observations cited in the foregoing chapters. Around the Upper Zambezi and Kasai, pre-colonial world market integration was clearly 'embedded' in a morality of personal relations and reciprocal exchange, even in negotiations with foreign traders.

Three possible, not mutually exclusive, interpretations offer themselves. Firstly, it could be argued that this was a phenomenon of prolonged transition to a 'real' market society, perhaps resulting from location (remoteness from market centres) and particular historical conditions (insecurity, absence of central government). One could anticipate a gradual transformation of older rules of 'balanced reciprocity' into a system of market prices, as soon as these conditions were overcome. But similar moralities of exchange can still be observed in the region today, one century on, and throughout they seem to have been relatively efficient not as resistance against 'the market', but in accommodating new interests, including to some extent those of the market agents themselves. It is very likely, however, that older indigenous rules underwent considerable adaptations and changes in the

---

[14] See the first volume, second part, 6th chapter in his 'Economy and Society'.
[15] Polanyi 1957; Bohannan and Dalton 1962

process. For example, the emphasis on making 'gifts', i.e. the creation of obligations on others, which had presumably been a show of strength in earlier times, seems to have shifted gradually towards the demanding of 'gifts' and related transfers. The lapse of time between present and counter-present was often reduced to a morally indispensable minimum, and credits were increasingly taken from rather than given to foreign traders. These moves may have also been precautionary measures against 'defaulting', and the implication of inferiority was probably alleviated by the fact that the creditors were foreigners and arising obligations therefore more restricted.[16] But this change clearly indicates that power over people came to depend more and more on an accumulation of material goods.

This raises, secondly, the question of whether local rules of reciprocity were merely an ideology, used or invented to cover fairly straightforward utilitarian interests of buyers and sellers. The central utilitarian interest, within the margins set by the world market, were of course the 'terms of trade'. The evidence suggests that the prevalence of credit arrangements and the rule of fixed equivalences between standard barter units cushioned the impact of world market price fluctuations in the interior for most of the period. This would have been to the producers' disadvantage with improving world market terms of trade over much of the 19th century, had they not found indirect means to increase their prices. What angry foreign travellers experienced as an 'invention of many claims', as 'extortions, exactions and vexations' could in fact be seen as a skillful adaptation of indigenous rules of reciprocity and jurisdiction: 'friendship', 'hospitality', 'generosity' and often forged accusations were the most typical claims towards the visitor, which, it was hoped, would pay off sooner or later. They often did, since attempts to escape from such obligations invariably led to legal prosecution and excessive demands for compensation, backed up by considerable military power and threats of boycott.

Opportunities to apply such strategies were of course not equal. Chiefs with their rights of hostship and arbitration and their greater control over food and armed forces probably benefited most from such indirect 'price increases'. But the scatteredness and independence of their 'subjects' enabled even small local headmen to enjoy similar rights and powers vis-a-vis foreign caravans. The authority of chiefs and headmen among their followers and dependants, however, depended to a considerable extent on their ability to bargain favourable exchange rates for them, guarantee prices etc. In addition, the same kind of 'friendships', 'debts' and 'compensations' that were transacted between chiefs and caravan leaders also occurred regularly between ordinary village men and women on the

---

[16] Cf.Miller 1988: 50

one hand, and simple caravan members. At any rate, it is possible that as long as world market demand was favourable (until the early 1900s), through these means the inhabitants of the Upper Zambezi and Kasai were able to improve the terms of trade between coast and interior, between traders and producers, in their favour.[17] Any quantification of unequality in market exchanges, however, is made difficult by the fact that both 'use-value' and 'exchange-value' of imported goods were very different in the interior of Africa and in industrializing Europe.

Negotiations and struggles between traders and producers, however, were never just about the terms of trade in a utilitarian sense, but also about the morality of exchange itself. There is evidence that rules and rituals of exchange were often presented to foreign visitors as 'traditional', while in reality they were continually changed and flexibly adapted to new situations. This may illustrate that 'invention of tradition' did take place well before the colonial period; but the caveats that have come up in this debate must also be considered.[18] Notably, this case demonstrates that there was no hegemonic social interest behind this 'ideology'; rules of reciprocity were accepted - or reinterpreted - by different, often opposing groups. Experienced traders and middlemen were frequently prepared to satisfy even allegedly impudent demands, because they knew that 'friendship', 'hospitality' and peace were worth more than the often modest amounts of export goods or food received in immediate return. Yielding to indigenous thinking, they tended to grant 'gifts' (bonuses) on top of their payment for goods rather than explicit price increases. They knew that to secure any decent profit they depended on reliable personal relationships of 'trust' with local inhabitants as the infrastructure of their business: for example as a kind of insurance against losses through credit defaulting, runaway slaves or deserting carriers, and to avoid costly delays in search of export goods, food, carriers and guides.

The producers themselves, especially the stronger and better-off, were also apparently not unwilling to forego immediate benefits in favour of more long-term claims. They needed the traders' loyalty sometimes for support in their local political ambitions, but in any case for a secure and direct access to the market on which they and their dependents relied for imported 'wealth'. Physical access to the market, apart from any question of the terms, was what commodity producers in this remote region had to struggle for first and foremost, right from the beginning of market integration. During the pre-colonial period, this access was embodied for most producers by foreign traders, and much effort was invested in

---

[17] Contrary to the assumption of Clarence-Smith 1979a
[18] See Ranger 1993

establishing personal links with them. This did not prevent producers from adopting a completely different, hostile attitude towards those foreigners (African middlemen, later resident Europeans) whom they saw rather as competitors or inhibitors of this access, or as breaching compacts of 'trust'.

Commodity relations in general probably develop regularly in some sort of synergism with, not in opposition to, forms of gift exchanges and reciprocal personal relations.[19] In this particular case, the attempts by pre-colonial commodity producers and traders to build such an overarching morality of exchange, notwithstanding or even because of their otherwise differing interests, seem to have had particular importance because market relations were so particularly precarious. Without some success in this enterprise, the remarkable dynamic of market integration in the area would hardly have been possible. The 'moral economy' thus obtained, or at least envisaged, was, at any rate, very different from that propagated by the European 'explorers', missionaries, conquerors and administrators who followed the routes of pre-colonial long-distance traders. (See epilogue, Part F)

---

[19] Elwert 1991

Part F
EPILOGUE

Humanist 19th century travellers like Livingstone spent some time on ideas how to improve what they experienced as 'utter hopelessness in many cases of the Interior', especially the 'evils of slavery' and 'the people of the country being most shamelessly greedy and unreasonable in their demands'.[1] Livingstone's concepts reveal a somewhat contradictory assessment of transformation in the region of the Upper Zambezi and Kasai. On the one hand, he attributed such undesirable phenomena to the 'approach to a market' and hoped for a possibility to make the inhabitants return to 'the ancient law [of hospitality] towards strangers', and to the 'idea of presents being reciprocal'.[2] On the other hand, he was deeply convinced of the healthy effect of market production, and saw 'long-continued discipline and contact with superior races by commerce' as the only 'prospect of the negro'.[3]

The fairly detailed 'development plans' Livingstone derived from this second idea read to some extent like a prophesy of what subsequently was to happened in the region, at least from the Portuguese end. His main recommendations included a network of safe, direct communication with the coast, based on cheap ox-drawn transport to exclude demanding African carriers and middlemen; the punishment of 'outrages' by potentates along the road; a prohibition of price control, and the reduction of the inhabitants of the interior to pure commodity producers. Prosperity, based on 'good food and a fair amount of work', he hoped, would in the end also desiccate the roots of slavery.[4]

This programme would, by and large. also have suited the interests of Portuguese speaking and Boerish traders who flocked to the region in increasing numbers, especially with the rubber boom, and suffered from the 'exactions and extortions' discussed above. The ox-wagon (called *mulemba* by the inhabitants) gradually became the most important means of long-distance transport, until, in the 1920s, the Benguela railway substituted the old 'watershed' caravan route.[5] But the traders remained ambiguous about the advance of Portuguese administrative control, because of their own partly unlawful status and practices. Nevertheless, when the new situation finally arrived in the 1890s,[6] they profited from it, for example by assuming local administrative powers. On the other side, the Governments motives for the military occupation of what was to

---

[1] Livingstone 1963: 243, 72 and 109 [1854/55, especially on Chokwe and Luvale]
[2] *Ibid.*: 96, 253
[3] *Ibid.*: 243
[4] *Ibid.*: 117-120
[5] The first such wagon was reported from the Mbunda country in 1854 (Livingstone 1963: 33); around the turn of the century, they frequented the main 'watershed' route (Lemaire, 1902: 134)
[6] See introduction, chapter A 3

become the Moxico District in the remote east of Angola were apparently not so much to gain the support of traders against their African competitors and the demands of their suppliers, as to forestall British and Belgian forces in the 'scramble for Africa'.[7]

This military and diplomatic advance until 1904 resulted in the trisection of the region of the Upper Zambezi and Kasai by a set of most artificial boundaries (see map 1), which made each part a periphery of another European colony. Lines of communication in the ancient 'Atlantic Zone' were completely redirected: in the east towards Katanga (Shaba), and in the south-east towards South Africa. Economic interests, however, clearly also played a role on the three European sides. While the interests of Portuguese mercantile capital remained somewhat closer to Livingstone's ideal of the diligent African export producer (mainly rubber), the concession companies of the 'Congo Free State', and the mining trust ('British South Africa Company') of Cecil Rhodes were more interested in another old export commodity of the region: labour, to be put to work not as slaves, but as wage workers.[8] In all cases, the main lever of Government intervention in the local economy was taxation, in Angola first in kind (rubber), in the British territory from the beginning in cash, which in most cases forced taxpayers to seek temporary employment outside their home region.

This brings us back to the question addressed at the beginning of this study as to the origins and chances of 'peasantization' in a region that was incorporated in the periphery of Southern African migrant labour economies. After the preceding analysis, this question must now be asked in a more specific way: How stable were the conditions and forms of pre-colonial market production in a broader, more long-term perspective ? To what extent did the colonial conquest mean a break, as is often assumed, and how far did earlier forms of market integration prepare a colonial peasantry ?

This is not the place for a comprehensive assessment of the effects of the transition to colonial rule on the rural economy of the Upper Zambezi and Kasai. That will be attempted in future studies, and a few remarks must suffice here.[9] A basic assumption is that changes in rural African production and markets cannot simply be deduced from colonial state interventions, just as little as these simply represented long-term interests of capital. Specific local factors such as effective market demand, local

---

[7] See Pélissier 1977: 395ff
[8] Cameron suspected already in 1875 that some of the slaves sold by the Ovimbundu to Bulozi might reach the South African diamond fields as 'labourers' (1877: II 141).
[9] Preliminary results are found in von Oppen 1990 and forthcoming

administrators' ambitions and the strategies of producers themselves have to be considered.

The interventions of the new local administration itself were contradictory; their impact on the regional economy was often retarded and not very strong. It is little known, for example, that not only the Portuguese and Belgian, but also the British local administration in the region initially tried to expand rubber production. The British administration's primary concern, similar to the others, was to find supplementary local revenues (taxes, royalties) as long as incomes from labour migration were low, in order to recover Government expenditures in this remote area. Success was small, however, at least on the British side, as native rubber producers refused to work for or sell to European traders and preferred to cross the border to Angola where they obtained better prices and bonuses (*matambwishi*).[10]

British and Belgian officers made continued attempts to interrupt these old trade links to the west, especially by intercepting caravans suspected of carrying slaves. But their control began to become more effective only after 1913/14, when the new international boundaries were actually demarcated. *Mambari* and Luvale traders carrying calico and beeswax continued to cross the border regularly, at least until the late 1920s, despite threats of arrest, and were protected by villagers.[11] Beeswax, probably the oldest export product of the region, continued to be produced, with minor interruptions, up to the present day.

Enthusiasm for labour migration among young men of this region, on the other hand, was comparatively low throughout the colonial period, but particularly in the beginning, also because they still feared being enslaved on the way; their reluctance reflected an appalling death rate in the mines and on the road.[12] Tax evasion, assaults on messengers and the desertion of entire gangs of recruits from Balovale were frequent until about 1920.[13] When, subsequently, interest in labour migration increased, urban wages were apparently not seen as an alternative to local income-generating activities, but as a way to create preconditions for them.

Population movements in general remained a significant indicator of prospects for regional commodity production. Up to the end of the rubber boom, around 1910, large numbers of people fled from the more systematic grip of the British administration into Angola. After that date, the main stream of cross border migration was reversed, in consequence

---

[10] Annual Report Barotse District, NAZ KDE 8/1/2; interview Y.Samakayi, 24.10.1986
[11] Annual Reports Balovale District 1917/18 and 1928/29, NAZ KDE 8/1/8 and 8/1/19; interview Y.Samakayi 24.10.1986
[12] Annual Reports Balovale, 1916/17 and 1917/18
[13] Annual Report Balovale District 1917/18, NAZ KDE 8/1/8

of a series of uprisings by Mbunda, Luchazi, Luvale and Chokwe in Angola, culminating in 1916/17.[14] The main targets of these uprisings were resident Portuguese-speaking traders and rubber buyers, who had sometimes been attacked on earlier occasions, but were increasingly resented because they also collected taxes (in rubber) on behalf of the administration. They often abused this right and benefited from their clients' increasing indebtedness.[15] The wider background of these struggles, however, was the collapse of world market prices for wild rubber, which soon brought the entire rubber trade to an end. After 1916, a systematic censusing and tax collection in cash money began also in Angola, which forced young men to seek employment in Katanga.[16] It looks as if the end of the rubber boom, combined with serious famines, marked the definite end of the pre-colonial economy, at least of regional commodity production.[17]

Economically, the 1910s were perhaps the most difficult years of the last two centuries in this region. But in retrospect, the early colonial period appears as an only temporary setback for commodity producers. The main way out of this crisis was food production, which had already been expanded for pre-colonial markets. New opportunities for growing sales of staple crops and fish arose again primarily from foreigners and their staff, who were now resident in the region. Missionaries, labour recruiters and administrators relied largely on the local food market. The loyalty of both recruits and local Government employees depended to some extent on a generous distribution of rations by their employers. Especially on the Northern Rhodesian (now Zambian) side of the border, food imports from European dominated farming areas, in Southern Rhodesia and increasingly the Line of Rail, were impossible because the Upper Zambezi was virtually cut off from the rest of the territory, and up to 1941 could be reached only by very costly river transport through Livingstone. In what was to become the Zambezi and Kabompo Districts (then Balovale) the British administration was lucky in finding a rural population, continuously swelled by kindred immigrants from neighbouring Portuguese territory (Angola), which was capable of and most interested in producing substantial amounts of food for sale.

In the north, on the Angolan side of the boundary, additional external demand was apparently created by the Benguela railway line and an increasing transit travellers, similar to the pre-colonial pattern.[18] A

---

[14] Annual Report Balovale District 1912/13, NAZ KDE 8/1/4
[15] See Pélissier 1977: 408ff
[16] Annual Report Balovale District 1916/17, NAZ KDE 8/1/8; interview Sondoyi,
[17] See above, chapter C 5
[18] No systematic collection of historical data on this part of Angola after about 1920 has been made yet.

probably bigger new market, however, arose in the south. The Lozi had used to grow maize, but the collapse of earlier modes of production and excessive labour migration, aggravated by a series of catastrophic harvests, meant that enormous quantities of relief supplies had to be imported regularly from neighbouring areas. The inhabitants of Balovale were more than willing to become the main suppliers. What they supplied to both their own administration and Bulozi ('Barotseland') was overwhelmingly their traditional surplus crop, cassava. Between 1923 and the early 1960s, Balovale peasants (comprising a total of around 50,000 adults) exported up to more than 1,000 tons of cassava meal per year via official channels to Bulozi, mainly for Government and labour recruitment agencies. During the late 1920s and 1930s, administrators in Balovale came to appreciate this exceptionally positive response of peasants to the new market, which they also saw as an alternative to labour migration which had been sharply reduced during the Great Depression. They proudly called their district the 'granary of Barotseland'.[19]

But new outlets for dried fish, the other traditional sales' food, were also found. As soon as a 650 km road was built from the Upper Zambezi to the towns of the 'Copperbelt', fishermen began to organize transport and to export substantial amounts of dried fish. Less bulky agricultural crops, especially groundnuts, were taken along the same way.

This view onto further developments in rural commodity production must break off here. Its purpose has been to show that there are in fact some striking continuities between the pre-colonial and colonial period. At least in that part of the region that now belongs to Zambia they have carried on up to the present.[20] Where historical continuities appear, however, their conditions must be named as well. Only one of these conditions has been mentioned so far: the emergence of new kinds of market demand that created certain, if modest, outlets for 'traditional' market products. But, as in the pre-colonial period, this alone does not explain the producers' remarkably strong responses to these newly arising marketing opportunities. Were there similar continuities in local structures and conflicts around market production ?

On a more theoretical level, such questions have been asked within the debate on 'peasants in Africa', but almost exclusively for the colonial and post-colonial period.[21] A definitional debate on whether 'peasants' already existed in the pre-colonial Upper Zambezi and Kasai or not would, in my opinion, be rather sterile. To me, it appears more fruitful

---

[19] AR Balovale 1935 (NAZ SEC2/71, vol.I)
[20] See introduction, chapter A 1
[21] See introduction, chapter A 2

and even necessary to take the criteria of peasant production that have been proposed as **questions**, and to examine them in a historical view.[22] As far as the pre-colonial period is concerned, this was the purpose of the foregoing analysis. For the colonial and post-colonial period, a comprehensive analysis of continuity and change in peasant production remains to be made. But there are indications that characteristic social structures and strategies of rural market production in the region, which had emerged in the course of the pre-colonial period, continued to shape responses to new economic conditions.

A few important examples for the colonial period should be mentioned here. There was a continuing interest among producers in productive innovations as long as these did not depend too much on outside intervention; cultivators, for example, continued to expand cassava production, but experimented at the same time with new varieties and with numerous more or less new crops that promised to find a market. One aspect behind this development was that the division of labour partly changed. With the greater involvement of men in agriculture, old rivalries with female producers now took place to some extent within agriculture. But the local circulation of complementary goods through gifts and trade, ideally between woodlands and plains, 'male' and 'female' production, continued to be of great importance for daily reproduction. For a long time, market producers apparently worked not so much for the consumption of a few manufactured goods as for the means of payment in various local transactions. As late as 1933, the administrator of Balovale complained that the inhabitants, especially women, wanted only cloth for their products.[23] 'Trousers' (European clothing) became universal only around the same time, through the migrant labourers' gifts when they came home.[24]

Another continuity was that at marketing stations large numbers of producers, both women and men, turned up with relatively small quantities of produce. The emphasis on cassava, still mainly a 'female' crop, and the abolition of slavery probably even increased the chances of equal access to markets during this period. Significantly, 'surplus' production was not adversely affected by the liberation of slave labour, while a lot of the new market for cassava resulted from the much more negative effects of the abolition of slavery in the neighbouring Lozi society. More than ever, assistance in production had to be solicited through the networks of inter-village exchange, which made any sustainable accumulation beyond certain limits difficult. The desire (and

---

[22] Such criteria are briefly mentioned in chapter A 2, under 'peasantization'.
[23] Annual Report, Balovale District 1933, NAZ 7/1/16/3
[24] Interview with Yowena Samakayi, 24.10.1986

possibilities) of small-scale producers to produce for the market themselves is perhaps the most serious indigenous obstacle for 'emergent farmers' in the region. It seems also to be significant that, to my knowledge, none of the regional chiefs was able to defend a privileged economic position he had held in the pre-colonial period, largely based on political authority, military power and slave labour, beyond the colonial conquest. New special revenues arose for some chiefs only in the 1950s, when the first Government programmes were launched to support (male dominated) 'progressive farming'.

Finally, there are clear similarities between pre-colonial and colonial 'modes of negotiation' by producers with traders (both African and European) and Government officials, at least in the British dominated area. Hard bargaining, evasion, attempts to establish personal relationships, boycott and outbursts of violence were such modes which could all be adopted more or less parallel to each other, according to situation and position of the partners. At least for the colonial period, an underlying attitude of distrust can be discerned, however, and significantly, the 'personal' relationships attempted to form with Government representatives were moulded in a 'father'/'children' rather than a 'friendship' kind of ideology.[25]

This short overview has shown that, besides some striking continuities, structures and strategies of market production also underwent transformations after the end of the pre-colonial period. But these changes can be expected to remain slow at least as long as two basic conditions are unchanged: remoteness, a relative abundance of open land, and an absence of any significant import of capital. Under these conditions, newly arising marketing opportunities, often mediated by state intervention in the form of development projects, are bound to meet with widespread interest and a similar set of characteristic responses.

These responses were described as contradictory in the opening chapter (A 1). The subsequent analysis has made it clear, it is hoped, that such inconsistent images are mainly due to an uncritical application of abstract concepts of society. The 'traditional subsistence economy', on the one hand, is often more innovative, dynamic and conflictive, and therefore opens wider entrances for market relations, than is widely assumed. 'Peasant commodity production' or 'small-scale farming', on the other hand, depend to a considerable extent on non-market social relations. The process of market integration between these poles is neither linear nor uniform; it can occur in very different forms and uneven at paces, and is influenced from both sides by the specific social actors involved, operating in specific historical time and space.

---

[25] See von Oppen, forthcoming

APPENDIX AND REFERENCES

Synopsis of travellers' reports on the Upper Zambezi and Kasai, 1794-1907

Author/ Journey (Edition)[2]	Date	Origin / Destination[3]	Sub-areas/groups covered (with year)[1] Chokwe Central	North	Luvale	South. Lunda	Luchazi/ Mbunda/ Mbwela
Silva Teixeira[4] (1940)	1794	Bihe- Lovar	(1794)		1794		(1794)
Vieira de Andrade (1940)	1799	Bihe- Lovar				1799	(1799)
Anony- mus (1840)	<1803	Bihe- Lovar		<1803		1803	1803
Baptista[5] (1873)	1805- 14	Mukari- Kazembe	1805		(1814)		(1808)
Graça (1890)	1843- 48	Bihe- Musumba	1846			1846	(Katende)
Silva Porto[6] (1942, 1986)	1847 48	Bihe- Bulozi					1847/48 [12-1]
Silva Porto (1938)	1852- 53	Bihe- Mushuku- lumbwe				[11-1]	1852/53
Magyar (1860)	1850 1851 1855	Bihe- ----- Musumba	1850 1855	1850 1851	1850 1851 1855		1851 1855

---

1 Year in (brackets): marginal remarks; other numbers in [brackets]: months of visit
2 Edition consulted (see bibliography below)
3 Neighbouring places only
4 Also Botelho de Vasconcellos, 1844
5 See also da Costa, 1873, the owner of Baptista and his companion
6 Journey was done by two agents of Silva Porto's

Synopsis of travellers' reports

Author/ Journey (Edition)	Date	Origin Destination	Sub-areas/groups covered (with year) Chokwe Central	North	Luvale	South. Lunda	Luchazi/ Mbunda/ Mbwela
Livingstone (1963, 1857)	1854-1855	Bulozi-　　　　　Kasanje	1854 1855	1854 1855	1854 1855	(1854/1855)
Cameron (1877)	1875	Luba-Bihe	1875		1875 [8-9]	
Pogge/Lux (1880)	1875	Malanje-Musumba			1875 [8]	
Capello/Ivens (1882)	1878	Ngangela-Kasanje	1878 [7]			
Pinto (1881)	1878	Mbandi-Bulozi				1878 [7]
Schütt (1879)	1878-79	Malanje-Mai Munene	1878 [11/12]			
Buchner (1883)	1879-1880	Malanje-Musumba	1879-1880			
Wissmann (1902)	1880	Malanje Mai	1880 [6/7]			
Silva Porto (1891)	1880	Bihe Mai	1880 [3-4]	1880 [4-6]		
Dias de Carvalho (1892)	1883-1886	Malanje-Musumba	1885-1886			
Capello/Ivens (1886)	1884	Bihe-Kaonde		(1884) [9]	1884 [7]	
Arnot (1969)	1884	Bulozi-Bihe				1884 [5-6]

Author/ Journey (Edition)	Date	Origin --- Destination	Sub-areas/groups covered (with year): Chokwe Central	North	Luvale	South. Lunda	Luchazi/ Mbunda/ Mbwela
Arnot (1969)	1885-1888	Bihe- ------- Bunkeya	1885 [11]		1885/6 [12/1] 1888 [5/6]		
Crawford (1912)	1889	Bihe- Bunkeya			1889 [9/10]		
Johnston (1893/ 1969)	1891	Bihe- Bulozi					1891 [10/11]
Coillard (1897)	1895	Bulozi- Kakenge			1895 [6]	1895 [6]	
Trigo Teixeira (1936)	1895	Bihe Moxico	1895 [5-9]				
Goold-Adams (NAZ)	1897	Bulozi			1897	1897	
Gibbons (1904)	1898-99	Bulozi- Lunda			1898 [9]	1899 [10]	
Lemaire (1903)	1899	Katanga- Dilolo			1899 [8-9]	1899 [9-10]	
Harding (1904)	1899	Bulozi- Bihe			1899 [1]		1899 [c.3]
Harding (1904)	1900	Bulozi				1900 [10f]	
Schomburgk (1925)	1904-1907	Kaonde- Kavungu				1904-1907[7]	
Frobenius (1988)	1905-06	Middle Kasai	1905-06 [fr.10]				

---

[7] Various journeys between Kabompo and Zambezi rivers

References

1. Oral sources[1]

Interviews conducted by myself

Chief Ishinde
(Senior Chief of the Southern Lunda of Zambezi/Zambia),
Mukandankunda Capital; audience on 25th August 1986
Chief Ndungu
(Senior Chief of the Zambian Luvale),
Mize Capital; audience on 23rd August 1985
Chieftainess Nyakulenga,
Nyakulenga Chief's Headquarter, Zambezi District;
interview and discussion on 23rd Oct.1986
Chifwisha, Mr., and Mr. J. Muwika
(Headman, peasants and canoe builders),
Chifwisha village, Zambezi District; interview 22nd October 1986
Chipoya, David, (peasant),
Kanema village, Dipalata area, Zambezi District; interview 14th October 1986
Chishinji, David,
(ex-trader, preacher, my assistant),
Dama village, Dipalata area, Zambezi District; interview 16th October 1986
(see fig. 16, right)
Chizombo, Lazaro,
(ex-teacher, expert on Southern Lunda history), Chitokoloki Mission, Zambezi District; interview on 30th Oct.1986
Finnegan, Mr. and Ms.,
(Missionaries CMML),
Dipalata/ Zambezi; interview 11th September 1986
Fishermen at Nyambingila Subchief's Headquarters,
Zambezi District; interview on 18th Aug. 1985
Kaloza, Lopi,
(trader and ox-cart transporter),
Chingalala area, Zambezi District; interview 22nd October 1986
Kandala, Mr., (fisherman, peasant),
Lungwevungu area, Zambezi District; interview on 5th Sept. 1985
Likomeno, Mr., (Fisherman),
Nyatanda/Zambezi-West; interview 13th August 1985

---

[1] See introduction, A 3.2.

Maseka Mbondu, Thomas,
Kanampumba [senior adviser]
and other Advisers to Chief Ishinde,
Mukandankunda Capital, Zambezi District;
interview and discussion on 25th Oct. 1986
Munyawu, Mr. (Headman, farmer), Dipalata Area, Zambezi District; interview on 8th Oct.1986
Muyembe, Mr., (Headman),
Muyembe/Zambezi-West; interview 26th August 1985
Munyawu, Gordon,
(son of the former, living with his father, farmer); interview on 9th Sept. 1986
Orr-Ewing, Mr.,
(ex-District Commissioner, Balovale),
Wye; interview 2nd November 1987
Sakutadika, Jonas, (farmer),
Dama village, Dipalata area, Zambezi District; discussion on 18th October 1986
Sakutohwa, Mr., (Fisherman),
Nyatanda/ Zambezi-West; interview 15th August 1985
Samakayi, Yowena Shirikose,
(ex-trader and beekeeper; peasant), Dama village, Dipalata area, Zambezi District; interviews on 21st and 24th October 1986
(see fig. 9)
Samungole, Mr.,
(farmer; transporter/trader; ex-parastatal employee; Ward Chairman Mwange-Nyawanda Ward),
Chinyama Litapi, Zambezi District; interview on 3rd Sept. 1985
Sondoyi, Mr.,
(ex-rubber producer and -peasant),
Dama village, Dipalata area, Zambezi District; interviews on 18th and 24th October 1986
(see fig. 16, left)
Women, group of, **Kanema** village,
Dipalata area, Zambezi District; discussion on 8th Oct.1986

Recorded by others

Chinyama, Thomas, 1945:
The early history of the Balovale Lunda, Lovedale Press
Sangambo, Mose Kaputungu, n.y.[2] [Second edition, 1985]:
The history of the Luvale People and their chieftainship, Mize Palace
[First edition 1979, edited by Robert J.Papstein and Art Hansen, Los Angeles: Institute for Applied Research]
Schönberg-Lotholz, Ingeborg, **1960**:
"Karawanenreisen der Tjiaka um 1900", in: *Memórias e Trabalhos do Instituto de Investigação Scientífica de Angola*, vol.2, 109-28
[results from a series of historical interviews with ex-Ovimbundu traders]

2. Written Sources[1] and Bibliography

Published Sources and other literature

Adelman, I., and Morris, C., **1973**:
    Economic growth and social equity in developing countries, Stanford

Alff, Ulrich, Achim **von Oppen** and Roland **Beck, 1986**:
    'Westbank Study'. Development possibilities in Zambezi District - West Bank. Eschborn (German Agency for Technical Development; unpubl.)

Almeida, Antonio de, **1965**:
    "The Yellow Bushmen (Kwankhala and Sekele)", in: *idem*: 1-11.

Almeida, António de, **1965**:
    Bushmen and other Non-Bantu peoples of Angola. Three lectures, Johannesburg (University of Witwatersrand Press)

Alpers, Edward A., **1975**:
    Ivory and slaves in East Central Africa. Changing patterns of international trade to the later 19th century, London (Heinemann)

Amin, Samir, **1972**:
    "Underdevelopment and dependence in Black Africa - origins and contemporary forms", in: *Journal of Modern African Studies*, vol.10,4, 503-24

Anonymus, **1940**:
    "Derrota de Benguella para o sertão", in: Felner (ed.): vol.II, 12-27 [by `um Certanejo'; Original from before 20th April 1803]

Antunes Cabrita, Carlos L., **1954**:
    Em terras de Luenas. Breve estudo sobre os usos e costumes da tribo Luena, Lisboa

Arnot, Frederic S., **1893**:
    Bihé and Garenganze, London

Arnot, Frederic S., [2]**1969**:
    Garenganze or Seven years of Pioneer mission work in Central Africa, London [new edition of the original from 1889, new introduction by Robert I.Rotberg]

Austen, Ralph A., and **Headrick**, Daniel, **1983**:
    "The role of technology in the African past", in: *African Studies Review*, vol.26, 3/4, 163-184

Austen, Ralph, **1987**:
    African economic history. Internal development and external dependency, London and Portsmouth N.H. (J.Currey and Heinemann)

Baptista, J., **1873**
    "Journey of the *Pombeiros*", in: Burton (ed.), 1873: 169-188; 198-200; 203-233

---

1   See introduction, A 3.2, and synopsis above

Bastin, Marie-Louise, **1966**:
"Tshibinda Ilunga: Héros civilisateur", Université Libre de Bruxelles (unpublished Ph.D. dissertation)

Bastos, A., **1912**:
Monographia de Catumbella, Lisbon

Baumann, Hans, **1932**:
"Die Mannbarkeitsfeiern bei den Tsokwe und ihren Nachbarn," in: Baessler Archiv, XV, 1, Berlin

Baumann, Hans, **1935**:
Lunda. Bei Bauern und Jägern in Inner-Angola. Ergebnisse der Angola Expedition des Museums für Völkerkunde, Berlin. Berlin (Würfel)

Beck, Josephine, and **Dorlöchter**, Sabine, **1987**:
"'Wahileyi' - Women's agricultural activities as a basis for subsistence and for their economic independence,"in: Crehan and von Oppen (eds.): B1-B116

Beck, Josephine, and **Dorlöchter**, Sabine, **1988**:
Frauen als 'Opfer der Entwicklung'? Strategien und Handlungsspielräume afrikanischer Kleinbäuerinnen zur Sicherung ökonomischer Unabhängigkeit. Zwei Dorffstudien aus der Nord-West-provinz Zambias. Berlin (Diplom thesis Institut für Soziologie der Freien Universität)

Beinart, William, **1982**:
The political economy of Pondoland, 1860-1930. Production, labour migrancy and chiefs in rural South Africa, Cambridge (Cambridge University Press)

Berg, Eberhard, et al. (eds.), **1991**:
Ethnologie im Widerstreit. Kontroversen über Macht, Gesellschaft, Geschlecht in fremden Kulturen (Festschrift for Lorenz G. Löffler), München (Trickster)

Bernstein, Henry, **1979**:
"African peasantries: A theoretical framework", in: *Journal of Peasant Studies*, 6, 4, 421-443

Bhila, H.K., **1982**:
Traders and politics in a Shona kingdom: The Manyika and their Portuguese and African neighbours, 1575-1902, Harlow, Salisbury (Longman)

Birmingham, David B., **1966**:
Trade and conflict in Angola, Oxford (Oxford University Press)

Birmingham, David B., and Phyllis M. **Martin** (eds:), **1983**:
History of Central Africa, 2 vols., London (Longman)

Birmingham, David, **1983**:
"Society and economy before A.D. 1400", in: Birmingham and Martin (eds.): vol.I, 1-29

Bisson, Michael, **1980**:
Pre-historic archeology of North-Western Province, in: Johnson (ed.): 53-66

Bley, Helmut, 1992:
Mombasa und sein Hinterland: Handel, Politik und Anpassung im 18. und 19. Jahrhundert (Lecture read in the University Lecture Series on 'Africa: Changing Appropriation of Nature' at the Freie Universität Berlin, Winter Semester 1992/93)

Bloch, Maurice, and Jonathan P. Parry (eds.), 1989:
Money and the morality of exchange, Cambridge (Cambridge University Press)

Bohannan, Paul and George Dalton (eds.):
Markets in Africa, Evanston (North Western University Press)

Bohannan, Paul, 1959:
"The impact of money on an african subsistence economy", in: *The Journal of Economic History*, vol.19, 4, 491-503

Bohannan, Paul, and Dalton, George, 1962:
"Introduction", in: Bohannan and Dalton (eds.): 1-26

Bontinck, François, 1974:
"Le voyage des pombeiros: essai de réinterpretation", in: *Cultures au Zaïre et en Afri*que, 5, 39-70

Bontinck, François, 1976:
"Les *Quimbares*: Note sémantique", in: *Africa (Rome)*, vol. 31, 1, 41-55

Botelho de Vasconcellos, Alexandre José, 1844:
[account of the kingdom of Loval and its road from Benguela, after report given to him by A. da Silva Teixeira on journey in 1795], in: *Annaes Marítimos e Coloniais*, 4a série, 159f [translation in: Burton (ed.),1873: 24/5, footnote]

Bowditch, T.E., 1824:
An account of the discoveries of the Portuguese in the interior of Angola and Mozambique, London

Brant Pontes, 1940:
"Memória...sobre a communicação das duas costas", in: Felner (ed.): vol.I, 248/49

Brun, Samuel, 1983:
"Samuel Brun's voyages of 1611-20", in: Jones (ed.): 44-95

Buchner, Max, 1883:
"Das Reich des Mwata Yamvo und seine Nachbarländer", in: *Deutsche Geographische Blätter*, vol. 1, 6, 56-67

Burton, R.F. (ed.), 1873:
Lacerda's journey to Cazembe, and journey of Pombeiros etc. London

Cameron, Vernon L., 1877:
Across Africa. 2 vols., London

Capello, Hermengildo, and Ivens, Roberto, 1882:
From Benguella to the territory of Yacca, 2 vols., London

Capello, Hermengildo, and Ivens, Roberto, 1886:
De Angola à contracosta, 2 vols., Lisboa.

Carvalhais, João Teixeira de Barros, 1915:
Uma diligência e expedição comercial à Mona Quimbundo em 1912, Loanda (Imprensa Nacional de Angola)

Chenery, H., et al., **1975**:
Redistribution with growth. London

Childs, Gordon, **1949**:
Umbundu kinship and character, London

Chilivumbo, A., **Milimo**, J.T., et. al., **1983**:
"Small farm sector study", in: Ncube (ed.): 335-357

Chrétien, Jean-Pierre, **1983**:
Histoire rurale de l'Afrique des Grands Lacs. Guide de recherches, Bujumbura/Paris (AFERA/Karthala)

Clarence-Smith, W. Gervase, **1979a**:
Slaves, peasants and capitalists in southern Angola 1840-1926, Cambridge (Cambridge Univ.Press)

Clarence-Smith, W. Gervase, **1979b**:
"The Myth of uneconomic imperialism: The Portuguese in Angola, 1836-1926", in: *Journal of Southern African Studies*, vol 5., 165-180

Clarence-Smith, W.Gervase, **1979c**:
"Slaves, commoners and landlords in Bulozi, c.1875 to 1906", in: *Journal of African History*, 20, 219-234

Clarence-Smith, W.Gervase, **1983**:
"Capital accumulation and class formation in Angola", in: Birmingham and Martin (eds.): vol.II, 163-199

Clay, G.C.R., **1945**:
History of the Mankoya District, Lusaka (Rhodes-Livingstone Institute)

Cock, J.H., **1985**:
Cassava. New Potential for a neglected crop, Boulder and London (Westview)

Cohen, David W., **1983**:
"Food production and food exchange in the pre-colonial Lakes' Plateau Region", in: Rotberg (ed.)

Coillard, François, **1897**:
On the threshold of Central Africa, London

Comaroff, Jean and John, **forthcoming**:
Of revelation and revolution, vol. 2. Chicago

Comaroff, Jean, **forthcoming**:
"Fashioning the colonial subject: The empire's old clothes", in: Jean and John Comaroff

Cooper, Frederick, **1977**:
Plantation slavery on the East Coast of Africa, New Haven (Yale University Press)

Cooper, Frederick, **1981**:
"Peasants, capitalists and historians: A review article", in: *Journal of Southern African Studies*, 7, 3, 284-314

Coquery-Vidrovitch, Catherine, **1977**:
"Research on an African mode of production", in: Gutkind and Waterman, (eds.): 77-92 [first published in 1969 in *La Pensée*]

Coquery-Vidrovitch, Catherine, **1985**:
Afrique noire. Permanences et ruptures. Paris (Payot)

Coquéry-Vidrovitch, Catherine, and Paul E. **Lovejoy** (eds.), **1985**:
The Workers of African Trade, Beverly Hills and London (Sage)

Costa Maciel, D. **da, 1948**:
"Quiocos - excerptos de uma monografía", in: *Mensário Administrativo*, no.15, 29-36

Costa, Francisco Honorato **da, 1873**:
[Letter by the 'Director of the Fair of *Casanje*' to the Governor of Angola], in: Burton (ed.): 200-202

Cowsey, D.G., **Shaw**, J.R., and **Leslie**, A., **no year** [c.1982]:
Report to the Development Bank of Zambia on a study to determine the feasibility of an extension of cassava production on a commercial scale in Zambia, Lusaka (unpublished)

Crawford, David, **1912**:
Thinking black. 22 years without a break in the long grass of Central Africa, London (Morgan and Scott)

Crehan, Kate, **1984**:
"Women and development in North-Western Zambia: From producer to housewife", in: *Review of African Political Economy*, no.27/28, 51-66

Crehan, Kate, **1985**:
"Production and gender in North-Western Zambia", in: Pottier (ed.): 80-100

Crehan, Kate, **1986**:
Production, reproduction and gender in North-West Zambia: A case study, Manchester university (unpubl. Ph.D. dissertation)

Crehan, Kate, and Achim **von Oppen** (eds.), **1987**:
Is small beautiful ? 'Small-scale producers', 'informal activities' and 'development' in their social and economic context. Five Case studies on rural economic activities and the impact of development projects in the Zambezi and Kabompo Districts (NW Zambia). Berlin (Arbeitspapiere zu Wirtschaft, Gesellschaft und Politik in Entwicklungsländern No.8a)

Crehan, Kate, and **von Oppen**, Achim, **1988**:
"Understandings of 'development': An arena of struggles. The story of a development project in Zambia", in: *Sociologia Ruralis* (Special Issue on *Aid and Development*), vol. 28, 2/3, 113-145

Crummey, D., and C.C. **Steward**, (eds.), **1981**: *Modes of production in Africa: The pre-colonial era*, Beverley Hills (Sage)

Cunnison, Ian, **1961**:
"Kazembe and the Portuguese, 1798-1832", in: *Journal of African History*, vol.2, 1, 61-76

Curtin, Philip D., **1975**:
Economic change in pre-colonial Africa: Senegambia in the Era of the slave trade, Madison (University of Wisconsin Press)

Dalton, George, **1971**:
Tribal and peasant economies: An introductory survey of economic anthropology. Reading, Mass. (Addison-Wesley)

Delachaux, T., and **Thiébaud**, C.E., **1934**:
Land und Völker von Angola, Neuchâtel and Paris

Delgado, Ralph, **1944**:
    Ao sul do Cuanza. Ocupação e aproveitamento do antigo Reino de Benguela, vol.I, Lisboa

Dellille, A., **1930**:
    "Besnijdenis bij de Alunda's an Aluena's in de streek ten Zuiden van Belgisch Kongo," in: *Anthropos*, XXV, 5-6, 851-858

Dellille, A., **1944**:
    "Over de Mukanda en Zemba bij de Tshokwe," in: *Aequatoria*, VII, 2, 49-55

Dellille, A., **1946**:
    "De Huwelijkstitel bij de Chokwe", in: *Aequatoria*, vol.9, 1, 9-12

Derricourt, R.M., and **Papstein**, Robert J., **1977**:
    Lukolwe and the Mbwela of North-Western Zambia, in: *Azania*, XI, 169-175

Dias da Silva, A., **1949**:
    "Algo acerca dos povos dos Luchazes", in: *Mensário Administrativo*, no. 24/25, 35-42

Dias de Carvalho, Henrique Augusto, **1890**:
    Ethnographia e história tradicional dos povos da Lunda (Expedição portugueza ao Muatiânvua, vol. 5), Lisboa (Imprensa Nacional)

Dias de Carvalho, Henrique Augusto, **1892**:
    Descripção da viagem à Mussumba, Lisboa

Dias, Jill, **forthcoming**:
    "Changing patterns of society in the Luanda hinterland", in: Heimer (ed.), forthcoming

Dias, Margot, **1962**:
    "Preparação da farinha de mandioca torrada (farinha dos musseques)", in: *Garcia de Orta* (Lisboa), 10, 1, 59-76

Diniz, Ferreira J.O., **1918**:
    Populações indigenas de Angola, Coimbra (Imprensa da Universidade)

Diniz, Ferreira J.O., **1925**:
    "Une étude de l'ethnographie d' Angola", in: *Anthropos*, vol. 20, 1-2, 321-331

Donge, van, Jan-Kees, **1985**:
    "Understanding rural Zambia today: The relevance of the Rhodes-Livingstone Institute", in: *Africa*, 55, 1, 60-76

Douglas, Mary, **1963**:
    The Lele of the Kasai, London (International Africa Institute)

Douglas, Mary, **1964**:
    "Matriliny and pawnship in Central Africa", in: *Africa*, vol. 34, 4, 301-313

Dupré, Georges, and **Rey**, Pierre-Philippe, **1973**:
    "Reflections on the relevance of a theory of the history of exchange", in: *Economy and Society*, vol. 2, [first published 1968 in *Cahiers Internationaux de Sociologie*]

Durkheim, Emile, **1893**:
  Sur la division sociale du travail. Paris

Ehret, Christopher, **1974**:
  "Agricultural history in Central and Southern Africa, c.1000 B.C. to c. A.D.500", in: *Transafrican Journal of History*, vol.4, 1.25

Ekholm, Kajsa, **1977**:
  "External exchange and the transformation of Central African social systems", in: Friedman and Rowlands (eds.): 115-136

Elwert, Georg, **1983**:
  "Der entwicklungspolitische Mythos vom Traditionalismus", in: Goetze and Weiland (eds.): 29-55.

Elwert, Georg, **1984**:
  "Die Verflechtung von Produktionen: Nachgedanken zur Wirtschaftsanthropologie", in: *Kölner Zeitschrift für Soziologie*, Special Issue 26, 379-402

Elwert, Georg, **1985**:
  "Märkte, Käuflichkeit and Moralökonomie", in: Lutz (ed.): 509-519

Elwert, Georg, **1987**:
  "Ausdehnung der Käuflichkeit und Einbettung der Wirtschaft - Markt und Ökonomie", in: *Kölner Zeitschrift für Soziologie und Sozial-Psychologie*, Special Issue No. 28,

Elwert, Georg, **1991**:
  "Gabe, Reziprozität und Warentausch. Überlegungen zu einigen Ausdrücken und Begriffen", in: Eberhard Berg *et al.* (eds.): 159-177

Elwert, Georg, and Roland Fett (eds.), **1982**:
  Afrika zwischen Subsistenzökonomie und Imperialismus, Frankfurt (Campus)

Essner, Cornelia, **1987**:
  "Some aspects of German travellers' accounts from the second half of the 19th century", in: Heintze and Jones (eds.): 197-205

Fagan, Brian M., **1970**:
  "Early trade and raw materials in South Central Africa", in: Gray and Birmingham (eds.),1970: 24-38

Fage, J.D., **1978**:
  A history of Africa, New York

Feierman, Steven, **1974**:
  The Shambaa-Kingdom: A history, Madison, Wisconsin (University of Wisconsin Press)

Felner, A. de Albuquerque (ed.), **1940**:
  Apontamentos sobre a colonização dos planaltos e litoral do sul de Angola, Lisboa (Ministério das Colónias),

Ferreira Ribeiro, M., **1885**:
  Homenagem aos heróes que precederam Brito Capello e Roberto Ivens na exploração da África Austral, 1484-1877, Lisboa

Ficalho, Conde de, [2]**1947**:
  Plantas úteis da Africa Portuguesa. Notas do Professor Rui Teles Palhinha, Lisboa (Agencia Geral das Colónias)

Figueira, Luiz, 1938:
Africa Bantú. Raças e tribos de Angola. Lisboa (Oficinas Fernandes)

Fisher, M.K., ²1984:
Lunda-Ndembu Dictionary. Ikelenge (Lunda-Ndembu Publications)

Flint, Eric, 1970:
"Trade and Politics in Barotseland during the Kololo period", in: *Journal of African History,* vol.11, 1, 71-86

Fodor, Istvan, c.1983:
Introduction to the history of Umbundu: L. Magyar's records (1859) and the later sources, Hamburg/Budapest (Buske/Academia Kiado)

Fonseca Cardoso, A., 1919:
"Em terras do Moxico. Apontamentos de Ethnographia Angolense", in: *Trabalhos da Sociedade Portuguesa de Anthropologia e Ethnologia* (Porto), vol. I, 1, 3-29

Fortes, Meyer, and E. E. Evans-Pritchard (eds.), 1940:
African Political Systems, London (Oxford University Press)

Friedman, J., und M. J. Rowlands (eds.), 1977:
The evolution of social systems (Proceedings of a meeting of the Research Seminar in Archeology and Related Subjects, held at the Institute for Archeology of the University of London), London: Duckworth

Frobenius, Leo, 1907:
Im Schatten des Kongo-Staates, Berlin

Frobenius, Leo, 1988:
Ethnographische Notizen aus den Jahren 1905 und 1906. III: Luluwa, Süd-Kete, Bena Mai, Pende, Cokwe (Studien zur Kulturkunde 87), Stuttgart (Steiner)

Gago Coutinho, Carlos Viegas, 1915:
"Impressões das duas viagens atravs d'Africa entre Angola e Mocambique", in: *Boletím da Sociedade de Geographia de Lisboa,* 33a série, 5-6, 181-208

Gamitto, António C.P., 1937:
O Muata Cazembe e os povos maraves, chevas, muizas, muembas, lundas e outros da Africa Austral. 2 vols. Lisboa (Agéncia Geral das Colónias)

Gann, Lewis, 1954:
"The end of slave trade in British Central Africa: 1889-1912", in: *Rhodes-Livingstone Journal,* no.16, 36-56

Geisler, Gisela, 1990:
Die Politik der Geschlechterbeziehungen in einer ländlichen Gemeinde in Zambia: "Be quiet and suffer" (Arbeiten aus dem Institut für Afrika-Kunde 66), Hamburg (Institut für Afrika-Kunde)

Geschiere, Peter, and Raatgever, Reini, 1985:
"Introduction: Emerging insights and issues in French Marxist Anthropology", in: van Binsbergen and Geschiere (eds.),1985: 1-38

Gibbons, Alfred St.Hill, 1904:
Africa from South to North through Marotseland, 2 vols., London / New York

Giblin, James Leonard, 1986:
Famine, authority and the impact of foreign capital in Handeni District, Tanzania, 1840-1940. (unpublished Ph.D. Dissertation in History), Madison (University of Wisconsin)

Giddens, Anthony, 1984:
The constitution of society. Outline of the theory of structuration, Cambridge (Polity Press)

Gluckman, Max, 1941:
Economy of the central Barotse plain, Lusaka (Rhodes-Livingstone Paper No.7)

Godelier, Maurice, 1963:
La notion de mode de production asiatique et les schémas marxistes d'évolution des sociétés, Paris (C.E.R.M.)

Goetze, Dieter, and Heribert Weiland (eds.), 1983:
Soziokulturelle Implikationen technologischer Wandlungsprozesse, Saarbrücken (Breitenbach)

Goody, Jack, 1969:
"Economy and feudalism in Africa", in: *Economic History Review*, 2nd series, vol.22

Gossweiler, John, 1907:
"Relatório da missão agrícola à região dos Ganguelas, Ambuelas e Luchazes", in: *Relatórios, Secção de Agricultura* (Luanda)

Gossweiler, John, 1939:
Carta Fitogeográfica de Angola, Lisboa (Governo Geral de Angola)

Government of the Republic of Zambia, 1979:
Third National Development Plan, 1979-1983, Lusaka (National Commission for Development Planning)

Governo Geral da Provincia de Angola, Repart.do Gabinete, 1910:
Relatório da missão de colonisação no planalto de Benguella em 1909, Loanda (Imprensa Nacional de Angola)

Governo Geral de Angola, 1918:
Relatórios 1907-09, Luanda (Imprensa Nacional de Angola)

Graça, Joaquim R., 1890:
"Expedição ao Muatayanvua. Diario de Joaquim Rodrigues Graça", in: *Boletim da Sociedade de Geographia de Lisboa*, 9ª Sér., 365-468

Grandvaux Barbosa, L.A., 1970:
Carta Fitogeográphica de Angola, Luanda (Instituto de Investigação Científica de Angola)

Gray, Richard, and Birmingham, David, 1970:
"Some economic and political consequences of trade in Central and Eastern Africa in the pre-colonial period", in: Gray and Birmingham (eds.): 1-23

Gray, Richard, and David Birmingham (eds.), 1970:
Pre-colonial African Trade. Essays on trade in Central and Eastern Africa before 1900. London (Oxford University Press)

Gutkind, P.C.W., and P. Waterman, (eds.), 1977:
African social studies: A radical reader, London (Heinemann)

Guy, Jeff, 1987:
"Analysing pre-capitalist societies in Southern Africa", in: *Journal of Southern African Studies,* 14, 1 (Oct.), 18-37

Guyer, J., 1981:
"Household and community in African Studies", in: *African Social Research,* 24, 2/3, 87-138

Guyer, Jane, 1988:
"The multiplication of Labour: Historical methods in the study of gender and agricultural change in modern Africa", in: *Current Anthropology,* 29, 2,

Hansen, Art, 1976:
When the running stops: the social and economic incorporation of Angolan refugees into Zambian border villages. (Unpublished Ph.D.dissertation, Cornell University)

Harding, Colin, 1904:
In remotest Barotseland, London

Harding, Leonard, et al., 1991:
Commerce et commerçants en Afrique de l'Ouest, Paris (L'Harmattan)

Harlan, J.R., J. de Wet, and A.B.L. Stemler (eds.), 1976:
Origins of African Plant Domestication, The Hague

Harlan, Jack R., 1982:
"The origins of indigenous African agriculture", in: *Cambridge Economic History of Africa,* vol. I, 624-657

Harms, Robert, 1975:
"The end of red rubber: A reassessment," in: *Journal of African History,* vol.16, 1, 73-88

Harms, Robert, 1979:
"Fish and cassava: The changing equation", in: *African Economic History,* 7, 113-116

Harms, Robert, 1981:
River of wealth, river of sorrow. The Central Zaire Basin in the Era of the Slave and Ivory trade, 1500-1891, New Haven (Yale University Press)

Harms, Robert, 1987:
Games against nature: an eco-cultural history of the Nunu of equatorial Africa, (Studies in Environment and History) Cambridge (Cambridge University Press)

Hartwig, Gerald W., 1976:
The art of survival in East Africa: The Kerebe and long-distance trade, 1800-1895, New York

Heidrich, Joachim (ed.), forthcoming:
Changing identities. Berlin (Das Arabische Buch)

Heimer, Franz-Wilhelm (ed.), 1973:
Social change in Angola, München (Weltforum)

Heimer, F.W. (ed.), forthcoming:
The formation of Angolan society

Heintze, Beatrix, 1979:
"Der portugiesisch-afrikanische Vasallenvertrag in Angola im 17. Jhdt.", in: Paideuma, 25, 195-223

Heintze, Beatrix, 1985:
Fontes para a história de Angola do século XVII, vol. I (Studien zur Kulturkunde 75) Stuttgart (Franz Steiner)

Heintze, Beatrix, 1989:
"A cultura material dos Ambundu de Angola segundo as fontes dos séculos XVI e XVII", in: *Revista Internacional de Estudios Africanos*, 10-11, 15-63
[Appeared also in German as "Zur materiellen Kultur der Ambundu nach den Quellen des 16. und 17. Jahrhunderts", in: Paideuma, 35 (1989), 115-130]

Heintze, Beatrix, and Adam Jones (eds.), 1987:
European sources for sub-saharan Africa before 1900: Use and abuse (special issue of *Paideuma*, vol.33), Stuttgart (Steiner)

Hermitte, Eugene, 1974:
An economic history of Barotseland, 1800-1940, North-Western University (unpubl. Ph.D.thesis)

Heusch, Luc de, 1972:
Le roi ivre, ou l'origine de l'état, Paris (Gallimard)

Heywood, Linda M., 1984:
Production, trade and power. The political economy of central Angola, 1850-1930, Columbia University (unpubl. Ph.D.thesis)

Heywood, Linda M., 1985:
"Porters, trade and power: The politics of labour in the Central Highlands of Angola, 1850-1914", in. Coquéry-Vidrovitch and Lovejoy (eds.): 243-268

Hobson, R.H., 1960:
Rubber - a footnote to Northern-Rhodesian history. Livingstone (Rhodes-Livingstone Museum Occasional Paper No.13)

Hogendorn, J.S., 1976:
"The vent-for-surplus model and African cash agriculture to 1914", in: *Savannah*, vol.5, 15-28

Honeybone, David, and Marter, Alan, 1979:
Poverty and wealth in rural Zambia, Lusaka (University of Zambia)

Hoover, J.Jeffrey, 1978:
The seduction of Ruwej : Reconstructing Ruund history. (The nuclear Lunda: Zaire, Angola, Zambia). Unpubl. Ph.D. dissertation, Yale University

Horton, A.E., 1978:
English-Luvale Dictionary. No place

Horton, A.E., ²1975 (¹1953): *A dictionary of Luvale*. Revised edition. No place (First edition: El Monte, California)

Hudson, R.S., 1935:
"The human geography of Balovale", in: *The Journal of the Royal Anthropological Institute*, vol. 65

Iliffe, John, **1979**:
A modern history of Tanganyika, Cambridge (Cambridge University Press)
Iliffe, John, **1987**:
The African poor, Cambridge (Cambridge University Press)
Isaacman, Allen, **1972**:
Mozambique: The africanization of a European institution. The Zambezi Prazos, 1750-1902, Madison (University Wisconsin Press)
Isaacman, Allen, **1990**:
"Peasants and rural social protest in Africa", in: *African Studies Review*, 33, 2, 1-120
Jaeger, Dirk, **1981**:
Settlement patterns and rural development. A human geographical study of the Kaonde, Kasempa District, Zambia, Amsterdam (Royal Tropical Institute)
Jaspert, Willem, **1929**:
Afrikanische Abenteuer. Auf der Walze durch Urwald Sumpf und Steppe, Berlin (Köhler)
Jewsiewicki, Bogumil, **1981**:
"Lineage mode of production: Social inequalities in Equatorial Central Africa", in: Crummey and Steward (eds.): 93-115
Johnson (ed.), D.S., **1980**:
Handbook to the Northwestern Province 1980. Lusaka (Zambia Geographical Association Handbook No.8),
Johnston, James, [2]**1969**:
Reality versus romance in South Central Africa, London (Frank Cass) [First edition 1893]
Jones, Adam, **1983**:
German sources for West-African histo- ry 1599-1669 (Studien zur Kulturkunde 66), Stuttgart: Steiner
Jones, William O., **1959**:
Manioc in Africa, Stanford (Stanford University Press)
Kjekshus, Helge, **1977**:
Ecology control and economic development in East African history. The case of Tanganyika 1850-1950, London etc. (Heinemann)
Klein, Herbert S., **1974**:
"The Portuguese slave trade from Angola in the eighteenth century", in: *Journal of Economic History*, 32, 4, 894-918
Klein, Martin A. (ed.), **1980**:
Peasants in Africa, Beverly Hills/London (Sage)
Klein, Martin A., **1980**:
"Introduction", in: Klein (ed.): 9-43
Kodi, Muzeng Wanda, **1976**:
"A pre-colonial history of the Pende people (Republic of Zaire), from 1620 to 1900", 2 vols., Northwestern University (unpublished Ph.D.thesis)
Konczacki, Z.A., and J.M. Konczacki (eds.), **1977**:
An economic history of Tropical Africa, London (Cass)

Koponen, Juhani, **1988**:
People and production in late pre-colonial Tanzania. History and structures, Helsinki (Finnish Society for Development Studies etc.)

Kubik, Gerhard, **1971**:
Die Institution *mukanda* und assoziierte Einrichtungen bei den Vambwela/Vankangela und verwandten Etnien in Südost-Angola. Wien (unpublished Ph.D. dissertation)

Kubik, Gerhard, **1981**:
Mukanda na Makisi. Circumcision school and masks (Commentary to a record), Berlin (Staatliche Museen Preußischer Kulturbesitz

Kubik, Gerhard, **1984**:
"Das Khoisan-Erbe im Süden von Angola, dargestellt anhand ethnographischer, linguistischer und musikologischer Fakten", in: *Wiener Ethnohistorische Blätter*, Heft 27, 125-154

Kun, Nicolas de, **1960**:
"La vie et le voyage de Ladislas Magyar dans l'intérieur du Congo", in: *Bulletin ARSOM*, vol. 6, 604-636

Kuper, Adam, [2]**1983**:
Anthropology and anthropologists. The modern British school, London etc. (Routledge & Kegan Paul) [first edition 1973]

Lacerda e Almeida, F.J. de, **1936**:
Travessia da Africa, Lisboa (Agência Geral das Colónias)

Lacerda, José Maria de, **1844**:
"Observações sobre a viagem da costa d'Angola à costa de Moçambique, 1787-1798 (extracto)", in: *Annaes Marítimos e Coloniais*, 198ff

Lemaire, Charles, **1903**:
"Les Wamboundous. Colporteurs noirs entre l'Atlantique et le Katanga", in: *Revue de Géographie (Paris)*, vol. 50 (June) and 51 (July, August), 50-68, 134ff

Livingstone, David, **1857**:
Missionary Travels and Researches in South Africa; etc., London (J.Murray)

Livingstone, David, **1960**:
Livingstone's Private Journals, 1851-53 [edited by Isaac Schapera], London (Heinemann)

Livingstone, David, **1963**:
Livingstone's African Journal, 1853-1856 [edited by Isaac Schapera], 2 vols., London (Heinemann)

Lopes de Lima, J.J., **1846**:
Ensaios sobre statística, vol.3, Lisboa

Lovejoy, Paul E. (ed.), **1981**:
Ideology of Slavery in Africa, Beverly Hills (Sage)

Lovejoy, Paul E. (ed.), **1986**:
Africans in bondage. Studies in slavery and the slave trade, Madison, Wisconsin (African Studies Press)

Lovejoy, Paul, **1983**:
  Transformations in slavery: a history of slavery in Africa, Cambridge (Cambridge University Press)
Lutz, Burkart (ed.), **1985**:
  Soziologie und gesellschaftliche Entwicklung, Frankfurt/Main (Campus)
Lux, Anton E., **1880**:
  Von Loanda nach Kimbundu. Ergebnisse der Forschungsreise im äquatorialen West-Afrika, Wien (Hölzel)
Maclaren, P.I.R., **1958**:
  The fishing devices of Central and Southern Africa. Livingstone (Occasional Papers of the Rhodes-Livingstone Museum, No.12)
Madeira Santos, Maria Emilia M., **1978**[1], **1988**[2]:
  Viagens de exploração terrestre dos Portugueses em Africa, Lisboa (Centro de Estudios de Cartografía Antiga)
Madeira Santos, Maria Emilia M., **1986**:
  "Introdução (TrajectÂria do comrcio do Bi)", in: Silva Porto 1986: 33-216
Magyar, Laszlo (Ladislaus), **1857**:
  Reisen in Süd-Africa, 1849-1857. vol.I. Pest (Repr. Kraus, 1974) [vol. II never appeared]
Magyar, Laszlo (Ladislaus), **1860**:
  "Ladislaus Magyar's Erforschung von Inner-Afrika. Nachrichten über die von ihm in den Jahren 1850,1851 und 1855 bereisten Länder Moluwa, Moropu und Lobal", in: *Petermann's Geographische Mitteilungen*, VI, 44; 227-237
Mainga, Mutumba, **1972**:
  Bulozi under the Luyana kings. Political evolution and state formation in pre-colonial Zambia, London (Longman)
Malaisse, F., **1979**:
  "L'homme dans la forêt claire zambézienne. Contribution à l'étude de l'écosystème forêt claire (Miombo)", in: *African Economic History*, no.7, 38-64
Malinowski, Bronislaw, **1970**:
  Crime and custom in savage society, London (Kegan Paul International) [First edition 1926]
Marter, Alan, **1978**:
  "The Small Scale Farmer in Zambia", in: *The University of Zambia Business & Economics Association Journal*, vol.3, 1-21
Marter, Alan, **1978**:
  Cassava or maize ? A comparative study of the economics of production and market potential of cassava and maize in Zambia, Lusaka (Rural Development Studies Bureau)
Martin, Phyllis M., **1986**:
  "Power, cloth and currency on the Loango coast", in: *African Economic History*, 15, 1-12

Marx, Christoph, **1988**:
> *Völker ohne Schrift und Geschichte. Zur historischen Erforschung des vorkolonialen Schwarzafrika in der deutschen Forschung des 19. und frühen 20. Jahrhunderts*, Wiesbaden (Steiner)

Mauss, Marcel, **1973**:
> *Sociologie et Anthropologie*. Paris (Presses Universitaires de France)

Mauss, Marcel, **⁵1973**:
> "Du don, et en particulier de l'obligation a rendre les présents", in: Mauss: 145-279 [first published in 1923/24]

Mbwiliza, J.F., **1991**:
> *A history of commodity production in Makuani 1600-1900. Mercantilist accumulation to imperialist domination*, Dar es Salaam (Dar es Salaam University Press)

McCulloch, Merran, **1951**:
> *The Southern Lunda and related peoples. (Ethnographic survey of Africa, West Central Africa part I.)* London (International Africa Institute)

Meillassoux, Claude, (ed.), **1971**:
> *The development of indigenous trade and markets in West Africa*, London (International African Institute / Oxford University Press)

Meillassoux, Claude, **1960**:
> "Essai d'interprétation du phénomène économique dans les sociétés traditionelles d'autosubsistance", on: *Cahiers d'Etudes Africaines*, vol.4, 38-67

Meillassoux, Claude, **1971**:
> "Introduction", in: Meillassoux (ed.): 3-86 [French and English]

Meillassoux, Claude, **1975**:
> *Femmes, greniers et capitaux*, Paris (Maspero)

Meillassoux, Claude, **1982**:
> "Historische Bedingungen der Ausbeutung und Überausbeutung von Arbeitskraft", in: Elwert and Fett (eds.): 17-28 [orig. 1979 in: *Current Anthropology*]

Meillassoux, Claude, **1989**:
> *Anthropologie der Sklaverei*, Frankfurt and Paris (Campus and Ed. de la Maison des Sciences de l'Homme) [orig.1986]

Mello Geraldes, Carlos Eugenio de, and Bernardo **d'Oliveira Fragateiro**, **1910**:
> *Le caoutchouc dans les colonies portugaises*, Lisboa (A Editora)

Mendes Corrêa, A.A., **1916**:
> "Antropologia Angolense: I: Quiocos, Luimbes, Luenas e Lutchazes", in: *Archivo de Anatomia e Antropologia*, vol. II, 323ff

Middleton, John, and David **Tait** (eds.), **1958**:
> *Tribes without rulers*, London

Miers, S., and I. **Kopytoff** (eds.),**1977**:
> *Slavery in Africa: Historical and anthropological perspectives*, Madison (University of Wisconsin Press)

Milheiros, M., **1948**:
> "Lundas e Luenas: posto de Caianda", in: *Mensário Adminstrativo*, nos. 15 and 16, 13-20

Milheiros, M., 1949:
"O direito gentílico nos Luenas", in: *Mensário Administrativo*, no. 17 and 19

Miller, Joseph C., 1970:
"Cokwe trade and conquest in the nineteenth century", in: Gray and Birmingham (eds.): 175-201

Miller, Joseph C., 1972:
"The Imbangala and the chronology of early Central African History", in: *Journal of African History*, vol.13, 4, 549-574

Miller, Joseph C., 1973:
"Slaves, slavers, and social change in nineteenth century Kasanje", in: Heimer (ed.): 9-29

Miller, Joseph C., 1974:
Cokwe expansion, 1850-1900, (African Studies Program, Occasional Paper No. 1) Madison (African Studies Press, University Wisconsin)

Miller, Joseph C., 1975:
"Legal Portuguese slaving from Angola. Some preliminary indications of volume and direction", in: *Revue française d'histoire d'Outre-Mer*, vol. 62, 226-27, 135-176

Miller, Joseph C., 1976:
Kings and kinsmen: Early Mbundu states in Angola, Oxford (Oxford University Press)

Miller, Joseph C., 1981:
"Lineages, ideology and the history of slavery in Western Central Africa", in: Lovejoy (ed.): 41-72

Miller, Joseph C., 1982:
"The significance of drought, disease and famine in the agriculturally marginal zones of West-Central Africa", in: *Journal of African History*, vol. 23, 17-61

Miller, Joseph C., 1983:
"The paradoxes of impoverishment in the Atlantic Zone", in: Birmingham and Martin (eds.): vol. I, 118-159

Miller, Joseph C., 1988:
Way of death. Merchant capitalism and the Angolan slave trade, 1730-1830, London/Madison (Currey/University of Wisconsin Press)

Ministério da Marinha e Ultramar, 1889a:
Estadistica Comercial da Provincia de Angola, Lisboa (Imprensa Nacional)

Ministério da Marinha e Ultramar, 1889b:
Relatório do Governador Geral da Provincia de Angola, Lisboa (Imprensa Nacional)

Ministério da Marinha e Ultramar, 1894:
Relatório do Governador do Districto de Benguella, Lisboa (Compagnia Nacional Editora)

Minster Agriculture Ltd., **1982**:
Farm Survey Kabompo District. Final Report. Thame/Eschborn (German Agency for Technical Development, unpubl. project document)

Miracle, Marvin P., **1966**:
: *Maize in Tropical Africa*, Madison (University of Wisconsin Press)

Miracle, Marvin P., **1977**:
: "The introduction and spread of maize in Africa", in: Konczacki and Konczacki (eds.): 41-51 [first published in 1965]

Mowat, Linda, **1989**:
: *Cassava and Chicha. Bread and beer of the Amazonian Indians* (Shire Ethnography), Aylesbury (Shire Publications)

Murdock, George Peter, **1967**:
: *Ethnographic Atlas*. Pittsburgh (University)

Mwondela, Willie Robert, **1972**:
: *Mukanda and Makishi. Traditional Education in North Western Zambia*. Lusaka (NecZam)

Myint, Hla, **1958**:
: "The 'classical theory' of international trade and the underdeveloped countries", in: *The Economic Journal*, vol.68, 317-37

Ncube, Patrick, (ed.), **1983**:
: *Agricultural baseline data for planning*, Lusaka (National Commission for Development Planning)

Newbury, Colin W., **1971**:
: "Prices and profitability in early 19th century West African trade", in: Meillassoux (ed.): 91-106

Newbury, Colin W., **1972**:
: "Credit in early 19th century West African trade", in: Journal of African History, 13, 1, 81-95

Northrup, David, **1978**.
: *Trade without rulers: pre-colonial economic development in south-eastern Nigeria*, London (Clarendon)

Oliver, Roland, **1978**:
: "The emergence of Bantu Africa", in: *Cambridge History of Africa*, vol. 2, 342-409

Oppen, Achim von, **1981**:
: Wanderarbeit, Unterentwicklung und Lebensbedingungen in einer peripheren Region Sambias: Der Kabompo Distrikt. Berlin (unpubl. Diplom thesis, Geographisches Institut der Freien Universität)

Oppen, Achim von, **1990**:
: Trust, reluctance and worldly demands. Peasant modes of negotiating agricultural development intervention in the history of North-West Zambia" (Paper presented to the XIVth Congress of the European Society for Rural Sociology, Giessen, July 1990)

Oppen, Achim von, **1991**:
: "Cassava, 'the lazy man's food' ? Indigenous agricultural innovation and dietary change in northwestern Zambia (ca. 1650-1970)", in: Food and Foodways, 5, 1, 15-38

Oppen, Achim von, **1992**:
: "'Endogene Agrarrevolution' im vorkolonialen Afrika ? Eine Fallstudie", in: *Paideuma*, 38, 269-296

Oppen, Achim von, **forthcoming**:
"Mobile practice and local identity. Changing moralities of rural marketing in Northern Rhodesia, 1930s-60s', in: Heidrich (ed.):

Oppen, Achim von, and **Dorlöchter-Sulser**, Sabine, **1989**:
"The sweating barrel. Historical notes on drinking and alcohol in the Upper Zambezi" (paper presented *in absentia* to the American Anthropological Association annual meeting 1989, Washington, Session *'Bread and Beer - The transformation of starches from nature to culture'*)

Oppen, Achim von, E.C.W. **Shula**†, Ulrich **Alff** *et al.*, **1983**:
LIMA Target Group Survey. Final Report. Kabompo (Integrated Rural Development Programme, unpubl.)

Palmer, Robin, and Neil **Parsons** (eds.), 1977:
The roots of rural poverty in Central and Southern Africa, London etc. (Heinemann)

Papstein, Robert J., **1978**:
The Upper Zambezi: A history of the Luvale people, 1000-1900. (unpubl. Ph.D.dissertation, University of California Los Angeles)

Papstein, Robert J., **1989**:
"From ethnic identity to tribalism: the Upper Zambezi Region of Zambia, 1830-1981", in: Vail (ed.): 372-394

Pausewang, Siegfried, *et al.*, **1986**:
Zambia - Country study and Norwegian aid review, Fantoft (Chr. Michelsen Institute)

Pearson, Emil, **1977**:
People of the aurora. San Diego (Beta Books)

Pearson, Harry W., **1957**:
"The economy has no surplus: Critique of a theory of development", in: Polanyi, Arensberg and Pearson (eds.): 320-339

Pélissier, René, **1977**:
Les guerres grises. Résistance et révoltes en Angola (1845-1941), Montamets (Pélissier)

Phillipson, D.W., **1982**:
"Early food production in sub-saharan Africa", in: *Cambridge History of Africa*, vol.I, 770-829

Pinto, Serpa, **1881**:
How I crossed Africa, 2 vols., London

Pogge, Paul, **1880**:
Im Reich des Muata-Jamvo, Berlin (Reimer)

Polanyi, Karl, **1944**:
The great transformation. London

Polanyi, Karl, **1957**:
"The economy as instituted process",
in: Polanyi, Arensberg and Pearson (eds.): 243-270

Polanyi, Karl, Conrad M. Arensberg and Harry W. Pearson (eds.), 1957:
Trade and market in the early empires, New York and London (The Free Press)

Post, Ken, **1977**:
"Peasantization in Western Africa", in: Gutkind and Waterman (eds.): 241-249

Pottier, Johan P., **1986**:
"The politics of famine prevention: ecology, regional production and food complementarity in western Rwanda", in: *African Affairs*, vol. 85, 339, 207-237

Pottier, Johan, (ed.), **1985**:
Food systems in Central and Southern Africa, London (School of Oriental and African Studies)

Provincial Planning Unit, **1986**:
Draft Provincial Development Plan 1986-1990, North-Western Province, Solwezi (unpublished)

Purseglove, J.W., **1976**:
"The origins and migrations of crops in tropical Africa", in: Harlan, de Wet and Stemler (eds.): 291-310

Raatgever, Reini, **1985**:
"Analytic tools, intellectual weapons: The discussion among French Marxist anthropologists about the identification of modes of production in Africa", in: van Binsbergen and Geschiere (eds.), 1985: 290-330

Ranger, Terence, 1971:
The agricultural history of Zambia, Lusaka (Historical Association of Zambia Pamphlet No. 1)

Ranger, Terence, **1978**:
"Growing from the roots: reflections on peasant reserach in Central and Southern Africa", in: *Journal of Southern African Studies*, vol.5, 99-133

Ranger, Terence, **1985**:
Peasant consciousness and guerilla war in Zimbabwe, London (Currey)

Ranger, Terence, **1993**:
"The invention of tradition revisited: The case of colonial Africa", in: Ranger und Vaughan (ed.): 62-111

Ranger, Terence, und Olufemi **Vaughan** (eds.), **1993**:
Legitimacy and the state in twentieth century Africa. Essays in honour of A.H.M. Kirk-Greene, Basingstoke, London (Macmillan)

Rauch, Theo, and **Weyl**, Ulrich,**1978**:
"Integrated Rural Development North-Western Province", Eschborn (unpublished)

Redinha, José, **1958**:
Etnossociologia do nordeste de Angola. Lisboa ('Atica Impr.)

Redinha, José, **1961**:
"Nomenclaturas nativas para as formações botànicas do Nordeste de Angola", in: *Agronomia de Angola*, n. 13

Redinha, José, **1968**:
"Subsídio para a história e cultura da mandioca entre os povos do nordeste de Angola", in: *Boletím do Instituto de Investigação Científica de Angola*, 1968, 95-108

Redinha, José, **1968**:
"Ethno-agricultura: Tradições, practicas e conceitos agrícolas entre os Quiocos da Lunda", in: *Trabalho*, vol. 23, 73-87

Reefe, Thomas Q., **1983**:
"The societies of the Eastern Savannah", in: Birmingham and Martin (eds.): vol. I, 160-204

Reefe, Thomas, **1981**:
The rainbow and the kings: a history of the Luba empire to 1891, Berkeley and Los Angeles (Univ. of California Press)

Rey, Pierre Philippe, **1971**:
Colonialisme, néo-colonialisme et transition au capitalisme: example du 'Comilog' au Congo-Brazzaville, Paris (Maspero)

Rey, Pierre Philippe, **1973**:
Les alliances de classes, Paris (Maspero)

Richards, Audrey I., **1939**:
Land, labour and diet in Northern Rhodesia, Oxford (Oxford University Press)

Richards, Paul, **1983**:
"Ecological change and the politics of African land use", in: *African Studies Review*, vol.26, 2, 1-72

Richards, Paul, **1985**:
Indigenous Agricultural Revolution. Ecology and Food Production in West Africa, London (Hutchinson)

Richards, Paul, **no year** [1986]:
On the South side of the garden Eden. Creativity and Innovation in subsaharan agriculture. London (unpubl. seminar paper, Dept. of Anthropology, U.C.)

Riechert, Ch., **1979**:
Study on promotion of bee-keeping as part of IRDP, Zambia, Eschborn/Hamburg (unpublished project document)

Roberts, Andrew, **1970**:
"Pre-colonial Trade in Zambia", in: *African Social Research*, X, 715-746

Roberts, Andrew, **1973**:
A history of the Bemba, London (Longman)

Roberts, Andrew, **1976**:
A history of Zambia, London etc. (Heinemann)

Robertson, Claire C., und Martin A. Klein (eds.), **1983**:
Women and slavery in Africa, Madison (Univ. of Wisconsin Press)

Roche, E., **1979**:
"Végétation ancienne et actuelle de l'Afrique centrale", in: *African Economic History*, no.7, 30-37

Rodney, Walter, **1972**:
Review of: Gray and Birmingham, 1970, in: *Transafrican Journal of History*, vol.2, no.1

Rodney, Walter, **1973**:
How Europe underdeveloped Africa, London and Daressalam (Bougle l'Ouverture and Tanzanian Publishing House)

Rotberg, Robert I. (ed.), **1983**:
Imperialism, colonialism and hunger: East and Central Africa, Lexington, Mass. (Lexington Books)

Sahlins, Marshall, **1974**:
"On the sociology of primitive exchange", in: Sahlins: 185-276

Sahlins, Marshall, **1974**: *Stone age economics*, London (Tavistock)

Saul, J.S., and **Woods**, R., **1971**:
"African Peasantries", in: Shanin (ed.)

Schachtzabel, Alfred, **1923**:
Im Hochland von Angola, Dresden (Verlag Deutsche Buchwerkstätten)

Schecter, Robert Edmund, **1976**:
History and historiography on a frontier of Lunda expansion: the origins and the early development of the Kanongesha, University of Wisconsin (unpublished Ph.D.thesis)

Schmitter, Uwe, **1988**:
'Joints and cracks' - Handwerk und Entwicklung. Kleine Warenproduktion und andere Formen der Produktion am Beispiel des Holzhandwerks in Zambias Nord-West-Provinz. Berlin (Unpubl. Diplom thesis, Institut für Soziologie, Freie Universität)

Schomburgk, Hans, [2]**1925**:
Wild und Wilde im Herzen Afrikas. 12 Jahre Jagd- und Forschungsreisen. Berlin (Deutsche Buchgemeinschaft) [first edition 1910]

Schomburgk, Hans, **1928a**:
Mein Afrika, Berlin (Axel Junker)

Schomburgk, Hans, **1928b**:
Fahrten und Forschungen mit Büchse und Film im unbekannten Afrika, Berlin (Deutsches Literatur-Institut)

Schönherr, Siegfried, **1979**:
LIMA small-scale farmer crop development. (Unpublished project report) Kabompo/Eschborn: IRDP/GTZ

Schütt, Otto, **1879**.
"Bericht über die Reise von Malange zum Luba-Häuptling Mai und zurück, Juli 1878 bis Mai 1879", in: *Mittheilungen der Afrikanischen Gesellschaft in Deutschland*, vol.1, 178-207

Schütt, Otto, **1881**:
Reisen im südwestlichen Becken des Kongo. Berlin (Reimer)

Servet, Jean-Michel, **1981**:
"Primitive order and archaic trade", in: *Economy and Society*, vol.10, 4, 423-450, and vol.11, 1, 22-59

Shanin, Theodor (ed.), **1971**:
Peasants and peasant societies. Harmondsworth etc. (Penguin)

Silva Porto, António Francisco Ferreira **da**, **1885**:
"Novas jornadas de Silva Porto nos sertões africanos", in: *Boletím da Sociedade de Geographia e da História de Lisboa*, 5a série, nos. 1,3,9, and 10, 3-36, 145-172, 569-586, 603-642

Silva Porto, António Francisco Ferreira da, **1891**:
Silva Porto e Livingstone. Manuscripto de Silva Porto encontrado no seu espólio, Lisboa (Typographia da Academia Real das Sciencias) [written in 1868]

Silva Porto, António Francisco Ferreira da, **1938**:
Silva Pôrto e a travessia do continente africano, Lisboa (Ministério das Colónias)

Silva Porto, António Francisco Ferreira da, **1942**:
Viagens e apontamentos de um Portuense em 'Africa. Excerptos do "Diario de A.F. da Silva Porto". Lisboa (Ministério de Colónias)

Silva Porto, António Francisco Ferreira da, **1986**:
Viagens e apontamentos de um Portuense em 'Africa. Diário de Antonio Francisco Ferreira da Silva Porto, vol.I, Coimbra (Biblioteca Geral da Universidade de Coimbra) [revised text with an extensive introduction (see Madeira Santos 1986) and numerous notes by Maria Emilia Madeira Santos]

Silva Teixeira, Alexandre da, **1940**:
"Relação da viage q~ fis desta Cidade de Beng.a para as do louar, no anno de 1794," in: Felner (ed.): vol.I: 236-237 [Original in AHU, Angola, cx. 80, No.66; first printed in *Archivos de Angola*, 1 (1933), 1, Documents XVII and XVIII]

Singleton Fisher, Walter, and Hoyte, Julian, **1948**:
Africa looks ahead. The life histories of Walter and Anna Fisher of Central Africa, London (Pickering and Inglis)

Singleton-Fisher, Walter, **1948**:
"Burning the bush for game", in: *African Studies*, VII, 1, 36-38

Soremekun, Fola, **1977**:
"Trade and dependency in Central Angola: The Ovimbundu in the nineteenth century", in: Palmer and Parsons (eds.): 82-95

Spittler, Gerd, **1987**:
"European explorers as caravan travellers in the West Sudan. Some thoughts on the methodology of journeys of exploration", in: Heintze and Jones (eds): 391-406

Spring, Anita, **1976**:
"Women's rituals and natality among the Luvale of Zambia", Cornell University (unpublished Ph.D. dissertation)

Spring, Anita, **1979**:
"Women's agricultural work in rural Zambia: from valuation to subordination. Agricultural changes in Zambia since the late 1930s", Los Angeles (African Studies Association 22nd Meeting, unpublished paper)

Spring, Anita, and **Hansen**, Art, **1985**:
"The Underside of Development: Agricultural Development and Women in Zambia", in: *Agriculture and Human Values*, vol. 2, 1, 60-67

Sundstrøm, Lars, **1974**:
The exchange economy of pre-colonial tropical Africa. London (Hurst & Co.)

Suret-Canale, Jean, **1964**:
"Les sociétés traditionelles en Afrique noire et le concept du mode de production asiatique", in: *La Pensée*, 177, 19-42

Teixeira de Azevedo, Frederico, **1918**:
"Relatório sobre a região do Moxico" and "Relatório sobre a região de Nana Candundo", in: *Governo Geral de Angola*: 49-68

Terray, Emmanuel, **1971**:
"Commerce pré-colonial et organisation sociale chez les Dida de Côte d'Ivoire", in: Meillassoux (ed.), 1971: 145-167

Terray, Emmanuel, **1974**:
"Long-distance trade and the formation of the state: the case of the Abron kingdom of Gyaman", in: *Economy and Society*, vol.3, 3

Thornton, John, **1981**:
"The chronology and causes of Lunda expansion to the west, c.1700-1852", in: *Zambia Journal of History*, no.1, 1-14

Thurnwald, Richard. **1916**:
"Bánaro Society. Social organization and kinship system of a tribe in the interior of New Guinea", in: *Memoirs of the American Anthropological Association*, vol. 3, no. 4

Thurnwald, Richard, **1932**:
Werden, Wandel und Gestaltung der Wirtschaft im Lichte der Völkerforschung (Die menschl. Gesellsch. in ihren ethno-soziologischen Grundlagen, vol. 3), Berlin, Leipzig (Walter de Gruyter)

Torday, E., **1925**:
On the trail of the Bushongo, London (Seeley Service and Co.)

Torday, E., and Joyce, **1922**:
"Notes ethnographiques sur des populations habitants les bassin du Kasai et du Kwango oriental", in: *Annales du Musée du Congo Belge*, 3, 2

Tosh, John, **1980**:
"The cash-crop revolution in tropical Africa: An agricultural reappraisal", in: *African Affairs*, vol.79, 79-94

Trapnell, C.G., and **Clothier**, J.N., [2]**1957** :
The soils, vegetation and agriculture of North-Western Rhodesia. Lusaka (Government Printer) [first edition 1937]

Trenk, Marin, **1991**:
Der Schatten der Verschuldung. Komplexe Kreditbeziehungen des informellen Finanzsektors, Saarbrücken (Breitenbach)

Trigo Teixeira, Frederico Cesar, **1936**:
"A ocupação do Moxico", in: *Cuadernos Coloniais*, vol. 12, 1-31

Turner, Elizabeth L.B., and **Turner**, Victor W., **1955**:
"Money economy among the Mwinilunga Ndembu: a study of some individual cash budgets", in: *Rhodes-Livingstone Journal*, XVIII,

Turner, Victor W., **1953**:
Lunda rites and ceremonies. (Occasional Papers of the Rhodes-Livingstone Museum, No.10). Livingstone

Turner, Victor W., **1957**:
Schism and continuity in an African society. A study of Ndembu village life. Manchester (Manchester University Press)

Turner, Victor W., **1969**:
The ritual process. London

Tylden, G., **1953**:
"The gun trade in Central and Southern Africa", in: *Northern Rhodesia Journal*, II, 1, 43-48

Vail, Leroy (ed.), **1989**: *The creation of tribalism in Southern Africa.* London and Berkeley (J.Currey and Univ. of California Press)

van Binsbergen, Wim M.J., **1981**:
Religion change in Zambia, London and Boston (Kegan Paul International)

van Binsbergen, Wim M.J., **1985**:
"From tribe to ethnicity in western Zambia: The unit of study as an ideological problem", in: Geschiere and van Binsbergen (eds.): 181-234

van Binsbergen, Wim M.J., **1992**:
Tears of rain. Ethnicity and history in central western Zambia, London, New York (Kegan Paul International)

van Binsbergen, Wim, and Peter **Geschiere** (eds.), **1985**:
Old modes of production and capitalist encroachment. Anthropological explorations in Africa, London etc. (Kegan Paul International)

van Horn, Laurel, **1977**:
"The agricultural history of Barotseland, 1840-1964", in: Palmer and Parsons (eds.): 144-170

Vansina, Jan, **1960**:
"Recording the Oral History of the Bakuba: II - Results", in: *Journal of African History*, vol.1, 2,

Vansina, Jan, **1962**:
"Long-distance trade routes in Central Africa", in: *Journal of African History*, vol. 3, 3, 375-390

Vansina, Jan, **1966**:
Kingdoms of the savannah. Madison (University of Wisconsin Press)

Vansina, Jan, **1978**:
The children of woot: a history of the Kuba peoples, Madison (University of Wisconsin Press)

Vansina, Jan, **1979**:
"Finding food and the history of pre-colonial equatorial Africa: a plea", in: *African Economic History*, vol.7, 9-20

Vansina, Jan, **1990**:
Paths in the Rainforests. Toward a History of Political Tradition in Equatorial Africa, Madison (University of Wisconsin Press)

Vellut, Jean-Luc, **1972**:
"Notes sur les lunda et la frontière luso-africaine, 1700-1900", in: *Etudes d'Histoire Africaine*, 3, 61-166

Vellut, Jean-Luc, **1975**:
"Le royaume de Cassange et les réseaux luso-africains (ca. 1750-1810)", in: *Cahiers d'Etudes Africaines*, 14, 117-136

Vellut, Jean-Luc, **1977**:
"Rural poverty in Western Shaba, c.1890-1930", in: Palmer and Parsons (eds.): 294-316

Vellut, Jean-Luc, 1979:
"Diversification de l'économie de cueillette: miel et cire dans les sociétés de la forêt claire d'Afrique centrale (c.1750-1950)", in: *African Economic History*, Spring 1979, 93-112

Vellut, Jean-Luc, 1989:
"L'Économie internationale des côtes de Guinée inferiéure au XIXe siècle" (Contribution for Reunião Internacional de História de Africa) Lisboa (Centro de Estudos de História e Cartografía Antiga)

Venning, J.H., 1955:
"Early days in Balovale", in: *Northern Rhodesia Journal*, vol. 2, 6, 53-57

Vieira de Andrade, Elias, 1940:
"Epanafora dos dias de viagem que se gastão desde a Libata do Sova de Caberabere denominado Quindombe the as terras do Lovar, Rios grandes q. se passão, nomes das Terras, e Sovas dellas &.," [by a '*negociante e morador do Sertão de Benguela*'], in: Felner (ed.): vol.I: 252/3

Watts, Michael, 1989:
"The agrarian question in Africa: debating the crisis", in: *Progress in Human Geography*, 13, 1-41

Wendorf, Horst, 1988:
'Make money from beeswax and honey'. Kleine Warenproduktion am Beispiel bäuerlicher Bienenhaltung in Zambia's Nordwest-Provinz (Zambezi District). Berlin (unpubl. Diplom Thesis, Institut für Soziologie, Freie Universität

White, Charles M.N., 1948:
Material culture of the Lunda-Lovale people. (Occasional Papers of the Rhodes-Livingstone Museum, No.3) Livingstone

White, Charles M.N., 1949:
"The Balovale peoples and their historical background", in: *Rhodes-Livingstone Journal*, no.8, 26-41

White, Charles M.N., 1953a:
"Notes on the circumcision rites of the Balovale tribes", in: *African Studies*, XII,2, 41-56

White, Charles M.N., 1953b:
"Conservatism and modern adaptation in Luvale female puberty ritual", in: *Africa*, XXIII, 15-24

White, Charles M.N., 1954:
"Notes on the *Mungongi* ritual of the Balovale tribes", in: *African Studies*, XIII, 4, 108-116

White, Charles M.N., 1955:
"Factors in the social organization of the Luvale", in: *African Studies*, XIV, 3, 97-112

White, Charles M.N., 1956:
"The role of hunting and fishing in Luvale society", in: *African Studies*, XV, 2, 75-86

White, Charles M.N., 1957a:
"Clan, chieftainship and slavery in Luvale political organization", in: *Africa*, XXVII, 1, 59-75

White, Charles M.N., **1958**:
"A note on Luvale joking relations", in: *African Studies*, XVII, 1, 28-33
White, Charles M.N., **1959**:
A preliminary survey of Luvale rural economy. (Rhodes- Livingstone Paper No.29), Manchester (University Press)
White, Charles M.N., **1960a**:
An outline of Luvale social and political organization. (Rhodes-Livingstone Paper No. 30), Manchester (Manchester University Press)
White, Charles M.N., **1960b**:
"A Survey of African Land Tenure in Northern Rhodesia", in: *Journal of African Administration*, vols. 11 and 12 (1959/60), 171-178 and 3ff
White, Charles M.N., **1961**:
Elements in Luvale beliefs and rituals. (Rhodes-Livingstone Paper No.32), Manchester (University Press)
White, Charles M.N., **1962a**:
"The ethnohistory of the Upper Zambezi", in: *African Studies*, XXI, 10-27
White, Charles M.N., **1962b**:
Tradition and change in Luvale marriage. (Rhodes-Livingstone Paper No. 34). Manchester (Manchester University Press)
White, Charles M.N., **Chinjavata**, J.C., and **Mukwato**, L.E., **1958**:
"Comparative aspects of Luvale female puberty ritual, in: *African Studies*, XVII, 4, 204-220
Wirz, Albert, **1984**:
Sklaverei und kapitalistisches Weltsystem, Frankfurt (Suhrkamp)
Wissmann, Herrmann von, [8]**1902**:
Unter deutscher Flagge quer durch Africa von West nach Ost, Berlin (Walter) [First edition 1889]
Wolf, Eric R., **1982**:
Europe and the people without history, Berkeley, Los Angeles (University of California Press)
Wolf, Eric, **1966**:
Peasants, Englewood Cliffs, N.Y.
Wolpe, H., **1972**:
"Capitalism and cheap labour power in South Africa: From segregation to apartheid", in: *Economy and Society*, vol I, 4, 425ff
Wright, Marcia, **1993**:
Strategies of slaves and women. Lifestories from East/Central Africa, New York, London (Lilian Barber, James Currey)
Yoder, John C., **1992**:
The Kanyok of Zaire. An institutional and ideological history to 1895 (African Studies 74), Cambridge (Cambridge University Press)

Unpublished Sources

- **NAZ :** Files kept in the National Archives of Zambia (Lusaka)
- **PRO :** Files kept in the Public Record Office (London)
- **AHU:** Files kept in the Archivo Histórico Ultramarino (Lisbon)

Note:

* Quotations in languages other than English have been translated by myself.
* Years and places given in [brackets] after references in the text refer to the time and area where the information was originally collected.

MAP 1

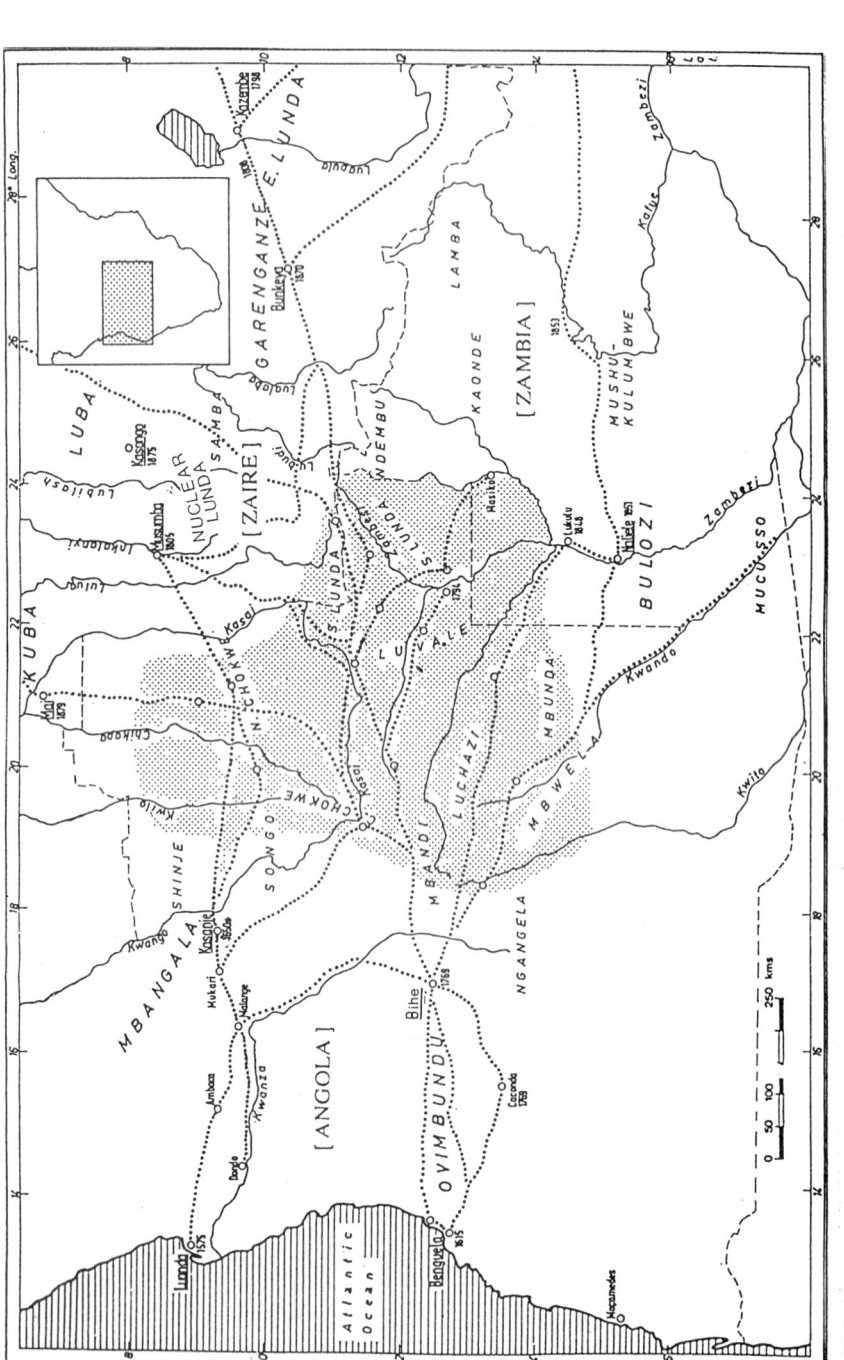

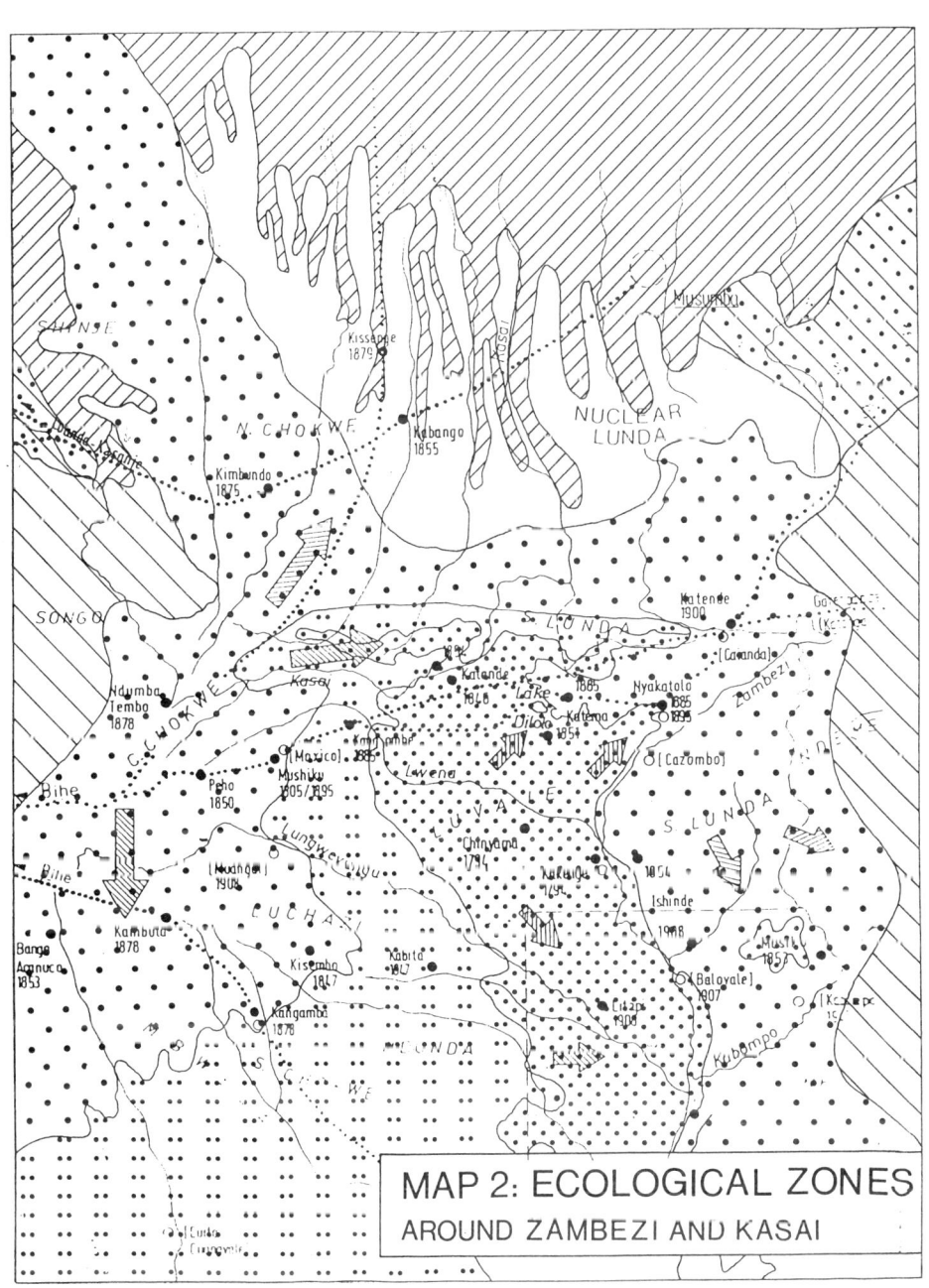

MAP 2: ECOLOGICAL ZONES AROUND ZAMBEZI AND KASAI

MAP 2/3 (key)

ECOSYSTEMS ON KALAHARI SANDS:

S: Woodlands
I: *musenge, mavunda*
V: *Brachystegia, Cryptosepalum*

S: Savannah-woodland mosaic (with gallery forests)
I: Lv. *litala (lito)*,
Ch. *kabengi (muchito)*,
LNd. *lusese (ito)*
V: e.g. *Landolphia*

S: Tree and shrub savannah
V: *Brachystegia, Burkea*

S: Grasslands, poorly drained, partly flooded during rains
I: *chana*; Lv. *chinema, kangungu*
V: *Loudetia* ssp.

ECOSYSTEMS ON CLAYEY SOILS:

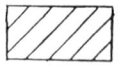
S: Forest-savannah mosaic with gallery forests
I: Ch. *usaki,muchito*;
Lv. *litungu, lito*);
V: *Marquesia, Berlinia*

S: Woodlands

S: Woodland-savannah mosaic

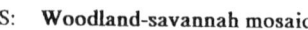

[S = scientific term
I = indigenous terms
V = typical vegetation]

• • • • •   Main transit routes of caravans from the west

●   Important chief's capital, and year of first recorded visit

○   Early colonial outpost and year of establishment

MBUNDA   Ethnic groups and main direction of migration

MAP 3

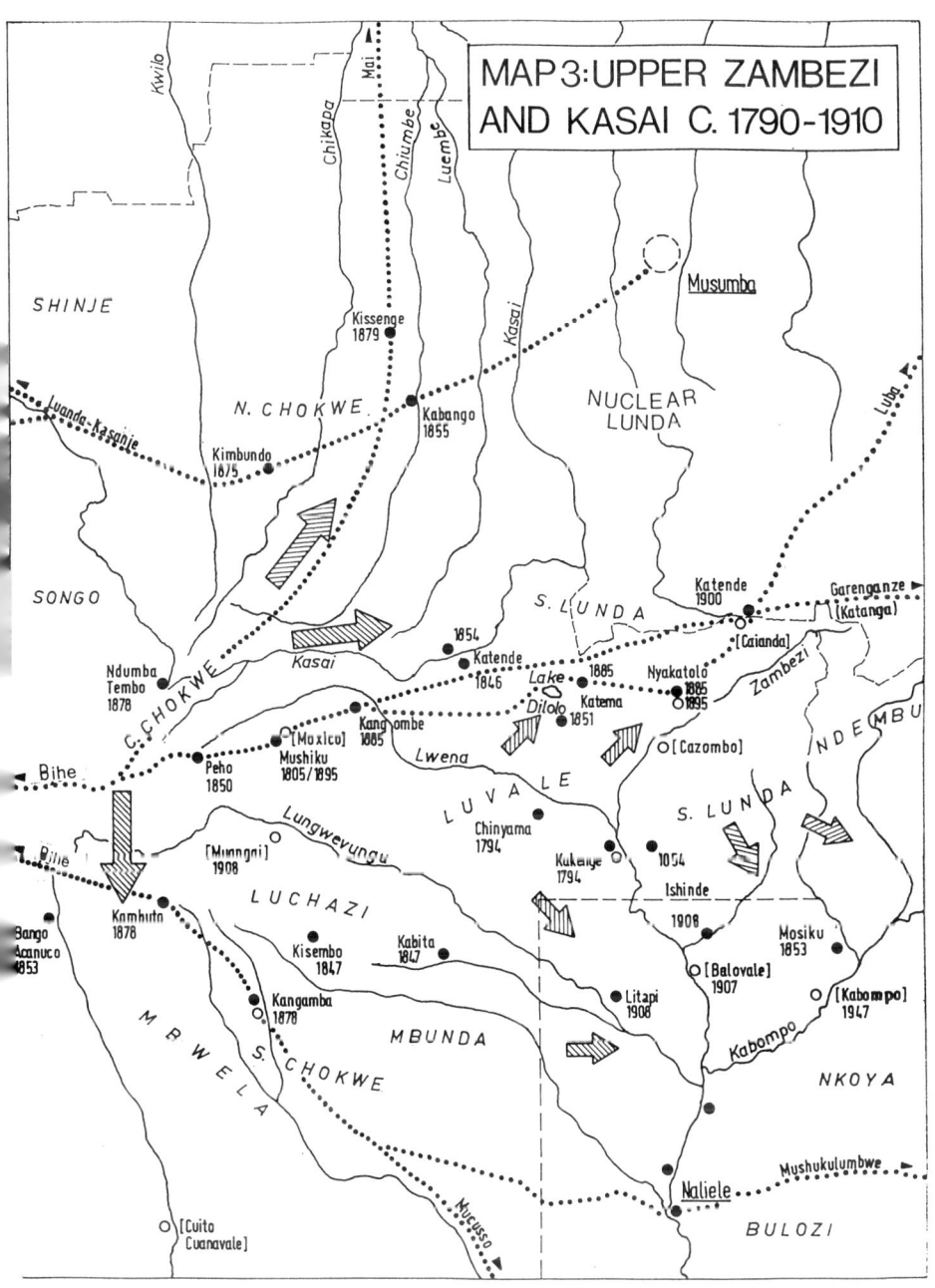